GREAT COMPOSERS

GREAT COMPOSERS

WHSMITH

EXCLUSIVE
·BOOKS·

Produced exclusively for WH Smith & Son Limited by
Marshall Cavendish Books Limited,
58 Old Compton Street,
London W1V 5PA

First printing 1989
2 3 4 5 6 7 8 9   99 98 97 96 95 94 93 92 91 90

ISBN 1 85435 201 6

Printed and bound in Hong Kong

Contents

FOREWORD BY
Antony Hopkins

There is an old nursery rhyme whose final line is 'she shall have music wherever she goes'. Today, 'she' has become 'we', for music is so much a part of everyday life that it is almost unavoidable: it accompanies us as we pick our way along the crowded aisles of the supermarket; it deafens us at cocktail parties; it marks time as we wait at airports; and it is even used in dentists' surgeries to calm our apprehension. The danger of such over-exposure is that we begin to treat music as one of those taken-for-granted amenities like electric light or central heating – we may be aware of it but we take little notice. We hear but we do not listen. Now it is true that a great deal of such music makes no real demands, even though the performances have a highly professional gloss. It has been described as 'wallpaper music' and, though wallpaper can be an asset to a room, it is scarcely a major art-form. But music of quality *does* make demands and it deserves more than casual listening, as it is a language of extraordinary power and subtlety. And it is a truly international language, for if you look in record shops in any of the five continents you will see many of the same works – works that are universally loved and that have retained their appeal over the centuries. Great music is also the nearest equivalent we have to a time machine, since every performance enables us to experience the emotions of people long dead; we can share Bach's faith, Haydn's wit, Beethoven's adversity, and Liszt's grand passions. While music of quality may make an immediate emotional appeal, our enjoyment will be greatly enhanced if we can cultivate a keener sense of period, for the language of music undergoes continual change. Mozart does not 'speak' to us in the same way as Brahms, though both composers may be concerned to express the same truths. To understand such differences, we need to know something about the background to composers' lives, their position in society, the reception accorded to their music, their loves, their triumphs and disasters. It is in these areas that GREAT COMPOSERS is so enlightening. Written in an eminently readable style, free from jargon and pedantry, this unique series sheds a clear light on all aspects of a composer's life, works and times, so that we know him like a personal friend. This greater knowledge and understanding will undoubtedly bring a fuller enjoyment and appreciation of music's riches, teaching us how much it has to offer if we *listen* rather than *hear*.

Antony Hopkins

Antony Hopkins is best known for his radio programme, *Talking About Music,* but he has also composed film scores, incidental music and operas. He holds an honorary Doctorate at Stirling University and Fellowships at Robinson College, Cambridge and at the Royal College of Music. In 1976 he was made a Commander of the British Empire.

Johann Sebastian Bach
1685–1750

In his own time, Bach was respected as a virtuoso organ player – now he is known and appreciated for the emotional depth of his Baroque music.

Ambrosius Bach (above), father of Johann Sebastian Bach, was a talented member of the musically gifted Bach family. In 1671 he became court trumpeter and director of music in Eisenach, where Bach was born in 1685. The portrait on the preceding page of Johann Sebastian Bach is one of only two existing authentic likenesses of the composer.

Johann Sebastian Bach was born in 1685 in Eisenach, Thuringia (in what is now East Germany), into a family firmly established locally as a musical one; it is reported that in some parts of Thuringia, the very word 'Bach' had come to denote a 'musician'.

Ambrosius Bach of Eisenach, Johann Sebastian's father, was a good violinist and trumpeter. From 1671 he was court trumpeter and director of town music in Eisenach.

By the time Sebastian was ten both parents had died and he was adopted by his eldest brother Christoph, organist of the Michaeliskirche in Ohrdruf, a small town near to Eisenach. Christoph was a skilled organist and Sebastian praised him as 'a profound composer'. Since no works by Christoph are known, Bach probably meant that he was a creative keyboard improviser. Certainly Christoph Bach exerted a profound influence on Sebastian. He taught him to play keyboard instruments and introduced him to the technique needed in music-copying. During this time Sebastian gained practical experience in organ-building, since the main Michaeliskirche organ was substantially repaired under Christoph's supervision.

Education in Lüneberg

By the time Bach was 15 accommodation in his brother's home was at a premium. His brother had two children and a third on the way; so Bach left the house to take up a chorister-scholarship at the Michaelisschule, in Lüneberg.

At Lüneberg, Bach became a member of the Mettenchor (Matins Choir). Members of this choir were usually boys from poor families. They received free schooling, board and lodgings and were paid a small amount depending on their seniority. They also received a share in fees for weddings and other

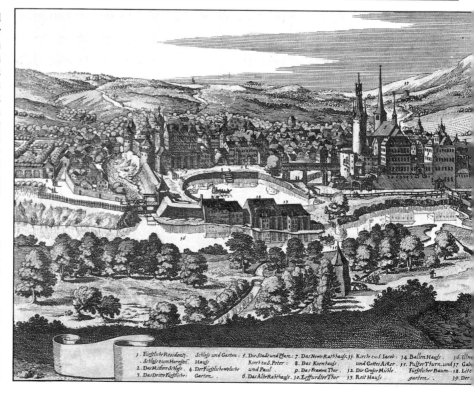

special occasions in which they took part.

Bach sang in the choir until his voice broke, changing from a treble to a bass baritone, then he became an instrumentalist. At school he studied Latin, Lutheranism, arithmetic, history and geography, German poetry, physics, heraldry and genealogy.

While he was at Lüneberg he heard the organist of the Johanniskirche, Georg Böhm, play. Böhm probably advised Bach to hear Adam Reincken, the distinguished organist of the Hamburg Catharinenkirche. Bach was impressed by both Reincken's showy playing and the church's organ itself.

From 1702, aged 17, Bach was on his own. In March 1703, after a few unsuccessful attempts to find work, he was employed at a minor Weimar court as a musician, but was paid as a 'lackey'.

Bach was 15 when he became a chorister–scholar at the Michaelisschule, the school associated with the Michaeliskirche (above centre).

While a student, Bach went to Hamburg to hear J. A. Reincken (above), the organist of the Catharinenkirche.

Bach spent nine years in Weimar (left) as a court musician.

In August 1703, he was appointed organist of the new Church in Arnstadt. In fact, the young Bach had first been approached by the church committee (the Consistory) of Arnstadt to examine the newly repaired organ earlier in 1703. He so distinguished himself that the church committtee offered him the job, over the head of a local man, Andreas Börner.

In Arnstadt, Bach's duties were comparatively light, but their specific nature was never clearly established, and later this gave rise to disputes. Bach had an excitable temperament and failed to gain the confidence of the local student musicians. He also irritated the Consistory which so generously urged his appointment, and was unpopular with his congregation. He was most roundly censured for extending approved leave from four weeks to nearly three months and, as a result, for leaving his assistant to play for Advent and Christmas 1705 and the New Year festivities of 1706. The Consistory found his explanation unsatisfactory, and they also complained that his accompaniments to chorales were too involved for ordinary congregational singing. There was also a complaint from the Consistory about the presence of a 'stranger maiden' in the organ gallery. However, this was his future wife, and he had permission for her presence from the parson.

The reason for his absence around Advent and Christmas can only have been for one purpose: to attend the celebrated evening sacred concerts *(Abendmusiken)* of Lübeck's Jacobikirche, organized by the famous Danish master-organist and composer Dietrich Buxtehude.

In midsummer 1707, Bach left Arnstadt to take up an appointment as organist of the Blasiuskirche in Mühlhausen. Despite the brevity of his stay in Mühlhausen – just over a year – it was an eventful time. He wrote his first cantatas as well as many works for the town council. It was also in Mühlhausen that he married his first wife, Maria Barbara Bach, a distant cousin and, like Sebastian himself, the child of a musical member of the Bach family. They had met while he was in Arnstadt, and were married in her home village of Dornheim in 1707.

Bach left Mühlhausen in 1708 to take up an appointment at the court of the Duke of Weimar.

Konzertmeister in Weimar

This offer of engagement – voiced as a command – had been issued by Duke Wilhelm Ernst of Saxe-Weimar, one of Thuringia's most important noblemen, whose court was of important cultural and theological standing. Bach worked under his patronage in Weimar from July 1708 to December 1717. At first he was court organist but from 2 March 1714 he was invested with the newlycreated title of *Konzertmeister*. In Weimar, Bach composed a large quantity of organ music, his harpsichord toccatas and a strikingly expressive series of cantatas for the Ducal chapel. One of his commissions, a birthday cantata for the pretentious Duke Christian of Weissenfels, marked the start of an association with the Weissenfels court which lasted until that Duke's death and the end of his line in 1736.

During his Weimar period, six of his children were born. Bach and his wife kept touch with friends and relations from Ohrdruf, Arnstadt and Mühlhausen by making them godparents to their children.

Bach's skill attracted students and from this time onwards he was never without pupils. He was offered an important organist's post at Halle when

Bach often travelled great distances to hear famous musicians perform. One of his more epic journeys was in the winter of 1705, when he walked from Arnstadt to Lübeck to hear the Danish organist Dietrich Buxtehude. He is thought to have attended a series of evening recitals, including one where the Castrum doloris (below) was performed. Bach overstayed his four weeks' leave and when he returned to Arnstadt three months later, was reprimanded by the church committee.

Handel's teacher, Zachow died. He did not take up the post because, when he asked permission to leave Weimar, the Duke created him Konzertmeister, and the employers at Halle could not match the salary which went with this new post. His relationship with Halle remained good and in 1717, was praised in print as 'the famous Weimar organist', by the influential Hamburg composer, Mattheson.

Particularly significant to 18th-century musicians was his visit to the Saxon capital city of Dresden late in 1717, where a contest was arranged by an influential nobleman. Bach and the great French keyboard-player and composer, Louis Marchand, were invited to play (and presumably to extemporize) in a harpsichord competition. There are various accounts of this event, or non-event, as it turned out, since Marchand, quit Dresden leaving Bach without an opponent. This was taken by many, then and later, to be a sure sign of the 'superiority' of German music over French.

A sour note at Weimar

Although his first years at Weimar had been creative, the last year of his employment there was disagreeable. Family feuds in Weimar's royal house and the unsavoury manipulation to find a new Kapellmeister were the causes of his dissatisfaction. As a result Bach decided to look elsewhere for a position as Kapellmeister. An offer came from Prince Leopold of Anhalt-Cöthen, so Bach sought his release again from Duke Wilhelm, and was again refused. When Bach again asked permission to go, the Duke placed him under house arrest from 6 November 1717 and then dismissed him in disgrace on 2 December.

Kapellmeister to Prince Leopold

Relations with his new employer were good. Prince Leopold was a musical young man and he gave Bach every encouragement to write all kinds of instrumental and secular vocal music.

In Cöthen, the last of Bach's children by his first wife was born, a son, named after Prince Leopold, who was his godfather. Sadly, the child did not live long.

Unlike most of the un-authentic portraits of Bach, this one (right), depicts him as a young Konzertmeister at the court of the Duke of Weimar in 1715.

Despite this sadness, Bach later wrote that in Cöthen he was generally very happy. He apparently composed very fluently here: to this period belong the sonatas for violin and harpsichord, the unaccompanied solos for violin and for cello, and the *Six Concertos* which we know as the 'Brandenburg' Concertos. The first book of the *Well-Tempered Clavier* and a number of vocal works written to honour the Prince's birthday and to express devotion to him at the opening of each new year date from this time in Cöthen.

However, from 1720–21, Bach suffered a series of setbacks. While he was away attending, with other musicians, the visit of the Prince to the spa at Karlsbad his wife, Maria Barbara, died.

Second, he failed to take up the post of organist of the Jacobikirche in Hamburg, either because he was

A Kantor (below left) directs a group of music students. In German cities, from the Reformation until the mid-18th century, this was a highly sought-after post. As Kantor of the Thomaskirche and Thomasschule (below) in Leipzig, from 1723 until his death in 1750, Bach was director of church and school music. Mendelssohn's sketch shows the Bach Memorial – which he donated – in the centre foreground.

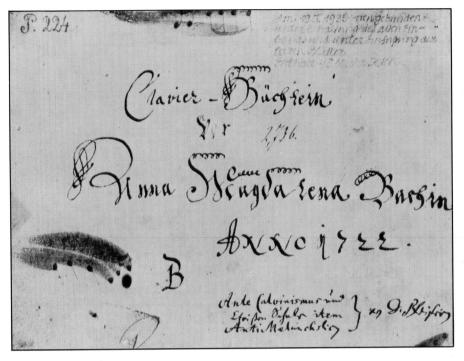

One of many music albums Bach made for members of his family, the Clavier-Büchlein (above) is dedicated to his second wife, Anna Magdalena. It contains some first drafts of Bach's compositions and some by his children.

involved him in no little expense. In any event, by March 1721 Bach was clearly angling for offers of employment elsewhere.

In December 1721 Bach married Anna Magdalena Wilken. Like Bach she was the child of a *Hoftrompeter* (Chief Trumpeter) and was herself a professional singer. She may also have wished him to move, but this is uncertain.

The mature years in Leipzig

As Kantor of the Thomasschule, Bach held one of the most important music posts in Lutheran Europe: only Kantor of Hamburg ranked higher. Bach was the town's most important musician, responsible for the music of four Leipzig churches and for any music which might be required for civic functions. The musical training of students at the school attached to Thomaskirche was also his responsibility. His main church duties extended to music for the principal services and feasts, as well as weddings and funerals, for which he received separate fees. He received a salary and payments in kind, of corn and wine, and was housed in the newly-renovated south wing of the Thomasschule. His first six years in Leipzig were demonstrably the most productive of his busy life. Until 1726, he composed elaborate music for his first choir. This was made up of the 12–16 best singers and was directed by Bach himself.

In 1728, he once again found himself in dispute with the church authorities; this time over the question of who should choose the songs to be sung before and after vespers. From this time his dealings with both council members and teachers at the Thomasschule were difficult. It seems that when confronted with what he saw as undue pressure, Bach reacted defiantly against the bureaucracy.

In 1729, after spending some time away from

unwilling or unable to donate to church funds the vast sum expected from successful candidates. So, the last chance he had of becoming the regular player of a really outstanding instrument of this kind passed out of his hands.

The third setback was the remarriage of Leopold on 11 December 1721 to his cousin, Princess Friderica of Anhalt-Bernburg, a lady who was not in any way artistically inclined. Possibly she was jealous of her husband's former love of music – which had

An imaginative 19th-century representation of the Bach family (right). It shows Bach at the keyboard, and other members of the family playing and singing. Bach married twice and had 20 children, but only 9 of them survived to mature ages. All the children received musical training from Bach and in 1730 he was proud to report that he could form a vocal and instrumental ensemble with his family. Three of his sons, Wilhelm Friedeman, Carl Philip Emanuel and Johann Christian, became composers.

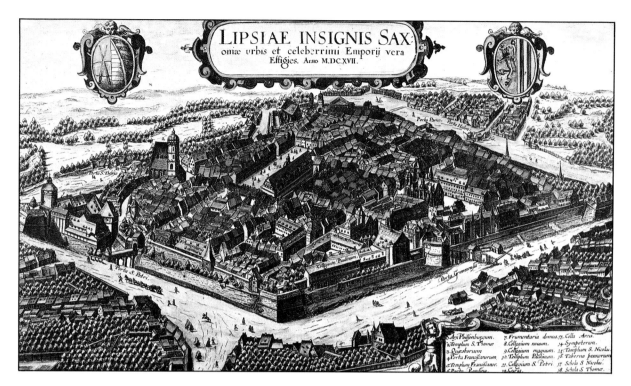

Leipzig at the Weissenfels court, he was given the title of court Kapellmeister of Saxe-Weissenfels. During this year he also returned to Cöthen to perform funeral music on the death of his former employer, Prince Leopold.

On his return to Leipzig he became director of the collegium musicum which had been founded by Telemann in 1704. This was a loose association of musicans and students which gave weekly public concerts. This gave him the opportunity for writing more secular music more declamatory in its style. His works were scaled for the larger numbers now at his disposal.

Although he was writing less sacred music his interest was as strong as ever and most of his major ecclesiastical works were written after 1730. Throughout his Leipzig period he provided performances of his cantatas every Sunday, and in 1731 the first performance of the St Mark Passion took place on Good Friday.

During a five-month period of national mourning on the death of Elector Friedrich August I of Saxony in 1733, Bach began writing the Kyrie and Gloria of his B minor Mass. Hoping that this would be the means of a new appointment at court, he presented them to the new Elector Friedrich August II in Dresden. They were probably performed at the Sophienkirche where his son, W. F. Bach, was working as organist, but the only title given to him was that of Hofkomponist.

In 1737 Bach resigned from the directorship of the collegium musicum and turned to keyboard music, working on the Well-Tempered Clavier and the third part of the Clavier-Übung. He probably also devoted more time to private teaching.

Bach once again took over as director of the collegium musicum in 1739, but withdrew in 1741 when Gottfried Zimmermann, the coffee-house owner in whose premises the collegium performed, died. In August 1741 Bach journeyed to Berlin to see his son, C. P. E. Bach, who in 1738 had been appointed court harpsichord player to Crown Prince Frederick of Prussia (Frederick the Great). He also

visited Dresden where he presented a copy of the Aria with 30 variations to Count von Keyserlingk for use by his resident harpsichord player Johann Gottlieb Goldberg. These were the 'Goldberg' variations.

From 1742 Bach composed only a few sacred cantatas and the Peasant Cantata of 1742 was his last secular work. He concentrated on performances of his major works and of those of other composers, such as Telemann and Handel. He also kept up his interest in organ building and examined and inaugurated many church organs.

In 1747, through Count von Keyserlingk he received an invitation to visit the court of Frederick the Great. He began his visit with a piano exercise in fugal improvisation on a theme given by the king. There followed on the next day an organ recital and chamber music recital where Bach again improvised.

On his return to Leipzig he began writing down and working on the King of Prussia's fugue theme. He turned this into a larger work, the 'Musical Offering', dedicated to Frederick which was printed in September 1747.

During his declining years, Bach struggled with failing eyesight. In 1749 an English eye specialist, John Taylor, performed an operation on him which was partly successful and a second operation left him very weak. Nevertheless in May 1750 he took on a last pupil, Johann Gottfried Müthel, but it is uncertain how much he was actually able to instruct him.

He received his last Communion on 22 July and died on 28 July 1750 at home, after a stroke. His second wife survived him by ten years, then died in poverty. Bach had left a modest estate, all of which was divided between his widow and the nine surviving children of both marriages.

Before he died, his music had become unfashionable, and for 50 years after his death nothing of his was published. However, later both Mozart and Beethoven found much to be admired in his music, but it was through Mendelssohn (from 1829) that Bach's works were once again revived.

Bach spent 27 years in Leipzig (above), as Kantor of the Thomaskirche and Director of Music of Leipzig. This was the most productive period of his life and he composed huge quantities of sacred music, including 6 cycles of cantatas – about 300 cantatas in all. As Director of the collegium musicum, he had the opportunity to produce music of a less religious nature. His great Passions, the St Matthew and St John Passions, were first performed in Leipzig and between Christmas Day 1734 and Epiphany 1735, the Christmas Oratorio was first heard.

Bach and the Church

Although the Protestant Church in Germany was divided between the differing views of Lutheranism and Pietism, Bach wrote church music as an expression of his own religious feelings – a blend of the two.

Bach's religious feelings grew in the new climate of religious toleration which evolved in the aftermath of the bitter Thirty Years' War (below) – a dynastic struggle focused on Germany which developed into a collision between the Catholic and Protestant Churches.

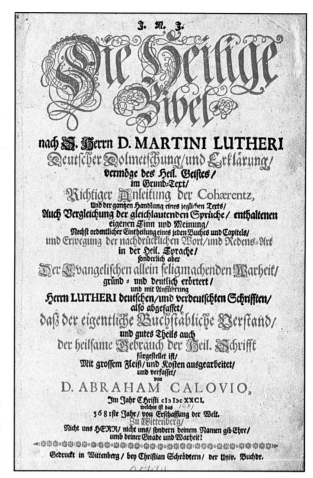

Martin Luther (far left) a German religious reformer, whose 'protestant' doctrines were the basis for Bach's religious upbringing.

The title page (left) of the Calov Bible, one of the many religious books in Bach's library. This edition of Luther's translation of the Bible was published in 1681 in three folio volumes with a commentary by the publisher, the Wittenberg professor of theology, Abraham Calov. Calov was one of the most prominent representatives of Lutheran high orthodoxy.

In many parts of Europe, only a century before Bach's birth in 1685, to reject the Catholic religion was to invite torture and even public execution. The power of the church was such that religion almost dominated everyday life. But during the following century – at least in northern Europe – matters changed rapidly and radically. Automatic allegiance to the Catholic Church, or to Catholic rulers, was brought into question by an increasing tide of 'unorthodox' religious feeling which shook the supremacy of catholicism. After 1530, the end of the Reformation in Germany, protestantism as pioneered by Martin Luther took root in many parts of Europe. But the development of differing religious identities of the nations of Europe was not easily won and gradually led to open hostility culminating with the conflict known as the Thirty Years' War (1618–1648). In essence this was a struggle for the balance of power between the Austrian Hapsburgs and the German Princes. Germany, then a collection of separate states, was divided by religious factionalism as well as dynastic rivalries and became the focal point of the long, drawn-out and debilitating war.

The depredations of this conflict left most of Germany in ruins. Only after peace was signed in Westphalia in 1648 could people anywhere in Europe look forward with any degree of optimism to a future where religious differences might not assume such great proportions.

Lutherans and Pietists
By the time Bach was born religious toleration was the order of the day. A new, more worldly and material, rather than spiritual, outlook was apparent in all aspects of life. Although music too, was freed from specific church use, many composers like Bach wrote both sacred and secular music with equal interest and enthusiasm. Bach was a deeply religious man and he expressed this in his music; nevertheless, in retrospect, his music can be seen as part of this general process of secularization.

Germany in the late 17th century was made up of over 300 little states, each with its own autocratic ruler and court, and each subscribing also to a church. In most of Germany that church was protestant, although by now it had divided into several denominations within the Protestant Church. In the north, where Bach lived for all his life, there were two major protestant denominations – Lutheran and Pietist. Protagonists of each were critical of the other, although they commonly lived as neighbours in the parishes and even attended the same church on Sundays.

Pietists, as their name suggests, preferred a distinctly more devotional attitude to life and their faith than most Lutherans. They were not as strict as true Puritans and their religious practice was by no means dour. They tended to emphasize the contemplative and more spiritual aspects of protestantism, regarding much of the rest of life as mere distraction. Martin Luther (a religious reformer and founder of Lutheranism) stressed the importance of faith (as opposed to good deeds or mere outward appearances) in religion.

Pietists, however, fervently wished to extend this idea into a personal and rather emotive relationship between Christ and a believer. The relationship was brought about by the believer's individual acknowledgement of Christ, rather than by the intervention of pastors. Such an experience was described by the man acknowledged as the founder of Pietism, Philipp Jakcob Spener (1635–1705), as a 'Christian awakening'. To the Pietists, therefore, music was a simple vehicle for fervent praise and rather sentimental devotion – and any elaboration of its was seen as a barrier to personal communication with God rather than an aid to it.

Lutherans, on the other hand, believed fundamentally in the God-given nature of talents, of creativity in all artistic forms, especially in music. Music itself could thus be a manifestation of praise, and the more excellent the composition, the greater the glory given to God.

Contemporary German church music

Musically, Germany in the 1680s was the meeting point of a number of influences. Form and formality in music were the main imports from France, while from Italy came a taste for panache and melody. Both were worked into the national preference for the baroque style and, in particular, the German love of counterpoint.

For more than 50 years prior to Bach's birth the major form in German music, both sacred and secular, had been the slow, formal 'hymn' called the *chorale*. Luther himself wrote many chorales that Bach was later to arrange and elaborate on. Chorales were also the basis for a variety of other forms. One of these variants was the *cantata*. It was defined as essentially a theatrical form by its first major proponent, Pastor Neumeister of Hamburg, in 1700, and as such the cantata was welcomed by the Lutherans who heard it – but the 'theatricality' was intolerable to the Pietists.

It was probably through such innovations as the

Eisenach (below), the town in which Bach was born in 1685 and where Martin Luther attended school. On the middle hill in the background is the Wartburg fortress where Luther took enforced refuge after the Diet of Worms, 1521 when he was placed under the ban of the empire by the Holy Roman Emperor, Charles V. While in the Wartburg Luther completed his translation of the Bible.

Philipp Jakob Spener (above) is acknowledged as the founder of Pietism, a spiritual movement for the revival of piety within the Lutheran doctrine in the 17th century. The Pietists were by no means dour in their devotion, but desired a more personal, direct contact with Christ, without the religious trappings which they saw creeping into Lutheran practices.

Schloß 4. Die Klag 7. Fürstl. Schießgraben. 10. S. Anna Spital. 13. S. Georgen thor. 16. Schloß und Vestung Wartenberg.
kirch. 5. S. Niclaus kirch 8. Prediger Closter 11. Frauwen thor. 14. Predigerthor. 17. Der Modelstein: da zuvor ein Schloß gestanden.
6. Das Klockenhauß 9. S. Maria Stifft. 12. Clacks thor. 15. Die Nüß und Herßel fluß. 18. Hie ist die Eysenacher burg gestanden.

cantata that the musical differences between the two denominations, Lutheranism and Pietism, became more and more perceptible, until finally church music for the two became incompatible. Pietists wrote virulent tracts about the interference caused to meditation by 'bursts of laughter' from screeching Italian sopranos, the total distraction from personal prayer through the 'clashing din of instruments' that drowned both word and thought, and the 'seduction of the ear' by 'carnal' use of intellectual brilliance. They also preferred small prayer-meetings of enthusiasts to formal church services. The Lutherans went on simply developing and enlarging on the sounds and instruments which to them, in their well-established and well-attended church services, constituted an increasingly satisfactory means of worshipping their God.

The separation between these two protestant denominations was regrettable since many people, including Bach, shared sympathies with both the Pietist and orthodox Lutheran points of view. Bach, for instance, as much of his music in later life makes

Bach (left) saw his music as the expression of his deep religious feelings. From 1708–1718 he worked for the Duke of Saxe-Weimar as chamber musician and court organist. For the Duke's daily devotions, which took place in the castle church, known as the 'castle of heaven' (right) he produced some of his best organ music.

quite clear, wanted a warm, personal relationship with his God. He owned many books and tracts based on Pietist sentiments, including one by Spener. However, he and his family held orthodox Lutheran views and attended Lutheran services whenever possible.

Bach's early years

This then was the society, with its religion and musical background, into which Bach was born in Eisenach on 21 March 1685.

Eisenach itself was a great centre of Lutheranism. As a schoolboy Luther himself had stayed in the town at the home of the Cotta family (now called the Lutherhaus). In 1521, because of his reforming activities, Luther was placed under the ban of the empire by the Holy Roman Emperor, Charles V. For his own protection, and under the orders of the Elector of Saxony, he took enforced refuge at the Wartburg just south of Eisenach.

Bach's religion was founded on the views taken in from his family and on the formal religious education he received at school in Eisenach. After the deaths of both parents his musical education continued in the house of his eldest brother Johann Christoph, in Ohrdruf. Johann Christoph was organist at the church of Ohrdruf so it was not surprising that music and religion went hand in hand for Bach.

He attended school at Ohrdruf, studying the *Compendium locorum theologicorum,* a sort of religious instruction course written by the orthodox Lutheran theologian Leonhard Hutter of Wittenberg (and first published in 1610). From Ohrdruf Bach obtained a scholarship to a choir attached to the

For the last 27 years of his life Bach lived and worked in Leipzig (right) where he was Kantor of the Thomasschule and civic music director. The first large-scale choral work which Bach wrote as Kantor was the St John Passion (a page of which is shown below). It was first performed at vespers on Good Friday 1724 in the Nicolaikirche.

Martinsschule in Lüneberg. Here he found himself surrounded by a tremendous wealth of church music past and contemporary at a formative time in his life.

It was probably at Lüneberg that he had his first taste of genuinely secular music. In his own music Bach never made a distinction between what he composed for the church and his compositions for his secular employers. For him, his music was always an expression of his own deep feelings. But here at Lüneberg he was entirely prepared to incorporate elements of influences from France and Italy into what he played and sang. Such 'foreign' innovations were intensely disliked by the Pietists, of course, and not even fully appreciated by the orthodox Lutherans at this time.

Bach's first church post was as organist and Kantor at Arnstadt. Part of his contract there stated that he was to 'take care of the organ, and to cultivate the fear of God, sobriety and a love of peace...' His actual duties were to play the organ for two hours on Sundays, at the Monday intercessions, and at matins on Thursdays; he was also responsible for a small choir at the Latin school.

It was not a happy time for him and for one reason or another his conduct came in for some strong criticism by his employers – the church committee.

From Arnstadt he moved to Mühlhausen where he secured the post of organist at St. Blasius's church. Within four months of taking up the appointment (in June 1707 at the age of 22), he married his first wife, Maria Barbara and settled down to the duties of playing the organ at all services. He was still determined, however, to introduce the new-style cantatas, modelled on Buxtehude's (for his own composing style had not yet matured). One of his first compositions here was *God is my King,* a cantata for the annual inauguration of the city council at the Mary's church. It was also at about this time that he wrote the motet (a form of chorale) *Actus Tragicus.*

Conflict at Mühlhausen

Unfortunately, he again ran into difficulties with his superiors. The pastor at St. Blasius, Johann Frohne, was a Pietist – and one with particularly strong views. It was at this time that Christian Wolff, a philosopher and protégé of Gottfried Liebniz, was becoming active at the town of Halle, a focus for progressive ideas in religion. His theories eventually led to being given the title 'Prince of Enlightenment', and being hailed as the prophet of the age of enlightenment, then about to dawn. His questioning of establishment views led directly to the reinforcement and spread of Pietism – and Pastor Frohne and his congregation were quickly and unreservedly affected.

One of the parishioners of Mühlhausen, Georg Ahle, even published a treatise condemning the very style of music that Bach was attempting to introduce. And although Bach became renowned for his virtuoso organ playing (and his expert advice on organ reconstruction during visits to neighbouring cities), his doctrinal – and therefore musical – differences with his employer caused considerable tension. Further-more, he was known to be on excellent terms with Pastor Frohne's much-disliked 'rival' in the city, the

music was considerable and Bach made special studies of the works of Vivaldi. But whereas such influences had previously inspired him to extravagance in writing and led to rebellion against church authority, now he was able to analyze more maturely what he heard, and even to try and improve upon it. Gradually, his music – just as his choice of themes had done – became less controversial, less ornamented and complex, though no less brilliant. As his style matured he omitted most of the exaggerated innovations on which he had insisted at Arnstadt and Mühlhausen.

From Weimar Bach went to Cöthen as Kapellmeister to Prince Leopold's secular court. While here, his wife Maria Barbara died. Her death came as a shattering blow. Suddenly he had four children to look after by himself. Plunged into grief, his renewed religious faith is expressed in his church music after 1720. It was also during his mourning that he buried himself in teaching the harpsichord to his sons and others. Eighteen months later, though, at the age of 36, he married Anna Magdalena, a singer in court and only seven years older than Bach's eldest daughter. This happy outcome of events after the death of his first wife increased Bach's gratitude to life in general as well as his reverence for God and the church in particular. His own private notebooks of the time are full of thoughts of love and death, and sentiments on scriptural themes.

The title page (far left) of one of a series of secular cantatas written by Bach for performance by the collegium musicum. He dedicated the cantatas to the new Elector of Saxony (below) who was crowned King of Poland on 19th February 1734. Bach probably hoped that he would be offered a position at court, but, in fact, only received a nominal title which involved writing occasional compositions.

orthodox Lutheran Archdeacon Georg Christian Eilmar of St Mary's, who became godfather to the Bach's first child in December 1708. By then, however, Bach had already resigned his post at Mühlhausen.

Organist at Weimar

He was lucky to find a vacancy as court organist to Wilhelm Ernst, Duke of Saxe-Weimar in Weimar. Duke Wilhelm was actually a fervent but rather dour Lutheran. The music he required at his daily devotions was strictly liturgical, and for these Bach wrote many of what are now his most famous cantatas. However, at the time, and perhaps conscious of his previous record, Bach was careful only to choose religious themes which were neither particularly Lutheran nor particularly Pietist.

In effect, Bach was in the process of devising his own personal religion, which was a combination of both Lutheranism and Pietism. Almost all the texts for his cantatas at that time were written by the orthodox Lutheran Salamo Franck – who shared Bach's liking for warm, personal expression of a relationship with God. Perhaps one of the most famous works by both Franck and Bach is the cantata *Komm, du süsse Todesstunde* ('Come, Thou Sweet Hour of Death').

In Weimar Bach began to put together what eventually became a surprisingly full and varied library of both Lutheran and Pietist books. However, although his personal religious commitment was taking firm shape, it was here he wrote cantatas which had a more secular starting point than those written for use in church. The well-known aria *Sheep May Safely Graze,* generally thought to refer to the Good Shepherd, is in fact part of a cantata extolling the Duke of Weimar's hunting prowess.

In music as well as in religion, then, Bach was aware of his own principles and standards and was able to use new influences in a more mature way. At the court, the influence of Italian and French styles of

The frontispiece (below) of the Musicalisches Lexicon written by Johann Gottfried Walther, a second cousin of Bach's, illustrates the atmosphere of the church concerts for which Bach composed.

The mature years

He left Cöthen in 1723 to become Kantor at St Thomas's in Leipzig. He was obliged to undergo a doctrinal examination in June 1722 and even before he got the job, to agree to some restrictive conditions imposed by the city councillors. The Kantor was the musical director for all five churches in the city; the population was generally Lutheran – but most of the clergy and also many of the Leipzig city councillors were Pietists.

At Leipzig, Bach settled down to write music for performance in the five churches under his direction. The first major work he produced during this period was the *St John Passion,* first performed in April 1724. During the next 20 years he is thought to have completed no fewer than 295 cantatas.

In this role it seemed that Bach could indulge his own enthusiasm for writing music in a fashion that related all the way back to the traditions of Luther himself. In particular, he could use the special combination of notes, chords or tempi according to the late medieval practices of 'musica theorica' and 'musica prattica': each musical figure was symbolic – one might represent the Trinity, another a specific aspect of Christ, and so on.

Even as he delighted in the musical theory of a bygone age – and was regarded as very old-fashioned for doing so – he was also refining his composition in a very contemporary way. His refinements, although suggesting a scenic background to the meaning of the words accompanying the music, resulted in a distinctly intellectual effect. This is evident in works like the *Christmas Oratorio* and the *Magnificat.*

In Leipzig, most of Bach's cantata texts were produced by the local Commissioner of the Post Office, Friedrich Henrici (who wrote under the name Picander). It was he who provided the text for the *St Matthew Passion,* first performed on Good Friday 1729. Although the work is thought of by many as the peak of Bach's church composition, the performance created a furore. Pietists in the congregation – all influential – hated it, finding it intolerably 'distracting'.

Bach enlarges his library

Whether a response to this reaction and criticism or not, at this time Bach greatly enlarged his collection of books on theology. He already possessed most of the works of Luther. In 1733 he purchased a version of Luther's Bible with a commentary, published in three volumes, by the theologian and mystic Abraham Calov of Wittenberg. His underlinings and marginal notes in the Bible make it clear that he gave it a very careful reading. Other spiritual publications Bach acquired at this time became the sources for later cantatas, though he occasionally changed the emphasis on these texts from strictly orthodox Lutheran to something between that and Pietism.

In the hope that he might obtain a position at court, Bach wrote two movements, the Kyrie and Gloria, of the *B Minor Mass* and presented them to the new Elector of Saxony, Friedrich August, who became King of Poland. Unfortunately, the only title he received was that of court composer.

Bach's life and work in Leipzig was often punctuated with disputes between himself and the church council. As before, these disputes usually arose because of differences between a strictly Lutheran and a Pietist approach to religious practice. Further Pietist condemnation came in 1737 from Johann Adolf Scheibe in Hamburg, who wrote scathingly about Bach's method of composition, although the controversy which followed ended with Scheibe being conciliatory and conceding that Bach was a skilled performer.

Whatever criticism he received in his time from those who did not share his religious views, Bach nevertheless continued to produce music which he saw as reflecting his own personal spiritual feelings.

Frederick the Great

Vain, sarcastic and cynical, Frederick II of Prussia was often outstandingly disagreeable. But his delight in culture and civilized values provided a lighter counterpoint to his dark soul.

With his father's example before him it was a wonder that Frederick the Great of Prussia had any interest in intellectual pursuits at all. His father, King Frederick William I, was one of the most determined and outrageous philistines ever to wear a crown. During the 18th century many of the rulers of the scattered principalities of divided Germany sought to add to their prestige by building palaces and opera houses, and by patronizing artists and musicians. But Frederick William was a maverick who abhorred all such cultural pursuits. He closed the Berlin Academy to economize, despised opera and classical learning, and devoted his reign to building a large, perfectly drilled army.

Because French was the language of literature and France the home of the arts, both were cordially loathed by this militaristic king, who expressed his distaste by dressing up condemned criminals in French fashions before sending them to the executioner. His idea of an evening's entertainment was to smoke and drink too much with a select circle of male friends before rounding off the day with an attack on the wretch whose duty it was to read the newspapers aloud. On occasions this servant – by all accounts a masochistic man – was set on fire, thrown out of the window, or hurled into the moat.

Father and son

Friction between this 'royal drill-master' and Crown Prince Frederick was assured. The king of Prussia loved to hunt and drink while his heir loathed both. The situation got far worse when it became apparent that the young Frederick loved French literature, adored music and longed to study the classics, and his father's treatment of him soon degenerated into an attempt to break his will by physical violence. As a youth Frederick was physically attacked, verbally abused in public and occasionally starved. Frederick William's brutal treatment reached its peak when he had Frederick's closest friend executed in front of his eyes for trying to help the crown prince escape from his odious court. But this horrific incident seemed almost to exhaust the king's malice towards his son, who was then allowed to marry and set up his own home at Rheinsberg.

Frederick William chose the young Princess

Though a difficult personality to his friends and family, Frederick the Great (left) was an excellent ruler who was idolized by the people of Prussia.

Frederick William I was most at home at his nightly tobacco evenings (right). But his sensitive and intellectual son found these rowdy, beer-swilling occasions an ordeal.

Frederick William I of Prussia (far left) was a fat and fierce little man who made his family's life a misery. His wife, Queen Sophia Dorothea (left), had a much gentler personality but she had little influence over her overbearing bully of a husband. A daughter of George I of England, she told everyone that her husband was mad and that she went in fear of her life.

When Frederick William found out about his heir's escape plan, he flew into such a temper that he was barely restrained from drawing his sword on young Frederick the Great (below). As a brutal climax to his punishment, Frederick was forced to witness the execution of the friend who had been his accomplice (below left).

Elizabeth of Brunswick-Wolfenbüttel as his son's bride, and although Frederick was not entirely enchanted by this choice he assented to the match. The old house at Rheinsberg was extensively re-modelled in the light and airy fashion of the day before Frederick and his wife were able to move in during 1736. After this there were almost five years during which the crown prince was able to follow his inclinations towards culture and learning on the tacit

In order to get a household of his own Frederick married Princess Elizabeth Christine of Brunswick-Wolfenbüttel (right), a shy woman who was devoted to him even though he had little interest in her. The newly-weds were given a charming country house at Rheinsberg (above). Here, Frederick was at last able to enjoy poetry, witty repartee, flute sonatas, wine and the company of fascinating foreigners without interference from his blustering father.

understanding that his way of life would never be unconventional enough to provoke his father. So although Frederick the Great was probably bisexual with his homosexual tendencies very much the dominant ones, he lived uncomplainingly with his dull wife and tried, unsuccessfully, to beget an heir. His father had promised him that he would be allowed to travel abroad once the succession to the throne was secure.

The years at Rheinsberg were to be a pleasant interlude in Frederick's life; the violence he experienced in his father's household was behind him and his own nature had not yet soured into bitter cynicism. Indeed he seems to have been motivated by a certain well-intentioned naivety, an idealism that would have made him snort with derision a few years later. He read a great deal and summed up his feelings and ambitions when he wrote to the Prince of Schaumburg-Lippe: 'Good intentions, love of mankind, and the hard work of a solitary can perhaps be beneficial to society and I flatter myself that I am not among its idle, useless members.'

An enlightened prince

In addition to Frederick acquiring a reputation for high-mindedness, he chose forms of relaxation that were a great deal more refined than those favoured by his oafish father. Every evening at Rheinsberg there was a concert unless the household performed a play. Chief performer at these concerts was Frederick himself who was an enthusiastic but somewhat erratic performer on the flute.

Witnesses conflict over Frederick's ability as a musician. He was certainly devoted to the flute and usually managed to practise for several hours every day. He also composed passably well and some of his pieces are still played, while his march 'Hohenfriedberg' is quite well known. On the other hand, many who heard him play recalled that his

music teacher, the composer Johann Joachim Quantz, coughed loudly whenever he played the wrong note and that this coughing was often rather frequent. Carl Philipp Emanuel Bach, who was recruited to the resident musicians at Rheinsberg as a cembalist, was said to have been literally tortured by his royal patron's dreadful playing. But plenty of disinterested members of his audience recorded that he was rather accomplished. Whatever the truth may have been, it is evident that music was a great entertainment and solace to Frederick throughout his life.

While he was crown prince Frederick was not rich but he was able to make modest attempts to patronize the arts. Many members of his household (in particular his cook) were French, and German was not used as a language by any of them. This arrangement, which would have provoked monstrous anger in Frederick William had he known of it, was at least partly in deference to the supremacy of French culture. Frederick was able to persuade the French painter Antoine Pesne to settle at Rheinsberg and he left many portraits of the crown prince and his small court. His favourite architect was the German soldier Georg Wenzeslaus von Knobelsdorff, who found his inspiration in the classic proportions of Ancient Greece.

This cultivation of the artistic side of life soon became known throughout Europe and Rheinsberg was visited by members of fashionable, international society, who would not have dreamed of staying at the court of the king of Prussia. As a final polish to the Rheinsberg idyll Frederick was able to begin a correspondence with François Marie Arouet Voltaire, the great sage of the Enlightenment.

'Your Humanity'

Voltaire's undoubted genius made him the most towering figure in contemporary European

Johann Joachim Quantz (above) was a composer and Frederick's music teacher. He improved the design of the flute, his royal master's favourite instrument.

Frederick was generally acknowledged to have been an accomplished flautist (above), although his timing was sometimes alleged to have been erratic. His compositions included flute sonatas (below), some of which are still played. In old age he lost too many teeth to be able to play and he consoled himself with an extra hour's sleep.

literature and a highly influential philosopher. Basically, Voltaire believed that tolerance and the exercise of humanity were both right and enjoyable, but he went rather further than earlier humanist philosophers had done because he ignored the traditional role of religion in morality. Indeed he was actively anti-religious, arguing that much cruelty and persecution sprang from religious bigotry. In addition to having these civilized ideals, Voltaire was a great wit whose sparkling conversation was famous and whose barbed plays and books had an enormous readership. Although he was highly honoured in France in his lifetime he was never to achieve a stable respectability because of his outspoken anti-clericalism and a rather sophisticated sex life, which was often considered immoral.

Frederick's unusually solemn opening letter to this brilliant Frenchman was siezed upon with delight. Voltaire had a number of little weaknesses of which snobbery and a rather grasping nature were among the most prominent. He was flattered to be sought out by a future king and, of equal importance, a king who would inherit one of the few full treasuries in Europe. He replied in terms of the highest praise and at a later stage in the correspondence he hailed Frederick as a prince-philosopher, referring to him as 'Your Humanity' rather than 'Your Majesty'. It was out of the question for Voltaire to visit Rheinsberg – as he was both immoral and French it would have caused some act of wild violence by King Frederick William – but through his letters he exercised considerable influence over the young crown prince.

An indication of this was Frederick's own start in literary composition, which culminated in the celebrated *Anti-Machiavel*. In this work Frederick criticized the ruthless philosophy of the Renaissance theorist, Machiavelli, and argued that armed aggression was immoral and that duplicity would

In 1736 Frederick began his famous correspondence with the great French man of letters, Voltaire (above). Voltaire thought it a 'miracle' that 'the son of a crowned ogre, brought up with the beasts of the field, should understand the subtleties of Paris'.

serve a ruler badly. All in all, Frederick gave a convincing impression of a decent, civilized man of cultivated tastes whose reign was likely to be wise and peaceful. Yet it was vanity as much as his love of learning that drove Frederick on (he rather liked the image of himself as a philosopher and wit), and when he came to the throne, this same vanity would make him adopt a very different character.

The accession

When King Frederick William died in May 1740 a great restraint was removed from his oldest son. A ruthlessly executed separation from his wife was almost Frederick's first concern. His queen was expected to live at Berlin during the winter and at Schönhausen during the summer while Frederick moved to Potsdam and rarely saw her, behaving with the utmost coldness whenever he did. The new king also wrote to Count Francesco Algarotti, a handsome Italian philosopher whose best-known work was a popularization of Newton's theories on optics called *Neutonianismo per le dame*, begging him to join him as soon as possible.

Combining scientific knowledge with a love of art and music, Algarotti had been a welcome visitor to Rheinsberg and he was now briefly to become an intimate friend of Frederick's. However, it was soon apparent that the king of Prussia and his boon companion could not be absolutely carefree in their behaviour. On a pleasure trip to the French town of Strasbourg both men adopted aliases which failed to deceive the town's governor, the Marechal de Broglie. The governor managed to end the escapade in a humiliating way by sending for Frederick and offering to receive him with full honours. This was Frederick's only visit to the country he regarded as the centre of civilization.

But the complications of his unorthodox emotional life did not stop Frederick from bringing some humane reforms to his kingdom. He abolished the torture of civilians, decreed tolerance of all religions and allowed complete freedom of speech and expression by ending censorship. The Berlin Academy was reopened and the French philosopher, Pierre Louis Moreau de Maupertuis, was made its president on the recommendation of Voltaire. (The two Frenchmen professed to be great friends at this stage, though they eventually fell out because of Maupertuis's involvement with one of Voltaire's mistresses.) Frederick found Maupertuis amusing but lacking the brilliance of his rival, whom he now contrived to meet. In 1740 the new king of Prussia and Voltaire met in the Duchy of Cleves, enjoying a three-day 'honeymoon' in each other's company.

The seizure of Silesia

In those first months Frederick seemed set fair to become the enlightened monarch his inclinations promised but at the same time there were hints that he was, after all, his father's son. Upon his father's death, Frederick disbanded the famous Giant Grenadiers, a regiment of freakishly tall soldiers that had been Frederick William's pride and joy. But far from being a gesture against militarism, this was in fact an economizing measure of real benefit to the Prussian army because the money saved was used to raise 10,000 fresh soldiers of the line and to increase the supply of munitions. And soon the new king showed his true colours.

Within five months of his accession, Hapsburg Emperor Charles VI died leaving his family lands in

Germany, Italy, Austria and Hungary to his young daughter Maria Theresa, as well as an agreement that her husband would be elected to his imperial title. All this had been solemnly ratified in treaties with the great powers, treaties to which Prussia was a signatory. However, Frederick's desire for the rich province of Silesia was so great and his longing for military glory so strong that he ordered his army into Silesia and siezed it from Maria Theresa. This started an episodic war which soon involved France and England and other German states, and which lasted, with long periods of peace, for almost two decades. The first round in the engagements ended for Prussia when Frederick faithlessly abandoned his allies and made a separate peace with Maria Theresa in June 1742. He had acquired all the territory he had gone to war for, a beautiful province about one-third the size of England, together with the reputation of a magnificent soldier and the character of an immoral cynic. 'Ambition, self-interest and the desire to hear my name spoken outweighed other considerations,'

On his accession Frederick disbanded the Giant Grenadiers, a regiment of super-tall soldiers (right) which had obsessed his 'drill-master' father.

the philosopher-king later confessed, 'and I decided for war.'

Far from feeling remorse, Frederick tended to revel in his new image as a hard-headed realist. His tendency to tease his chosen companions, to dwell on their weaknesses and to be disparaging about their motives became steadily more pronounced. But by 1742 these unpleasing characteristics were only beginning to develop and Frederick found it easy to attract the famous and artistic to his court as he turned his mind to the arts of peace.

Among the king's new friends was the Marquis Jean-Baptiste de Boyer d'Argens, whose passionate interest in painting and the theatre was infectious. He was made director of the Comédie-Française de Berlin. Pesne was commissioned to paint the ceilings of the palace of Charlottenburg and Knobelsdorff designed a fine opera house. Best of all, Frederick managed to attract Voltaire to Berlin, and the irascible Frenchman was so enchanted by the attention shown him – by the concerts, operas and things of beauty – that he proposed to make Prussia his permanent home. All this was most agreeable to Frederick but, in 1744, the dispute with Austria-Hungary flared up again and he was forced to

The Battle of Fontenoy (above) from the French point of view. Marshal Saxe, whose book on warfare was always by Frederick's bed, led the French forces to victory over the English at this battle in 1745. Fontenoy was a crucial fight in the long, episodic war that had started in 1740 after Frederick seized the Austrian province of Silesia. The Austrian empress, Maria Theresa (left), called Frederick a 'monster' but when she died in 1780 he claimed that though he had fought her, he had never been her enemy.

Frederick's dream palace at Potsdam, Sans Souci (right), was finished in 1747 and became his favourite home. Under the terraced greenhouses he grew the Mediterranean flowers and fruit that he loved.

mobilize his forces and, once again, go through the expensive business of making war.

Frederick in the field

By December 1745 the Prussian armies had gained enough crushing victories for Frederick to conclude another advantageous peace. His military reputation was very high indeed as he was an aggressive, confident commander who led the best equipped and most experienced force in Europe. In the kingdom of Prussia war was a deadly serious business for which the state was carefully prepared. Not all the great powers of Europe competed with quite the same dedication. The English tended to use their army as a holding centre for society's more violent misfits led by their most dangerous and least intellectual aristocrats, and the French frequently showed an insane adherence to outmoded concepts of chivalry.

Between them the French (who were Frederick's allies) and their English opponents mounted one of the 18th century's grimmer comedies at the battle of Fontenoy in May 1745. As the massed ranks of both sides approached to a lethal closeness, French and English officers capered about between the lines in an ecstasy of politeness, offering each other the honour of firing first. The English were quicker to tire of this pantomime and their grinning redcoats mowed down the French Guards with savage zeal. However, the last laugh lay with the French who won the battle handsomely; the English were so poorly led and badly trained that they were virtually incapable of large-scale manoeuvre – Frederick reckoned them and their commander no better than animals.

Great commander though he was himself, Frederick became less and less keen on fighting. As king of Prussia it was his habit to describe himself as the first servant of the state and it was evident enough that in most cases war was a damaging business for his people and country. At the end of 1745 he hoped that his territorial gains had been consolidated and

that his active military career was over. Once more he turned to building up his state and establishing a civilized way of life for himself.

The symbol of this lighter side of Frederick's life is the pleasure palace of Sans Souci (which translates as 'carefree'), which he and Knobelsdorff designed and built outside Potsdam. The pink and white building stands at the top of a slope, above terraces which are all glassed over so that they are reminiscent of a cascade. Frederick moved into Sans Souci in May 1747 and established an informal, almost entirely masculine court – the queen was never invited there.

The king now ran his life to a demanding schedule which made room both for long hours of work for the state and for his favourite diversions. He was always woken at 4 a.m., which he did not enjoy much, and his servants were instructed to throw cold water on his face if they found him dozing off. After he had enjoyed a brief musical session on the spinet, he turned to dealing with his voluminous mail. Next, he gave his day's orders to an aide and was ready by 10 a.m. to direct military exercises or catch up with his personal correspondence. He dined at noon and liked his company to be as entertaining as possible. In the afternoon he did administrative work and took exercises – usually a brisk walk. He practised the flute as much as four times a day which, despite his early start, ended late: supper was at 10 p.m. and this was usually followed by a concert.

It was an exhausting routine primarily dedicated to the service of the Prussian state and under this self-imposed slavery Frederick may well have felt himself entitled to his few hours of pleasure and entertainment. He imported wits, singers, actors, musicians and dancers to join his court. (The famous dancer Barbarina had a notable triumph in that she was reputed to have had affairs with both the king

The seductive Algarotti (above), to whom Frederick wrote when his father had died: 'I await you with impatience – don't leave me to languish.'

This Meissen centrepiece (right) was commissioned by Frederick in 1761. He was fond of fine porcelain and set up his own china factory at Berlin in 1763.

Sans Souci (left and far left) was a very personal palace where Frederick enjoyed the elegance that reminded him of Paris. Many of its interiors were decorated in the fashionable rococo style, which is characterized by the use of pale colours, including gold, mirrors, and naturalistic motifs such as clouds, foliage and birds.

Frederick's court was decidedly homosexual, for he liked to be surrounded by what one ambassador called 'he-muses'. The dancer La Barbarina (left) was one of the few women invited to Sans Souci.

and Algarotti.) Of his musical visitors the most distinguished was undoubtedly Johann Sebastian Bach who spent an evening at Sans Souci and later improvised a fugue on a theme given him by the king. While music was undoubtedly of great importance to the king, his chief pleasure was probably in witty conversation. But after all the promises and hesitations it was not until 1750 that Voltaire actually decided to make his home in Prussia. Once there, he and Frederick kept each other much amused for a short while until their relationship began to sour.

The Seven Years War
By 1756 Frederick was once more at war in the most disastrous, long drawn-out and desperate struggle of his reign. He was in the impossible position of fighting all the great continental powers at once with the English as his only allies. For this situation he could thank the misfiring of his cynical self-interest and his waspish wit. Maria Theresa had never forgiven him the robbery of Silesia and was able to make common cause with the king of France and the empress of Russia. Their hostility towards Prussia owed quite a bit to the stinging remarks which its king frequently made about them and which were freely reported to them. The English were delighted by the whole business and merely supported Frederick financially and with a minimum of troops while they overran France's overseas colonies.

The Seven Years War was a long torture to Frederick who was only just able to prevent the destruction of his state. His endless string of victories hardly dented the massive resources of his foes while his own army was constantly whittled away. Frederick's sombre letters to his friends reflect the nightmare he lived through in every desperate year until the death of the empress of Russia in 1762 dissolved the coalition against him. He survived this traumatic experience by 24 years but it left its mark on him, giving him an even sourer nature and a deep pessimism.

Frederick (centre) converses with Voltaire (in the lilac coat) and other cronies over dinner at Sans Souci. The king loved entertaining clever men and his visitors' accounts of him suggest that although he was capable of extraordinary rudeness, he was also a charming host in congenial company. Frederick the Great was always hardest on himself and was basically kind. As an old man he travelled extremely slowly in a battered carriage so as not to exhaust the elderly soldiers who formed his personal guard, and his last words were an instruction to his servants to throw a quilt over one of his dogs, which was shivering with cold.

Old Fritz

But this second half of Frederick's reign held achievements just as great as the military conquests and humane reforms of the early years. Prussia was able to flourish again after the ravages of the Seven Years War and she owed much of this to the tireless work of the man who became known as 'Old Fritz' to his people. He was very miserly over some things and became rather scruffy in appearance with his uniform covered in dog hairs and his boots unblacked. He drove himself hard with long hours of work, which he tried to continue into the last day of his life, and he was enormously popular with the Prussian people, although he always maintained that this meant nothing to him. At set times of the year he held military manoeuvres or visited parts of his sprawling domains. In fact it was a pouring wet day at army manoeuvres that brought on the fever that eventually killed him.

After his death in August 1786 Frederick became one of the heroes of Germany, immortalized as a brilliant and resourceful soldier as well as a tireless and unbending servant of the state. His constant self-denial and disinterested humanity certainly made him a remarkable ruler by any standards. He was often coarse and had a vitriolic tongue yet the solace that he found in the arts showed his commitment to civilized values, and his enlightened stewardship of Prussia raised the standards of European government.

George Frideric Handel
1685–1759

*Handel's search for a free musical climate took
him to England, a country he adopted as his home
and where he exercised his talents on a vast range
of vocal and instrumental works.*

One of the greatest composers of the Baroque period, George Frideric Handel was born on 23 February, 1685, in Halle, Germany. His father, Georg, a highly respected barber-surgeon, was 63 when his second wife, Dorothea Taust, gave birth to their son.

The young Handel soon showed a keen interest in music though he was not encouraged by his father, probably because he thought that a career in law would offer more prospects and stability.

Not much is known about Handel's early years, but Handel later told his first biographer that his father would not let him have access to a musical instrument. So he smuggled a clavichord up into the loft of the house – a small, gentle-toned keyboard instrument – on which he could practise secretly. Nevertheless, his talents must have been impressive for at some time during his childhood he was taken to the ducal court of nearby Saxe-Weissenfels, where the duke heard him play and advised his father to have him properly taught. This task fell into the hands of F. W. Zachow, organist of the Halle Liebfrauenkirche, who tutored Handel during his time as a pupil at the local grammar school. From this respected and gifted composer he received a basic grounding in the techniques of composition.

After his father's death in 1697, Handel continued his studies for a career in law, but by the time he was 17 he was an accomplished musician, a brilliant organist and harpsichordist, and had a number of compositions behind him. So when he entered the University of Halle he was at the same time appointed organist of the Domkirche in Halle. The composer Telemann was also a student at Halle and their friendship dates from this period.

Hamburg

In 1703, only a year after entering the University, he gave up his law studies and moved from Halle to the bustling commercial city of Hamburg. Unlike most German centres at that time, Hamburg was a free city, not dominated by a prince or ruler – and it had a public opera house. Handel made a living taking pupils and playing second violin and then harpsi-

Georg Handel (above), father of the composer, hoped his son would have a legal career. Handel studied law for a year at the University of Halle and at the same time was organist at the Cathedral. In 1703 he gave up his studies and job to make his way in Hamburg (right).

chord in the opera-house orchestra. He made many friends here, notably, Reinhard Keiser, the talented composer who directed the opera, and Johann Mattheson, a young composer and music commentator. Despite the fact that at one time Handel and Mattheson quarrelled, and even fought a duel, their friendship endured. Mattheson later recalled that Handel was a weak melodist, that he composed lengthy arias and interminable cantatas, but was a good writer of harmony and counterpoint. Mattheson also remarked that he found Handel to be a strong and independent character with a 'natural inclination to dry humour'.

Both young men applied for the post of organist at the nearby city of Lübeck. However, after visiting Lübeck it seems that both were put off by one of the conditions of the job: marriage to the unattractive daughter of the organist, Buxtehude.

Back in Hamburg, Handel began composing his first opera, *Almira,* which was enthusiastically received when performed in 1705. His second and third operas were less successful: the third was too long and had to be split into two operas, *Florindo* and *Daphne.* By the time they were produced in Hamburg Handel had gone to Italy, at the instigation of the son of the Grand Duke of Tuscany.

He arrived in Florence in the autumn of 1706 and

travelled to Rome soon after. Here he quickly made important friends among the Roman aristocracy. His first oratorio (a musical setting of a sacred subject) was composed and performed in Rome in 1707, and by May 1707 he was in the employ of the Marquis Francesco Ruspoli, as household musician. His chief duty was to supply cantatas for the Marquis's weekly concerts. His largest work for Ruspoli was an oratorio, *La Resurrezione,* performed at Easter, 1708. He also wrote a great deal of church music for Ruspoli including a brilliant and imaginative setting of the *Dixit Dominus.*

As his reputation spread, he received invitations to all the main musical centres of Italy. At the end of 1709 he visited Venice, where his opera, *Agrippina,* received great acclaim and was performed no fewer than 27 times. His visit to Italy was successful on many levels, above all because he became so fluent in the Italian operatic style, but he also made a number of important contacts. One of these was Prince Ernst August of Hanover, the brother of the Elector of Hanover, Georg Ludwig, the future King George I of England. Another was the Duke of Manchester, the English ambassador to Venice.

Both men encouraged Handel to visit their respective countries, and when he left Italy in 1710, he went to Hanover as head of music at the Elector's

One of the influential people Handel met in Italy was the Duke of Manchester, whose splendid arrival in Venice is shown above. The Duke was the English Ambassador to Venice in 1707. He told Handel much about England and strongly encouraged him to come and see it for himself.

court. One of the conditions Handel made before he took up the post, was that he should be granted 12 months' leave to visit London, which even at this stage seemed to be the place which attracted him most. His employer raised no objections – after all, he knew he himself was likely to be going to London as King when Queen Anne died.

First visit to London

Handel's visit to London lasted eight months. He arrived in London late in 1710 and, probably because of his Hanoverian connections, was warmly received at Queen Anne's court where he gave at least one concert. However, his sights were set on the opera, and his first London opera, *Rinaldo,* was produced in February 1711. It was a huge success, despite the ridicule of critics who thought the idea of performing Italian opera in England absurd.

Handel directed all the performances from the harpsichord, and dazzled the audiences with the

Handel's royal employer, the Elector of Hanover, was crowned King George I of England and Scotland (left) in 1714 on the death of Queen Anne.

The London to which Handel was attracted was a place where people took a lively interest in enjoying themselves. A great cross-section of people spent their leisure time in the relaxed atmosphere of the city's many parks and gardens, as reflected by this painting.

Handel's compositions, like the Suites de Pieces pour le Clavecin *(below), were published by a variety of people, not always with his permission. In 1720 Handel obtained a 14-year copyright privilege, but as this gave him little protection against pirate publishers, he dropped it in 1724. His problems were not only with publishers: some professional musicians gave performances of his works without consulting or paying him. His most successful way of stopping this practice was to revise and enlarge the original scores and then give performance of the 'new' works.*

brilliance of his playing. During this visit to London he met the assistant manager of the opera, J. J. Heidegger and his niece, Mary Granville, then aged 10, who became a life-long friend and admirer. He also attended many concerts and performed regularly at private concerts, among them those given by Thomas Britton, a music-loving coal merchant.

The London opera season finished in June and Handel hastened back to Germany. Apart from some time in Halle, visiting his family, he spent 15 months working in Hanover producing chamber and orchestral works before returning to England. He had agreed with Prince Georg Ludwig, the Elector, that he would return to Hanover within a reasonable period of time, but he had been learning English and was greatly attracted by the musical opportunities offered in London, so it is likely that when he arrived in London in the autumn of 1712 he had every intention of settling there. In fact, he spent the next 50 years living in London.

In London, Handel quickly produced two new Italian operas: *Il pastor fido* in 1712 and *Teseo* early in 1713. He dedicated the libretto (the text of an opera, written usually by a commissioned librettist) of *Teseo* to the young Earl of Burlington, a leading patron of the arts. From 1713 to 1716 Handel lived in Burlington House in Piccadilly. Here the earl and his mother entertained many of the important literary figures of the day, including Alexander Pope and John Gay. Handel spent his days composing and in the evenings played for the Burlington guests. During this time he also composed a number of church works, including a *Te Deum* and *Jubilate* to celebrate the Peace of Utrecht. He also wrote a birthday ode for Queen Anne which was performed in 1713, her last birthday.

Queen Anne died in August 1714, and was succeeded by George I, the Elector of Hanover from whom Handel had played truant. Much has been written about Handel's truancy and the King's

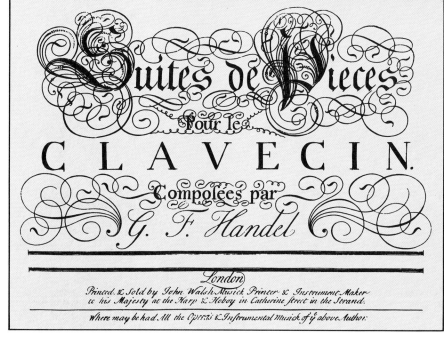

Suites de Pieces

Pour le

CLAVECIN.

Composées par

G. F. Handel

London

Printed & Sold by John Walsh Musick Printer & Instrument Maker to his Majesty at the Harp & Hoboy in Catherine street in the Strand.

Where may be had All the Opera's & Instrumental Musick of ÿ above Author.

supposed anger. One anecdote suggests that the *Water Music* was composed to pacify the monarch who, it is said, found himself being serenaded from a neighbouring barge during a water party on the Thames. Another story has it that the Italian violinist Geminiani helped restore Handel to favour by insisting that only Handel could accompany him when he played before the King.

In fact, George I was probably not in the least cross with Handel: within days of his arrival in London he heard some of Handel's music, and one of his first actions was to double Handel's salary as royal music master. Whether or not there was a water party with music in 1715, such an event did take place two years later and it was probably then that the well known *Water Music* was composed.

In 1716 Handel made a brief visit to Germany to see his family in Halle. He also went to Ansbach where he met an old University friend, J. C. Schmidt, and invited him back to London as his copyist and secretary. Schmidt, or Smith, as he soon became, and his son remained Handel's faithful friends and assistants to the end of his life, although there were times when Handel was not always well disposed to the elder Smith.

London becomes an opera centre

By the end of 1716 Handel was back in London supervising the revival of two of his operas. In the summer of 1717 he moved out of London to Edgware, when he became resident composer of the Earl of Carnarvon (later the Duke of Chandos), at his splendid country house, Cannons. Handel was there until 1720, during which time he composed 11 anthems for the chapel as well as two dramatic works: the pastoral serenade *Acis and Galatea,* and the first of his dramatic works on biblical subjects in English, a musical treatment of the story of Esther. There was no opportunity for writing opera at Cannons but it was still uppermost in Handel's mind.

Up to this time, though operas were frequently performed, no permanent opera centre existed in London. But many wealthy patrons of the arts were interested in creating one. Their discussions resulted in the establishment of the Royal Academy of Music, a commercial as well as artistic venture. The King was a patron and many leading noblemen, including Burlington, supported it. Handel was appointed the musical director and early in 1719 he went to the continent to sign up a team of singers. He made a brief stop in Halle (Bach went there to see him, but Handel left before he arrived!) but his main port of call was the court of Dresden where he persuaded several of the leading soloists to work in London.

Handel's career over the next few years reflects the ups and downs of opera in London as it came into and went out of favour.

Handel's activities from 1720 to 1728 centred around the King's Theatre in the Haymarket, which was the home of the Academy. During this time he composed a series of operas, including many of his finest works. In 1723 he moved into a handsome house in Brook Street, near Grosvenor Square and in 1726 became a naturalized British subject. The

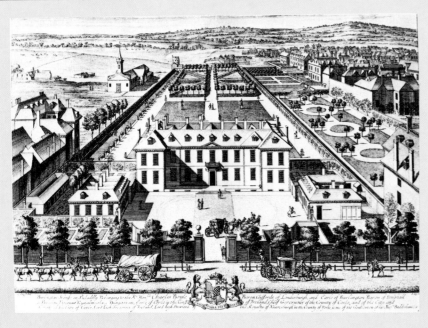

Handel lived at Burlington House (left) in Piccadilly from 1713 to 1716 as the guest of his friend, the young Earl of Burlington. Then aged 18, the Earl was already one of the leading patrons of art and literature in London.

A caricature (above) of some of the resident singers engaged by Handel for the Royal Academy of Music. Seen here (left to right) are Senesino, Cuzzoni and Berenstadt.

The first opera Handel wrote for his London début was Rinaldo *(top centre, painting of Rinaldo under the spell of Almirena by Tiepolo). The scenario was drafted by Aaron Hill, a dramatist and the manager of the Queen's Theatre, Haymarket where the opera was first performed on 24 February 1711. It was a huge success and received a further 15 performances during the season.*

following year he was commissioned to write anthems for George II's coronation in Westminster Abbey. One of these anthems, *Zadok the Priest,* has been performed at every coronation since then.

Collapse of the Academy

However, not everything went smoothly for the Royal Academy of Music. Its directors were often at odds with each other and there were increasing financial problems. There were scandals and public scenes involving some of the singers, which damaged the prestige of the Academy and the audiences frequently behaved badly – their cat calls and disturbances hardly added to the atmosphere. As a result, the Royal Academy of Music ran out of money in the summer of 1728.

Handel did not suffer much from the demise of the Academy, since he was a salaried employee, not the proprietor. He also received salaries from the Royal family and since 1723 had been employed as a composer to the Chapel Royal. However, he still wished to have his operas performed, so he entered into a contract with the former opera house manager, J. J. Heidegger and the Director of the Academy agreed to let the King's Theatre to him for five years. Some of his new operas met with mild success though his singers did not always impress the audience.

Handel's last year of tenure at the King's Theatre saw the formation by a group of noblemen and musicians of a rival opera company called the Opera of the Nobility. Heidegger let the King's Theatre to his new group in 1734, and Handel transferred his own opera company to a newer theatre in Covent Garden. In the summer he visited Oxford (he was offered a doctorate in music, but declined to accept it) and gave oratorios including the new *Athalia,* in the Sheldonian theatre.

He continued to direct his energies and his genius, primarily towards opera and early 1735 saw the production of two of his supreme operas, *Ariodante* and *Alcina.* It was not until 1737 that the crash came, and both Handel's opera company and the Opera of

John Christopher Smith (above) or Johann Christoph Schmidt as he was originally known, was a friend from Handel's university days. In 1716 Handel persuaded him to leave Ansbach, where he was involved in the wool trade, and come to London to work for him as copyist and secretary.

the Nobility closed – financially devastated by lack of popular support.

Just before this, Handel had suffered what might have been a stroke or an attack of severe rheumatism. Partly paralysed, he made a journey to Aix-la Chapelle, to take the baths.

By October he made an amazing recovery and within a couple of weeks was at work on a new opera. His old impresario colleague, Heidegger, who had briefly defected to the Nobility, was now back at the King's Theatre and he engaged Handel as composer and Director. However, although Handel composed

The portly Handel (above) was known for his vast appetite, but the cartoon (left) by Goupy upset him. Handel is depicted as a pig, because after a frugal meal together, during which Handel told Goupy of his financial difficulties, he saw Handel drinking Burgundy on his own! Goupy left the house angrily and published this cartoon a few days later.

of six had been published in 1738), were intended for performance between the acts of oratorios. Indeed, Handel's playing of organ concertos became one of the attractions at his oratorio performances from this time on.

Dublin and Messiah
Handel's last operas, given in the 1740–41 season, were total failures and from then on he withdrew from the opera scene. His English works given about the same time had scarcely more success so it was not surprising that rumours became rife that he was planning to leave England. Whether Handel intended to leave England or not, an invitation from Dublin, to give performances came opportunely, and during summer, 1741, he prepared himself by writing a new work. He had, it seems, been asked to prepare a work for a performance in aid of Dublin charities and for this he chose a sacred topic: the coming of the Messiah. He also composed *Samson,* a new oratorio partly based on the poems of Milton.

Handel arrived in Dublin in November 1741. Just before Christmas, he embarked upon his first six-concert subscription series which were greatly enjoyed. In a letter home to Charles Jennens, the man who had compiled the texts for *Messiah* and other works, Handel expressed his delight with his Dublin success. However the climax of his trip to Dublin came on 13 April 1742 with the first performance of *Messiah.*

Oratorios in London
Handel was back in London at the end of summer 1742, with a welcome success behind him after the tribulations of the preceding years. From now on his life took a more regular pattern. He had given up opera (though he had tempting offers to return to it), and now pursued an idea that may have been suggested by the success of his subscription series in Dublin. He directed almost all his energies towards organizing an oratorio season, each Lent, at Covent Garden. That of 1743, with *Samson* as its main attraction, was a success, although the inclusion of *Messiah* did it

Handel's activities at the Queen's Theatre (later King's) ended in 1734. He moved to a new theatre (above) in Covent Garden managed by John Rich. An organ belonging to Handel (seen in the picture) was installed in the theatre and in his will he left the instrument to Rich, but it was destroyed in a fire in 1808.

a few more operas he was more interested in writing oratorios – which had a more appreciative audience than opera. His public, which now included members of the middle classes, was not keen on the 'exotic and irrational' notion of opera in a foreign language and preferred instead to hear familiar biblical stories in English and to be uplifted by the power of Handel's music. In response to this demand, he performed *Saul* and *Israel in Egypt* in 1739 (the first was a success, the second failed). That year he also composed the famous Twelve Grand Concertos for strings, op. 6. These, like the organ concertos (a set little good – London audiences were suspicious of the idea of an oratorio with biblical words in a theatre. In fact, *Messiah* became popular in London only in 1750, when Handel started performing it (as he had in Dublin) in aid of charity.

The pattern of performances was established, but the pattern of the music to be performed was not. For the 1744 season, Handel included a new work that was neither oratorio nor opera; *Semele,* designed for concert rather than stage performance, and on a classical rather than Biblical theme – and a highly profane one at that, dealing with the love affair between Jupiter and Semele. It was unsuccessful; the new audience must have been puzzled by it, for it offered none of the enlightment or moral uplift that they had come to expect. He presented the same formula the next year, with *Hercules,* another classical drama; both this and *Semele* (which was revived the next season) were poorly received, and Handel almost had to cancel his season. His new biblical oratorio, *Belshazzar,* was also received with indifference. This particular season was given at the King's, rather than at Covent Garden; perhaps these works' limited appeal to the opera audiences had something to do with their relative failure.

But things improved. In 1746, circumstances were on Handel's side: the 1745 rebellion had been firmly put down, and the nation was in patriotic mood – and

the mood is caught in Handel's *Occasional Oratorio* and his *Judas Maccabaeus,* the new works of 1746 and 1747.

Encouraged by their success, Handel seems to have been in good spirits and full of creative energy in the late 1740s. He wrote two new oratorios in each of the summers of 1747 and 1748, those of the latter year, *Solomon* and *Susanna,* being among his finest works. 1748 was also the year of the treaty of Aix-la-Chapelle, which ratified the succession of Maria Theresa, to the Austro-Hungarian throne. As this was settled in favour of his allies, George II decided it ought to be publicly celebrated; Handel was invited to write the music to go with a firework display – the Music for the Royal Fireworks.

With a substantial oratorio repertoire built up, Handel, now over 60, eased up somewhat on composition. The new oratorio in 1750 was *Theodora,* which had only modest success – Handel is reported as saying, ironically, that the music sounded better in an empty hall.

Ill-health and failing sight

In summer 1750, Handel made his last journey to Europe. We do not know where he went; he may have visited friends and relatives in Halle. In 1751, back in London at work on a new oratorio, *Jephtha,* he began to be seriously troubled by his failing sight; he wrote into the score that he was forced to stop work, just at the passage where the chorus sing 'How dark, O Lord, are Thy decrees, all hid from mortal sight'. *Jephtha* was, however, completed and had its first performance the following year; it was his last complete original composition.

In 1759, he was still able to give an oratorio season; but his health was failing. Five days after the season ended, in April, he added a final codicil to his will, including a request for burial in Westminster Abbey. He died three days later. At his funeral 3,000 Londoners were present and the funeral anthem was sung by the choirs of the Chapels Royal, St Paul's and Westminster Abbey.

Many contemporaries left accounts of events in Handel's life. He was a big man with a vast appetite; he was quick to anger and impatient, but witty too. He never married and although he was a social man with many friends in the upper strata of London society, there are gaps in our knowledge of his personal relationships. Perhaps it is best to look to the warmth, vivacity and drama of his music to appreciate the sort of man he was.

Handel's last codicil to his will provided for a sum 'not exceeding Six Hundred Pounds' for his own monument, by Roubiliac, in Westminster Abbey.

Handel took the waters at many spa towns including Aix-la-Chapelle, Bath and Cheltenham. The last spa town he visited was Tunbridge Wells (above) in August and September 1758. He made plans to return to Bath in April 1759 but was too weak to make the journey. He took to his bed and died on 14 April in his house in Brook Street.

Handel's London

A city and a society of extreme contrasts, Handel's London was the metropolis of Dr Johnson and his circle, of coffee-houses and pleasure gardens, and of a buoyant commercial life.

The kings whose reigns spanned Handel's career in London: George I (top left) became king in 1717 even though he couldn't speak the language – something which prompted the development of cabinet government. Although his son, George II (top right), did speak English, he was an equally 'stupid but complicated' person. He was succeeded by his grandson, George III, his son, Frederick, having died from a chill caught while playing tennis.

By the 1750s London was already a great city, a 'metropolis' as it was then usually called. No longer just an overgrown town, it boasted fine houses and streets and squares in classical style, which made it an elegant place in which to live and to visit.

London consisted of the City proper and what is now central London. In the 18th century the City (as now) stretched from Temple Bar in the Strand to the Tower. Those who lived there were the poor and the tradesman-class, known as the 'Cits'. High society had already moved out of the City and lived west of Temple Bar – beginning to form what we now know as the West End. Temple Bar itself, an imposing edifice which inconveniently narrowed the street, was regularly the scene of one example of the age's morbid streak: until 1776 the smart could hire spy-glasses to view the rotting heads of traitors that had been stuck on top since the 1745 Jacobite rebellion.

The 'West End' occupied only a few square miles, with part of the lived-in district dribbling along the Thames down to Westminster. Here, the House of Commons was not the relatively orderly place we know today. Many booted and spurred members in greatcoats could be seen stretched out asleep on the benches, or eating oranges and cracking nuts, while a debate was in progress.

Although many of the houses of London were grand, the streets were often filthy. They did, however, teem with life: strollers and people on

Visually, Georgian London was the height of elegance. But the fine clothes, splendid architecture and serene landscapes, for which this period is renowned, were only part of a larger, and far less rosy picture. The streets of London were filthy and dangerous (right) and the people seemed cruel and rowdy.

business; sedan-chairs and carriages. Street-traders' cries vied with the noise of iron-rimmed wheels on the cobbles. Although sedan-chairs made no noise the chairmen were often loud, rude and rough – deliberately pushing their poles into passers-by and splashing them with dirt.

Practically policeless and, at night, poorly lit, London had an incredibly high crime-rate – and relatively few criminals were brought to justice. Even in daylight people of all classes were threatened, robbed, beaten-up and murdered. Apart from countless humble citizens, victims of thuggery included the Prince of Wales, the Prime Minister and the Lord Mayor. At night, bells were rung so that revellers from Piccadilly could assemble to be safely escorted back to Kensington Village and foot guards were employed to see people home from the pleasure gardens at Vauxhall and Ranelagh. But the public generally relied only on watchmen, constables and a few Bow Street runners, the forerunners of policemen. But danger lurked even when precautions were taken – the link-boys who lit customers home by torchlight were often in league with robbers.

The first Georges

Georgian London was a city relatively free from the turbulence of the 17th century and the social and intellectual ferment of the 19th. Its apparent stability and prosperous complacency were revealed in politics, religion, commerce, letters, and in the lifestyle of the first Hanoverian kings. The reigns of both George I (1714–27) and George II (1727–60) exhibited an external, though superficial, calmness that rested on the settlement of old quarrels at home and expanding power (naval and commercial) overseas.

George I knew no English when he came to the throne at the age of 54. He acceded by virtue of the Act of Settlement of 1701, which had been passed to prevent a return of the Stuart line, and which had made his mother Sophia, the Electress of Hanover in

Germany, the heir to Queen Anne's throne. But George I had ruled as an autocrat in Hanover and he had little interest in the English people. He was not partial to their liberal consititution and so he left the day-to-day running of affairs to his ministers, most notably Sir Robert Walpole. Like his father, George II was also more interested in Hanover than England and at Dettingen in 1743 he was the last English monarch to lead his army into battle in Europe. Both George I and George II spent much of their reigns out of England, so that the House of Hanover did not become fully naturalized until the reign of George III (1760–1820), who did think of himself as English and who declared that he 'gloried in the name of Briton [sic]'.

Despite the fact that the first two Georges were dull and often boorish kings, the royal court at St James's Palace remained an important social and political centre. Because he had divorced and shut away his queen, George I had no consort to grace his court (though he did have several mistresses). The Prince of Wales, later George II, had a stormy relationship with his father, which may have been partly due to his resentment of the way in which his mother had been treated, but the tension between the king and his heir had a positive social effect.

It meant that the Prince and Princess of Wales's household became a stimulating rival to the actual court, attracting younger, livelier and more ambitious people. The Princess of Wales, Caroline of Anspach, was, moreover, a formidable woman who loved company and gossip, and an infinitely more cultivated personality than George I. But that was not saying very much, for the only art that interested Caroline and George II was music. Indeed, music was George's one delight and he had a passionate interest in opera. It is due as much to George II as anyone that Handel secured the encouragement which led him to settle in England.

George III was another dull king and since he

Dr Johnson (right), the famous conversationalist and leading light of London society, was a frequent visitor to tea- and coffee-houses (bottom right). These all-male ' establishments were popular throughout the 18th century.

Robert Walpole (above), who was Prime Minister from 1721 to 1741, led an efficient but corrupt administration. The 18th-century parliamentary scene was generally riddled with intrigue, rowdiness, and the worst excesses of careerist politics. In Hogarth's 'Election Entertainment' (left) the voters are being fêted by a candidate.

acceded to the throne before he had an heir, restless socialites did not have the compensation of a rival junior royal household. George III was home-loving, parsimonious and morally very correct, and so too was his queen, Charlotte. Even her very first party, given in 1761, was a meagre affair which set the tone for a long reign.

Manners and morals

An invitation to a 'rout' (party), a ball or an assembly in one of London's great houses was far more important to society than one to the fuddy-duddy palace. In these houses people could expect a good time, mingling with celebrities of one kind or another. And here they found what 18th-century society admired most: wealth, wit, taste, cynicism, humour and style.

But high society did not necessarily mean polite society in Handel's London, for a relatively coarse attitude to life and gross manners were general. The language of even the most illustrious citizens, both men and women, was as uninhibited as it was unrefined. Dukes thought nothing of becoming disgustingly drunk in public and fashionable young men – 'rakes', 'Bloods' and 'Nerves' – were particularly addicted to rowdy behaviour in private and in public.

And it was the young men who often attracted the most attention as trendsetters in fashion. They were conspicuous on account of their beautiful manners as well as their outrageous clothes, and they were a gift to caricaturists. Many such dandies may have had homosexual preferences, a 'vice' that was more openly prevalent in the 18th century than most people realize.

However, the extent of this 'vice' was nothing compared with the enormity of female prostitution in 18th-century London. High-class courtesans charged as much as 500 guineas for a night. Less well-off men could afford the very cheap attentions of countless girls and women, especially in Covent Garden where there were plenty of brothels and available women in taverns. Green Park at night was a notorious open-air brothel. The authorities locked the gates at dusk but since at least 6,500 people had keys this hardly mattered.

Clubs and coffee houses

For indoor socializing of another kind, there were the gentlemen's clubs, most of which were born in the 18th century, as well as establishments for those functions down the social scale. Men of rank and

position met, ate, talked, gambled and relaxed in elegant new premises in St James's or in Pall Mall. Many lesser clubs were held in a room in a tavern. Intellectuals went to debating clubs and the anti-religious joined the notorious 'Hell-Fire' club. More favoured in lower-circles were the 'cock and hen' clubs, the haunts of tarts and villains.

Almac's (later Brooks) was renowned for its excessive gambling, which was in fact a virulent disease all over London. Anything and everything were grounds for a bet and for the rich the stakes were very high. The statesman and orator, Charles Fox, would lose £500 an hour at the gaming tables, while even a poor man would cast away his week's meagre wages at the throw of a dice. The government sponsored state lotteries while a favourite

game in private houses was gold- or silver-loo.

Excessive drinking was another problem in a city where gin was as cheap as a penny a pint and signs outside gin-shops offered an opportunity to get drunk for twopence. Among the poorer citizens, men and women alike, the ravages of alcoholism were most vividly exposed in Hogarth's prints *Gin Lane* and *Beer Street*. Although these savage indictments of the original 'mother's ruin' were executed in the 1750s when government action against cheap drink had commenced, the same state of affairs persisted until the end of the century. Among the upper classes 'two-bottle' men were famous; port was also a very popular drink. In addition to alcohol, Handel's London was also awash with new stimulants as tea, coffee and chocolate

On summer evenings, a favourite pastime for Londoners was a visit to a pleasure garden. The most popular was at Vauxhall (left, illustrating this title page) where people wandered in the spacious grounds and listened to music provided by an orchestra. There were many other forms of entertainment, too, not the least of which was the possibility of a romantic rendezvous.

Although enjoying the genteel side of life, people were, on the whole, very insensitive to the plight of others. Society women, for instance, considered a visit to the lunatics at Bedlam (below) an amusing outing.

One of the plays enjoyed by the fickle London theatre-goers of the 18th century was John Gay's The Beggar's Opera *(left). Audience participation, as often as not, involved hurling abuse – or indeed whatever was at hand – at the actors. But for the most part, as Hogarth has caricatured (below), the audience was usually more interested in flirting.*

became popular beverages at home as well as in the coffee-houses.

'My face is very well known at the Grecian' wrote James Addison, the essayist and poet, in 1711. He was referring to a coffee-house, the first of which opened in London in 1652. Queen Anne's reign (1702–14) saw the houses' heyday but they were popular throughout the 18th century. Less élitest than the gentlemen's clubs, they were haunts where men could drink coffee and tea, talk politics and indulge in gossip; smoke, play cards and read newspapers.

The pleasure gardens

One of the 18th century's most delightful innovations was the pleasure garden. Including spas, and taverns with bowling-greens, Georgian Londoners had about 50 such 'gardens' – from Hampstead in the north to St Helen's in the south – to choose from. The most fashionable were Vauxhall and Ranelagh, neither of them in what was then London 'proper'. Vauxhall was in the village of Chelsea and Ranelagh just south of what is now Vauxhall Bridge. Both included tree-lined walks (at night, hung with coloured lights), arbours, grottoes, pavilions and refreshment rooms. Ranelagh, the more sophisticated garden, boasted a magnificent Rotunda where people could promenade, listen to music, eat and drink. At Vauxhall there were

fancy-dress balls, and dancing often went on all night. The spa at Sadlers Wells (the theatre was built in 1765) catered for 'lower-class lasses, sailors and other young people dancing'. They were also entertained by pantomines and women wire-walkers.

London's parks have always been the envy of other capitals. Charles I had opened Hyde Park to the public in 1637 and a century later George II added Rotton Row (corrupt pronunciation of *route du roi*), where the fashionable could ride. Green Park was also open to all ranks. Cricket, which was first organized on a county basis in the 18th century, was played at White Conduit Fields in Islington and bare-fist boxing could be enjoyed at Mr Stoke's Amphitheatre in the Islington Road. There were cock-fights at the 'Royal Cock-Pit' in Birdcage Walk, which was patronized by the nobility as well as the riff-raff, all betting heavily, while bear-baiting could be witnessed at 'The Bear-Garden' at Hockey-in-the-Hole.

'The house of the Devil'

The Londoners of Handel's day amused themselves in boisterous ways. It was not until the 1780s that the capital's theatres provided anything like the well-conducted entertainment we are familiar with today. Only when the old custom of allowing members of the audience to sit on the stage was stopped in 1762

done thing to attend the chapel at Magdalen Hospital (in fact, many now famous hospitals were built in the Georgian era, notably Guy's, the Foundling and St. Thomas's.)

The Established Church was in a very complacent state and Protestant dissenters and Catholics were excluded from the universities as well as many public offices unless they paid allegiance to it. Many Anglican bishops carried out few pastoral duties, preferring to dispense favours and patronage, and living richly, while the over-worked lower clergy suffered. Secure in its monopoly, this Established Church upheld a bland and unquestioning view of Christianity and in such circumstances it was not surprising that the most important religious movement of the 18th century was the evangelical revival led by John Wesley (1703–91).

The London of Handel's day was a city of extreme contrasts, a true metropolis where squalor and magnificence, poverty and wealth, cynicism and piety, violence and *joie de vivre* all jostled alongside one another. It was a city which could not be ignored and which aroused strong feelings, such as the often repeated opinion of Dr Johnson, who declared that 'when a man is tired of London, he is tired of life; for there is in London all that life can afford'.

The contempt Hogarth felt for the Established Church can be seen clearly in his 'Sleeping Congregation' (below), where he fiercely ridicules the apathetic and lackadaisical attitudes of both clergy and congregation alike. Like many other Londoners, however, he was relatively unimpressed with the evangelical fervour of John Wesley (left) that was gaining popularity in other parts of Britain.

did the 'house of the Devil' even begin to be more respectable. Even so, few people stayed for the whole evening; many attended only to make assignations with lovers or prostitutes. Audiences rarely went to see one play or concert: they also expected a farce, a pantomime, a ballet and some music. But opera was more exclusive. Most music was written by foreigners who, although living in London remained foreign; only Handel was considered to be a Londoner.

The best shops in 18th-century London were scattered far and wide across the capital, though certain trades still congregated in particular districts. Apart from some luxury shops in Bond Street and St James's, there were no shopping streets as such and many shops were still in the City. The rich went to George Seddon for furniture and mirrors; to Henry Clay for *papier mâché,* and old book shops (often also publishing houses) were still in St Paul's Churchyard and Fleet Street, though new ones gradually opened in Pall Mall and Piccadilly. There were goldsmiths in Cranbourne Street and perfumiers in Shire Lane and it was smart to eat strawberries at Netty's Fruit Shop in St James's Street. Shop-keepers and assistants cringed to the 'carriage trade' and other prestigious customers who were carried from their own front doors to the front door of the shops in silk-lined leather sedan-chairs.

The rise of Methodism
Like entertainments and shopping, religion was also largely a matter of taste and means, and certain churches were deemed more fashionable than others. Thus high society favoured such new churches as St Martin-in-the-Fields (in what is now Trafalgar Square), St Mary-le-Strand and St George's in Hanover Square. And if a famous clergyman such as the Reverend Dodd were preaching there, it was the

Wolfgang Amadeus Mozart
1756–1791

Mozart – impish, childlike and irrepressibly cheerful – maintained a staggering output of inspired composition throughout his short life. He was, without doubt, the most extraordinary musical genius of his time.

Young Mozart was taken by his father on a series of exhibition tours which introduced him as a genius to the nobility of Europe. Mozart later found the master-servant relationship with employers too stifling, and so set out to make his way as a freelance musician.

Wolfgang Amadeus Mozart is regarded as the greatest musical artist of the latter part of the 18th century. From an early age his great talent was obvious. If he had not been born into music he might have been a mathematician or linguist – as a child he covered the walls of his home with chalked calculations and easily picked up Italian, French and English. Portraits of the little prodigy in grand clothes and wig have china-doll faces and give very little indication of the extraordinary versatility and personality of this diminutive genius.

Although musically mature at an early age, Mozart seemed immature in character, and even when grown up, displayed a lack of responsibility and an inability to come to grips with the harsh reality of the world. During his childhood he was thought to be in general a serious, solemn child, dedicated single-mindedly to his art, but with a mischievous gaiety that bubbled repeatedly to the surface.

Until he set out to fend for himself, he had had no need to take any initiative on his own behalf, nor had he need of a sense of self-sufficiency, his father being so much in control of his life.

However, when he needed to display all the shrewdness and control provided by his father, it was obvious that he did not have the capacity or discipline to organize his own life, and so in essence, remained a child, unable, except through his music, to act for himself.

His father Leopold Mozart (1719–87), was the son of an Augsburg bookbinder. His education was broadly based in the sciences and arts – organ and violin playing and singing were among his accomplishments. He was expected to become a priest, and went to the Benedictine University of Salzburg where he passed examinations but did not complete the course, he or his directors no doubt recognizing music as his true profession.

Leopold was shrewd in making the right moves for entering 'service' and became a chamber musician in the establishment of the Salzburg dignitary, the Count of Thurn and Taxis. Aged 24 he secured a higher appointment as violinist in the Court Orchestra of Sigismund Christoph von Schrattenbach, Prince-Archbishop of Salzburg, and was admired for some of the pieces he wrote for it. But he achieved fame on an international scale when he published the first important book on violin playing, which was translated into several languages.

He married Anna Maria Pertl in 1747 and they settled permanently in Salzburg. Their daughter Maria Anna (known as Nannerl), born in 1752, four years before Wolfgang, showed early ability as a keyboard player, but was soon over-shadowed by her brother. (When only four, Mozart could play all the pieces his father had collected for Nannerl.)

In the 18th century Salzburg (left) was ruled by independent prince-archbishops, and it was thanks to one of these, Count Sigismund Schrattenbach (above) that the Mozarts were able to travel widely.

The young Mozart (left) and his sister Nannerl (with her brother, below) were brought up in a richly musical environment. Their remarkable talents were nurtured from the first by their father, Leopold, who took them through Europe to perform together as child prodigies. Leopold Mozart was an established court musician and composer who had achieved international acclaim in 1756 with the publication of his great work on the theory of the violin, Versuch gründlichen Violin-schule (title page, below).

a round of exhibition tours to the courts of Europe began. For the next ten years the Mozart family was involved in showing off the genius of the child prodigy, Wolfgang, to the society of the day: he was rapturously received by his audiences.

Exhausting conditions of travel, performances which might last long into the night and the children's occasional illnesses have brought the accusation that, however eager the boy was to perform during this period, Leopold was exploiting him. He simply referred to the exhibitions as 'business', but his dream was to raise the family status and to secure for Wolfgang fame and fortune greater than his own.

In December 1771 the last Italian tour of Leopold and Wolfgang was brought to an end with the news that Leopold's tolerant employer Archbishop Schrattenbach had died. He was succeeded by the former Bishop of Gurk, Count Hieronymus Colloredo, a man reputed to be sour-natured, but who officially confirmed Mozart's position as *Konzertmeister* at his court, a position he had in fact held in an honorary capacity for three years already.

Working under Colloredo

Count Colloredo, when congratulated by members of the Bavarian court on his *Konzertmeister* remained silent and shrugged his shoulders. He himself was a good enough violinist to recognize great talent, but to him the Mozarts seemed to be taking too much advantage of their position.

Sacred music occupied Mozart a good deal in the following years; more than a dozen short liturgical pieces plus four masses and two litany settings were written between 1771 and 1773. Among his Salzburg instrumental works some of the loveliest are the violin concertos with their uniquely tender vein of youthful yearning; but piano concertos had already become the most fashionable of concert pieces. Mozart's first original one (K.175) with festive trumpets and drums is more brilliant than profound, yet it was worth keeping handy as a certain winner for other audiences. Only the last two of the six piano concertos he wrote at this time are often heard – the last, the jolly one for two pianos, and the remarkable fifth (K.271).

Under his father's teaching Wolfgang's education advanced far beyond that of boys sent to school. He revelled in it and was never forced or punished. On one occasion at least Leopold tried to restrain Wolfgang's musical sprinting, as we hear from the Salzburg trumpeter and violinist, Andreas Schachtner, who had joined a few colleagues to try some new works at the Mozart home. Someone had given the young Mozart a little violin on which he experimented before having lessons. He wanted to play it with the others, but was told to run away and stop bothering everyone. He began to cry. Schachtner said: 'Let him play seconds with me.' Leopold relented: 'Play with Herr Schachtner, but so softly that we can hardly hear you, otherwise you'll have to go.' After a few moments Schachtner stopped playing for, with irregular fingering, the five-year-old held his part through six trios. It was Leopold's turn to show tears, but of pleasure and wonder. He determined that all Europe should witness such miracles.

The exhibition tours

Leopold took leave of absence from his post, and from 1762, when Wolfgang was six and Nannerl ten,

In 1780 the Elector of the Palatine, Karl Theodor (left), commissioned Mozart to write an opera for performance in the Carnival season in Munich (above). The result was Idomeneo (title page of vocal score, right), which established Mozart as the greatest dramatic composer of his age. Its première on 29 January 1781 was greeted with rapturous applause.

The Archbishop was an exacting task master – and although fair enough about money he was ungenerous over leave. But as he himself was taking holidays with his imperial relatives from July to September 1773, the Mozarts were allowed to visit Vienna. Their decision was sudden, and as they knew that the Viennese nobility had left for their estates it was rumoured that some vacancy, death, or other turn of events was known to Leopold who imagined prospects for Wolfgang. If so he was disappointed. His letters mention artistic contacts but no financial gain.

In 1777 the Archbishop wanted all his musicians present for a visit to Salzburg by Joseph II and flatly refused a request, made by Mozart after the performance of the *Jeunehomme Concerto,* to visit Paris. Leopold offered his resignation but stayed on. Wolfgang however was struck off the pay-roll. Now aged 21 he hoped to travel alone and find a suitable position, but his father mistrusted his son's volatile nature and ordered his mother to accompany him.

Munich, Mannheim and Paris

In August mother and son set off, first stopping in Munich. There the Elector spoke kindly but had no vacancy. Next they went to Augsburg and then on to Mannheim. He had hopes of gaining an appointment here, since the Elector, Karl Theodor, had established academies, art galleries and museums, and had a deep interest in music. However, he eventually made it clear that there was no post for Mozart. It was during this time in Mannheim that Mozart met and fell in love with a 16-year-old soprano, Aloysia Weber and wrote home enthusiastically suggesting that he should travel with her and her father. Leopold was so exasperated on receiving news of his son's leisureliness that he ordered him, with his mother, onwards to Paris. After a miserable nine-day journey Mozart and his mother arrived there in March 1778.

Unfortunately they found that there was little chance of work for the operatic stage while literary Paris was enjoying the pamphlet battle about the

Mozart inherited his high spirits from his mother, Anna Maria (below left), whose vivacity was heightened in the son to alarming proportions. Even at the age of 22 his father deemed him too unruly to travel alone and Anna Maria accompanied him on his 1778 visit to Paris (bottom). While Mozart entertained the fashionable salons and was fêted by the beau monde, his mother remained homesick and neglected in their lodgings. In June she contracted a fever, and two weeks later she was dead. Deeply concerned about the effect the death would have on his father, Mozart wrote a letter (below) to an old family friend, the Abbé Joseph Bullinger, asking him to break the news gently to Leopold.

rival merits of Rameau's and Gluck's operas. However, the Baron Grimm befriended Mozart, lent him money and advised him on job offers. During this period Mozart had one resounding success with performances of the *Paris Symphony* in the Tuileries. Soon afterwards his mother became ill and died. She had been unhappy and ailing for several weeks, with what affliction we do not know. Wolfgang moved into Grimm's house and tried to delay the shock for his father, first telling him of a 'serious illness', then asking a family friend to proceed from 'little hope' to the bitter truth.

Within a few weeks came an unexpected demand for his return. At Salzburg both the organist and the *Kapellmeister* had died; Count Colloredo would appoint Leopold to the latter high office on condition that his son accepted the former on better terms than formerly. Baron Grimm wisely advised a return via Strasbourg where Mozart was well paid for some concerts. He could not resist a detour to the Webers, but Aloysia had cooled towards him.

The end of servitude

Between January 1777 and May 1781, the last years Mozart was to spend under his increasingly callous employer, only a few works heard at Salzburg revealed Mozart's full powers.

Having promised to release Mozart for commissioned operas, Colloredo could not offend Carl Theodor by denying Mozart leave for *Idomeneo* at the 1781 Munich Carnival. *Idomeneo* was Mozart's first truly great opera, not only in its crowd scenes but in the tragic dialogues filled with pathos. Mozart was truly 'lionized' by Munich and its ruler.

Leopold and Nannerl came to witness the reception of *Idomeneo,* enjoy the carnival and visit their Augsburg relatives. Their three weeks' leave extended to more than three months until a peremptory command came from Colloredo for Wolfgang to go to Vienna. Here Mozart's casual attitude succeeded in annoying his tyrannical employer to such a degree that he subjected Mozart to almost impossible working and living conditions – and finally the threat of dismissal. This was exactly what Mozart wanted and he promptly handed in his resignation. Fortunately this did not affect his father's position and Leopold retained his Salzburg office.

Vienna's rising star

Wolfgang found lodgings with the Webers. Herr Weber had died and his first love, Aloysia, had married an actor, Joseph Lange, but his name was soon to be linked with the third of the Weber daughters, Constanze, who was training as a singer.

In April 1771 Count Colloredo (right) replaced Count Schrattenbach as ruler of Salzburg. Unlike his predecessor, who had encouraged Leopold Mozart to travel, Colloredo required the presence of his musicians at Court. A disagreement between Colloredo and Mozart resulted in the composer's resignation in 1781.

Her mother, now in reduced circumstances, welcomed a lodger of known achievements and even greater promise; his and Constanze's mutual affection, encouraged by her mother, developed into a love that demanded the fulfilment of marriage. Leopold was disappointed that his son should be marrying beneath him but it seems that Constanze and Mozart were well suited and extremely happy.

During the winter (1781–82) Mozart's prospects brightened. The publisher Artaria accepted a selection of his piano sonatas and duets, including the popular one in D for two pianos; they had a good sale. On Christmas Eve the Emperor invited him to a contest in piano playing with the London piano maker, Clementi, then at the height of his fame as a performer. The contestants showed mutual esteem and good humour. We imagine that they 'tied' in sight-reading and performing known works, but that Mozart excelled in improvising variations on a given theme; but what we know for certain comes only from their own reports. Clementi wrote generously; he had 'never heard anyone play with such intelligence . . . and was overwhelmed by an *Adagio* and some extempore variations'. Unfortunately Mozart's comments are 'bitchy' but may have been made so to please his father, for they come in a letter acknowledging Clementi as a brilliant technician – 'a *Mecanicus* . . . no feeling'.

Financial anxiety before his marriage was dispelled by work on *Il Seraglio.* Joseph II had established a theatre for German musicals and its manager found Mozart's *Seraglio,* with its eastern setting, particularly suitable. Playing first in Vienna to crowded houses in January 1782, it spread Mozart's fame in other cities. Unfortunately it did not bring royalties since composers, unless they made special arrangements, had only an initial fee from managers.

The happiest years

Without approval of their families Mozart and Constanze were married in St Stephen's Cathedral in Vienna on 4 August 1782, Baroness Waldstatten, one

of Mozart's rich pupils providing 'a princely banquet'. Fate granted them only nine years together but they were happy years, in spite of a profusion of unfounded rumours caused by Mozart's merry nature, love of dancing, parties and banter with the opposite sex. But Mozart remained punctiliously religious – 'I never prayed so fervently nor confessed and communicated so devoutly as with her', he once wrote.

Their first child died in infancy just before their visit to Salzburg, where Leopold and Nannerl received Constanze with cold politeness. We inherit the magnificent C minor Mass which Mozart had vowed to compose for the occasion.

During this time in Vienna Mozart met Joseph Haydn, 24 years his senior, who spent nearly a year

In 1781 Mozart broke free from the patronage of the Viennese Court and took lodgings in the house (bottom left of picture below) of Frau Weber (top right). He had already met Herr Weber and their second daughter Aloysia (right) a few years earlier. Mozart had fallen in love with the 17-year-old girl, but to Frau Weber's disappointment she married an actor.

In Vienna Mozart supported himself by teaching and by giving concerts. The ticket (above) is a rare relic from one of the subscription concerts he gave during 1774.

there, 1784–5, and participated in chamber music, chiefly in Mozart's house. He played first violin and Mozart viola. When Leopold made his first visit to the married Wolfgang, he heard Haydn's famous declaration: 'Before God . . . I tell you that your son is the greatest composer known to me.' Leopold could not dismiss the vision of high imperial employment, for the Emperor had already granted Mozart a small annuity as court composer without specific obligations. However, operas by the imperial *Kapellmeister,* Salieri, did seem to delay production of Mozart's in Vienna. It is true that Salieri had an envious nature, but the story that he poisoned Mozart is unsubstantiated. Even so, Mozart's fortunes declined as Salieri's rose.

A biography of Mozart's last five years becomes

Unaware of the fact that he was being manipulated into marriage by his landlady, Mozart quickly succumbed to the charms of her daughter Constanze (below left). The marriage contract (below right) was signed on 3 August 1782 and the wedding took place in St Stephen's Cathedral on the following day. She was 19; he was 26.

success. In society ballrooms music from the opera was turned into dance tunes, and became all the rage: 'they talk of nothing but *Figaro;* scrape, bow, sing and whistle nothing but *Figaro*'. At a concert between opera performances Mozart performed a new symphony, written especially for the occasion, which became known as the *Prague.*

At the end of May 1787 Leopold died and Mozart renounced his share in the estate to his sister, Nannerl, for a payment of 1000 gulden.

Soon after the success of *Figaro* Prague wanted another Mozart opera, about which Mozart was approached by Count Thun and the pianist-composer Dušek, but the city had to wait for it until the end of October 1787, when the composer directed the first performance of *Don Giovanni.* The full title

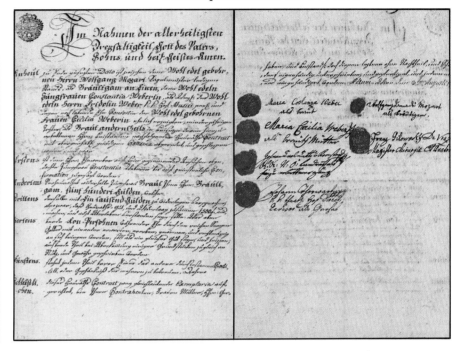

largely a list of masterpieces. He wrote what his artistic conscience commanded. His public triumphs were with opera, the genre requiring maximum preparation and minimum financial return.

Operatic works

Mozart found his librettist in Lorenzo Da Ponte, a sexual and financial adventurer who, having caused scandals in most European cities, eventually became a teacher of Italian in an American college.

Experience taught Da Ponte exactly what was or was not effective in musical drama. He suggested to Mozart a version of the second comedy, *Le Mariage de Figaro* in Beaumarchais' trilogy which begins with *Le Barbier de Seville.* The play was banned for its satire on aristocratic morality but Da Ponte assured the Emperor that political allusions had been excised. Despite crowded and enthusiastic houses *Figaro* could run only until the next scheduled opera followed. Later Vienna performances were not paid for. With two young children and another soon expected the Mozart family could not make the trip to England, as planned, especially after Leopold's sarcastic comments on the proposal that he should accept 'a payment for looking after the children and two servant-wenches'. (Even at the age of 30 Mozart could be foolish in practical matters). Instead they set off to Prague in 1787. *Figaro* had a 'sensational'

Of the six children born to Constanze and Wolfgang in their nine years of marriage only two survived infancy: Karl Thomas and Franz Xaver (right and left). Both were musically gifted but only Franz Xaver made music his career.

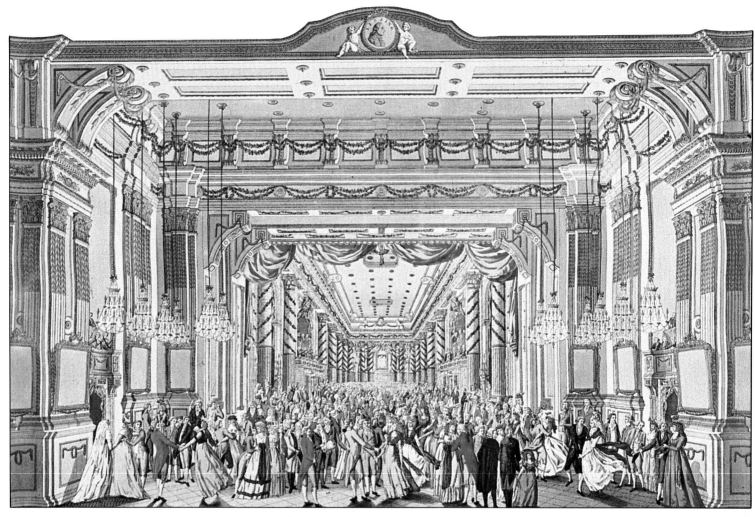

was *Il dissoluto punitio, o sia il Don Giovanni,* and even Mozart, before Prague raved over it, wondered how its mixture of terror, pity and comedy would be received.

It is said that the overture was completed during one of the opera's last rehearsals, which is an extraordinary achievement. As far as we know, Mozart more than other great composers had the ability to carry a new work about with him 'in his head', so nearly perfect in all details that the score rarely showed alterations. The English composer Thomas Attwood who lodged with the Mozarts in Vienna, tells us how, after a meal, Mozart might fold and unfold his napkin, then go into another room and write out a complete movement.

Back in Vienna Gluck had died and Mozart received from the Emperor the small annuity reserved for the office of court chamber musician, but *Don Giovanni,* with alterations demanded by some of the singers, was not the success it had been in Prague. After a short run it was not revived until after Mozart's death. The Emperor declared it 'even more beautiful than *Figaro* . . . but no food for the palate of my Viennese'. It is from this year, 1788, that the begging letters to his good friend Michael Puchberg a merchant, freemason and musician begin.

Cosi fan tutte, (Thus they all do,) was the third Mozart-Da Ponte collaboration, and was greatly enjoyed by the Viennese audiences from its first performance in January 1790. The orchestral textures of this delicious fantasy are generally considered to be the composer's most admirable score for *opera buffa.* But it did little to improve his financial state.

A regular income as court composer did not help Mozart out of his financial difficulties, though he was careful to disguise the fact by dressing well (above). Though his opera Don Giovanni *(title sheet above right) met with success when it was first performed in Prague in 1787, his fortunes did not change. In 1791 it was received indifferently at the coronation of Leopold II (top).*

Illness and declining months

Finding it difficult enough to pay for the 'cures' at Baden, necessary for Constanze, Mozart himself began to suffer from rheumatism and headaches which were symptoms of the kidney disease which killed him. The unfinished portrait by his brother-in-law, Joseph Lange, shows Mozart with his eyes fixed on the music he is playing at the piano and reveals the slight bulge characteristic of uraemia. He had only a year to live. Joseph II had died and the new Emperor was to be crowned at Frankfurt. Mozart thought he would recoup his fortunes by going there during the festivities. He was certainly applauded there and at other cities where he gave concerts, yet the expenses of the journey greatly reduced the takings. At home he fulfilled commissions for chamber works and supplied dances for the court before he entered the last year of his life.

Alone at home Mozart forgot his troubles while engaged on a project suggested by the actor-manager, Emanuel Schikaneder. This was *The Magic Flute*, but work was interrupted by another commision. The new Emperor required a serious opera during the festivities of his second coronation as King of Bohemia. Mozart set off for Prague with his wife and, it is said, worked on the opera *La Clemenza di Tito* while travelling. The gala performance brought none of the acclaim given to *Don Giovanni* a few days before. He returned home exhausted and in rapidly declining health in the September of 1791.

The requiem

During his last months Mozart was plagued with images of doom. A mysterious gaunt messenger, who he fancifully regarded as Death personified, called to ask for a Requiem Mass with which a certain nobleman wished to honour his wife's death. The all classes, ceremony or expenditure or even large gatherings for funerals. It was so unpopular an edict that it was revoked within a year, but Mozart died while the ban was in force. The Emperor subscribed handsomely to funds which enabled Constanze to have money in hand after paying debts. Further funds were raised by a benefit concert arranged soon after the funeral which was attended by courtiers and music lovers. Directing Mozart's famous last symphonies in London, Haydn wept on hearing of the young composer's death.

Haydn himself was now 'free' in his old age but not even secret poverty had led Mozart to abandon his artistic freedom. We can conceive of no music that he might have composed if he had lived in the freedom of Beethoven's and Schubert's Vienna. They were to enjoy patrons as friends, not as masters. It is a remarkable fact that this last towering musical genius of the 18th century had, in his time, anticipated not only this freedom of life but the artist's right to personal sincerity.

This scene (left) is from Act II, Scene 19 of Mozart's last opera The Magic Flute. *The extraordinary richness of the music unites an equally extraordinary mixture of solemn ceremony based on Masonic rituals, and light-hearted comedy. It was an instant success when first performed on 30 September 1791.*

mystery is now cleared. Count Walsegg – Stuppach's messenger was Anton Leutgeb, son of the mayor, whose portrait shows him to have been unusually cadaverous in appearance. By the end of November Mozart's faintings, vomiting, stiff limbs and swellings on the hand and feet were pronounced incurable. From his bed Mozart heard miniature rehearsals with his pupil Süssmayr at the piano. Increasing paralysis forced him to leave parts of the Requiem for Süssmayr to finish, which he did at least competently. A merciful coma eased Mozart's passing in the early hours of 5 December 1791.

It is commonly believed that Mozart's sparsely attended burial in an obscure grave showed that he was no longer appreciated, but among the 'enlightened' Emperor's orders was one forbidding to

In July 1791 a 'mysterious stranger' commissioned a requiem from Mozart. The 'stranger' was actually the son of the Mayor of Vienna, but Mozart became convinced that he was an agent of divine providence — and that the requiem he was to write was to be his own. He worked on it right up to his death, spending his last day working on the Lachrymosa (right).

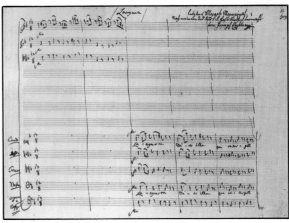

Captain James Cook
and the age of exploration

During Mozart's lifetime the last great landmasses of the globe were finally charted from the foundations laid down by a short but productive burst of exploration.

By the year 1600 Columbus and Cabot had reached North America, Vasco da Gama had rounded the Cape of Good Hope en route to the lands of the East, and Drake had circumnavigated the globe. Most of the great continents, if not yet explored, were at least known. Yet even in the 18th century, huge tracts of land and ocean remained undiscovered – the full extent of the globe still a mystery. But within 100 years, the situation was to become substantially different. Pushed on by the spirit of 'Enlightenment', which above all encouraged enquiry and question, Europeans set out to try to complete the global picture.

The Great Southern Continent
Until the 18th century, the twin arms of European exploration – across the Atlantic to the Americas and round the Cape of Good Hope to Asia – had not met. Colossal areas of the Pacific ocean, which lay between, remained unexplored. Although the western shores of the Pacific were known and Dutch sailors had, in fact, advanced as far as the north-west coast of Australia, accurate maps of the day still left much of the Pacific – almost half the earth's surface – as a tantalizing blank space.

Throughout Europe, however, there was a persistent and cherished belief in the existence of a Great Southern Continent – Terra Australis Incognita – which lay somewhere in the southern hemisphere. Commonsense, as well as the contemporary belief in natural symmetry, suggested that there must be such a continent to balance the known landmasses of the north. So, despite the fact that Spanish and Dutch explorers had already whittled away the possible size of this mysterious continent, by increasing the known area of ocean around it, the idea continued to flourish.

The promise of riches that such a continent might bestow upon its discoverer were too enticing for men to let it remain long as a mapmaker's fantasy. In an age of great commercial competition, the two maritime powers of Britain and France were particularly keen to locate Terra Australis Incognita and be the first to establish lucrative trading links there. Because of this rivalry, both Britain and France regularly paid for government-sponsored voyages of exploration in the Pacific. Captains such as Anson, Byron, Wallis and Carteret plied the oceans, competing for public acclaim with outstanding contemporary personalities such as Bougainville and James Cook.

It is a measure of Britain's commitment to funding

new discoveries that, as early as 1714, an Act of Parliament was passed to officially offer a prize of £20,000 – a staggering sum in those days – for the inventor of a means of 'accurately determining longitude at sea.' After almost 50 years of false hopes and unsuccessful experiments, the prize was won in 1764 when John Harrison invented a marine chronometer. This device made it possible to establish longitude to within half a degree and so chart voyages with greater accuracy; this was to help considerably the eventual success of Captain Cook.

The scientific incentive
These 18th century voyages had a scientific goal that went far beyond purely commercial considerations and was fostered by the intellectual climate of 'Enlightenment Europe'. Travel books were widely popular and novels such as Daniel Defoe's *Robinson Crusoe* (1719) became best sellers. This was a period that saw the development of modern science while natural history became the 'hobby' of many educated people and was accepted as respectable

The three epic voyages of Captain James Cook (left) took him to the ends of the earth. On his first voyage he charted the east coasts of Australia and New Zealand; on the second he explored the Antarctic and charted many South Pacific Islands; and on his third tragic voyage he discovered Hawaii and probed northwards to the Bering Straits – helping to re-draw the map of the world (top).

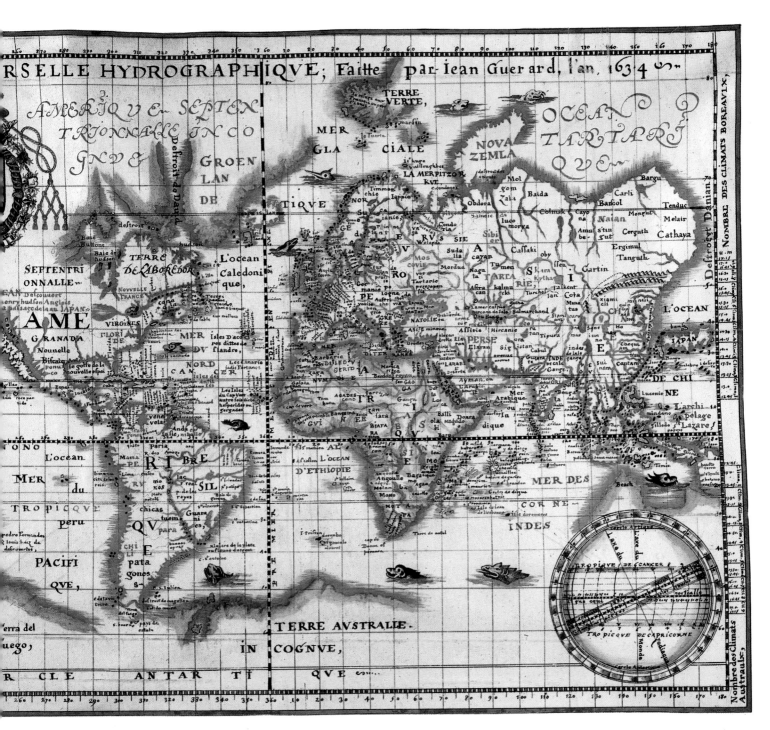

RSELLE HYDROGRAPHIQVE; Faitte par Iean Guerard, l'an, 1634

The explorer Louis Antoine de Bougainville.

conversation for the drawing room.

For the first time men of learning were considered essential members of any expedition. Botanists and zoologists were especially valued because the gathering of new flora and fauna not only satisfied public curiosity, but held out the promise of important new commercial enterprises, such as the trade in coffee and tea. Scientific gentlemen, added copious new details to the system of classifying plants and animals that was founded by Carl Linnaeus in 1735. His *Systema Naturae* provided a truly international framework and, because it was based on Latin, it removed the kind of confusion and duplication that arose from arbitrary classification in each discoverer's native tongue.

Great prestige was attached to the activities of these scientists and collectors. Sir Joseph Banks, who

accompanied Cook on his first voyage in 1768, was acutely conscious of the importance of his position. Indeed, he refused to accompany Cook's second voyage because there was no room on board for his entourage of 13 people, including musicians to play for him as he dined each evening. He even refused to compromise by taking less than two trumpeters!

The French, too, had their colourful heroes. The naturalist Philibert de Commerson, who sailed with Bougainville, seemed at first glance a quiet character. The crew of Bougainville's ship, *La Boudeuse,* saw nothing unusual about the friendship between Commerson and the lad who served as his assistant and shared his cabin until the ship reached Tahiti. Only then was it discovered that the assistant was female; it must be judged quite an achievement on the part of Commerson and his lover that they

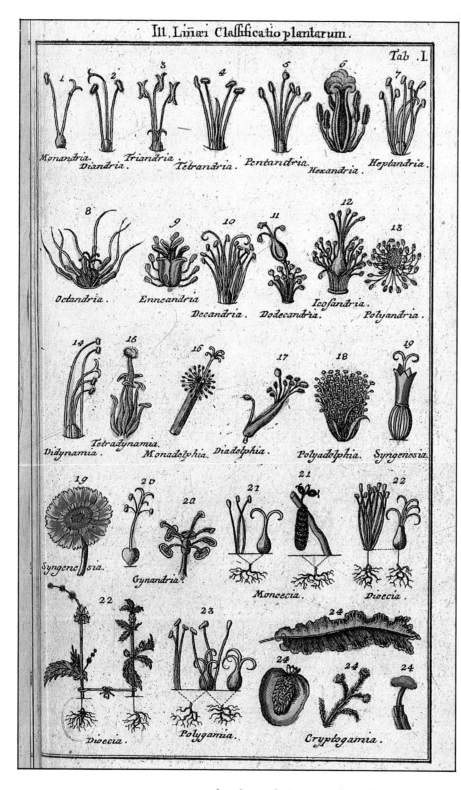

Ill. Linæi Classificatio plantarum.

Tab. I.

1 *Monandria.* 2 *Diandria.* 3 *Triandria.* 4 *Tetrandria.* 5 *Pentandria.* 6 *Hexandria.* 7 *Heptandria.*

8 *Octandria.* 9 *Enneandria.* 10 *Decandria.* 11 *Dodecandria.* 12 *Icosandria.* 13 *Polyandria.*

14 15 *Didynamia.* 16 *Tetradynamia.* *Monadelphia.* 17 *Diadelphia.* 18 *Polyadelphia.* 19 *Syngenesia.*

19 *Syngenesia.* 20 *Gynandria.* 21 *Monoecia.* 22 *Dioecia.*

22 *Dioecia.* 23 *Polygamia.* 24 *Cryptogamia.*

In 1735 the first edition of a mammoth work, the Systema naturae, *by Swedish naturalist Carl von Linné (Linnaeus) appeared in Europe (left). His system of classifying plants – according to the number and structure of their stamens and pistils – was quickly taken up by botanists around the world. Linnaeus also introduced a consistent principle for naming all living things, using a Latin double-name to give the genus and species; it was this scientific approach which laid the foundation for all future classifications.*

managed to keep their secret from the entire ship's crew for some 17 months!

The ravages of scurvy

Long distance voyages were plagued by the threat of scurvy. This debilitating disease caused by lack of vitamin C supplied in fresh fruit and vegetables, was an occupational hazard for sailors in the Pacific. Indeed, the ravages of scurvy and starvation were largely responsible for the fact that the Pacific was still unexplored up to the 18th century. The Portuguese, the Spanish and the Dutch had all organized voyages of discovery to the South Seas but

the distances involved were so vast that supplies always ran out. For any chance of success, expeditions needed a supply-base somewhere at the heart of the unknown area.

In 1776, a British expedition, led by Samuel Wallis in the *Dolphin* and Philip Carteret in the *Swallow,* came upon an island that was to prove the answer to this problem. When the two ships became separated in the Pacific, Wallis came upon Tahiti and its island group (which he called the Society Islands). He also discovered some of the Tuamotu and Marshall islands. Carteret sailed further south and discovered Pitcairn Island. On his return to England, Wallis

In the interests of science, ships' crews were kept busy taking a variety of measurements, including the earth's magnetism (left), the sea's temperature and the pressure of the atmosphere. Cook was also helped, on his second voyage, by the Harrison chronometer (below) which could measure longitude with great accuracy.

Among the many celebrated scientists associated with 18th century expeditions, Sir Joseph Banks (left) was one of the most distinguished. He not only accompanied Cook's first voyage, but also created the botanical gardens at Kew and was President of the Royal Society from 1778 to 1820.

Cook and his crew were fascinated by the strange new flora and fauna they encountered on their voyages to Australasia: the extraordinary kangaroo on the right was sketched for posterity by the expedition artist, Sydney Parkinson.

loss of Canada and the failure to secure the Falkland Isles from the British.

However, Bougainville came from a titled family and was prepared to bear much of the cost of expeditions out of his own pocket – even at this time good enough qualifications to command voyages of exploration. Bougainville was also a man of character, learning and culture and he made a valuable contribution to his country's future interests in the South Seas. He had a steely determination to press ahead no matter what, and the openness of mind and depth of learning (he had published a work on mathematics) which were typical qualities of 'gentlemen' of the 18th century.

Setting off on his first great voyage, in December 1776, Bougainville had a tall order ahead. He was charged with discovering the true size of the supposedly 'giant' natives of Patagonia and with locating the 'southern continent'. On the way, he was expected to seek out all possible ports of call, laying claim to any new lands for the King of France, to bring back drawings and specimens of new discoveries and also to return with valuable spice plants that would help improve the flagging French economy.

Not surprisingly, he met with mixed success. He quickly established that the Patagonians were not giants and his colleague, the naturalist Commerson, collected some 40 boxes of previously unrecorded specimens. He was quite undiscriminating in laying claim to any land he passed, though little benefit came to France from this exercise. Bougainville even claimed the island of New Britain, though he knew perfectly well that it had been discovered by the British in 1700 (and had a commemorative plaque on the beach to prove it). In all, Bougainville 'took possession' of seven island chains but only two of them – the Tuamotus and Society Islands – eventually came under French sway.

The main purpose of this ambitious expedition were never fulfilled. No southern continent was found and no commercially valuable spice plants were discovered. Little comfort was derived from its one important scientific achievement: a detailed log with accurate longitudinal readings which helped to establish the total width of the world's greatest ocean.

Captain Cook

The only navigator who really conquered the South Pacific as a whole was Captain James Cook. His first epic voyage (1768–1771) when he circumnavigated New Zealand and sailed along the treacherous reefs of eastern Australia (New South Wales and Queensland), made the greatest addition to Europe's stock of geographical knowledge since the discoveries of Columbus. On the second voyage (1772–75), Cook sailed far enough south to finally prove that there was no Great Southern Continent, and on the third voyage (1776–79), he explored the northern ocean and confirmed that there was no navigable water linking the North Pacific to the North Atlantic.

Cook was a self-made man with both vision and practical skills. The son of a Scottish labourer, he was born in Yorkshire in 1728 and apprenticed to a grocer and draper when he was 17. After only 18 months he decided that the sea was his true vocation and, from 1746 to 1755, he served in the merchant marine. During his apprenticeship, working on ships engaged in the North Sea coal trade based at Whitby, Cook learned many of the basic skills that would one day help him to master the Pacific. He also developed

recommended that Tahiti would make a suitable point for gathering fresh supplies and would provide a welcome resting place for weary sailors.

The voyages of Bougainville

Hardly had Wallis left Tahiti than the island was visited again, by the French explorer Bougainville. In many ways, Louis Antoine de Bougainville was distinguished by his poor qualifications to command a lengthy voyage into unknown seas. He was not a professional sailor and had never been given any naval training. He had also played an honourable but significant role in two major French disasters – the

While Cook is rightly remembered for his heroic efforts in the South Pacific, his third and final voyage took him far from its sun-soaked islands. The John Webber scene above shows the Resolution *'beating through the ice', with its consort the* Discovery *'in the most eminent danger in the distance', during Cook's exploration of the waters around Alaska. The purpose of this expedition was to find a sea route from the Atlantic ocean to the Pacific and, although Cook was unsuccessful, he did discover Hawaii and other North Pacific islands which served as vital bases for future Arctic expeditions.*

a particular affection for the broad-bellied, blunt-bowed collier vessels peculiar to the Whitby coal trade. It was this type of ship he chose for all three of his great voyages of exploration.

In 1755, Cook joined the Royal Navy to fight in the Seven Years War with France. After service in a succession of ships, he was rapidly promoted to master and, in 1759, was charged with the daunting task of charting a natural zigzag, known as the Traverse, along the St Lawrence River approaches to Quebec. When the war was over, he continued with surveying work along the coasts of Newfoundland and was so successful that, despite his humble origins, he was chosen to lead an expedition to the South Pacific in 1767.

Endeavour and Resolution

Scientific interest was deeply aroused throughout Europe by an important astronomical event that was due to take place on 3 June 1769. On that day, the planet Venus would pass across the face of the sun. It was hoped that calculations based on the transit time as observed in widely differing parts of the world, would enable scientists to calculate the precise distance of the Earth from both the sun and Venus itself. Many nations participated in the preparations for this great event; the Russians, for example, despatched explorers to hitherto unknown parts of Siberia and the British sent Captain Cook to the newly discovered island of Tahiti.

There was, however, much more to Cook's public brief than the simple observation of an astronomical event. He had secret instructions to search for the Great Southern Continent and to explore and chart as much of New Zealand's coast as might prove practicable. His ship, a Whitby collier rechristened the *Endeavour,* left Plymouth in August 1788 with supplies on board for a two year voyage.

As an explorer, Cook had resolute determination and, as a captain, he was exceptionally conscientious in following the accepted but often ignored principles for ensuring the health of his crews. By taking supplies of lime juice (from which the nickname for the British – Limeys – comes), for example, and stopping over at the newly discovered base of Tahiti, he conquered the horror of scurvy. It

says much for his qualities of leadership that, having survived the rigours of one Pacific voyage, a number of the crew on the *Endeavour* signed on for Cook's second voyage in the *Resolution*.

Most important for posterity was that Cook's journals and charts were more accurate than any previously kept. He combined his skill as a seaman with a sound knowledge of both mathematics and astronomy. He recorded his experiences and impressions in a daily journal which gives personal insight into the character of this public hero. The account of his weighty decision to abandon any further search for the cherished Great Southern Continent, after the discovery of the frozen landmass of Antarctica, shows remarkable candour and concern for the safety of his crew.

'I, who had ambition not only to go farther than anyone had been before but as far as it was possible for men to go, was not sorry at meeting with this interruption; as it, in some measure relieved us; at least shortened the dangers and hardships inseparable from the navigation of the southern polar regions.'

Cook's ships, Resolution and Adventure (left) dwarf the native canoes as they take anchor in Matavai Bay, Tahiti. Cook visited Tahiti in the summer of 1773 and again the following spring, to take on supplies and give his men a well-earned rest. The island was so delightful that sailors tried to jump ship. Cook had some sympathy, writing that, in Tahiti, a man could 'injoy all the necessaries and some of the luxuries of life in ease and Plenty'.

Noble savages

Though neither a 'gentleman' nor an aristocrat like Sir Joseph Banks or Bougainville, Cook was just as much a product of the enlightened attitudes of the 18th century. Like them, he was fascinated by the lifestyle and customs of the peoples he discovered on his voyages and was familiar with the prevailing philosophy of the virtues of the 'noble savage'.

For some time, European philosophers, most notably the controversial Frenchman Rousseau had been preoccupied with the seemingly destructive effects of civilization and technical progress on society. Rousseau argued that, if only man could remain in a state of nature, he would still be living in the equivalent of the Garden of Eden. His book, *Origin and Foundation of Inequality among Men* was published in 1755 and had lasting impact.

'The first man who, having enclosed a piece of ground, bethought himself of saying This is mine, and found people simple enough to believe him, was the real founder of civil society. From how many crimes, wars and murders, from how many horrors and misfortunes might not anyone have saved mankind, by pulling up the stakes and filling up the ditch, and crying to his fellows, Beware of listening to this impostor; you are undone if you once forget that the fruits of the earth belong to us all, and the earth itself to nobody'.

The awesome spectacle of a Tahitian war fleet (above) preparing to sail forth in an attack on the nearby island of Mo'orea was witnessed by Cook and his men in 1774. The fleet included some 160 war canoes – their chief resplendent in his battle-dress on the foremost craft – as well as numerous smaller boats in support. Warriors, armed with spears and clubs, fought from platforms built over the hulls, while unarmed oarsmen propelled each galley into battle.

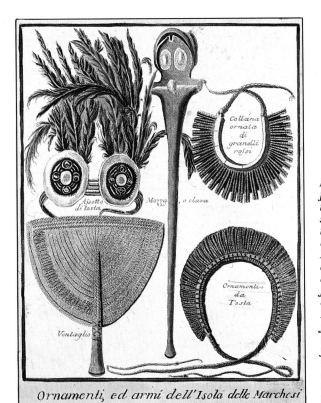

Ornamenti, ed armi dell'Isola delle Marchesi

Illustrations of the finely worked crafts that Cook and his men saw in Polynesia found their way into travel books throughout Europe. Here, a page displays the ornaments and arms of people from the Maquesas, one of the Society Islands' group. A feather headdress, necklets of seeds and fibre, a carved club and a fan of plaited coconut busk fibre together show the impressive skill of the islanders.

Bougainville, too, was well acquainted with the theories of Rousseau and, during his brief stay in Tahiti, was vividly reminded of the philosopher's theme. The Polynesian lifestyle seemed delightfully easy and unmaterialistic. Simple wood-framed houses thatched with leaves were in scattered homesteads connected by shaded walks. Farming and fishing provided food and, because of the fertile soil and warm climate, little effort was needed for success in either of these activities. The main preoccupation of the people seemed to be keeping themselves clean and well groomed for the purpose of making love.

There was a darker side to the islanders, however, a side that Bougainville saw little of during his seven-day visit. Widespread infanticide, human sacrifice and gruesome warfare practices provided a sharp contrast with the otherwise idyllic daily routine.

Cook had the benefit of a far more extended visit than Bougainville and also had a more critical manner. The difference between the two explorers' attitudes is reflected in their dealings with one constant source of friction between them and the islanders – the inveterate pilfering of vital equipment. Bougainville believed that the islanders must be innocent of theft because they had no notion of property, but Cook was not so deceived. He developed a successful strategy of kidnapping, but not harming, important islanders, and returning them only in exchange for the stolen goods.

The rosy European view of a South Seas paradise was, sadly, far from the truth. While the people were, generally, hospitable and good-natured, they also indulged in fearsome inter-island warfare and made human sacrifices to their gods (right). In keeping with the scientific spirit of their day, Cook and some of his officers visited a Tahitian temple to observe the ritual killing of an unfortunate victim. Skulls piled high in the background emphasise the frequency of such gruesome practices.

Neither captain used violent measures in their dealings with the people. In open clashes with hostile groups, the 18th-century explorers in the Pacific generally showed a restraint and moderation that would have been completely alien to their Victorian successors. Bougainville forbade his men to fire on a group that had tried in vain to attack his party. He felt it would have been shameful to kill these lightly armed peoples with superior European weaponry. In the same way, Cook did not take revenge on the New Zealand Maoris who killed and then ate ten British sailors from his sister ship, the *Adventure.* The sailors who remained were horrified by the act of cannibalism but, with a cool detachment, Cook wanted to understand why it had been committed and actually went along to witness another ritual involving an islander.

The end of an era
Captain Cook was stabbed to death during a sudden outbreak of fighting between Hawaiian islanders and their European visitors in 1779. The violence arose out of a petty dispute which Cook would probably have settled peacefully, if he had not been on the beach at the time. It was a bitter and ironic tragedy that he should have been killed in this way, particularly since he was perceptive enough to recognize that the contact between Europe and the South Sea peoples would bring little benefit to the islanders. But the untimely death of Cook did

Throughout the 18th century, artists and writers alike idealised life in the South Pacific. The French philosopher Jean Jacques Rousseau (above) identified closely with nature and advocated a simple life free from the trapping of 'civilisation'. His ideas had a profound effect on contemporaries and many of the paintings of native people reflect the romantic appeal that these 'noble savages' held for Europeans. In John Webber's portrait of the Ra'iatean princess Poetua (right), Polynesian grace and beauty is personified.

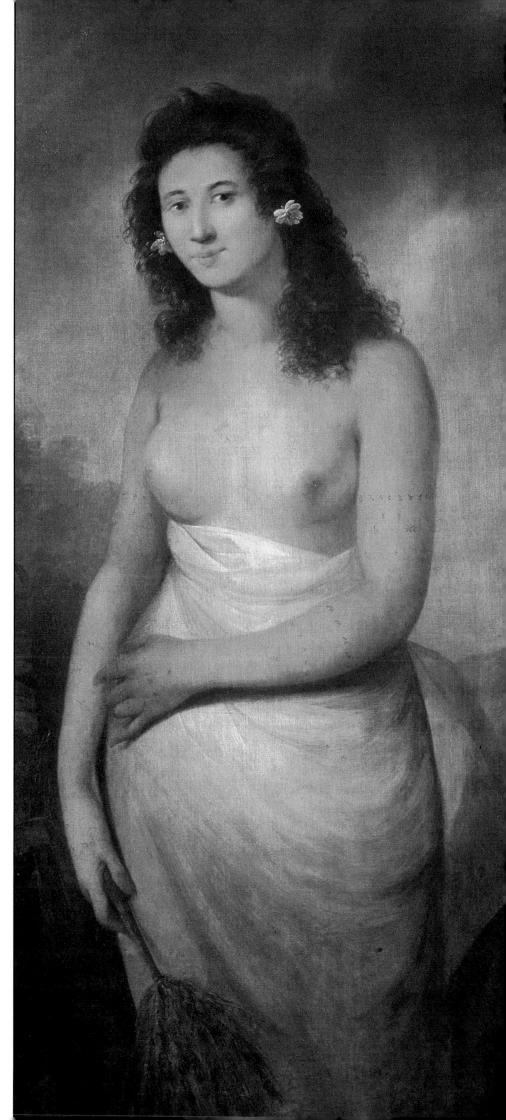

nothing to detract from the popular impression of a South Seas paradise. The descriptions of Tahiti, from both Cook and Bougainville, caught the imagination of Europe in a way that the cultures of North America never had. 'Noble savages' were brought back to London and Paris, where they were treated as celebrities and helped to fuel a blissful myth that remains to this day.

Islanders like Aotouru, who came back with Bougainville, and Omai, who was brought back with Cook after his second voyage were regarded as distinguished visitors. Omai was presented to King George III, taken on a grand tour of Yorkshire in the company of Sir Joseph Banks and even painted by Joshua Reynolds before being returned home with Cook on his third voyage.

Cook's death marked a turning point in the history of exploration. He charted thousands of miles of ocean and island groups and determined the size and limits of the earth's habitable areas. After him, transglobal trading routes became commonplace but no-one bettered his monumental achievements.

The democratic tendencies of the 18th century and the continued rivalry between Britain and France had a profound effect on the future of both countries. In 1783, Britain was forced to recognize the independence of her colonists in North America after they had successfully defeated her armies with the help of French financial support, while the Europe of 1789–1815 was dominated by the French Revolution and subsequent rise of Napoleon Bonaparte. An era of imperialism had begun.

After his second voyage Cook, the national hero, was presented to King George III, taking with him an islander called Omai (left). Omai took London by storm, reinforcing the ideal of the 'noble savage' but, on Cook's third voyage, reality caught up with Europe's dreamers. The expedition put into Hawaii for fresh supplies and was troubled by a series of petty thefts. Cook went ashore to take a hostage (for release on return of the goods). His landing-party was halted by a crowd whose mood darkened with the rumour that the English had killed a chieftain. In the ensuing fracas, Cook was set upon (below) and, before his men could save him, the Captain had been cut down and killed.

'Our worthy brother'
Mozart the Freemason

Mozart's naturally philanthropic feelings, his enjoyment of the achievement of perfectly expressive music for his fellow men and his love of ritual, all were deepened and fulfilled during his years as a member of the Order of Freemasons.

'Who did not know him? Who did not esteem him? Who did not love him? – our worthy Brother Mozart . . .'

These words from a Masonic oration on his death show how highly Wolfgang Amadeus Mozart was regarded by his fellow Freemasons. From his initiation into the small Viennese lodge, Beneficence, on 14 December 1784 until his death seven years later, Mozart was an active member of the Order. During this time he composed much music for lodge ceremonies – in fact, his last completed work was a Masonic cantata, and his last opera, *The Magic Flute,* is a Masonic allegory.

The spread of Freemasonry in Europe
The 18th century quasi-religious cult of Freemasonry had its origins in the medieval stonemasons' guilds. In the 17th century rituals and symbols of ancient religious and chivalric orders were added to those already associated with the craft guilds. In outward form Freemasonry has changed very little since Mozart's time. It is still an exclusively masculine secret society with elaborate ritual based on ancient Greek and Egyptian mysteries. Freemasons of today would recognize much of the ritual from Mozart's day including the secret passwords, the blindfolding of a candidate for initiation and the symbolism derived from medieval stonemasonry. Today, few would regard Freemasons as dangerous or subversive, yet in Europe during the latter part of the 18th century, although tolerated at first, they were eventually banned and persecuted.

The first Grand Lodge was established in England in 1717, with the aim of being 'the means of conciliating true friendship among persons who must otherwise have remained at a perpetual distance.' Freemasonry was not a political force in England, but when it spread to France in 1725 it became associated with the ideals which were the forerunners of the revolution of 1789.

Wolfgang Amadeus Mozart (above), was initiated as a Freemason into the Viennese lodge, Beneficence, in December 1784. In 1785 Beneficence merged with two other lodges. The new lodge was called Newly Crowned Hope. Despite the controls imposed on Freemasons in Austria by Emperor Joseph II, Mozart was an active member of the order until his death in 1791.

Since the foundation of Freemasonry in the 18th century most of the ritual involved has remained the same. Although the dress would differ from today's, Masons still undergo initiations like that shown here.

1 The Master.
2 Senior Warden.
3 Junior Warden.
4 Candidate.

PLATE 1. *A Meeting of Freemasons, for the reception of Apprentices. The Junior Warden introducing in the Lodge the Candidate to be Initiated an entered Apprentice.*
Published Jan: 30.th 1809, by Tho.s Palser, Surry Side Westminster Bridge.

5 Speaker.
6 Secretary.
7 Treasurer.
8 Tyler.

In 1738 and 1751 papal bulls (edicts) banning Freemasonry were issued but enforcement in Roman Catholic states depended on whether or not the individual heads of state were pro- or anti-Masonry. In Austria, for example, the Empress Maria Theresa at first tolerated the Masons – probably because her husband, Francis of Lorraine, was one. She was, however, suspicious of Masonic activities and on one occasion is said to have entered a lodge disguised as a man. On another occasion she ordered her soldiers to make a raid on the lodge of which her husband was a member. After Francis' death she did suppress the lodges though many of them continued their activities in secret.

On her death in 1780 her more liberal son, Joseph, revoked the papal ban and even seemed to favour Freemasonry. During the early part of his reign Freemasonry flourished and the majority of Viennese intellectuals – mostly Catholics – belonged to the Order. Indeed, during this period, it was very fashionable to be a Freemason. Caroline Pichler, the daughter of a Viennese councillor who was a Mason, wrote:

'The order of Freemasonry pursued its course with an amount of publicity and ostentation which was almost ludicrous. Freemasons' songs were composed, published and sung everywhere. Their symbols hung on watch-chains; ladies were presented with white gloves by novices and associates, and various articles of fashion were christened à la franç-macon. Others had less pure intentions, for it was useful to belong to the order, the members of which were everywhere and had acquaintances in every circle.'

The situation changed rapidly before the end of the decade because of the spread of revolutionary ideas from France and the growth of various other societies, namely the Rosicrucians and the Illuminati. In Bavaria the Illuminati had gained control of several Masonic lodges. The Illuminati were not revolutionary, nor were they anti-religious but they did advocate far-reaching social changes and were therefore viewed with suspicion by the authorities and especially by the Catholic church. In 1784 a Jesuit-led campaign with the backing of the Rosicrucians resulted in the persecution of the Illuminati and the eventual banning of all secret societies. The Bavarian Government pressed the Austrian Emperor Joseph II to ban the Illuminati in Austria. He refused, but he did introduce measures to control the activities of the Freemasons in 1785. He ordered the eight Viennese lodges to be reduced to not more than three, and as a result two lodges, Truth and Newly Crowned Hope were formed.

After his death the repression of the Order grew worse, ending in a reign of terror under Francis II and his chancellor, Metternich. Eventually all secret societies were banned and in Austria from 1808 to 1918 it was illegal to be a Freemason.

Mozart and the Order

Mozart's conversion to Freemasonry was no sudden event; he had had connections with the Order from an early age. As an eleven-year-old boy he was treated for smallpox by Dr Wolff, a prominent Mason, in the town of Olomouc in Moravia. A year later in Vienna the Mozart family were introduced to Dr Anton Mesmer, the celebrated hypnotist – also a Mason. And it was in his garden that the young Wolfgang's first opera *Bastien und Bastienne* was performed.

When he was 17 Mozart was asked by a leading Viennese writer Tobias von Gebler, to compose music for his play, *Thamos, King of Egypt*. Gebler was a Mason as well as being a member of the Illuminati and in the play Masonic ritual and symbolism are presented.

A few years later another Masonic member of the Illuminati, Otto von Gemmingen, invited Mozart to write music for a melodrama on an Egyptian theme, based on Voltaire's play *Semiramis*. Both text and music are unfortunately lost but the work undoubtedly had Masonic significance, and Mozart was so delighted about this commission that he offered to compose the music free of charge.

It was probably Gemmingen who later persuaded Mozart to join the Order of Freemasons. He,

Once initiated, Mozart would have worn a Masonic apron, like that shown below, to all lodge functions. All the objects represented on the apron are important in Masonic ceremony. The temple in the centre is the Temple of Solomon and in the foreground are the tools of a working stonemason, as well as a beehive – the symbol of industry.

The Hapsburgs – Empress Maria Theresa, her husband, Francis I, and their son, Joseph – all had a part to play in the history of Freemasonry in Austria. The Empress, although she was a devout catholic, did not impose a papal ban on Freemasons because her husband was himself a Freemason. Nevertheless, on his death the ban was enforced and persecution of Masons followed. Her more liberal son, when he became Emperor Joseph II, revoked the ban and during the early part of his reign Freemasonry flourished.

Gemmingen, was the Grand Master of the lodge, Beneficence, in which Mozart was initiated in December 1784. Mozart may have attended meetings of the Illuminati in Salzburg long before he took that final step. The Iluminati met in a lonely grotto in the mountains near Salzburg. This romantic spot must have made a deep impression on the young composer – after his death his widow, Constanze, said that he had drawn up plans for a secret society called The Grotto. In any case Mozart, usually happy in the company of people who forgot rank in the pursuit of making and enjoying music, was probably naturally attracted to the Masonic ideals of brotherhood and philanthropy.

Ignaz von Born

In 1781 Mozart left Salzburg for Vienna where he quickly made many friends among Freemasons, including a leading member of the Illuminati, the scientist and writer, Ignaz von Born. A contemporary wrote of Born:

'I know of no one whom people would rather meet, or hear with greater interest. He has not written much but everything he says should be published, for it is always witty, relevant, and his satire is without malice.'

One of his satirical writings was directed against the 'monkish orders' – clerics whose fanaticism he strongly opposed. In 1785 he resigned from the Bavarian Academy of Sciences as a protest against the persecution of the Illuminati in Bavaria, declaring that 'the words Jesuitry and fanaticism can be equated with roguery and ignorance, superstition and stupidity.'

Contemporaries believe that Born was the model for Sarastro, the wise priest of the Sun-God in *The Magic Flute*. He was an authority on Egyptian mysteries and most probably gave Mozart excellent advice on the ritual scenes in the opera. Born was the founder and Grand Master of the lodge, True Harmony, sister lodge of Beneficence, with which it shared a temple. Among its members were many leading Viennese intellectuals – writers, artists, scientists and musicians. Mozart often attended its meetings and was promoted to the Second Grade of Masonry there on 7 January 1785 'with the accustomed ceremonies'. Joseph Haydn, perhaps influenced by his friend Mozart, had already applied for membership of the lodge, saying that it was his 'sincerest wish to become a member of that Order, with its humanitarian principles.' His initiation was due to take place on Friday 28 January but had to be postponed since he did not receive his invitation to the ceremony in time. Haydn visited Mozart two days after his initiation to hear the last three quartets which the younger composer had dedicated to him. In April 1785 Mozart's father Leopold was initiated in the lodge Beneficence and promoted to the Second

This highly decorated Masonic certificate (left) was issued to one of Mozart's contemporaries, Bartholmäus Zitterbarth, when he became a member of The Three Fires lodge on 1 December 1785. Zitterbarth was a merchant and a great theatre-lover. He became a theatre proprietor and for many years collaborated with Mozart's friend and fellow Mason, Emanuel Schikaneder.

The signs and symbols of Freemasonry were not confined to use in lodge ceremonies. Everyday objects such as plates and figurines, like the Meissen porcelain piece (left), although full of Masonic meaning, were made to adorn the homes of Masons. Here the column and set square denote the architectural symbols, while the pug dog shows that this particular figure is of a Mason belonging to a mock order of German Masons, known as Mops, formed by a group of bored courtiers.

The Grotto of Aigen (right) near Salzburg was the meeting place of the Illuminati, a secret society, many members of which were also Masons. It is likely that this place is the inspiration for the 'Cavern of Water' – one of the scenes in Mozart's opera The Magic Flute.

Grade in True Harmony. Mozart composed the song *Fellow Craft's Journey* for the occasion.

Masonic music

Fellow Craft's Journey was the first of many works composed for the brotherhood after Mozart became a Freemason. Several of his earlier works, though, like the unfinished cantata *Hymn to the Sun* express Masonic ideas.

Music was very important to the Freemasons. They believed that it could 'spread good thoughts and unity among members'. Meetings began and ended with a simple folk-like song, usually in three parts with organ accompaniment and always scored for male voices.

Freemasons used a special musical symbolism to denote parts of the ritual. The number three has Masonic significance – the 'Three Knocks' made at the door of the lodge by a candidate for initiation were represented by a triple rhythmic figure. Pairs of slurred notes indicated the ties of brotherhood. Mozart naturally used much of the symbolism to good effect and developed it, giving it greater depth and expressiveness.

One of his most popular Masonic works was the cantata, *Masonic Joy* which was performed for the brothers of the lodge in honour of Ignaz von Born. The Emperor had honoured Born for his metallurgical discoveries and the brothers of the lodge invited members of other lodges 'to a friendly and joyous repast . . . with the intention of expressing their sentiments in conviviality, through the arts of poetry and music.'

Towards the end of 1785, Mozart wrote two songs for the lodge, Newly Crowned Hope, which had been formed in accordance with the Emperor's decree. Apart from the reorganization of the lodges in Vienna the Emperor ordered that records of meetings and membership be submitted regularly to the police. The changes were not accepted without controversy and many resigned from the lodges.

Mozart joined the lodge Newly Crowned Hope – of which one of his old friends, Tobias von Gebler, was the Grand Master. The two songs, *For the Opening of the Lodge* and *For the Closing of the Lodge* praise the new leaders and express hope for the future of Freemasonry. Sadly, because of the difficult times ahead, these hopes were not realized. Rumours circulated that the Illuminati were promoting revolutionary ideas from France, and spies and informers were everywhere. Books were seized and arrests made.

Many documents from this period, including some of Mozart's letters, were destroyed. Some do survive though, including a letter to his father, just before his death in 1787, where Mozart exhorts him to look on death as 'man's best friend' according to Masonic teaching.

There are further Masonic allusions in the pathetic begging letters to his fellow Freemason, Michael Puchberg, a wealthy merchant:

'I take you to be a man who, if he can do so, will,

like myself, certainly assist a friend, if he be a true friend, or his Brother, if he be indeed a Brother.'

Mozart frequently helped his fellow Masons, even when in want himself. He often performed at benefit-type concerts to assist needy fellow Masons, and the proceeds of his cantata, *Masonic Joy,* when published, were devoted to 'the relief of their (the Masons') needy fellow-men.' He lent money to Anton Stadler, the gifted but unscrupulous clarinettist, (to whom he dedicated the clarinet quintet and concerto); and to Count Lichnowsky (later Beethoven's patron), with whom he travelled to Berlin in 1790. Lichnowsky left Mozart stranded in Potsdam – 'an expensive place', without repaying the 100 gulden he had borrowed.

Last years

After 1785 Mozart wrote no more openly Masonic music until 1791, the last year of his life, when he seemed to gather fresh courage to face the difficulties caused by his own and his wife's illnesses, by increasing poverty, and by the stresses of the

Music was very important to Freemasons: they felt it could 'spread good thoughts and unity among members.' The title page (far left) for Mozart's cantata **Masonic Joy** *shows Ignaz von Born, the Master of the Lodge, as a bearded figure crowned by the goddess of Wisdom. The cantata was performed when Born was honoured by Joseph II for his metallurgical discoveries. Mozart not only wrote music for special occasions but also for regular lodge ceremonies. Most Masonic songs were collected and published in book form (left).*

political situation. After a period during which he composed comparatively little, he produced a number of masterpieces which are serene and confident, as though he had suddenly turned a corner and seen a light. Several of these works have Masonic influences, especially his opera, *The Magic Flute*.

In the spring of 1791 an actor-manager called Emanuel Schikaneder invited Mozart to compose the music for a fairy-tale opera for his theatre in the suburbs of Vienna, where he planned to give a season of light entertainment. The story goes that Mozart agreed to try his hand at it, though he had never before attempted anything of the sort. The libretto was to be based on an Oriental fairy-story, and was to contain spectacular elements and magical effects likely to please a popular audience, with plenty of comedy and a part for Schikaneder himself — that of Papageno, the bird-catcher.

In the end the opera turned out quite differently. It was probably Mozart himself who was responsible for turning it into a Masonic allegory. (Schikaneder, though formerly a Freemason, had been expelled from the Order.) A few years earlier, on a visit to

The lodge in the anonymous painting (above) was identified in 1980 by H Robbins Landon as that to which Mozart belonged — Newly Crowned Hope. The members of the lodge are taking part in the initiation ceremony of a blindfolded candidate. The Master of Ceremonies, in the centre foreground, is thought to be Prince Nicolaus Esterhazy. Mozart is seated on the end of the right-hand row of lodge members.

Prague, Mozart had been welcomed by Masons forming a guard of honour and singing *Masonic Joy*; he had thanked them, saying that he intended to pay tribute to Freemasonry in a better way. He fulfilled that promise in *The Magic Flute*.

The opera is full of Masonic symbolism, verbal, visual and musical. The spoken dialogue is often directly taken from Masonic ceremonies; the frontispiece to the first edition contains Masonic symbols; the 'Three Knocks' are clearly heard in the overture, and the opera as a whole must have surprised the audience, if they came expecting to see a pantomine.

It is not necessary to understand all the symbolism

to enjoy *The Magic Flute.* Goethe, himself a Freemason, said that 'the majority of spectators will enjoy it; the initiated will understand its higher meaning.' Mozart, however, was upset by a friend who made fun of the 'higher meaning' of the opera.

At the time when the opera was written – two years after the French Revolution – Freemasonry was under attack from its enemies. It required great courage and conviction to present a work in which the ideas of equality and fraternity were so clearly expressed, even though disguised in a fairy-story. Mozart went further than his Masonic Brothers by extending the principles of liberty, equality and fraternity so as to embrace the whole of humanity, women as well as men. The Freemasons excluded women from their lodges, but in *The Magic Flute* Pamina is admitted to the company of the Enlightened on equal terms with Tamino.

Masonic cantatas

Two other works composed in his last year express the same humanistic message.

While he was still at work on *The Magic Flute* Mozart received an unusual commission from another Freemason. A Hamburg merchant, Franz Ziegenhagen – a follower of Rousseau – had written a book suggesting that a society based on equality of race, religion and sex could lead to the happiness of the human race, in a world free from want and war. He proposed to found a colony near Hamburg to put his ideas into practice, and invited Mozart to write a cantata, (K. 619) to be sung at meetings in this colony.

His last completed work, *A Little Masonic Cantata,* was composed in November 1791, for the opening of a new temple for the lodge, Newly Crowned Hope. He conducted the work himself, and it was enthusiastically received. 'How madly they have gone on about my cantata! If I didn't know that I'd written better things, I should think this my best work'. In this joyful cantata Mozart reaffirmed his belief in the humanistic ideal of Freemasonry.

Mozart fell ill soon after the performance of his cantata and was unable to finish a Requiem commissioned by a mysterious stranger. Mozart believed he was writing the Requiem for himself – in fact the commission was from a nobleman who wanted to present the work as his own.

Although the papal bulls of 1738 and 1751 banned Freemasonry, it was not inconsistent for a Catholic to be a Freemason, and Mozart never renounced his faith. However, when his sister-in-law, Sophie Haibl, tried to find a priest to administer the last sacraments she had difficulty in persuading 'one of those clerical brutes' to go to the dying composer, whose associations with the Illuminati and Freemasons were well known.

As he lay dying his mind was frequently on *The Magic Flute.* According to one report, on the eve of his death in his fevered imagination he thought he was at the opera, and whispered: 'Hush! Hush! Now the Queen of Night is taking her high B flat!'

The opera was becoming more and more popular, in spite of attempts by the enemies of Freemasonry to get it banned. Sadly, Mozart did not live to enjoy its success; he died on 5 December 1791, and was buried in a pauper's grave.

When Mozart first joined the Order he had been glad of the chance to exchange ideas with liberal-minded people; no doubt he enjoyed the Masonic feasts and concerts; the mysterious rituals, too, attracted him, for he always loved codes and riddles. Above all he believed in the Order's humanitarian principles, which he upheld to the end of his life.

'He was a diligent member of our Order: brotherly love, a peaceable disposition, advocacy of a good cause, beneficence, a true, sincere sense of pleasure whenever he could help one of his Brethren with his talents: these were his chief characteristics.'

Wolfgang persuaded his father Leopold Mozart (above) to become a Freemason. Leopold was initiated in the lodge Beneficence on 1 April 1785 and he was promoted to the Second Grade in the lodge True Harmony ten days later. Before he left Vienna he was promoted to the Third Grade in a ceremony at which Born presided. Wolfgang composed the song Fellow Craft's Journey *to mark the former occasion.*

THE GREAT COMPOSERS
Joseph Haydn
1732–1809

Recognized in his lifetime as a composer of genius, Haydn, throughout his long musical career, was a central figure in the growth and development of the mature Classical style.

Regarded by his contemporaries as the father of modern instrumental music, Joseph Haydn was the first composer to recognize and develop the full potential of the evolving musical forms of the symphony and the sonata.

Born in 1732 he was the son of Mathias and Anna Maria Haydn. His father was a master wheelwright and a market magistrate (Marktrichter) and although an important man in the bureaucracy of the town of Rohrau – on the borders of Austria and Hungary – he was not well off. Joseph was the second of twelve children of whom only six survived infancy.

Neither of his parents had any musical training but his father loved folk songs and played the harp 'without knowing a note of music'. Joseph joined in the family's musical evenings and by the time he was five could sing many of his father's favourite songs with him – to the delight of family and friends who were all aware of this growing musical talent.

His first chance of advancement came when a relative, Johann Mathias Franck, visited the family in 1738. Franck was headmaster at the school in Hainburg and organist and director of music at the parish church of St Philip and St James. Hainburg itself was not much bigger than Rohrau, but it was decided that it would benefit Haydn to receive an education there. Although fascinated by the new sights and sounds around him the young Haydn did not have a very happy childhood in the Franck household, nor did he have an easy time at school under Franck's tutelage since Franck's preferred teaching method was to bash knowledge into the heads of his pupils.

Despite the unpleasant aspects of life in Hainburg Haydn did make musical progress. He learned to play every musical instrument and became a good singer. Although he never forgot the bad times in Hainburg he always regarded Franck's teaching as important. Long after he left Hainburg he recorded his debt to Franck:

I have to honour this man (Franck), even though he is long dead, for teaching me so many different things, even though I got more thrashings than food in the process.

When Haydn was seven, a second opportunity for

St Stephen's Cathedral, Vienna (right) where Haydn was a choirboy for eight years. He was recruited to the choir by Georg Reutter, the Kapellmeister at the Cathedral. Reutter had heard Haydn singing in the town of Hainburg where he received his early schooling.

A view of the Kohlmarket, Vienna (below), the area where Haydn lived after he was expelled from the cathedral choir in 1749. He rented a garret at the top of the Michaelerhaus, the large building on the right. In the left foreground are the premises of Artaria, who later became Haydn's publishers.

change in his musical education cropped up. He wrote in his autobiography:

When I was seven Kapellmeister von Reutter (of St Stephen's Cathedral in Vienna) passed through Hainburg and quite by accident heard my weak but pleasant voice. He forthwith took me to the choir house (of St Stephen's), where apart from my studies, I learned the art of singing, the harpsichord, and the violin, from very good masters. Until my eighteenth year I sang soprano with great success, not only at St Stephen's but also at Court. Finally I lost my voice.

When his voice changed he was no longer of any use to Reutter, who sought a pretext to dismiss him. When Haydn mischievously cut off the pigtail of a fellow-chorister Reutter expelled him.

Vienna is the city most associated with Haydn, but in fact, after his initial studies at St Stephen's Cathedral and his subsequent years of near starvation from 1749–1757, Haydn did not live in Vienna again until the last years of his life. When he was thrown out on the streets as a young boy of 18 he almost perished. Although he was lucky enough to meet and

Pietro Metastasio (above) an Italian poet, was one of the influential and successful literary and musical figures whom Haydn met when he was trying to earn his living in Vienna.

At first Haydn struggled as a freelance musician and teacher of music. Later, through his acquaintance with Metastasio and the composer Nicolo Porpora, his fortunes changed. Haydn was introduced to a world where he was able to make contact – at musical gatherings such as the one shown below, where he is represented playing the keyboard – with potential patrons.

share lodgings with Michael Spangler – an impoverished singer and music teacher – he led a very meagre existence. Gradually he made his way as a freelance musician – playing, teaching and composing diligently.

Through one of his pupils he met the Italian writer and poet Metastasio. At much the same time he met Nicolo Antonio Porpora, an Italian composer and became his valet and factotum. From Porpora he learned the true fundamentals of musical composition. As his assistant he had social access to the nobility – the only people in 18th-century society who could advance his career.

First court appointment

At one of the social and musical events to which Porpora introduced him he met an Austrian noble-man, Karl Joseph von Fürnberg. Von Fürnberg invited him to his country house in 1757 to take part in performances of chamber music. During this visit Haydn wrote his first string quartets, which were received with great enthusiasm. Von Fürnberg also recommended Haydn to Ferdinand Maximilian, Count von Morzin of Bohemia, who appointed Haydn his Kapellmeister in 1758. This was Haydn's first permanent musical post and he was paid 200 florins a year and received free board and lodgings. Haydn's duties were to organize all the music of the Count's orchestra of 16 musicians who played in Vienna during the winter and at his country estate in Lukaveč in the summer. Haydn's early quartets and symphonies dating from this period were very popular and were circulated in manuscript form throughout the Austrian Empire. His First Symphony was written for and performed by Count von Morzin's orchestra in 1759 – one of the guests at the performance was Prince Paul Anton Esterhazy – a wealthy nobleman who was to be Haydn's future employer.

An unsuccessful marriage

With some financial security behind him Haydn's thoughts turned to marriage. He had fallen in love with one of his pupils, Therese Keller, the daughter of a wig-maker in Vienna. It is thought that she did not return his affection and in 1756 she entered the convent of St Nicholas in Vienna. Haydn wrote this first major work, *Salve Regina in E major* for her induction. Whether he felt under an obligation to the family or was put under some pressure by them is not known, but in November 1760 he married Therese's older sister, Maria Anna. The marriage was not a success. It soon became evident that Maria Anna was ill-natured, indifferent to music and unsuited to domestic or family life.

According to reports from musicians who worked for Haydn she was always doing things designed to irritate him. They said that she used his manuscripts as lining paper for her pastry tins and paper for hair curlers. Whatever the truth of the matter she devoted much of her time to the church and Haydn turned to his music as an escape. Haydn enjoyed the company of women and given the unsuccessful nature of the marriage found companionship with a number of other women. Of his many women friends the most celebrated were the singer Luigia Polzelli (engaged to sing at Esterhazy in 1779) and Maria Anna von Genzinger, wife of one of the Esterhazy doctors.

Due to financial difficulties Count Morzin was forced to disband his orchestra in 1761 and Haydn

had to look for another post. Hearing that Haydn was unemployed, Prince Paul Anton Esterhazy offered him the post of Assistant Kapellmeister. One of the most powerful and wealthy Austro-Hungarian families, the Esterhazy family spent the summers at their palace in Eisenstadt and the winters in Vienna. Haydn was in charge of a small but brilliant orchestra and, on condition of giving satisfaction, was promised the post of Kapellmeister on the retirement or death of the incumbent, Werner.

For the next thirty years Haydn was involved at the court of the Esterhazys. In 1762 Prince Paul Anton died and was succeeded by his brother Prince Nikolaus, an extremely cultured man, who continued his brother's efforts to expand and modernize the Esterhazy musical repertoire. Haydn remained in his service until Nikolaus died in 1790. During this time Haydn wrote in every musical genre, both vocal and instrumental, and gained a reputation that made him the most famous composer in Europe.

Kapellmeister at Eszterhaza

The year 1766 was a turning point in Haydn's musical development. Werner, the Kapellmeister, died and Haydn was appointed to the post. This meant that he had total responsibility for all musical performances at court and was again able to compose church music (formerly this had been Werner's preserve).

Also in 1766 Prince Nikolaus moved the court to a palace which he had built on one of the family estates in Hungary at a place called Süttör. The palace, from 1765 known as Eszterhaza, was said to rival Versailles in beauty and splendour.

Two of the new facilities at Eszterhaza were a marionette theatre and an opera house. For both of these venues Haydn created successful and original works, but for the opera house he also rehearsed and performed works by other composers. Most of his own operas were written to celebrate special occasions like marriages, royal visits and name days.

At Eszterhaza Haydn was isolated from his musician friends in Vienna. The palace itself was remote and only visited by those invited by the Prince. Haydn, however, realized that the isolation was ultimately beneficial to him.

The theatre at Eszterhaza was opened in 1768, and as the Prince's interest in opera increased, the opera season was greatly extended. In 1786 there were 125 performances and 17 operas were staged.

In 1779 the opera house together with the collection of music which was housed in it, was destroyed by fire. Fortunately, Haydn kept the autographed scores separate from the performance material so the music was not lost. A more magnificent theatre was rebuilt in 1781 but Haydn wrote only three more operas for Eszterhaza.

Also in 1779 Haydn established a firm contact with the Viennese publishers, Artaria. Up until this time only one of Haydn's works had been published with his permission. Editions of his work which had appeared in other countries were probably published without his permission or even without his knowledge. In any case, prior to 1779 Haydn's compositions were really the property of Prince Nikolaus. Now, due to the terms of a new contract between himself and the Prince, Haydn was free to supply publishers with his work, and from 1780–1790 he entrusted most of his principal compositions to Artaria. Both he and the publishers made a good deal of money from the transactions and his reputation abroad grew at an astounding pace.

Haydn's relationship with the young singer Luigia Polzelli blossomed in 1779 when, together with her violinist husband, she was engaged at Eszterhaza. Luigia's marriage, like that of Haydn, was not a happy one and Haydn seemed to lavish on Luigia the affection he had not felt for his wife. Although Luigia seemed to have a sincere affection for Haydn, she was quick to see the benefit that the Kapellmeister's affection might have for her. When the orchestra was disbanded in 1790 Haydn and Luigia continued their friendship by letter. When Haydn's wife died in 1802

Prince Nikolaus Esterhazy (above left) succeeded his brother, Prince Paul Anton – Haydn's first Esterházy employer – in 1762. Prince Nikolaus was Haydn's patron and employer for nearly 30 years until his death in 1790. He was a cultured and artistic man who never grudged any money spent on splendid occasions. Before he succeeded to the title he spent much of his time at a hunting lodge which he had inherited at Süttör. He used it as a summer residence but enjoyed being there so much that he decided to rebuild it as a palace. From 1765 it was known as Eszterhaza and from 1766, the new palace (above) became his main court. It was here at Eszterhaza that Haydn's musical activities were centred.

he signed a declaration that if he remarried it would only be to Luigia. However, Luigia returned to Italy when her husband died and shortly before Haydn's death married an Italian singer. It was rumoured that her second son, Antonio, born at Eszterhaza in 1783 was Haydn's illegitimate son.

In 1785 Haydn was accepted as a member of a Viennese lodge of Freemasons and probably through this contact (Mozart, too, was a Freemason) his friendship with Mozart grew. At a private evening concert in Vienna Mozart played three of the set of six new quartets which he dedicated to Haydn. After the performance Haydn told Mozart's father, Leopold, that he thought Mozart was the greatest composer he knew.

Haydn's last important works written at Eszterhaza were the Twelve Quartets, Op. 54, 55 and 64, written for Johann Tost, a violinist in the Eszterhaza orchestra. In 1790, Princess Elizabeth Esterhazy died in February and her husband, Haydn's patron, died seven months later. He was succeeded by his son, Anton, whose interests were more political than artistic and who had no interest in music. He disbanded the orchestra and the choir and though Haydn was retained, he remained as choir master in name only. He received a handsome pension from the estate of Prince Nikolaus but as there was nothing to keep him in Eszterhaza, he was free to travel and he decided to return to Vienna.

In Vienna he received an offer of employment from the King of Naples but, glad to have his independence once more, he was reluctant to take up the offer of a court post. A visit from Johann Peter Salomon, a German born violinist and London concert promoter, gave him another option. Salomon engaged him for a series of concerts in London.

The London visits

Haydn took leave of his friend Mozart at a farewell luncheon during which they both wept and Mozart was filled with a premonition that they would not see each other again – a feeling which sadly proved true. Haydn, who had travelled very little indeed and had never even seen the sea, set off with Salomon for England on 15 December 1790.

Under his contract with Salomon Haydn agreed to travel to London to conduct twenty concerts, each one to include a first performance of one of his own compositions. He would receive £300 for a new opera, £300 for six new symphonies as well as a further £200 for their copyright, £200 for his participation in the 20 concerts and a further £200 guaranteed for a benefit performance.

The first of the Salomon season of concerts took place on 11 March 1791, and it received a rapturous reception in the press and from the public. A rival

As court composer Haydn was required to produce church music, operas, symphonies and works for the baryton (the Prince's favourite musical instrument). Some of Haydn's operas were written and performed for name-day celebrations of members of his patron's family, or in celebration of special visits. L'incontro improvviso (below) was first performed in August 1775 when the Austrian Archduke Ferdinand and the Archduchess Beatrice, accompanied by the imperial court visited Eszterhaza.

concert organization known as the Professional Concerts had realized that a celebrity such as Haydn might win the entire London audience if there was no opposition. They promoted a series of concerts engaging another European musician, Ignaz Joseph Pleyel, who had been a pupil of Haydn's, as a counter-attraction. Both Haydn and Pleyel refused to take part in the rivalry which was being fostered and soon, after hearing both musicians, the London public was able to judge from performances which was the supreme genius of the two.

Haydn became a favourite of London society and many hoped that he would settle permanently in London. He was received by the Prince of Wales and was persuaded to stay in London for a second season. While in London, Oxford University conferred on him the title of Doctor of Music.

Haydn noted down everything which seemed quaint and unusual – London prices, English habits and customs, notes about people and music which he heard. He went to Ascot to watch the races and in November 1791 stayed with the Prince of Wales and his brother, the Duke of York, at Oatlands in Surrey. His closest friend in London was Rebecca Schroeter, widow of a German pianist and composer. She took piano lessons from Haydn and a strong friendship developed between them. Haydn kept her letters and in his old age showed them to a friend saying:

Those are from an English lady who fell in love with me. She was a very attractive woman, and still handsome, though over sixty; and had I been free I should certainly have married her.

At the beginning of 1792 Haydn heard the sad news of the death of his friend Mozart, aged 35. Later that year Haydn left London to return to Vienna. En route he stopped at Bad Godesburg where a young court composer submitted a cantata to him for his assessment. Haydn praised the cantata and promised to be the composer's teacher if he ever came to Vienna. The young composer was Beethoven and he took up the offer later that year when he came to Vienna. There were difficult moments in their relationship – Haydn once remarked, 'You give me the impression of being a man who has several heads, several hearts and several souls.'

Haydn was greatly affected in 1793 by the death of

The Hanover Square rooms, in the left background (above) saw Haydn's London's success.

Haydn's most important duty for his third Esterhazy patron, Prince Nikolaus II, was the composition every year of a new mass to celebrate the name-day of the Prince's wife, Princess Maria Hermenegild (left).

The crowning achievement of Haydn's old age was his oratorio, The Creation, *first performed in public in 1799. On 27 March 1808 a special performance (below) was given in the hall of the Old University in Vienna, to mark Haydn's 76th birthday. Haydn by this time was very frail and was carried into the hall from his coach.*

The last few weeks of Haydn's life were disturbed by the French bombardment of the Vienna suburbs (right).

his great friend Maria Anna von Genzinger. He found life in Vienna was not as stimulating as the cultural life he had experienced in England, so in 1794 he set off again for London. This time he took with him his servant and copyist, Johann Elssler. His second London visit was even more successful than the first.

Haydn was introduced at Court and the King, George III, asked him to stay in England – the Queen even offered him a suite in Windsor Castle. Haydn gave the proposition serious thought but felt that he wanted to spend his remaining years in his home country. He was also probably alarmed by the increasing violence of the Napoleonic War, threatening to isolate England from the Continent.

The mature years in Vienna

However, in Austria his patron Prince Anton Esterhazy had died and his successor, Prince Nikolaus II requested Haydn to return as he had decided to reconstitute the princely band and choir. In August 1795 Haydn bade farewell to his many English friends and returned to Vienna. In England his art had expanded greatly and it seemed that not only was he inexhaustible but that his inspiration was unlimited. London broadened his horizons and he returned to Vienna a thoroughly sophisticated 18th-century gentleman.

In between his two London visits Haydn had purchased a house in a suburb of Vienna called Gumpendorf and it was to this house, newly enlarged in 1793, that he returned in 1795. His patron had abandoned Eszterhaza and established his summer residence at Eisenstadt. Haydn's duties, apart from the normal admistrative duties of Kapellmeister, were to produce a mass once every year for the name-day of Prince Nikolaus II's wife, Princess Maria Hermenegild. The series of six masses he wrote in celebration of his patroness, of whom he was particularly fond, are proof of his astonishing creativity. However the crowning achievement of

Haydn's old age was his oratorio, *The Creation.* He spent the whole of 1797 and part of 1798 working on this composition. His librettist Gottfried van Swieten organized a group of Viennese aristocrats who agreed to sponsor a private performance, each guaranteeing Haydn a sum of 500 ducats. This took place at the Schwarzenberg Palace on 29 and 30 April 1798. The work was so successful it had to be repeated on 7th and 10th May. After revisions the work had its first public performance at the Burg Theatre on 19 March 1799. Haydn conducted it and Salieri, the Emperor's Kapellmeister, played the pianoforte. The atmosphere was electric and the work was a resounding success.

Probably fired by the great success of *The Creation* Haydn and von Swieten decided to collaborate again on another oratorio. The text chosen was a poem by James Thomson, *The Seasons.* Haydn worked on the first part of *The Seasons* in 1799 but ill health hindered his progress and he left the last sections until 1801. The first performance was sponsored in the same way as *The Creation* and the first public performance took place at the Redoutensaal.

His unhappy marriage came to an end in 1802 when his wife died, but it was too late for him to think of remarriage. At this time, he began to put his affairs in order and in 1805 with Elssler drew up a thematic catalogue, the *Entwurf-Katalog.*

Although he had no close female companion in his old age, his patroness, Princess Maria Hermenegild, saw that he was comfortable and Prince Nikolaus's doctors attended him as he became more frail and ill. In the days preceding his death the French attacked Vienna and during one of the bombardments a cannon ball fell near the house. When the French took and occupied Vienna Napoleon placed a guard of honour at Haydn's door. Haydn died on 31 May 1809 of old age and exhaustion. He was buried in the cemetery at the Hundsturmer Linie but his body was reburied in 1820 by Prince Nikolaus at Eisenstadt.

'Vive la Nation'
Revolution in France 1789

When the French people rose against their king, Louis XVI, in 1789 the shock waves caused by the forces of revolution were felt in almost every country in Europe.

At about half past ten at night, on 20 June 1791, King Louis XVI and Queen Marie Antoinette of France, together with their two children, the King's sister Madame Elizabeth, and the royal governess, slipped out of the Tuileries Palace by an unwatched door and into a waiting carriage. The King was wearing the clothes of a valet; the Queen was dressed to look like a governess; and the six-year-old dauphin was dressed up as a little girl. The governess, for the moment alias 'Baroness Korff, appeared as the employer of these royal servants and mother of the boy and girl, and the coachman was none other than Count Fersen, a handsome young Swede who was devoted to the Queen and who had been involved in drawing up the escape plan.

At the gates of Paris the getaway party changed into a heavier coach, prepared for a long journey, and at a slow pace took the road east. The little town of Varennes was reached between 11 and 12 on the night of 21 June. More than once in their slow progress the royal family had been recognized but allowed to pass on. Apart from the ineffectiveness of

their 'disguises' – the King's face was on every assignat, the new paper currency – the spanking new green and white coach, drawn by six horses, was also very conspicuous. That they had managed to reach Varennes was a matter of luck, given the Queen's insistence that the family travel together, for this decision prevented the use of a smaller, faster vehicle. It was the delays that were to prove fatal for the fugitives.

By stealing out of Paris this way the King was turning his back on the revolution that had started in 1789. He was heading eastwards to set up the royal standard at Metz, and to meet the Marquis de Bouille who was in command of an army with royalist sympathies. With the help of the other monarchs of Europe, particularly his brother-in-law, the Emperor Leopold of Austria, and the King of Prussia, Louis then hoped to defeat the revolutionaries and reconquer France for the *ancien régime* and to restore himself as an absolute monarch. However, these hopes were never to be fulfilled and Louis was destined to lose both his crown and his life.

On July 14th 1789 an
armed mob, made up
of Parisian craftsmen
and shopkeepers,
stormed the Bastille
(far left). And
despotisim, as
symbolized by this
great prison fortress
was overthrown with
the collapse of its
defences – the
Revolution had begun.

From the seclusion of
his magnificent
chateau in Versailles,
Louis XVI (left) felt
answerable only to God
in the way he ruled his
people. But his was a
kingdom wracked with
problems about which
he was tragically ill-
informed. It was a
country divided by a
rigid class system,
weighed down by
oppressive taxes and
brimming over with the
anger of the oppressed
poor – ideal fuel for
revolution.

The monarchy and the revolution

Unlike his predecessors Louis XIV (the Sun King) and Louis XV, Louis XVI was not an imperious autocrat, but he was very stubborn and woefully ill-informed. And from the seclusion of the royal chateau he had been blind to the true state of the nation and the plight of his people. When revolution came in 1789 Louis was not swept away; instead the revolutionary forces offered him a revised role – that of constitutional monarch who would reign by sanction of a national assembly of elected representatives. In a bid to cling to his throne, Louis at first went along with this, but in truth he did not see why he could not carry on as before – ruling alone by divine right rather than being merely the mouthpiece of an elected parliament. When finally the Assembly looked to re-structuring the clergy, Louis' will to continue with the new order broke.

He was intensely religious and he disliked the revolutionary idea that the property of the church belonged to all believers, not just the clergy, and that it was at the disposal of the nation. Still less did he like the new laws, enshrined in the Civil Constitution of the Church which the Assembly passed in 1790, whereby bishops and priests were to be elected. By this new arrangement the lower clergy benefitted from a doubling of their incomes, to be paid by the state, and by the destruction of the old aristocratic monopoly on senior appointments such as bishoprics. Then a further decree, passed early in 1791, required all holders of clerical offices to take an oath of allegiance to the state, and the King's misgivings were confirmed and supported when the Pope condemned outright the whole Civil Constitution in March and April. From then on Louis' resolve to flee hardened.

In secret, he made moves towards armed intervention by his fellow monarchs and began his plans to escape in order to martial counter-revolutionary forces.

Marie Antoinette

In less troubled times Louis had enjoyed nothing better than to retire to his workshop and forge, where he used to indulge his favourite hobby of lockmaking, and he would come down to his wife's parties, and scoldings, with forge-blackened hands. Whereas Louis on the one hand was too mild and dull a character to manage a great historical crisis, his more assertive wife, was dangerously susceptible to dramatic initiatives.

The story of Marie Antoinette's 'Let them eat cake' response to the plight of the bread-starved people of Paris has a very dubious basis in fact but, like many such stories, it does reflect a historical reality. Long before the revolution began Louis XVI's unhappy queen had acquired great unpopularity. Much of her bad image was very unfairly based on the fact that she was Austrian, the living symbol of an unpopular alliance through marriage between France and its traditional enemy, Austria. No sooner had she arrived at Versailles than the young Hapsburg princess had to run the gauntlet of various court factions who were hostile to the Austrian connection. But Marie Antoinette was not a conciliatory person, and she responded by withdrawing into a private little world and mingling only with her intimates.

Marie Antoinette was a pleasure-loving and extravagant queen and she made it too obvious when she was bored with some of her royal duties. Her

The French 'parliament' – for what it was worth – was divided into three estates: the aristocracy, the clergy and the middle-class professionals and businessmen who represented the masses. The Third Estate, as the latter group were known, fearing they could always be outvoted, demanded a large percentage of the votes. It was their political awakening (below) that spelled disaster for the King.

REVEIL DU TIERS ETAT.

dislike of stuffy court ceremonies was such that her mother, the Empress Maria Theresa, often tried to warn her about the consequences of such behaviour.

I know very well how tedious and futile is a representative position; but believe me, you will have to put up with both tediousness and futility, for otherwise you might suffer from much more serious inconveniences than these petty burdens – you more than most rulers, since you have to rule over so touchy a nation.

When the revolution happened Marie Antoinette was to realize just how touchy her subjects were. But she had no political sense and a disastrous habit of making enemies out of the people who could have helped her and her mild-mannered husband. Of the shrewd statesman Mirabeau she wrote disdainfully, 'We shall never be so wretched, I believe, as to be reduced to the painful extremity of having recourse to Mirabeau.' Yet his advice to the royal pair was sound. He told the King to accept the moderate revolutionary constitution, which did leave him with considerable powers such as the right to veto legislation, and to stand by the people and their parliamentary representatives as a constitutional king. Likewise advised General Lafayette, the liberal aristocrat who had fought for the Americans during their recent revolution. Lafayette also believed that there was a role for the King in the new France, if he

After their daring but ill-fated escape to Varennes, the King and his family were brought back to face the angry crowd of Paris (left). Their flight had destroyed once and for all, any possibility of retaining a constitutional monarchy.

In 1789, General Lafayette (below), presented a declaration of rights to the National Assembly. It was based on the American Declaration of Independence. (He had taken a major part in the American war) but his struggle for order and humanity was in vain.

The deputies of the Third Estate declared themselves to be the representative National Assembly and for solidarity took an oath (above left) which bound them to remain in session until their demands were met and they were joined by the other two Estates.

played his cards right, but he too was spurned. In April 1791 Mirabeau died, despairing of a monarchy that he believed was doomed. Then the Queen, ardently encouraged by her intimates, began to make plans, not for a compromise with democracy but for escape and revenge.

Disaster at Varennes

Just before the cumbersome coach reached Varennes its occupants had been recognized by a staunch young patriot.

In the coach there was a woman whom I thought I recognized as the Queen and on the seat in front of her to the left was a man. I was struck by the resemblance of his face to the likeness of the King printed on an assignat which I had with me at the time.

This was a posting master named Drouet (the posting station was the stage where carriages on long journeys changed postillions and horses) and he acted promptly on his hunch. Riding in pursuit, he learned of the coach's forward route and galloped across the countryside quickly enough to close the road. Varennes was actually within easy reach of Bouille's army and safety but, because of incompetence and bad luck, by the time the troops he had sent to meet the royal family arrived in the town the King had already been arrested and the fugitives were surrounded by bands of hostile peasants. Even then, Bouille's troops could have saved the day if they had challenged the King's captors because the revolutionaries' guns were not loaded. Drouet refused the substantial reward offered by the Assembly after Varennes but a year later he got himself elected as a deputy.

From Varennes the tragic return journey began. It took three and a half days because of the roundabout route adopted in order to avoid hostile crowds and all the while the royal coach needed the protection of National Guards and the presence of several deputies. Slowly, ignominiously and painfully the royal family arrived back at the palace that they loathed, surrounded as it was by the truculent citizens of Paris and cut off from the joys of hunting and the pleasures of the Petit Trianon. In the course

of this sad week the young Queen aged rapidly and it was said that her hair turned grey.

The counter-revolutionary menace

As yet it was only the King's status, not his life, that was endangered by the flight. So despite the fact that Louis had left behind a signed document repudiating all the measures he had accepted during his 'captivity' and despite the fact that royal fleurs-de-lis crests were being defaced in the streets, the Assembly still believed that the King was necessary and desirable as the head of state – they even put about the fiction that, far from having fled his people, the royal family had been 'abducted'. And although the King was temporarily disgraced by being suspended from his duties and rights, the new

The Paris crowd stormed the Tuileries (right), residence of the royal family, on August 10th 1792. Louis' Swiss Guard, ordered to cease fire by the King, were massacred.

The Marseillaise (below) was composed in 1792 by a French captain of engineers and amateur musician. It was sung by revolutionary troops marching to Paris from Marseilles – and was later named after the city.

constitution adopted in October 1791 duly installed him as the head of state.

Still Louis hoped that his court in exile, *France extérieure,* would deliver him as the escape fiasco had drawn international attention to his situation. Europe did seem to be resounding with denunciations of the revolution and little congregations of aristocratic émigrés, dedicated to a restoration of all their privileges and the King's former powers, were gathering around France's frontiers. Koblenz in Germany, where the King's brother, the Comte d'Artois, had installed himself, was full of such émigrés and they were confident of the military support of the outraged monarchs of Europe. The émigrés urged officers in the French army to desert their regiments and the women sent little dolls to titled gentlemen remaining in France as tokens of their contempt for anyone who compromised with the Revolution.

But the other European powers were in fact lukewarm as far as action against revolutionary France was concerned. They were more worried about what Catherine the Great was up to in Poland and some countries, like Britain, considered it quite useful that France's internal turmoil distracted her from military activity in the rest of Europe. But eventually Marie Antoinette's brother, Leopold of Austria, stirred himself. In August 1791, at Pilnitz, he and the King of Prussia undertook to avenge any offence against the French royal family and take joint action to restore order in France *if* the other powers would join them. But since there was no question of

Louis' final words – 'that he had wished for nothing but good for his people' – fell on deaf ears. Cheers of 'Vive la Nation' rose from the blood-crazed crowd as the King was executed and his severed head held up for all to see (right).

such a united front, this declaration was a hollow threat.

Attack on the Tuileries
Marie Antoinette saw through Leopold's cynical gesture immediately but the Pilnitz Declaration was seen by the people of France as an insult and an ultimatum. The country was gripped by a nightmare image of Austrian and Prussian armies, led by the émigrés and supported by traitors within, descending on them to crush the gains of the revolution. Some deputies began to argue that France should declare war first, attack being the best defence. Besides, the democratic refugees from neighbouring countries who thronged Paris, reassured the Assembly that their peoples would welcome the revolutionary armies – 'The French people will utter a great shout and every other nation will answer its call.' It was also hoped that the war effort would help to stabilize popular commitment to the revolution. In April 1792 the Assembly approved a declaration of war against Austria.

As the Austrian and Prussian armies mobilized tension mounted in France, particularly in the unruly capital city which had led the revolution. The King and Queen were in an impossible situation, for Louis was still the head of revolutionary France and the advancing enemies were his friends. So while Louis signed the decree that initiated the war, Marie Antoinette was secretly sending details of the French military plans over the border, and both King and Queen were praying for a counter revolutionary victory.

'La patrie en danger' (The country in danger) became the call throughout France as a state of emergency was declared, and those with faltering courage were roused by the sight of the men of Marseilles marching to their new patriotic song, the *Marseillaise*. But the royal family's situation grew more and more precarious as the fraught summer days passed. In one incident a mob swarmed into the palace and forced the King to don a cap of liberty and drink to the nation's health. The King handled this potentially ugly confrontation with great composure, but future crowds would be less easy to humour, less willing to trust him. Unfortunately, it was possibly the relative harmlessness of this crowd that disinclined the King to pay attention to Lafayette's new escape plan.

The Parisian crowd's mood was to change drastically with the Brunswick Manifesto of August 1792. The Duke of Brunswick was the commander of the counter-revolutionary allies and though his manifesto's contents derived from proposals first put forward by Louis and Marie Antoinette, he had allowed the émigrés to word it in the most provocative way possible. It ordered Paris to submit at once to the King upon pain of an 'exemplary and ever memorable vengeance' and the delivery of the city to 'military punishment and total destruction'. Once again the King had not been particularly well served by his friends for nothing could have been more calculated to identify the monarchy with the invader and concentrate anger against the throne.

On 10 August the Tuileries Palace was attacked by a huge and extremely hostile crowd. Recognizing the peril of their situation, the royal family fled for protection to the National Assembly. But in the ensuing riot in the Tuileries more than 1,000 people were killed – shot or trampled underfoot. The King was now stripped of all his remaining constitutional powers as anti-royalist feeling in Paris ran high. Many of the deputies in the Assembly sincerely believed that the Tuileries rising had saved Paris from an aristocratic plot designed to coincide with the counter-revolutionary invasion. But the rising meant

After a three-day trial, looking worn out and far older than her years, Louis' pleasure-loving and extravagant queen was sentenced to death. With her head shorn and wearing a simple white dress, Marie Antoinette rode to her place of execution in a cart.

the end of the constitutional monarchy, from now on France would be a republic. This meant that anyone who wished to restore the monarchy was a traitor, because they were also necessarily wishing for a national defeat at the hands of foreign powers and the émigrés.

The September massacres

By 2 September Verdun, only 140 miles from Paris, was taken by the invaders. The wildest rumours now circulated in the panic-stricken city. It was widely believed that when the invading forces were within reach of Paris, a 'fifth column' of priests and aristocrats would break out of the prisons to strike at peaceful citizens and murder the families of the men who had marched to the frontiers to defend *la patrie*. This was tinder for the appalling 'September Massacres', a series of gruesome incidents in which the inmates of Paris's prisons were slaughtered by hysterical crowds while the national security forces turned a blind eye. In one particularly shocking murder the Princess Lamballe, a one-time favourite of the Queen's, was struck down, killed and mutilated. Her head was then stuck on a pike and paraded before other political prisoners.

The grisly September Massacres were the beginning of a phenomenon that was to evolve into the 'Reign of Terror'. It was not long now before the guillotine – so named after Dr Guillotin who had recommended it as a humane means of execution because of the speed with which its blade fell from a great height – would begin to rise and fall, and one of its first prominent victims was to be the King.

Execution of the King

Revolutionary confidence shot up with the first military victory at Valmy at the end of September, but this did not make the Assembly (now the Republican Convention) feel any more charitable towards the King. Since the attack on the Tuileries, the King had been redundant and, ever mindful of

Maximilien Robespierre (right), labelled the 'incorruptible', dominated the Committee of Public Safety during its brief period of power which included the Reign of Terror.

the temper of the uncomfortably close Parisian crowd, the deputies argued and debated about what was to be done with him. Did the abolition of the monarchy mean the elimination of the King, and if not what should be done with him? Should he be impeached for crimes against the people, or was this even necessary if kingship itself were considered a crime? Finally, the deputies decided that some sort of trial was in order and the King, now confined in the grim tower of the Temple, was brought before them.

Standing at the bar, Louis denied that he had ever wished to shed the blood of his people but he never challenged the Convention's right to try him. His timid defence was then completely undermined when an iron chest containing royal private papers was found in the Tuileries. Here was the desperate correspondence between Louis (and Marie Antoinette) and foreign powers, between Louis and Mirabeau, and so on. Unmistakable evidence of his double dealing, there was no shadow of a doubt now as to the King's guilt. The Tuileries correspondence proved to be the King's and ultimately the Queen's, death warrant, for the deputies now voted by an overwhelming majority for his execution.

On the morning of 21 January 1793 'Louis Capet, last King of the French', was publicly executed. The guillotine was placed in the Place de la Revolution (now Place de la Concorde) and surrounded by soldiers and representatives of the local Paris

French citizens celebrate a festival in honour of purity (above). Festivals prompted by Robespierre and his followers played an important part in maintaining revolutionary fervour among the people of Paris.

Bearing the symbols of the French worker, the poster shown below carries the bold message of revolution – liberty, equality, fraternity or death!

assemblies. Louis was taken to the scaffold in the mayor's carriage, with the curtains drawn, and he bore himself with quiet dignity. He tried to make a final speech but his words were so drowned by the roll of drums that it was impossible to catch what he said. As his severed head rolled automatically into a sack it was retrieved by the executioner and held up for all to see. Many of the gathered citizens defiantly shouted *'Vive la Nation'* and many rushed forward to dip pieces of cloth and paper in the King's blood.

The Reign of Terror

Although the execution of the King provoked a great storm of outraged protest abroad – London went through a period of general mourning – in France itself there was surprisingly little reaction. The war was distracting and the fact that France was now threatened by virtually every power in Europe encouraged a desperate 'we'll show 'em' attitude. But despite the many achievements of the revolutionary armies, they were over-extended and a serious reversal of fortunes had set in by March. At the same time, the Vendée, a region on the west coast, flared up in revolt against the revolution, particularly its religious legislation. The struggle against this rising and the renewed war effort brought with it more economic hardship, and to meet the crisis the Convention appointed a Committee of Public Safety in the summer of 1793. The men on this committee, notably Robespierre, did succeed in driving foreign armies from France, in crushing the royalist threat in the Vendée, stabilizing the economy and alleviating distress from hunger. But it achieved this at a great price in the form of the bloodiest phase in French history, the Reign of Terror.

The death of the Queen

The Terror, which lasted until the Committee was overthrown a year later, claimed the lives of an estimated 40,000 'enemies of the revolution' in the name of national security. And those who suffered first were the nobles who had not yet fled France, and who were now rounded up and thrown into the gloomy dungeons of the notorious Concièrgerie Prison. Here the widowed Queen herself was brought to await a three-day trial and in October 1793 Marie Antoinette was guillotined. It is a tiny measure of the hardened fanaticism of this period that she was brought to the scaffold not in a carriage like her husband but in a cart. She had cut off her hair herself and wore a simple white dress. The Queen looked haggard but met her death with the haughty composure that had always characterized her.

Louis' Queen was 38 years old when she died. After Marie Antoinette's execution Marie Grossholz, a talented young wax-modeller, was brought to the prison where the Queen's body had been carried in a handcart. There she was asked to make a death-mask of the features she had known in those far-off days of royal Versailles. Later, as that intrepid business-woman and survivor, Madame Tussaud, Marie made her waxworks into the basis of a 'chamber of horrors', which was to become a highly commercial and grisly memorial to the violent consequences of mass paranoia.

Marie Antoinette was soon followed to the scaffold by her pious sister-in-law, Madame Elizabeth, and in 1795 her young son, styled Louis XVII by his exiled subjects, died in captivity. The eight-year-old boy was said to have died of a kind of tuberculosis, and he had been a delicate child, but foul play was suspected. His sister, Marie-Thérèse, was more fortunate. After the overthrow of the Committee of Public Safety in July 1794 Austria managed to secure her release in exchange for some members of the Convention who were their prisoners. And by a strange twist of fate these prisoners included the Deputy Drouet, the quick-thinking posting master who had been responsible for the King's arrest on that dreadful night at Varennes.

Epilogue

With Robespierre and his followers gone – either deported or victims of the guillotine that had dispensed so effectively with thousands of their opponents – the Terror finally ended. The coup that overthrew the Committee of Public Safety came as a result of mounting hostility towards Robspierre's independent authority and his puritanical vision of a 'Republic of Virtue'. The Committee itself had already been weakened by divisions in its ranks over the wars that were being waged with most of the major powers of Europe.

These had been years of confusion and chaos, and in a bid for stability the Convention submitted a new constitution. They recommended that they should be replaced by a new legislative system, but retained the right of automatic re-election of two thirds of their members, and that their main rivals be disenfranchized.

The royalists, who had until then been hoping for a chance to restore the monarchy, rose in revolt to prevent the new constitution coming into effect. Royalists bourgeoisie and aristocrats converged on the Convention, but the rebellion was successfully crushed, the Convention and the republic saved by a young Corsican artillery officer who took it upon himself to step in and take charge. His name – Napoleon Bonaparte.

When in-fighting threatened to destroy the gains made by revolution and the establishment of the Republic, Napoleon (below) stepped in and took control by force. In defeating the foreign powers threatening France, Napoleon instilled confidence in the French people and in turn he was regarded as their saviour.

Ludwig van Beethoven

1770–1827

Beethoven's story is one of personal triumph over tragedy and supreme musical achievement. A complex and brilliant man, no composer before or since has exerted greater influence.

*Beethoven was the archetypal Romantic artist.
Scarcely any significant composer since his day
has escaped his influence or failed to
acknowledge the continuing power of his work.*

Beethoven was born in this house, at 515 Bonngasse, Bonn, on 17 December 1770. Not surprisingly, his place of birth has been a focus of interest: this pencil drawing was made in 1889 by R. Beissel, 58 years after the death of the composer.

A modern photograph of the same house now accorded the status of a shrine, in addition to its main function as a Beethoven museum. The only major structural changes made since Beethoven was born, have involved enlarging it on the garden side and altering the roof.

Ludwig van Beethoven is generally considered to be the greatest composer the world has ever known, even by people for whom he is not a personal 'favourite'. But why should he be held in such regard?

Consider these facts: no other composer's work has contained as large a proportion of established master pieces; Beethoven took music out of the 18th century and gave it a radical new direction, and in doing so broke many rules which were considered sacrosanct – but always for good musical reasons. Moreover, despite all that has happened since his death, his music continues to influence composers today.

Early years

For someone who was destined to be lionized by the aristocracy of his time, Beethoven's start in life was inauspicious. He was born in Bonn on 17 December 1770, the son of an obscure tenor singer in the employ of the Elector of Cologne. His father was said to be a violent and intemperate man, who returned home late at night much the worse for drink and dragged young Ludwig from his bed in order to beat music lessons into the boy's sleepy head. There are also stories of his

ther forcing him to play the violin for the amusement
his drinking cronies. Despite these and other abuses
which might well have persuaded a lesser person to
athe the subject – the young Beethoven developed a
nsitivity and vision for music.

When, despite his father's brutal teaching methods,
idwig began to show signs of promise, other
achers were called in. By the age of seven he was
ivanced enough to appear in public. A year or so later
ie composer Christian Gottlob Neefe took over his
usical training, and progress thereafter was rapid.
eethoven must have felt immense pride when his Nine
ariations for piano in C minor was published, and was
sted later in a prominent Leipzig catalogue as the
ork of 'Louis van Betthoven (sic), aged ten years'.

In 1787 Beethoven met Mozart. Beethoven was
siting Vienna, a noted musical centre, and must have
lt a little out of his depth for he was clumsy and
ocky; his manners were loutish, his black hair unruly
id he habitually wore an expression of surliness on
is swarthy face. By contrast the great Mozart was
ipper and sophisticated. He received the boy
oubtfully, but once Beethoven started playing the
iano his talent was evident. 'Watch this lad,' Mozart
eported. 'Some day he will force the world to talk
bout him.'

eparing for greatness

ith the death of his wife the last steadying influence
n Beethoven's father was removed. The old singer
nhesitatingly put the bottle before Ludwig, his two
ounger brothers and his one-year-old sister. The
tuation became so bad that by 1789 Beethoven was
orced to show the mettle that was to stand him in
ood stead later in life. He went resolutely to his
ither's employer and demanded – and got – half his
ither's salary so that the family could be provided for;
is father could drink away the rest. In 1792 the old
ian died. No great grief was felt: as his employer put
, 'That will deplete the revenue from liquor excise.'

For four years Ludwig supported his family. He also
iade some good friends, among them Stephan von
reuning, who became a friend for life, and Doctor
ranz Wegeler, who wrote one of the first biographies
f Beethoven. Count Ferdinand von Waldstein
ntered Beethoven's circle and received the
edication of a famous piano sonata in 1804.

In July 1792 the renowned composer Haydn passed
irough Bonn on his way to Vienna. He met Beet-
oven and was impressed, and perhaps disturbed, by
is work. Clearly, he felt, this young man's talent
eeded to be controlled before it could be developed.
onsequently Beethoven left Bonn for good early in
lovember 1792 to study composition with Haydn in
ienna. However, if Haydn had hoped to 'control'
eethoven's talent he was fighting a losing battle.
eethoven's music strode towards the next century,
eavily influenced by the strenuous political and
ocial tensions that ravaged Europe in the wake of the
rench Revolution. Haydn, who had been a musical
endsetter himself in his youth, found that Beethoven
as advancing implacably along the same radical path.

Those first weeks in Vienna were hard for Beet-
oven. Opportunities were not forthcoming; expecta-
ons were unfulfilled. In addition it must have irked
im, fired as he was by the current spirit of equality, to
ave to live in a tiny garret in Prince Lichnowsky's
iansion. Soon, however, the Prince gave him more
pacious accommodation on the ground floor, and,
iindful of the young man's impetuous behaviour, in-
tructed the servants that Beethoven's bell was to be

*A highly idealized
portrait of Beethoven
(above), painted in 1819
by Joseph Carl Steiler,
when the composer was
49 years old. He is shown
at work on the score of
the Missa Solemnis. By
this time he was already
totally deaf.
Beethoven was deeply
attached to his mother
Maria Magdalena (left),
referring to her as his
'best friend'. She died in
1787 of tuberculosis,
when Beethoven was 17.
A pious and conven-
tional woman, she tried
to shield Beethoven and
her other children from
their drunken father's
worst excesses.*

Joseph Haydn (above), the great classical composer, attempted to guide the young Beethoven's talent; the latter, however, would have none of this and later claimed to have learnt little from his mentor. The miniature (above right) shows Beethoven in 1803, while he was composing the 'Eroica' Symphony.

answered even before the Prince's own!

Impetuosity was also a feature of his piano playing at this time. In those days pianists were pitted against each other in front of audiences to decide who could play the more brilliantly and improvise the more imaginatively. Beethoven's rivals always retired, bloodied, from such combat. While he made enemies of many pianists in Vienna, the nobility flocked to hear him. Personally and professionally his future looked bright. Compositions poured from him and he gave concerts in Vienna as well as Berlin, Prague and other important centres. His finances were secure enough

for him to set up in his own apartments. He was the first composer to become a freelance by choice, as opposed to depending on patrons. However, it was his skill as a pianist rather than as a composer that brought him recognition during his twenties.

The onset of deafness

Beethoven's career as a virtuoso pianist was, however, soon to be terminated. In a letter written to his friend Karl Ameda on 1 July 1801, he admitted he was experiencing signs of deafness.

How often I wish you were here, for your Beethoven is having a miserable life, at odds with nature and its Creator, abusing the latter for leaving his creatures vulnerable to the slightest accident ... My greatest faculty, my hearing, is greatly deteriorated.

Apparently Beethoven had been aware of the problem for about three years, avoiding company lest his weakness be discovered, and retreating into himself. Friends ascribed his reserve to preoccupation and absentmindedness. In a letter to Wegeler, he wrote:

How can I, a musician, say to people "I am deaf!" I shall, if I can, defy this fate, even though there will be times when I shall be the unhappiest of God's creatures ... I live only in music ... frequently working on three or four pieces simultaneously.

Many men would have been driven to suicide. Beethoven may indeed have contemplated it. Yet his stubborn nature strengthened him and he came to terms with his deafness in a dynamic, constructive

Therese, Countess von Brunswick (right), was Beethoven's pupil and developed an 'intimate and warm-hearted' friendship with him. She also gave him this portrait. This gesture has been suggested as evidence that she was his 'Immortal Beloved': the great and secret love of his often stormy life.

ay. In another letter to Wegeler, written five months fter the despairing one quoted above, it becomes lear that Beethoven, as always, stubborn, unyielding nd struggling against destiny, saw his deafness as a hallenge to be fought and overcome:

ree me of only half this affliction and I shall e a complete, mature man. You must think of ne as being as happy as it is possible to be on his earth – not unhappy. No! I cannot endure it. will seize Fate by the throat. It will not wholly onquer me! Oh, how beautiful it is to live – and ive a thousand times over!

With the end of his career as a virtuoso pianist nevitable, he plunged into composing. It offered a nuch more precarious living than that of a performer, specially when his compositions had already shown hemselves to be in advance of popular taste. In 1802 is doctor sent him to Heiligenstadt, a village outside 'ienna, in the hope that its rural peace would rest his earing. The new surroundings reawakened in Beethoven a love of nature and the countryside, and hope nd optimism returned. Chief amongst the sunny works of this period was the charming, exuberant Symphony o. 2. However, when it became obvious that there vas no improvement in his hearing, despair returned. 3y the autumn the young man felt so low both physically and mentally that he feared he would not urvive the winter. He therefore wrote his will and left nstructions that it was to be opened only after his leath. The 'Heiligenstadt Testament', as it is known, is long, moving document that reveals more about his tate of mind than does the music he was writing at the ime. Only his last works can reflect in sound what he hen put down in words.

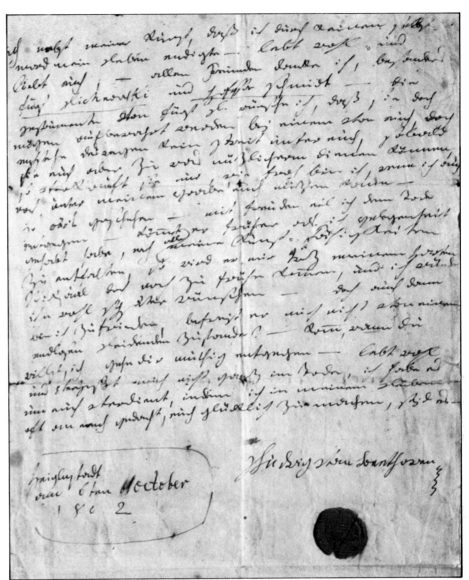

The last page of the 'Heiligenstadt Testament' (above), which Beethoven intended to be both a will and a statement of his personal philosophy. By now his deafness was developing and he felt he was soon to die.

O ye men who accuse me of being malevolent, stubborn and misanthropical, how ye wrong me! Ye know not the secret cause. Ever since childhood my heart and mind were disposed towards feelings of gentleness and good will, and I was eager to accomplish great deeds; but consider this: for six years I have been hopelessly ill, aggravated and cheated by quacks in the hope of improvement but finally compelled to face a lasting malady . . . I was forced to isolate myself. I was misunderstood and rudely repulsed because I was as yet unable to say to people, "Speak louder, shout, for I am deaf" . . .

With joy I hasten to meet death. Despite my hard fate . . . I shall wish that it had come later; but I am content, for he shall free me of constant suffering. Come then, Death, and I shall face thee with courage. Heiglnstadt (sic), 6 October, 1802.

During the summer of 1802 Beethoven stayed in Heiligenstadt (left), a little village outside Vienna.

Just how bad was Beethoven's plight? At first the malady was intermittent, or so faint that it worried him only occasionally. But by 1801 he reported that a whistle and buzz was constant. Low speech tones became an unintelligible hum, shouting became an intolerable din. Apparently the illness completely

swamped delicate sounds and distorted strong one
He may have had short periods of remission, but fo
the last ten years of his life he was totally deaf.

Beethoven in maturity

The mature Beethoven was a short, well-built man. H
dark hair went grey, then white, but was always thic
and unruly. Reports differ as to the colour of his eye.
His skin was pock-marked, and his mouth, which ha
been a little petulant in youth, later became fixed in
grim, down-curving line, as if in a permanent expres
sion of truculent determination. He seldom took car
of his appearance, and, as he strode through the street
of Vienna with hair escaping from beneath his top ha
his hands clasped behind his back and his coat cross
buttoned, he was the picture of eccentricity. Hi
moods changed constantly, keeping his acquaintance
guessing. They could never be sure that a chanc
remark might be misconstrued or displease the maste
in some way, for his powerful will would admit of n
alternative view once he had made a judgement.

By nature, Beethoven was impatient, impulsive, un
reasonable and intolerant; deafness added suspicio
and paranoia to these attributes. He would ofte
misunderstand the meaning of a facial expression an
accuse faithful friends of disloyalty or conspiracy. H
would fly into a rage at the slightest provocation, and
he would turn on friends, dismissing them curtly a
being unworthy of his friendship. But, likely as not, h

One of Beethoven's most important patrons was the Russian Ambassador to Vienna, Count Razumovsky, to whom he dedicated a number of pieces. Beethoven is shown here playing for the Razumovsky family. On the right is their palace in Vienna.

A portrait of Beethoven painted by Ferdinand Schimon in 1818–1819, when the composer was at the height of his fame.

would write a letter the next day or so, telling them how noble and good they were and how he had misjudged them.

A tempestuous life

After his return from Heiligenstadt, Beethoven's music deepened. He began creating a new musical world. In the summer of 1803 he began work on his Third Symphony – the 'Eroica'. It was to be a paean of glory to Napoleon Bonaparte and, like its subject, it was revolutionary. It was half as long again as any previous symphony and its musical language was so uncompromising that it set up resistance in its first audiences. It broke the symphonic mould, yet established new, logical and cogent forms. This was a miracle Beethoven was to work many times.

Stephan von Breuning, with whom Beethoven shared rooms, reports a thunderous episode in connection with the 'Eroica' Symphony. In December, 1804, the news arrived that Napoleon, that toiler for the rights of the common people, had proclaimed himself Emperor. In a fury, Beethoven strode over to his copy of the Symphony, which bore a dedication to Napoleon, and crossed out the 'Bonaparte' name with such violence that the pen tore a hole in the paper. 'Is he, too, nothing more than human?' he raged. 'Now he will crush the rights of man. He will become a tyrant!'

For the next few years in Vienna, from 1804 to 1808, Beethoven lived in what might be described as a state of monotonous uproar. His relationships suffered elemental rifts, his music grew ever greater, and all the time he was in love with one woman or another, usually high-born, sometimes unattainable, always unattained. He never married.

His Fifth and Sixth Symphonies were completed by the summer of 1808. The Fifth indeed 'takes fate by the throat'; the Sixth ('Pastoral') is a portrait of the countryside around Heilingenstadt. These and other works spread his name and fame.

In July 1812 Beethoven wrote a letter to an unidentified lady whom he addressed as 'The Immortal Beloved'. It is as eloquent of love as his 'Heiligenstadt Testament' had been of despair:

*My angel, my all, my very self – a few words only
today, and in pencil (thine). Why such profound sorrow when necessity speaks? Can our
love endure but through sacrifice – but through
not demanding all – canst thou alter it that
thou art not wholly mine, I not wholly thine?*

So moving an outpouring may well have resulted, at last, in some permanent arrangement – if the lady in question had been free, and if the letter had been sent. It was discovered in a secret drawer in Beethoven's desk after his death.

His brother Casper Carl died in November 1815. The consequences brought about something that neither the tragedy of deafness nor Napoleon's guns could achieve: they almost stopped Beethoven composing. Beethoven was appointed guardian of his brother's nine-year-old son, Karl – a guardianship he shared with the boy's mother Johanna. Beethoven took the appointment most seriously and was certain that Johanna did not. He believed her to be immoral, and immediately began legal proceedings to get sole guardianship of his nephew. The lawsuit was painful and protracted and frequently abusive with Johanna asserting 'How can a deaf, madman bachelor guard the boy's welfare?' – Beethoven repeatedly fell ill because

Among the exhibits in the Beethoven Museum in Bonn is his piano (above). He was a celebrated virtuoso on the instrument until his increasing deafness forced him to abandon playing.

As he strode through the streets of Vienna, deep in thought and unkempt in appearance, Beethoven was the picture of eccentricity and a delight to caricature. Some sketches such as the one (right) by Lyser were able to capture that determination which so strongly characterized the composer.

of the strain. He did not finally secure custody of Karl until 1820, when the boy was 20.

The Ninth Symphony ('Choral') was completed in 1823, by which time Beethoven was completely deaf. There was a poignant scene at the first performance. Despite his deafness, Beethoven insisted on conducting, but unknown to him the real conductor sat out of his sight, beating time. As the last movement ended Beethoven, unaware even that the music had ceased, was also unaware of the tremendous burst of applause that greeted it. One of the singers took him by the arm and turned him around so that he might actually see the ovation.

The final days
In the autumn of 1826 Beethoven took Karl to Gneixendorf ('The name,' said Beethoven, 'sounds like the breaking of an axe') for a holiday. A servant there has left a graphic picture of Beethoven the possessed genius as he worked upon his last string quartet:

At 5.30 a.m. he was at his table, beating time with hands and feet, humming and writing. After breakfast he hurried outside to wander in the fields, calling, waving his arms about, moving slowly, then very fast, then abruptly stopping to scribble something in his notebook.

In early December Beethoven returned to Vienna with Karl and the journey brought the composer down with pneumonia. He recovered, only to be laid low again with cirrhosis of the liver, which in turn gave way to dropsy. His condition had deteriorated dramatically by the beginning of March and, sensing the

At 3 pm on 29 March, 1827, Beethoven's funeral took place in Vienna. The Viennese turned out en masse: at least 20,000 people crowded into the square in front of the Schwarzpanierhaus – Beethoven's last residence. There were eight pallbearers, dozens of torchbearers and a choir who sang to the accompaniment of sombre trombones.

orst, his friends rallied round: faithful Stephan ought his family and Schubert paid his respects. Beethoven's final moments, if a report by Schubert's end Hüttenbrenner are to be believed, were amatic in the extreme. At about 5.45 in the after- on of 26 March, 1827, as a storm raged, Beethoven's om was suddenly filled with light and shaken with under:

ethoven's eyes opened and he lifted his right t for several seconds, a serious, threatening pression on his face. When his hand fell back, half-closed his eyes . . . Not another word, not other heartbeat.

Schubert and Hummel were were among the 20,000 ople who mourned the composer at his funeral ree days later. He was buried in Währing Cemetery; 1888 his remains were removed to Zentral-friedhof Vienna – a great resting-place for musicians – where lies side-by-side with Schubert.

erword
ethoven revolutionized classical music, breaking any rules which had been considered inviolate for nturies. He influenced every succeeding major com- oser. It's possible that he did not personally share the fty ideals later generations have attributed to his usic: indeed, at the height of his powers he shows a ghtening self-centredness, saying 'Strength is the orality of the man who stands out from the rest, and is mine.' But his work – the most powerful and portant body of music ever to be put together by e composer – is eternal.

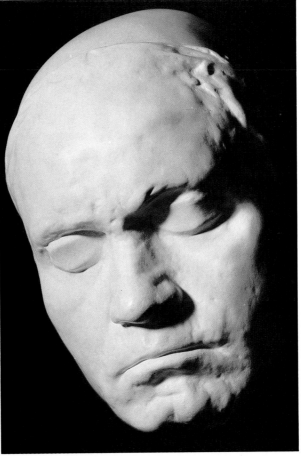

Two days after Beethoven's death the young painter Danhauser took this death mask of the composer. Parts of the temple bones had been removed at the post-mortem the previous day, giving the head a curious formlessness.

German Romantic Art

The haunting landscapes of Friedrich, the heroic panoramas of Koch and the spiritual allegories of Runge reflect in exciting and original ways the dramatic developments in German Romantic music.

Mozart, Beethoven and Schubert are well known to us. What we tend to overlook at times is that the works of these great composers form part of a rich flowering that ranged throughout the arts and sciences in the German-speaking countries. German culture was undergoing a rebirth around 1800 which seemed to affect almost every aspect of human achievement. Apart from music, this can be seen most strikingly in philosophy, where Kant opened up crucial new avenues of thought, and in literature, where Goethe dominated the contemporary European field.

The visual arts played a full part in these developments. While not quite as rich in achievement as the music, philosophy and literature of the period, they reflected many of the same interests in original and exciting ways. Furthermore, there was one painter, at least, who was of the first rank. This was the landscape artist Caspar David Friedrich. Born four years later than Beethoven, his art came to maturity at the time when that composer was writing his most celebrated concertos and symphonies. The two never met. Nor do they appear to have shown any particular interest in each other's work. Yet they often seem close in their attitudes, and sometimes in the effects that their creations produce. The sense of individualism, fascination with innovation, with the heroic, and with an

1 (above) Carstens: 'Night with her Children Sleep and Death'. Chalk. *The subject for this design was taken from the Greek poet Hesiod, and the figures are endowed with the still nobility of classical sculpture. For the great writer Goethe, Carstens was the artist 'with whom one gladly begins the new epoch of German art'.*

2 (above right) Koch: 'Schmadribach Falls'. Watercolour. *Koch, like Carstens, had a heroic vision, which he expressed through his gift for landscape painting. His celebrated Alpine scene is conceived on a grand scale, and reflects Carstens' view that high mountains inspire similar sensations to a Michelangelo.*

intense, near-mystical appreciation of nature — all these are tendencies that they share with each other and with many of their contemporaries.

Heroic genius

Perhaps the attitude that is most commonly found among artists at this time is the new view of creative genius. We are all familiar with the hackneyed image of the Romantic artist — unkempt, obsessed with his own greatness, living outside the conventions of society, and scorning the 'philistine' public. Nowadays, such an image is often used as a mask for mediocrity. But at the time when it first emerged, around 1800, it provided a genuine release. In the frightening and exciting decades that followed the French Revolution of 1789, it seemed that the artist had a new and important role to play. No longer was

he to be a 'servant', performing duties for Church, monarchy and the privileged. Using his unique gifts he could stimulate awareness and provide guidance to people at a time when many of the traditional supports seemed to have rotted away.

In Germany, this image of the artist was crystallized most succinctly by the poet Friedrich Schiller. Throughout his career, Schiller used his powers as a writer to promote the image of a responsible and honourable society, and oppose the kind of feudal oppression that he himself had suffered as a youth. His attitude aroused much support. Beethoven subscribed to it when he incorporated the poet's *Ode to Joy* – with its stirring phrase 'all men will become brothers' – into the final movement of his Ninth Symphony. Schiller also discussed his views in theoretical writings. The most

influential of these was his *Letters on the Aesthetic Education of Mankind* (1795). Written at a time when the 'Reign of Terror' that followed the Revolution in France was at its height, these letters asked the question of what value was art for people in a time of political crisis. The answer that Schiller gave was that people could only achieve true and responsible political freedom when they had developed the sense of judgement that comes with an appreciation of beauty. It was the duty of the artist to provide society with uplifting creations that would stimulate such awareness.

In the visual arts, the person who seemed to embody Schiller's ideal most completely was the North German, Asmus Jacob Carstens (1754–98). The son of a miller who was orphaned at the age of 15, Carstens struggled against tremendous odds to realize his ambition of becoming an artist. He had to endure seven years as an apprentice cooper before he could begin his art studies. From the start he wanted to be a 'history' painter – one who depicted important subjects, usually of a morally uplifting kind, using grand, idealized figures. He believed – like most other people of the day – that such an artist could only succeed if he based his art on the noble,

3 (above) Runge: 'Morning'. (Small version). Oil.
Runge rejected the 'heroic' vision of painters like Carstens and Koch in favour of an imagery of a more spiritual kind. This colour sketch is part of a series that Runge planned, but never completed, showing the 'Times of Day'. The tiny child lying in the dewy fields immediately recalls the infant Christ. With arms outstretched, in a gesture of rapture, he receives the gift of light – the liberator of the soul. Above him hovers the beautiful figure of Aurora, the bringer of dawn, whose spirits scatter rosebuds on the ground.

classical forms of ancient Greek and Roman sculpture and the paintings of the great artists of the Italian Renaissance like Raphael and Michelangelo Buonarroti, who both worked in Rome. He therefore determined to go to Rome, where he could study such art at first hand.

He set out to walk there from North Germany – but had to give up when he got to northern Italy because of lack of funds. He was 38 before he was financed by the Berlin Academy, who supported him on the understanding that he would return after two years to teach for them. However, when this time was up he refused to come back, declaring, 'I do not belong to the Berlin Academy, but to mankind, which has a right to demand the highest possible development of my capabilities . . . .' In the years of life that remained to him he stayed in Rome, working in the midst of the art of his idols. He never received the commissions he craved for, to do vast paintings on the scale of Michelangelo's *Last Judgement.* All he left behind him were some modest oil paintings, and a large quantity of designs for the pictures that he would have liked to have made.

Some of these drawings, however, do convey in a most moving way the heroic qualities that he felt to be at the core of great art. His *Night with her Children Sleep and Death* (illustration **1**) depicts a group of mythological characters as described by the Ancient Greek poet Hesiod. The figures are powerful, yet calm and balanced. Their grandeur is given poignancy by the pathos of the theme. Night, sleep and death are concepts that arouse feelings of meditation, fatalism and sadness. By clothing them in noble forms, Carstens seems to be implying that human dignity can be maintained even in the face of the frightening and the unknown.

Carstens' idealism, and his legendary intransigence, made him a focal point for other German artists who sought to paint heroic works. Closest to him was Joseph Anton Koch (1768–1839), a Tyrolese painter who arrived in Rome in 1795, after having broken away from the rigorous academic training in the Karlsschule in Stuttgart. For some years Koch continued Carstens' work in a direct way. He even made etchings after his hero's designs. After 1800, however, he turned increasingly away from figure painting and developed instead his gift for landscape painting. Carstens' sense of grandeur can be felt in a most stimulating way in many of these. Koch became one of the leading exponents in Rome of a new 'heroic' landscape, in which the classical compositions of the great 17th-century landscape painters – notably Claude Lorrain and Nicolas Poussin – were revised in the interests of a more vigorous, muscular kind of scenery. His most celebrated work is the mountain view, *The*

4 (left) Runge: 'The Huelsenbeck Children'. Oil.
Runge never liked portraiture, he considered it a trivial genre. However, his portraits are some of the most penetrating of his times. This painting shows the children of his brother's business partner with an almost disturbing directness. They are vigorous creatures of instinct; one brandishes a whip, another clutches at a leaf, only the older girl acts as a restraining influence. Their figures are made even more vital and monumental by Runge's use of scale. He places us at the children's level, underneath the towering sunflower.

5 (left) Kersting: 'Caspar David Friedrich in his Studio'. Oil.
Friedrich was the greatest of the German Romantic painters. For him, landscape elements were symbols of the spiritual world: standing quietly before a blank canvas in his bare studio, he would only begin work when the image 'stood lifelike in his mind's eye'.

6 (below) Friedrich: 'Cross in the Mountains'. Oil.
This startling painting – an altarpiece for a private chapel – caused an uproar when it was first exhibited. One critic called it 'a veritable presumption if landscape painting were to sneak into the church and creep onto the altar'.

largely dependent upon the generosity of his brother Daniel, a merchant in Hamburg.

Runge's ideas came to maturity while he was studying at Dresden between 1801 and 1804. It was here that he came into contact with a group of writers and critics who were seeking to turn away from classical models. One of their number, the critic Friedrich Schlegel, was the first to use the word 'romantic' to define the modern age. It was an age, he felt, that lacked the perfection of the classical world, but was more dynamic, and richer in spiritual potential. For Runge, the ecstatic feelings that he experienced before nature gave the most vivid intimations of this state. His cycle of the *Times of Day* – which was to include representations of Morning, Evening, Midday and Night – was intended to communicate a sense of the mystery and inner harmony of creation. Although he made designs for all four pictures, only one, *Morning,* came anywhere near completion. The coloured sketch for it (illustration 3) can give some idea of his objectives.

The picture shows a sunrise over a flat North-German plain. It is no ordinary sunrise, however, for the scene is peopled with allegorical figures. On the ground, in the foreground, lies a small child – reminiscent of the infant Christ – who opens out his arms to receive the gift of light. The place where the sun should be is dominated by the classical figure of

Schmadribach Falls in the Alps. The watercolour sketch (illustration 2) gives some idea of its scale. Painted in 1811, just a few years after Beethoven's Third Symphony, the *Eroica,* it is itself a kind of heroic symphony of nature, conveying a sense of the vastness and power of natural creation. It surveys a large expanse of Koch's native alpine scenery, moving from silent, snow-capped mountains to bare rocks and a torrential waterfall; and then below to dense woodlands, pasture and a gentle mountain stream. All these different moods are held together by the firmness of the design and the precision with which each form is depicted. It is in this sense of controlled immensity that Carstens' influence is perhaps most strongly felt.

Nature and mysticism
Both Carstens and Koch represented the new 'heroic' form of artistic vision. However, they were still quite traditional in the way they used classical forms to embody their ideas. And younger artists were beginning to find such imagery irrelevant: 'We are no longer Greeks and Romans, and when we contemplate their perfect works of art we can no longer feel the totality in the way that they did.' The man who wrote this was the painter Philipp Otto Runge (1777–1810). As his words suggest, he felt the perfection of the classical world to have little relevance for the modern era. Instead he sought to achieve an uplifting image using the more complex and intangible sensations that he felt epitomized the present age.

Like Carstens, Runge was an artist who never realized his grand ambitions. He died of tuberculosis at the age of 33 with only a fragment of his scheme completed. Like Carstens, too, he had some difficulties in establishing his career. Coming from a merchant family in the North-German Pomeranian town of Wolgast, he was 22 before he could gain his parents' permission to study to be an artist. The obscurity and originality of his ideas meant that he received little patronage. For most of his life he was

Aurora – the bringer of dawn. Around her are scattered small *genii* (spirits). Some of them bear rose petals – classical symbols of the dawn – to earth. The picture is surrounded by a frame in which pure white lilies are shown being brought to flower by the effects of light.

Light is, in fact, the unifying force in this complex picture. This point can perhaps be brought out most clearly if one compares it with Koch's *Schmadribach Falls*. Koch's heroic scene is based upon an actual place, and its effect depends upon the clear delineation of form. Runge's picture relies upon the realism of its light effects to conjure up a specific point in time, the moment at which light floods onto the earth and darkness is dispelled. It is typical of Runge that he should associate this moment with the birth of Christ. For he shared the belief of the Dresden Romantics that it was Christianity which had brought a new era of spiritual awareness.

While Runge's work is evidently a fantasy, it is based upon the most careful and probing study of natural effects. His diligence also made him an exceptionally fine portraitist, as such works as his *Huelsenbeck Children* (illustration 4) show. Runge disliked painting portraits – it seemed to him to be too menial and mundane a task. He never worked as a professional portraitist, but he did occasionally do pictures of his family and friends. The Huelsenbeck children were the offspring of a business colleague of his brother Daniel. He shows them playing in their garden. The baby grasps instinctively at a leaf, the boy rushes impulsively forward. Only the girl shows any concern for others, as she looks back towards the baby. They are in no way sentimentalized, but are shown as elemental, animal-like forces at one with the world of nature.

7 (above) Schinkel: 'Gothic Cathedral by a River'. Oil. *Schinkel, an important Prussian architect, developed an interest in landscape painting following the impact of Friedrich. Here, the Gothic cathedral, darkly silhouetted against a luminous sky, is intended as a political symbol of national regeneration.*

Caspar David Friedrich (1774–1840)

Runge's achievements – like those of Carstens – remained fragmentary. His visionary approach to nature was shared by another artist, however, who had a long and fulfilled career.

Like Runge, Friedrich came from the extreme north of Germany – in his case the Pomeranian town of Griefswald. Like Runge, too, it was his contact with the self-styled 'Romantics' in Dresden that brought about the development of his art. He went there in 1799 – after having studied at Copenhagen Academy – and was to remain based there for the rest of his life.

Friedrich's belief in the 'inner' vision of the artist is made clear in his advice to painters: 'Close your bodily eye so that you may see your picture first with the spiritual eye. Then bring to the light of day that which you have seen in the inner darkness so that it may react on others from the outside inwards.' Friedrich does actually seem to have created his pictures with his 'inner' eye, conceiving them in his mind before drawing them out on his canvas (illustration 5). But this does not mean that he was inattentive to nature. Almost every form in his paintings, down to the smallest leaf, is based upon something that he had studied. The job of the 'inner' eye was to combine these forms in new ways that brought out a deeper meaning.

Friedrich had originally trained as a topographical artist, producing views of his native Pomerania.

When he first came to Dresden, he made his living selling such works. Gradually, however, under the influence of the Dresden Romantics, he became more ambitious and began to design works with symbolic content. By 1808 this process was fully developed. This was the year in which he painted the *Cross in the Mountains* (illustration 6). The picture created a sensation when it was exhibited in the artist's studio. To conventional critics – notably a local writer called the Freiherr von Ramdohr – it seemed to break all the rules of painting. The first, and most glaring infringement is the use for which the work was intended. It was designed to be an altarpiece – for use in the private chapel of the castle of Tetschen in northern Bohemia. Normally an altarpiece would show religious figures, such as Christ, the Virgin Mary or some saints. But Friedrich has shown instead a landscape. The point that he was making was that he felt the contemplation of nature was as spiritual an experience as the contemplation of saints or stories from the Bible. 'The divine is everywhere' he once argued, 'even in a grain of sand.'

The picture is so dramatic in its effect that it might at first sight seem unnatural. However, in central Europe it is common to see crucifixes on the tops of mountains. The real drama of the picture comes not from its imagery, but from the way in which Friedrich has presented it. We are shown nothing but the tip of the mountain, and this is viewed in such a

8 (above) Schinkel: 'The Hall of Stars of the Queen of the Night'. Engraving after design for Mozart's 'Magic Flute'.
Schinkel's design perfectly complements the mysterious, masonic intentions of Mozart's opera. The magical effect is produced by the overwhelming symmetry of the scene. As one critic said: 'So much can be achieved by simple ingenuity'.

9 (left) Friedrich: 'Two Men Contemplating the Moon'. Oil.
This painting has political overtones. The two men wear 'Old German' costume – the dress associated with revolutionaries. The figures have been identified as Friedrich himself and one of his pupils.

way as to form a striking silhouette against the evening sky. Here again the conventions of picture making had been flouted. At that time landscapes were normally expected to have foreground, middleground and background. But Friedrich cuts all this away to arrive at a dramatic and compelling image.

Such original uses of scenery soon made Friedrich a notorious figure. A few years later, in 1810, he had a major success when he sent a pair of large landscapes to be shown at the academy exhibition in Berlin. One showed a monk wandering along a barren shore, the other a funeral taking place in a ruined abbey surrounded by barren oak trees, the whole scene lost in the dusk. Once more Friedrich achieved his effects by his striking use of silhouettes and lighting, making natural forces seem charged with heightened meaning.

These two pictures were bought by the Crown Prince of Prussia. Friedrich's success now seemed secure. However, the fascination with his striking, unusual style of painting was to some extent dependant upon the special circumstance of his times. A great surge of national feeling had been stimulated by the invasion of Germany by Napoleon in 1806. This invasion was eventually repulsed in 1814. In the intervening years there was a great taste for those works of art that appeared to have a natural flavour, and which kept alive the image of the German people as a vigorous spiritual force. Friedrich's images – with their emphasis on northern landscapes and mystical effects – seemed particularly relevant. He was, in fact, extremely patriotic. Like Runge – who designed an allegory on the *Fall of the Fatherland* – he painted works which had direct political associations. One depicted a French huntsman lost in a German forest of evergreens. It was shown in 1814 in an exhibition that celebrated the defeat of the French.

Friedrich's impact

It is hardly surprising that Friedrich's pictures should at this time have inspired other artists. In Berlin the great architect Karl Friedrich Schinkel (1781–1841) turned to landscape painting. This was largely because the privations of the Napoleonic Wars had brought about a cessation of most building projects in Prussia. Schinkel was deeply impressed by Friedrich's dramatic use of lighting. He used a similar type of effect in his *Gothic Cathedral by a River* (illustration 7). Painted in 1814, this picture also had political overtones. The splendid cathedral, soaring above a river, was seen as an image of national regeneration. This picture was a fantasy, but a few years later such a project was actually put into practice. Under the protection of the Prussian king, the medieval cathedral of Cologne was completed and became for many Germans a symbol of their nation's restoration.

Since 1806 Schinkel had also been working as a scene painter. At first he painted *dioramas* (illuminated scenery), but after 1815 he was also employed as a designer by the Berlin Royal Theatre. In this capacity he experimented with that inter-

10 (below) Friedrich: 'The Arctic Shipwreck'. Oil. *Here Friedrich depicts the classic Romantic theme of man at the mercy of the elements. Turner chose such subjects to highlight the human drama, but Friedrich concentrates on the inevitable conclusion, as the ship is crushed by great pyramids of ice.*

relationship of the arts that had so fascinated Runge and other romantic theoreticians. His interest in the association of pictorial scenery with music and poetry was most fully engaged in his designs for opera. For Mozart's *Magic Flute* he conceived a series of designs in 1815 that seemed a perfect accompaniment to the opera's mysterious intentions. The overwhelming symmetry of the *Hall of Stars of the Queen of the Night* (illustration **8**) is the most remarkable of these. As with his *Gothic Cathedral by a River,* these designs had a political meaning. The performance of *The Magic Flute* for which they were intended was a celebration of the restoration of peace. In this context Mozart's mystical fable became an affirmation of the Prussian state's triumph over the tribulations of the Napoleonic period.

After the Napoleonic Wars, Friedrich's art began to fall out of favour. His painting now came to be regarded as eccentric. Furthermore, his own political views isolated him. Friedrich was not only a nationalist. He was also a liberal, who wanted the overthrow of the feudal régimes of the German principalities. In the years following the defeat of Napoleon, most German governments became increasingly reactionary. Friedrich never took part in any overt protest against these. But his pictures often contain hints of his beliefs. His *Two Men Contemplating the Moon* (illustration **9**) shows two men in 'old German' costume, a style of dress that was associated with liberals and revolutionaries. The figures have been identified as Friedrich himself, and one of his pupils.

During these years Friedrich's art changed. He moved away from the depiction of monks, ruins and crosses, and painted instead contemporary scenes, such as the *Arctic Shipwreck* (illustration **10**). This is one of a number of shipwreck scenes that he painted in the 1820s. Like his contemporary, the English painter Turner, and other Romantic artists, Friedrich was fascinated with natural disasters for the way in which they pitted man against the elements. This picture, which shows a ship being slowly ground to pieces in an ice-bound sea, seems to suggest that the struggle is a futile one. But in the background is a calm blue sky and a burst of light – indications of the promise of eternity beyond this life.

The medieval revival
At the same time that Runge and Friedrich were developing a visionary form of landscape, other German artists were looking in a different direction, and modelling their art on that of the middle ages. They were inspired by Romantics like Friedrich Schlegel, who believed that the modern world had become unbearably pagan and materialistic. Such people looked to the middle ages as an age of humble faith, when spiritual values dominated society. For Germans there was an added attraction to this period. It had been a time when Germany had enjoyed political unity, under the Holy Roman Empire. This contrasted with the present age, when it was divided into a mass of small states.

In the early years of the 19th century, groups of artists imitating the styles of medieval art sprang up throughout Germany – particularly after 1806, when Napoleon's invasion gave a new spurt to nationalism.

11 (left) Overbeck: 'Franz Pforr'. Oil.
Overbeck and Pforr were the leaders of the 'Nazarenes', a brotherhood of artists who harked back to the middle ages as a time of simple Christian faith and values.

Great Composers

12 (below) Schwind: 'The Symphony'. Oil. *Schwind's painting forms a direct link between music and the visual arts. Indeed, his gently flowing line has been compared with the lyrical effect of music. In this ambitious work, Schwind combines a number of scenes in a way that reflects the different themes in a piece of music. In the lower scene a concert is actually taking place, and Schubert can be spied in the left background.*

The most influential group emerged in Vienna. This was the 'Brotherhood of St Luke', which was founded in 1808 by some students of the Vienna Academy. As can be seen from the portrait by one of the leaders, Friedrich Overbeck (1789–1869) of the other, Franz Pforr (1788–1812) (illustration **11**), they took their medievalism very seriously indeed. They tried to use the simple forms and bright colours that they associated with medieval art. And they also affected a medieval lifestyle, growing their hair long, wearing flowing robes and living for a time in a quasi-monastic community. In 1810 they moved to Rome, to be closer to examples of medieval art and to the centre of Christianity. Here their long hair gained them the nickname 'Nazarenes' – that is, people who had a Christ-like appearance. As they grew more famous, their art became more pious and stilted. They never achieved their aim of restoring the values of medieval society, but they were to remain influential among religious painters for more than half a century.

It is hard to see many connections between this group and the principal developments in the music of the period. But the medieval revival did involve music in other ways. One was through the renewed interest in folk culture, which was seen as a living, vernacular, branch of medieval art. Indeed, collections of ballads, fairy tales and folk-songs were widespread at this time. The most famous product of this interest was the Grimm brothers' collection of Fairy Tales (1812–22). In music this interest led to the practice of including folk-tunes in pieces – something that Beethoven did at times. It also led to the development of *Lieder* – lyrical songs which drew upon the traditional themes and forms – a musical form perfected by Franz Schubert.

Moritz von Schwind (1804–71)

In painting, some artists also turned to folk art and legends for their inspiration. The most important of these was Moritz von Schwind (1804–71) who frequently illustrated fairy tales painting pictures with a strong lyrical mood. It has often been remarked that the flowing 'melodic' line evident in Schwind's designs has a musical character.

A Viennese by birth, he was a close friend of Schubert's. He was himself a highly gifted violinist, and once remarked that one should have a 'mouthful of music' every day. He attempted to reproduce the effects of music in several of his pictures. One of his most ambitious works was entitled *The Symphony* (illustration **12**), and brought together a group of scenes in a way that he felt mirrored the association of themes and motifs in a musical composition.

Interesting though such connections are, they do have their limitations. Schwind is always in danger of becoming the mere illustrator of musical effect. While his pictures have a lyrical charm that is reminiscent of Schubert, they hardly have the subtlety, profundity and emotional breadth of the works of that composer. They are, perhaps, a warning against using one art form too closely to imitate the qualities of another. Paradoxically, more telling parallels between art and music emerge when each is exploring its own properties. From this point of view Runge and Friedrich share more of the qualities of the German music of the early 19th century. For they were each concerned with radically rethinking the basis of their art – discovering new ways of using form, light and colour to express their dramatic and original visions.

The Napoleonic age

Few events have determined the course of world history as much as the French Revolution and fewer still have thrown up such a monolithic figure as Napoleon – visionary, tactician and despot.

The young Napoleon embodied the Romantic ideal of individual struggle and heroism. But after more than a decade of bloody campaigns his image changed to that of a ruthless despot.

In the bloodbath years following the storming of the Bastille the French constitution was vandalized by successive, well-meaning, but quite unworkable, attempts at government. From 1789 to 1791 the deputies in the Constituent Assembly, as the new governing body was now called, set about the task of creating a new France. The most intractable problem concerned the fate of the Catholic Church and the massive debt inherited from the Bourbons. The immense landed wealth of the Church was seized and used, through the introduction of a new form of currency, the *assignat,* to pay off the debt. But there remained the problem of the relationship between the assembly and the king – and that of the relationship between the assembly and the popular movement.

In 1791 the king still had important powers – he could in fact veto legislation passed by the assembly – the power had not yet passed to the people. In that year, in a fit of panic, the royal family made an abortive attempt to escape from France and, in doing so, made a mockery of the 'constitutional monarchy'. And then a month later a demonstration of republicans was repressed with some bloodshed by the National Guard. It seemed that both the king and the majority of the poor were unsatisfied with the Revolution's reforms. The Constituent Assembly gave way in 1791 to a completely new body, the Legislative Assembly.

The new body was not averse to war. Its leaders favoured a revolutionary crusade to unite an increasingly divided nation. In April 1792 war was declared on Austria and Prussia – powers that threatened to overthrow the revolution.

Patriotic revolutionary forces were unleashed by the war and the Parisian crowd stormed the Tuileries palace where the king had been kept virtually a prisoner since 1791. The overcrowded prisons were invaded and over 1000 suspected traitors were killed – no government could now afford to ignore the potentially explosive force of the Parisian crowd. For the remainder of the Revolution events would be dictated largely by two factors – the quality of the harvest and success or failure on the field of battle.

The king was executed in January 1793 and by March – repelled by the new direction the revolution was taking – the region of the Vendée in western France exploded in a spontaneous outburst of hostillity. The government (now the National Convention) was faced with defeat abroad and civil war at home. The Jacobins, dominated by Maximilien Robespierre, seized power, drove foreign armies from France, quashed the royalist threat in Vendée, and launched the revolution on its expansionist phase.

Though the economy was stabilized and the hungry were fed the Jacobin period was one of quickening fanaticism. Two thousand 'traitors' in and around Nantes were killed, 5000 'counter-revolutionaries' in Lyons were liquidated. The Reign of Terror had begun.

Many regions of France were teetering on anarchy in 1793, but Robespierre and his colleagues in the Committee of Public Safety gradually centralized power. Opposition was mercilessly crushed; one-time leading lights of the revolution were led to the guillotine – Danton and his followers and Robespierre and his. They became the last noble victims of the terror after a political coup by the so-called 'Thermidoreans' in July 1794.

With the end of Robespierre and the Terror, power shifted yet again and by 1795 the bourgeoisie had the whip hand rather than the Parisian crowd. With the threat of royalist terrorism mounting, the Constitution of 1795 vested power in a Directory of five, a compromise between a fragile democracy and total dictatorship. The Directory lurched from one crisis to the next. Governed by officials who were at best cynical, at worst corrupt, and overwhelmed with the problems of spectacular military expansion, in 1799 the Directory finally succumbed. A young Corsican general seized power and began to clear up the debris of a decade of revolution. Napoleon Bonaparte was at the centre of the stage.

The rise of Napoleon

Napoleon was, it has been argued, 'the most powerful genius who ever lived', scourge of kings and defender of the great ideals of the French Revolution; a statesman of principle and an administrator of unparalleled ability; a spectacular warrior, yes, but one driven time and again into battle by the enmity of the reactionary forces ranged against revolutionary France.

To those who feared and hated him he was the sleek-haired 'Corsican ogre', and a generation of English nursemaids would terrorize squealing children with the awful warning that if they did not stop crying 'Boney' would come and devour them. He was a ruthless tyrant, cold, manipulative and indifferent to the sufferings he inflicted on humanity.

Born on 15 August 1769 Bonaparte completed his schooling at the Ecole Militaire in Paris in 1785. He then embarked on what was to become the greatest military career in history.

Like his military tactics, Napoleon's career was marked by breathtaking speed and resolute doggedness. In 1791 he was promoted to lieutenant and the following year to captain. For Napoleon, 1793 was to

be a critical year: the Revolution was rapidly turnin bloodier, Louis XVI and Marie Antoinette had bee executed, France had thrown down the gauntlet at th feet of the world's powers while internally she wa torn by rebellion in several provinces.

The Revolutionary government recoiled in shoc when Toulon, a significant naval base, defected fron the Republic and admitted an Allied force unde Admiral Hood. All attempts to take the town had bee repulsed, until Napoleon, as fate would have it, too over from a wounded gunner. It was a propitiou moment; the young officer applied his vast energy an military inventiveness to the siege of Toulon. Unde his direction the town was reoccupied by Frenc forces and as his reward Napoleon was mad Brigadier-General. His age was just over 24.

Appointed to the army in Italy he was a decisiv factor in the French victory at Loano in 1794. Bu there followed a greater opportunity which h grasped with characteristic speed. In October 179 the Paris mob rose against the Directory and it fell t Napoleon with his salvoes of cannon, his so-calle 'whiff of grapeshot', to quell the rebellion. His succes won for him instant praise and, ten days late promotion to Commander of the Army of the Interior.

Whatever else Napoleon Bonaparte may have beer he was first and foremost a soldier, and it was as a artillery officer in the armies of revolutionary Franc that the young Corsican first distinguished himsel From 1792 onwards, France was constantly at war wit various combinations of her continental neighbour aided and abetted by Britain – all of them apalled b what they saw happening in France and fearful of th implications of such upheaval. Quite apart from th understandable horror inspired by the thud of th guillotine blade, such ringing phrases as 'the Rights o Man' and *'Liberté, Fraternité, Egalité'*, sent tremor through the aristocratic societies of the late 18t

On 21 October, 1805, Nelson lay dying on the deck of his flagship (below). But Britain had won the battle of Trafalgar and had secured naval supremacy for the rest of the wars.

Napoleon fell passionately in love with Josephine (right). She was his mistress for a few months before they married in 1796. During Napoleon's long absences abroad, Josephine dabbled freely in love affairs and the marriage looked ready to collapse. But finally it was her failure to produce an heir that decided Napoleon to divorce her. In 1810 he married Marie-Louise, daughter of the Austrian Emperor.

century which reverberated all through Europe.

Bonaparte rose at lightning pace through these campaigns, to take command of the Army of Italy (the French army designated for action in Italy) in 1796, at the age of 27. The campaign that followed made him a national hero: a *blitzkrieg* through northern Italy where he scored a dozen resounding victories in as many months. He was then given command of the Army of England, and promptly set about planning the downfall of France's most dangerous enemy – as she had been for the past hundred years. After careful examination of the possibilities Bonaparte concluded that a direct assault across the English Channel would fail, so he chose instead a most audacious indirect form of attack – through Egypt to India, which would both demoralize Imperial Britain and cripple a vital area of her commerce.

The French expeditionary force which set sail from Toulon in May 1798 met with initial success – first Malta, then Alexandria and the Nile delta falling before it. But a crushing defeat at the hands of Horatio Nelson in the Battle of the Nile of 1 August ruined the grand design, and Bonaparte eventually escaped back to France leaving his army behind.

The failure in Egypt did nothing to diminish his ambitions, nor indeed to harm his prospects – within a month he had conspired successfully to stage a bloodless *coup d'état,* from which he emerged as First Consul. He would go on to promote himself to First Consul for Life in 1802 and finally crown himself Emperor of France in 1804, but from this moment in November 1799 he was effectively master of France.

There was only the briefest of pauses while Napoleon consolidated his power and reorganized the military forces now at his sole command, and then in the spring of 1800 he struck at northern Italy again, where an Austrian army was beseiging Italy. Having made their way through the snow covered St. Bernard

Wellington did far more than lend his name to a boot. He hounded Napoleon throughout the Iberian Peninsula and finally defeated him at Waterloo.

Napoleon achieved the pinnacle of his career and the height of his formidable arrogance on 2 December, 1804, when he declared himself Emperor. Although the Pope was brought to Paris for the ceremony Napoleon placed the crown on his own head.

Pass, the French fell upon and defeated the Austrians at Marengo on 14 June. A further shattering defeat at the hands of a French army in Germany later that same year knocked Austria right out of the war – leaving Britain and France glaring hatred at each other across the Channel but with neither able to do much about it. Fulminate as they might against the dreadful 'Boney', there was no way the British could challenge his supremacy on the Continent. Scheme as he did to bring down 'the nation of shopkeepers', the British Fleet still stood between Napoleon and complete victory. It was stalemate, and on 25 March 1802 the two nations signed a peace treaty at Amiens. The opening phase of the Napoleonic wars was over.

Invasion plans

There was never any realistic hope that the Peace of Amiens would last for long: it was no more than a temporary armed truce between irreconcilable enemies. In May 1803, after a mere 14-month respite, the war was resumed, and resumed in such a way as to give the British nation a terrible fright. With no one left on the Continent with the stomach to fight him, at least for the time being, Napoleon was free to concentrate the entire weight of his military machine on a cross-channel invasion. Over the next two years a huge army – the Grand Army – was assembled at the Channel ports, and some 200 flat-bottomed boats were built capable of transporting fully 200,000 battle-hardened soldiers to the south coast of England.

However, the prerequisite for invasion of England was, as always, control of the Channel. Napoleon's strategy was chess-like in its complexity, but basically it involved luring the British fleet into the Western Atlantic, so that a combined French and Spanish fleet could sweep unopposed up the Channel to Boulogne, there to rendezvous with the invasion flotilla. Britain's fate would be sealed.

What happened in fact was that the French fleet under Admiral Villeneuve was hounded back and forth across the Atlantic by Nelson, and finally driven to ta refuge in Cadiz. On 19 October 1805 Villeneuve ve tured forth to do battle – against his better judgeme but on the express order of an incensed Napoleo Two days later, on the 21st, his fleet was annihilated Cape Trafalgar in one of history's most celebrated nav engagements. The great invasion scare was lifte although an end to hostilities was as far away as eve

More French victories

Crushing victories over the Austrians at Ulm, and ov combined Austrian and Russian forces at Austerlitz 2 December 1805 made it plain enough once again th on land, the French were still invincible. Prussia w rash enough to enter the fray belatedly the followi year, only to have her armies destroyed on 14 Octob at Jena and Auerstädt. And if there was still any dou as to who was master of Europe it was settled in th summer of 1807, at Friedland, where the Grand Arr inflicted 25,000 casualties on the Russians.

At this stage Napoleon the soldier gave way Napoleon the diplomat. In his celebrated meeting or July 1807 with Tsar Alexander I, on a raft anchored the Nieman river in northern Prussia, he succeeded prising Russia away from the alliance with Britain. the Treaty of Tilsit, Napoleon and Alexander effective divided the Continent into two great spheres influence, Russian in the east and French in the we This was probably the high point of Napoleon's fo tunes, and it freed him once again to direct his aw some energy and willpower to the destruction Britain.

Trafalgar had ended conclusively any dream naval supremacy and invasion. The only way bring Britain to her knees was by destroying h commerce, and the only way to destroy her commer was to establish a 'fortress' Europe – a Europe continent from which British trade was total excluded. This in turn implied sealing off the enti coast of western Europe, Atlantic and Mediterranea

it was that Napoleon turned his gaze for the first
[ti]me on the Iberian peninsula, and in particular on
[Po]rtugal, Britain's traditional ally. Given the unlimited
[sca]le of his ambitions, and the intransigence of Britain
[in] the face of them, the logic of this step was probably
[in]escapable. And yet it was here, at the height of his
[su]ccess, that Napoleon set off on the long road to
[W]aterloo.

It was easy enough to march through Spain and
[oc]cupy Lisbon, towards the end of 1807, and to topple
[th]e Spanish crown the following year – where
[Na]poleon installed his brother Joseph as king. The
[pr]oblem, and it was one he had not encountered before,
[wa]s that the Spanish and Portuguese populations rose
[in] arms against the French invader. Years of inter-
[mi]nable, savage guerilla warfare lay ahead, and even
[wo]rse from the French standpoint the chaos enabled
[Br]itish forces to form a bridgehead on the Continent.

Arthur Wellesley, later Duke of Wellington,
[as]sumed command of the British army in Portugal in
[18]09, and, while for several years the Peninsular War
[re]mained a bloody sideshow to the greater theatres
[of] war to the east, it was from there that Wellington
[wo]uld eventually return in triumph to London – by
[wa]y of Paris.

[Wa]r with Russia

[If] Napoleon's attempt to subjugate Spain and Portugal
[wa]s a mistake, his break with the Tsar and attempt
[ac]tually to conquer Russia was a calamity. The Treaty
[of] Tilsit, on the face of it an admirable arrangement for
[bo]th sides, could not long be sustained. Aside from
[fe]ar of provoking Napoleon's wrath, the Tsar had no
[in]centive to stamp out trade with Britian, and he
[be]gan to turn a blind eye to his merchants' evasion of
[th]e regulation banning that trade – the so-called
[Co]ntinental System. Moreover, Russia had designs on
[Po]land and the Balkans, which Napoleon would not
[to]lerate. On both counts, therefore, the Tsar had to be
[br]ought to heel, and in the spring of 1812 Napoleon

amassed a force of half a million men.

Contrary to his expectations, such a show of force
did not intimidate the Tsar, and towards the end of
June the Grand Army struck out for Moscow. Seventy-
five miles short of the goal, on 7 September 1812, one
of the goriest engagements of the entire Napoleonic
era was fought to a standstill – The Battle of Borodino.
Technically a French victory, in that the Russians
withdrew, leaving Moscow undefended and indeed
deserted, it was a victory that cost Napoleon as dear as
any defeat could have done. He held an empty Moscow,
but he had not destroyed the Russian army, and could
no longer escape the dreadful conclusion that he had
won nothing at all, and that he must retreat before the
onslaught of Russian winter. So began one of the most
ghastly episodes in the annals of warfare. Starving,
freezing, stumbling through blinding snow storms;

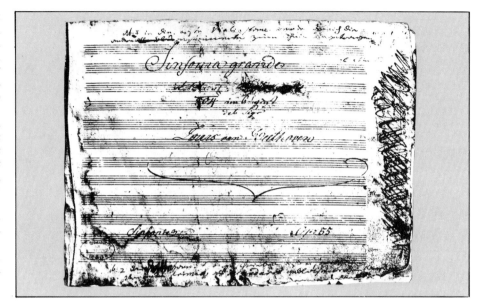

Beethoven's 'Eroica' symphony was almost certainly inspired by the ideal of Napoleon as champion of freedom, but the intended dedication was scrawled out (above).

After what was perhaps the goriest battle of the Napoleonic wars – the indecisive battle of Borodino, 1812, Napoleon occupied a near-deserted Moscow. In the end he had no option but to begin the long retreat (below).

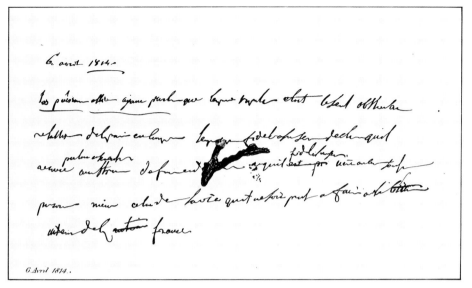

6 Avril 1814.

Napoleon's unconditional abdication of 6 April, 1814 (above). A month later, with a guard of 600 soldiers, he was on his way to the island of Elba and exile. But within a year he'd escaped and was back mustering another army.

harassed on all sides by Russian snipers and decimated by the icy torrents of the river Beresina, the tattered remnants of the Grand Army straggled back towards Poland. Of the 600,000-odd troops who entered Russia little more than 100,000 returned. It was to be a turning point in the Emperor's career.

The disastrous Russian campaign doomed Napoleon – and not least because it shattered the myth of invincibility that had so long surrounded him. Russia, Austria and Prussia were now all ranged against him in the east, while Wellington was advancing remorselessly from the south-west.

At the Battle of Leipzig in October 1813, what was left of the Grand Army was smashed beyond repair; Wellington crossed the Pyrenees in November; in December the Prussians advanced across the Rhine. Twist and turn Napoleon might, in a dazzling series of defensive manoeuvres, but the trap was sprung and there was no escape. On 31 March 1814 the victorious allies entered Paris; Napoleon was forced to abdicate – an unconditional surrender, in fact – and he was exiled with a retinue and pension to the Mediterranean island of Elba.

Waterloo

For the allies to leave Napoleon in relative comfor close to home, considering how much they had suffe at his hands, may strike modern observers as be unduly generous to a vanquished foe. It certai proved dangerous. At the beginning of March 1815 staged a dramatic escape from Elba, rallying supp on all sides from peasants and ex-soldiers as marched triumphantly north to Paris. So began famous 'Hundred Days', the desperate last throw man who could not countenance defeat and who co still inspire fierce loyalty even in a palpably lost cau Obviously the allies would not stand idly by, Napoleon characteristically went straight over to offensive, marching his Old Guard into Belgium confront the British and Prussian armies marshall against him. On 16 June he defeated the Prussian Ligny, but two days later at Waterloo Wellingto army, reinforced at a critical moment by the Prussi brought this extraordinary chapter of European hist to a close. And this time the allies took no chanc They exiled their enemy thousands of miles away the south Atlantic island of St. Helena.

The Europe he left behind would never be the sa again, however keen the victorious powers might to reverse the currents set in train by the Frer Revolution and the massive upheavals caused by years of warfare. For however dreadful the carnage had wrought in pursuit of his military ends, Napolo had in fact been responsible for implanting many the ideals of the Revolution as far and wide as conquests had taken him. Or, looked at another w he had torn apart so much of the fabric of an old order that it was quite impossible ever to restore it

The map of Europe itself had been irreversi changed. To take only one example, Germany in 18 had been a patchwork of 396 petty principalities a free cities, a hold-over from medieval times. Napolo reduced it to 40, and this was an essential step the development of a modern Germany. Wherever French armies passed, they left behind the Frer Civil Code – which embodied concepts like individ liberty and equality before the law. Reactionary for might show little enthusiasm for such ideals, but th would prove remarkably difficult to stifle.

Finally defeated at Waterloo Napoleon sails (right) on the HMS Bellerophon for the distant island of St Helena from which there was to be no escape. He spent his last years dictating memoirs and contemplating what might have been. He died there on 5 May, 1821, aged 51.

Franz Schubert
1797–1828

***Short, chubby and bespectacled, Schubert may
have lacked glamour, but his musical talents
were much respected and his warm, friendly
nature made him loved by all who knew him.***

*hubert (above)
ranscended the trials of
s often unhappy life to
mpose ethereal,
arkling music that in
s wit, charm and range
feeling, truly reflected
e humanity of his
nius.*

Many composers of the Classical and Romantic eras
wrote intensely personal music, but few wrote music
so endearingly human as Franz Peter Schubert.
Mozart's music is magical but gives little impression of
the man; Haydn's shows a craftsman at work. Yet with
Schubert it is as if we were standing at his shoulder,
watching him at work and sharing his innermost
thoughts as a composer.

The first thing we learn about Schubert from the
writings and letters of his friends and acquaintances is,
as we would hope from knowing him only through his
music, that he was greatly loved, though by no means
uncritically, by those who knew him. All his friends
were fiercely loyal, although sometimes he did not
realize it. The playwright Eduard von Bauernfeld, a

close friend, remembered him as 'the most honest soul
and the most faithful friend' and later, in an obituary
poem, wrote:

*So true and honest, not of common clay,
So free from artifice, so skilled in art.
A single mind his guide through all the days,
Which made him thoughtful, yet did joy impart.*

The writer also tells us, however, that he was 'more
taciturn than other mortals'. It seems that Schubert
had a warm, friendly nature that had to be discovered
behind a natural shyness and reticence. His artist
friend Moritz von Schwind remarked in retrospect:
'The more I realize now what he was like, the more I

Franz Theodor Schubert, (left), the composer's father, loved music and always encouraged his son's musical talent. They would often have musical evenings together when young Franz would gently correct Papa's mistakes.

see what he has suffered'. From these and oth
comments we begin to get a picture of a man who w
dominated, sometimes unwillingly, by the force of l
genius and yet desperately unable to make the best u
of his gifts – at least in a worldly sense. The warmth
his nature is reflected in his music but the shyness th
came partly from his humble origins made him t
timid to challenge the musical establishment, so th
throughout his life Schubert saw much lesser m
than himself gaining all the honours.

His friends found him very stubborn at times. I
would fall out with those who could and would ha
helped him, squandering many chances that were p
his way. This partly accounted for his lack of success
the competitive world of the theatre. Lack of effort
hardly a fault to pin on one who wrote so much in
comparatively short life, yet unfinished works a
frequent and several have movements half sketch
but never completed.

Very little is known about his working hours, f
these he spent very much alone. In the evenings, in th
coffee houses and taverns, he became cheerful a
outgoing. But there is little doubt that he was of
depressive nature rarely able to escape from h
reclusive tendencies without the help of alcohol. A

The Imperial and Royal School in Vienna (right), where young Schubert was a choirboy and pupil for five years from 1808 until 1813. By the time he started at the school at the age of 11, he was already a prolific composer and a talented pianist and violinist. Teachers found there was little they could teach him about music.

Pages from Schubert's diary (left) for 13th June, 1816, a day made unforgettable for him by a performance of a Mozart quintet. 'A light and bright, beautiful day,' Schubert writes, 'I shall remember it throughout my whole life – I still hear as if from afar, the magic sound of Mozart's music . . . Oh! Mozart! Immortal Mozart, how many visions of a brighter and better world you have imprinted on our souls!' They were indeed firmly imprinted on Schubert's soul, and Mozart's influence can be heard in many of his works.

While at the Imperial and Royal School, Schubert made a great impression on the eminent composer Antonio Salieri (above) who gave him lessons in composition.

then he would over-indulge his liking for good wine, which he refused to dilute with water, as was the Viennese custom, often becoming boisterous and even violent and, in the final stages, morose and brooding. Schwind believed that Schubert did much to damage his health by his heavy drinking and thus hastened his early death. There were many embarrassing scenes before his friends helped him back to his room in the small hours of the morning. Having slept it off, he would work in solitude all the next day and then emerge again for yet another riotous evening.

Physically, Schubert had little on his side. He was very short in stature, standing about five-feet-one, and plumply built so that his friends gave him the nickname of *Schwammerl* – 'the little mushroom', or, to put it into English schoolboy terms 'Tubby'. He had a round, fat face, short neck and not too high a forehead. Those searching for some redeeming features in their description mention well-shaped (though thickish) lips and a dimpled chin. According to his friend Sonnleithner he had 'a mass of brown and naturally curly hair, round shoulders and back, chubby arms and hands with short fingers – and, if I remember rightly, grey-blue eyes'. He walked in a hunched-up sort of way and his expression was 'generally obtuse and inclined to be sullen'. However, everyone seems to agree that when he was interested in a conversation or listening to music his face became alive and he had a sweet-natured smile.

We have the benefit of several portraits of Schubert painted by friends during his lifetime and, though they do not entirely agree and some cannot resist the obvious temptation to romanticize, there is no getting away from the short stumpy nose and the short-sighted eyes (his sight was bad from boyhood) behind the ill-fitting spectacles which are still kept in the

Schubert museum in Vienna. In later years when Moritz von Schwind was asked to sum up his appearance he described him as 'a drunken cabby'. Others have added their mite of deprecation by describing him as 'a Bavarian peasant' and 'undistinguished'.

In the end, of course, these things matter very little. They all loved their small, shy, gentle friend; and posterity does not demand that those who write like angels should necessarily look like them.

Early years in Vienna
It is strange that of all the great composers whom we think of as Viennese through their association with the city, Mozart and Beethoven among them, only Schubert was actually born there. He was the son of a poverty-stricken teacher who ran a private school in a Viennese suburb, and an erstwhile cook. Living in inadequate conditions and rarely well-fed, his parents had attempted to raise no less than 11 children before Franz Peter came on the scene. Of these only the first, Ignaz, and the last two, Ferdinand and Franz Karl survived into adulthood.

Franz Peter Schubert was born on 31 January 1797, in a small room used as a kitchen, and was duly baptized as a Catholic. Little is known of his early childhood but we imagine a stocky but unathletic child, short-sighted and intellectually inclined, who studied at his father's school from around 1803. Father Franz did all he could to interest his children in music, and the elder brother Ignaz, by then about 17 and teaching at the school, attempted to nurture Schubert's obvious early talents. He soon admitted that his pupil had natural abilities that went far beyond his own and that he could teach him nothing. Schubert began writing compositions for the family and by the age of ten he was the leading singer in the local church

Despite his quietness, Schubert's presence was much valued on social occasions and it is not surprising to see pictures of him on a picnic – an open-air 'Schubertiad' – with his friends (right).

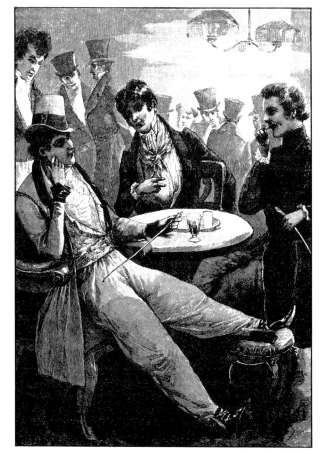

Many evenings found Schubert sitting in the cafés of Vienna like the one above, drinking wine (not diluted with water unlike the Viennese custom) until he staggered home late at night.

choir and was writing music to be performed there.

In 1808, he was admitted to the Court Chapel choir at the Imperial and Royal School. If there was some initial excitement at the donning of the military-styled uniform there was also the sudden realization of the rather bleak regime that such a life entailed. It was very much a round of hard work with school lessons all day, music lessons in the evening and very few weekends when there was not some concert or service; and visits from his family were rare. There were many typical schoolboy notes from Schubert asking for a little more pocket-money and some food to enhance a meagre diet: 'After a so-so lunch we've to wait eight and a half hours for a rotten supper'.

He did reasonably well at his general studies and, of course, found the musical studies no trouble at all. 'A very special musical talent' said his report at the end of the second term. The grounding and opportunities were unsurpassable. As well as singing in the choir, Schubert played in the school orchestra and became familiar with the music of composers such as Haydn and Mozart with occasional sorties into the work of the 'moderns' like Beethoven. Fellow pupils remembered Schubert as 'shy and uncommunicative' and he would spend most of his spare time composing and practising in a deserted room.

In truth, Schubert's father had some doubts about the wisdom of a musical career and would have preferred his son to follow his own calling as a teacher. Schubert's mother died in May 1812 and at this time father and son were drawn much closer together. When Schubert's voice broke in July he had to leave the choir, but his father agreed that he could stay at the school for another year if he would work hard at his academic studies as well as the music. It was to be a fruitful year. Schubert was taken on by Kapellmeister Antonio Salieri as his special pupil in harmony and counterpoint and they got on well. Schubert was

Schubert fell in love with Therese Grob (above) and would have married her had he not been so poor – her parents insisted she married a wealthy baker.

ways proud to call himself 'a pupil of Salieri'; while e master, like everyone else, simply proclaimed that e found that Schubert 'knew everything there was to ow about music' without much help from him.

reluctant schoolmaster

this time Schubert was offered a scholarship by the nperor but, as music was given least priority in the ourse of studies offered, he declined it and decided to mour his father by joining the family school as a nior master. There was much family rejoicing, but hubert loathed the work. It was not at all easy for a rson of his nature and was very poorly paid. His ther had remarried and Franz got on well with his epmother who helped him with money. He stayed at e school until 1816 and, in spite of its demands, his ree years as a teacher proved to be fruitful ones. uring this time he wrote around 400 compositions cluding his first three symphonies, some of his early tempts at opera, string quartets, masses and some 50 songs in which he gradually found his true style. e had his first considerable success with a song *retchen am Spinnrade* ('Gretchen at the spinning-heel'), a setting of words by Goethe which was ssed around among his friends and sung at many nateur concerts.

Schubert was at this time making the acquaintance a brilliant young pianist Mme Jenny and his oughts at this time were occasionally directed ward the fairer sex. He fell in love with Therese rob, the young daughter of a friend of the family who d sung in his Mass in F at the local church. The affair ontinued for a while but as an impoverished hoolmaster he was in no position to marry and ventually she wed a wealthy baker.

By early 1816 he had grown thoroughly tired of pping with unwilling pupils and decided to gain his eedom. He wrote for the vacant post of Music

Director in Laibach, citing Salieri as his reference. However, Salieri was not entirely to be trusted. He recommended another pupil and Schubert was turned down. Throughout his life he was to find similar difficulty in obtaining official support and it made him ever more reluctant to seek it. However, Schubert buried his resentment and wrote a cantata to celebrate Salieri's 50th birthday.

In his diaries he ruefully remarks that 'Man is the plaything of chance and passion – to some it is given and others have to struggle.' With the fair Therese in mind he finds 'the idea of marriage full of terror for the single man'. He continued to take his daily walks in the country and refresh his mind with its beauties. And he proudly notes, on 17 June 1816: 'I composed today for the first time for money. Namely a cantata for Professor Watteroth's name day to words by Dräxler. The fee is 100 Viennese florins'.

The young composer

So Schubert stepped out into the world to become a composer. Leaving home he lodged for a while with his friend Josef Spaun. Through him he now met a another medical student, Franz von Schober, whose rich Viennese family were keen patrons of the arts and lived an unconventionally Bohemian life. In the autumn, Schober persuaded Schubert to move into the family home and tried to help him in every way. It was there that he met the famous singer Michael Vogl (whom he had heard singing Gluck) and diffidently showed him one of his songs. Vogl declared it was not bad but secretly he was greatly impressed and soon became a great champion of Schubert's music. His performances of the songs did a great deal to get Schubert known in Vienna.

By 1817 he had written some of his most attractive songs such as *Die Forelle* ('The Trout') and *An die Musik* ('To Music'), so essentially Schubertian in their

Schubert's friends were very important to him, not only for company, but because they did everything they could to promote his music. He is pictured above with his two associates, Anselm Hüttenbrenner and Johann Jenger.

melodic grace and flow, as well as dramatic pieces like *Der Tod und das Mädchen* ('Death and the maiden'). He worked on his 4th Symphony which had a definite flavour and style of Beethoven about it, and composed the carefree 5th Symphony, which is infused with the spirit of Mozart. Although his music was still considered daring and unconventional he was gradually being taken up by the fashionable 'Biedermeier' society of the day; the drawing-room society people who lived their cultural and intellectual lives in a careful avoidance of the controversial political and revolutionary stirrings of the times.

In fact, Schubert himself often grew tired of the endless socializing and he was glad to be offered employment for the summer of 1818 as a music tutor to the two young daughters of Count Esterházy a hundred miles from Vienna in Zseliz. It was his first long journey outside Vienna and he enjoyed the leisurely life as well as a mild flirtation with a pretty lady's maid called Pepi. But even this began to pall and he was glad to return to Vienna for the winter. Through influential friends he now got his first commission for a one-act opera for which he was paid some 50 pounds.

In the summer of 1819 he went for a trip into the Austrian countryside with Michael Vogl as his companion. It was one of the happiest periods of his life and, while staying with an old friend Albert Stadler he wrote a sparkling piano quintet for the local musical society with a variation movement based on his *Die Forelle* – the happily inspired 'Trout' quintet. Back in Vienna for the winter of 1819–20 he was almost involved in an unpleasant brush with the authorities. He was at a party when his friend Johann Senn was arrested (he later spent a year in prison); the inoffensive Schubert was allowed to go free.

By 1821 he was becoming reasonably well-known as a composer and was given a job at the Court Theatre. But his unpunctuality and lack of cooperation soon put an end to this. His income came mainly from the modest fees that he could command for his drawing-room appearances. At these he would perform his duties well enough but refused to socialize and hated the praises and speeches at the end. He was happy enough being left to improvise at the piano while the young people danced. But his work was still not published and some of his friends thought it high time that it was. Sonnleithner, Josef Hüttenbrenner and others got together and persuaded the publisher Diabelli to put out some of Schubert's best songs on a sale or return basis. The first was *Erlkönig* in April 1821 and others quickly followed. It brought him a small but regular income from his music at last.

Illness and despair

In 1822, probably after one of the customary drunken evenings, Schubert was persuaded by some of his drinking friends to visit a brothel. It was typical of his luck that he was the only one to suffer from this, contracting a serious dose of syphilis which was to have tragic consequences. The disease and the ensuing painful mercury treatment made him desperately ill and he spent the early part of 1823 in hospital. It weakened an already unstable constitution and he was a long while recovering. It was at this time that he wrote: 'There is no man in the world as wretched and unhappy as I'; it was a bleak time after what had seemed a hopeful period. His 'Unfinished' Symphony, written at the end of 1822, seems to be born from the depths of personal tragedy.

By this time even the happy world of the Schubertiads (as the evenings with his friends were known) was beginning to disintegrate. From now on it was a life that alternated between occasional hope and happiness and deep depression., His friends scattered (even his great ally Vogl was now in retirement). He kept in touch sporadically, writing to Kupelwieser the painter in 1824:

Imagine someone whose health will never be right again, and whose sheer despair makes things ever worse rather than trying to improve matters; imagine someone whose highest hopes have been dashed and to whom the happiness of love and friendship brings only pain; whose enthusiasm for all things beautiful threatens to forsake him – and I

A rather fanciful pictu of Schubert at the piar (above) painted by Gustav Klimt around 1900 but it creates a wonderful impression the gentle gaiety of Schubert's music.

A tragic end

In the darkest of moods Schubert sat down and wrote his song-cycle *Winterreise* ('Winter Journey'). He warned his friends that they would be shaken by it; and they were. The bitterness and sense of despair in the songs made even the optimistic Schober feel gloomy. Yet, in all his grief, Schubert was still to write some of his most beautiful and often profound music – the two glorious Piano Trios and the great String Quintet included; and various offers from publishers induced a small degree of optimism again. He revised the score of the C Major Symphony for the *Musikverein* but they found it too difficult to play and it was not performed until 1839. There was a very special pleasure for him in a concert of his music on 26 March, 1828 when the E flat Piano Trio was played. Yet even this was marred by public attention being turned to the magical violin playing of the great Paganini who had given his first concert in Vienna just before. The papers were so full of the Italian 'comet' that there was no room for any mention of Schubert's music.

That year, Schubert had been studying Handel's music and decided to arrange lessons in counterpoint. 'Now for the first time I see what I lack.' But before he could start the lessons, he fell seriously ill again and moved into his brother Ferdinand's house so that he could have the comfort of a little attention. In October, 1828, he went for a short holiday to Eisenstadt where he brooded long over the grave of Haydn. Returning to Vienna his sickness grew worse but he managed to take walks and to work a little until 11 November, when he took to his bed. He tried hard to regain his strength, but on the 16th he suddenly deteriorated and a nervous fever was diagnosed. On the afternoon of the 19th, with Ferdinand and the doctor at his side, Schubert suddenly grasped at the wall and, murmuring 'This is my end', he died.

Attended by heart-broken friends and family his body was taken to the cemetery at Wahring and buried in a grave next to Beethoven's. On his tombstone an epitaph by Grillparzer, a contemporary poet, was engraved: 'The art of music here entombed a fair possession, but even fairer hopes'.

...sk you if such a one is not a wretched and unhappy ...eing? Each evening when I retire to bed I hope I may ...ot wake again; and each morning brings back ...esterday's grief.

Vienna pays tribute to Schubert, one of its greatest sons, in this statue in the Stadtpark (right). But the grim, imposing statue seems far removed from the human, gentle 'Schwammerl'.

Yet despite his doubtful health and moods of gloom ...nd despondency, his friends would often find him ...usy and wrapped in his work, turning out the sunny ...ctet and, in the summer of 1825, probably writing ...he great and glorious C major Symphony. Even the ...rigins of this are clouded in surmise. That summer of ...825 he went to Hungary with Vogl and repeated ...ome of the pleasures they had experienced on their ...rst trip together. In 1826 his friends again made ...arious efforts to get him an official post but all of ...hese failed.

Fashion in Schubert's time

Schubert himself dressed rather scruffily, though his lifetime coincided with a rich succession of new fashions. Some were ludicrous, some sensible, but all testified to the quickening pace of life in the early 19th century.

...e beguiling Madame ...camier (left) was a ...lebrated 'pin-up' of ...st-revolutionary ...ance. In her white ...emise-dress with its ...unging neckline, she ...udes all the charm of ...e empire look from the ...b of her neo-Grecian ...airstyle to her suitably ...re feet. Her saffron-loured shawl is ...aped gracefully on ...r lap – the wearing of ...is garment was now an ...t in itself.

Schubert's lifetime (1797–1828) coincided with many profound political and economic changes, and, as is often the case, these great changes were reflected in everyday life, particularly in the clothes worn by fashionable people. Then, as until recently, Paris was the capital of fashion. Inevitably, the ideals of the French Revolution (1789–99) and the glories of Napoleon's career, which harked back to the austere values of classical civilization, affected what Parisian trend-setters wore. So the great ladies of Napoleon's empire who dressed in simple cotton, or muslin, dresses (known as *robes en chemises*) were consciously reacting against the extravagant styles of Marie-Antoinette's day.

In addition to these political stimuli, there was also an economic basis for the 'empire' look. The increasing activities of England's East India Company in the 17th century had led to the import of fine printed cottons from India. The lightness, colour and variety of this textile made it fashionable among the rich both for dress and furnishings. Bearing in mind that earlier cloths, with the exception of ultra-luxurious silk, had been relatively coarse, heavy and dull, the instant appeal of Indian *calicoes* was not surprising. In the 18th century cotton-growing on a

large scale commenced in the southern USA in order to feed the pioneering British cotton 'industry'. (In fact the British cotton industry *was* the early industrial revolution.) With mass production prices came down and then British cotton conquered the world.

Another important factor to account for the vitality of fashion in this period, particularly the speed with which new trends were disseminated, was the invention of the fashion plate in the late 18th century. Published all over Europe, fashion plates enabled ladies and gentlemen in great cities such as Vienna and St Petersburg to copy immediately the very latest *modes de Paris*. Previously, fashionable women had been dependent on access to the mannequin dolls dressed in the latest styles that were laboriously carried about Europe, with an inevitable time-lag, by such enterprising folk as Marie-Antoinette's dressmaker.

The empire look

The white, high-waisted 'empire' gowns with their short, puffed sleeves were so light that it is remarkable that more women did not die of pneumonia, for especially dedicated followers of this influential fashion even dampened them to make them more

...though children in ...hubert's day (right) ...nefited from a new ...nphasis on freedom ...nd simplicity, as well as ...e arrival of cheap and ...eerful cottons, they ...ere still dressed far ...ore elaborately than ...ildren are today. ...ese boys and girls ...re wearing miniature ...rsions of their ...rents' clothes.

clinging. Pink or white stockings were often wor
beneath as a gesture, and gesture is the word, o
modesty, and the necklines were so low that the
often revealed more of the bosom than they covere
Madame Hamelin was, like Madame Récamier, o
celebrated pioneer of the 'empire' look. She one
went to the opera in a dress that exposed her bod
from one breast to the opposite hip, and she als
walked bare-breasted in the Champs Elysée
Although he admired chic women – the Empre
Josephine was very stylish – Napoleon tried to restrai
the more daring ladies of his court by bricking u
fireplaces in the hope that the resulting chill woul
encourage a degree of modesty.

In their shape dresses continued to be variations o
the empire theme until the 1820s. By then significar
details had intervened to reduce the purity of th
severely classical outfits pioneered by the likes o
Madame Récamier and Madame Hamelin. Althoug
the very high waist persisted, dresses began to b
tailored to accommodate the bust rather than pushir

*Ladies inspect the wares in a textile shop (left). Once
the material was purchased and the latest fashion
plates were studied, it was up to the ladies
themselves or, if they were well-off, their
dressmakers, to hand-sew their outfits. The woman
below is putting the finishing touches to her satin
wedding dress with the help of a maid. The sewing
machine was not available until the 1850s.*

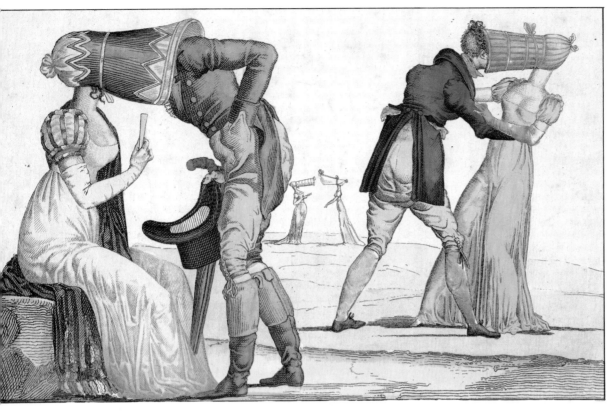

'Les Invisibles en Tête-à-tête'. This French caricature mocks the poke bonnets with exaggeratedly long brims that were in vogue during the 1820s – a period that saw a virtual explosion of millinery styles. Significantly, the men who are here taking advantage of the women's outlandish hats are wearing breeches. Long pantaloons, or trousers, were about to become regulation dress for gentlemen.

up into an unnaturally high position, and the still floor-length hems began to sprout flounces, embroidery and even ruffs of fur. The little puff sleeves were lengthened and ruffled or pleated, with the leg-o-mutton shape becoming established as a favourite style.

Gradually, too, the fashion for very thin, filmy materials waned and traditionally rich fabrics such as silk, velvet and satin (with coarse printed cottons for the less wealthy) came back into their own, as did colours other than white. Out with the light cottons went the classical-style sandals that went with them and in their place came dainty slippers with low sides and no heel, made of satin or soft leather. The toes were short and rounded and often decorated with a small bow or embroidery. (Needless to say, small feet were admired as a sign of refinement.) In due course, when hems began to rise just a little, these delicate slippers were replaced by shoes and ankle boots.

The arrival of underwear

By the 1820s the traditional feminine shape was re-emerging, as the skirt's width was increased and a greater fullness was introduced at the hips to emphasize the waist. This tendency necessarily required the intervention of that enduring device for female self-exploitation: the corset. This tortuous garment started beneath the bust and ended at the hips. Up until the early 19th century no other underwear, other than petticoats and occasional fads such as the bustle, had been considered necessary – undergarments would, in any case, have ruined the effect of the light chemise dresses. But with the heavier gowns drawers came on the scene. They were usually made of linen, for cotton was considered to be socially inferior for this purpose until later in the 19th century. Drawers were very long and it was considered most indecent to let them be glimpsed beneath the hem of one's dress. Gradually, these pioneering under-garments evolved into relatively tight-fitting pantalettes, fastened just below the knee.

Some commentators considered drawers to be indecent and unhealthy and all sorts of tirades were launched against them: 'In high life many women and girls wear drawers, an abominable invention which produces disorders in abundance.' Poor, unfashionable women, however, were spared this abominable invention until much later in the century.

Although considerations of climate had not troubled the wearers of empire gowns unduly because they generally travelled in carriages and lived in comfortable, warm houses, the fashion had nonetheless given rise to all sorts of compensatory outer garments. In one form or another, these outer clothes were destined to stay for a considerable time. Shawls, for example, were now an indispensable item in every woman's wardrobe and wearing one's shawl in a feminine and becoming way was an essential accomplishment. The most prestigious shawls originally came from Kashmir in India but soon Scottish manufacturers were profiting from the successful imitations of them made in Paisley. The pelisse, normally a three-quarter-length coat-gown with raglan, fur-lined sleeves, also made its appearance, as did the pelerine, a cape tied around the shoulders. A version of the male greatcoat known as the redingote, with several overlapping shoulder capes, also arrived to ensure the continued health of fashion-conscious women. A single-breasted jacket from England known as the spencer, which was a small neat-fitting buttoned garment that covered just the bodice of the gown, was also popular.

Accessories and headwear

The fashionable woman paid as much attention to her accessories as she did to the cut of her gowns, for then, as now, they were an all-important element in achieving a total look. At the end of the 18th century mob caps were favoured by day with turbans by night: turbans were often made in the same fabric as the gown and adorned with an ostrich plume. Indeed,

Schubert's lifetime saw an unprecedented cult of headgear, with a virtual explosion of millinery styles in the 1820s. Bonnets of all shapes and sizes were popular, as were straw hats, and they were imaginatively decorated with flowers and ribbons. For hairstyles the empire look had favoured curls. By the 1820s, however, these natural styles had given way to much more complex hairdos, with topknots often elaborated to form bizarre rolls, wings and even horns. Hat-makers had a daunting task designing edifices to sit on these styles.

Gloves and a parasol were important accessories, particularly the latter item, which, when it was not serving as a walking stick, helped to maintain the fair complexion that was the hallmark of gentility. Large fur muffs were also worn and in the evening fans were an all-important female device for communication as much as for ensuring that one glowed gently rather than perspiring. One long-term consequence of the chemise-dress was the arrival of the handbag's ancestor in the form of the reticule, or 'ridicule' as it was humorously known. First seen in the 1790s, these small purses served as the pocket which the light chemise-dresses could not sustain. By the 1820s they had diversified into soft leather purses with drawstrings and handbags with flaps and buckles.

German peasant household (left). The occupants of this rustic cottage are plainly and sensibly dressed as they go about their daily business. The spinning-wheel on the left and their wooden clogs indicate that, far from following the whims of fashion, their clothes are literally home-spun.

Despite their odd hats and the absence of good shoes, these men (left) are quite fashionable, as almost all of them are clean-shaven and in trousers, while the storyteller in their midst sports a tattered frock-coat and a topper.

The English look

While the ladies of Europe's capitals looked to Paris for the lead in fashion, well-dressed gentlemen were orientated towards England. Just as French ladies had rejected the powdered wigs and stiff satin gowns of the old order in favour of the initially simple empire look, their male counterparts' quest for simplicity took the form of Anglomania. England was seen as the land of liberty and the sombre style of the English country gentleman seemed right for post-revolutionary Europe. Accordingly, wigs, lace ruffles, embroidered coats and silk stockings were abandoned at the end of the 18th century in favour of a smartened 'interpretation' of English country clothes. Schubert's lifetime was in fact the hey-day of the English dandy, whose influential 'king' was George Bryan, or Beau Brummell (1778–1840). The well-dressed Englishman became the ideal man of many a fashionable young lady's dream. Into the head of one of his female heroines the French writer Gautier put this vision:

Sir Edward was so splendidly the Englishman of her dreams. The Englishman freshly shaved, pink, shining, groomed and polished, facing the first rays of the morning sun in an already perfect white cravat . . . Was he not the very crown of civilization?

Until the rise of the dandy even aristocratic male clothes were not designed to fit well, but now the cut and fit of a man's clothes, particularly his jackets and coats, were all-important. The frock-coat, or tail-coat, worn from the time of the French Revolution for both formal or informal wear, ruled the fashionable man until the 1820s. Though styles varied there were, in the main, two quite distinct types: one was cut across at the waist like today's tails and the other was taken at an angle from a very high waist. Both Napoleon and George III adopted this style and with Napoleon in particular a most distinctive profile was created. But there were, of course, many subtle variations on the shape of this basic male 'uniform'.

The waistcoats and breeches that went with these coats were designed to emphasize the waist, and the waistcoat was often laced at the back to facilitate the rather feminine silhouette that was thought desirable. (It is interesting that at a time when fashionable women went around in a state of white near-nudity, their menfolk were relatively colourful and restricted.) The breeches were most often in plain cream, yellow, sage green, or striped, and the waistcoat was in a contrasting colour. Breeches were worn with tight stockings, either plain or patterned, and, for indoor wear, soft black leather pumps decorated with silver buckles, or a small ribbon. Boots

served for a gentleman's outdoor footwear.

But the breeches gradually disappeared and then the more trouser-like pantaloons became the universal item of men's dress throughout Europe, notwithstanding considerable variations in cut and length. For daywear they were usually full-length and strapped under the foot like today's ski pants. For evening wear they tended to be a little shorter and were sometimes open-seamed from the calf down and fastened with a row of gold buttons. Pantaloons were sometimes cut loosely over the thigh and then tight from the knee — again emphasizing the feminine silhouette. Over the frock-coat was worn a calf-length cloak for evening, or, for day, the single-breasted great coat with shoulder capes.

Romantic style

Except for a few stubborn oldsters, wigs were dropped by the end of the 18th century, as were queues (pigtails) and manes. Now men's hair was kept fairly short and, for those who fancied themselves as Romantics, it was maintained in a style of rather studied disorder. Although light sideburns were popular, on the whole men were clean-shaven in Schubert's day. By the end of the 18th century the universal three-cornered hat, or tricorne, had been

Several key accessories, including a gentleman's cane and a lady's reticule, feature in this 1824 fashion plate (above right). The elegant dandy in the foreground has clearly paid the required attention to his cravat. As men's fashions became more sober such importance was attached to the details of the cravat's many folds (right) that their order was seen as a clue to the wearer's personality and status.

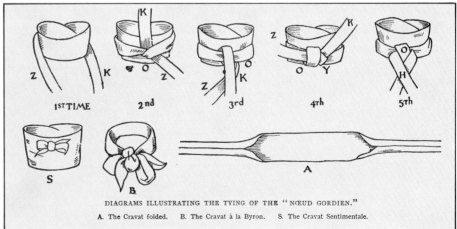

DIAGRAMS ILLUSTRATING THE TYING OF THE " NŒUD GORDIEN."

A. The Cravat folded.   B. The Cravat à la Byron.   S. The Cravat Sentimentale.

The wealthy Grosvenor family (below) illustrate trends in fashion that were becoming established around the time of Schubert's death (1828). With their very elaborate coiffures – ringlets cascading down the sides of the face were especially popular – and their rich dresses, the Grosvenor women contrast with their more soberly dressed menfolk. From behind, the adult ladies would have presented a back view similar to this detail (right) from a contemporary fashion plate.

abandoned in favour of the bicorne, always associate with Napoleon, and an early version of the top hat. B by 1825 the bicorne was passé and the top h evolved so that its sides were parallel and sometim splayed out towards the top. Like wigs, dress swor had all but disappeared by the time of Schubert's bir and in their place came sword sticks, cunning disguised as canes. Tight-fitting gloves becam fashionable in the 1820s, though, unlike those of t ladies, they were only wrist-length. Other vit accessories included a silver-topped cane and quizzing glass – a small rectangular magnifying glas The lorgnette, a pair of spectacles held by the hand into which they were folded when not in use, was als a popular upper-class accessory from the late 18 century. The art of using a lorgnette was, like the use the fan, a highly complex social game and a tru fashionable gentleman aimed to have all the lorgnett in his vicinity 'turned' upon him.

It is extremely unlikely that Schubert ever carried quizzing glass since he always wore glasses – even bed. But the composer was, like all respectable men his day, at the mercy of his tailor. Indeed, one of t reasons why England was such an important pac setter for men's fashions in the late 18th century w

ecause of the expertise of her tailors. Even though chubert led a gay social life in the coffee houses of ienna and at private gatherings of writers, poets and rtists, where a certain eccentricity of dress was no oubt tolerated, by 1821 he had incurred debts with oth his tailor and his shoemaker.

But the composer was not unduly concerned with ne refinements of up-to-the-minute fashion: he could ot have afforded it. On his death, at the age of nearly 2, he left three cloth coats, three frock-coats, ten airs of pantaloons, nine waistcoats, one hat, five pairs f shoes, two pairs of boots, four shirts, nine eckerchiefs and pocket handkerchiefs and 13 pairs of ocks. For the times and the sort of company that chubert kept, this was really a very minimal rardrobe. He appears to have had not a little difficulty rith dress since his appearance has been described as nat of 'a drunken cabby's'. His great friend, the painter Moritz von Schwind, recollected arriving one norning to take Schubert on an excursion: the omposer hurried to finish his dressing and was ummaging in his chest of drawers for a pair of socks. ut, however much he rummaged, every pair turned ut to be hopelessly torn to pieces. 'Schwind', said chubert at the end of this forlorn inspection,

'Schwind, now I really do believe that whole ones are not knitted any more.'

The all-important cravat

Most portraits of Schubert show that he wore a neckerchief or cravat in the style of the time, but clearly he did not waste the time upon it that more elegant gentlemen considered necessary. This most important feature of Romantic dress inspired in the year of Schubert's death the publication of *The Art of Tying the Cravat* with its 32 different methods, accompanied by the illustrations of the author, H. Le Blanc. The social implications of how one wore one's cravat were not to be ignored – by the ambitious at any rate:

When a man of rank makes his entrée into a circle distinguished for its taste and elegance, and the usual compliments have passed on both sides, he will discover that his coat will attract only a slight degree of attention, but that the most critical and scrutinising examination will be made on the set of his Cravat. Should this unfortunately not be correctly and elegantly put on – no further notice will be taken of him; whether his coat be of the reigning fashion or not will be unnoticed by the assembly – all eyes will be occupied in examining the folds of the fatal Cravat.
His reception will in the future be cold, and no one will move on his entrance, but if his cravat is savamment *and elegantly formed – although his coat may not be of the latest* cut – *every one will rise to receive him with the most distinguished remarks of respect, will cheerfully resign their seats to him, and the delighted eyes of all will be fixed on that part of his person which separates the shoulders from the chin – let him speak downright nonsense, and he will be applauded to the skies; it will be said – 'This man has critically and deeply studied the thirty-two lessons on the Art of Tying the Cravat'.*

That the cravat was such an item of the period and reflected social mores as well as anything else is perhaps summed up by the visitor one morning to the abode of Beau Brummell who found him with his valet

The mounted peasants in Gustave Courbet's painting of 1855 illustrate the slower pace of changes in dress among ordinary people, especially rural people, in the 19th century. Apart from their hats, they would not have looked very different in the 18th century. But the rather grotesque man with the pig is equipped with an umbrella, an accessory that was not at all common until the end of the century.

amid a pile of crumpled cravats. When the visitor enquired, he was told, ruefully, by the valet, 'Sir, those are our failures.'

Children's wear

Upper-class children – boys and girls alike – were usually clothed in dresses of contemporary adult style, until virtually the end of the 18th century. Family portraits abound showing five-year-old boys in waisted, full-skirted dresses and swords, which cannot have afforded them any greater ease of movement than their sisters in their constricting, floor-length dresses. (Boys were usually put in adult-style breeches from about the age of five or six.) Although Schubert was the twelfth child of a poor family, he was nevertheless subject to the rigours of a very formal school uniform. When he was admitted in 1808 at the age of 11 to the Imperial and Royal School his uniform consisted of a brown coat with one epaulette, white breeches, shoes with buckles and a three-cornered hat trimmed with gold braid.

On the subject of children's clothes the great Enlightenment philosopher, Jean-Jacques Rousseau wrote:

The limbs of a growing child should be free to move easily in his clothes; nothing should cramp their growth or movement; there should be nothing tight, nothing fitted closely to the body, no belt of any kind.

Although the old custom of swaddling babies was dying out in Schubert's time it was only in the 20th century that such liberal notions had a practical influence on the clothes of older children.

By Schubert's day fashion had evolved into a symbol of status that was more related to general wealth than to birth, for the French Revolution put an end to aristocratic society as the only 'society': the banker's wife could now successfully vie with the princess. In all ages, however, the dress of peasants and workers has changed less markedly than that of people with leisure and money to indulge in the latest fashion. Many of the ordinary women of Schubert's day, particularly countrywomen, would have been wearing their traditional dirndls, the national dress of the Bavarian and Swiss Alps, with its wide skirt, coloured or white apron, and its distinctive, tight-fitting bodice. Even so, the textile revolution and the great improvements in communication did affect what ordinary folk were wearing in the early 19th century. So although lower-class women wore simple bonnets or caps that were immune to the millinery styles of the big cities, they generally wore simpler, and in summer, cooler clothes than their grandmothers. Their plain skirts and aprons, and their short capes, contrasted with the bulky outfits worn in the 18th century.

All in all, Schubert lived in an age when women's fashion was more simple and less extreme than it had been before his time while for men, a sober and conservative look was adopted which has survived until the last few decades.

These assured ladies of the 1830s are partaking of afternoon tea from suitably exquisite porcelain cups – such rituals were integral to refined lifestyles. Despite the continuing popularity of Paisley shawls, the almost severe simplicity of the classical look has now given way to a much more sumptuous style. Note the threesome's positively sculpted hair and their satin dresses, which boast higher necklines, lower waistlines and fashionable leg-o-mutton sleeves.

Schubert's Vienna

Schubert's cosy and middle-class Vienna concealed a more sinister and repressive one: a police state that tried to stifle creativity and place a tight lid on the city's simmering discontent.

While the rest of Europe was still recoiling from the violence of the Napoleonic wars, its old order bloodied and shaken, the Viennese were hastily whitewashing over the recent events. Kings had been executed, thousands had been slain and Vienna itself had been occupied by the conquering French, but soon after the Congress of Vienna (1815) which redrew the map of Europe, the Viennese middle class were behaving as though nothing had happened.

Presided over by the clever political manoeuvering of the Austrian Chancellor, Prince Metternich, the Congress tried to write off the French Revolution and to restore the old established values: respect for kingship, material wealth, the social hierarchy and the integrity of the family.

And it was in Vienna itself that this policy was pursued most carefully. Emperor Francis I and his obedient government lulled the Viennese into a gentle slumber, while at the same time, anything which threatened to disrupt the system – such as a free press or student political groups – was subjected to strict censorship, and watched over by an elaborate network of police spies. Out of a period of post-war confidence, and under the machinery of a police state,

One aspect of Vienna was the popular middle-class pastime of promenading through the city's resplendent formal gardens – a far cry from the rigid censorship and police activity that prevailed.

Austria entered the period that came to be known, somewhat insultingly, as 'Biedermeier'.

Biedermeier

This word was coined around 1850 as Austria was becoming industrialized and entering the modern world. People looked back on the period after 1815 as a time of sleepy domesticity and 'Biedermeier' became their condescending label for that epoch. Biedermeier was made up from the German adjective 'bieder' meaning plain or inoffensive, and Meier – one of the commonest German surnames. (The English equivalent might be 'the style of the conservative and rather boring Mr. Smith'.)

At first, Biedermeier was a mocking reference to the domesticated and dull cultural life of Austria between the Congress of Vienna in 1815, and the revolution that finally shattered the tranquillity of Vienna in 1848. But later, people came to admire the simple style and décor and the humane quality of family life at this time: Biedermeier became a general term to describe Austrian culture during that time – particularly the style of Vienna.

The living-rooms of the well-to-do during the period known as Biedermeier (1815–1848) were comfortably decorated with parquet floors, clear colours and a host of ornaments (left).

A household typical of the time (below left): a large musically inclined family steeped in domesticity.

The preoccupation of the Viennese with the family unit and the display of financial security is emphasized in this painting by Waldmüller (below) – during this period the best known of Vienna's artists.

In 1815 it was declared that 'peace is the citizen's first duty'. Excluded from politics, the middle class looked for fulfilment in music, the theatre, and above all in family life and domesticity. It was a way of life which dominated the middle class in Vienna, and which also shaped the lifestyle of the aristocracy and the working class.

It presented the working class with the ideals of thrift, hard work, and love of order to follow. And it turned the aristocracy away from a total obsession with extravagance or with success at court. They began to pursue a more humane and modest way of life, seeking their greatest joy within the family. As Adalbert Stifter, Austria's greatest novelist of the time expressed it: 'pure family life is our greatest happiness, a happiness which appears inexhaustible.' But it was above all in the style of the middle-class home that Biedermeier values were seen most clearly.

The home and music

The living-room became the focal point of the home: it was a room to be lived in and enjoyed by the whole family. All trace of pomp and formality was banished.

The preference was for bright, clear colours on the walls, often with a delicate floral pattern. The furniture was light and unoppressive – it was never taller than the height of a standing person. This was a vivid contrast to the heavy 'Empire' style of furniture in France where large dark pieces of furniture would dominate the room. To give the room a cosy, feminine quality, chairs were covered in colourful patterns, and flounce-like draperies were hung over the arms and back rests.

Harmony with nature was a feature of the Biedermeier style. Plants and floral designs were incorporated into the living-room – from a simple stand for a potted plant to elaborate *jardinières* which included goldfish bowls and bird cages. The conservatory became a customary feature of middle-class homes, so that nature could be enjoyed during the winter. Around April it was common for the better-off families to rent a villa in the beautiful wooded suburbs of Vienna for the spring and summer months.

The dining-room was the next most important room, dominated by a large expandable dining-table, surrounded by chairs. The sideboard was becoming a common piece of furniture and stood along one wall. The larger houses also had a study for the master of the house, and a dressing room for the lady as well as a bedroom for the parents, rooms for the children, and accommodation for the servants. But within the living-room there was often a special working area for the housewife, containing a small sewing table and a seat. More well-to-do households would have a music corner in the living-room, with instruments that suited the talents of the family, as making music together would be one of the principal joys of the typical Biedermeier household.

In the musical circle that surrounded Schubert we can see a specially gifted group of young people, but engaged in music in a way that was typical of the Biedermeier household. At first, Schubert's father and his three sons played together as a string quartet. As the group expanded, they moved to the house of a friendly merchant, and then to the home of a violinist friend, Otto Hatwig, who became the leader of the orchestra.

Memoirs from this time record music groups in the homes of a university professor, a general, senior civil servants, a brewer, a calligrapher, wholesale merchants and retail traders. Both Schubert and the greatest poet of this period, Franz Grillparzer, attended the musical soirées of the banker Johann von Geymüller. Legend has it that Geymüller's home contained five pianos: one for each of his exceptionally musical daughters.

Schubert set some of Grillparzer's poems to music and both were bewitched by the intelligent and spirited singing of these sisters. When one of this lively and constantly changing group was particularly struck by a song 'our Schubert' had written, he would make a copy and show it to friends, or send it to Salzburg or Munich. Through these informal musical groups, Schubert's work circulated around Vienna and Austria; Schubert himself was never over-concerned about getting his work published.

Painting

Painting in Austria at this time provides an interesting mirror reflecting the values of Biedermeier society. While artists in France, Germany, and England were being drawn towards the themes of nature that had a violent, transcendental quality, the painters of Vienna

concentrated on family life and on flowers.

In England, Turner was painting landscapes wher the light battered the viewer like a physical force. I Germany, Casper Friedrich was creating alpine view that had the intensity of a religious vision. But i Austria, landscape painting remained picturesque an precise and never hurled itself into the Romanti abyss. Instead, the themes that came to epitomiz Vienna during its Biedermeier phase – bourgeoi simplicity in place of aristocratic pomp, the cos home in place of the palace, the lovable details o everyday life in place of the big moments of historica conflict – found an apt form of expression in the work of the typical exponents of Austrian art.

The greatest artist of this time, Ferdinand Geor Waldmüller, developed his own style of luminou intensity to paint both landscapes of great clarity, an simple paintings of family groups where the figure harmonized with their background in a way that wa both elegant and natural.

But though Waldmüller's art is now acclaimed a totally characteristic of Biedermeier Vienna, in hi own life he fought a series of tedious and ultimatel dangerous battles with the artistic establishment. H did not fit in either with the classically inspire painters, or with the Nazarenes (the Austrian versio of the pre-Raphaelites). Instead, he argued agains 'chewing the cud of things handed down' and becaus of his critical attitude towards tradition he wa relieved of his teaching job at the Academy of Fin Arts in Vienna.

Instead, Waldmüller obtained a job as a curator of gallery, but was pensioned off after writing memorandum on reforms needed in the teaching o art: he had not sent his criticisms through the correc channels. By the time that he died, Waldmüller's wor fetched no price at all. His life is a good example of th Viennese tradition of stifling talent and ultimatel ignoring it.

Theatre
The world of theatre also tells us how people wh were tormented and even destroyed by the attitude of their time, were later remembered as personifyin

In his choice of subject-matter the Viennese artist von Engert epitomized the spirit of homeliness: an enclosed flower garden with a vine pergola, hollyhocks and sunflowers (above). Among these suburban images a woman sits knitting and reads what is almost certainly a Bible.

Outside Vienna, painters like Caspar David Friedrich scorned the pedestrian Biedermeier style and chose a totally different mood and subject. The sense of the infinite is hauntingly portrayed in Friedrich's Moon rising over the Sea *(right).*

l the things that Vienna symbolizes: romance, gaiety, nd a love of life.

Ferdinand Raimund was the greatest dramatic figure the period. He was stage-struck at the age of 13 and orked his way up through a troupe of travelling ayers, until, by the age of 18, he had begun to tablish himself on the Viennese stage as a new kind comedian: one who could be both subtle and ntle. Raimund fell in love with Toni, daughter of a offee house proprieter, but her parents were too obbishly middle-class to accept an actor as a son-in- w. Against the wishes of their daughter, they jected Raimund's suit. In despair, he had a brief rtation with an actress who happened to be the ughter of his director and patron, who forced m to marry the girl. Raimund was now in double ouble. He had to obtain a divorce from a wife he did ot love, and somehow retain the affection of his eloved Toni and win the approval of her parents. rprisingly, Raimund was also a deeply religious atholic, and after obtaining his divorce he did not el himself free to re-marry. Instead, over a small rine in a vineyard in the Vienna Woods, he and Toni vore a vow before God to be true to each other.

While enduring such a complicated and unhappy rivate life, Raimund wrote a series of plays that made im the comic genius of his time. Yet beneath the ocial satire there was a sad and haunting perception f life passing people by. In his most famous work — *as Mädchen aus der Feenwelt oder Der Bauer als illionär* ('The Girl from Fairyland or the Peasant urned Millionaire') — Raimund himself played a mple peasant, Fortunatus Wurzel, who in a flash is ansformed on stage from a vigorous youth into a ent and almost senile 'Aschenmann', a dustman who ollects wood ash while singing a sad little song with a norus: 'All is ashes, all is ashes.'

After nine years of painful devotion to his beloved oni, the girl's parents finally relented and allowed the ouple to live together in their home. But this torment ad taken its toll of Raimund's spirit. In 1836 he was itten by a dog, and for some reason Vienna's greatest omic genius convinced himself that the dog was bid and he was about to contract the disease, so he

For the Viennese middle class, going to the theatre was a chance to parade their prosperity (left). But beneath this opulent veneer lay a sense of stagnation and time passing by which was cleverly satirized by Vienna's most popular actor, Ferdinand Raimund (above with actress Constanze Dahn).

Emperor Francis I (above) and his Chancellor, Prince Metternich (above right) collaborated on a policy that diverted attention away from Europe's political ferment. Although Vienna seemed free of unrest it was at a price – in 1801 the Austrian Ministry of Police took over the administration of censorship.

Metternich and his ministers reformed th
curriculum. Controversial areas such as philosoph
were allowed to rot, while the study of science an
technology was encouraged. 'Anyone can philosophi.
and criticize as the spirit moves him, but positiv
science must be learned,' as Metternich's chief aic
Friedrich von Gentz put it. Any university lecture
teaching the doctrine of free thought was relieved
his job. Any student suspected of belonging to
political association could be put under detention an
deported to the provinces. These policies were
success for Metternich and the universities remaine
quiet. Meanwhile, an elaborate network of polic
informers watched over the people of Vienna.

When Schubert died in poverty in 1828, th
circumstances of his burial bore some resemblance t
Mozart's, who was buried in a pauper's grave. On
interesting difference was a sentence in the municip
report which asked 'Whether there were books amon
the property of the deceased and whether a repo
about them had been made to the Imperial Boc
Revision Office'. This was standardized procedure fc
uncovering any subversive pamphlets that might b

picked up a gun and committed suicide.

The theatre provided a rich source of interest and gossip for Vienna, and the Austrian police recognized the value of the theatre during periods of public tension. When closure of the theatres was suggested, the Police Department replied: 'People are accustomed to theatrical shows. In times like these, when individuals are affected by so much suffering, the police are more than ever obliged to cooperate in the diversion of citizens by every moral means. The most dangerous hours of the day are the evening hours. They cannot be filled more innocently than in the theatre.'

The theatre was not just for the wealthy or the middle class. It also faithfully reflected the attitudes of working class and petit bourgeois audiences, and enjoyed the loyalty of all Vienna. In 1813, a fortnight after an army commanded by the Austrian Prince Schwarzenberg defeated Napoleon at Leipzig, a new hit appeared on the Vienna stage, written by a clever young journalist Adolf Bäuerle. It was *Die Burger in Wien* ('Citizens of Vienna') and the character who made the play a sensational success was Staberl: a whining embodiment of the 'little man'; an umbrella maker; a buffoon; the despair of his friends; and yet one of life's survivors. All of his speeches and complaints ended despairingly 'I wish it did me some good . . .'.

It was an apt 'catch' phrase for a nation that had been defeated by Napoleon, allied to Napoleon through marriage, and had finally vanquished Napoleon. A nation which was told by a benevolent dictator of an emperor not to worry about politics, and to concentrate on domestic life. 'I wish it did me some good . . .' was the cry of Vienna's man in the street every time he got entangled in some wild idea that went wrong.

The police state

The price to be paid for all this domestic bliss was nothing less than a highly organized police state. Metternich knew that what he was trying to keep out of Austria was the *Zeitgeist* or 'spirit of the age'. Nationalism, the Romantic Movement, talk of revolutionary political ideas, were all sweeping across Europe, and for Metternich censorship and a well organized police system were the best defence.

To keep the universities as quiet as possible,

nong the deceased person's possessions. In 1830 the stem was further tightened up because revolution d driven the French king from his throne, and reatened to contaminate Austria.

An unsuccessful attempt was made to halt the flood people from the countryside into the city. From the ench experience it was realized that a mobile orking class was the most likely group to cause olitical trouble and the word 'proletariat' was iported from France to describe this new and ingerous social force.

Emperor Francis I passed laws to restrict the iilding of new houses. Casual workers had to obtain iecial marriage permits from the police in an attempt > prevent the working class from reproducing too pidly, and for a time a complete ban was placed on :w factories being established in Vienna.

ie City

ienna had grown to embrace a population of 326,000 :ople by 1830. About a quarter of these lived in the :ntre still surrounded by the medieval walls of the :ty. The rest lived in the suburbs which increased rapidly despite Imperial attempts to keep the lid on the population.

Such rapid growth, unsupported by any major building programme, did not produce a healthy environment. Schubert died in 1828 of typhus at the age of 31, the same disease that had killed his mother. Typhus, dysentery, and tuberculosis were rife in the city, and the infant mortality rate was high.

Schubert's father had fourteen children from his first two marriages – only five children survived. His brother Ferdinand married twice and had 25 children – only 12 survived. In 1831 half the Viennese who died were under 20 years old. In real terms, the population of the city was actually falling because of the high death rate. It was only the constant arrival of new workers from the Austrian Empire which made Vienna appear to grow in population.

Evidence from the courts and from police records shows that there was real misery bordering on starvation for the working class. And corruption was common among the poorly paid lower clerks of the public services, as they tried to supplement their meagre wages with bribes.

Student uprisings (below) were the inevitable reaction to a repressive regime, though in Vienna they never attracted the same fanatical support given to the other similar demonstrations that were taking place throughout Europe.

Not far from Vienna's glorious palaces there were ramshackle streets peopled by the city's destitute (left). Such poverty was not, of course, peculiar to Vienna, but in a city where complacency ruled it seemed more of a disgrace.

Since the published word was strictly censored few had the courage to speak out against the establishment. However, the poet Grillparzer (right) was a notable exception.

When unskilled workers in a village near Vienna went on strike, their leaders were sentenced to hard labour in chains. When bakers' shops were looted during the bread riots in 1805 the cavalry were required to clear the streets, leaving ten dead behind them. In 1811, over 1500 shoemakers demonstrated in Vienna until military strength dispersed the march. Even as conditions improved after the war, a quick rise in the price of some basic item such as candles was enough to trigger off a dangerous state of unrest in the poorer quarters.

Although the official message of the Biedermeier period was that 'happiness in a quiet corner' was the best policy for the good citizen to follow, numerous accounts tell us how aware people were of their extremely limited freedom: freedom which amounted to being able to sit at home, think of nothing much and enjoy a quiet life.

The French

The poet Grillparzer was a patriotic youth who took part in the defence of Vienna against Napoleon's bombardment in 1809. But while the French were actually occupying the city, they were hardly regarded as a hated invading army. If anything, they inspired admiration. The French officers with their experience of revolution, their military success, their political sophistication, seemed to come from a world very different from the humdrum and quiet life of Vienna. The poet Grillparzer tells us how obsessed he became by Napoleon at this time:

I myself was no less an enemy of the French than m father, and yet Napoleon fascinated me with a mag power. I had hatred in my heart, I had never been addicted to military displays, and yet I missed not one of his reviews of troops. I still see him before m running rather than walking down the steps of Schönbrunn [the huge palace on the outskirts of Vienna] and then standing there like cast-iron to survey his troops on the march past with the unmoved look of the lord and master. He put me under a spell as a snake does a bird. My father mus have been little pleased by these unpatriotic excursions but he never forbade me.

Napoleon was finally defeated and for 15 years th Viennese lived in a state of apparent Biedermei tranquillity. But in 1830 two years after Schuber death, disturbing news reached them of anoth revolution in France. Once again the French ha shown what being in control of your own politic destiny could mean.

In his Journal Grillparzer wrote:

The French have driven out their king who tried to break the constitution and turn them into a variet of Austrian, which civically and politically, seems t be the worst fate that could happen to anyone. I wis I were in France. It is still better to live in the dange of democracy than to have the spirit defeated and th noblest human needs sacrificed to an abominable system of stability.

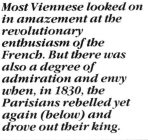

Most Viennese looked on in amazement at the revolutionary enthusiasm of the French. But there was also a degree of admiration and envy when, in 1830, the Parisians rebelled yet again (below) and drove out their king.

Felix Mendelssohn

1809–1847

A child prodigy, remarkable for his depth and sensitivity as well as his precocity, Mendelssohn flowered into one of the most celebrated – and best-loved – composers of his time.

Felix Mendelssohn does not conform to the popular idea of a struggling Romantic composer. He did not write by the guttering flame of a candle in an unheated garret or die, unrecognized, in poverty. He was born into a wealthy and cultured family who did all they could to encourage his prodigious musical talents. By the age of nine he was an acclaimed performer; at 16 he had proved his genius as a composer. Artist, poet, traveller and even mountaineer, he was a man of great sensitivity and charm who numbered among his friends the great and famous and the literary and musical giants of his day.

As a young boy he won the heart of Goethe; in his prime he captivated Queen Victoria. When he died – at only 37 – two nations went into mourning, for the composer, and the man. Although Mendelssohn had much music still to give, he had already laid the cornerstone for modern musical appreciation in the Western world.

A cultured background

The influence of Mendelssohn's family on his life and works start with his grandfather, Moses Mendelssohn. Born in Dessau, into poverty and under the severe restrictions imposed on Jews by 18th-century Prussia, Moses took his destiny into his own hands. At the age of 14 he walked 80 miles to Berlin, where he taught himself languages, mathematics and philosophy. He became one of the great thinkers and teachers of the Enlightenment period and his writings were translated into 30 languages. He was a champion of religious tolerance and fought in particular for Jewish emancipation. Both his philosophical ideals and his talent for making money were passed on to his son Abraham, who became a banker and married the musical and highly-educated Lea Salomon.

The young couple settled in Hamburg, where their eldest child, Mendelssohn's beloved sister, Fanny, was born in 1805. Lea noted with uncanny foresight that the baby had 'Bach fugue fingers' – and indeed, had the convention of the time allowed, there is little doubt that Fanny would have become a composer of distinction. As it was, she contented herself with writing songs and performing recitals of other people's music. The composer of the family was to be Felix, born in February, 1809. He was followed by two more children, Rebekka and Paul.

Two years after Felix was born, the family uprooted. Abraham, like many other bankers and merchants of Hamburg, had managed to dodge Napoleon's trade restrictions and had become very rich indeed. Like them, he was now faced with a more direct threat from the occupying French troops. The Mendelssohns fled to Berlin.

Mendelssohn at 20, newly arrived in London. Charming, gracious and debonair, he immediately won the hearts of the English. They were not only moved by the warmth and sentiment of his music, but also found him to be the perfect gentleman.

The happy, comfortable and enlightened environment in which the young Mendelssohn grew up was made possible by the courage and determination of his grandfather, Moses (right). As a boy, Moses, a poor hunchback Jew, had walked the 80 miles to Berlin, in the hope of making a better life for himself. There, against a background of prejudice, he prospered, winning a name for himself as a philosopher and champion of Jewish emancipation.

Mendelssohn at 12 (below) – a brilliant child who captivated everyone he met.

In Berlin, Abraham made a significant contributio to the defence of Prussia by equipping voluntar soldiers and financing a military hospital. After th victory over Napoleon he was rewarded with position on Berlin's Municipal Council and elevated status not usually accorded to a Jew. Part out of Christian conviction and partly to cement the new standing, the family added the name Barthold which had been adopted by Abraham's brother, their own.

Musical beginnings

In this illustrious setting, the young boy's genius too root and flourished. He was given a rounded educatio under Berlin's most prestigious teachers. His princip music tutor was Carl Zelter, a colourful man who coarse behaviour and unconventional dress we more suited to his previous occupation as stonemason than to his post as the Director of Berlin Singakademie.

Zelter's pupil went from strength to strength. nine he was performing, as a pianist or conducto before an admiring circle of family and friends including some of Germany's foremost writers, poe and philosophers – Heine, Hegel, Humboldt and Jakc Grimm were among those who heard him play. At tc Felix began to compose; a young friend witnessed th scene:

I found him on a footstool, before a small table, writing with such earnestness. On my asking what I was about, he replied, gravely, 'I am finishing my new Quartet for piano and stringed instruments.' looking over his shoulder [I] saw as beautiful a scor as if it had been written by the most skilled copyist. was his first Quartet in C minor. Then, forgetting quartets, . . . down we went into the garden, he clearing high hedges with a leap, running, singing and climbing trees like a squirrel.

The boy's energy amazed all who knew him. I studied; he composed without ceasing; at the age of 1 he even started his own newspaper. His mother, wii her usual intuition, wrote that 'his impulsivene: sometimes makes him work harder than he ought to his age.' Mendelssohn would always work harder tha he ought to – and one day it would kill him.

At the age of 12 Zelter's protégé so impressed hii that he proposed to introduce him to Goeth scientist, sage, poet, and Germany's foremc philosopher and thinker. When Goethe agreed to sc him, his family were thrown into a state of excitemen but Felix was not overawed and reported in a lette home:

He was in the garden and just coming round a hedge He is very friendly, but I don't think any of the pictures are like him. One would never take him fo 73 but 50.

And later he told of their daily routine:

I play here much more than I do at home: rarely les than four hours, sometimes six or even eight. Goeth sits down beside me and when I have finished . . . I ask for a kiss or take one. You cannot imagine how goo and kind he is to me.

It was the beginning of a friendship that was to la: until Goethe's death and spanned five significant visit The relationship deepened Mendelssohn's love fc classical literature, and assured its importance in th composition of his music. For his part, Goethe was nc only entertained and amused by his youn

ompanion, but prompted to a greater appreciation of
lassical music, though he never managed to share
Mendelssohn's enthusiasm for Beethoven.

After the visit to Goethe the family, with its
entourage of tutors, embarked on a tour of
Switzerland. Felix absorbed each new impression
voraciously; once awakened, his passion for travelling
would never die. As on later journeys, he sketched or
painted views that struck him with their beauty, and
wrote copious letters and poems, often illustrating
them with amusing cartoons. He also commented on
the native taste in music – yodelling:

*his kind of singing sounds harsh and unpleasant
when it is heard nearby, or in a room . . . in the
alleys, mountains and woods, when you hear it
ingling with the answering echoes, it sounds
eautiful.*

This is early evidence of the critical awareness of
the music of others that made him determined to
bring good music to the people – to teach musicians to
play and the public to listen – which was to be one of
his major achievements.

Germany's new composer

Meanwhile, the budding composer delighted his
teacher with a one-act opera, *The Uncle from Boston.*
After its performance Zelter addressed the audience

Carl Zelter (left) was an inspired choice as Mendelssohn's music teacher. Something of a rough diamond, he was renowned for his lack of tact, and could be relied upon to lower the tone of conversation. Yet, despite his boorishness, Zelter was a man of utter integrity, and, in Goethe's words, one of 'subtle and diamantine genius'.

Mendelssohn, the child prodigy, plays before the illustrious Goethe at one of the regular Sunday morning musical parties organized by his family (below). The young boy was to strike up a surprisingly close friendship with the 73-year-old writer and philosopher – then struggling to complete part II of Faust.

In addition to his many talents – composer, poet and even mountaineer – Mendelssohn was also an artist of some ability. He painted this charming view of Lucerne (above) while on a trip to Switzerland, inspired by the serenity of the landscape.

One of Mendelssohn's greatest triumphs was his rediscovery and revival of Bach's St Matthew Passion *(right). Prior to this Bach had been regarded by the public as 'a powdered wig stuffed with learning.' Now Mendelssohn created a whole new wave of interest in the Baroque composer. 'To think', he exclaimed, 'that ... a Jew should give back to the people the greatest Christian music in the world.'*

and congratulated the 14-year-old: 'My dear boy, from this day you are no longer an apprentice, but a full member of the brotherhood of musicians. I hereby proclaim you independent in the name of Mozart, Haydn and old father Bach.'

But Abraham still needed convincing that music was the right career for his son. He took him to Paris to see the composer Cherubini, who was Director of the Paris Conservatoire. The verdict was decisive: 'Your boy is talented, he will do well. He has already done well.' Barely a year later, Cherubini was proved right. At the age of 16, Mendelssohn completed his String Octet, op. 20, which was partly inspired by lines from Goethe's *Faust*. It is recognised as his first fully mature work, and some critics claim it is an unparalleled achievement for a 16-year-old; not even Mozart or Schubert produced music of such brilliance so young. Germany had a new composer.

His next work was another masterpiece, his overture to *A Midsummer Night's Dream*. Again the inspiration came from classical literature, and it has been said that no other music has so successfully captured the essence of Shakespeare. Mendelssohn's friend, the pianist Ignaz Moscheles, declared when he heard it that 'this great and still youthful genius has once again made gigantic steps forward.' Mendelssohn was progressing in other fields too. Having translated Terence's Latin comedy *Andria,* he was awarded a place at the University of Berlin, where he studied aesthetics under the philosopher Hegel.

Mendelssohn next turned his attention to the work

Johann Sebastian Bach, for many years neglected by the listening public. He spent several years working on the score of *St Matthew Passion,* and when the work was released, it caused a considerable stir in the music world. Tickets for the first performance were sold out within minutes, and some members of the audience were so moved by the music that they wept openly.

Success in Britain

Armed with his now considerable reputation, the 20-year-old set out to conquer more distant lands. He had already made the acquaintance of Sir George Smart, the founder of the Philharmonic Society, and he went to stay in London with the hope of being invited to play there. He was introduced to the pleasures of London life by Moscheles and another friend, Klingemann, both of whom had settled there.

The gaiety and excitement of London after the narrow and stuffy atmosphere of Berlin turned his head and won his heart: it was the beginning of a life-long love affair with England. After three days he wrote home: 'I hardly remember the chief events. Things toss and whirl about me as if I were in a vortex, and I'm whirled along with them. Not in the last six months in Berlin have I seen so many contrasts and such variety as in these three days.' He spent his time living in Hyde Park, delighting in operas, concerts and balls and the charming young ladies he met there, and marvelling at the thickness of the fog and the even greater density of English plum pudding.

When he made his début, it was to deafening applause and the highest critical acclaim. One reviewer noted 'scarcely had he touched the keyboard than something that can only be described as similar to a pleasurable electric shock passed through his hearers and held them spellbound.' He set the seal on his success and established himself as the darling of the British public with a charity concert for the people of Silesia, who had been made homeless by floods. He was fêted everywhere as a musician of transcendent talent and, no less important to the English, a perfect gentleman.

In July, Mendelssohn and Klingemann travelled to Scotland. The young composer was vividly impressed with the romantic scenery of the Highlands: 'When God himself takes to landscape painting, it turns out strangely beautiful . . . everything looks so stern and robust, half-enveloped in mist or smoke or fog . . .' It inspired him to write his 'Scottish Symphony', and also to take out his drawing pad. During a journey to Fingal's cave, already immortalized a decade earlier by Keats, the first bars of the *Hebrides* Overture occurred to him.

Mendelssohn was less impressed with British folk music. He found the sound of bagpipes offensive to his ear, and when the pair moved on to Wales he wrote: 'Dear me, a harper sits in the hall of every reputed inn, playing incessantly so-called national melodies; that is to say most infamous, vulgar, out-of-tune trash, with a hurdy-gurdy going on at the same time.'

Brotherly love

By the end of August, Mendelssohn was ready to return home. His sister, Fanny, was to be married and he wanted to be at the wedding. But he was prevented from going by a carriage accident that injured his knee. From his sickbed he wrote her a desperate letter.

This then is the last letter you'll receive before your marriage. For the last time I address you as Fräulein Fanny Mendelssohn-Bartholdy . . . There's much I would like to say to you, but I'm not really able . . . I feel as if I had lost the reins with which formerly I was able to guide my life. When I think about everything which is now going to change, and take a different shape, everything which I have long taken for granted, then my thoughts become unclear and half wild.

The love between brother and sister had always been passionately strong. Felix inevitably showed his compositions to Fanny before anyone else and relied on her advice. In his letters he had addressed her ardently. She made him feel 'quite giddy'. He called her his 'angel', his 'darling little sister' and declared,

In 1829 Mendelssohn travelled to London, where he was immediately plunged into its dazzling social whirl (above). It made Berlin seem positively provincial.

Throughout his life, Mendelssohn shared a deep love and understanding with his sister Fanny (left) – there is no doubt that she was the most important single influence on his life. Their correspondence testifies to the intimacy and, sometimes, intensity of their relationship. When Fanny died – she was suddenly seized by a paralytic stroke while playing the piano – Felix was heartbroken. He collapsed on hearing the news of her death and never fully recovered.

'My sweet, I love you terribly.' On her side, Fanny was no less vehemently attached to her brother. When he left Berlin she wrote 'all will be mute and desolate'. Felix constantly appears in her diary – far more entries are devoted to him than to her fiancé, Wilhelm Hensel. Of him she wrote 'a bridegroom is no more than a man'. Felix's other sister, Rebekka, reported that Fanny fell asleep in Hensel's company – she was bored because he was not there, and on her wedding day she wrote:

I have your portrait before me, and ever repeating your dear name and thinking of you as if you stood at my side, I weep! Every morning and every moment of my life I'll love you from the bottom of my heart, and I'm sure that in doing so I shan't wrong Hensel.

They must have been well aware that the intensity of their love was dangerous. Fanny's marriage was a timely escape. By the time Mendelssohn returned to Berlin for his parents' silver wedding anniversary – having written an operetta for the occasion – she was Frau Hensel.

In 1830 at the age of just 21 Mendelssohn was offered the chair of music at Berlin University, but he refused. He had just begun to compose his 'Reformation' Symphony, and was totally absorbed by it; he wanted to travel; perhaps he also felt it was a mistake to stay too long in the neighbourhood of Fanny and her new husband. His travels were to take him, via a last visit to Goethe, to Austria, Italy, Switzerland and France. He travelled light, taking with him 'three shirts and Goethe's poems'. He met Chopin, Liszt, Berlioz, Paganini, Meyerbeer, Dorothea von Ertmann, who had been a close friend of Beethoven's, and the dramatist Karl Immermann, with whom he intended to collaborate on an opera. His trip to Italy inspired the wonderful 'Italian' Symphony – his Symphony no. 4.

In March, 1837, Mendelssohn married Cécile (above), who bore him five children. The marriage was a very happy one – Cécile was, in Fanny's words, 'a fresh breeze, so bright and natural'.

A pen drawing by Mendelssohn of Birmingham (above) where he travelled to conduct the triumphant first performance of his oratorio Elijah *in 1846, just over a year before his death.*

Later achievements

In the spring of 1832, deeply saddened by news of the deaths of Goethe and Zelter, Mendelssohn returned to England. Here his performances drew capacity crowds, but he was called back home by his father, who wanted him to apply for Zelter's post as Director of the Singakademie. In the event he was not disappointed when Zelter's deputy got the job – he had further engagements in London and had been invited to conduct the 1833 Music Festival in Düsseldorf. Here he instituted an important revival of Handel's works besides conducting an impressive series of operas. But neither the audience nor the orchestra lived up to his expectations. He had administrative difficulties and no time for composing. Frustrated beyond endurance, he tore the score of Beethoven's *Egmont* in two during a rehearsal and when, in the summer of 1834, he received an invitation to take over Leipzig's Gewandhaus Orchestra, he accepted with alacrity and relief.

Here in the cultural capital of Germany he had a free hand to organize the city's music and plenty of time in which to compose. During his ten-year stay in Leipzig, he achieved a great deal. He built a first-rate orchestra out of what began as an undistinguished collection of musicians: no doubt they were as encouraged by the enthusiasm of their conductor as by the handsome salary increase he won for them. As usual his repertoire was wide and varied and he introduced the public to works that had hitherto been ignored – including Beethoven's Fourth, and later, his Ninth. He also premièred Schubert's last symphony; Schumann had unearthed the manuscript in Vienna and saved it from almost certain destruction. Another achievement was to invite the leading soloists of the day to perform at the Gewandhaus: all this added up to the tremendous success of his concert seasons, bringing an increased public enthusiasm for music that has formed the basis of all modern musical appreciation.

Short-lived happiness

In 1837 Mendelssohn crowned his happiness by falling in love and getting married. His bride was the

...ptivating Cécile Jeanrenaud. It was eight months ...fore Cécile and Fanny met, and Mendelssohn must ...ve been greatly relieved that Fanny found his wife 'a ...esh breeze, so bright and natural'. The marriage was a ...ppy one, and there were five children.

In 1840 the death of the repressive King of Prussia ...omised the dawn of a new era in Berlin, and his ...ccessor persuaded Mendelssohn to take a post as the ...pital's music director. The composer left Leipzig ...ith a heavy heart. In Berlin he met with bureaucratic ...ifficulties and gradually withdrew from his ...bligations. His next achievement was to found the ...eipzig Conservatory, which he built into Germany's ...remost academy of music. In the meantime he ...ontinued his visits to England, which he always ...garded as his second home, and became a firm ...vourite with Queen Victoria and Prince Albert who ...dmired his urbanity as well as his compositions. In a ...pical burst of energy he composed his oratorio ...*lijah* in a matter of months for the Birmingham Music ...estival of 1846.

All this tireless activity was taking its toll. Public acclaim had never been more tumultuous, but Mendelssohn was driving himself too hard. In May 1847, as he was making his way home from his tenth visit to England, broken and exhausted, he was shattered to learn of the death of his beloved sister, Fanny. He never recovered from the blow. In October he had a slight stroke, and on 4 November he died. He was buried next to his sister. Amidst the public mourning, Cécile was alone. A few days after her husband's death she wrote:

There are corners of my mother-in-law's garden where I must martyr myself to be able to grasp what has happened. Here are the same trees, bower, branches, there is the ruined fountain, and they all still exist. Felix's grave bears a marble cross with his name. Behind it I have planted a lilac and a rosebush. I wanted to keep the mound free and green, it's always heaped with flowers and wreaths. I placed my tributes at his feet.

Six years later Cécile died, utterly inconsolable, at the age of 36.

In the last decade of his life, Mendelssohn focused his activities on the Leipzig Gewandhaus (below). Here, with typical energy and enthusiasm, he built up a distinguished orchestra, which became a model for all Europe. Under his leadership, they performed many major works that had previously been ignored – including Schubert's last symphony – and were graced with some of the finest soloists of the age. Through such selfless work, Mendelssohn created a lasting musical legacy, increasing the public's enjoyment of music.

A model for the nation
Victoria and Albert

Despite demanding public roles, Victoria and Albert enjoyed an idyllic family life and were at one with their subjects in their enthusiasm for, among other things, Felix Mendelssohn's delightful music.

Sketch
140 ℒ 1839

he term 'Victorian' has come to mean all things roper and restrained, heavy with solemnity and atus. But Queen Victoria, in her early years at least, as not like that at all. When she married her distant ousin, Prince Albert of Saxe-Coburg-Gotha (a small erman duchy), she married for love. To the 20-year-d Queen, Albert was an incredibly handsome and harming, even 'incomparable', man. She felt a deep hysical passion for him, which she expressed quite benly in her letters, and though he was a rather more eserved person, he was totally dedicated to her.

They had many things in common, not the least of hich was a love of family life that was partly due to the ct that they had both endured scandal and disruption their own childhoods. Albert never saw his mother ter the age of five when the Princess Louise of Saxe-oburg-Gotha ran off with another man, and Victoria's ther had died when she was a baby. Mindful of lbert's wayward mother and of Victoria's two hocking uncles – George IV and William IV – the oyal couple shared a desire, almost raised to a sacred bligation, to set new standards of respectability.

model family

the early years of their idyllic marriage Victoria and lbert set about initiating an exemplary style of royal ving. Despite a stifling emphasis on etiquette and ormality on public occasions, daily family life was

Though still girlish and fun-loving, the 20-year-old Victoria (far left) had clear ideas about marriage. It had to be a love match and her partner had to come up to high standards of male beauty.

Albert might have been tailor-made: he fulfilled all of the Queen's hopes with his 'beautiful blue eyes, an exquisite nose, & such a pretty mouth with delicate moustachios & slight but very slight whiskers'. She was happy to propose (left) in October 1839, and when he accepted they immediately fell into each other's arms. They were married in February 1840 (below) and within a year the first of their many children, Princess 'Vicky', was born.

The 'new and much admired' royal 'pear' (above). Victoria and Albert were exemplary newly-weds.

characterized by a refreshing informality. An artist engaged to paint frescos at Buckingham Palace observed how, after their diplomatic and political work, the young couple would stroll out into the grounds, 'evidently delighted to get away from the bustle of the world to enjoy each other's society in the solitude of the garden . . . Here too the royal children are brought out by the nurses, and the whole arrangement seems like real domestic pleasure'. There is no doubt that the royal household was a very happy one. Victoria never disguised her distaste for tiny babies and she confessed that too many pregnancies – she had nine children in 17 years – had made her 'so worn out' and 'so miserable', but she was a devoted mother.

Despite her distaste for childbearing, a process she always referred to with typical delicacy as *die Schattenseite* (the shadow-side) of marriage, Victoria was lucky in that she was as vigorously healthy as she was fertile. Her first baby was born three weeks prematurely and though the immediate reaction was one of disappointment at the failure to produce an heir, this was the only blot on an otherwise perfect birth. 'Oh Madam,' said the doctor in charge, 'it is a princess.' 'Never mind', was the matter-of-fact Queen's reply, 'the next one will be a prince.' After her 12-hour labour she found herself in no pain whatsoever and she had a good appetite. 'Dearest Albert hardly left me at all and was the greatest comfort and support.' In view of the fact that even until recently fathers were kept well away from the labour room, Prince Albert's involvement is all the more surprising, and touching. During all of Victoria's

Prince Albert, like his wife, was also a fond and conscientious parent. He introduced decorated 'German' trees as an element in the royal family's Christmas. The innovation was a congenial reminder of the Prince Consort's foreign-ness and, as this Victorian Christmas card's theme shows, the custom soon caught on in Britain and elsewhere.

amily life at Windsor above). Victoria and Albert saw a great deal more of their nine children than many other aristocratic Victorian parents, but they relished their evenings alone together. The Queen disliked small babies, but she was a loving mother of her children as they grew beyond the 'frog-like' stage. Her own sketches, Prince Arthur (left) and Princess Beatrice (far left), reveal her absorption with them. Beatrice was born with the help of 'soothing, quieting and delightful' chloroform, a fact that helped to make the use of anaesthetics in childbirth popular.

confinements he alone lifted her from her bed to her sofa and for this purpose he would come instantly from any part of Windsor Castle.

Albert was, moreover, a paragon of Victorian fatherliness. Though strict and rather pompous in his expectations, he was never unapproachable. The royal children were seen and very much heard, and saw their parents far more than many aristocratic children of the day. One lady-in-waiting observed that 'the beloved parents have nothing so much at heart as the right training of these precious children.'

Although Albert could not, as a foreigner and a consort, take part in the monarchy's constitutional role, he certainly did what he could to run Victoria's household well. He saved thousands of pounds by abolishing many outdated or downright wasteful customs. The Queen had never seen a fire in the dining room at Windsor Castle, for example, because according to old court rules the Lord Steward had to lay the fire, and the Lord Chamberlain had to light it. As a result, she had always eaten in the cold. This was the sort of thing Albert put a stop to.

Prince Albert's management of the household

economy included also the running of the farm and estates at Windsor and elsewhere. He was quick to implement the most modern techniques and was much admired as a resourceful and efficient farmer. All the bulls were named after members of the royal family – one was even named Fitzclarance after an illegitimate son of William IV – and this touch indicates that Albert was not, contrary to contemporary opinion, entirely lacking in a sense of humour.

'Home sweet home'

In his role as the ideal husband and father Albert also devoted a great deal of energy to the various royal family homes: first Osborne, on the Isle of Wight, and later Balmoral in Scotland. Victoria and Albert found Windsor Castle too oppressively grand, but Osborne was relatively 'cosy'. This seaside house was purchased in 1845 and rebuilt according to the royal couple's, or rather Albert's, specifications. Here was a purpose-built setting for an idyllic family life. An entire Swiss cottage was erected in the grounds for the children to play in and their father regularly joined them in hide-and-seek games in the surrounding woodland, even demonstrating the art of turning somersaults in the haystacks – undoubtedly to the delight of the royal children.

Throughout Osborne House the entwined initials V

and A still speak of that happy Victorian marriage – everywhere, that is, except over the smoking-room door, whose function as a male sanctum is indicated by a single A. The interiors at Osborne can still be seen. They are heavy, ornate and loaded with bric-à-brac: every surface is covered by paintings and family portraits, or littered by items such as hand-painted china ornaments and replicas, cast in silver or bronze, of dead family pets. Osborne was an enormous version of the kind of home that every respectable middle-class family aspired to create. Indeed the Queen was also very typical of her age in her taste for collecting.

This love of material things had started early in her life with a collection of dolls, perhaps begun as a consoling substitute for brothers and sisters. In every establishment Victoria owned there were boxes and cupboards filled to capacity with china plate, silver objects and clothing, as well as accessories for every conceivable occasion. Later in life she took to having every room setting photographed, and every object catalogued, and in her widowhood she would enjoy thumbing through these volumes, as if to ensure that the past with all its mementoes would never slip away.

Almost everything the royal family did, their respectable subjects imitated – and so Scotland and all things Scottish did well out of Albert and Victoria's love for the Highlands. While Osborne served well as a family home, it was still near London. But Scotland was less accessible, and there Victoria and Albert could more definitely escape the cares of state. They welcomed the seemingly relaxed attitude of the Scots to royalty and the unpretentious, wholesome atmosphere of the Highlands. The growth of the

railway system greatly enhanced the possibility of getting away from it all. Victoria was much impressed by the speed and privacy that trains offered, and first used a train to travel from London to Windsor in 1842. She later availed herself of her own private carriage, built in 1869, to transplant her to Balmoral, the chosen Scottish base, overnight. Victoria and Albert had the castle rebuilt – complete with towers, castellated gables and turrets – in 1853, in order to have space for their large family and the inevitable visits of government ministers.

Balmoral was situated amid a stunningly romantic landscape and its interior was a positive riot of colour, for 'tartanitis' was a royal ailment. Lord Rosebery was heard to comment that he thought the drawing room at Osborne was the ugliest place he had ever seen until he saw the equivalent at Balmoral. 'Here everything is Scotch – the curtains, the carpets, the furniture, are all different plaids, and the thistles are in such abundance that they would rejoice the heart of a donkey if they happened to look like his favourite repast, which they don't. I am told it is *de rigueur* to clothe oneself in tweed directly.' But Lord Rosebery was in a minority. The royal mania for all things Scottish was sufficient to stimulate a boom for manufacturers of tweed and tartan, internationally as well as nationally.

As might be guessed, the Queen and the children learned Scottish dancing; while Albert engaged in 'manly' pursuits such as deer-stalking. Sometimes the royal couple went out into the Highlands for picnics, or travelled incognito, with perhaps just a couple of attendants. In her journal the Queen recorded her

Albert reformed the administration of the royal household with such economizing zea[l] that Osborne on the Isl[e] of Wight (right) and Balmoral (below right) were bought out of the resulting savings. Purchased in 1845, Osborne was rebuilt as [a] family holiday home and was easily accessible by rail. Victoria and Albert enjoyed travelling by train and are shown (below) in their luxurious private saloo[n] car with King Louis-Philippe of France.

for want of trying on Albert's part, and the country had much to be grateful for. Victoria was almost absurdly ignorant of her people and she had very little knowledge of the great changes being brought about by the industrial revolution. She fretted about the increasing number of working-class people swelling the new cities of her realm. During her lifetime the vote was gradually extended so that by 1867 some working-class men were enfranchised, but the Queen continued to regard democrats and socialists as dangerous trouble-makers. She herself was an ardent Whig, supporting the party that represented the old landowners, churchmen and their political and commercial interests.

But Albert was more realistic and more aware of the adjustments that great social and economic changes required in the monarchy's role and style. The Prince's interest in the 'industrious classes' turned Victoria's thoughts more charitably in their direction and she helped him with speeches to such worthy bodies as the Society for the Improvement of the Labouring Classes. Albert also saw to it that the Queen played an important part, above the whirl of electoral politics, in promoting industry and influencing foreign attitudes towards Britain. The success of the Great Exhibition of 1851 was largely due to Albert's vision and his hard work in organizing it. But his openness to modern developments in technology and the arts still militated against spontaneous popularity. The shrewd King Leopold of Belgium, Victoria's uncle and one of her father-figures, was provoked to warn his niece about the undesirability of Albert's interests. 'These dealings with artists, for instance, require great prudence. They

:static delight in open-air outings and rough suppers
 country inns, although often the party would be
:cognized and sent on its way with a cheer.

The Queen's own account of her Highland life, *.aves from a Journal of our Life in the Highlands*, .as subsequently (1868) published. Illustrated with :r own sketches and bound in moss-green covers .lorned with golden antlers, it sold 20,000 copies at ice and quickly went through several editions. Some reign and domestic critics groaned at Victoria's iildlike style, while others, such as the astute Prime inister Disraeli (himself an accomplished novelist) .w it as a chance for rank flattery – he gratified the ueen's ego by addressing her as 'We authors . . .' But .e general public were, as ever, drawn to the ersonality of the Queen, so open, honest and heart- arming.

bert's image
'ith the exception of the period when she was the :cluded 'Widow of Windsor', Victoria was extremely opular as a monarch and a personality. But though lbert was respected he was never regarded with the ime affection. His prowess in horse-riding and 1ooting could not make up for the fact that he was a :ry serious, high-minded person. The English ristocracy was extremely suspicious of his .itellectual interests and the people suspected him as 'foreigner'. It was even suggested, at the time of the :rimean War, that Albert was involved in handing ver state secrets to Russia, and two London :ewspapers actually reported that the poor man had :een accused of high treason and sent to the Tower.

Victoria, who declared that her husband 'always *iscinates* wherever he goes', was offended all her life y the fact that Albert never seemed to be accepted or)ved freely by the populace and the court. It was not

are acquainted with all classes of society, and for that very reason are dangerous.' If Albert had been stupid, flirtatious and lazy, he might have been adored and appreciated by many more than his wife.

In Victoria's case, Leopold's warning was not necessary: she quite liked to sing and to play the piano, but she avoided the company of intellectuals and once said that she never felt quite at ease when reading a novel. She enjoyed playing cards, loved charades, riddles, or games of that sort, and simply adored dancing. Luckily Albert enjoyed this too, and the Queen was blessed with a husband with whom she could waltz away – in total propriety! Her prowess as a dancer was always remarked on, and she continued to be lively until well into her 40s. Although she disapproved of heavy drinking, she always attended the servants' balls at Balmoral. When these reached the wildest stage, with bodies falling under the table, Victoria would simply pretend that nothing out of the ordinary was happening.

She could take the art of ignoring the awkward to extraodinary lengths. Her servant-companion of later years, the gillie John Brown, was notorious for his intake of Scotch. When on one occasion he fell to the ground in a drunken stupor, Queen Victoria maintained that she had felt a 'slight earthquake shock'. But where she felt it necessary she would observe the strictest rules. She hated smoking – so much so that, at Windsor Castle, guests of high rank would be seen lying on the floor of their bedrooms, in pyjamas, blowing the smoke up the chimneys in order to avoid detection.

A 'wonderful genius'

In addition to their shared love of their chidren, country life and dancing, Victoria and Albert both enjoyed music. The Queen had a beautiful singing voice, but her tastes were fairly low-brow. She preferred the Italian operas and light pieces by Rossini to choral works by Handel. But Prince Albert had been tutored in a rather more rigorous way and he liked to play Bach at the organ. Losing himself in his world of music, seated at the organ at Windsor Castle, was one of the ways in which he consoled himself in the early years of his marriage for the loss of his country, his family and his friends. (For political reasons he was not allowed to bring any close retinue with him to his marital home in England.)

It was not surprising, therefore, that Felix Mendelssohn – a German, handsome, a perfect gentleman, and the creator of comfortable, homelike music – suited the royal tastes entirely. Mendelssohn himself was spiritually at home in England. He spoke the language well and was warmed by the public's enthusiasm for his music. His first important work was based on Shakespeare (*A Midsummer Night's Dream Overture*); his Scottish Symphony was dedicated to Queen Victoria, and the *Hebrides Overture* (Fingal's Cave) has always remained one of the most popular pieces of his work in Britain.

Mendelssohn first met the Queen and Prince Albert five years after their marriage. He played for the Prince and the Queen, Albert then played a chorale for him and Victoria sang one of his songs. The composer then

Albert plays to a thoughtful Mendelssohn and an enchanted Victoria (right). Victoria and Albert were sincere Mendelssohn fans and the composer was twice 'summoned' to meet them at Buckingham Palace. The Queen, he wrote to his mother, 'is gentle, courteous and gracious. She speaks good German and knows my music well'.

Infatuated with Highland life, Victoria and Albert stimulated a great vogue for all thing Scottish. The whole family, including the Queen, learned 'Scotch reels' (above left); the royal children were dressed in 'Highland things'; while Albert, wi the help of an intimidatingly huge dictionary, applied himself with typical diligence to the learnin of Gaelic.

entranced his royal audience by improvising on two themes, which he asked them to suggest: Rule Britannia and the Austrian National anthem. Mendelssohn wove these two into a little piece and somehow managed to blend in the themes from the songs that Victoria had sung, thus demonstrating his genius and his charm. In a letter home to his mother after the event, Mendelssohn was happy to say that the pleasure and attentiveness of Victoria and Albert 'put me in better humour than usual when I improvise for an audience'.

The composer visited the court again two years later. His many happy experiences in the country moved him to give the first public performance of his oratorio, *Elijah,* to open the Birmingham Music Festival in 1846. Oratorios had been favourite works in England since the time of Handel and they suited the high religious feeling of the Victorians. Mendelssohn came to England to supervise rehearsals, and again to conduct the work on subsequent occasions. Victoria and Albert attended the second London performance, and invited the composer to perform at Buckingham Palace. The Queen also

attended a concert with the London Philharmonic, at which Mendelssohn played a Beethoven concerto. In her typically simple style, she noted in her journal:

It was so full of feeling and soul & his touch was wonderful. He played entirely by heart, which, when doing so with the orchestra must be most difficult. He is a wonderful genius & is deservedly an amazing favourite here . . .

'Mr Mendelssohn's' popularity with the royal family was reflected in the fact that in 1858 the Queen's eldest daughter left her marriage ceremony to the strains of his Wedding March and as an old lady Victoria is said to have boasted that the charming composer had 'taught' her singing. The Queen's claim was somewhat exaggerated, but was a tribute to the success of her meetings with the composer.

The master in the house
On many matters of taste Victoria and Albert were at one with their middle-class subjects, but in one area in particular their marriage had a profound influence. Though Victoria was the Queen, Albert was most

From Balmoral Victoria and Albert enjoyed trips to local beauty spots, which climaxed with elaborate picnics. But the trip to Cairn Lochan in 1861 (above) was the last such outing to include the Prince Consort, who died in the same year.

147

definitely the head of their family. While Victoria may have started out married life full of enthusiasm and a certain tolerance, she gradually became more severe and disapproving of impropriety. No divorced woman could enter the court, and no re-married widow either. She also abdicated a great deal of personal freedom, deferring to Albert on many issues, public and private, during their married life. Given that she was single when she acceded to the throne and showed remarkable agility then in handling her own affairs, this passive attitude must have been inculcated by Albert. She once wrote to King Leopold, 'We women are not *made* for governing — and if we are good women, we must dislike these masculine occupations.' And dislike them she did.

But it would be wrong to form the impression that Albert and Victoria were a perfectly bourgeois royal family. This was not the case. From the start they both shared a deep belief in the importance of the monarchy. Even if their family life was a model to lesser folk, Victoria and Albert were perfectly matched in their high aspirations and regal self-consciousness. This quality was evident on Victoria's visit to France in 1855 (she was the first British monarch for several generations to travel abroad). Standing alongside that paragon of French chic, the new Empress Eugènie, the English queen was, as usual, unfashionably attired — Albert was no help at all in this respect. Some French dignitaries were amused by Victoria's outfit. She wore an enormous bonnet and a dress patterned with vivid geraniums that would have done credit to a window-box. A crude green parasol shielded her and she carried a huge handbag embroidered with a white poodle, which had been a present from one of her daughters. But despite these ludicrous accessories, and the unfavourable contrast between her tiny, stout

figure and that of the slender, pace-setting, Empress Eugènie, there was no doubt in the Parisian public's mind as to Victoria's status. An almost serene regal composure attended her down to the last detail.

In 1861 Prince Albert died, quite suddenly, of typhoid. He was only 42 and Victoria was overwhelmed by grief. Now she was on her own as the widowed head of a large, and still young, family and the occupant of a role that gave few allowances for such distress. She suffered from the temporary physiological changes that modern drugs can alleviate. She felt cold and she lost weight; she could hardly walk and she suffered from dreadful headaches. Together her 'symptoms' added up to what might be described, and better understood, today as a nervous breakdown. For five years she became the secluded, and therefore unpopular 'Widow of Windsor', devoting her time to the commemoration of her husband in every conceivable way. Even so, the length of her mourning period, and the somewhat morbid expressions of it, were not so outlandish in an age when small children were often dressed in black after the death of a remote relative. The problem was that Victoria had an 'outside' duty to perform — people expected the royal show to go on.

When she finally emerged, in 1866, she had a new man, literally, to lean upon — Her Majesty's Highland Servant John Brown — and his platonic, supportive presence helped her back into her public position as the Queen of England. Then, she seemed indestructible. Her 50th anniversary in 1887 marked the high tide of her popularity, and in 1897 the Diamond Jubilee — for the longest reigning English monarch — was equally magnificent. It was 1901, 40 years after the death of her 'dear Angel', before she was laid to rest alongside Albert at Frogmore.

Clad in deepest mourning, Victoria and Princess Alice sit despondently around a bust of Albert. The Queen was desolated by his early death: 'My life as a happy one has ended. The world has gone for me.' In her immense grief she devoted herself to commemorating him in every possible way. She even had a plaque erected on the spot where he had shot his last stag and for 40 years fresh clothes continued to be laid out in his room every evening, together with hot water and a clean towel.

Fryderyk Chopin
1810–1849

Behind the dazzling virtuoso and inspired composer lay another Chopin – a patriotic Pole, a tormented lover, a man who was terrified by large audiences and one who was racked by a terrible illness.

Chopin at the age of 19 – and by now recognized as a national composer - playing before distinguished guests in the salon of Prince Radziwill in Berlin. Radziwill, himself a cellist and tenor, took a keen interest in Chopin's career.

More than that of any other composer, the name of Chopin has become associated with one instrument – the pianoforte. At a time when Europe was well provided with keyboard virtuosi, Thalberg, Kalkbrenner, Moscheles and Liszt among them, Chopin's reputation was widely considered to stand above them all, despite the fact that he had no love for the concert platform and in his whole lifetime gave scarcely 30 public performances.

Although Poland at the time of Chopin's birth was enjoying a period of comparative calm in terms of its political struggles with Russia, national pride was strong, and in his music Chopin forged a spiritual link with his country and its people that distance and years of exile could never destroy. The national identity asserts itself not only in the pieces based on Polish dance forms (the polonaises and mazurkas), but in the use of elements from Polish folk music and in the pervasive strain of melancholy that seem to linger beneath the surface even in the most serene passages of his work.

Chopin's letters to his Polish friends reveal a lively intelligence and ever-present sense of humour. His accounts of the musical and social occasions he attended are incisive and witty; but though he was quick to scorn social and musical pretentiousness of all kinds in private correspondence, his behaviour was always kind, courteous and infinitely considerate. No one, having met Chopin, could fail to like him, and it is interesting to note how many of his pupils became staunch companions and helpers in later life when his own physical powers were fading. His foibles, such as his indecisiveness in matters great and small (whether to leave Poland, which jacket to wear for a concert),

France to seek his fortune, served in the Polish National Guard, became a tutor of French in Polish aristocratic circles and, in 1810, was appointed as teacher of French at the Warsaw Lyceum; soon after he took a part-time post teaching French at the Military School as well. He had married Justyna Krzyzanowska (born 1782) in June 1806. Their daughter Ludwika had been born in 1807, and Isabell (1811) and Emilia (1813) were soon to follow.

Fryderyk's childhood, despite the recent political upheavals in Poland, was a secure and happy one. The family moved from Zelazowa Wola to Warsaw in October 1810 so that Nicolas could take up his Lyceum post and were allotted a large apartment in the former Saxon Palace which also housed the school. Justyna was able to supplement Nicolas's small income by taking in boarders, some of whom became Fryderyk's most devoted friends.

From his earliest years Fryderyk showed a precocious gift for music – he was playing duets with his elder sister Ludwika before he had had any formal training – and also for drawing caricatures, writing verses and, with his sisters, devising comedies which they performed to celebrate family anniversaries. When he was six, Fryderyk began taking lessons from a local piano teacher, Wojciech Zywny, an eccentric 60-year-old Czech. A violinist by training, composer and occasional conductor, Zywny channelled Fryderyk's outstanding natural ability, both physical and interpretative, into the German classical repertoire – Bach, Haydn, Mozart and Beethoven – as well as guiding him through pieces by popular contemporary composers such as Hummel, an early influence on Chopin's own compositions, and the great virtuoso Kalkbrenner.

Fryderyk constantly improvised pieces of his own

Chopin's parents, Justyna and Nicolas (above) were married in 1806. They settled down in a house on the Zelazowa Wola Estate (below) near Warsaw, and it was here that Chopin was born four years later.

seemed trivial in the light of his other traits, for he was a constant friend, an affectionate son and brother, a sympathetic colleague and a generous, patient teacher.

Early evidence of genius

Fryderyk Franciszek Chopin was born at Zelazowa Wola, near Warsaw, on either 1 March 1810 (as Chopin himself believed) or, as his certificate of baptism states, probably erroneously, 22 February 1810. The 1 March date is now generally accepted. His father was Nicolas Chopin, born in Marainville, Vosges, in 1771. As a young man, Nicolas had left

coming in a quarter beat behind each other.' It would not be long before he felt the need to go abroad in search of wider, more enriching musical experience. Meanwhile, under Elsner's sympathetic eye, he continued composing for the piano. Attempts to conform to classical structures were less successful as were his efforts at orchestration, in which Elsner always encouraged him. But works such as the flamboyant *Là ci darem* variations, op. 2, which exploited his own gifts as a pianist, revealed how fast he was moving towards his mature style. His distinctively fluent and flexible treatment of melody and elegant use of keyboard configurations were already much in evidence.

An opportunity to visit Berlin arose, giving Fryderyk a chance to widen his musical horizons, yet although he found himself present at the same function as Zelter, Spontini and Mendelssohn (only a year older than Chopin, but already a prolific and widely acclaimed composer) he lacked the courage to speak to them. A year later, in 1829, he managed to get to Vienna to supervise publication of some early works, and on 11 August made his true professional début at the Kärtnertortheater, where his performance of his *Krakowiak*, op. 14, and op. 2 Variations, both with orchestra, had a tumultuous reception. Even better received, however, was his improvisation on a Polish drinking-song. A second concert followed a week later,

A view of Warsaw (left) around the time of Chopin's boyhood. At the age of eight, he gave his first concert here at a charity fête in the Radziwill Palace.

His feet well clear of the pedals and his face set in concentration, the young Chopin entertains his friends with his precocious piano playing (below).

which, at first, Zywny would note down for him. A Polonaise in G minor was published in 1817, and the Warsaw press commented with pride on the child's achievements, both pianistic and creative: 'Geniuses are born in our country also, but the lack of publicity hides them from the public.' Fryderyk's fame spread fast, and local ladies showered him with invitations to play at their homes. Hailed as a second Mozart, he gave his first public performance at the Radziwill Palace in 1818, aged eight, playing a piano concerto by Gyrowetz. In 1821 Fryderyk wrote a farewell Polonaise for Zywny, who admitted that there was nothing more he could teach the boy, and soon began taking composition lessons from Jósef Elsner, director of the new Warsaw Conservatoire.

In the summer holidays Fryderyk, always physically frail, was sent to the village of Szafarnia for country air, food and exercise. Here he heard traditional Polish folk-music – a lifelong influence – and sketched some of his first mazurkas. After three years at the Lyceum (1823–26), Fryderyk enrolled at the Conservatoire. His Opus 1, a Rondo in C minor, was published in June 1825, and his public performances while a student included demonstrations on the aelopantaleon and eolomelodicon (hybrid organ/piano instruments). Tsar Alexander I gave him a diamond ring after hearing him perform on the latter.

As a student, and ever after, Fryderyk avidly attended as many musical evenings, concerts and operas as he could. He admired Rossini's *Barber of Seville* and Weber's *Der Freischütz,* but even though he had never heard a first-rate company he realized that performances by the Polish National Opera left much to be desired. In 1828, after seeing *Der Freischütz,* he observed: 'The choir kept missing their cues and

As an adolescent, Chopin (right), when he was not composing, tried his hand at caricatures. Above is one of a Polish peasant as seen through the young composer's eyes.

and then, fired with his success, he returned to Warsaw determined to find a way of establishing his reputation outside Poland. His last year (as it turned out) in his native land was marked by a series of largely abortive plans to tour abroad, his love for a young mezzo-soprano, Konstancia Gladkowska (a student at the Conservatoire) and the composition of his two piano concertos – the first of which (no. 2 in F minor) had a slow movement inspired by his passion for Konstancia.

Chopin leaves Poland
On 11 November 1830, Chopin left Poland – initially for Vienna, but stopping en route at Dresden where he improvised for the Court. This time, however, Vienna was less interested in the young Polish genius; during eight frustrating months there he gave only two performances (4 April, 11 June), neither of which had anything like the impact of his earlier concerts. Otherwise he spent this time hearing as much music as possible, including opera, and in completing an impressive body of work: mazurkas, waltzes (including the Grande Valse Brillante, op. 18 in E flat), his B minor Scherzo and his last orchestrated work, the Grande Polonaise in E flat. He also sketched out his first ballade (G minor).

When he left Vienna, it was for 'London, via Paris', according to his passport: years afterwards he would jokingly remind his Paris friends that he was just

When Chopin arrived in Paris in mid-September 1831, he discovered a city of quaint gentility (right). But a few months later, in February 1832, he was whisked into the glitter of Parisian high life when he gave his first and much-acclaimed Paris concert.

assing through. En route in Stuttgart he heard that a ew Polish revolt had been bloodily suppressed by the ussians, and that Warsaw was in Russian hands. His rief for his homeland overwhelmed him, and it has ften been suggested that the news could have inspired is turbulent Étude op. 10 no. 12 ('Revolutionary').

A week later in Paris (September 1831) Chopin took odgings at 27 Blvd Poissonière. The city had become he political refugee club for half Europe as well as a ecca for artists of all types and nationalities. Through is compatriots – the only people with whom he could el completely at ease – Chopin came to meet leading gures of the Romantic movement, while Liszt, Mendelohn, Osborne and Hiller – all pianists – and the cellist ranchomme became his closest musical associates.

Despite being part of such an influential circle, it vas five months before he made his Paris début, at the alle Pleyel on 26 February 1832. There he played, vithout orchestra, the F minor Concerto and *Là ci arem* variations, as well as taking part in a 6-piano xtravaganza by Kalkbrenner. For Chopin the concert vas an artistic triumph. The critic Fétis wrote: 'an bundance of original ideas, . . . His inspiration paves he way for a fundamental change of form [in piano ompositions]'. The performance was not a financial uccess, however. Money was a problem, despite the act that he had acquired a few pupils from the Polish ommunity, and Chopin described himself at this time

as suffering from 'consumption of the purse'. Soon, however, with his appearance at a Rothschild soirée, matters improved dramatically: now that his reputation as a brilliant musician was acknowledged in fashionable society, he became the most sought-after piano teacher in Paris. Mme de Rothschild herself was one of his pupils.

By 1832 he was said to be the lover of the rich and musically talented countess Delfina Potocka, who was separated from her husband. Chopin dedicated to her the F minor Concerto that Konstancia Gladkowska (now married) had partly inspired two years earlier. (Much later he would also dedicate to Delfina his Waltz op. 64 no. 1, the so-called 'Minute Waltz'.) He found it easier to work, however, when Delfina was not in Paris to consume his time and his emotions. At the time his Etudes op. 25 were his main concern, but he was also writing nocturnes and mazurkas, completing work on his G minor Ballade and sketching out some preludes. Liszt had been playing some of his études, to the composer's wholehearted approval: 'I wish I could steal from him his manner of playing my études', he remarked to Ferdinand Hiller in a letter dated 20 June 1833.

The concerts in which Chopin participated that year (he was not the principal performer) did nothing to further his career; his 1834 performances were likewise few and insignificant, and 1835 saw two performances, in April (4 and 26) which confirmed Chopin's aversion to playing in public concerts: the first, which included the Paris première of his E minor Concerto, was damned with faint praise, and although the second, featuring his Andante spianato and Grand Polonaise in E flat (op. 22), was far better received, the hurt of the earlier experience was not forgotten.

Chopin had neither the temperament nor the physical constitution for the life of a concert pianist. He suffered agonies before public concerts:

I wasn't meant to play in public. . . Crowds intimidate me, their breath stifles me, their stares petrify me, their strange faces throw me into

The drawing-room of Chopin's apartment in Square D'Orléans (above) where he moved in 1842. George Sand lived next-door-but-one and she wrote, 'we are for ever running in and out of each other's houses at night.'

As a student and later when in Paris, Chopin was strongly influenced by Rossini's Barber of Seville, for which the costume (below) was designed.

When Chopin stopped in Dresden (right) in 1825, he intended to renew a boyhood friendship with the son of the Wodzińska family. Instead, he began a courtship with the 16-year old Maria (above) which soon became a passionate – though short-lived – love affair.

confusion. But it's different for you: if you can't captivate them, you dominate them.

That summer Chopin travelled – first to Carlsbad to meet his parents, for the last time, then to Dresden where he fell in love with the 16-year-old Maria Wodzińska. He wanted to marry her, but the match was not encouraged by her parents and the romance was eventually to peter out. From Dresden he went to Leipzig to meet Mendelssohn, who introduced him to the young Clara Wieck – at 15 already established as a concert pianist. It was at her home that Chopin first met Robert Schumann, the man who had honoured him in 1830 with the famous exclamation: 'Hats off gentlemen, a genius!' The two were never close. Chopin was embarrassed by the fulsome praise Schumann lavished on him in reviews: 'He exaggerates so much he makes me look ridiculous.' As he did not much admire Schumann's music, he could not return the compliment, either, though he did dedicate his second ballade to him (op. 38). Clara's interpretation of his own work was another matter: Chopin was most favourably impressed.

Affair with George Sand

In October 1836, at the home of Liszt and his mistress Countess Marie D'Agoult, Chopin was introduced to the prolific novelist George Sand (Aurore Dudevant). He was not instantly attracted to her ('I did not like her face . . . There is something off-putting about her'). George Sand was fascinated by genius of all kinds, however, and musical enough to want to share in Chopin's creative life in some way. She invited him

George Sand's drawing-room in the secret love-nest at Nohant (left) in the heart of France. Here, in the warm climate, that suited his ever-precarious health, Chopin wrote many of his finest pieces and enjoyed a satisfying domestic life with George Sand.

ften to meet her circle of friends – Alfred de Musset, Heine, the Polish poet Mickiewicz and the artist Delacroix, among many others. While he resisted the convention-flouting siren – who not only smoked cigars and wore men's clothes in public but was none too discreet about her many lovers – she began to experience a deep longing for Chopin.

The following summer he refused her invitation to join her and several of his compatriots at her country house in Nohant. Indeed, most unexpectedly, but perhaps because of his depression after the breaking of his engagement to Maria Wodzińska, he left with his friend Camille Pleyel for a two-week visit to London. Here he maintained the lowest profile possible: he played only once, at the house of the piano manufacturer James Broadwood, where he was introduced as M. Fritz. A mere bar or two of his playing was, however, enough to reveal conclusively his true identity.

In the summer of 1838 Chopin at last yielded to George Sand's love – a selfless devotion fired not only by passion but by her desire for a family life (she had two children, Maurice and Solange, by her husband Casimir Dudevant). Always discreet about their liaison, they decided to spend their first winter together in Majorca, where, they had assumed, the climate would have a beneficial effect on Chopin's health. At first, when they arrived on 8 November, the Mediterranean landscape, day-long sunshine and relaxed atmosphere combined to give Chopin a feeling of well-being and he embarked upon several new compositions. But with the arrival of the damp and windy winter weather his tubercular symptoms reappeared. He had been very ill in 1835, and the *Warsaw Courier* had issued a denial of his death in 1836; now, once again, he was coughing violently and spitting blood. He had a low opinion of the Majorcan doctors: 'The first said I was going to die,' he recalled, 'the second that I had breathed my last, the third that I was already dead.'

In mid-December, evicted from their first lodgings, they moved to an isolated monastery at Valldemosa, to which a Pleyel piano was at length delivered from Paris. There, while George coped with the domestic chores, Chopin worked on his C sharp minor Scherzo, C minor Polonaise and F sharp Impromptu, as well as completing his 24 Preludes. In February 1839 they left for Marseilles then spent the summer at Nohant.

A productive period

Life fell into a pattern: summers they usually spent at Nohant, otherwise they each maintained a Paris apartment. Chopin had given no public concerts since March 1838, when he played his E minor Concerto at Rouen to honour a compatriot, the conductor Orlowski; in the same month he had played before Louis Philippe at the Tuileries. He was to give another command performance for the royal family in October the following year, this time at St Cloud with the Prague-born pianist Moscheles. Moscheles had at first thought Chopin's music 'rather cloying' and 'unmanly', but had since become an ardent admirer. Shortly afterwards Chopin played him his first mature sonata, in B flat minor.

When he was not giving lessons or composing, Chopin spent much of his time with George Sand and her children, frequently entertaining at either his place or hers. Besides the usual Polish émigrés, guests included the novelist Balzac, the composers Meyerbeer and Berlioz and the great Romantic painter Delacroix. Though at the height of his creative powers, in the salons of the nobility Chopin tended to be held in higher regard for his gifts as a pianist, improviser and

Chopin (left) painted in 1848 – a year before his death. It was in this year that he performed his last concert in Paris at the Salle Pleyel and saw George Sand for the last time, quite by accident. He was, by this time, seriously ill.

impersonator – of, for example, familiar figures such as Liszt and Kalkbrenner – than for his composing.

He and George were very close at this time: he was a great comfort to her when her first dramatic venture, *Cosima,* failed, and when she accompanied their friend, the mezzo-soprano Pauline Viardot, on a concert trip he and her children stayed behind to look after each other and mourn George's absence.

Rift with George Sand

His health was ever precarious; though 5 feet 8 inches tall, he weighed only six stone thirteen pounds at this time – little more than the 12-year-old Solange. None

Maurice Sand (below right) as drawn by his mother George Sand (below left) before he had grown into an irresponsible and conceited young man with a fierce jealousy of Chopin. He was largely instrumental in bringing the lovers' relationship to its bitter and premature end.

In 1848, after an exhausting round of concerts and lessons in London, Chopin stayed in Edinburgh (above). Increasingly sick and frequently coughing blood, he gave a concert which created so little enthusiasm that Jane Stirling (above right), his devoted admirer, bought a batch of tickets and gave them away.

the less, he suddenly decided to yield to his friends' urgings and give a public performance. Then began 'the Chopinesque nightmare' of doubts, fears and indecision. He tried to cancel the concert when he learned that their beloved Pauline Viardot could not appear with him, and he forbade the printing of posters and programmes. As Marie d'Agoult had once remarked, 'Chopin keeps changing his mind. The only constant thing about him is his cough.'

With George's support, the concert, held on 26 April 1841, was less of an ordeal than Chopin had feared. It was a dazzling occasion, producing excellent reviews ('Chopin has done for the piano what Schubert has done for the voice') and the fantastic sum of 6000 francs in revenue. Another performance, again at the Salle Pleyel, was given the following February, with Pauline Viardot and Auguste Franchomme. Again the occasion was a triumph, audience and reviewers united in their rapture ('sheer poetry superbly translated into sound'). It was Chopin's last but one performance for six years.

His relationship with George Sand began to break down partly when, as her children became young adults, Chopin became caught in the cross-fire of parent-offspring quarrels, and partly because of an extraordinary novel George wrote which plainly mirrored their own relationship as she saw it. In her story the actress Lucrezia Floriani – a virtuous lady, devoted to her children – is destroyed by the jealousy of Prince Karol, the lover whom she has nursed through near-fatal sickness. The implications of this tactless literary venture were obvious to all: George had had enough of her Polish lover. Yet if anything, it was Maurice, George's son, who could most fairly have been accused of jealousy: now an adolescent, he violently resented Chopin's relationship with his mother and had been trying to break it up.

Eventually, after a bitter row in which Chopin tried to arbitrate between Solange, her new husband Clésinger and George, the nine-year friendship was over. Having sent him, on 28 July 1847, a letter of farewell, George was never to seek a reconciliation.

Failing health

From this moment Chopin's health and spirits were on a downward spiral. To give him something other than

his pain and misery to think about his friends aga persuaded him to give a public concert. He agree and on 16 February 1848 at the Salle Pleyel he ma aged to walk unaided to the piano and play not on many of his own compositions but also, to start t concert, Mozart's Trio K496 in E.

A former pupil, Jane Stirling, had been his mainst and administrator, during the agonizing pre-conce period. Recognizing his need for someone to depe upon, which for so many years George Sand had bee she willingly offered herself in the hope that he wo in due course make her his wife. Like George, she w six years older than Chopin, but there the similar ended. Chopin was grateful to her for her devot exertions on his behalf but at no time does she appe to have stirred his emotions.

He had long been planning another trip to Englan and on 20 April 1848, with no thought of the possib risk to his health, he crossed the Channel. Soon, London, he embarked upon a punishing schedule social engagements and even went to the opera. I played before Queen Victoria and Prince Albert at glittering evening at Stafford House, home of the Du and Duchess of Sutherland.

Desperately ill, Chopin lacked the strength to res when Jane Stirling suggested a trip to Edinburgh. Th left London on 5 August 1848. Neither the 12-ho train journey nor the raw Scottish air did him a good: 'I can hardly breathe,' he wrote to an old frien 'I am just about ready to give up the ghost.' Yet survived to give a concert in Manchester (28 Augus and to play in Glasgow (27 September) and Edinbur (4 October). Otherwise his performances were co fined to the genteel drawing-rooms of Scottish ladies all of whom commented that his music sounded 'li water', Chopin reported, while at the same tim describing these ladies' own efforts at the keyboar 'they all look down at their hands while playing a

lay the wrong notes with feeling.' Jane Stirling both
bored and irritated him, and at last, with the utmost
diplomacy, Chopin was able to convey to her, via a
relative, that there could be no marriage. Soon afterwards, providence gave him an excuse to return to
London: a charity concert in aid of Polish exiles, held
at the Guildhall on 16 November. Though turning out
that night was nearly the death of him, he was little
appreciated by the audience and virtually ignored by
the press. Using the English climate as a pretext for
leaving 'beastly London' as soon as possible, he arrived
home in Paris, after a seven-month absence, on
24 November.

A brief remission gave him a few more months'
relative happiness surrounded by his friends. Some of
the inspiration which had deserted him on his break
with George Sand briefly returned, and he produced
two mazurkas which were published posthumously
(op. 67 no. 2, op. 68 no. 4). But then came the
inevitable relapse. His friends moved him to Chaillot,
then outside Paris, for the summer, from where he
wrote asking his sister Ludwika to visit him.

She was with him when, at 12 Place Vendôme, he
died on the morning of 17 October 1849.

An elaborate funeral took place at the Madeleine on
30 October, with a full performance of Mozart's
Requiem – as Chopin had requested.

When he had been buried, three miles away at the
Père Lachaise cemetery, Ludwika took his heart back
to Poland with her, in accordance with his final wish,
and, carefully wrapped, all the letters he had received
from George Sand.

*A daguerreotype of
Chopin in 1849. His
artistic life in that year
seemed to be as
suffocated as his
tortured breathing.
Barely 39, he wrote two
mazurkas but had not
the strength to make
legible copies of them.*

*Chopin, in 1849, left his
tiny apartment in the
Square D'Orléans, first
for the cleaner air of
Chaillot and then, in
August, for a lavish
apartment in Place
Vendôme (left). To begin
with he was well enough
to take an interest in the
furnishings and décor,
but a relapse in
September was to prove
fatal and on 17 October
he died.*

The two faces of Paris

For the talented and successful, the Paris that Chopin knew provided unrivalled opportunity and stimulus. For the less fortunate, however, it was still a city of great hardship and poverty.

In 1831 Chopin arrived in Paris, the city where he was to spend most of his remaining years and, at that time, the undisputed centre of political and artistic activity for all Europe. Scene of both the 1789 revolution and the recent 'July Revolution' of 1830, which set up Louis Philippe as 'citizen king', Paris seemed to embody the spirit of political struggle and to represent all that was progressive in art and thought. It was a place that held a magnetic attraction for refugees and exiles of all kinds, but especially for creative artists, and it provided an ideal setting for the formulation of the ideals of the Romantic movement.

The capital represented opportunity and enterprise. Paris had shrugged off its Imperial past and the years 1830–50 witnessed a rapid expansion in industry and trade and a dramatic increase in the power of the middle class – acquisitive, materialistic and socially ambitious.

Gifted personalities

Chopin was not the only aspiring celebrity of the day to be setting his sights on Paris: 1831 was the year that Aurore Dudevant (better known by her pen-name – George Sand) arrived to lead a new life, away from her husband and, she hoped, in a free and stimulating environment that would prove conducive to her forging a career as a writer; Mendelssohn, too, chose this year to return to the city where six years previously Cherubini had given his blessing to the brilliant 16-year-old's ambition to become a professional musician; others, like the young writer Balzac, had been settled in Paris for some years waiting to make the hoped-for breakthrough with 'a pretty woman he has never met, (whose) name is Fame'.

These three were only a few of the personalities with whom Chopin was to meet in Paris. Soon after his arrival in September 1831 he reported to a friend that he had met Rossini, Cherubini, Baillot (a rival of Paganini's), and the pianists Herz, Hiller, Kalkbrenner and Liszt, and he had seen Meyerbeer's first major success, *Robert le diable:* 'a masterpiece of the modern school . . . I doubt whether anything so magnificent . . . has ever before been done in the theatre.'

Meyerbeer had waited some years for his Paris success. What made *Robert le diable* such a triumph was that it provided in abundance the thrills and spectacle sought by the bourgeois audience of the Opéra. Titillation and conspicuous expense, rather than its impressive and often original orchestration, gave the work an irresistible appeal that had somehow eluded Meyerbeer in his previous attempts to please the Parisian public; now he had the right formula his

Painted in 1831, the year Chopin arrived in Paris, the watercolour (right) shows a typical Parisian scene. As Chopin wrote about the city at this time, 'Paris is whatever one chooses to make of it. In Paris you can divert yourself, or be bored, laugh or cry, do whatever you like; nobody so much as looks at you, for there are thousands doing the same, each in his own way.'

Paris in the 1830s and 40s was a centre of artistic creativity. Many of the gifted writers, artists and musicians were also friends and met frequently. Chopin (far left) counted among his contemporaries (from left to right) Delacroix, a major painter of the Romantic movement whose famous self-portrait this is; Lamartine, one of the key literary and political figures of the day; de Musset, celebrated writer and former lover of George Sand, and finally Berlioz, whom Chopin esteemed as a friend but detested as a composer.

Parisians found many ways of entertaining themselves, depending on their social class and interests. The better-off might attend a musical evening in a salon as shown in this unfinished sketch (right). Standing in front of the hearth is the painter Delacroix with the poet de Musset beside him.

new-found fame was secured.

George Sand's experience as a novelist and playwright was in some ways comparable: her first success, *Indiana* (1832), seemed to suggest that women should desert their husbands and children and forget about marriage; the explicitly erotic *Lelia* (1833) furthered her reputation as a daring new talent. These books established Sand as one of France's most popular writers, overshadowed though she was by her contemporaries such as Victor Hugo (*Notre Dame de Paris,* 1831), Balzac (*Eugénie Grandet,* 1833), Stendhal (*Le Rouge et le Noir,* 1830) and the poet Lamartine.

The poet Alfred de Musset, who with Hugo, Lamartine, Vigny and Chateaubriand would be classed among the great literary figures of the Romantic movement in France, was one of George Sand lovers before she met Chopin: they travelled to Ital together in 1833–34, just as Sand and Chopin were t seek privacy by deserting Paris for Majorca a few year later, and their relationship provided each with ra material for novels.

The literary and artistic circle of Paris was a close knit one in many ways. They met constantly in eac other's homes to discuss the issues of the day – socia political and cultural – and almost always there woul be music in some form or other to help pass the evenin as pleasantly as possible. Chopin was amazed by th number of pianists ('I do not know if any place ha more'), and his reaction was echoed by Mendelssoh who noted in a letter to a friend that he had 'ca himself headlong into the vortex' of sightseeing an

Less formally, those from a humbler background are diverted by a puppet show (below).

e strenuous social whirl: 'Moreover the musicians
re are as numerous as sands on the sea-shore, all
ting each other; so each has to be visited
dividually, and one has to be highly diplomatic
cause they are all gossips.'

Mendelssohn's favourite theatre was the Théâtre
ramatique, which seems to have staged what would
w be recognized as variety shows, but he dis-
pproved of the fact that politics and sex were so
ominent an ingredient of all the acts. He was,
wever, enchanted with the Italian dancer Taglioni,
hom he saw in *La Sylphide* at the Opéra. The work
self perfectly reflected, in its story of a search for an
attainable ideal, the spirit of the age. Chopin's
usic, de Musset's poems, Delacroix's paintings and
ugo's novels did the same: the city seemed to breed
eative artists of the highest calibre, and to provide an
nbience in which their work could flourish.

e salon

t the centre of this brilliant section of Parisian society
as the salon, a name which literally means drawing-
om, but which here is used in a wider context to
fer to select social gatherings. It was not enough for
tists to produce works of art: they had to be seen by
e opinion-formers of the day, to be part of the
fluential inner circle.

When Chopin first met George Sand, in 1836, it was
. the presence of Liszt and his mistress Marie
Agoult, the Polish poet Adam Mickiewicz and the
riter Sainte-Beuve. And when, about a month later,
hopin invited her to an evening at his apartment in
e rue de la Chaussée d'Antin, it was in the company
f not only Liszt and Marie but of the pianist Pixis, the
eat tenor Nourrit, the German poet Heine, and
veral eminent Poles.

Elegant chairs and a Pleyel grand piano furnished
hopin's drawing-room, which had heavy grey
rtains and dove-grey wallpaper. On the polished
or, which reflected the light from the candle-lit
iano, lay one or two rugs. Liszt played, Nourrit sang
d Chopin improvised on some themes from
eyerbeer's latest triumph, *Les Huguenots;* George
nd, it was noted, said little on this occasion, but sat
y the fire and smoked a good deal. After the music, tea
as served and for the rest of the evening Liszt did
ost of the talking.

While such *soirées,* or evening gatherings, were
mparatively intimate affairs held in private homes,
e salon of the musician and piano manufacturer
amille Pleyel was nothing less than a small concert
all: a large room with a stage, hung with thick velvet
rtains and bedecked with flowers. This was the
ene of several of Chopin's Paris concerts given
efore the élite of society, who were in Liszt's words
e most elegant ladies, the most famous artists, the
chest financiers, the most illustrious lords, . . . a
mplete aristocracy of birth, wealth, talent and
eauty.'

Chopin, as much as anybody, enjoyed doing the
cial rounds of the aristocracy, visiting the opera and
sociating with talented people. During his courtship
f Maria Wodzińska, Chopin had been warned by her
arents to avoid, for the sake of his health, late nights
the Paris salons, but he seems not to have heeded
e advice.

How could he? He was building his reputation as a
usician and, although since the Revolution the
tistocracy no longer supported their own music
aff, reputations still rested largely on the opinion of
gh society. In Paris, this meant the residents of the

The poorer side of Paris is evident in this picture (left) of a coffee seller chatting to her neighbour on the corner of the Porte St Denis.

Masked Parisians (below) enjoy the freedom of Carnival time at midnight.

*Markets were a focal
point for Parisians. The
most famous of all was
the vegetable, fruit and
meat market of Les
Halles shown in this
painting (right) of 1835.*

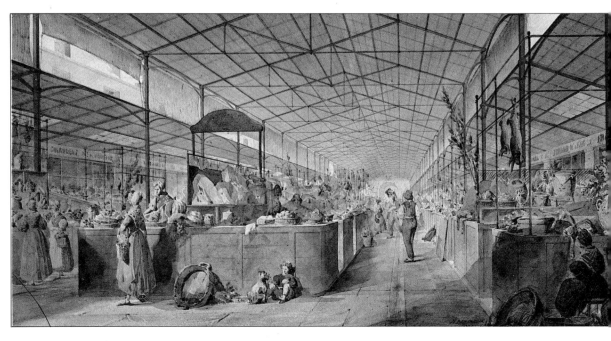

Faubourg St Germain, and everyone knew and
accepted this as a fact of life.

As the German poet Heine observed wryly:

*The triumphal march of the piano virtuosi is
especially characteristic of our time and testifies to
the victory of the machine over the spirit . . . Like
locusts, the pianists invade Paris every winter, less
perhaps to earn money than to make a name for
themselves here, from which they can then profit all
the more richly in other countries. Paris to them is a
huge hoarding on which their fame is spelt out in
giant letters . . .*

However, Chopin, lacking the constitution of Liszt,
could never have lived the life of a touring concert
virtuoso. He was also temperamentally unsuited to
such a career, preferring to play for small numbers.
His very occasional concert performances, despite the
high prices charged for tickets, would never have
provided him with sufficent income to live in the style
necessary for those who wished to be accepted in the
salons of the nobility – and it was in these very salons
that Chopin made the contacts he needed to attract
wealthy pupils. Teaching was his main source of
income throughout his adult life, and he depended on
being able to command a high fee for lessons.

Among the other expenses Chopin had to meet was
that of an apartment well enough furnished and
decorated to be suitable for teaching pupils from well-
to-do backgrounds, and in an acceptable district. Then
there was his carriage, and the hire of a coachman.
Perfume was another necessary luxury. There may
appear to be an element of dandyism in these
extravangances, but this was common to all the
members of Chopin's circle.

The other Paris

There was, of course, another Paris – the Paris of the
ordinary people, who got up at five every morning and
trudged through the mud and filth of the unpaved city
streets to dingy workshops and offices in which the
smell of the streets permeated the atmosphere and
where outbreaks of cholera often spread like wildfire.

Chopin took great delight, as a newcomer to Paris,
in walking the streets and observing all aspects of the

city that Balzac had summed up as 'mud studded wit
diamonds', a vast and exciting place in total contrast t
Warsaw. He noticed that once dusk had fallen:

*. . . all you hear is street vendors shouting out the
titles of the latest pamphlets, and you can often buy
three or four sheets of printed rubbish for a sou, such
as 'How to Get and Keep a Lover', or 'Priests in
Love', or 'Romance of the Archbishop of Paris and
the Duchesse de Berry', and a thousand similar*

*The flower market on the
banks of the Seine (right)
was a place where the
well-to-do mingled with
ordinary working
people.*

obscenities very wittily put together.

Crime, of course, increased as darkness gathered. Robbery and murder on the streets was a common occurrence, which the police tended to ignore. To be out of doors on foot after dark was to run a great risk, and most of the young men carried weapons.

Chopin was well aware of the different facets of life in Paris:

You find here the greatest splendour, the greatest filth, the greatest virtue and the greatest vice; at every step you see posters advertising cures for venereal disease – there is shouting, uproar, noise and mud past anything you can imagine. You can get lost in this swarm – and that's no bad thing: no one enquires how anyone else manages to live . . .

The most common form of transport, still, was the horse. Carriages were owned only by the rich. However, the omnibus had been introduced in areas where the roads were passable. The Champs-Elysées at this time was still a country road, with sewage ditches at either side. When Chopin first arrived in Paris, it was used for grazing cows, and sometimes for soldiers' encampments, though by 1848 about half of it had been built on.

The legacy of Napoleon was everywhere – in the 60 new streets, including those near the Louvre and the Tuileries and in the new bridges over the Seine. On 15 December 1840 the cry of *'Vive l'Empereur!'* was once again heard in Paris, when the French honoured his memory by bringing his remains back from the island of St Helena where he had died nearly 20 years previously. Nostalgic for past glories, the people were

about to re-gild the Napoleonic myth, and it seemed as if most of them had turned out that bitter winter's day to watch the funeral procession pass down the Champs-Elysées.

End of an era

Even as this ceremony took place, the nephew of the dead emperor, languishing in prison in northern France after an unsuccessful attempt to overthrow the so-called 'July Monarchy' of Louis Philippe, was

Street entertainers are still popular with crowds in Paris. The juggler shown above was painted in 1832, the year after Chopin arrived in Paris.

In 1840 the remains of Napoleon were brought back from St Helena and buried with great ceremony at Les Invalides (left). This was in accordance with Napoleon's wishes to be buried on French soil 'in the midst of the French people whom I have loved so well.' In commemoration of the occasion Mozart's Requiem was sung. It was rarely performed in Paris and the next time would be at Chopin's own funeral in 1849.

plotting his campaign to seize the office that he regarded as his by right. Louis Napoleon Bonaparte's day was not so far away.

There had always been an undercurrent of political unrest in Paris, and political discussion was by no means confined to intellectual circles. The Paris police were more concerned with political offences than with street crime, so that those who read the newspapers in the cafés made sure that they read all of them, in order that their political persuasions should not be generally known.

Gradually the general unrest became, throughout France, stronger and more focused. The frenzy to construct new railways had overreached itself, leaving 50,000 railway workers unemployed in France alone, and this – together with the negative effects of the Industrial Revolution (which was slow to affect France), the economic depression and the failure of the harvest – had made unemployment a major issue.

In early 1848 riots broke out. The National Guard was used to suppress them, but on 22 February, a week after Chopin's last Paris recital at the Salle Pleyel, the Tuileries were stormed. Louis Philippe had already fled. The direct outcome of the uprising was the installation in December that year of Louis Napoleon as President. He would later be known as Napoleon III, after a democracy lasting less than four years, and France under the Second Empire would be run according to principles which had much in common

with those of both the first Napoleon's dictatorshi and the autocratic rule of Louis Philippe.

For Chopin and his colleagues, the immediat outcome of the 1848 Revolution was that he no longe had any means of making a living. As Berlioz observe in his *Memoirs:*

Who thinks of art at such a time of frenzy and carnage? Theatres shut, artists ruined, teachers unemployed, pupils fled; pianists performing sonatas at street corners . . . painters sweeping gutters, architects mixing mortar on public buildin sites . . .

It was the end of an era. Liszt gave up his concer career and became director of music to the Duke Weimar. George Sand remained at Nohant. The ailin Balzac returned briefly to Paris the following year t die. Victor Hugo, who at first held office in the ne régime, fled to Brussels in 1851, the year of the cou d'état.

Chopin's Paris was no more, though he did not liv long enough to suffer directly from the soci consequences of the uprising: his suffering, i England, Scotland and finally in Chaillot and Paris, wa to take another form. Perhaps it was as well. The ne order – to be known as the age of the bourgeoisie an epitomized in the novels of Zola as Philistine, selfis and money-grubbing – was not one in which a talen such as his could easily have flourished.

Robert Schumann
1810–1856

*Schumann – composer, critic and intellectual –
lived a turbulent yet at times brilliantly creative life.
A complex character, his decline was foreshadowed
in his increasingly erratic behaviour.*

*obert Schumann
(above) was the essence
f the Romantic
omposer. But though he
ailed against the
onservatism of
receding generations,
e was a generous and
upportive critic of
oung composers.*

Schumann was a prime-mover in the advancement of 19th century Romanticism; in his capacity as founder and editor of the famous German musical periodical *Neue Zeitschrift für Musik,* he was decisively influential in promoting the music of other young Romantic composers, among them Chopin and Brahms.

Strange as it may seem today, Schumann's music itself was less well-known in his day than were his activities as a writer. His music was the product of a nature so sensitive, and it spoke in so personal an idiom, that it was many years before it began to be accepted by the public.

Personality and appearance

As a young man, Schumann already showed two clear facets to his character. On the one hand he was extrovert, good company and energetic in his pursuit of new experiences, on the other, his avid passion for literature, especially Jean Paul Richter, E. T. A. Hoffman and the classics, encouraged the poetic side of his nature and turned him into a sensitive, retiring, thinker. A by-product of this second facet was a secretive trait, revealed in his penchant for pseudonyms and the so-called cyphers or coded messages he habitually hid in his music.

He also adopted two parallel pseudonyms for

As the precocious son of one of Zwickau's leading citizens, young Robert Schumann (left) starred easily at musical and literary gatherings in his hometown. He was largely self-taught, however, and did not receive formal musical training until he was 18.

himself: Florestan, the passionate hero, and Eusebius, the gentle introvert. These two 'characters' converse together in his diaries as early as 1831, when he was 21, and they soon enter into his music reviews. Later, they are named side-by-side as the actual composers of his music.

Sometimes he would display the most outrageous bad manners, especially if he had been subjected to what he considered to be bad music, or indeed any music badly performed. On these occasions he would speak his mind without restraint, or leave the company without a word. With hindsight, we may see in these general dual aspects of his nature the beginnings of the mental problems to which he was to fall victim in his last years.

Contemporary reports portray Schumann as a solidly-built man, upright but with a looseness about his stride almost as if his broad shoulders were boneless. He tended to narrow his blue eyes in an attempt to alleviate his short-sightedness, for which he habitually carried a *lorgnette* (a pair of glasses on a handle), and mischievous dimples appeared in his cheeks when he smiled. Long dark brown hair framed, and sometimes partly obscured, a face described as handsome in youth but ruddy and unhealthily chubby in his 40s. His dress was conservative and with time became more so: he usually wore black in later years.

Early years

Robert Alexander Schumann was born in Zwickau, Saxony, on June 8, 1810, the youngest of the five children of the bookseller, publisher and author August Schumann. His education, at first in a private school and later at Zwickau Lyceum, was supplemented by exposure to as much good literature in his father's bookshop as he could find the time to read, and by piano lessons from a local organist.

In 1826 Schumann experienced major grief with the deaths in quick succession of his only sister Emilie, whose suicide at the age of 19 released her from life as a total invalid; the composer Weber, with whom Schumann had planned to study composition; and of Schumann's father, who had succumbed at the age of 53 to a 'nervous disorder'. Some say that Schumann's later illness was inherited from his father.

However, Robert was soon to know happier times:

August Schumann (below right) died when Robert was 16 leaving his widow (below left) to steer her intense son, into a safe career in law. But Robert's nervous temperament was alarmingly reminiscent of that of his father, and her efforts were in vain.

Hans Thoma's vision of the Rhineland (above). In 182 Schumann enjoyed a dissolute holiday there, though he kept up his piano practice by pretending to be an interested customer in a piano shop.

to Leipzig and his re-establishment as Wieck's pupil in Leipzig, whose house he shared for a while from October 1830. Wieck had written to Schumann's mother to the effect that if the young man were to study tenaciously for three years he would become a great pianist, but he frankly doubted Schumann's mental ability to sustain such a discipline. He suggested a six-month trial period and Schumann's mother agreed, thereby at last releasing him from all pretence at studying law. Wieck's attention, however, was not upon Robert Schumann. His daughter Clara, 11 years old, had become a brilliant pianist under her father's tuition and he now took her off on an extended concert tour.

Schumann filled the time by composing, writing, and inventing 'new and more suitable' names for his friends and acquaintances. Wieck became 'Meister Raro', the conductor Heinrich Dorn, who took over from Wieck as Schumann's music tutor, became 'The Music Director', and Clara Wieck became 'Zilia' (short for Cecilia, the patron saint of music). By July 1831 Schumann was calling himself 'Florestan and Eusebius'.

The independent composer

By the spring of 1832 Schumann had reached a turning-point. Lessons with Dorn and with Wieck had ceased, he had become financially independent on his 21st birthday due to his accession to a large part of his father's fortune, and he realized at last that his dream of becoming a great concert pianist would never become a reality. Amid circumstances that have never satisfactorily been explained, he had damaged one, or perhaps two, fingers on his right hand. He is known to have invented a sling device to strengthen the weak fourth finger and this has been blamed for permanently crippling his hand. Another theory, for which there is not much evidence, to account for the damage is that a treatment for syphilis had induced mercury poisoning

young ladies started to become important to him. Happy he was, too, when drinking champagne, which he consumed in prodigious quantities from the age of 17 onwards.

Career

In 1828, Schumann was pushed into law school by his mother and his guardian. Once ensconced as a law student at Leipzig University, Robert made earnest endeavours to avoid every lecture. Instead, he spent his time at his desk concocting literary fantasies in Jean Paul Richter's manner, or at the keyboard practising and improvising. Exposure to Schubert's songs encouraged him to write a number of songs at this time. In August 1828, four months after his enrolment as a law student, Schumann began piano lessons with Friedrich Wieck in Leipzig.

Schumann's next act was to persuade his mother to allow him to transfer for a year to Heidelberg University. This was ostensibly to continue his law studies amid more stimulating surroundings and 'with the most famous professors'. But in reality it was so that he could be with an old friend, Gisbert Rosen. A bonus at Heidelberg was the presence of the 'famous professor' Anton Thibaut – who also just happened to be an enthusiastic musician! Schumann arrived in Heidelberg in May 1829 after a Rhineland holiday that left him penniless but happy.

Much of his year in Heidelberg was spent in socializing and living the unfettered life of an eligible young artist. Again, law studies were low in his priorities. His departure from Heidelberg led him back

J. P. F. Richter (left), better known by his pseudonym of Jean Paul, was Schumann's great literary hero. 'If everybody read Jean Paul,' wrote Schumann, 'we should be better but more unhappy.' Here Richter is shown at work in his garden, a suitable study for a great Romantic visionary.

From a very early age, Clara Wieck (right), was one of Europe's most outstanding pianists and her ambitious father's pride and joy. Friedrich Wieck's resistance to his brilliant daughter's betrothal to Schumann is understandable, because Clara became engaged just at the point in her career when her father was beginning to reap the financial rewards of his daughter's talent and his dedicated tuition. The form it took was, however, inexcusable.

The marketplace at Leipzig (below), a lively university town. Here, it was all too easy for an arch-romantic student such as Schumann to ignore lectures and 'drop out' into a congenial world of wine, women, song and endless passionate discourse on the arts.

that affected his extremities. Whatever the truth of the matter, his damaged hand precluded a concert career, and Schumann turned instead to composition, mainly for solo piano. He also attempted, and nearly completed, a symphony, the first movement of which was played on 18 November 1832, in Zwickau, and again, in greatly revised form, at Clara Wieck's *Grand Concerts* on 29 April 1833, in Leipzig.

Severe depression set in during 1833. That summer he suffered from persistent fever, and in October his brother Karl's wife, 25 year-old Rosalie, died, and his brother Julius died in November. In letters to his mother he appears to take pleasure in wallowing morbidly in his grief. It was a self-centred grief that Schumann displayed, perhaps an attitude typical of one who could write in his diary the portentous line: ' was obsessed by the thought that I might go mad.'

Schumann the journalist

Fortunately, a constructive influence entered his life at this time: the pianist Ludwig Schunke, a hearty and pleasant optimist, came to share Schumann's rooms and in 1834 he was among the group, headed by Schumann and including Wieck, who launched the twice-weekly musical periodical *Neue Zeitschrift für Musik*. Most of the editorial chores fell to Schumann and he became happily immersed in the work. His group of friends were the living equivalent of the *Davidsbündler*, or 'Band of David', an imaginary brotherhood devised by the composer to fight Philistinism and the mediocre in music. The members were, naturally, Florestan, Eusebius and Meister Raro, together with any exalted musical spirit – Mozart's Berlioz's – who happened by. The *Davidsbündler* fought out its battles in the pages of *Neue Zeitschrift für Musik*.

Much of Schumann's life revolved around the Wieck household, a centre for the 'real' *Davidsbündler* and a meeting place for composers visiting Leipzig, the attraction, of course, being the widely admired young pianist Clara. Schumann had become engaged in 183 to Ernestine von Fricken, but a development in the Wieck house caused him to disentangle himself: Clara was growing up, and she and Schumann began to see each other's company more and more.

he Wieck family war

larmed at what he considered an ill-advised, if not nhealthy, match between the wayward Schumann nd his 16-year-old daughter, old Wieck resisted with very weapon at his disposal. A letter forbidding chumann to call at his house was the first shot, and he nformed his daughter that there would be real shots if ne composer disobeyed. Clara herself was confined to ne house and told that all the money she had earned uring her concert tours was held in trust until her 1st birthday, and not one penny would be hers if she narried before then without his consent.

For her part, Clara was profoundly distressed, for ne reciprocated the love Schumann so ardently xpressed. The couple managed to exchange notes nd even the surreptitious kiss at rare, secret neetings. For Robert, this was not enough. In esperation, he wrote to Wieck imploring him to elent and make two young people happy. At the ubsequent meeting, the old man so confounded chumann by parading a host of conflicting arguments, nalicious insults, doubtful concessions and ccusations before him, that the composer retired in lmost suicidal depression.

At length the whole sad business was referred to the ourts. The slow-moving legal wheels were further etarded by Wieck's refusal to attend hearings. Meanwhile, he did his best to ruin the considerable eputation Clara had built for herself by writing nalicious, and often falsely-signed, letters to everyone ne could think of. It is difficult to believe that any ather could bear such vicious malice towards a

The Schumanns seven years into an idyllic marriage that took place after a nerve-racking courtship. There were strains on the union, however, due to the competing requirements of their separate careers – she could not practise while he composed, and his pride was wounded by her greater fame as a pianist.

Compared with Leipzig, Dresden (below), where the Schumanns moved in 1844, was a stuffy and conservative place, but initially it had a calming effect on Schumann's already precarious mental state.

daughter as Wieck did to Clara.

The court duly heard Wieck's objections and on 4 January, 1840, a decision was made. All of Wieck's objections were overruled save one: that concerning Schumann's excessive drinking. This charge Wieck was required to prove, but since he failed to do so within a specified time, the final decision in favour of Schumann and Clara was made in August 1840, four years after Wieck's declaration of war. By a stroke of ironic timing, the wedding took place at Schönefeld, near Leipzig, on 12 September 1840; the very next day, her 21st birthday, Clara would have been legally free to marry whomsoever she pleased!

Creativity

Schumann's composing energy had been severely sapped by the long battle, but in 1840 he turned from writing for solo piano to produce a whole host of songs, among them his famous *Liederkreis, Frauenliebe und -leben, Dichterliebe,* and many more. When this mine of songs became temporarily exhausted, Schumann turned to the orchestra. His 'Spring' Symphony was written in the depths of winter (23 January to 20 February 1841) and performed in March, and in May he completed his *Fantasie* in A minor for piano and orchestra which was later to become the first movement of his Piano Concerto. Two other substantial orchestral works were to appear before the end of the year, but his restless creativity, stimulated by the sublime happiness of his new life with Clara, was pushing him into new spheres: 1842 was to see his two greatest chamber works, the Piano Quintet and the Piano Quartet.

On the road with Clara

Meanwhile, Clara followed her own career. This inevitably led to conflicting engagements; in March 1842 the couple were parted, Schumann in Leipzig,

Even dull Dresden did not escape the revolutionary fervour of 1848–49. But when the barricades went up, Schumann, unlike Wagner, did not man them. During the fighting he took refuge with his family outside Dresden.

completed in June. The year also saw a reconciliation between Clara and her father and an uneasy truce between the old man and Robert. The first half of 1844 was taken up with a successful concert tour of Russia by the couple. However, it was only successful as far as Clara was concerned, since her fame had preceded her, but Schumann, despite directing his own 'Spring' Symphony in St Petersburg and attending a performance of his Quintet in Moscow, with Clara playing the piano part, was conscious of taking a second place to his wife's concert achievements.

Upon their return to Leipzig Schumann relinquished editorship of *Neue Zeitschrift* in order to concentrate upon a new passion: opera. All that issued from his tired brain were some pieces based on Goethe's *Faust*, and even this effort, meagre in comparison with the years 1840–42, cost him dearly in mental stamina. The strain of the Russian tour, with its attendant professional frustration, and a general feeling of depression, abruptly crystallized into a total nervous breakdown. Even music, he reported, 'cuts into my nerves like knives'. For a week he was unable to sleep and could barely walk; doctors were powerless to help except to recommend a complete change of scene. Consequently, the family moved to Dresden in December 1844 and slowly Schumann's health began to improve.

During 1845 he completed the Piano Concerto and began work on another symphony, but the latter took almost a year to complete, and it was during this time that new menaces assailed him: vertigo, and deterioration of his hearing – further signs of the

Clara in Copenhagen, while Wieck gleefully put about the rumour that the marriage had collapsed. Alone, Schumann gazed into beermugs and studied counterpoint, sometimes simultaneously. Clara's career, however, was to be punctuated by pregnancies. The first child, a daughter, had arrived on 1 September 1841, and seven more children were to follow up to June 1854.

It was the turn of choral music in 1843, but only one work emerged: *Das Paradies und die Peri*, an oratorio,

Before moving to Düsseldorf (right), Schumann had been perturbed to learn that the town boasted a lunatic asylum, for he disliked hearing anything that reminded him of insanity. His misgivings proved sadly justified because his mental condition deteriorated seriously in Düsseldorf.

This posthumous portrait of Robert Schumann (1859), though probably idealized, still conveys the despair of a man gripped by acute nervous crises beyond the competence of contemporary medicine.

After a final breakdown in 1854, Robert Schumann was committed to Dr Richarz's private asylum at Endenich near Bonn (below), where he died in 1856.

progressive collapse of his nervous system. A two-month holiday at Norderney, a North Sea island, brought temporary respite, and in November 1846 the couple set off on tour for Vienna in a new mood of optimism. It was misplaced.

The audiences there applauded Schumann's music dutifully, but seemed to have forgotten how welcome they had made Clara some years before. She was still a wonder, but no longer a wonder child. In Prague, however, where the couple gave two concerts on their journey home, they were enthusiastically received, and a subsequent trip to Berlin also encouraged them. Further operatic endeavours occupied Schumann during 1847 and 1848 (*Genoveva,* more work on *Faust,* and the overture *Manfred*), and he entered the most productive period of his life.

Late inspiration

From this time, music literally poured out of him for some six years. Even the revolutionary unrest of May 1849 failed to stem the flow completely, but it did force the family to flee Dresden for two months after a last-minute escape through a back door to avoid Schumann's conscription into a hastily set-up militia.

Clara continued giving concerts and Robert's music was gaining recognition, but attempts to consolidate his position in Dresden were unsuccessful, as was his application for the post of music director at Leipzig. However, in September 1850 the family moved to Düsseldorf; Schumann had accepted the post there of municipal music director. After a period of adjustment, and despite further mental and physical debility early in 1852, his composing urge returned. He also had quarrels with the authorities over his running of the city's musical activities. Schumann was temperamentally unsuited to maintain the training and discipline of his musicians, a fact betrayed by a serious lowering in artistic standards.

The end

The trouble in Düsseldorf and a number of working visits to other musical centres during 1853 finally destroyed nerves made frail by prolonged overwork. In February 1854, hallucinations and 'very strong, painful aural symptoms' occurred and his nights were filled with heavenly and hellish dreams. Convinced that his fears of insanity were at last vindicated, he threw himself into the Rhine, but was rescued and brought home in a fearful state of mental derangement. Doctors forbade Clara to see him, and on 4 March 1854 he was taken to a private asylum at Endenich, near Bonn. Clara did not see him until more than two years later, by which time he was unable to utter intelligible words.

During those two final years he experienced periods of relative stability and corresponded with Clara and with several friends. He even accepted visitors, Brahms among them. Schumann's mind was still spasmodically active: he continued to compose, though nothing important emerged, and towards the end Brahms disturbed him obsessively making alphabetical lists of towns and countries.

On 29 July, 1856, at 4pm, he died in his cell. His span of 46 years was over.

Schumann's music did not break barriers, neither was he ahead of his time. On the contrary, it tended to ignore the formal confines of the classical period in the interest of self-expression, and it was emphatically of its time in that it wholeheartedly adopted the Romantic fervour generated by authors, poets and painters early in the 19th century.

Leisure in Schumann's Germany

Schumann's Germany witnessed the rise of a new middle-class phenomenon – leisure time. And although, for many, survival itself was the main consideration, the wealthy continued to entertain on a lavish scale.

Leisure has become something we now take for granted: time to spend with our family, time to read, time to write letters, time to relax and pursue hobbies. Yet leisure is very much a modern invention – a late by-product of the industrial revolution. If we read between the lines of letters and diaries in early 19th-century Germany, we can see many modern leisure activities in a primitive form, as well as the remains of earlier social systems going back to the middle ages.

Germany in 1800 was much closer to the middle ages than France or Britain. While England advanced into industrialization, the political convulsions in Paris set a pattern that influenced the rest of the world. Germany did not exist as a country. It was a patchwork of states connected by dreadful roads. After the Napoleonic Wars, the German Confederation was set up with 39 separate principalities, but even within the state of Prussia, the largest state, there were numerous customs zones: a traveller going from Hamburg to

Berlin had to pass through 63 frontier posts. And the roads were so bad that to travel, in 1815, from Brunswick to Lübeck, about 130 miles, took three days.

Communications were almost non-existent across large areas of the countryside. Over 90 per cent of the population lived in farms and small villages. The great majority of people lived and died without ever seeing a town, let alone attending a theatrical performance or buying a magazine. Villagers would refer to a place three miles away as 'abroad'. Ironically, one result of these primitive conditions was a high degree of hospitality. Travellers in early 19th-century Germany were made welcome and pumped for news of the outside world simply because people felt so cut off.

Peasant life
One of the key leisure activities in these isolated rural communities was centred around the spinning room.

In fine weather the bee[r] garden (right) was a popular family attraction, providing a[n] opportunity to eat and drink, show off one's be[st] outfit and hear the loc[al] musicians.

By today's standards, life in Germany during the first half of the last century was serene and uncomplicated – at least, for those above the poverty line. The timeless and classless pleasure of lakeside fishing was a pastime enjoyed by many.

During the long winter months, when there was no agricultural work to be done, the villagers – men and women, married and unmarried – would gather in the larger rooms to spin together, and to sing and gossip as they spun. This social habit continued to be popular after hand spinning was no longer a vital activity.

If any traveller passed through the village, he was encouraged to visit the spinning room and tell of his travels. If he had any books or newspapers, he was encouraged to read them aloud. The spinning room became an important social centre around the time of the Reformation, and the custom persisted until well into the 19th century.

In fact, as young people began to leave the land and head for the city and as village society disintegrated, the spinning room became a last bastion of the old way of life. They sang of how much better off they were in the countryside, the songs becoming more idyllic and sentimental.

The spinning room was attacked both by the clergy and the police – because there the peasants socialized without anyone in authority over them. The Church denounced the spinning rooms as dens of iniquity because young, unmarried men and women would drink together, sing songs together, and perhaps even worse . . . Certainly the spinning room functioned as an unofficial marriage market and as a centre for allowing romance to blossom.

It was a spinning room that provided the starting point for Wagner's opera *The Flying Dutchman*: it is there that Senta and her maidens sing of the haunted ship and its ghostly crew. In the spinning room Senta conceived the idea of saving the soul of the Flying Dutchman.

Other accounts of peasant life in the early 19th century suggest scenes from the middle ages. As one

The hub of rural community social life for gossip, news, romance and conversation was the spinning room (above left). But to the police and the clergy it represented a potential hot-bed of agitation and moral degeneracy. The authorities considered there was little to fear, however, from the musical soirées favoured by the middle class (above).

The coffee house (left) was the middle-class equivalent of the spinning room – except that it was strictly a male preserve. The coffee drinkers caught up on the news and exchanged views on the constantly changing political scene.

Westphalian peasant of the time remembered it:

'Two or three times a year the peasants had permission to play games in the main hall of the farm. They played blind man's buff and games like that. They were jumping and singing and falling all over the place, shouting and laughing. Until at the appointed hour, the head man appeared, like the figure of Fate himself, and ordered them all to go to bed.'

The leisure time of the lower classes was supervised as much as possible. One book of advice to the lady of the house suggested:

'Servant girls are not supposed to go to dances if their morality is threatened, but you must tell them that when you hire them. It is better to compensate them with money or with innocent pleasures. You must never forget that you have a duty to supervise the morals of the servants. It is incomprehensible why some ladies give little knick-knacks to their maids, and thus encourage their vanity, and so the maid can be led into sin.'

The middle class

For the lady of the house, leisure was increasing as the extended family shrank during the 19th century. Around 1800 it was common for a rural household to contain several generations, as well as the servants and the apprentices that worked with the master. During the 19th century this was gradually whittled down to the nuclear family we are used to: parents and children. These shrinking households gave the lady of the house more time for her own amusement, and more time to spend with the children. Among this new middle-class, and mainly female, audience there was a craze for reading popular novels.

Goethe's *The Sorrows of Young Werther* made him famous overnight in 1774 with the tragedy of a young hero who is not only disappointed in love, but also feels alienated from the world around him. With its intense emotional aura, and its vivid account of the growth and despair of love, *Young Werther* established a new uniform for sensitive young men of means all over Europe: a blue coat worn over yellow breeches. Napoleon was reported to have read the novel at least seven times; and several young men actually committed suicide in careful imitation of the book's doomed hero. The novels of Jean Paul Richter also achieved a huge popularity, and his lush romantic style strongly influenced the prose of Robert Schumann.

There was no shortage of critics who complained that young women were ruining their minds by reading too many frivolous novels. A more uplifting type of book began to appear at this time: detailed accounts of household management to tell young wives how to set up and run their establishments. From these books it becomes clear how many activities that are now part of shopping and a consumer society used to take place inside the middle-class home. Hair dressing, making soap and candles, brewing beer, cultivating indoor plants, and the massive task of stocking the larder for the winter months with pickles and preserves are all explained within these manuals.

The attitude towards children in these works is quite sensitive and imaginative – a long way from the clichés of a strict 'Germanic' upbringing that might be expected. In the early 19th century several children's classics were published based on older sources – the Brothers Grimm's fairy stories from German folklore, and the more grotesque stories of *Struwwelpeter* by Heinrich Hoffmann. The fact that these books are still

Street entertainers like the organ grinder (left) brought popular melodies to the very front doors of urban dwellers. In the same vein travelling fairs with booths and sideshows provided a cheap form of entertainment for the populace.

In this painting by Spitzweg a German family is gently satirized taking a Sunday stroll. But walking was a serious matter: for many it was not only a free and readily available pleasure, but also their only means of getting about.

popular with children today suggests that the emphas on domestic happiness was not totally witho foundation.

After 1848 the passion for reading romantic fictic began to diminish and the reading craze move towards a new type of magazine. Technic improvements in printing made magazines cheaper an enormous print runs possible. One massive but typic. success was called *Gartenlaube* ('Garden Bower') an first appeared in 1853. At the end of the first year it ha attracted 5000 readers. Twenty years later it ha a circulation of 380,000 with its combination c romantic fiction and domestic advice. Improvemen in printing and distribution had created a new mark for a new type of magazine – the forerunners of th women's magazines which today sell in their million

The theatre

A country consisting of few towns, bad roads, and littl cultural unity will not quickly give rise to a thrivin theatre. Over a period of 70 years, from th appearance in the 1770s of Germany's first dramatis of world stature, Gotthold Ephraim Lessing, th German theatre struggled heroically on to the stag By the year 1840 there were reckoned to be 6 theatres in German-speaking countries, employin about 5000 actors, musicians and singers.

This theatre was created out of several earlie traditions but chiefly from the touring German theatr companies which had been thriving since about 1700

For the well-heeled, artistes from Italy wer bringing opera to the courts and also occasional work of mime deriving from the *comedia dell'arte* traditio – the popular improvised comedies of 18th-centur Italy. These highly trained troupes often brough sophisticated stage effects with them, so that citie could appear to be consumed by fire, and chariot could ascend into the sky.

The association between students and hell-raising is not confined to this century. Duelling, though officially outlawed, was widely practised among students as a demonstration of personal valour and defiance against the establishment.

as the master of dramatic form, an influence discernible in the historical works of Goethe and Schiller which were staged at Weimar.

Goethe worked hard to improve the social standing of actors and to improve their discipline as a troupe: performers were fined if they missed their cues; one actress who absented herself for a week was punished on her return by being confined to quarters under military guard.

A visitor to the Weimar theatre noticed that the middle class and students sat downstairs, the courtiers and officials in the balcony, and the masses in the top gallery. The students could be particularly troublesome in the summer, especially during the cherry season: they would eat fruit in the stalls and bombard the actors with cherry-stones. Although Goethe invited the actors to his home and attempted to improve their social standing, he did not find this easy. A contract for one troublesome married couple laid down that they should separate if Herr Burgdorf continued to create scandals by assaulting his wife in public!

It was a disagreement with a difficult actress which finally led Goethe to resign from the theatre. While he was temporarily absent in April 1817, Karoline Jagemann (who had become the mistress of Weimar's ruler, Karl August) staged a production of the play *Aubrey de Mont Didier's Dog* which featured a performing poodle in the lead role. Since Goethe had worked so hard to increase the cultural prestige of theatre, and raise the social status of actors above that of circus animals, he was deeply upset and left the direction of the theatre to Fräulein Jagemann.

A third strand was provided by academics and writers who were looking for a way of forging a distinctly German drama by the mid 18th century. By 1800, several German towns had companies which they would call a 'National Theatre' to distinguish them from travelling players, and from the foreign companies maintained by the courts.

Goethe's role
Of great importance in creating a German Theatre was the work done by Goethe at the court of Weimar, where he directed a company of professional players from 1791 to 1817. Here the emphasis moved away from French convention towards emulating Shakespeare

Mid 19th century theatre
By 1840 the leading actor-managers of Germany, such as Iffland in Berlin, lived in sumptuous villas and were as celebrated as Garrick in London. The dominant form of drama was historical and heroic, under the

Dramatists and critics and all those who wanted to see the German theatre grow in stature may have taken the art form with great seriousness, but for the theatre goers themselves it was a chance to be as boisterous as they liked.

influence of Schiller: 'Subject – historical with a marked preference for Germany in the middle ages. Hero – very heroic, and in tragedy, unmistakably guilty. His character is usually free from complications, with no hidden depths. Certain historical combinations occur again and again', is how one critic tartly put it. And the audience was still fragmented. An English visitor to Berlin's theatre commented: 'You see travelling strangers from every country, young people from the middle class when a celebrated actor appears, and on opera nights the upper class, but the real people you never see.'

Of course most of the 'real people' were still in the countryside. In 1850 there were only five towns in German-speaking countries with a population over 100,000. One English gentleman, who was touring through Germany in 1840, described a travelling fair near Frankfurt which was probably typical of the occasional entertainment enjoyed by the 'real people':

'The booths in the fair were devoted to eatables, prints, books and plaster casts, all suited to the lowest class of person. Shooting with an airgun was the favourite amusement – sometimes it was a figure in motion; or else it was a wonderful cottage which opened its doors as soon as it was struck and displayed all of its internal arrangement, from the

cellar to the attic. There was a wonderful troupe of apes from Holland, a circus, a family of acrobats from Hamburg, an Egyptian wizard, a white Negress, a Swiss giantess. In the booth of acrobats I found an elevated stage, a row of musicians in front and several tiers of seats around the circumference. The audience was quiet and observant and much delighted with the jests of Mr. Merryman whose humour was of the very broadest kind.'

The upper class

Since poor communications and lack of mobility curtailed the leisure activities of most people, it is not surprising that the one class that was spectacularly mobile was the aristocracy. Visiting spas in summer and enjoying the hospitality of relatives all over Europe – no matter how remote – were key features of

Well-provisioned picnic – with wine rather than beer – were among the many pursuits enjoyed by Germany's aristocra who had the time and resources to take their pleasures in the countryside at a gentle pace.

For those who had the money, hand-tinted books were available for the children. Depicting typical children's games, they also had educational uses, for example in learning to count.

his luxurious way of life.

Because the principalities of Germany had been reduced from more than 300 independent territories in the late 18th century to a mere 39 separate states after the Congress of Vienna in 1815, a class of aristocrats was created who retained their titles but no longer had any territory to rule over. They were known as the 'mediatized princes' and one solution to the difficulty of possessing a noble name but no kingdom, was to travel and stay with one's family – family included not only the most distant cousins, but also their connections via marriage.

So a young, impoverished, mediatized prince could potentially enjoy the hospitality of an extremely extended family. When Prince Chlodwig von Hohenlohe visited Paris he was wined and dined by noble households every night of the week, although he was in no position to reciprocate their hospitality. While in Berlin he dined every week with the King of Prussia himself, whom he regarded as merely his equal in rank. This degree of hospitality could be enjoyed all over Germany, but not in Vienna, where the court remained curiously uninterested in strangers and made little effort. The Prussian military attaché to Vienna, Prince Kraft von Hohenlohe-Ingelfingen, arrived in 1854 and was disappointed to receive almost no invitations in the months that followed. Fortunately, the mobilization of the Austrian army during the Crimean War resulted in a dearth of male dancing partners at balls: 'And so I danced myself rather than introduced myself into the society of Vienna,' he later wrote.

Life in Royal courts

The quality of life in the courts of German-speaking countries varied enormously. Weimar, the capital of Saxe-Meiningen, acquired great cultural prestige because of its association with Goethe, but it remained a town of only 6000 people and many visitors commented on its village-like atmosphere.

At the other end of the scale, Berlin, the capital of Prussia organized its court functions along highly military lines. The guests at a large State function would be divided into categories and entertained according to their rank. For example the women would be grouped as: wives of the nobility; wives of other guests; unmarried girls who had been presented at court; and girls who had not been presented at court. Surprisingly, the formal style of day-to-day life at the Prussian court could also be extremely frugal. Extravagance was only sanctioned on very special occasions, such as a wedding or a Jubilee. At an ordinary dinner, it was quite normal for Kaiser Wilhelm I solemnly to mark with a pen the level of the wine bottle at the end of the meal, before returning it to the cellar in readiness for the next meal.

The impulse towards a cultured life in Germany often came from the middle class, rather than from the

The last & Newest Fashions for the Opera, Evening Parties & the Theatres.

court. Schumann discovered this to his cost when he moved from Leipzig, the commercial centre of Saxony, to the relatively dull routine of court life in Dresden, the seat of Saxony's kings. When Mendelssohn arrived in Leipzig in 1835 to take over as musical director of the Gewandhaus, their concerts had already been famous for 50 years, and it was the wealthy textile merchants of Leipzig who subsidized them. In 1843 this commercial patronage also founded a Conservatory, which increased Leipzig's prestige. Goethe and Lessing had been students at the University and Leipzig was also the centre of the growing German publishing industry. All this cultural activity led Goethe to describe the town affectionately as 'der

In an age of mass-produced newspapers and magazines the fashion plate was used to mirror high-society's obsession with its public image. The one above claims it illustrates 'the latest fashions for opera, evening parties and the theatre'.

The artist Georg Kersting
has delicately captured
the simplicity of life for
the middle-class
German of this time in
his painting The
Embroiderer. The guitar
on the sofa hints again
at the importance of
musical ability as a
domestic diversion.

The hungry years

For many Germans in the early 19th century leisur
remained a remote dream. Through railway
industrialization, and Prussia's political ambition,
fragmented and backward territory was slow
turning into the most powerful state in Europe. B
the most acute writers of the time all described th
process with a premonition that something sinist
was happening. Shortly before his death in 183
Goethe remarked that a war 'like the Thirty Years Wa
appeared to be imminent.

To some extent commentators were driven by th
knowledge that the population was increasing rapidl
without any increase taking place in the supply
food. So pauperism and hunger became more wid
spread in the 1830s. The following decade was know
as 'the hungry forties' because a series of disastrou
harvests threatened some areas of the country wi
famine. One response to this was massive emigratio
from Germany to the United States. (Perhaps as man
as one million Germans emigrated to America betwee
1820 and 1860.) Another response, in literary term
was a new type of journalism trying to describe ho
the poor really lived. Heinrich Bettziech in hi
description of Berlin wrote in 1846:

*'Not a bed nor a table, without firewood, clothes or
shoes. No money, no potatoes, no prospects, hope
only of the workhouse or a miserable death in the
Charité [poor house]. Only rags and straw and dirt
and vermin, and hunger howling in their entrails.'*

It was a situation that led the poet Heine to sum u
German society in the sinister sentences: 'In Germar
there are two species of rats: fat rats and hungry rats
Until prosperity and industrialization had transforme
Germany by the end of the 19th century, simpl
physical survival remained the major preoccupatio

klein Paris' (little Paris).

By contrast, in Dresden many of the most distinguished artists and intellectuals had been drawn
from all over Germany to the court of the autocratic
King Friedrich Augustus II, where they were
smothered by rigid protocol. At first Schumann
regarded this dearth of culture as a challenge. 'Here
one can get back the old, lost longing for music, there
is so little to hear!' he wrote to one friend. But
gradually he was worn down by the spirit of
amateurism in the place and after the insurrection in
1849, Schumann left Dresden without regrets.

The splendour of a
household that knows
little of poverty or
hardship: the places are
set and the silver tureen
promise the entering
guests a sumptuous
meal. Wining and
dining on such an
extravagant scale were
vital events on the socia
calendar of the
aristocracy.

Franz Liszt
1811–1886

*Virtuoso extraordinary, passionate lover, man of
religion and composer of genius, Liszt's sensational
career embodied the ambitions, contradictions and
achievements of the Romantic movement.*

Carl Czerny (right) was Beethoven's most brilliant pupil and, in turn, one of the young Liszt's most important teachers in Vienna. He was also a composer of repute, though today he is best remembered as a composer of several instructive works for the piano.

Liszt (below) at the age of 16. By this early stage in his long and eventful career, Liszt was already an acclaimed and experienced piano virtuoso.

Franz Liszt, or Ferencz, as he was christened, was born in the small village of Raiding in Hungary on 22 October, 1811. It was the year of the Great Comet and the gypsies who camped nearby foretold a dazzling future for the baby. His father, Adam Liszt, was a land steward on the estates of Prince Esterházy: Haydn had served at the Esterházy court for 30 years: Mozart's pupil Hummel had been Kapellmeister there; and Cherubini had been a visitor. Adam himself could play most instruments and bought his son a piano as soon as he was big enough to sit on a piano stool.

Under his father's tuition the boy made outstanding progress. At the age of nine he made his first appearance in public, stealing the thunder from a titled blind pianist who was top of the bill. Shortly afterwards he caused a sensation with a solo performance at the Esterházy home. The Princess was so impressed that she gave him Haydn's name book — unfortunately for posterity, the child promptly lost it. His first newspaper review declared his playing 'beyond admiration'. A group of local dignitaries formed a committee and provided the young genius with a six-year stipend so that he could study.

Adam was so ambitious for his son that he resigned his post and, with his wife Anna, left Hungary for Vienna, the musical capital of Europe. Here he tried to engage the services of Hummel as a teacher, but found him too expensive. Instead, he settled for Salieri, the man who had been responsible for so much of Mozart's misfortune, and the composer Czerny, who was Beethoven's greatest pupil. Czerny was so amazed at the potential of the young Liszt that he refused to accept any fee. He noticed with astonishment that 'Nature had produced a pianist.' Liszt could play anything at sight and improvised brilliantly though he knew nothing of harmony. He was such a sickly child (this was attributed in part to the fact that his mother had fallen down a well shaft when she was pregnant) that his exertions nearly made him fall off the piano stool; and he had the most alarming habit of 'flinging his fingers all over the keys'. Czerny set out to give the boy what he lacked — control and discipline — but the

'flying fingers' remained a hallmark of his playing, an an innovation, because until Liszt pianists had playe in the same way as organists, with their fingers curle under like claws.

'It is Mozart himself'

At this time Liszt was presented to Beethoven. A intermediary persuaded the musical giant of the day t attend one of Liszt's concerts, and though there i some doubt as to whether Beethoven would hav accepted, being very deaf, Liszt himself often told th story of how, when he had finished playing, Beethove got up on to the stage and embraced and kissed him Ungenerous critics have dismissed this symboli encounter as pure invention. But Liszt needed no suc publicity: his Viennese concerts brought a rash of rav

very latest design which permitted rapid repetition of one note. Thus equipped, Liszt took Paris by storm. 'Since last night I believe in reincarnation . . . It is Mozart himself. His tiny arms can scarcely reach both ends of the keyboard, his feet can hardly touch the pedals . . . yet he is the first pianist in Europe,' enthused the press. He played to the French royal family, he was lionized by the noblest ladies of the land and his picture was on sale in every shop. Such was the tumult around him that his mother, a simple countrywoman, decided to return to Austria to live with her sister.

In 1824 Liszt made his London début. The pianist Moscheles, who had every reason to be jealous, generously affirmed that 'in strength and in his conquest of difficulties he surpasses anything hitherto heard.' Exhausting tours of France and Ireland followed, culminating in a royal command performance before George IV at Windsor.

By the time he was 16, Liszt had been in the limelight for seven years and the strain was beginning to tell. He and Adam took a sea cure at Boulogne. Liszt turned for strength to religion, as he was always to do, but his father, also weakened by their travels, fell ill with typhoid and died. His last words to his son were 'Je crains pour toi les femmes' (literally, 'I'm afraid for you and women'). Adam Liszt had a presentiment that women would be his son's undoing or rather that his passion for women would be greater than his dedication to music.

First loves

After the death of his father Liszt was disillusioned by stardom. Believing that his art was 'debased to not much more than a trade . . . labelled as entertainment for fashionable society', he gave up performing and

reviews. 'A young virtuoso has dropped from the clouds,' they gushed, 'There is a god amongst us.'

When Liszt was 12, Czerny declared there was no more he could teach him and recommended that he should continue his studies at the Paris Conservatoire. Before travelling to Paris Liszt gave a farewell concert in Budapest and repaid the sum he had been donated. Then there was a triumphant tour of Germany: in Munich he received a second portentous kiss, this time from the monarch.

Initially, Paris was disappointing. Cherubini, director of the Conservatoire, upheld the rule that foreigners were not to be admitted. But there was a compensation: Sébastian Erard, the famous piano manufacturer, had heard of the young Liszt's prodigious success and with an astute sense of the value of publicity he gave him an instrument of the

A Romantic vision of a gypsy family (above). Similar images inspired Liszt's Rhapsodies, *for though the composer – dressed in Hungarian style on the right – left his homeland when he was a boy he never forgot his 'roots'.*

George Sand and her coterie (below). Among the men depicted around this highly individual and brilliant woman are the painter Delacroix, who stands behind Sand and the unmistakable Liszt, and the bearded dramatist Félicien Malefille, who is declaiming on the right. Chopin, George Sand's current lover, is represented by the brightly coloured bird perched upon her knee.

went to live quietly with his mother, who had returned to Paris. His teaching brought in enough money to keep them both.

It was at this time that he first fell in love. Caroline de Saint-Cricq was his pupil, a girl of his own age from an aristocratic family. When the music lessons spilled over into poetry readings her father forbade him to see her again: she was duly married to a diplomat. To Liszt the loss was a severe blow – he suffered an emotional and religious crisis that was to last for two years. (This Caroline was to be the only former love he remembered in his will.) He refused food and felt a strong conviction that his vocation lay with God rather than in music. He suffered cataleptic fits and once, when he was unconscious for two days, a Paris newspaper announced his death and printed an obituary.

In 1830 revolution broke out in Paris. 'The guns have cured him' announced Liszt's mother as her son was aroused from his lethargy. Within the next exciting year he met the three men who were to have a lasting influence on his music: Paganini, Berlioz and Chopin. Paganini's supposed alliance with the devil fascinated the young pianist, as did his uncanny virtuosity. In Berlioz he found another tormented Romantic who had extended the range of the orchestra just as Paganini had extended the range of the violin. Liszt determined to do as much for the piano.

Chopin's influence was different: he calmed Liszt's nerves and introduced him to his first great affair. At an impromptu party at Chopin's home Liszt played into the small hours to a select company of artists: Heine, Delacroix, Rossini, Meyerbeer and George Sand. A sixth guest, Marie d'Agoult, was deeply affected. 'His flashing eyes, his gestures, his smile, now profound and of an infinite sweetness, now caustic, seemed intended to provoke me to an intimate assent.'

The reign of Marie
The Countess Marie was a 28-year-old mother of three children. She was estranged from her husband, a man of limited outlook some 20 years older than herself, and she led an independent life devoted to the serious pursuit of literature and philosophy. Her liaison with Liszt, whose mercurial nature inclined him towards passing affairs and involvement in long-term relationships only with women made of sterner stuff than himself, lasted for 10 years.

To begin with the affair was difficult and scandalous and caused both of them a great deal of anguish. But in 1835 they broke for ever with convention and settled in Switzerland, where their life together became more ordered. There, their first baby, Blandine, was born. Under Marie's influence Liszt studied Goethe and Dante and applied himself to composition. These were the years of the *Années de pèlerinage,* lyrical evocations of his travels with Marie. While he gave free lessons to the young ladies at the Geneva Conservatory, paying as much attention to their charms as to their musical talents, Marie taught him the airs and graces of the fashionable world. In due course, he grew restless to be back among it.

In 1837 in Italy, a second daughter, Cosima, was born. (She was destined to marry first her father's favourite pupil, Hans von Bülow, then the composer he supported and admired so much, Richard Wagner.) Shortly after Cosima's birth Liszt found the excuse he needed to escape from the domestic setting that was becoming increasingly claustrophobic to him. He heard news of floods in the Danube and rediscovered the meaning of the word 'homeland'. 'O my wild and distant country! O my unknown friends! Your cry of pain has brought me back to you.'

The Countess Marie d'Agoult (left). Until her relationship with Liszt, by whom she had three children, 'her reputation hadn't a blemish.'

On the road again

He rushed to Vienna and gave 10 concerts to relieve the homeless. He also visited Hungary for the first time since his boyhood and heard once more the music of the gypsies, which had fascinated him since his youth. After a long absence from the stage the adulation he received went straight to his head. Not surprisingly, this was the beginning of the final rift between Liszt and Marie. Although he returned to her, the taste of fame was too sweet and after the birth of their third child, Daniel, he set off on a glittering series of tours that took him all across Europe.

He raised money for a monument to Beethoven, he raised money for charity, and he earned a personal fortune. Everywhere he received the highest accolades: he was welcomed with frenzied enthusiasm; his concerts were a sensation; his presence required speeches and banquets; he was presented with swords, medals, a title; and his departure was attended with solemn ceremony. His coach was often escorted miles out of town by bands of students. If he had to wait five minutes for a train, the station piano would be dragged out onto the platform so that he could perform to the crowd that always surrounded him.

His social success was equally brilliant, for Liszt's prodigious musicianship was matched by his sex appeal. When his face assumed its remarkable agony of expression, mingled with radiant smiles of joy, and his playing reached an impassioned high, ladies would scream and faint, or rush the stage to be nearer his soulful gaze 'like poor little larks, at the feet of a

The Swiss scenes and sounds encountered by Liszt on his 'honeymoon' with Marie in 1835 inspired his Années de pèlerinage, *a sort of musical diary.*

terrible enchanter'. At one concert two Hungarian countesses fell upon each other and rolled over and over on the floor to gain possession of Liszt's snuffbox. At another, a lady retrieved the stub of his cigar – she kept it in her bosom for the rest of her life.

As the superstar of the day, he was the darling of courts and salons and wrote to Marie of his conquests. There was Bettina von Arnim, close friend of Goethe and Beethoven: 'an imp of magnetic intelligence'; Charlotte von Hagn: 'the odalisque of two kings'; Princess Belgiojoso; the singer Caroline Unger; the pianist Camille Pleyel; and Mariette Duplessis, la Dame aux Camélias. Sometimes his affairs got out of hand. His liaison with the tempestuous dancer Lola Montez (later the mistress of mad King Ludwig of Bavaria) ended when he locked her in their hotel room and beat a hasty retreat out of town.

The mass hysteria that surrounded him – 'Lisztomania' as it was termed – may have done little for Liszt's character as Marie's faithful partner, but it did, once and for all, change the status of the musician in society. Previously, a pianist had been little more than a servant; his playing, background music that filled awkward gaps in the conversation of the audience. Now he was a person to be courted, whose talent entitled him to celebrity status.

But by 1847 the long-suffering Marie had had enough. She ended their relationship in a letter. 'What have I to do with a charming good-for-nothing, an upstart Don Juan, half mountebank, half juggler, who makes ideas and sentiments disappear up his sleeve and looks complacently at the bewildered public that applauds him? Ten years of illusion! Is that not the very sublime of extravagance? Adieu, my heart is bursting with bitterness!' Under the pseudonym of Daniel Stern she wrote a novel, *Nelida* (an anagram of their son's

Liszt performs the Galop Chromatique, *the virtuosic stunt with which he nearly always ended his concerts. Addicted to the limelight he returned to the hectic life of a travelling virtuoso in 1839.*

name), in which she portrayed him in a clear an unflattering light. Liszt denounced the book as a unjust attack by a scorned woman, but Marie fictional account of her lover's weaknesses is mor accurate than the fondness his contempora admirers would allow.

The reign of Princess Carolyne

With Marie eclipsed by other loves, there was no room in Liszt's life for another authoritative woma and in 1847, at the age of 36, he met her. She wa Carolyne Sayn-Wittgenstein, a 28-year-old Polis princess who, like Marie before her, was married bu separated from her husband. Though Liszt admire her for her title and her wealth, they shared dee religious feelings (Carolyne was also a piou Catholic), a love of literature and a passion for cigar For the princess it was love at first sight, 'I kiss you hands and kneel before you, prostrating my forehea to your feet, laying, like the Orientals, my finger on m brow, my lips and my heart . . .' She declared tha henceforth her whole being existed only to glorif him, and she was as good as her word.

In 1839 Liszt visited Hungary for the first time since his boyhood. He played at Budapest and Poszany, and proposed the foundation of a Hungarian national conservatory. On this, and on his further visits in the 1840s, he was greatly acclaimed. The programme (above) was for a concert given in 1846.

She whisked him off to her romantic castle at Woronince in southern Russia. There, while the snow whirled outside, her servants serenaded the lovers to the playing of the balalaika. In this congenial setting Liszt made a major decision. He renounced his life as a travelling virtuoso and, under Carolyne's encouragement, resolved to devote himself to composition. With this end in mind he went in 1848 to Weimar, where he had had a musical appointment since 1843, to live there permanently on a modest salary as musical director.

There Liszt was joined by Carolyne, who eventually reached Weimar after a dramatic chase to the Russian border, which she crossed only moments before officials closed it at the command of the tsar. (It was difficult for Russian subjects, even aristocrats, and especially independent-minded women, to leave Russia without government permission.) On her arrival, Liszt was obliged to take his leave of the woman who was sharing his hotel room. He joined Carolyne and her daughter, to whom he was more fatherly and affectionate than he was with his own children, in the large villa on the edge of town that was

There was hardly a country in Europe to which Liszt's tours did not extend. 1847 found him in Constantinople (below), where he admired the views up the Bosporus and impressed the Sultan.

Lola Montez (above) was one of Liszt's most exotic admirers. She once stormed into a banquet where he was present and danced on the table.

to be their home for the next 12 years. Some visitors did not take kindly to the 'irregular' ménage, but, as usual, the criticism was mainly directed at Carolyne. 'She has ensnared him by his vanity, she strews incense about him perpetually, without proportion and without scruple,' observed one, and Liszt's royal employers continued to address all official correspondence to the hotel where he had initially stayed.

But the tough and cultivated princess was more than financially supportive of her genius. Under Carolyne's influence Liszt composed the majority of his best piano works, including the piano concertos. She understood him very well. 'It is not genius that he lacks, but the capacity to sit still — industry, prolonged application. Unless someone helps him in this respect he is impotent, and when the consciousness of his impotence takes possession of him he has to resort to stimulants.' This was the period of his musical maturity and, most important, he used his status there as Europe's foremost musical celebrity to promote the work of other composers, especially that of Richard Wagner. In addition, anybody could attend the free classes he gave three times a week, and everybody did as hordes of aspiring pianists and musicians flocked to Weimar for an 'apprenticeship' under him.

When the divorce proceedings initiated by the princess finally came to a head in 1860, Carolyne went to Rome to get the sanction of the Vatican for their marriage, which was to take place there on Liszt's 50th birthday. But on the eve of the wedding, when the church was already bedecked with flowers, a hooded messenger arrived while Liszt and Carolyne were at prayer and, in true operatic style, announced that the princess's in-laws (her husband was quite equable about the divorce provided his cash settlement was sufficient) had put forward a further objection to the union. The ceremony was duly cancelled. This was a stroke of luck for Liszt, because as his daughter Cosima suggested, it would have been like 'a burial service' to a man who sensed that he had another vocation.

This episode marked a turning point in both their lives. The faith that had united them, now parted them. They were no longer lovers, though they remained close friends. Carolyne took a separate apartment in Rome and, with a supply of cigars at her side, began writing religious works, including an interminable project expressing her disillusionment with the church. It was called *The Interior Causes of the External Weaknesses of the Church in 1870* and ran to 24 volumes. This daunting work took her 25 years to complete, during which time she lived the life of a hermit. Two weeks after she wrote the last word, in 1887, she died.

Retreat to religion

In 1862, the year after the marriage débacle, Liszt's daughter Blandine died in childbirth, and this and the loss of Carolyne turned his thoughts again to religion. Liszt had undergone phases of religious intensity, as a child and – at intervals and with interludes – throughout his life, so the reinvigoration of his faith at this stage in his hectic life came as no surprise to those who knew him well. In 1865 he solemnized this life-long commitment by taking four minor orders of the Catholic church. (A further three vows were required before full ordination as a priest 'licensed' to hear confession and say mass.) He soon moved into an apartment in the fabulous Villa d'Este just outside Rome, where the beauty of the gardens and the famous fountains gave him a perfect environment for composition.

Liszt's new, black-clad and tonsured image as a devout abbé added to his mystique as well as his personal happiness but he was to be disappointed by the reception given to his sacred music: Catholics found it too innovative and in Protestant countries it was regarded with suspicion. Of his new life, he wrote to a confidante, 'I have not changed, it is only that my life is ordered more simply'. That he was the same man was to be proved by the fact that the serene Villa d'Este was the setting for his last dramatic affair.

A young Russian, the 'Cossack Countess', Olga Janina, came to Rome to seduce him. At 19, she already had a colourful past behind her. Her childhood had been devoted to bloodsports and she had lived among thoroughbred horses. She was married at 15. On the morning after her wedding she horsewhipped her

Carolyne and her daughter (right). Liszt's relationship with her ended in Rome (above), where he acted on his vocation to be an abbé. But his faith was as aesthetic as it was spiritual.

husband and left him. At 16 she bore a daughter. Then she went to study the piano and became infatuated with Liszt's music, and, inevitably the man himself.

Knowing Liszt's weakness for luxury she rented a fantastic apartment and bought a complete wardrobe from the Parisian couturier Worth. Liszt the former womanizer was impressed, but he said, 'Never speak to me of love: I must not love.' Cleverly, she allowed him to retire to the Villa d'Este and gave him enough time to grow lonely in his meditations. Then she appeared at his door dressed as a gardener's boy and bearing a basket of flowers. 'He showed such joy that I could see how terribly solitude weighed upon his soul that was so passionately in love with the world and its homage.' Their relationship was tempestuous. Liszt repented of his lapse from celibacy and refused to see her; Olga threatened to kill them both, to take poison, to slash her wrists; after a week he was again her lover.

The end came when Olga, a would-be concert pianist, bungled three attempts at a recital. Liszt was so harsh with her that the audience was saddened and embarrassed; the poor girl returned home to take a dose of laudanum (tincture of opium) and remained unconscious for 48 hours. She threatened to shoot them both, but he persuaded her to leave. Olga, like Countess Marie, consoled herself by writing a book about Liszt, revealing the division in his personality.

A 'three-cornered existence'

Towards the end of his life Liszt began a strenuous regime, a 'three-cornered existence', dividing his year between Rome, Weimar and Budapest and devoting his time to music, religion and love, not necessarily in that order. The arrangement was satisfactory, but exhausting. Cosima had married von Bülow in 1857 but in 1864 she married Wagner, after a protracted liaison in the course of which she had two children by him. When the scandal first broke Liszt was loyal enough to his first son-in-law to sever relations with Cosima and Wagner for five years. Eventually, however, he was reconciled with them and Wagner's death in 1883 came as a great blow.

It was en route for Bayreuth in 1886 that he caught his death of cold. He was sitting in a train with a honeymoon couple who were admiring the moon through the open window – not a situation a great Romantic would complain about. Once in Bayreuth he fell ill with pneumonia, and died painlessly on 31 July.

As the grave Abbé Liszt, the composer's image in old age was that of the artist as a benign patriarch. Here he is shown in his study (below) where he devoted much of his last few years to composing sacred music (above) and at Bayreuth (left) with Cosima and Richard Wagner. He died there in 1886.

Like men possessed
The great virtuosos

Lionized by society, hero-worshipped by audiences, the virtuosos were the superstars of the age. Through their extraordinary technical brilliance they exalted music into new realms of popularity.

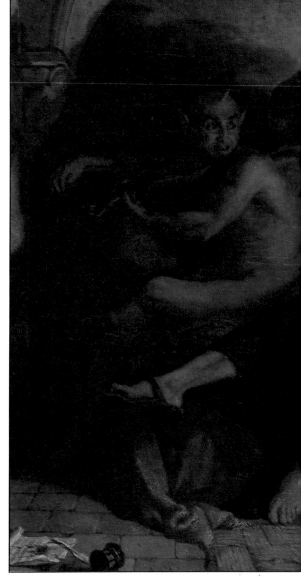

With his powerful hands and sunken, distorted face – the result of successive jawbone operations – it is easy to see how Paganini's (left) uncanny virtuosity was often perceived as diabolic. This legand echoed the career of the great Tartini (d.1770) an 18th century virtuoso violinist. Tartini (right) wrote his famous Devil's Sonata *after a dream in which the devil had played the violin with 'consummate skill'.*

When Niccolò Paganini played the violin, people said they could see the devil standing at his elbow; when Franz Liszt stormed up and down the keyboard, the audience went hysterical. Between them these two great virtuosos inspired, hypnotized, entranced and awed a whole generation. Yet towering though Paganini and Liszt were, they were not the only virtuosos to set aflame the hearts of contemporary audiences, nor yet necessarily the most technically accomplished.

The fervid imagination of the romantics, which seemed to embrace the rising middle class, demanded heroes. Pianists should not simply be accomplished musicians, but knights of the keyboard. And pianists from all over Europe seemed to spring up to meet this demand. There was Liszt's great rival, Sigismond Thalberg, who people swore must have three hands; there was the Bohemian titan Alexander Dreyshock with his startling octaves; Alkan the recluse; de Meyer the clown, who played with his elbows; the Viennese dandy who took America by storm, Henri Herz; Louis Gottschalk; and many others, not to mention the great

composer pianists such as Mendelssohn and Chopin.

There had of course been virtuosos before, from Vivaldi to Mozart, but never had they been in the public eye in such a way before. In the days when serious music was the reserve of the wealthy patrons, the virtuoso was appreciated by just a handful of connoisseurs. As the middle class grew, however, and patronage began to decline, music was forced to reach an ever widening audience – indeed, anyone with the price of a concert ticket in their pocket.

What this new audience demanded more than anything was pianists. During the early decades of the 19th century, the piano had found its way into nearly every well-to-do household in Europe. it was not just a musical instrument; it was an integral part of social life. Few soirées would be complete without a musical interlude around the piano. Like fine needlework and light conversation, playing the piano – or singing to it – was an essential social accomplishment for any young lady of good breeding. Naturally, it was pianists people wanted to see, and pianists are what they got.

From 1815 onwards pianists began to travel all over Europe, and sometimes beyond, playing cities and towns, big halls and small. Not only were there many pianists, but the popularity of the piano as well had opened the way for many talented players. New conservatoires, founded in Paris (1795) and London (1822) for example, were turning out a score of graduates a year all relying more and more on public concerts to earn a living.

As the audience constantly demanded fresh excitement, in the form of new players, it was no good a pianist staying in one place – audiences would soon decline. It was essential to keep on the move.

Liszt (right) was so impressed by Paganini performances with the violin that he resolved do the same for the piano. Like his virtuose mentor, he acquired a demonic reputation, although he was also likened to a god. Playin like a man possessed, Liszt also 'possessed' b audiences, especially *their female members, with his electrifying showmanship.*

Although many gravitated to Paris, which was blessed by a phenomenal wealth of pianistic talent and remarkably appreciative audiences, few stayed for long periods. Even the frail Chopin undertook a punishing tour of England and Scotland. The age of the touring virtuoso had begun.

The touring virtuoso

Touring was by no means easy. The railway network was not established until the 1840s, and travel was slow and exhausting, especially in winter. Few concert halls existed, and there was little in the way of management and organization to run the business side of the concert circuit, from booking halls and musicians to printing programmes and arranging accommodation for the soloist. Even in Paris, François Habeneck did not establish the *Société des Concerts du Conservatoire* until 1828. Advance notice of the event would often be nothing more than the gossip of travellers arriving slightly ahead of the performer. The travel-worn virtuoso would probably have to perform, without rehearsal, on an indifferent instrument – with even more indifferent musicians, hurriedly assembled for the performance. Ignaz Moscheles, for instance, an older contemporary of Liszt's, found himself in Liverpool in 1825 with eight strings and 'four halting wind instruments' for his concerto accompaniment. Yet Moscheles was at that time a major virtuoso, on a par with Kalkbrenner and Hummel. He lived long enough, until 1870, to become an anachronism, but in 1825 his star was high. Although he had started off as a bravura pianist, by this time he was a dedicated 'pure' musician, the first touring virtuoso to try to bring Beethoven and other quality music to the public and a major figure in the transition to the high Romantic virtuoso – someone who could perform the best music on offer.

The kind of touring schedule the virtuosos undertook would be considered demanding even with today's organization and transport. The violinist Paganini, for instance, played 112 concerts in less than a year when he toured the British Isles between the spring of 1831 and 1832. As there was little time for rehearsal, pianists would naturally tend to choose a few favourite pieces. In 1818, the pianist Johann Tomaschek wrote:

Never settled in one place, always touring, always busy preparing programmes for concerts, they never have time to study anything new. As a result, most of their programmes are mostly repetitions of earlier programmes, except that pieces may be presented in a different order.

Up until 1830, touring was intense, but fairly low key. Then, however, two events changed the picture. First, there was the gradual fanning of the Romantic flame right across Europe. People began to expect more of the virtuoso. He took on more and more the aura of the hero, the warrior, the great Artist – in Schumann's words 'a daring fellow, whose fate is to conquer and rule, not with the dangerous tools of combat, but with the peaceful tools of art'. They looked to be thrilled and inspired by the skill and passion of the virtuosos. People began to go to virtuoso concerts not simply to listen to great playing, but to be enthralled, amazed, overcome.

Paganini

Second, and not entirely disconnected, there was Paganini. Paganini had long been recognized in his

native Italy as a talented violinist, but when, at the age of 45, he began to tour Europe in 1828, the effect was cataclysmic. During the next four years, Paganini played in all the major cities of western Europe, and his tour was more than just a tour, it was a triumphal progress that left everyone, musicians and public, awestruck in its wake.

Technically, Paganini was undoubtedly brilliant, combining many different strands of virtuosity in a way no one had done before. He played scale passages and arpeggios at breakneck speed – Michelangelo Abbado observed that he played his *Sonata a mouvement perpetuel* at an incredible tempo of 12 notes a second at his Paris concert in 1832. He made phenomenal use of harmonics, pizzicato, bow tricks and lefthand plucking – in his variations on *God Save the Queen,* he would play the melody complete with double stops with the bow, while plucking the bass line with his left hand! And his speciality was melodies played on the G-string alone.

Even this was not crucial, however, other virtuoso violinists could perform equally dazzling feats, though few could perform quite as many. What was crucial was the effect Paganini had on his audience.

When he began touring, Paganini, by then in his mid 40s, was a spectral, riveting figure. Suffering from syphilis and other health problems, he had had all his teeth removed shortly before his appearance in Paris. And his dishevelled hair hung in two lank locks at either side of his pallid, hollow face, while one gaunt shoulder sat higher than the other. His very ugliness combined with his intense personality and the dark eyes that blazed hypnotically from their deep sockets gave him a magnetic, demonic quality that few could ever forget. Few people could see him without feeling that there was something a little frightening about him. Berlioz describes his first meeting with him, after a performance of the *Symphonie Fantastique* in December 1833:

Liszt caricatured as a superstar (left). His besotted lady fans provided forms of audience participation – clapping, fainting, ogling and showering him with flowers – that contrasted dramatically with the haughty lack of interest of earlier audiences.

. a man waited for me alone in the hall, a man with *ong hair, a keen eye, a strange and ravaged face – a ossessed genius, a colossus among giants, whom I ad never seen, and the first glimpse of whom 'isturbed me deeply . . . it was Paganini!!*

Even the sober Charles Hallé describes the 'striking, we-inspiring, ghost-like figure of Paganini' and how e sat spellbound, 'a shudder running through me *henever his uncanny eyes fell upon me'.

When Paganini took to the stage in his black tailcoat nd began to play, the effect was hypnotic – few could ter give a dispassionate account of his performance. ll were carried away by the frenzied intensity of his laying. People talk of the supernatural, dreamlike uality, how they felt – very little about the erformance. Even the critic of the serious *Leipziger lusikalische Zeitung* was moved to talk about 'a vorld we may have experienced before, but only in *reams*', and about a 'hidden cloven hoof'.

No wonder people began to talk about pacts with ne devil and how some even believed they could see ne devil at his elbow guiding his arm. He seemed to be ne very epitome of Faust, who was then becoming a ult figure through the influence of Goethe's novel and *hristopher Marlowe's play. Faust is the conjuror who persuaded by the devil's agent Mephistopheles to ell his soul to the devil in exchange for power and nowledge. The idea of this devilish talent and the lost oul had tremendous fascination for the Romantics – iszt himself wrote many pieces on the theme. And aganini seemed to be Faust, Mephistopheles and the *)evil all rolled into one.

Of course, for a long while, Paganini did little to ispel these fancies – even the rumours that suggested e had murdered his mistress (or her lover) and that e now used her intestine for his fourth string. It was aluable publicity. And it is in this that Paganini's nfluence lay. It showed the great advantages of

In the days before recording technology, concert tours (and teaching) were a vital source of income for virtuosos. But poor roads, bad publicity, inadequate instruments and unrehearsed accompanists were regular occupational hazards between venues such as Rome (below) and Paris.

publicity, how personality was as important as technical skill for the virtuoso, and, above all, the importance of putting on a show. It is no coincidence that Paganini inspired a merchandizing operation comparable in its scope to some of those of the 20th century – people flocked to buy hats, dresses, perfumes, gloves and walking sticks *à la* Paganini.

Thalberg

When people went to a concert, they expected to see a show, to be excited, or to see a great personality; they rarely went just for the music. Some virtuosos, like the high-minded Clara Schumann, insisted on

Ignaz Moscheles (below) brought a crisp and incisive touch to his own piano-playing, but he found the effects of some other virtuosos, notably Chopin, too showy.

Dreyshock's (above) virtuosic speciality was octaves. When he played in Munich it was said that his octaves – which needed 16 hours of practice a day – could be heard in Paris.

that is astonishing. Everything is so calculated an so polished, and shows such assurance, skill and superlative effects . . . he is unique.

However, Mendelssohn's use of the word 'cal lated' is significant – for that indeed is what approach to music seemed to be. It seems that desp his dazzling technique, he was lacking in poet Chopin wrote a succinct and clever summary Thalberg in 1830:

As for Thalberg, he plays excellently, but he is n my man. Younger than I, pleases the ladies, make pot pourries from La Muette [an opera by Auber], g his soft passages by the pedal, but the hand, takes tenths as easily as I take octaves – has diamond sh studs – does not admire Moscheles.

Nevertheless, for a while, Thalberg seriou rivalled Liszt, and while Liszt was away from Paris w Countess Marie d'Agoult, Thalberg was denting I crown. On his return, Liszt was spoiling for a fig After writing a scathing review in the *Gaze Musicale,* Liszt wrote to George Sand that he h wanted to make a study of Thalberg's complete wor 'so I shut myself in for a whole afternoon to study th conscientiously'. Thalberg could be equally cutti There is a story that Liszt suggested a two-hand concert, to which Thalberg replied, 'No . . . I do r like to be accompanied.'

Finally, the eccentric Princess Belgiojoso manag

giving serious music concerts without a hint of showmanship, but most others not merely succumbed but positively revelled in the 'showbiz' possibilities of the piano virtuoso.

Flamboyance was the order of the day, and each virtuoso struggled to outdo the next in the extravagance of their effects. Rivalry was not merely fierce, but cultivated – it was useful publicity. Audiences loved to think of the idea of two or even more titans of the keyboard battling it out. While Henri Herz was touring the United States at the same time as Leopold de Meyer, they conducted a protracted battle in the columns of local newspapers in long letters addressed 'To the Public'. The incident that provoked it – de Meyer's pianos were left in the concert hall that Herz was due to play in – was remarkably trivial, but they both made the most of the controversy, which the American public thoroughly enjoyed.

One of the more popular events was a showdown between two – or more – colossi of the piano. Of these by far the most eagerly awaited was the battle between Sigismond Thalberg and Liszt.

Thalberg was a completely different character from Liszt and he cultivated the idea of achieving the most spectacular of pianistic effects with the minimum of visible effort. He would sit at the piano virtually motionless while dazzling audiences with a technique that seemed to rival Liszt's. His speciality was a sequence that sounded as if it could not possibly be played with less than three hands – every virtuoso had to have a trick like this. Thalberg's was achieved by playing the melody with his thumbs while accompanying it with arpeggios, both above and below. It was this that gave him his nickname 'Old Arpeggio'.

Of Thalberg's playing, Mendelssohn, who was quite a pianist himself, wrote that it was:

an accumulation of the finest and most exquisite effects, a crescendo of difficulties and embellishments

arrange a play-off between the two giants in her [sa]lon on 31 March, 1837. Everyone who was anyone [in] Paris was there. It was quite an affair. Not only were [Li]szt and Thalberg there to fight it out – so too were [C]hopin, Herz, Czerny (Beethoven's pupil and Liszt's [te]acher) and Pixis, all major virtuosos. When it came [to] the crunch, Thalberg played brilliantly and dazzled [hi]s audience – but there was no contest; Liszt was king.

Spectacular events like this were the order of the [d]ay. When Henri Herz made his first performance in [E]ngland on 2 July 1838, he performed, with other [m]usicians, Czerny's *Concertstücke,* arranged for no [fe]wer than 8 pianos and 12 harps.

[T]he showmen

[H]enri Herz was an elegant pianist but an out and out [s]howman with no pretence. He was probably out to [m]ake money – and this is just what he did. Herz had a [b]eautiful house in Paris, earned four times as much as [a]ny other virtuoso, set up his own piano-makers and [b]uilt a concert hall. He probably toured more than any [o]ther virtuoso, and when he went to the United States, [n]ot untypically, he used a press agent called Bernard [U]llman who once said to Herz:

[I] will take care of the announcements of your [c]oncerts. I will have your programs printed, I will see [t]o it that everything is in order in the hall where you [w]ill give the concert, I will bring you to the attention [o]f the newspapers. The papers are the nerves of [a]rtistic success, just as money is the nerves of war.

Sigismond Thalberg's audiences craned their necks to view his celebrated 'three-handed' effects at the keyboard. Unlike Paganini, however, Thalberg (right) was a polished aristocrat with a smooth and dignified demeanour.

At venues such as the Hanover Square Rooms (below), London's music-lovers enjoyed the virtuoso phenomenon.

Anton Rubinstein (below) was the first great European virtuoso to tour America. Rubinstein's 'Historical Recitals' covering the entire development of keyboard music were legendary.

Silentium

Adagio con sentimento

Passagio chromatico

Fuga del diavolo

Forte vivace

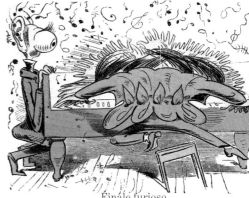

Finale furioso

These caricatures of a virtuoso in action illustrate how the star pianist enslaved his audiences with displays of pianistic 'fireworks'. Indeed, the great virtuosos were sometimes revered more for their agility and versatility as performers in the widest sense of the word, than for the quality of the music produced.

And this is just what Uilman did, organizing ever more spectacular publicity for Herz. One of Ullman's ideas was a concert lighted by 1000 candles, which greatly delighted the public and was an instant success. Another was for a massive event with speeches, giant choirs and a Grand March arranged for 40 pianos – all on an American nationalist theme. In the end, Herz just played the March with 8 pianos, but the event was also a success. The age of publicity and showmanship was here to stay.

Another man out to dazzle – if not deafen – the audience but perhaps little else was Alexander Dreyshock. He must have been quite a pianist, for when he arrived in Paris in 1843, a reviewer began to talk about a new trinity of piano virtuosos with Liszt the Father, Thalberg the son and Dreyshock the Holy Ghost. But Dreyshock was anything but ghostly – his playing was reckoned loud enough to wake the dead. Heine suggested that people in Paris could hear him playing in Munich if the wind was right. He was to Heine a 'god of thunder' whose octave playing was truly spectacular – he was apparently able to play Chopin's *Revolutionary* Etude replacing the left-hand passages – with octaves – an impressive feat.

Dreyshock, like many other virtuosos on the circuit, was giving the public what they wanted. Even Liszt, who could really play poetically when he wanted to, regarded himself as a servant of the public and would give the public what they wanted – bravura display, fantasies on popular operatic themes and pot-pourris of familiar tunes.

Liszt, like so many virtuosos, relied on the strength of his personality to make his impression on the audience. This was not only showmanship, it was musically important as well. As Schumann says, 'If Liszt were to play behind the scenes, a considerable part of the poetry would be lost.'

Liszt himself, like Paganini, deliberately cultivated

the Mephistophelian mystery he seemed to possess it was an important part of his effect. All the majo virtuosos seemed to throw themselves at the pian trying to work themselves and the audience into frenzy of passion. The hysteria of the audience and th intensity of their performance must have sometim taken them over so that for a few moments the played, as they fantasized, 'like men possessed'.

Liszt's influence on the succeeding generation pianists was enormous. Indeed, every buddir virtuoso in Europe wanted to come and learn his cra at the Master's classes in Weimar – among them th brilliant Carl Tausig, reckoned by some to be the mo complete virtuoso of all time. Another was a your Russian who looked like a reincarnation of Beethove Anton Rubinstein. Rubinstein as a boy emulated Liszt dynamic, showy style and travelled to see Liszt in 184 and enrol as a pupil. But for some reason, th perenially generous Liszt told him to 'win the goal his ambition by his own unassisted efforts'. And that precisely what Rubinstein did in a way perhaps nev contemplated by Liszt – the greatest virtuoso of th them all.

Bravo—Bravissimo

Jacques Offenbach
1819–1880

*Of German-Jewish origins, Offenbach – dubbed
'Monsieur 'O' de Cologne' – expressed his own
chirpy zest for life in the witty and typically French
world of operetta which he created.*

One of Jacques Offenbach's first best-selling songs A toi *(the title page of which is shown above) was dedicated to Herminie d'Alcain, the daughter of a Parisian society hostess at whose soirées Offenbach had played. In 1844 he married Herminie and later had four children – (from left to right) Marie, Berthe, Pepita and Jacqueline.*

Offenbach was a small, eccentric-looking man with thin Jewish features, dandy whiskers and pince-nez. He had a birdlike quality about him – a bright chirpy zest for living. He was a witty talker and personally provided the source of much of the humour in his works to his librettists. He was also a compulsive worker, forever pressing his librettists for their material and driving everyone into a fever of activity. All of this was expressed in the liveliest examples of his music. Yet there is more to Offenbach than this exuberant front suggests at first sight. Underneath his lively exterior he was by nature a romantic personality, and woven into his music are characteristically tender and lyrical melodies and songs.

Though of German origin, Offenbach became as French in character as his works, yet he never mastered the French language. His musical ancestry was in the music hall song, the folksong, the opéra comique and possibly in Rossini and Mozart. In fact, it was Rossini who summed him up best and most flatteringly when he called Offenbach 'the Mozart of the Champs Elysées'.

From Germany to France

Offenbach's grandfather, Juda Eberst, a singer and music-teacher had settled in what is now a suburb of Frankfurt – Offenbach-am-Main. Juda's son Isaac inherited his father's musical inclinations, and when he left home at the age of 20 it was to a precarious life as an itinerant singer and violinist. Eventually, in 1802, Isaac settled in Deutz, a suburb of Cologne, finding there fairly regular employment with light orchestras and dance-bands. Given the nickname of 'Der Offenbacher', he adopted the name of Offenbach feeling that it had more of a musical ring to it than Eberst. In 1805 he married a local girl called Marianne Rindskopf and together they managed to

make a living and raise a large family.

There were 10 children in all, and Jakob (later Jacques) born in 1819, was their seventh child. He grew up happily, went to the local school and was taught the violin by his father. It soon became clear that he had exceptional musical talents. By the time he was eight he had started to compose and at nine had chosen the cello as his special instrument. His first teacher was an eccentric Cologne professor, Josef Alexander.

Together with his brother Julius on violin and sister Isabella on piano, he formed a youthful trio and played in the local dance-halls and cafés. Their father acted as manager, and naturally enough anything they earned helped the family finances.

Isaac was determined that his children should be given every opportunity to develop their talents, so he decided to move Jakob to another teacher, Bernhard Breuer (to whom in 1833 Offenbach dedicated his Opus 1). Then, when Offenbach was 14, his father decided to send both sons to Paris to study music. An audition was arranged for them at the famous Paris Conservatoire. The Conservatoire had strict rules forbidding entry to foreign students. However, the director – Luigi Cherubini – was so impressed by Jakob's talents that he agreed to take both of the young Offenbachs as students.

However, Offenbach's interest in music more popular than that offered by the strict curriculum of the Conservatoire was strong, and he found the teaching dull and irksome. The Conservatoire was ideal for students with more serious intentions like

asked to contribute a waltz to their repertoire. Offenbach also returned to the cello, lucratively exploiting his talents as a virtuoso performer in the salons of the nobility. For these occasions he wrote his own music and in January 1839 gave his first public concert. Later that year he was asked to write the incidental music for a comedy *Pascal et Chambord* but the production was a failure and the commission led nowhere. Luckily for the two boys their father visited them in Paris: he advised his sons to take up a plan to travel in Europe as virtuoso performers. But before this the brothers returned to Cologne for a family reunion.

Jacques returned to Paris and Jules took up a post in Bordeaux, but by the end of 1840 they were in Cologne again, this time because of more unfortunate circumstances – their brother had died and their mother was ill. Sadly, she too died while they were there.

Marriage and success

Back in Paris Offenbach fell in love with a charming girl called Herminie. But her parents were keen to see some tangible proof of his suitability as a husband and provider. He therefore organized larger concerts in Paris and introduced more of his own works, including a song that became very popular — *A toi,* (aptly dedicated to Herminie d'Alcain). He arranged tours in France and Germany and then, in 1844, went for the first time to London. Here he took part in concerts at Her Majesty's Theatre and played at Court for Queen Victoria and Prince Albert. He returned from his London success a wealthy young man and was accepted by Herminie's parents as a suitable husband for their daughter. Offenbach and Herminie began what was to be a long and happy marriage on 14 August 1844. Herminie remained at his side throughout, providing a happy family life and

those of Charles Gounod, Offenbach's almost exact contemporary, who became a student there in 1836. He had already obtained his Bachelor of Arts, was a winner of all the prestigious prizes and full of the earnest urge to write masses and grand operas. His first opera, *Sapho,* when it appeared in 1851 was highly praised by Berlioz. Offenbach, however, had no such intentions and dreamed of writing for the theatre.

After only a year's study at the Conservatoire under Cherubini, Jakob departed without distinction, and found himself jobless in the battle-torn city of Paris. His cello skills helped him to one or two temporary jobs and eventually a regular post in the orchestra at the Opéra-Comique. He also continued to study the cello privately under the well-known cello virtuoso Louis Norblin.

The leading opera composer of the day was Fromental Halévy and Offenbach played in the orchestra for several productions of his operas. Offenbach attended the opening of Halévy's masterpiece *La Juive* as the composer's guest. Halévy was impressed by the enthusiastic young man and gave him some lessons in composing and orchestration. Back at l'Opéra-Comique, he was gradually given his head and allowed to write some incidental music. He also did some of the hack work for another up-and-coming young composer Friedrich von Flotow and his opera *Martha.*

In the dance-halls the leading names were those of Musard, Tolbecque and Jullien and the young Offenbach, now known as Jacques, was occasionally

Jacques Offenbach was born on 20 June 1819 in Deutz, a suburb of Cologne (above). His natural musical ability found an early outlet in the trio he formed with his brother Julius and sister Isabella. They played in the local dance-halls and cafés, helping considerably to swell the family finances.

Charles Gounod (right), a French composer and Offenbach's exact contemporary, entered the Paris Conservatoire in 1836, but unlike Offenbach was an exemplary student, winning the **Grand Prix de Rome** *in 1839. The success of his opera* Faust, *first performed in 1859, gave Gounod access to the Opéra, and won him musical respectability.*

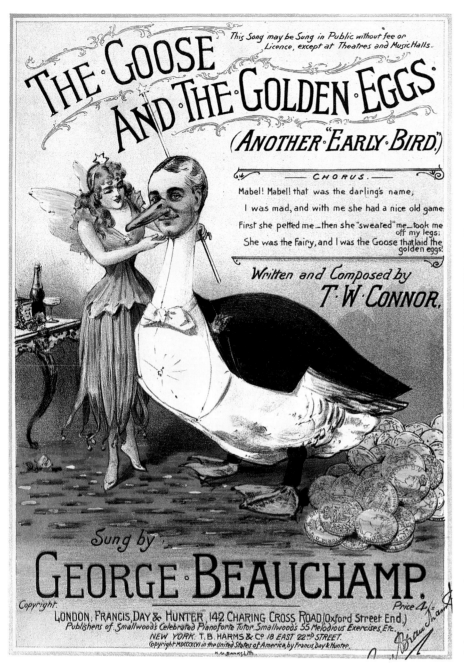

found Cologne itself in revolutionary turmoil. Once the situation in Paris had stabilized Offenbach returned, calling himself Jacques once again, and resumed his crusade to become a writer for the theatre. In 1850 he was offered the job of musical director and conductor at the Comédie Francaise. Here he did much to improve musical standards but tended to quarrel with other members of the company who didn't like the orchestra getting so much attention. However, backed by Arsène Houssaye the director they revitalized the theatre. Although his own compositions found outlet between acts of the main performances his ambition to compose solely for the theatre was continually thwarted.

Working in Paris at the same time was another young operetta composer, Florimond Roger, known by his pen-name of Hervé. Younger than Offenbach, he had solved the problems of finding outlet for his work by founding his own theatre 'Les Folies Nouvelles'. Hervé commissioned a work from Offenbach under the strange title *Oyayaie,* and this had a modest success when produced in June of 1855. Encouraged, Offenbach began to think about founding his own theatre and as it happened that very year proved the turning point for his venture.

Les Bouffes-Parisiens

It was the year of the great Paris International Exhibition and with Paris full of foreign visitors all looking for a good evening's entertainment the time was exactly right for bold new artistic ventures. With a little financial help from his friends, Offenbach took the lease on a very small theatre in the Champs Elysées, called it Les Bouffes-Parisiens and advertised his first production for 5 July 1855. The theatre could only hold an audience of 50 and then only by the use of seats that were so steeply stepped that the audience appeared to be clinging to the rungs of a ladder.

Finding his ambition to compose solely for the established theatre continually thwarted, Offenbach opened a theatre of his own – Les Bouffes-Parisiens. Here he innovated a form of comic opera in which his own sense of humour and brand of music played a central role. An important influence on this came from British music halls which Offenbach visited in London in 1856. The title page (above) of a popular contemporary music hall song gives an idea of the comic nature of these productions.

ignoring his mild flirtations with famous actresses. She was a shadowy but important figure who inspired the tender side of his creations and went on to outlive him by seven years.

The next five or six years saw Offenbach achieve a measure of musical success but as far as his ambitions as a composer went these years proved cruelly frustrating. He was fated to see other composers who had no greater talent than his own becoming more and more famous. When he was commissioned to write operettas there was always something which prevented their production. The final straw came in January 1848 when the revolution of that year stopped the production of an operetta commissioned by Adolphe Adam for the Théâtre-Lyrique.

Offenbach has been criticized for his actions during this period. He left his Paris house, as he was destined to do again later, during the Franco-Prussian war, and fled with his wife and daughter to Cologne where he changed his name back to Jakob and behaved like a good German, particularly as he

The success of Orpheé aux Enfers *in 1858 gave Offenbach instant international fame. The scene above is from the first Vienna production in 1860 with the great Johann Nestroy (winged) as Jupiter.*

La Périchole *(title page above right) was more of a romantic tale and less of a 'normal' Offenbach satire.*

Hortense Schneider, the singer (above), as she appeared in the title role of The Grande-Duchesse of Gerolstein. *Her admirers included many of the royal visitors (right) to the 1867 Paris world exhibition.*

Offenbach became an entrepreneur as well as composer and director of the new theatre. The show was such a success it outlived the Paris Exhibition, which had been one of the reasons for starting it, and Offenbach moved the company to a small theatre in the Passage Choiseul for the winter. This was eventually to become the company's permanent home, and Offenbach spent a great deal of time refurbishing it. Meanwhile, Offenbach gave up his conducting job at the Comédie Francaise and began to concentrate on writing.

The first winter season opened on 29 December 1855 with a substantial and effective work called *Ba-ta-clan,* set in a Chinese province where an ex-Parisian rules. The work was highly amusing – Halévy invented a splendid new 'language' for the plot. Even from these early beginnings the pattern for future Offenbach scores, with a mixture of naively senti-mental waltzes and vivacious can-cans, was clearly discernible. Offenbach was aware that he was creating a new – more national – genre, and therefore playing a part in forming an original style, rather than simply bowing to or borrowing from the established Italian style of opera that was prevalent at the time. He also realised his ambition of reviving the tradition of opéra-comique. In the early days of the Bouffes-Parisiens Offenbach auditioned the young Hortense Schneider. She was an instant success in *Le Violoneux* in August 1855 and during the next 12 years starred in most of Offenbach's major operettas.

In 1856 Offenbach and his directors announced a competition. The prize offered was 1200 francs and a medal for a one-act operetta in the style set by Les Bouffes. The panel of distinguished judges included Auber, Halévy, Thomas, Scribe and Charles Gounod, the latter a respected member of the musical establishment (but who had yet to write his greatest masterpiece, *Faust*). An eliminating test produced six candidates from a field of 18 entrants. They were asked to set to music a libretto called *Le Docteur Miracle* written by Halévy and Leon Battu. The result was a draw between Lecocq and Georges Bizet – two composers set for distinction at a later date.

For the new summer season, Les Bouffes-Parisiens moved back again to the Champs Elysées and continued to thrive. After this it moved back,

From this point dates the beginning of a fruitful collaboration with a young writer called Ludovic Halévy who wrote the words for the entertainment *Entrez, Messieurs, Mesdames,* which opened Les Bouffes on that historic night. The evening's entertainment included a ballet with Rossini's music arranged by Offenbach and two one-act operettas – one of which *Les Deux Aveugles* (The Two Blind Beggars) became Offenbach's first established piece. The two actors who played the beggars on the first night were so hilariously funny that it made them, the operetta and Les Bouffes-Parisiens famous overnight. Parisiens and foreign visitors heard of this diverting new venue and the demand for the limited number of seats was huge.

permanently, to the theatre in the Passage Choiseul.

In London in 1857 he was welcomed back as conductor and composer rather than as the virtuoso cellist he had been on his first visit. The season was organized by a relative of Offenbach's parents-in-law, John Mitchell, and the season was so successful that Offenbach sent for the rest of the company in order to extend it further.

Wealth and fame

Back home in Paris the family finances were in such a good state that they were able to move to a very respectable house in the Rue Lafitte, near the Rothschilds. This house became the hectic musical centre with Friday evening parties attended by Bizet, Delibes and Gustave Doré.

Offenbach's lavish hospitality at home and the generous amount of money he spent on his theatre, always keeping it spick and span, put pressure on him to produce new and greater productions. So in 1858

Offenbach's rather eccentric appearance was caricatured to great effect by cartoonists of the day. In the cartoon by Gill (below) – drawn for the cover of a satirical magazine – he is shown astride his cello, surrounded by characters from his operettas.

The Villa Orphée (above), the holiday home built for the family in Normandy, was paid for from the proceeds of Orphée aux Enfers.

he embarked on his first substantial show. The archaic licencing laws which had only allowed him a small cast of four were lifted and the way was open for as lavish a production as the small theatre would allow. The amusing account of the frantic behind-the-scenes activity at Les Bouffes Parisien in the Paris magazine, *Journal Amusant,* gives us a glimpse into the chaotic way Offenbach and his company worked. This describes the general scene of the first day of production of *Orphée aux Enfers* (Orpheus in the Underworld) where there were actors demanding new costumes, friends asking for free seats, a shortage of musicians, the bailiffs arriving and having to be pacified, a burst gas main, and a list of cuts from the censor.

Orphée was a hard-hitting lampoon, on one level of a classical story, on another, of classical music. Many critics were deeply offended at Offenbach's irreverent use of Gluck's works, but most found it a sharp satire which they secretly enjoyed but publicly deplored as bad taste. People were a little dubious about being seen there and business was slow. Possibly the show would have won through on its own eventually because of its splendid music but matters were brought to a head by an all-out attack launched by a prominent critic, Jules Janin, who was deeply shocked and found it 'a profanation of holy and glorious antiquity'. This, however, proved to be its making – the very suggestion of something shocking did the trick. The demand for seats grew overwhelmingly and it seemed that all Paris wanted to see and talk about *Orphée.* Above all the new brand of music that Offenbach had to offer was now able to show itself to the full and his works found their way abroad where they influenced composers in Vienna, London and New York.

In 1860 the Bouffes Parisien was accorded the honour of an entry in small book in a series of guides to the Paris theatres – a signal of acceptance. At last

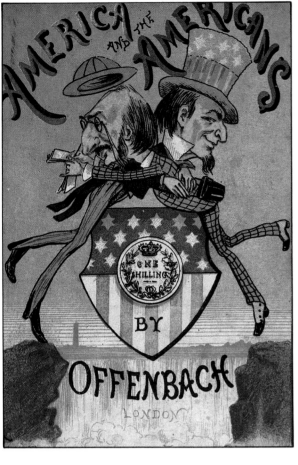

In 1876, due to a variety of circumstances, Offenbach found himself in financial difficulties. Consequently, although he was in poor health, he was tempted by the offer of $30,000 to conduct a concert tour of America. The tour, celebrating the Centenary of the Declaration of Independence, was a great success. On his return to France Offenbach wrote an account of his journey, Orpheus in America. *The English edition of 1876 (cover, left) was entitled* America and the Americans.

related to his intake of good food and wine.

The theatre housing Les Bouffes Parisiens was rebuilt to accommodate larger audiences and in 1864 it saw a triumph in the same league as *Orphée – La Belle Hélène*. Although *La Belle Hélène* attracted large audiences, the critics felt it was another desecration of antiquity. Nevertheless, the ensuing years were fruitful – *Barbe-Bleue* (Bluebeard) appeared in 1866, followed by the most scintillating of all his works *La Vie Parisienne* which evokes the sophisticated spirit of the Paris which everyone imagines. Next, and coinciding with the great Paris World Exhibition of 1867, came the greatest international success – *La Grande-Duchesse de Gérolstein*. Hortense Schneider was so supreme in this role that she acted her part of the Grande-Duchesse off-stage as well as on-stage.

The last years

There were a few halting steps in Offenbach's success though. *La Périchole,* for example, his most romantic operetta, was not quite scandalous enough to be a major success despite containing one of Offenbach's finest arias, the famous Letter Song, which Hortense Schneider put over with artful simplicity. And the Franco-Prussian war appears to have cut the flow of his inspiration in 1870 and for most of 1871, but by now his operettas were flourishing abroad. *The Princess of Trebizonde* opened in London in 1870 and Offenbach went over to see the production.

Offenbach retreated from Paris as the Republic was declared and his work, denounced as 'Prussian' because of his German origins, immediately went out of favour. Lecocq, a jealous rival, declared that the reign of Offenbach was no more popular abroad than in his own country. In response Offenbach re-wrote many of his operettas for the Théâtre de la Gâité, but they were often over-inflated and not so popular. He suffered some financial losses with this series of works and was forced into bankruptcy. With his fortunes so low, Offenbach felt obliged to restore them by accepting with reluctance (for he was unwell) an invitation to visit America for the World Exhibition in Philadelphia. The Americans obviously expected a wicked Parisian figure who would dance the can-can on the platform. Instead he cut a small, forlorn and rather serious figure, homesick for his family and France. His concerts in Philadelphia were well-attended, and his music became established in America.

Back in France, Offenbach continued to write – *Madame Favart* produced in 1878 was a pleasant *succès d'estime* at l'Opéra-Comique, the old fortress he had so often tried to storm. From 1877 onwards Offenbach had been obsessed with a desire to write a Grand Opera and as his theme settled on some of the fantastic *Tales of Hoffman*. On this work, thin and tired, he toiled away in what was to be his last year of life. Sadly there were endless delays in the progress of the production of this, but in the meantime he managed one more first-rate operetta – *La Fille du Tamobur Major*. Finally, in September 1880, he was able to attend a rehearsal of 'The Tales' and in October he played the score through to the cast.

The next day he had a choking fit and lapsed into recurrent bouts of unconsciousness. On the morning of 5 October 1880 he died of gout of the heart. An old comedian friend called to see him and was told by Monsieur Leonce, the porter: 'Monsieur Offenbach died without knowing it.' 'He will be surprised when he finds out!'

Offenbach's work reached l'Opéra – a ballet, *Le Papillon* choreographed by the great Taglioni and featuring a new star Emma Livry. It was an enormous success at the time and although the ballet unaccountably disappeared from the repertoire, until revived in modern times, its main tune, the 'Valse de Rayons' lived on as one of Offenbach's best known melodies. By 1862 the bad health that was to plague Offenbach's later years began to show itself. Some of the symptoms were due to overwork but the severe attacks of gout he suffered were directly

Offenbach's lasting contribution to French popular music of the 19th century was his restoration of the Gallic traditions of wit and vivacity in the Opéra-Comique (below), when it was in danger of being swamped by Italian influences.

The siege of Paris
and the Franco-Prussian War 1870–71

With the strains of Offenbach's music still ringing in the streets, Paris prepared for battle with Prussia. Offenbach escaped, but Parisians went on through the bloodiest phase in their history.

The two main protagonists in the Franco-Prussian War of 1870–1871, Otto von Bismarck (above) and Napoleon III (above right). Napoleon's vainglorious notion of stemming the growing might of Prussia led the French, and Parisians in particular, into dark days of defeat and civil strife.

When France took the decision to go to war against Prussia on 19 July 1870, an easy victory was confidently expected. Within one week such illusions were shattered as early defeats left France's northern provinces of Alsace and Lorraine open to invasion. In declaring war, France had unleashed a catastrophic train of events which in less than a year would swell the pages of history. Between July 1870 and May 1871 France saw the end of the Second Empire, the establishment of a republic and a humiliating military defeat. She suffered a Draconian peace settlement and a seige of her capital on two occasions: first by Prussian troops and secondly, following the outbreak of civil war, by troops of the new French Republic. The two seiges make interesting comparison: the defence of the city against

Prussia was a heroic but futile struggle, while the second was a tragic episode. Of the second seige, *The Times* wrote, 'The French are filling up the darkest page in the book of their or the World's history.'

The road to war
Just as the groundswell of nationalism in Italy in the 1850s saw the creation of a united state, so the 1860s witnessed the rapid development of German national feeling. The decade was punctuated by wars of unification fought against Denmark and Austria. Following victory in this latter conflict, the growing strength of Prussia presented a serious challenge to the European balance of power and to French security. Gripped by an outburst of patriotism, French public opinion feared that Bismarck (the

Prussian Chancellor) would unite Germany by merging the Bavarian states into the Prussian dominated North German Confederation. Many felt that to allow this would be an irrevocable abdication of France's greatness. The feeling grew that war between France and Prussia was inevitable: this fatalism precipitated events in 1870.

Since the end of the Austro-Prussian war, the ailing French Emperor, Napoleon III, had sought in vain for an ally against the growing might of Prussia. He had also lost much support at home for failing to obtain territorial compensation for French acceptance of Prussia's victory. His failing powers and lack of diplomatic acumen were to let him down again as France slipped over the precipice into a costly war sparked by a minor diplomatic incident.

French ministerial and public opinion was infuriated when the Prussian royal family, the

abridged version of the telegram to the press in the hope of provoking France into an ill-considered response. Bismarck's version suggested an acrimonious exchange had taken place between William and Benedetti. Outraged French public opinion demanded war. By prolonging the affair the French had played into the hand of Bismarck, who had succeeded in goading France into a war which he calculated would enable him to put the finishing touches to German unification. But the responsibilty for war was not all Bismarck's. French ministers did nothing to pacify public opinion and there was plainly a lack of calm and balance on their part. They had made a false move in pressing for a guarantee and feared to draw back, being swept along by a floodtide of partisan sentiment.

Preparations for siege

Despite her optimism, France was in no state to fight a major war. She could only muster a force of 250,000, she underestimated the power of the Prussian army and failed to appreciate the importance of artillery. The French forces were outmanoeuvred by the better-commanded Prussians. Paris was stunned by this string of early setbacks, especially as rumours had been rife that the army of the Crown Prince of Prussia had been captured. (The rumour had started in a successful attempt to rig the Stock Exchange.) Reluctantly, the city prepared for siege as the

The Ems Telegram (left) which sparked the conflict. The original was sent by Kaiser William I of Prussia to his Chancellor, Bismarck, informing him of a diplomatic exchange between himself and the French Ambassador to Berlin, Benedetti.

Hohenzollerns, nominated a candidate for the vacant Spanish throne. France regarded Spain as her own sphere of influence and was appalled by the prospect of Leopold von Hohenzollern ruling Spain. Benedetti, the French ambassador to Berlin, however, success-fully persuaded Kaiser William I to withdraw the nomination. (The idea had been Bismarck's, and William was not enthusiastic about it.) But instead of accepting William's word, the French were driven on by bellicose opinion at home and disastrously overplayed their hand. They demanded a formal guarantee that the candidacy would never again be renewed. William refused and, from the holiday spa of Ems, sent a telegram to Bismarck informing him of his intentions. On receiving the communication, Bismarck took the initiative – he released an

prospect was hard to grasp. Paris saw itself as the centre of civilization – the cosmopolitan capital of the world. As recently as 1867, the city played host to hundreds of thousands of visitors who flocked to the city to visit the Universal Exhibition, to admire the marvellous boulevards of Baron Haussmann, and to watch Napoleon III's splendid military parade in the Bois de Boulogne. Entertainers and whores flocked to the Exhibition – Paris was not only the centre of culture, but of fun as well. Opera and ballet flourished. Visitors were regaled with the music of Offenbach, and Strauss – never one to miss an occasion – contributed a new waltz, *The Blue Danube*. What a contrast, then, in that September as over 3000 heavy cannon were brought to the city, transforming Paris from a city of pleasure to a

Paris prepares for siege (above) in the early days of the war, transforming itself from a city of pleasure, gaiety and music into a massive fortress. Here, troops are shown encamped in the gardens of the Tuileries.

The war went badly for France from the start and the French army soon found itself besieged at Metz. In her capacity as Regent, Napoleon's wife, Empress Eugenie (right), ordered the last remaining strong force, under General MacMahon, to relieve the army trapped at Metz. Her decision was disastrous, as the ensuing Battle of Sedan proved.

Empress Eugenie, however, feared for her husband's life. With the authority of Regent, she instructed MacMahon to relieve the French army besieged at Metz. The decision was foolhardy – she had sent MacMahon, her husband and an army of 84,000 to their capture, at the ensuing Battle of Sedan. No disaster in French history was more complete or humiliating.

Political consequences soon followed: in a bloodless coup on 4 September, the Second French Empire was overthrown. The Empress fled to London, to be joined by Napoleon the following year. The Emperor died in 1873, a broken man.

The siege begins

Soon after Sedan the Prussians arrived outside the gates of Paris – the first siege was about to begin. Despite the increasing hopelessness of the military situation, nationalistic pride, together with enthusiasm at the prospect of establishing a radical republic, made Parisians eager to continue the fight. Parallels were drawn with a similar situation during the great French Revolution when, faced with an invading foreign army, France was saved by her people. Though the new Government of National Defence consisted mainly of conservatives, uncertain about carrying the fight to Prussia, it was driven on by ardent Republicans, such as Gambetta and Rochefort who dreamt of a *levee en masse* (conscription) which would stem the tide. The Prussians, however, were similarly determined. Bismarck felt that victory with substantial territorial gains would make German unity irresistible. There could be no compromise – it was 'war to the knife'.

Only a fortnight into the siege the food supply was seen to be dwindling. Although the only problem for the wealthy was whether their diet had been adulterated with horse flesh, the poor found meat difficult to find at all. Butchers refused to sell at prices fixed by the government, which provoked violent scenes. People began queueing (a new word, first coined at the time) at 2am in the hope of getting provisions. Bread was still plentiful, but eggs, vegetables and fish were scarce and greatly overpriced.

massive fortress. A quarter of a million sheep were brought into the Luxembourg Gardens, and 40,000 oxen put out to grass inside the city walls. But the authorities did not expect the siege to last into winter. Stocks of flour and coal were insufficient, and so too was the provision of dairy stock.

The war continued to go badly for France. By late August the largest French force of 173,000 under General Bazaine was pinned down at the northern town of Metz. The only notable army remaining was at Chalon under the command of MacMahon. This catalogue of defeats left the feeling in Paris that the end of Napoleon's Empire was nigh. The Governor of Paris, General Trochu, insisted that Napoleon – fighting alongside MacMahon – return to Paris. The

In the catalogue of disasters and defeats that make up the pages of French history in the war, the Battle of Sedan (right) ranks as the most catastrophic. Napoleon, along with General MacMahon and an army of 84,000, suffered humiliating defeat and capture. Meanwhile, in Paris, a coup overthrew Napoleon's Second French Empire, and later he and Eugenie escaped to London. Napoleon, a broken man, died soon after.

With the Prussian blockade complete, Paris's only means of communication with the rest of France was by balloon or carrier pigeons. The birds carried microfilm, used to practical effect for the first time. Gambetta made several sorties by balloon in the hope of organizing resistance and a provincial army to come to the relief of Paris. Meanwhile, Parisians launched great public subscriptions to pay for more arms. Victor Hugo, now returned from exile, donated the entire proceeds from his first magazine to the national cannon fund. These new weapons, though, could not assist the French forces outside the city. An aurora borealis which lighted the night

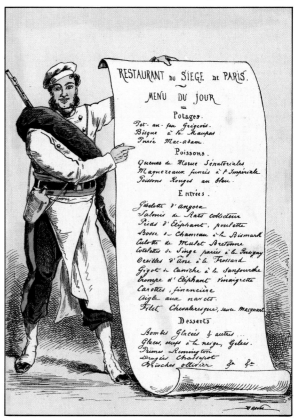

Soon after Sedan the siege of Paris began in earnest. Despite preparations food supplies quickly ran desperately short. Butchers' shops were filled with strange meats, for those that could afford it (above); restaurants offered the most 'exotic' of dishes – elephant trunk vinaigrette, donkey, and angora giblets (above right); and the poor were reduced to raiding the drains in the hope of catching a rat or two (right).

sky in late October turned out to be a harbinger of bad luck – news arrived the next day that Metz had fallen. Still the Parisians demanded *'une resistance à outrance'* (war to the end), in the hope that Gambetta's efforts to raise an army would be fruitful. Initially their perseverence seemed rewarded; news arrived by carrier pigeon that the Army of the Loire had relieved the town of Orleans, defeating the Prussians at the Battle of Couloniers. Paris was ecstatic and talk grew of breaking out of the city to link up with the Army of the Loire. Indeed, the only alternative to breaking out, since Parisians were not prepared to surrender, was starvation.

Provisions grew scarcer by the day. In November the daily mutton and beef ration was reduced to 35 gms (1/6 oz) for an adult, and half that for children. 40,000 horses had already been earmarked for slaughter. Cats were displayed in butchers' shops with coloured ribbons and paper frills and described as 'gutter rabbits'. Seasoned and boiled, they were said to be quite tasty. Visitors to the sick were commended to take a dead cat as a welcome alternative to flowers! Outside the famous Hotel de Ville there was even a rat market.

Driving through the Prussian lines, then, seemed

Pioneered by Frenchmen some years earlier, ballooning (right) proved the only means, other than carrier pigeon, for Parisians to communicate with the outside world during the siege. Here, Gambetta makes a night-time sortie to organize a resistance movement and the formation of a provincial army to come to the relief of Paris.

In a divided atmosphere charged with bitterness and emotion, Paris surrendered and the government collapsed. To make matters worse the Prussians were permitted by the newly elected Assembly to hold a victory march along the Champs Elysées (right).

the only course of action. Gunfire on the night of November 27 announced the attack, but any hope of catching the Prussians off-guard was dashed. French forces reeled under the weight of a massive dawn counter-attack. The battle raged for six days with casualties high amongst the French National Guard. In Paris people waited in the grip of breathless anticipation: great crowds gathered along the Avenue du Trone, but when at last the news came, it was shocking – 12,000 were lost. Ironically news reached Paris just as the orchestra at the opera struck up the triumphal march of Wagner's *Tannhauser*. Three days later the depression was complete: dismayed faces bent over newspapers in Paris which announced the defeat of the Army of the Loire and the recapture of Orleans.

And still Paris refused to surrender. Food shortages forced people to supplement their diets: 'The consumption of dogs, cats and rats is considerable,' wrote one newspaper. Some restaurants offered their clientele more exotic fare. Zebra, buffalo, yak, camel and elephants found their way on to menus thanks to the entrepreneurial spirit of the director of the Jardin d'Acclimatation. Though food was scarce, there was plenty of wine. Many took to drink hoping to conquer hunger and banish care. The end of December ushered in a new ally to the Prussian cause: the cold. The last week of 1870 was the coldest in living memory with temperatures falling to −12°C. The trees which lined the splendid Bois de Boulogne and Bois de Vincennes were felled when supplies of coal expired. Firewood was rationed to 75 kg a week – not enough to heat a room for a single day during such a bitter winter. Firewood depots were raided by Parisians, while in the Elysée district, telegraph poles were felled. As an act of charity, the Rothschilds supplied the poor with clothes for

48,000 children, but even this was not enough. Some newspapers hit upon novel sales gimmicks, claiming they could be worn as an undershirt which 'could be worn for a consecutive month without ceasing to be comfortable.'

As the odds stacked higher against Paris, the Prussians played a new card: artillery bombardment. During the first week of 1871, 25,000 shells fell on the city yet casualties were fairly light. But the real ace in the Prussian pack was simply to wait. To add to the miseries of cold and malnutrition came their inevitable concomitant: disease. The siege had forced the people to take drinking water from the polluted River Seine. An epidemic of smallpox and typhoid spread rapidly in the poorer districts to add to the many victims of pneumonia. Mortality was greatest among infants and the elderly.

Breaking point had been reached. The population again clamoured for military action against the Prussians. The military knew such a venture had no hope, but the generals callously felt that national honour would be well served by a last great attack. Indeed, this was what Paris wanted. As the Governor of the city, Trochu, put it, 'Paris must die on her feet.' Coldly and dispassionately, preparations were made for the futile, bloody slaughter of Buzenval Park, launched on January 19. That morning Paris awoke to a new decree ordaining the rationing of bread, but announcing the fresh attack:

'Those of us who can offer their lives on the battlefield will march against the enemy. Those who remain will submit to the bitterest sacrifices.

Prussian soldiers were entertained in the homes of the Paris bourgeoisie (right) and the government was accused of capitulation with the enemy. This further exacerbated the already divided opinion between the new Assembly and those Parisians who wanted the republic to take a stronger line.

Let us suffer, let us die if necessary. Vive la Republique!'

The attack was doomed from the outset as heavy rains turned roads and fields into swamps. Confusion reigned among the French troops which resulted in the accidental shooting of Trochu's escort by his own men. The gloom into which Paris was cast by the appalling debacle was deepened by the news that the last remaining provincial army of General Chanzy had been defeated at Le Mans.

These defeats, and the belief that after four months of siege Parisians would not oppose them, convinced the Government and Army that capitulation was inevitable. Rumours of surrender led hoarding shopkeepers to bring out the last of their hidden provisions, but only the rich could afford them. Cases were reported of people dropping dead in queues outside foodshops. Mortality among children was appalling. One observer wrote, 'At every step you meet an undertaker carrying a little deal coffin.' There were no longer any horses left to transport the dead to their burials, all had been eaten.

Defeat and surrender

The Government decided to seek an armistice. Their representative, Jules Favre, met Bismarck at Versailles. After negotiating an armistice, Favre, with the pride of his defeated capital in mind, told Bismarck that any attempt to disarm the National Guard would be resisted. The German Chancellor uttered this prophetic warning: 'You are making a blunder. There will be heavy reckoning, leaving rifles in the hands of fanatics.' The two sides agreed the bombardment and counter-bombardment cease at midnight on January 26. Bismarck agreed that Paris be allowed the last defiant shot.

The despised Thiers (left), the head of the new Assembly based at the old monarchist seat of Versailles, frustrated the hope held by many Parisians that a new radical republic would emerge from their defeat and the fall of the Second Empire.

After the fall of Paris, the Prussians offered the French Government a 21 day armistice on condition that a new National Assembly be formally elected on 8 February. Feeling inside Paris was passionately divided. In the election a violent campaign was organized against the 'men of the capitulation', the Government of National Defence. Workers and Extremists were elected along with Republicans. Out of 43 deputies returned, all but 6 were in favour of continuing the war. The result indicated the highly charged emotional state in the capital. Yet the elections in the provinces were overwhelmingly in favour of peace. Not for the first time in French history, the will of the capital and that of the provinces stood out in sharp relief.

The new Assembly on balance was essentially a monarchist, conservative and provincial affair. It was headed by the 73 year old Thiers, a man whom Parisians hated. As Minister for the Interior in 1848, he had been held responsible for the massacre of Rue Transnovian, when Paris workers had been gunned down by government troops. His appointment rubbed salt into the open wounds of Paris. A series of acts by the new Assembly soon caused the city's latent tendency to insurrection to flare up in exasperation. To begin with, the new government chose to meet at Versailles, the old Bourbon (royalist) centre of government. Paris felt that the hope of a radical Republican administration had been frustrated. To make matters worse, Thiers permitted the Prussians a victory march along the Champs Elysées, and allowed the new German Empire to be declared in the Hall of Mirrors at the Palace of Versailles. Since the suppression of the workers' revolt of 1848 in Paris, many workers had harboured a deep class hatred of the bourgeoisie in general, and of their politician in particular. Adolphe Thiers failed to

defuse the time-bomb in Paris – a volatile situation had been exacerbated by the arrival of 40,000 evacuees in the wake of the Prussian advance. Many prosperous Parisians (including Offenbach) had left before the siege, making Paris more a city of the poor than it had ever been. The final straw came when Thiers announced that all rent arrears built up during the siege be paid in full, and that the National Guard, who had heroically defended the city, would no longer be paid. Many guards relied up on their 1.50 francs a day for basic subsistence. When the government demanded that 200 guns, which had been paid for by public subscription and hidden from the Prussians, be handed over, the National Guard refused. As Bismarck had foretold, Thiers had committed the cardinal blunder of depriving the guards of their pay without having first disarmed them. When two generals of the National Assembly were seized by rioters at Montmartre and hanged, matters quickly got out of hand. The new government felt that revolutionary elements were in control of Paris, threatening to deny their authority while the Prussians looked on.

The Paris Commune

Thiers withdrew, leaving a vacuum filled by the Commune of Paris, which took its name from the Jacobin dominated assembly of 1793. While the governments of the day and many writers subsequently regarded the Commune as inspired by organized left-wing groups, it was rather a populist uprising – a manifestation of outraged patriots, and of general exasperation. The name served as a common

rallying point for many disparate groups. If it had one central motive force, it was the manifestation of the living tradition of radical Republicanism. There was thus civil war, and Paris was shortly to undergo its second siege within 6 months – this time by the new French government.

The second battle for Paris began on Palm Sunday, when a government army captured and executed five Communards. The Commune responded by launching a disorganized assault on Versailles which ended in the loss of 1000 prisoners. At this stage the government side had fewer guns and men than the Commune, but Paris failed to press home the advantage. The population, weakened by the first siege were intoxicated by the suddenness with which freedom had come. They could be neither effectively mobilized nor governed. Soldiers turned up for duty much as they pleased while citizens obeyed instructions only when it suited them. Parisians were forever debating, petitioning and celebrating. Lenin later described the Commune as 'a festival of the oppressed'. Theatres and opera went on much as usual, and life went on with far less disruption than during the Prussian siege. Communal legislation was generally moderate. No attempt was made to seize the Bank of France, and private property was not confiscated. The 'Law of hostages' provided for the arrest of those thought to be pro-Assembly, but fighting during the first few weeks was sporadic with relatively few casualties.

The Communards clearly failed to press home their initial advantage. The strength of the Versailles forces grew steadily, while Parisians indulged in the

jubilant destruction of the symbols of the old regime. Such acts as the destruction of the Vendôme column, bearing a statue of Lousi XIV, were no substitute for the effective defence of a city surrounded by enemy troops. On 8 May, the bombardment of Paris began afresh. The forts to the south of the city fell one by one. On 21 May, a large section of the city wall was found unguarded, and by nightfall the Versailles army had men inside Paris.

Delescluze, the veteran Jacobin radical of 1848, proclaimed a war of the people, not commanded by officers and discipline, but by the people – rifle in

As Thiers did nothing to defuse the tension between the Assembly and its opponents, the latter set up their own counter-assembly – the Paris Commune (bottom). This was the signal for civil war. To quell the rebels, the Assembly's troops attacked those of the Commune's in the streets of Paris itself (left) – the second siege of Paris was on. As the Versailles troops gained the upper hand, forcing the Communards ever further back behind their barricades, and closed in for the kill, terrible reprisals began. Communards were slaughtered or shot in their thousands by execution squads (below left) until there was no resistance left.

Thiers (shown above as the butcher of the Commune) had won a sordid victory in taming Paris. Never again did Paris alone decide the fate of France.

Put to fire and the sword by fellow Frenchmen as well as by Prussia, Paris (represented in the cartoon below) ended 1871 on her knees, defeated and broken by the dogs of war.

hand, cobblestone underfoot, and behind the barricades. Only when all was lost did the Commune resolve to fight seriously. Faith in street fighting was unreal. It needed much better organization than a siege operation. Once inside Paris, the Versailles troops, hidden behind buildings and 110,000 strong could only be countered by a planned, watertight defence. Barricades were easily by-passed in the labyrinthine streets.

Bloody week had begun. What was to follow, after the gaiety and lightheartedness of the liberation, was like some appalling fatal accident at the end of a school trip to the seaside. The Versailles troops shot all hostages and generally fought with greater barbarity than the Communards. To the horrors of hand-to-hand fighting was added fire, incendiary shells from the Versailles troops, and the burning of buildings by the Communards to clear lines of fire. The beautiful Tuileries Palace was fired by the rebels as a final act of defiance.

The final few days degenerated into uncoordinated acts of heroism or barbarity. Delescluze, in the dress of a deputy of 1848, top hat, frock coat, girt with his tricolour sash, all being lost, bade his comrades goodbye, and walked quietly down an enfiladed street. In a final act of desperation, he climbed the barricade at the end, stood there a second, then fell forward, shot dead. The novelist, Emile Zola, spoke in horror of 'heaps of bodies piled under bridges – a mass of human flesh dumped at random with heads and limbs jumbled in gross dismemberment.' The last battle took place in the cemetary of Pere-Lachaise, and there on the next day, against a wall that was later to become another shrine of bloody memory in which Paris is too rich, 147 men were shot. Valin, leader of the Commune, was executed after a farcical court marshal. By any standards, the ferocity of retribution is hard to comprehend, let alone condone. As *The Times* of 29 May put it:

The laws of war are mild compared to the inhuman laws of revenge under which the Versailles troops have been bayonetting and ripping up prisoners, women and children. So far as we can recollect, there has been nothing like it in history.

About 20,000 perished in the second seige – more than during the Reign of Terror. Casualties on the government side were light – about 1000. Doubtful of the enduring loyalty of their troops, their leaders moved cautiously, keeping casualties low and morale high. Soldiers were manoeuvred into positions where obedience was the easiest and least dangerous course of action.

Thiers had won a sordid victory. He had tamed Paris. Never again did it decide the fate of the rest of France. The respectable world rejoiced. The fine ladies of Versailles, who had seen Paris burning from the terraces of the palace screamed for more blood. The execution squads were busy. Blood was on the grass like dew. The illusions conjured by the events of Paris's history – 1789–1792 and 1848 – had drawn the people into the most merciless and bloodiest of its defeats. Napoleon III's empire had ended with Paris besieged and France defeated at the hands of the Prussians. But to France's eternal shame, it was an assembly of French monarchists, under a conservative republican head, that first provoked and then put to fire and sword the people of Paris in the bloodbath of May 1871.

Johann Strauss II

1825–1899

Almost all the Strauss family played a part in making Vienna the home of the waltz, but it was Johann Strauss II who was destined to be remembered as the 'Waltz King'.

The child who was destined to eclipse his famous father, Johann Strauss senior, as 'waltz king' was born in Vienna on 25 October 1825. Named after his father and nicknamed 'Schani', he was the eldest of the five surviving children of his parent's marriage. His mother, Anna Strauss, was a woman of strong character and exceptional capabilities, which were later put to the test when her wayward husband departed from the family home to live with his mistress Emilie Trampusch.

Family life

Although there must have been tensions between their parents, there is no record that the young Strausses had unhappy childhoods. Their father was not ideally suited to family life – he was happiest as the dashing public figure of music-maker and conductor. Also, he spent much time away from Vienna and the family, establishing his own reputation and that of his orchestra, abroad.

The family moved twice during Johann's childhood, eventually settling in a large communal house in Vienna, the Hirschenhaus, where they occupied two sets of rooms. To escape from the noise of children, Johann Strauss senior had his own rooms, where he worked and which were often filled with musicians rehearsing his latest compositions.

Summers were spent with the children's maternal grandmother in the suburb of Salmannsdorf. During one of these holidays when he was six Johann composed his first waltz tune, which his mother wrote down and called *Erste Gedanke* (First Thoughts).

The three Strauss sons – Johann, Josef and Eduard – all displayed musical talent early in their lives but their father would not hear of them becoming professional musicians. He probably wanted his sons to follow more professional and conventional careers than his own. Although he allowed them to learn the piano he actively discouraged them from any other musical pursuits. Their mother, on the other hand, was greatly encouraging and supportive of their ambitions.

Johann Strauss the younger, ever since he could remember, had wanted to play music just like his father. With his mother's backing Johann began to take lessons in secret from his father's first violinist Franz Amon.

After he turned 11 Johann was sent to the Schottengymnasium, one of Vienna's best secondary schools, which he attended for four years. His father had plans that Johann would enter a banking career, so after the Schottengymnasium he studied at the commercial department of the Polytechnikum.

When his father left the family home and moved in with his mistress, it was clear to Johann that he would probably have to work to support his mother and brothers and sisters. Abandoning the proposed career in banking, he wrote to tell his father that he felt it his duty to support his mother, and that this meant following in his footsteps to become a dance musician.

He resumed his violin studies in earnest and in the open, with the ballet master of the opera, Johann

Anton Kohlmann. He studied theory with a composer of church music, Joseph Drechsler, who naturally enough tried to influence him to become a composer of less secular music.

In the late summer of 1844 Johann felt confident enough to begin his musical career in public and applied to the Vienna magistrate for a licence 'to perform dance music, opera selections and concert pieces, depending on the demands'. He received his licence early in September 1844, formed an orchestra of 24 musicians and then set about finding a venue for his first performance.

Début at Dommayer's

Most of the proprietors of Viennese dance and music establishments had been warned by Strauss senior that they would incur his wrath if they allowed his son to perform in what he liked to think of as his sole preserve. However, with the help of his mother, Johann's début took place at the fashionable and prestigious venue, Dommayer's Casino, in the smart suburb of Hietzing.

Before the performance began most of those present had taken sides – either for father or for the son – but by the end of the evening the audience was completely won over and the Casino reverberated with calls for repeats. Overnight the son became the

Frau Anna Strauss (left) gave her son Johann Strauss II the backing and encouragement he needed to become a professional musician. His estranged father (above, left, shown with his musical contemporary Josef Lanner) did not want his sons – Josef, Johann and Eduard (below, right) to follow him in musical careers. Despite this, all three became closely involved in music-making which was part and parcel of sophisticated society life in 19th-century Vienna (above, centre).

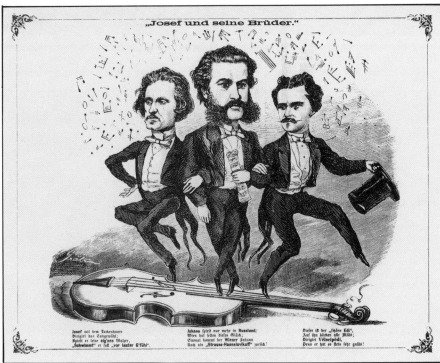

„Josef und seine Brüder."

only serious rival to his father and for several years their already strained relationship was to be made more difficult by Johann's success. Sometime later, after a reconciliation of sorts Strauss senior, still unhappy that his son was a competitor, asked him to join his orchestra. Young Johann decided against this, mainly in the interests of his mother with whose help and encouragement he had succeeded in his ambitions, and with whose support he had been able to follow his own path.

Despite his initial success, Johann did not find it easy to support himself and the family in Vienna, so he took his orchestra on tour to the outposts of the Hapsburg empire, thereby laying the foundations of his future widespread popularity. The revolution of 1848 added a political colouring to the conflict within the family. Although neither father nor son adhered to any serious political persuasion, it was perhaps natural that the elder man should accept the established order, while the younger sympathized with the rebels and students, many of whom were his own staunch supporters and friends. Schani's part in the revolution did not go far beyond the composition of a *Revolutions-marsch,* although he was arrested by the Police for performing *La Marseillaise* in public! The revolution was quickly put down and the young Emperor Franz Joseph ascended the

Johann Strauss II made his musical début on 15 October 1844 at the fashionable and favourite haunt of many Viennese, Dommayer's Casino (right), in the smart suburb of Hietzing. Overnight he became the only serious rival to his father.

throne. Vienna began to settle down to a comparatively peaceful life-style.

Early in 1849 Strauss senior set off on yet another successful and tiring tour abroad. He returned to Vienna in July 1849 and was soon giving concerts with his usual untiring verve to admiring Viennese audiences. In September he conducted the première of the *Jellachich March* at a concert lasting four hours, which left him exhausted and suffering with a fever. Despite feeling unwell he continued working but a few days later was overcome by the illness. Scarlet fever was diagnosed – he had been infected by the youngest daughter of his mistress Emilie. The child had returned from school ill and had sought comfort from her father, thereby inadvertently infecting him.

Complications set in and on 25 September 1849 Strauss senior died. His mistress disappeared with children, animals and all the goods she could carry away with her, leaving Strauss's corpse naked and untended in a bare room. Anna Strauss and her sons were summoned to the scene by anxious neighbours. Johann was devastated by the scene of his father's death and although through his music he brought joy to himself and countless others, it was said that he was forever after haunted by the morbidity of death.

After the initial shock of the early death of Strauss senior, the Viennese gradually accepted that the son was truly a worthy successor, although not before Johann appealed to public opinion through the columns of the *Wiener Zeitung*.

A meteoric rise

In 1849 Johann merged his father's orchestra personnel with his own and thus began a meteoric rise to international fame. The demand for Johann Strauss and the combined orchestras in the ballrooms of Vienna accelerated, and he was soon obliged to

Johann took Viennese society by storm with his marriage on 26 August 1862 to Henriette Chaluptzky, or 'Jetty' Treffz as she was better known. Jetty (right), several years his senior, was a former singer, who for the preceding 19 years had been the mistress of a wealthy banker, Moritz Todesco. Whatever misgivings there might have been about the bride, she nevertheless proved to be a good wife who brought welcome calm and order into Johann's chaotic life-style.

After his father's death in 1849 Johann took over the conductorship of his father's orchestra and merged it with his own. He was soon in such great demand that he had to employ sufficient musicians to play several venues at once throughout the city. He is shown (far right) conducting one of his orchestras at a Viennese ball, and using his violin bow as a baton.

Although he held no strong political views, it was perhaps natural that during the revolutionary period of 1848 Johann should align his sympathies with the rebels and students. His own part in the revolution, however, did not go beyond the composition of the Revolutions-Marsch, the title page of which is shown above.

employ sufficient musicians to play at several venues throughout the city, while he dashed from one to the other with his violin at the ready to lead a few items at each, thereby justifying the announcements: *'Heut spielt der Strauss!'* – Strauss plays here today! The constant round of composing and rehearsing by day, and playing to an adoring public for half the night eventually took its toll on his health, and in the summer of 1853 he was finally obliged to take a rest cure in the fresh mountain air of Bad Gastein. To ensure the orchestra's continuance with a Strauss at the helm, Johann and his mother persuaded Johann's brother Josef to deputize as interim conductor. Unwillingly, but out of loyalty to the family, Josef left his successful career as an architect and designer. Extremely talented he was no mere second-rate substitute – in fact, he proved so successful in his new role that he never returned to his drawing boards. He died young, aged 43, but in his 17-year musical career produced close on 300 original compositions, none of them in any way inferior to those of his brother.

The following summer saw Johann again recuperating in Bad Gastein, and there he was approached by the directors of a Russian railway company who proposed that he should direct the concerts at Pavlovsk, about 30 kilometres from St Petersburg. The concerts were to take place at the rail terminus, set in a magnificent park, and the plan was to attract more visitors, thus making the railway line from St Petersburg a profitable concern. It was not until the summer of 1856 however, that Johann travelled to Russia to take up this engagement, leaving Josef in charge of 'the Vienna branch of the family business'. The season marking the first of 12 subsequent visits to Russia, was a great success. Not only were his concerts there successful in terms of popular appeal but they were also highly profitable. It was there in 1869, that Johann and Josef shared not only the conducting, but also combined their talents to produce the famous *Pizzicato Polka*. By that time, their youngest brother, Eduard, was also established as conductor and composer in partnership with his brothers.

Romance and marriage

It comes as no suprise that the handsome and successful Johann Strauss enjoyed a number of love affairs, and it was in Russia that he first took one of them seriously enough to contemplate marriage; but the aristocratic parents of the lady in question, Olga Smirnitzky, would not hear of it. Unabashed, Johann transferred his affections elsewhere. Two years later on 26 August 1862, Johann's friend and publisher Carl Haslinger received a note from him:

Dear friend Haslinger, shameless fraudulent soul of a book printer! Will you come to my place at 7 o'clock tomorrow morning, to support me at my marriage one hour later? Answer immediately, you inky-fingered music dabbler! Jean.

The one-time Schani had become known by the

more fashionable name of 'Jean' and his bride to be
was Henriette Chalupetzky, formerly a renowned
singer known professionally as 'Jetty' Treffz. Jetty
was the mother of several children and for the
preceding 19 years had lived as the mistress of the
wealthy banker Moritz Todesco. The Strauss family
and all Vienna were astounded by the news, but
whatever the misgivings Jetty proved to be a good
wife, secretary, manager and artistic adviser. She
brought order into Johann's hitherto hectic lifestyle, encouraging him to take more time over
composition and to delegate more work with the
orchestra to his brothers. Thanks in part to Jetty's
steadying influence during the 1860s Strauss created
many of his greatest waltzes, such as *Morgenblätter*
(Morning Papers), *Künstlerleben* (Artist's Life) and
Geschichten aus dem Wienerwald (Tales from the
Vienna Woods). A year after his marriage to Jetty,
Johann was granted a title he had sought many times
and which his father had held before him: that of K.K.
Hofballmusikdirector (Director of Music for the
Imperial and Royal Court Balls).

In 1864 relations between Strauss and his
publisher, Carl Haslinger, deteriorated over financial
matters. For a time Strauss may have considered
entering publishing himself. Haslinger tried to
persuade other publishers to boycott all three
Strauss brothers, but finally C. A. Spina broke the
boycott and became Strauss's new publisher.

Every year at Carnival time the Strausses were in
great demand and the season of 1867 was no
exception. The renowned Vienna Men's Choral
Society, the Wiener *Männergesangverein* wanted a
new work to present at their annual *Narrenabend*
(Fool's Evening). Reminded of an earlier promise to
write something for this choir, Strauss set about
reworking a rough draft he had found among his
papers. By tradition the Fool's Evening was a riotous
affair in fancy dress, but in 1867 the mood of Vienna
was comparatively subdued. The populace was still
reeling from the military defeat of Austria by Prussia
at Königgrätz. The Imperial Court Ball that year was
replaced by a formal concert and the *Männer-*

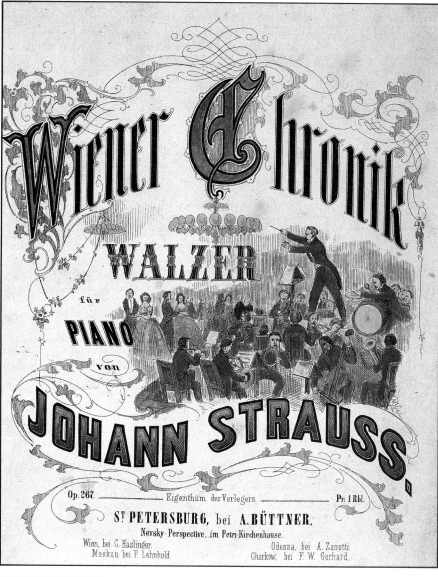

During the 1860s Strauss wrote many memorable waltzes including The Blue Danube *and the* Wiener-Chronik *waltz (title page shown above).*

During the autumn of 1867 Johann and Jetty visited London to take part in a season of Promenade Concerts which were performed at the Royal Italian Opera, Covent Garden (left). The season was a huge success with uproar and exultation at the end of every performance of waltzes.

Every year at Carnival time in Vienna Strauss was in great demand. Traditionally the festivities were riotous fancy dress affairs, like the Fool's Evening of the Vienna Men's Choral Society (below). In 1867, however, suiting the subdued mood of a defeated country, the festivities took on a a more formal aspect. Strauss wrote The Blue Danube *waltz for the concert which, that year, replaced their fancy dress evening.*

gesangverein followed suit.

Strauss's composition – *The Blue Danube* – which was his first choral waltz, started the second half of a mixed programme on 15 February at the Dianasaal. It was well received but wasn't accorded the half-dozen or more repetitions that so many Strauss works received. It was, however, destined to become his most popular waltz and with it he established his reputation in Paris later in 1867.

Strauss abroad

Strauss chose to make his début in Paris during the World Exhibition of 1867 and although the Strauss Orchestra was committed to engagements at home under the direction of Josef and Eduard, Johann reached an agreement with the German conductor, Bilse, who undertook to provide an orchestra in Paris and to share the conducting with Strauss. In Paris,

Johann and Jetty quickly established contacts that were to ensure the most prestigious engagements. Of all the social events held in connection with the Exhibition, the most lavish was the Gala Ball given at the Austrian Embassy by the Ambassador's wife, Princess Pauline Metternich. Jetty wrote home to Vienna:

Jean is the lion here, there has been no comparable success here for years, it is a fever, a tremendous triumph. Proposals are coming in, America is already in view – fabulous, fabulous!

One proposal that Johann immediately accepted came from London. The 25-year-old Prince of Wales had been impressed by the Waltz King's music and personality, and had apparently recommended him to Mr John Russell, who was to present a season of Promenade Concerts in London during the autumn of 1867. The 'classical' repertoire would be conducted by Giovanni Bottesini, the virtuoso double-bass player, and Strauss would conduct several of his own compositions at each of the 63 concerts scheduled to be given from 15 August to 26 October at the Royal Italian Opera, Covent Garden.

Jetty Strauss was no stranger to London – she had appeared there as soloist with Johann Strauss senior during his visit in 1849. Although she had long ago given up her stage career, she sang at ten of the Covent Garden concerts, sometimes accompanied by Johann at the piano, her repertoire including *Home, Sweet Home,* some Scottish songs, and arias by Mozart and Mendelssohn. We also learn from Johann's diary, in which he kept a detailed record of the London concerts, that the *Annen Polka* achieved no fewer than 82 performances during the season, its closest rival being the *Tritsch-Tratsch Polka,* played 38 times.

Johann and Jetty must have been well satisfied with their visit to London, for Johann closed his diary with the words: 'Splendid jubilation such as I have *never* known in my life!!! The most beautiful concert of my career! Vivat the English from the bottom of my heart!'

No doubt influenced by his encounter with Offenbach's stage works and encouraged by his wife and friend Max Steiner, the director of the Theater an der Wien, Strauss began to compose for the theatre after 1870. Of the many operettas he wrote, at least 13, including Der Zigeunerbaron *(left), had their first performances at the Theater an der Wien (centre). Many were successful but lacked good librettos, and as a result it is mainly the music, rather than texts, which has survived.*

Great Composers

On returning to Vienna, Johann retained more than a pleasant recollection of his London concerts, he regarded them as a pattern on which to re-style his Soirées, and began a new series of concerts at the Floral Hall of the Vienna Gardens Association. So much did England impress Strauss that when in 1869 he bought a house at Hietzing, near Dommayer's, he furnished and decorated it as if it was an English home.

A new direction

In 1870, aged 45, Johann was at the peak of success and popularity when he suffered the loss of his mother, who had always been the influential guiding star of the 'family business'. Less than six months later, his brother Josef, the shy, retiring, reluctant

genius of the family, died after collapsing while conducting in Warsaw. The principal conductorship and day-to-day management of the Strauss Orchestra passed to the youngest brother, Eduard, who was to uphold the tradition until he disbanded the orchestra in 1901. Leaving Eduard to direct the family orchestra freed Strauss to accept invitations to conduct outside Vienna, and he took up offers in London, Budapest and Paris. More importantly, though, it freed him to pursue a new musical direction – with operetta – but he had to be pushed into it.

Strauss had already come across, and admired, the operettas of Offenbach. Indeed, Offenbach had even advised him to try his hand in this sphere. But Strauss was not keen to start. He knew himself well enough to know that he had no innate ability when it came to working with words and drama, and he appreciated that it demanded a particular talent to combine words, music and theatre successfully. With hindsight his reluctance seems justified as nearly all his ensuing operettas were let down by his poor choice of librettos. Nevertheless, he was eventually persuaded by Jetty and Maximilian Steiner, the director of the Theater an der Wien, to compose for the stage.

In 1872 Jetty and
Johann attended the
World's Peace Jubilee
and International
Music Festival in
Boston, USA (left).
Johann conducted a
vast orchestra and
chorus before an
audience which he
estimated at 100,000.

*Strauss's third and
greatest operetta,* Die
Fledermaus *(title page
of one of the waltzes
from it, far left) was
produced in 1874.*

*In order to obain a
divorce to marry his
third wife Adele Strauss
(left), Johann had to
become a Protestant,
give up his Austrian
citizenship and take
on that of the Duchy of
Saxe-Coburg-Gotha in
1886. Nonetheless
Strauss's music
continued to reflect the
gaiety and glamour of
his beloved city of
Vienna (above).*

Strauss writes for the stage

In May 1870, Johann entered into a contract with the Theater an der Wien, the first fruit of which was the operetta, *Indigo und die vierzig Räuber,* (Indigo and the Forty Thieves). The première was fixed for 10 February, 1871; Maximilian Steiner's co-director, the popular soprano Marie Geistinger, sang the leading role and Strauss conducted. The house was sold out and the management had even improvised some additional seating. As in the case of some of the subsequent operettas, the text did not make good theatre, and only the music survived the success of the first few years.

Before completing his second operetta *Der Carneval in Rom* (Carnival in Rome) he and Jetty set sail for America in June 1872. Their destination was Boston, where the impresario Patrick S. Gilmore had organized a World's Peace Jubilee and International Music Festival. Johann's role was to conduct a vast orchestra and chorus before an audience which he estimated at 100,000! The outcome was hardly artistic, but the rewards, both financial and in terms of prestige were considerable.

By the end of January 1873 'Carnival in Rome' was in rehearsal at the Theater an der Wein. It was followed in 1874 by *Die Fledermaus.* Although its first season was not entirely smooth, *Die Fledermaus* was a masterpiece. There were frequent interruptions in the run to allow for previously scheduled appearances at the Theater an der Wien of the renowned singer Adelina Patti, and eventually, after the 49th performance of the operetta, it was taken off due to illness among the cast.

According to some sources Jetty and Strauss entered a difficult time in their marriage. Jetty who was in her 60s was no longer the vivacious hostess of former times, nor did she go out much. There appeared also to be disagreements over finances. In April 1878, however, Jetty Strauss suffered a stroke and died. Johann was stunned and at first unable to cope alone with any aspect of life that was not directly connected with music, yet within two months he was married again: this time to 28 year-old Angelika ('Lilli') Dittrich. It was a disastrous union and it ended in separation after four years. His third marriage was to a young widow, Adele Strauss (the daughter of the family financial adviser). In order to marry Adele who was Jewish (he was a Catholic), he had to renounce his Austrian citizenship. Consequently he took citizenship of the Duchy of Saxe-Coburg-Gotha in 1866, became a Protestant, and therefore obtained a divorce.

Happy last years

His last years with Adele and her daughter Alice brought him the peace and contentment that his highly strung temperament needed. He continued to compose not only operettas, the greatest of which after *Die Fledermaus* was *Der Zigeunerbaron* (The Gypsy Baron) in 1885, but also some of his finest independent concert waltzes, including the coloratura *Frühlingsstimmen* (Voices of Spring) and the magnificent *Kaiser-Walzer* (Emperor Waltz). There was also an opera, *Ritter Pasman,* that was produced at the Vienna Court Opera but withdrawn after only nine performances.

Throughout his last years, honours of all kinds were showered on the 'waltz king', who all the while remained modest and unaffected. He liked to pass the time when not composing in a game of cards or billiards with some of his close friends, among whom were the pianist Alfred Grünfeld, the surgeon Theodor Billroth, the sculptor Victor Tilgner, the great operetta comic Alexander Girardi, and of course, Johannes Brahms.

In May 1899, Johann caught a chill which very soon developed into the double pneumonia that was to end his life. He took to his bed but continued to write music, working on his only full-length ballet score, *Aschenbrödel* (Cinderella). He never finished but after his death the score was completed by Josef Bayer, the director of ballet at the Court Opera.

On the afternoon of 3 June 1899 Adele persuaded her husband to try and sleep a little; he replied: 'I will certainly do that . . .' At a quarter past four he died, peacefully sleeping.

After a funeral procession through Vienna he was buried on 6 June in the Central Cemetery in a grave near to those of the city's other great musical luminaries – Brahms, Schubert and Beethoven.

*The silhouette
caricature (left) drawn
after Strauss's death
shows him conducting
a celestial waltz. Not
only are the musical
cherubs enchanted by
his music, but so are
some of the other
musical inhabitants of
heaven. Those who
cannot help joining in
the waltz are Haydn,
Schumann, Mozart,
Bruckner, Handel,
Bach, Liszt, Wagner,
von Bülow, Brahms,
Chopin, Schubert and
Beethoven.*

The Mayerling Scandal

The music of Johann Strauss is indelibly linked with the image of a gay resplendent Vienna, but in 1889 Viennese society was rocked by the scandal of the century – the tragedy at Mayerling.

Prince Rudolf (above), the heir to the Austrian throne who died at Mayerling, shooting first his young mistress, Mary Vetsera, and then himself.

On the night of 29 January 1889, Crown Prince Rudolf, the 30-year-old heir to the Hapsburg Empire of Austria-Hungary, shot first his teenage mistress, Mary Vetsera, and then himself in a bedroom in his small hunting lodge at Mayerling, deep in the wooded country surrounding Vienna. Early in the following morning the bodies were discovered and the horrific news was rushed to the imperial palace, the Hofburg, in Vienna. No one could face telling the emperor, so the Empress Elisabeth, whose Greek lesson had to be interrupted, was told before him of the heir apparent's death. At first she wept bitterly, but then, drawing herself up with remarkable composure, she went to tell her husband, the Emperor Franz Joseph.

The scandal of the century

At the imperial family's request, the police, the prime minister (Count Taaffe) and the court doctor immediately went into action, their first priority being to cover up the most scandalous aspects of the Crown Prince's sudden death, namely the fact that it had been caused by suicide, and the presence of Mary Vetsera's corpse.

Mary Vetsera's furtive funeral was a macabre, inhuman affair. When she had been dead for a day and a half, her body, which had neither been washed nor laid out, was propped up in a carriage between two of her uncles and taken along icy roads at night to the nearby village of Heiligenkreuz. There, the local abbot had been persuaded to agree to her burial in the graveyard under his jurisdiction, despite Catholic scruples about burying suicides in consecrated ground: Mary's official death certificate stated that she had taken her own life, for it could hardly read 'shot dead by the Crown Prince Rudolf'. On the next morning a howling gale delayed the actual digging of the grave – Mary's uncles had to help the gravediggers – but the authorities were satisfied that the whole operation had gone ahead without attracting undue notice. This satisfaction was premature, however, for although there were no journalists in the vicinity, the locals could not help noticing all the curious comings and goings, and Mayerling was to become one of the hottest news stories of the century.

Love and death

In Vienna the first official announcement in the morning newspapers stated that the crown prince had died of a heart attack, but nobody believed this. Apart from his age, it was generally thought (incorrectly) that Rudolf had been in reasonable shape physically, and so far more interesting rumours immediately began to circulate about how, why and with whom he had died.

A day later, the emperor authorized a second official announcement, informing the public of at least part of the truth. This second statement said that the Crown Prince had taken his own life with the aid of a revolver and it mentioned a 'malformation of the skull' to suggest that he had done so under acute mental strain – this was the only way of guaranteeing Rudolf a full Catholic funeral, for a suicide could only get such treatment if he were proven to have been of unsound mind.

But, coming after the heart attack story, this announcement was just too straightforward to be believable, and the very fact that such a different version of things had been officially announced first encouraged further speculation. Also, too many of

The lovely, vivacious but rather empty-headed daughter of the wealthy Baltazzi family, Mary Vetsera (right), was barely 18 years old when she went to Mayerling to die with the prince she adored too much.

the people involved with the cover-up at Mayerling and Mary Vetsera's funeral talked, and within a week of the tragedy aspects of Mary's involvement had begun to percolate out into the sea of rumour and gossip that now absorbed Vienna. Despite the fact that there had only been two short official announcements, and that was to be all, and the fact that Mary Vetsera was not mentioned in either of these statements, what had happened at Mayerling soon became common knowledge. But interpretations of the tragedy differed according to people's sympathies, or their proximity to direct sources of information.

Even today, a precise reconstruction of the events leading up to Mayerling is a matter of guesswork because the findings of the court commission of inquiry and the official autopsies on the bodies have never been found, and because many of the central participants in the aftermath lied in their accounts of what happened in order to exonerate themselves from any blame. But the simplest and most obvious 'explanation' for the events at Mayerling went as follows.

Rudolf and Mary were deeply in love but he was unhappily married to Crown Princess Stephanie and, as the Hapsburg heir apparent and a Catholic, was unable to obtain a divorce to marry Mary (who may have been pregnant). Therefore, like the Tristan and Isolde of Wagner's new opera, which was all the rage

Rudolf and Mary died together on the night of the 29 January 1889. Less than 24 hours later, Rudolf's body was taken hastily from Mayerling under cover of night (left) and carried to the Hofburg in Vienna. Later the following day, 31 January, Mary's body was propped up in a coach between two of her uncles and taken, again under cover of darkness, to be buried in a local churchyard. But these attempts to cover up the real nature of the tragedy were doomed to failure.

News of the Crown Prince's death rocked Viennese society and on the morning of the 31 January, the streets of the city buzzed with men and women exchanging gossip and passing comment (right). No-one really believed the official explanation – that Rudolf had died from a heart attack – and rumours about the involvement of Mary Vetsera soon began to circulate.

THE ILLUSTRATED LONDON NEWS.

No. 2600.—VOL. XCIV.   SATURDAY, FEBRUARY 16, 1889.   TWO SIXPENCE
WHOLE SHEETS

SOME OF THE IMPERIAL FAMILY OF AUSTRIA.

ARCHDUCHESS STEPHANIE, WIDOW OF THE LATE CROWN PRINCE RUDOLF.   ARCHDUCHESS ELIZABETH, ONLY CHILD OF THE LATE CROWN PRINCE RUDOLF.

ARCHDUKE KARL LUDWIG, HEIR PRESUMPTIVE TO THE AUSTRIAN CROWN.   ARCHDUKE FRANCIS, ELDEST SON OF KARL LUDWIG.

The tragedy at Mayerling was hot news not only in Austria, but all over Europe, and over two weeks later The Illustrated London News *was still supplying readers with stories on the background to the tragedy (right). On this front page is part of Rudolf's family: his wife Stephanie, his only child Elisabeth and his Uncle Karl and cousin Francis.*

at the time, the lovers decided to take their own lives rather than end their relationship, or endure its continuation in secret.

This romantic interpretation is probably the one Mary would have hoped for. Not yet eighteen and head over heels in love with her prince, it is quite likely that she offered to die with Rudolf because the alternatives were too unbearable. Since she couldn't live without him, she would die with him.

But Rudolf was well-known as a bit of a rake and it seems unlikely that 'the little Vetsera' would have been a major passion. In fact, less than 48 hours before his death, he had been sleeping with another woman, Mitzi Caspar, a former dancer and singer of light songs at the opera who had become a prostitute. Rudolf was one of Mitzi's 'regulars' and, according to her, he had once asked her to join him in a death pact too. So, for Rudolf, a less romantic explanation had to be sought.

The Wittelsbach madness

Ironically, the expedient 'unsound mind' that ensured a full church funeral for Rudolf does appear to have had some basis in truth. Several latent conflicts in Rudolf's life – involving politics, marital difficulties, family tensions, excessive drinking and general ill health – probably combined to demoralize him so thoroughly that he lost all sense of proportion and went ahead with the deed he had frequently talked of. There is some evidence, too, from the diaries and reminiscences of people who knew him and letters he wrote, that Rudolf often feared he was on the brink of madness, and that he

Rudolf's mother, the Empress Elisabeth (far left) loved her husband, the Emperor Franz Joseph (near left) dearly, even though their marriage had been arranged. But she found the Viennese court unbearably claustrophobic and her liberal political views made her a liability to her husband. Elisabeth was allowed to 'escape' from court life and spent much of her life travelling yet she continued to influence her son. Her uncertain position and her volatile nature undoubtedly contributed to Rudolf's emotional instability.

often spoke of his death as the only 'honourable' way out of the personal problems he felt overwhelmed by. Moreover, a fear of hereditary insanity stalked the imperial family, particularly Rudolf's mother the Empress Elisabeth who was herself a very unstable person.

Elisabeth was one of the Wittelsbachs, the Bavarian royal family, who were so intermarried with the Hapsburgs that the empress and emperor were first cousins, and their children only had half the usual number of grandparents. 'Mad' King Ludwig of Bavaria was one of Elisabeth's cousins and she lived in dread that the family weakness would manifest itself again. (Elisabeth did in fact blame the tragedy at Mayerling on the Wittelsbach affliction).

The empress had been brought up in a relatively happy-go-lucky household that did little to prepare her for the rigours of her married life as the first lady in the most ancient and protocol-ridden court in Europe. She was an extremely beautiful woman – no portrait was said to do justice to her allegedly 'supernatural beauty' – and Franz Joseph worshipped her. But after the birth of her third surviving child (Rudolf was the second), the only way in which Elisabeth could cope both with her imperial responsibilities and her in-laws, notably her over-bearing mother-in-law, the Archduchess Sophie, was by frequent 'travelling'.

In contrast to his wife, and ever mindful of his survival of the revolutions in the year of his accession, Franz Joseph was as intensely conservative and unimaginative as he was shy and conscientious. Acutely aware of his responsibilities as the head of the 600-year-old Hapsburg dynasty, he worked incredibly hard, far harder than any of his civil servants, but had little time for new ideas. It seemed to him that the old ways were tried and true, and as a result the Hapsburg court was the stuffiest in Europe. Despite this conservatism, however, Franz Joseph was a kindly and compassionate man, an old-fashioned 'gentleman' to the core.

For Rudolf, Franz Joseph's conservatism was

stifling. He had had a far more liberal education than his father and had a natural curiosity in new ideas. And from his wayward mother, he had inherited a love for travelling and a sympathy for the Hungarian nationalist cause which could only bring him into conflict with his father. Indeed, he often found his political differences with his father and his father's political advisers so frustrating that he would act as a 'mole' on official policies to journalists, leaking information about government tendencies he disapproved of and sometimes writing articles anonymously. The political straightjacket of his role as heir to the throne could only exacerbate his natural instability.

A disastrous marriage

Neither did Rudolf's marriage, which had been arranged with purely dynastic and religious considerations in mind, help. Despite the shrewd misgivings of the Empress Elisabeth, Franz Joseph had pursued the only match he could condone for his son, marriage with one of the few remaining catholic-born princesses of late 19th century Europe – Princess Stephanie of Belgium. By all accounts, Stephanie was rather stupid, bossy and plain, hardly compatible with the highly educated and fastidious Rudolf who, though not considered to be handsome in a conventional sense, was nonetheless rated as a charming and 'pale and interesting' personality.

Rudolf and Stephanie were married in 1881 when she was just sixteen and he was twenty-three, and he allegedly became a noticeably gloomier person from the time of the marriage onwards. In the years before Mayerling, it was noticed that he seemed to become less and less well. Early in 1886 he became mysteriously ill and a retrospective analysis of his symptoms and the treatment suggests strongly that he was afflicted with syphilis. A year later he became very ill with bronchitis and could only contain violent fits of coughing by taking 'injurious' doses of morphine. In the following spring inflammation of the eyes assailed him, and kept him from shooting parties, and in the summer of 1888, after a riding accident, he began to suffer from severe headaches.

The treatment for syphilis was painful and, in those days, seldom completely effective. But Rudolf's complaint was called cystitis and peritonitis, and poor Stephanie was not told otherwise. She only found out the true nature of Rudolf's affliction, when she succumbed to the disease herself. Naturally enough, discovery of the true nature of the illness, and probably the realization that it meant no more children (their only child was born in 1883), did little to ease tension within the marriage.

Such 'dynastic' marriages, like Rudolf and Stephanie's, where the object was to create a bond between families, rather than individuals, were quite common. And under such arrangements husband and wife often agreed to go their separate ways within the marriage – but not so Stephanie. Unlike other royal wives – Britain's Princess Alexandra, for example, who managed the playboy Prince of Wales's indiscretions without rancour – Stephanie was reluctant to turn a blind eye to Rudolf's infidelities. She did not accept his amorous deviations as a fact of royal life and was apparently furious at the blatant way in which the affair with Mary Vetsera was conducted. Stephanie was one of the few people to whom Rudolf sent a farewell note, and it allegedly began:

Dear Stephanie,
You are rid of my presence and tiresomeness; be
happy in your own way . . .

A fatal 'crush'

If Crown Princess Stephanie's attitude upset Rudolf, his affair with the young Mary Vetsera was hardly likely to restore his equilibrium. She was barely educated, completely spoilt and brought up to think only of clothes, horse racing and pleasure. When she was sixteen (the age when she probably first met Rudolf), her mother began to take her out to society gatherings and she immediately attracted attention because of her ravishing 'oriental' beauty and her vitality; the Prince of Wales (later King Edward VII), who met her at a race meeting in 1888, found her pretty and charming.

Mary's mother, Baroness Helene Baltazzi-Vetsera, was the daughter of a Levantine banker who had amassed a great fortune in Constantinople and then settled in Vienna. She was an extremely ambitious woman socially and was considered, in the jargon of the day, to be rather 'fast'. (In fact she was once suspected of having amorous designs on Rudolf herself.) By marrying a minor diplomat she had climbed up a rung on the social ladder, but she was determined that Mary should secure their position with a really brilliant match. And, in the late 1880s, it looked as if her hopes would be realized, for Mary was surrounded by aristocratic suitors, including the Duke of Braganza. Rudolf, too, seemed interested and, provided this didn't go too far, could only enhance Mary's prospects. But the baroness reckoned without Mary's consuming passion for Rudolf, and her skill in keeping the details of the affair from her family.

Long before she met him properly, Mary had developed an enormous 'crush' on Rudolf. She seldom kept her eyes off him at social gatherings and her obsession had become a Vetsera family joke. And since Rudolf liked to conduct his amorous affairs on the principle of the newer the better, it was

Insanity seemed to run in the interbred Hapsburg family, and it may have been fear of going mad that drove Rudolf to take his own life. His mother Elisabeth's cousin, for instance, was 'Mad' King Ludwig of Bavaria (right) who drowned in mysterious circumstances – possibly as a result of suicide.

The closing years of the Hapsburg Empire were beset by tragedy. In 1898, it was poor Elisabeth, 'the vagabond empress', who was the victim. Boarding a steamer in Geneva, she was attacked by a wild-eyed young man, the Italian anarchist Luigi Luccheni (far left). After the attack, with immense willpower, she walked onto the boat, saying nothing of the stab wound inflicted by her assailant. But the knife had pierced her heart – within an hour she was dead. Despite her errant nature, she was much loved by her husband and by the people of Austria, and her funeral in Vienna (near left) was a grand state occasion.

inevitable that he eventually responded to the extremely flattering attentions of this beautiful young woman.

Several months after the Mayerling affair, Helene Baltazzi-Vetsera had a brochure privately published in which she gave her account of the circumstances that had led to Mary and Rudolf's deaths. The tragedy had ruined her socially and in this work she was attempting to defend herself from accusations that, by turning a blind eye to her daughter's liaison because of her hope of using the imperial connection in some advantageous way, she had somehow been responsible for what happened.

In her defence Baroness Vetsera reproduced her daughter's farewell letters, which clearly showed a determination to do something mysterious and serious, but she protested that she was ignorant of the extent of Mary's involvement with Rudolf and of her fatal intentions. She dated the actual seduction to about two weeks before Mayerling and accounted for Mary's conspicuous obsession with Rudolf during the previous year by maintaining that this was still only the 'crush' stage of the affair. But the wordly baroness must have known more; for example, she could hardly have failed to notice the expensive presents Mary received from her princely paramour. It is more probable that the baroness was quite used to sailing close to the wind propriety-wise, and that she hoped to retrieve Mary before she became too entangled. Helene Baltazzi-Vetsera would not have approved of a full-blown affair because there was absolutely no hope of a marriage, and she would probably have been genuinely horrified had she known that at some stage late in 1888 Mary became Rudolf's mistress. (Indeed, it is quite possible that Mary bolted for Mayerling because her mother had just discovered the full story and was endeavouring to end the whole relationship).

The road to disaster

The tragedy at Mayerling began on the evening of 27 January, when the whole of Viennese high society, including the Baltazzi-Vetseras and members of the imperial family, were gathered at a reception given by the German ambassador in honour of the Kaiser's birthday. At this function Rudolf took the opportunity to plan a shooting trip with his friend Count Hoyos. He asked the count to arrange with Prince Philip of Coburg (Rudolf's brother-in-law) to be in Mayerling for breakfast on the 29th. Mayerling was the Crown Prince's private hunting lodge, 2½ hours from Vienna. Lit by oil lamps and decorated with hunting trophies, it had excited little interest from Crown Princess Stephanie, who seldom went there.

When the hunting party assembled on the morning of the 29th, Rudolf excused himself from the day's activities because of a cold. Then Rudolf must have rejoined Mary, who had 'disappeared' from her home the day before.

Mary had vanished while her chaparone, Countess Larisch, was in a shop and she had been left sitting in a carriage outside. According to contemporary gossip, Countess Larisch had herself once been in love with the Crown Prince, and she so resented his marriage to Stephanie that she was only too willing to act as Rudolf's 'go between' with Mary Vetsera, frequently acting as her young charge's alibi or escorting her to places where propriety demanded a married lady as a companion.

But on this particular shopping expedition, when the countess returned to the carriage to find Mary gone, she was sufficiently alarmed – Mary had been behaving strangely and dropping dark hints about her intentions in the previous days – to alert Helene Baltazzi-Vetsera. Convinced that Mary was with Rudolf at Mayerling, they went together to the Police Chief Krauss, who was known to be in charge of

On 28 June, 1914, yet another Hapsburg met an untimely end when the Archduke Franz Ferdinand was shot and killed in Sarajevo by Gavrilo Princip, photographed here as he was led away from the scene of the assassination (right). Ferdinand's death became the final trigger that launched Europe into the Great War, a war that was to complete the destruction of the house of Hapsburg.

'minding' Rudolf. But Krauss explained that the hunting lodge was the Crown Prince's personal property and therefore beyond his jurisdiction. Even so, he quickly informed the prime minister, Count Taaffe. Taafe was sceptical about Baroness Vetsera's sudden motherly concern about her daughter's activities and, far from seeing a murderous situation developing, only considered the possibility of something mildy risqué happening.

On the evening of the 29th a family dinner party was scheduled to take place at the imperial palace in Vienna to celebrate the engagement of Rudolf's sister Valerie. Philip of Coburg duly left Mayerling to attend this party, arranging to return early in the following morning to continue the shoot. Meanwhile Rudolf simply sent a message to Stephanie, asking her to excuse his absence due to a heavy cold. In fact he dined that night with Count Hoyos, who later claimed that the prince had had a good appetite and had seemed in good spirits despite his cold. At around nine o'clock the friends said goodnight, and retired to their respective quarters (as an old crony of Rudolf's, Hoyos probably suspected that he had a ladyfriend somewhere on the premises). But early next morning a valet found Rudolf and Mary's bodies slumped in their bedroom, and by midday a distraught Count Hoyos had reached Vienna with the terrible news.

A portentous tragedy

By eight o'clock on the morning of the following day the coffin containing Rudolf's body had reached the Hofburg. Now the emperor knew from the court doctor the full horror of Rudolf's death and, wearing full uniform with sword and gloves, he went to see the body. A full autopsy began that evening, and on the following morning the way in which Rudolf had really died was told in the second official announcement to the public.

The funeral took place on 5 February, on a cold and grey winter afternoon. The coffin was taken from

the Hofburg, where the body had been lying in state (with cosmetic wax filling the huge hole in the skull made by the bullet wound), through the narrow streets of the old city of Vienna, to the Church of the Capuchins. When the ceremony was over it was carried down to the crypt and Rudolf was laid to rest among his Hapsburg ancestors. By the imperial family's request, no other crowned heads were present apart from the King and Queen of Belgium, Stephanie's parents. Franz Joseph managed to contain his grief until he followed the coffin to the crypt, where he broke down and wept – the empress had been too distraught even to attend the funeral.

Franz Joseph's courage and dignity throughout this time earned him universal admiration and sympathy. Typically, he coped by retiring even deeper in to his official shell and surrounding himself with even more work, reserving his affection and confidences only for his family, a very small entourage and his great friend, the actress Katharina Schratt. But the death of 'our dear Rudolf whom we shall never forget' hurt him profoundly and then, in 1898, there came another great blow – his beloved wife, the Empress Elisabeth, was stabbed to death by a lone wolf anarchist while on one of her trips abroad.

These unhappy events seemed portentous to many people in Vienna. It was widely believed that when 'der alte Herr' (the old Gentleman) died, so too would the Hapsburg Empire of Austria-Hungary. Furthermore, the untimely death of Crown Prince Rudolf, with his go-ahead inclinations and modern-mindedness, was of shattering significance for Austria-Hungary. The new heir apparent, Archduke Franz Ferdinand, was not very popular and when he was assassinated at Sarajevo in 1914 the First World War, which resulted in the disintegration of the old empire, was precipitated. Mayerling was more than a great human tragedy, it was also of immense political import, for on that bleak January night Austria-Hungary not only lost a crown prince, it also lost its future.

Johannes Brahms
1833–1897

Cautious and shy by nature, Brahms found it difficult to show his true feelings. It was only through his music that he was able to express his warmth of heart and utter sincerity.

Brahms was born in Hamburg on 7 May, 1833. His father, Johann Jakob Brahms, was an orchestral double bass player who married a woman 17 years older than himself. But Christiane, although 41 when they married, soon gave him three children of whom the composer, Johannes Brahms, was the second.

The Brahms household seems to have been happy and respectable, though poor. Johannes was sent to a private school and later to a grammar school. Outside his academic studies his two passions seem to have been his collection of toy soldiers (which he kept into adulthood) and – of course – music. In 1840 he began piano lessons with a teacher called Friedrich Wilhelm Cossel, and within three years Cossel had unselfishly passed him on to his own distinguished teacher

Eduard Marxsen. Marxsen seems to have known from the first that he was dealing with genius, or something very like it, and although his first aim was to turn his pupil into a brilliant pianist he soon recognized that an exceptional creative gift also had to be encouraged and guided.

His piano-playing skill did, however, lead the young Brahms into some experiences that were to leave a kind of scar on his adult life. From around the age of 13 he used to play, for food and minimal payment, in the dockland bars near his home which were effectively sailors' brothels. The atmosphere into which this highly sensitive teenager was inevitably drawn seems to have been sordid in the extreme; sometimes he tried to block it out by putting a book of poems on the

A tender portrait of Brahms (above) at the age of 20 (1853). In his youth he had a rather delicate face framed by long flaxen hair. As one lady-friend put it: 'He had the face of a child, which any girl could kiss without a blush.' It was perhaps to hide his rather effeminate looks that Brahms later grew the distinctive white beard which gave him his familiar, avuncular image.

The young Brahms came into contact with Hungarian folk music (above), following the influx into Hamburg of refugees after the 1848 Hungarian uprising.

The house where Brahms was born (right) – a cramped tenement building in the poor area of old Hamburg.

Brahms c.1860 (left) – an intensely romantic young man. If he had not been so short, Brahms would have been a very imposing figure, with his high brow, penetrating blue eyes and finely-chiselled features.

Throughout his life, Brahms had a deep love of the countryside, delighting in the natural beauty of the Swiss and Austrian scenery (right). For him, it was not only a welcome refuge from the pressures of city living, but also a lasting inspiration for many of his compositions.

music stand in front of him and simply playing h popular tunes mechanically. He never forgot th experience, and sometimes talked about it bitterly later life.

A career begins

At the age of 17, Brahms was already on the threshol of a successful musical career. He got to know Hungarian-Jewish violinist called Eduard Remény Reményi was three years older than Johannes, colourful character who specialized in playir brilliant gypsy-style music as well as the standar classics; he was also a bit of a revolutionary whos extensive travels had at least partly been caused by h need to evade the police.

He and Brahms set off on a joint concert tour earl in 1852 and during the trip Reményi introduced h companion to another and more distinguishe violinist, Joseph Joachim, who served the King Hanover as principal violinist. Joachim was impresse by Brahms's playing and even more so by his pian compositions, which at this time included sona movements and a powerful Scherzo in E flat mino This, he later declared, was music of 'undreamt-o originality and power'. Joachim arranged for the tw travellers to play to the King, offered Brahms (but no it seems, Reményi) a special open invitation to retur at any time, and provided a letter of introduction t the great pianist-composer Franz Liszt.

At the Court of Weimar, whose music he directe Liszt received Reményi and Brahms graciously. To shy to play himself, Johannes was both astonished an admiring when Liszt took his Scherzo manuscript an

sight-read it with great aplomb, meanwhile offering a complimentary running commentary. In turn, Liszt did his listeners the very considerable compliment of playing for them his own recently completed Piano Sonata in B minor – all the more of a privilege in that this greatest among living pianists no longer gave public recitals. Brahms must surely have been impressed. But perhaps because of his natural shyness, he was less than extravagantly fulsome in his praise. Whether Liszt felt offended we may only guess. But Reményi, the more practised courtier (and probably the shallower musician) was angry, feeling that his young partner had alienated a celebrated musician whose goodwill was of much professional value to him. He told Brahms that their association must end.

Brahms had no money. Was he to return dejectedly to Hamburg, where his father had already plainly indicated his wish to see his gifted son successfully standing on his own feet? Instead he wrote to Joachim: 'I can't return to Hamburg without anything to show . . .' Might he, please, visit Joachim, who was to spend the summer at the university town of Göttingen attending some of the lectures? An immediate 'yes' brought the two young musicians together again, and a long-lasting friendship and musical understanding developed.

The Schumanns

For some time Brahms had respected the reputation of the composer Robert Schumann, without knowing a great deal of his music. During 1853, however, both Joachim and other musical friends had brought him a wider knowledge of Schumann's work and Joachim urged him to visit Schumann at his home in Düsseldorf.

Finally Brahms overcame his hesitation and made up his mind. On 30 September, 1853 he knocked on Schumann's door, was welcomed and at once taken to the piano to play his C major Sonata. But he had not gone far when Schumann stopped him. 'Clara must hear this', he cried and went from the room to fetch his pianist wife. We have Clara Schumann's own diary account of what happened after this:

He played us sonatas, scherzos etc. of his own, all showing exuberant imagination, depth of feeling and mastery of form. Robert says there was nothing he could tell him to take away or add. It is really moving to see him sitting at the piano, with his interesting young face, which becomes transfigured when he plays, his beautiful hands, which overcome the greatest difficulties . . . what he played to us is so masterly that one can only think the good God sent him ready-made into the world. He has a great future before him, for he will find the first true field for his genius when he begins to write for orchestra.

Robert Schumann's reaction to his young visitor was like that of his wife, immediate and wholehearted. A diary entry for the day of their first meeting reads simply, 'Brahms to see me – a genius'. Johannes was virtually taken into the Schumann household and throughout October 1853 enjoyed an artistic environment of a richness such as he had never known before. As for Schumann, he was determined that Brahms's name, and his music too, should at once become more widely known.

Brahms (seated) with the distinguished violinist, Joseph Joachim (below). The two became firm friends and developed a sympathetic and fruitful musical partnership.

Tragedies and passions

Schumann's support and friendship were a magnificent stimulus, and Brahms rejoiced with them. But his close involvement with the older composer and his family was to draw him into a tragic situation. Schumann was a manic-depressive with a long history of mental illness, generally believed to have been due to syphilis. He had for some time been alarming Clara by long brooding silences and even hallucinations. Then on 27 February, 1854 he left his house and threw himself into the River Rhine. He was dragged out by a boat crew, but remained in a state of mental confusion. Within a few days he had been declared insane and was removed to an institution where he was to remain until his death two years later.

As soon as he heard the news, Brahms rushed to Clara's side. Prostrated by her husband's tragedy, and halfway through a pregnancy, she came to depend heavily on the support of her devoted young friend. Since she was not allowed to visit Schumann for fear of over-exciting him, Brahms acted as an occasional go-between, visiting her husband, who had some lucid periods. It must have put an immense strain on a deeply sensitive young man, particularly as he had fallen in love with Clara.

In the meantime Clara Schumann, with seven children to feed, had to work to earn a living. She, together with Brahms and Joachim, gave a series of concerts, and she made a point of playing Brahms's music. He, too, gave piano recitals in Bremen, Leipzig and his native Hamburg. But on the whole he was not a tremendous success: it seems that the 'flavour' of his big sonatas, sternly romantic as they were, was not to everyone's taste. His residence was now in Düsseldorf, near Clara, and he may have hoped to be offered the municipal directorship of music formerly held by Schumann. But that hope came to nothing. In the meantime, however, he remained in Düsseldorf, where it was soon clear that he was doing little to advance his career as a composer. His parents, and his old teacher Marxsen, became worried.

Some, if not all, of the reason for Brahms's residence in Düsseldorf must have been his growing love for Clara Schumann. She was ten years younger than her dying husband and still an attractive woman only approaching her mid-30s. 'I wish I could tell you how deeply I love you', he wrote to her in a letter. No one knows whether their relationship ever took a physical form, but most people think it unlikely. Clara took her role as a soon-to-be-widowed young mother very seriously. She became friendly with Brahms's mother, assuring her that she would stand by Johannes 'always, with true affection'. In theory, the idea of marriage to Clara may have attracted him. But when Schumann died and this became actually possible, he decided instead to leave Düsseldorf. He remained a devoted friend to Clara and her children, but there was to be no more talk of love between them.

Detmold and Vienna

From 1857 to 1860 Brahms held a court appointment as Director of Music to the princely court of Detmold, 60 miles south-west of Hanover. He taught the princess the piano and conducted a choir; as well as this he played the piano at concerts and had a number of private pupils whose fees augmented his salary. There was a court orchestra for which he composed two serenades. At this time also he completed his very un-courtly First Piano Concerto (1858), a stormy work which had occupied him since Schumann's illness and which almost certainly reflected his

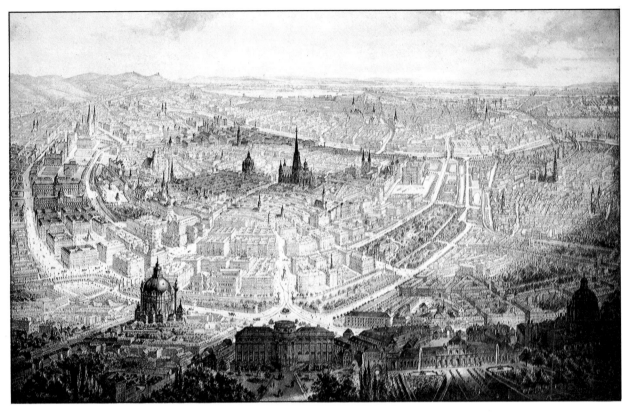

*rahms first visited
enna (right) in the
ring of 1863 and
mediately felt the
arm of the Austrian
pital. He wrote to a
iend: 'The gaiety of the
wn, the beauty of the
rroundings, the
mpathetic and
vacious public: how
imulating these are to
e artist! In addition we
ve in particular the
emory of the great
usicians whose lives
nd works are brought
aily to our minds.'
ater, in the early 1870s,
e was to make the city of
eethoven and Schubert
s permanent home.

rahms's own musical
stes were wide-
anging and refreshingly
ee from intellectual
obbery. He loved the
usic of Vienna's waltz-
'ng, Johann Strauss –
'ayed here by an all-
male orchestra (left) –
ist as much as he had
ved the Hungarian
ppsy music in Hamburg.
e once admitted that
e would have given
nything to have written
e Blue Danube.

rahms quickly settled
own to the lively social
fe in Vienna (below),
njoying the food and
rink as much as the
ompany.*

turbulent feelings at that time. It had its first performance in Hanover on 22 January, 1859, with Joachim as conductor and the composer himself as soloist; and Brahms played it again a few days later in Leipzig. But the audience reaction was cool, even hostile. Brahms wrote to Joachim: 'It will please one day . . . after all I'm still trying . . . all the same, the hissing was a bit much.'

Detmold and court duties were agreeable and well paid, but they occupied Brahms for only a few months of each year. He still spent part of his time with his family in Hamburg, but now acquired a house of his own in an attractive suburb. In Hamburg he founded a women's choir, which he conducted and trained; he composed music for them as well. Perhaps it was inevitable that this young man, still in his mid-20s, should have been attracted to one of his singers, called Bertha Porubsky. She was actually a visitor from Vienna, and Brahms liked to hear her sing her native Austrian folk songs. The romance, if such it was, ended when she returned to Vienna and married. But she and her husband remained friendly with Brahms, and it was for her first-born child that the composer later wrote what must be his most famous song, the *Cradle Song*, a tender and lilting lullaby.

Another woman in his life was also a singer. Agathe von Siebold was the daughter of a university professor at Göttingen, where Brahms had gone to stay with friends. She seems to have loved him, and he her: they enjoyed music-making together, and going for long hill walks. His friends were all certain that their engagement would soon be announced. But it never happened. 'I love you', he wrote to Agathe: 'I must see you again. But I *can't* wear chains. Write and tell me if I can return to take you in my arms'. She was deeply hurt, and Brahms too had the grace to feel guilty about his apparently callous behaviour. After that he was more cautious in his relationships with women. In fact, of his sex life nothing whatever is known for certain — even if he had one at all. Some of his biographers suggest he may have patronized prostitutes, associating sex indissolubly with the Hamburg of his childhood, but remaining unable to enter into more serious attachments. Certainly he never again got close to marriage, and found himself forced to make a joke of it: namely that when he wanted to marry he could not afford it but when he finally had enough money no girl would have him. A remark by Nietzsche to the effect that Brahms's music betrayed 'the melancholy of impotence' may have hinted unkindly at something more. For as a young man Brahms had a high-pitched voice and almost

feminine prettiness, as well as small stature; it may have been to disguise this that he later grew a large beard.

Meanwhile, as he approached 30, his music was becoming better known. Clara Schumann played the piano works, Joachim played the violin in his chamber music and conducted orchestral pieces, and a singer called Julius Stockhausen took the Brahms songs into his repertory, sometimes with the composer himself playing the piano. The particular style of his music, too, was beginning to be appreciated and to take its place in the scheme of things. But the critical response was distorted by the musical infighting of the time and his music only gained recognition slowly.

From 1862 Brahms made his home in Vienna. There he conducted a choir and enjoyed the pleasures of a city that still remembered Beethoven and Schubert. He met Wagner too and was not too proud to help copy out orchestral parts of *Die Meistersinger* for a Viennese performance of part of that opera. Leading players of chamber music seized on Brahms's music, and one called him 'Beethoven's heir'. He played his

own *Handel Variations* for piano with success, an the Viennese also heard his orchestral serenade Somehow, what with the various strands of his music activity, he managed to make quite a comfortab living. When his parents separated, he helped h mother to set up in a small flat of her own in Hambur and he was heart-broken, from all accounts, when sl died in 1865. Her death at least partly inspired him complete the *German Requiem,* first heard thre years later. It was the *German Requiem* that mac Brahms's name and established him financially.

The routine of Brahms's life, centring on h Viennese home, was gradually established. Tl autumn and spring often found him on concert tou as a pianist and conductor. In the winter he was musi making and composing in Vienna, and in the summe he liked to holiday at Lichtenthal, where Cla Schumann kept a cottage and where the old frien could meet and exchange memories and news.

The last decades
It was in 1876 that Brahms finally completed his Fir Symphony. The idea for such a work had haunted hi since the time of his first encounter with tl Schumanns long before, and he had shown Clara son sketches in 1862. He found the big horn solo of tl symphony's finale in a 'shepherd's horn' idea in 186 which he passed on to Clara complete with 'alpin words perhaps of his own invention. The symphony première in 1876 came after a four-year 'orchestra period following his appointment in 1872 as directo of the Vienna Philharmonic Society, which had als seen the successful performance of his *Requiem* and ' Anthony' Variations under his direction as well a much other old and new music. This golden period Brahms's 40s and early 50s saw the creation of some his most important orchestral works: three mo

The mezzo-soprano Hermine Spies (below), who wa Brahms's close friend during his middle age (his dear 'Herminchen'). Her considerable talent and fun-loving nature inspired a rich outpouring of nei songs from the composer.

Brahms happily poses with two daughters of a friend (below), during a summer visit to Gmunden.

In 1853, Brahms called
on the celebrated
composer Robert
Schumann (far left).
Schumann's reaction to
the young Brahms was
immediate and whole-
hearted. He hailed the
young composer as a
'genius', and became his
staunch friend and most
vociferous champion.

No less enthusiastic was
Schumann's wife, Clara
(left), a famous pianist
in her own right. Brahms
developed a desperate
love for Clara – 14 years
his senior – and was by
her side throughout her
husband's tragic illness
and death in 1856. Later,
this youthful infatuation
matured into a devoted
friendship.

An imposing portrait of
Brahms (below) at the
age of 58.

ymphonies (the Fourth, his last, dates from 1885), as
well as the Violin Concerto and the Second Piano
Concerto. There was also the *Academic Festival
Overture* written in 1880 for the University of Breslau
which gave the composer an honorary degree. This
was a time of both artistic and material success:
together with his publisher of the Viennese years,
Simrock, Brahms now earned a considerable income
from his music. He also had influence and was able to
help a gifted young composer, Dvořák, by helping him
to find a publisher just as Schumann had done for him
years before.

But he continued to live fairly simply, in relatively
modest lodgings. He kept up with his old friends, like
Clara Schumann, and with newer ones like the
amateur pianist Elisabeth von Herzogenberg whom he
got to know well in 1874 and to whom he wrote
fascinating and artistically revealing letters. With
other friends, relations were sometimes less easy. He
offended the pianist and conductor Hans von Bülow,
one of his strongest supporters, by conducting his
Fourth Symphony in Frankfurt just before Bülow and
his own orchestra were to perform it in the same city.
There was trouble, too, with one of his oldest and most
loyal friends, Joachim, when Brahms took his wife's
side in a marital upset. Brahms had written to
Joachim's wife expressing his belief in her innocence
following her jealous husband's accusation of
adultery; when the case came to the divorce court,
Joachim's suit was defeated partly on the evidence of
Brahms's letter which was read aloud. Shattered,
Joachim denounced his 'disloyal friend' and broke off
relations with him. Later they patched matters up, not
least with the Double Concerto for Violin and Cello
(1887) in which Joachim played the violin at the
première.

The concerto was Brahms's last orchestral work. He
had entered into an autumnal period. Although only in
his 50s, he found things changing about him. He put on
weight and travelled less far and less frequently. He
wrote fine shorter pieces for piano and his Clarinet
Quintet, but the *Four Serious Songs* (1896), with their

Great Composers

A familiar sight in Vienna: Brahms striding purposefully towards his favourite eating place at dusk, hands behind his back (above). In this typical pose, he has been captured by a caricaturist (above right) – who seems to have been familiar with Brahms's eating habits. The hedgehog alludes to the 'Red Hedgehog' restaurant, while also hinting at Brahms's prickly nature.

think, and without delay, about his own end.

Re-established in Vienna, Brahms sought coura geously to pick up the threads of his working and social life. But he was clearly unwell: his face began to take on a yellow tinge and friends became anxious Finally he saw a doctor, apparently asking, with a hollow humour, not to be told 'anything unpleasant Jaundice was diagnosed, and he was sent to a spa town Karlsbad, to 'take the waters'. But the doctors told hi friends a different story. Brahms was seriously ill. Lik his father before him, who had died in 1872, Brahm had cancer. He was never told, but it was clear that he knew himself to be doomed. He lost weight alarmingly and became very tired. Finally, lovingly watched ove by his landlady and friend, Frau Truxa, he died in hi bed on 3 April, 1897.

Personality and achievement

Like Beethoven, Brahms was short, less than five fee six inches in height. He was fair, with bright and penetrating blue eyes and a high-pitched voice which in later life he disguised by gruffness. He grew hi distinctive beard in 1878, became grey soon after 50 and finally grew fat (until his last, wasting illness). He enjoyed his food, but was not extravagant or exotic in his gastronomic tastes, and his clothes, though clean were somewhat untidy and unfashionable. In company he could be offhand and even rude, though i seems to have been uncouthness rather than malic that led to such incidents: like Beethoven, who could also offend, the character of the man (and of course hi genius) ensured that his friends uncomplainingl endured temporary slights of which Brahms himsel was often unaware. With children, and animals too, he was more at ease: they liked him and he them Children often followed him about while he was o holiday, and he encouraged them to do so. Once when a girl gave him a rose, he asked, 'Is that sup posed to represent my prickly nature?' She had n idea what he meant; but she, and many others like her

Biblical texts, must be songs of farewell. His sister Elise and his friend Elisabeth von Herzogenberg both died in 1892, von Bülow in 1894, and Clara Schumann in 1896. He heard this last news while on holiday and rushed to be at Clara's funeral at Frankfurt. He arrived too late for the service and had to travel on to Bonn, where Clara was to be laid beside her husband. The 36 hours of lonely, brooding travel took their toll, however: Clara had meant more to him than any woman save perhaps his mother, and her loss was perhaps even more of a shock than he had expected. The *Four Serious Songs* which he had composed only weeks before had been concerned with mortality: indeed, the third of them begins with the words 'O Death, how bitter art thou!'. Now it was time to

Brahms celebrating the wedding anniversary of his friends the Fellingers in the summer of 1896 (right).

One of Brahms's greatest pleasures was travel. He visited Italy no less than eight times between 1878 and 1893. His enthusiasm for the country was immense. As a friend related: 'Brahms bubbles with desire to speak Italian, has studied grammar for months and learnt all the irregular verbs.'

new that Herr Brahms was essentially a kindly man who made a careful choice of toys or sweets for resents, and above all had patience with his younger iends.

Quite early in life, Brahms seems to have lost any rthodox Christian faith. Yet the composer of the *German Requiem* and the *Four Serious Songs,* or for hat matter the Alto Rhapsody of 1869 with its deeply erious text by Goethe, was clearly very conscious of he eternal questions of life and death. He faced his wn death with something like stoicism, though his nwillingness to hear the harsh truth from his doctors, referring a fiction which could be kept up until the ery last, is rather touching. His evident human ulnerability, and tenderness too, always lay beneath a cautious, sometimes even suspicious surface personality: but where Brahms gave his affection and trust it was given wholeheartedly and (as far as he was concerned) for life.

Whether or not we understand Joachim's description of his friend as 'pure as a diamond, soft as snow', we may agree with what that perhaps implies, a quality which stands out in all Brahms's music and which may make it especially valuable in today's uncertain world – namely its utter sincerity. Brahms may have found it hard to express individual human love in a relationship such as marriage; but his warmth of heart found expression in his music, informing every piece he wrote, particularly the mellow later works. For that we shall always be grateful.

A fond picture of Brahms, taken towards the end of his life by his friend Maria Fellinger. It was to be the last photograph of Brahms. He was seriously ill with cancer and died on 3 April, 1897.

Following Brahms's death, his friends at Gmunden (with whom he had spent many happy summers) transformed their house into an affectionate memorial to him (left). Notice the portrait of the composer on the house's façade.

The iron chancellor
Otto von Bismarck

While Brahms was striving towards musical maturity his fragmented homeland, Germany, was unified through 'iron and blood' by a Prussian political genius: Otto von Bismarck.

The diplomats who met in Vienna in 1814 (below) were staunch conservatives, dedicated to the restoration of the pre-Napoleonic status quo. They sought to maintain European stability by balancing the territorial rights of the great powers so that no single state could become so large as to have a de-stabilizing strength. But the compromises reached at Vienna were eventually swamped by the unstoppable tide of nationalist and democratic forces.

In 1815 Germany was a loose federation of 39 states. They owed a vague allegiance to Austria and her Hapsburg royal family as the strongest state in the German world. This world consisted of underdeveloped kingdoms connected by a few rivers and apallingly bad roads: Germany had no coherent economic or political shape.

By 1871, however, Germany had been transformed into the strongest nation in Europe. This new Germany was dominated by the state of Prussia and ruled by her royal family, the Hohenzollerns. Militarily, she had defeated Austria and France decisively. Economically, she was threatening to overtake Britain as the most industrialized nation in Europe. More than any other nation, the new Germany was the creation of one individual: Otto von Bismarck. His dramatic career changed the life of Europe forever and most Germans could not help but be impressed by his short-term success. Johannes Brahms believed that the two most important events of his lifetime were the completion of the *Bachgesellschaft Edition* (the publication of Bach's complete works) and the creation of the German state by Bismarck. Brahms usually travelled

Two figures dominated central European politics for most of the 19th century. Metternich (above) frustrated plans for a united Germany, but Bismarck (above right) later built a German Empire under Prussian control.

with a volume of Bismarck's speeches in his luggage which he would read for daily inspiration.

Metternich's 'patchwork' Germany
Bismarck's unification programme undid the careful arrangements of Prince Clemens von Metternich, the Austrian master-diplomat who had presided over the Congress of Vienna in 1814–15.

At this congress, Europe's senior statesmen had met to redraw the map of Europe after the final defeat of Napoleon. Four great powers – Britain, Russia, Prussia and Austria – dominated the proceedings. They were

Federal Diet (assembly) was set up in Frankfurt where representatives of the 39 members of the Confederation could meet to discuss common political and economic questions. Of course, Metternich's intention was that they would discuss how to keep change out of Germany, not how to unite it, and for 30 years the system worked well.

This system depended on strict censorship and a strong police presence, keeping a particularly close watch on student activities. So the German Confederation survived 1830 – a year of revolutionary activity all over Europe – with comparatively little damage. Although a few states introduced more liberal constitutions, Metternich's system endured until the next 'year of revolution', 1848, and then it fell apart quite dramatically.

In 1848 there were uprisings and disturbances all over Germany, while a revolution in Vienna even forced Metternich, the personification of established order, to flee from his own capital. Quite abruptly, Frankfurt became the site of an attempt to convene a German parliament. Through direct male voting, representatives from all of Germany were elected to discuss a German constitution. This was the newly emerging middle class expressing their desire for a more liberal style of government: about 200 of the representatives were lawyers and judges; 100 were professors and teachers; and there was just one peasant. The Frankfurt delegates were as liberal as Prussia was conservative.

The economic catalyst

Metternich's system had been destroyed by forces that not even the cleverest statesman could contain: industrialization and economic change. Because of the political tumult that convulsed continental Europe until 1815, industrialization occurred in Germany very late and very fast. The country had been divided not just into principalities, but also into numerous trading zones, criss-crossed with borders and frontier posts

ooking for a system of stability that would keep the lid on the potentially explosive ideas which the French army had helped to spread across Europe – nationalism and republicanism.

After all, reasoned Metternich, if every people demanded their own state, what would happen to the mighty Austrian Empire? Within its boundaries were Hungarians, Italians, Poles and Slavs, as well as the German-speaking Austrians who were the ruling class and provided the government bureaucracy. Austria's size and strength made her by far the most powerful country in the German-speaking world. From the capital, Vienna, the empire's main strength lay to the east and the south-east across Europe to the border with Russia, and south into Italy as far as Milan.

What we know as modern Germany was a complicated patchwork of kingdoms, principalities, free ports and duchies with one major power, Prussia, in the north. There had been over 300 of these tiny territories at the end of the 18th century and Napoleon's armies tore through them like a whirlwind. The very act of being invaded had awakened some of these states from their almost medieval existence. And the necessity of fighting the French had forced some of these rulers to co-operate with each other, and in some cases even to promise their people some kind of constitution. By the time the dust had settled and Napoleon had been despatched to St Helena in 1815 – the year of Bismarck's birth – Germany had been somewhat 'rationalized'. What Metternich proposed was a German Confederation of 39 separate states, ranging from the two superpowers, Austria and Prussia, to city-states like Frankfurt.

Of the many territorial changes made at the Congress of Vienna one was to have enormous significance: Prussia assumed control of the Rhineland and Westphalia. This meant that Prussia was now responsible for defending Germany's western border against the French. And as the 19th century progressed, the Ruhr with its vast coalfields became one of the most powerful industrial zones of Europe. The strategic and economic implications of the Rhineland were to be greater than anyone could have anticipated in 1815.

The year of revolution

Metternich knew that if Austria were to retain her role as the chief power among German-speaking countries, then Germany would have to remain divided. A

The meeting between King William I of Prussia and Otto von Bismarck in 1862 (left), at the height of a constitutional crisis, was to change the course of European history. Despite his status as Prussia's 'iron chancellor', Bismarck's attitude towards the king remained characteristically calculating. An aristocrat himself, he considered the royal family, the Hohenzollerns, to be 'no better than my own'.

In 1848 a wave of revolution swept across Europe. There were uprisings in every German state, and the fighting in Berlin (left) was particularly bitter and bloody.

unification, of Germany was the building of railways. And the railways revealed what conservative country Prussia was, dominat politically and economically by the great landowne the *Junkers.* The estates of the *Junkers,* lay to the e of the Elbe – an area which is part of Poland and Rus today. There, the landowners' rule was absolute, a their sons became the officers of the Prussian ar and the administrators of the civil service. (Bismarc background and upbringing were classically *Junk* He was despatched from the family estates to educated in Berlin and though committed to st service of some kind all his life, he also maintained responsibilities as a landowner.)

Initially, the *Junkers* were hostile to railways, just they were hostile to all forms of modernization. But the 1840s two obvious advantages of the railw system changed their minds: they realized that th could get their agricultural produce to wider mark more quickly, and therefore more profitably, and t railways could revolutionize the conduct of w bringing enormous advantages to any army that had extensive and swift transport system. As Germany w drawn together by economic forces, the great politi questions that this process posed were: was it to b federation or a centralized state? And what role wo Austria play?

Bismarck takes the stage

At Frankfurt, in 1848, the liberal and profession classes tried to answer these questions. They drew a constitution for all the German lands, and th offered the crown of German Emperor to Frederi William IV, King of Prussia, who refused it. He argu

charging a complicated tariff system, which impeded the flow of goods. With a view to administrative efficiency rather than a conscious desire to encourage commerce, Prussian civil servants gradually drew most of the German states into a free trade area, which was formalized as the *Zollverein* (customs union) in 1834. Austria remained outside the system to protect the trade within her own empire, so the effect was to draw the rest of Germany into an association with Prussia in the north.

But the economic innovation which did most to accelerate the industrialization, and eventual

The well-meaning men who met at the Frankfurt National Assembly in 1848 (right) were divided on the question of the shape the future Germany should assume. The principal split was between the pro-Prussian and pro-Austrian nationalists. Lacking internal unity, the Assembly was a government in name only. Without revenue or armed forces, it collapsed when Germany's counter-revolutionary rulers recovered their nerve. The way was then clear for Bismarck's strategy of achieving unity – not through elections and constitutions, but through 'iron and blood'.

...uring the 1850s
...ermany finally evolved
...to an industrial
...ciety. Wealth shifted
...om farming (above) to

*industry (right). This
economic development
did more to change the
social order than
revolution and debate.*

he was supposed to represent the policies of his seniors in Berlin, and report back to them. Instead Bismarck began to implement his own policies, sending reports off to Berlin instructing the government on what to do. Bismarck had seen through the whole tangled question of German unification and his solution was simple: Austria had to be totally ejected from the sphere of German politics and left to concentrate on her empire in south-eastern Europe. The way would then be clear for Prussia to take control of the German Reich – on her own terms.

But Bismarck's single-handed strategy was not

The Danish decision to make the duchy of Schleswig an integral part of Denmark presented Bismarck with the chance to take the first step towards uniting Germany. Bismarck made great political capital from Prussia's swift military victory (below).

...at a king ruled by divine right and therefore could ...ot pick up a crown offered by a parliamentary mob. ...is was a clear statement that Prussia was not ...terested in unification based on a liberal or broadly ...tionalist appeal, and Bismarck supported the old ...ng's refusal.

At the Frankfurt parliament Otto von Bismarck first ...epped on to the national stage and in his opening ...eech he presented himself as the most reactionary ...presentative of a reactionary class. He was a huge ...an, powerfully-built, well over six foot, and he ...sulted most of the delegates with his opening ...marks. When uproar broke out, he calmly stood and ...ad a newspaper until it had subsided. It was a ...markable performance but it left a misleading image ...Bismarck. He may have been a *Junker*, but he was ...rdly a conservative. As a political operator he was ...obably the most radical statesman of his time. What ...smarck possessed was an extraordinarily rapid and ...btle grasp of any political situation. He could foresee ...e multiple implications of any initiative, and could ...provise, or bluff, or threaten his way out of any ...uation. As an opportunist, he was a genius. He ...ossessed total faith in his abilities, and he operated ...ry much as a loner. He used political parties or ...liticians while they suited his plans, and then ...opped them. He had no time for cabinets or ...lleagues or committees. He did not accept the ...ancellorship until he was certain he had total ...ntrol, and then he used it ruthlessly, ordering the ...ng around as sternly as any civil servant.

...smarck in limbo
...ter his remarkable parliamentary début at Frankfurt, ...smarck was given the job of representing Prussia at a ...-convening of the German Confederation. As such,

One by one, Prussia's rivals fell before her victorious armies. In 1866, it was the once-proud Austrian Empire that suffered, as the Hapsburg troops were routed in the Battle of Königgrätz (above).

appreciated by his political bosses and eventually he was sent off to languish as the Prussian ambassador to St Petersburg. 'I am being put into cold storage on the Neva,' he commented sardonically. In Berlin, the liberals and the conservatives argued endlessly about the future of Germany inside Prussia's parliament, but all through the 1850s things were going quietly Bismarck's way.

The Prussian railway network doubled its range; coal production virtually trebled; and the production of textiles, iron, and steel all increased in proportion. At the Great Exhibition of 1851 in London, one of the most talked about exhibits was a six-pound gun which had been cast by an iron-maker in the Ruhr, Alfred Krupp. Herr Krupp and his guns would also play an important part in Bismarck's plans for a greater Germany dominated by Prussia.

The currents of nationalism continued to erode the power of the Austrian Empire. In Italy, Count Cavour (the only statesman whose skill could compare with Bismarck's) made a pact with Napoleon III of France which enabled the Italians to throw Austria out of Lombardy, the richest province of the Austrian Empire. The defeat of the Austrian army at Magenta and Solferino was noted by Bismarck with interest.

Finally, in 1862, Bismarck's moment of destiny arrived. King William of Prussia, who had succeeded Frederick William IV in 1861, became locked in conflict with the Prussian parliament over the allocation of funds for the army. The king wanted to increase national service from two years to three, but parliament refused to pay for this. Neither side would give way, and the king was on the verge of abdicating

until he was persuaded to consult Bismarck. Bismarck convinced the king that he could handle parliament and also push through the army reforms; he emerged from this meeting as acting chief minister, minster-president, and foreign minister.

Iron and blood

Bismarck had virtually no knowledge of, or interest in domestic matters. What motivated him was a vision of the greater glory he could achieve for Prussia. One feature of the Prussian constitution that Bismarck understood very well was that parliament had no real power over ministers. Ministers were appointed by the king alone, and they appeared before parliament to explain their policies. Parliament could exert financial pressure, but if the prime minister was determined to ignore parliament and he retained the confidence of the king, there was nothing that could be done.

In October 1862 Bismarck explained his policy to parliament: 'Prussia must gather together her forces, conserving her strength for the favourable moment which has been missed several times already. Prussia's frontiers as drawn by the Congress of Vienna do not favour a healthy political existence. The great questions of the day will not be decided by speeches and majority votes – that was the great mistake of 1848 – but by iron and blood.'

This policy was put into practice in three wars that Bismarck initiated during the next eight years. Each had a specific political objective. Each was a work of political genius since each time Bismarck went to war he had succeeded in isolating the enemy and neutralizing other forces so that they could not take

principle was quite simple. Bismarck was trying to find a way of provoking a war with Austria.

It was a considerable gamble, because Austria had pulled herself together considerably since her defeats in Italy and indeed other European nations thought that the Austrians would win without difficulty. Saxony, Hannover, Bavaria and most of the secondary German states allied themselves with Austria, dimly realizing that if Prussia declared war on Austria she was in effect declaring war on all of Germany. This was to be the decisive battle and years later Bismarck recalled the moment before the conflict as 'the time when I was as close to the gallows as to the throne'.

On July 3, 1866, Prussia decisively defeated Austria on her own territory at the battle of Königgrätz. The troops of both armies fought ferociously, but the planning and leadership of the Prussian campaign was far superior. Von Moltke's maps and timetables won the day. The rest of Europe was stupified by the news of Austria's defeat, and Pope Pius IX uttered a famous cry: 'Casca il mondo!' ('The world is disintegrating!')

Having won his gamble, Bismarck took great care to limit the victory and to avoid humiliating Austria. The only territory lost by Austria was Venice, which Bismarck had promised to the Italians in return for military support in the south. Franz Joseph had to agree to Prussia's annexation of the hostile German states she had marched through – Hannover, Kassel and Nassau, as well as the wretched territories of Schleswig-Holstein which had been in limbo ever since Bismarck and the Austrians had fought a war over them. The Austrian emperor had to agree to the dissolution of the German Confederation and to the setting up of a new confederation of German territories north of the Main, which was controlled by the Prussian Hohenzollern monarchy and which excluded Austria.

dvantage of the conflict. And each time he won. All ismarck's strategy depended on was an army that vould not fail him, and in this respect he was ortunate: the Chief of the Prussian General Staff, Helmut von Moltke, was a brilliant commander. He ravelled incessantly, making maps wherever he went. He had carefully modernized and re-equipped his rmy. He had made extremely thorough preparations hrough studies of communications, logistics, and – specially – railway timetables. Elaborate plans were rawn up to control the transport of troops, guns, upplies, wherever they might be needed in Europe.

In 1864 Bismarck went to war with Denmark, vhich was trying to annexe the duchy of Schleswig. Bismarck presented himself as the defender of German nationalism, and he persuaded the Austrian mperor Franz Joseph to join him. Obviously Austria ould not let Prussia invade alone, and so these two eaders of the German people defeated Denmark. Franz Joseph then proposed that the two principalities in question – Schleswig and Holstein – should become independent members of the German Confederation, but Bismarck prevaricated, proposing that Schleswig be placed under Prussian administration, and Holstein under Austria. A series of extremely complicated political wrangles followed, but the underlying

Unification depended upon national pride in military victories, a pride that pervaded even children's games, as in 'Episodes in the German-Austrian War, 1866' (above). Victory over the French was crucial, and when Prussian troops entered Paris in 1871 (below), unification was complete.

comic map of Europe n 1871 (below) depicts Napoleon III's France

attempting to rebuff the designs of a belligerent Bismarck.

King William I of Prussia was proclaimed ruler of a unified Germany at Versailles in 1871. But he was unhappy at the ceremony because instead of 'German Emperor', he had wanted the less democratic title 'Emperor of Germany', and he left the hall without glancing at Bismarck (centre). The fact that all the dignitaries present are wearing uniforms is an indication of the fatally 'Prussian' character of the new Germany. Its brilliant military architect, von Moltke, stands to the left of Bismarck.

The final triumph

Bismarck's third and final war was waged with France in 1870. Again, this was preceded by an extremely complicated political wrangle in which Prussia proposed a Hohenzollern as a candidate for the throne of Spain. Napoleon III of France objected and Prussia seemed to back down, but at the last moment Bismarck succeeded in provoking a declaration of war by editing a telegram which described the French ambassador's meeting with the King of Prussia to make it appear as if the French had been grossly insulted. It was known as the 'Ems telegram' and it was a trivial pretext for a war that was to cast an extremely long shadow over the next 100 years.

Again, Europe expected a Prussian defeat. Bonaparte's invincible armies cutting across Europe were still a living memory and his nephew, Napoleon III, was believed to possess a similar style of military audacity. It was still not realized how carefully Bismarck and von Moltke had prepared for war, and just how confused the French politicians were.

France declared war on July 19, 1870. On September 1 Napoleon III and his army surrendered. A second French army of 173,000 men under Marshall Bazaine was beseiged at Metz, and they surrendered at the end of October. The city of Paris managed to hold out during a grim siege which lasted four months; by the end, the population of Paris was starving and hunting for rats and mice to eat. They surrendered in

January, but two weeks earlier, on January 18, 1871 King William I of Prussia was proclaimed German Emperor in the Palace of Versailles: the symbol of France's glory was the site of her greatest humiliation. The purpose of this highly efficient war had been to draw the remaining southern German states into union with Prussia, and to formalize this new union as the German Empire. It was the final act which completed Prussia's annexation and domination of the rest of Germany. In Vienna, Brahms composed his *Triumphlied* (Song of Triumph) as a celebration of this most glorious moment of German history.

At no point was this new German state based on anything except Prussia's military strength. The institutions that make up a modern democracy - parliamentary debate, a free press, an independent judicial system – never had a chance to develop. After the 1863 elections, Bismarck fined parliamentary candidates who had criticized the government in their election speeches, and civil servants with the wrong opinions were dismissed. Bismarck believed that strong government consisted of rewarding your friends and obstructing your enemies. It was more than a coincidence that the only man of outstanding ability with whom Bismarck collaborated closely was the army Chief of Staff, von Moltke. From 1871 until 1945 Germany continued along the road first mapped out by Bismarck, and her history was decisively shaped by her military and industrial might.

Pyotr Tchaikovsky
1840–1893

Tchaikovsky was neurotic and deeply sensitive, and his life was often painful and sometimes agonizing. But through the pain shone a genius that created some of the most beautiful of all Romantic melodies.

yotr Il'yich Tchaikovsky was born on 7 May 1840 at otkinsk in Russia, the second son (of five sons and ne daughter) of Il'ya Petrovich Tchaikovsky, a ining engineer, and his wife Alexandra Andreyevna. was clear very early in his life that he had an xtraordinary musical talent. At the age of four, with he help of his younger sister Sasha, he composed a ong for his mother.

Tchaikovsky's extreme sensitivity was also evident ght from infancy. He would over-react to any riticism and so strongly was he affected by music that ometimes the memory of a phrase would keep him wake at night. After one musical evening he was und sitting up in bed crying, 'This music! This music! 's here in my head and won't let me sleep.' A bright hild, he learned French and German from a French overness employed by the family, and when he arted piano lessons with a local teacher he fast vertook her in his ability at music.

School and Music

When Tchaikovsky was eight, the family moved to St Petersburg where the boy was to spend an unhappy time at the fashionable Schmelling School. It was here that he started his first piano lessons but his musical education was interrupted by a severe attack of measles from which he took six months to recover. As soon as he recovered, in May 1849, the family moved again, to Alapayevsk, but the following year Tchaikovsky's mother sent him back to St Petersburg to enrol in the preparatory class of the School of Jurisprudence as a boarder.

The parting from his mother was one of the most agonizing experiences of his life – he had to be forcibly wrenched away from her, and the horror of that moment stayed with him to the end of his life. The death of a schoolfriend from scarlet fever upset the sensitive boy even more. During an epidemic at his school Tchaikovsky lodged with the boy's family and,

Tchaikovsky was born into a well-to-do middle-class family in their elegant house in Kamsko-Votkinsk (below) – a town in the remote Vyatka province just west of the Urals.

Tchaikovsky's father Il'ya (above), described by the composer's younger brother Modest as being 'jovial and straightforward', was a prosperous manager of an iron mine. He married Alexandra Assier, the composer's mother (above right), in 1833. The influence she had on her son proved to be long and profound.

When Tchaikovsky was eight his father resigned and the family moved to St Petersburg where winter entertainments included horse and reindeer racing on the frozen river Neva (below and below right).

convinced that he had introduced the disease into the household, believed he was responsible for the death.

In 1852 the family came back to join him in St Petersburg, but his happiness lasted only two years. In June 1854, his mother succumbed to cholera and died. Tchaikovsky, who was very dependent on his mother, was shattered.

His emotional refuge was music. He took singing and piano lessons and through Luigi Piccioli, an Italian singing teacher, learned more about Italian opera. He even toyed with the idea of writing an opera himself, but his first published work was an Italian-style *canzonetta* (short song) called *Mezza notte*.

A musical career

After graduating from the School of Jurisprudence in 1859, Tchaikovsky began working as a clerk for the Ministry of Justice. He hated law, and began seriously to consider a career in music. He attended classes given by Nikolay Zaremba of the Russian Musical Society, soon to become the St Petersburg Conservatoire, and in 1862 started composition lessons with Anton Rubinstein, its first director. The following year, bored with his work at the Ministry, he resigned and joined the Conservatoire as a full-time student.

As well as classes in harmony and composition

Tchaikovsky took piano and flute lessons – the latte so that he could play in the Conservatoire orchest In 1865 he had the good fortune to have a perfe mance of his *Characteristic Dances* conducted Johann Strauss, at Pavlovsk, and in the same year made his first appearance as a conductor in performance of his Overture in F.

The same year Rubinstein's pianist brother Nikol who was about to found the new Moscow Co servatoire, offered Tchaikovsky a job as teacher harmony. This he accepted, moving to Moscow January 1866 to lodge with his employer.

Life in Moscow

The gregarious, larger-than-life figure of Nikol Rubinstein was to dominate Tchaikovsky for mai years. Homesick, and aghast at the thought of living Moscow 'for years . . . perhaps for ever', he four Rubinstein's lifestyle, with its constant 'open house' little overwhelming, and resented his 'looking aft me as if he were my nurse'. No doubt the older ma was concerned that his nervous, lonely house-gue and protegé should settle in well, and therefore too pains to introduce him to as many people as possibl

Yet when, in 1868, Tchaikovsky announced that I was in love with the soprano Désirée Artôt, the visiting with an Italian opera company, Rubinstein w among several of his friends who disapproved probably recognizing that, due to his homosexualit Tchaikovsky was unlikely to make a satisfacto marriage.

Fortunately, perhaps, for Tchaikovsky, Desire married another singer, and Tchaikovsky's flirtatio was halted – though they remained close friends.

In the meantime, he had composed his Fir Symphony, which nearly cost him a nervo breakdown. Both of his former teachers, Anto Rubinstein and Zaremba, were among its detracto But the nationalist group of composers in Petersburg, nicknamed the 'Mighty Five' (Balakire Rimsky-Korsakov, Cui, Borodin and Musorgsk approved of the first movement when it was heard 1868. His operas *The Voyevoda* and *Undin* composed shortly after, met with less success.

Nevertheless, Tchaikovsky was beginning to mal his mark on Russian musical society. He had met th music critic Stassov and also Balakirev, leader of th 'Mighty Five', in Moscow in 1868. Balakire conducted his symphonic fantasia *Fatum* in 1869 an also prompted and advised the composer on th creation of *Romeo and Juliet*.

The beauty of the Russian countryside which Tchaikovsky knew as a boy remained important to him throughout his life. Echoes of the songs and dances of rural Russia can often be heard in his music.

creative period

y now Rubinstein had moved to a larger house, along ith Tchaikovsky, and the stream of visitors ontinued unabated. Balakirev, Borodin and Rimsky-orsakov were among the guests, but Tchaikovsky as still consumed with loneliness: what he wanted as an intimate friendship with one special person, nd a family atmosphere. He always loved the ompany of children, and his summers fell into a outine of visits to his married sister Sasha or to his ealthy friend Vladimir Shilovsky at Usovo, and oreign travel. All his life he longed to be elsewhere; et if he travelled abroad, he was homesick and could ot wait to return to Russia. This was, perhaps nother aspect of his search for emotional fulfilment hat was never to be satisfied.

By the middle of 1871 he had composed a success-ul string quartet and was well advanced with *The Oprichnik,* his next operatic work. He also left Rubinstein's household and took a small flat of his own n order to concentrate on composition and he began is Second Symphony.

Professionally, he was doing very well, despite his ate start and, had he not been a natural spendthrift, iving away, or financing foreign trips with, whatever ncome he received, he would have been comfortably ff. But he was in torment about his homosexuality. He

At the age of 21, Tchaikovsky joined the St Petersburg Conservatory, where he studied, among other instruments, the flute and organ. During these lean years he supplemented his income by taking on piano and music theory pupils. In 1865, Tchaikovsky (left) graduated and moved the following year to take a teaching post at the Moscow Conservatory.

Great Composers

had begun to keep a diary, in which he made fran[k?] references to 'this', or 'Z', as well as to his drinking an[d] health.

Returning after a long trip in Europe in 1873 h[e] quickly sketched a new orchestral work, *The Tempes[t]* and revelled in the beauty of the Russian countrysid[e] All his life, however far he was from his homeland, th[e] thought of rural Russia filled him with patrioti[c] nostalgia. He once wrote, while in Switzerlan[d] 'Surrounded by these majestically beautiful views, an[d] feeling all the impressions of a traveller, I still long fo[r] Russia with all my soul, and my heart sinks as I imagin[e] its plains, meadows and woods.'

Back in Moscow, the longing for a true soul-mat[e] returned. There was no one to whom he was real[ly] close, though his next orchestral work, *Francesca d[a] Rimini,* his Second and Third String Quartets, his Fir[st] Piano Concerto and the opera *Vakula the Smith* wer[e] to keep him busy over the next few years.

In 1875, Tchaikovsky began writing his Thir[d] Symphony and a ballet commissioned by th[e] directorate of the Imperial Theatres in Moscow: *Swa[n] Lake.* The ballet suffered from a poor first performanc[e] in 1877; the orchestra found the work difficult i[n] comparison to the trifling pieces they normally playe[d] as dance accompaniment, and the audience of the da[y] did not appreciate the brilliance of the score. It wa[s] not until after Tchaikovsky's death that *Swan Lake* wa[s] to emerge as a great classic.

By his mid-30s, Tchaikovsky had reached a peak o[f] creativity in musical terms, but became more an[d] more troubled by the yawning emotional gap in hi[s] life. Seeing marriage as the only way to break with hi[s] homosexuality, for which he felt such shame, he wrot[e] to tell his brother Modest, also homosexual, of hi[s] decision. He had no idea who his marital partner wa[s] to be, but as ill-luck would have it, a candidate wa[s] soon to present herself. Yet just before his impendin[g] disastrous marriage Tchaikovsky had embarked on a[n] extraordinary relationship with a woman that was t[o] last for 14 years.

Romantic relationships

Tchaikovsky had begun to correspond with a[n] immensely rich widow named Nadezhda von Meck i[n] 1876 while composing his *Variations on a Rococ[o] Theme.* Her husband, an engineer, had made a fortun[e] out of Russia's new railway network, largely due to he[r] business acumen. Now a virtual recluse, Mme vo[n] Meck saw almost no one outside her family circle - which, however, often included a 'house' musicia[n] (the young Debussy was to be one of them). Afte[r] Tchaikovsky had executed her first lucrativ[e] commission they began to write to each othe[r] frequently, soon revealing their feelings and thought[s] to each other in a way that neither could have done t[o] anyone else.

Each was determined, because of this intimacy-by[-] letter, never to meet the other. This arrangement wa[s] ideal for Tchaikovsky, for it meant he need never ris[k] the possiblity of entering into a relationship requirin[g] physical passion. It suited her, too, because as long a[s] she never met Tchaikovsky her illusions about him, a[s] her ideal man, could never be destroyed.

Two works occupied Tchaikovsky at this time: hi[s] Fourth Symphony, the first of his three great works i[n] this form, which he was to refer to as 'our' symphon[y] in future letters to Mme von Meck, and the oper[a] *Eugene Onegin.*

Distressed by the difficulties he was having with th[e] Symphony, he was surprised one day to receive [a]

The famous Tatyana Letter Scene (above), from Tchaikovsky's opera Eugene Onegin, *parallels a crucial incident in the composer's own life. In May 1877, he had received an unexpected love-letter from a pupil at the Moscow Conservatory, Antonina Milyukova. More letters followed and eventually, in a state of emotional confusion, Tchaikovsky agreed to meet her. Perhaps mindful of the tragic story of Tatyana, whose love for Onegin is harshly repulsed, Tchaikovsky was moved by Antonina's declarations of love, and married her in July 1877 (right).*

love-letter from a woman he did not know, Antonina Ivanovna Milyukova, who claimed to be an admirer of his music. More letters followed, with earnest requests that she should be allowed to meet him.

Eventually, perhaps because he was so wrapped up in the tragic story of Tatyana in *Eugene Onegin,* whose love for Onegin is brutally repulsed, Tchaikovsky agreed to meet her, particularly because by this time Antonina had threatened to commit suicide if he refused. Though he told her, when they met, that he could never love her, he later reflected that he had acted thoughtlessly – before he knew what was happening, he had proposed to her and been accepted.

The marriage, which began in July 1877, was a disaster. Antonina's very presence quickly became abhorrent to Tchaikovsky, and to escape her he fled to the Caucasus on the pretext of taking the 'cure'. Mme von Meck, despite her sympathetic letters when he revealed to her his true feelings, was bitter about the marriage, and only too pleased to lend him money to allow him to get away from Antonina.

When he returned, briefly, Antonina boasted of her many former admirers, confident no doubt that her charms would soon have the desired effect upon Tchaikovsky. Yet when Nikolay Rubinstein and Tchaikovsky's brother Anatoly came to inform her that he was a mental and physical wreck, and an immediate divorce was necessary, she received the news with unnatural calm. Her reaction foreshadowed the mental instability which was shortly to assert itself: her sexual obsessions were to result in a succession of illegitimate children by various fathers, and she was to spend the last two decades of her life in a mental asylum.

The divorce, only permissable on the grounds of adultery, was finally granted in 1881, when the first

In 1876, Nadezdha von Meck (above), a resourceful 6-year-old widow, commissioned Tchaikovsky to write an arrangement for violin and piano. She was enraptured with the results and so began a curious patronage and a relationship which virtually excluded their seeing each other. Their prolific correspondence was therapy for them both and totalled 1100 letters.

The city of Florence (below) afforded Tchaikovsky relief from his recurrent bouts of depression. He moved there in 1878 and enjoyed briefly a life of unaccustomed contentment in an apartment rented for him by Mme von Meck. He left the city in 1879 and began a restless nomadic existence, travelling constantly between Russia and the rest of Europe.

child – not the composer's – was born, but Tchaikovsky was to fear public exposure of his homosexuality by Antonina for the rest of his life.

Emotional problems

The mental breakdown he suffered shortly after marrying her was severe. After a bungled suicide attempt, he fled to St Petersburg where he spent two days in a coma. However, the Conservatory granted him a sabbatical and Mme von Meck helpfully bestowed an annuity of 6000 roubles on him to ease any money problems. Anatoly took him off to western Europe for a holiday, where he began to recover his equilibrium. 'Henceforth', he wrote to Mme von Meck, 'every note that emanates from my pen shall be dedicated to you.'

Although he finished *Eugene Onegin,* his finest opera, in San Remo in January 1878, and went on to write his fine Violin Concerto in April, Tchaikovsky was about to enter into a creative doldrums. For years he led an unsettled life, travelling between Russia and western Europe and composing many pieces simply because he had been commissioned to do so rather than from an inner compulsion. The highly popular *1812* Overture was one of these; Tchaikovsky said of it that it was loud and noisy, 'I've written it without affection and enthusiasm', and he feared that there was 'probably no artistic merit in it'.

For almost four years he struggled to begin composing a new symphony. His life fell into a routine. He was now living in a rented house at Maidanovo, near Klin, from which he would sally forth every afternoon after working in the morning. He would take a notebook with him on these 'creative walks', then sort out his ideas during an evening work-session from five to seven. It was Balakirev who inspired his next symphonic work, *Manfred,* based on Byron's verse dream. Tchaikovsky became very depressed while he was working on this but was very pleased with it when he finished it in September 1885.

In 1887 he overcame his fear of conducting enough to conduct, despite agonizing mental strain, the first

When life in Moscow seemed more than Tchaikovsky could bear, the house of the Davidov family at Kamenka (above) provided a much-needed retreat.

Tchaikovsky's sister married Lev Davidov – a renowned revolutionary – in 1861. Of all the beloved Davidov family the composer was most fond of his nephew Bob (front row, near right).

hurt, especially at the implied assertion that their friendship depended on financial support. He wrote immediately to tell her so, but there was no reply. It later transpired that the story of financial ruin was untrue, and it appears that her action was probably triggered by a mental illness from which she suffered for some years. Whatever the reasons, Tchaikovsky's peace of mind was destroyed and he never recovered.

Last years

The following year he began work, without much enthusiasm, on a commission: a ballet based on E. T. A. Hoffman's *The Nutcracker and the Mouse King*. Then, suffering from nervous depression, he set off for Paris, before sailing for New York, to begin a conducting tour. In the French capital he read of the death of his beloved sister Sasha. Arriving depressed and homesick in America, Tchaikovsky's wretched state was relieved a little by the kindness and consideration shown to him by the American people.

In 1893, the last year of his life, Tchaikovsky enjoyed success, popularity and respect to a degree unusual for any composer. He was also at the height of his creative powers, composing the masterly *Pathétique* Symphony during the spring, and completing it, after problems with the orchestration, in August. He was very happy with the work, which he regarded as 'the best of all', and on 28 October he conducted its première in St Petersburg.

A few days later, on 6 November, he was dead. The fear of the public exposure of his homosexuality that had haunted him for so long was finally realized. The threat came, not from Antonina as he had expected, but from a member of the Russian aristocracy with whose nephew Tchaikovsky had had a homosexual liaison. A 'court of honour', including several of Tchaikovsky's contemporaries from the School of Jurisprudence, had decreed that to avert the scandal of exposure Tchaikovsky should commit suicide. Meanwhile, a story was circulated that he died of cholera after drinking unboiled water. He was buried in the Alexander Nevsky monastery in St Petersburg.

The demanding social life of St Petersburg and Moscow (above left) ran counter to Tchaikovsky's yearning for an unmolested life of tranquillity. But he found some peace at Sokolniki, (above right), a cab ride from the city. Here, 'grateful to the Muscovites for not caring for nature' he could take solitary walks.

Tchaikovsky (far right) died under strange circumstances, for long a source of great controversy. Did he die of cholera after drinking unboiled water? Or did he poison himself at the command of a 'court of honour'?

performance of *Cherevichki* ('The Slippers'), and the revised and re-named version of his opera *Vakula the Smith*. In March and November he conducted concerts in St Petersburg and Moscow that consisted entirely of his own works, and they were highly praised. Suddenly, it seemed, he had triumphed over his self-doubts and found the confidence to emerge as a first-rate master of the baton. In 1888 he undertook the first of his conducting tours of western Europe. Hailed everywhere as a great celebrity, he met Brahms and Grieg in Leipzig, Dvořák in Prague and Gounod, Fauré and Massenet in Paris.

Back in Russia he wrote his next masterpiece, the Fifth Symphony and the next year he embarked upon a second international conducting tour and the composition of his second great ballet score, *Sleeping Beauty*, which was first performed in St Petersburg in January 1890.

Tchaikovsky's brother Modest was the librettist of his next opera, *The Queen of Spades,* and like *Eugene Onegin,* the inspiration was a Pushkin tale, with Fate playing a major role in the story. But Fate, too, was once more to intervene in Tchaikovsky's life – again in the form of a letter. This time it was from Mme von Meck, who reported that she was on the verge of financial disaster and could no longer provide his annuity; their friendship must therefore end immediately. Tchaikovsky was amazed and deeply

Life under the Tsars

In a single decree in 1861, Tsar Alexander II granted freedom to 40 million serfs. Russia had finally accepted the ideal of individual freedom, but had also sown the seeds of revolution.

Defeat at the hands of the French and British armies in the Crimean War (above) meant that Russia was left with no part to play in general European affairs. A humiliated Russia looked for an answer to this national disaster and discovered that society was in need of great social reform.

The Crimean War ended in 1856, and defeat left Imperial Russia with an acute crisis of confidence. Her pretensions as a great military power were exposed as sham; her smug belief in the stability of her unique institutions lay in tatters; her plain backwardness in a rapidly changing world was starkly revealed. The chill of despair went wide and deep, and provoked even in the most conservative quarters the realization that things were not as they should be.

It was not that the loss of this particularly inane war left Russia threatened with dismemberment or the yoke of foreign domination. Nothing of the sort. The ramshackle empire stretching from the Arctic to the Caspian, and from the shores of the Baltic to China and beyond to the wastes of Siberia and even across the Bering Straits to Alaska, emerged from the Crimean fiasco pretty well intact. The trouble was that no one who took a serious look at Russian society in th[e] middle of the 19th century could fail to see that th[e] national humiliation was an inevitable consequence [of] national ineptness. The principal casualty of th[e] Crimean War, in other words, was Russian self-estee[m] and in its wake came a clamour for reform.

Russia's internal problem

It was not difficult to identify the failings of Russia[n] society, and indeed many of them were not unique t[o] Russia but only magnified by the sheer scale of th[e] place – a huge and cumbersome bureaucratic machin[e] that was at best irksome and at worst stultifying; a[n] unfair legal system, backed up by secret police, an[d] rife with corruption at every level; an overa[ll] economic performance that was pitiful by advance[d] European standards and steadily deteriorating as th[e]

...dustrial Age swung into full stride.

There was, however, one respect in which Russian ...ciety was uniquely badly organized. The over...helming majority of the Tsar's subjects were not free ...en or women but existed in bondage, either to the ...nd-owning aristocracy or to the state itself. Serfdom, ...ong with black slavery in the United States — the ...ost glaring abuse in the western world — lay at the ...eart of the Russian malaise. Its harmful effects ...rmeated every aspect of national life, and it was ...escapable, therefore, that the drive for reform ...ntred on its abolition.

It is difficult even to begin to grasp the magnitude of ...e serf problem. At this time the total population of ...uropean Russia was 60 million. Of these, nearly 50 ...illion were peasants, and 40 million of the peasants ...ere serfs; that is, they were agricultural labourers ...ho were, to all intents and purposes, the private ...roperty of those who owned the land on which they ...orked.

Russians, even those who detested serfdom, were ...uick to dispute the parallel between serfdom and ...avery, and there were some important differences. ...ut it is surely revealing that the wealth of land...wners was commonly expressed in terms of the ...umber of serfs they possessed, rather than in terms of ...ncome, capital or acreage. A large landlord would ...wn hundreds of 'souls', and a great one, thousands. ...he greatest of all, the state itself, owned roughly half ...e entire serf population, 20 million 'souls'.

...fe of the serf

...s with slavery, the conditions of life facing a serf ...aried depending upon the accident of his location ...d the temperament of his master. He was tied to the ...nd — where he was born he remained. Everywhere, ...owever, certain rules governed his existence.

If he ran away and was caught, and an internal ...assport system and stiff penalties for harbouring a ...gitive pretty well ensured his capture, he would be ...ogged at his master's pleasure — just as for other ...ffences, real or imagined, since there was no legal ...course for him. Forty lashes with the birch or 15 ...lows with the stick were stipulated as maximum

Though agriculture was the usual work of the serf, many were hired out to work in mines and factories. Others had to eke out their existence by scavenging for coal (above). They were in bondage to their owners and could be bought and sold like cattle. In the painting **The Bargain** *(below) a serf is cheaply bought by a noble.*

punishment, but a landlord with a mind to do so could ignore these limits with impunity. Only if he gained a reputation for the most outlandish brutality need he fear any sort of official rebuke. If a landlord considered a particular serf incorrigible, he could have him transported to Siberia or force him into the army, again without legal restraint.

The serf's working life was split between farming he did on his own behalf, or rather on the behalf of the peasant commune of which he was a part, and farming or other labour he did to meet his obligations to his master. These obligations were of two kinds: labour and money, and the relative weight of each depended on the type of estate and the inclinations of the landlord.

At one end of the scale, a landlord who had an abundance of fertile land and took a keen interest in farming would want to extract the maximum labour from his serfs, and might well waive entirely any money dues. Another landlord might have more serfs than he needed to work his own fields, in which case he would allow them, or some of them, to hire themselves out elsewhere for wages, demanding in return a fixed yearly sum. At the far end of the scale, a landlord might prefer not to farm at all, in which case he would turn the whole of his arable lands over to the serf commune, contenting himself with the profits from the sale of produce.

Such a system was obviously open to the grossest abuses, but to suggest that the general lot of the serfs was ceaseless toil punctuated by savage beatings would be wrong. An enlightened or even a prudent landlord, and there were many, would not wish to ruin his peasants. He would set feasible conditions of servitude, and as long as they were met he and his serfs would rub along amicably enough.

The serf would have a house for his family, a vegetable patch, a little bit of livestock and poultry, a share of the communal land and, since the landlord was in a sense responsible for his serfs, a degree of protection from any bullying or meddlesome officials.

In return for this he would provide, either himself or through his sons, an amount of labour that did not prevent him from attending to his own small farming operation. A serf in such conditions might well have viewed abstract concepts like freedom and liberty with indifference or downright scepticism, if, for example, he had compared his lot with that of a contemporary English farm labourer.

Nevertheless, in the manifold abuses of the institution of serfdom its fundamental immorality stands out blatantly. Many landlords were purely rapacious, and, if to meet their demands serfs were reduced to abject poverty, so be it. Others were absentees, enjoying the fleshpots of St Petersburg or better yet Versailles, and to pay for an extravagant lifestyle they would bring irresistible pressure to bear on their stewards to squeeze ever more revenue from their estates, regardless of the consequences. Some had no natural connection with their estates at all, but had bought them as pure investment, in which case they wanted the maximum return in the minimum time. Finally, not a few were sadistic brutes who despised the peasantry and saw it as their duty, or pleasure, to treat them in a sub-human fashion. Unwittingly, of course, they were creating a bedrock of unshakeable resentment that would soon find voice.

On becoming Tsar in 1856, Alexander II (right) embarked on a programme of social reform. Within a decade he had freed the serfs, remodelled the legal system, introduced a form of local government, created a free press and granted a measure of academic freedom to the universities.

In 1856, in the same year as his coronation (below), Alexander II made his momentous statement to the nobility of Moscow. 'It is better to abolish serfdom from above than to wait until it begins to abolish itself from below.'

peasant, by sad contrast, was notorious for his sloth, and left to his own devices would do the barest minimum to keep body and soul together. Without the discipline of the serf system he would actually slip backward from his existing level of poverty to utter destitution.

This pessimistic analysis was equally unsparing of the Russian landlord. His counterpart in England, it argued, could thrive in a competitive free market because he too was industrious and ambitious. He was keen to master new techniques for improved output and, as a consequence of generations of material advance, he had the capital to apply these techniques. The typical Russian landlord was not of a practical turn of mind and never had been, hence he had neither the skills not the accrued capital to regenerate Russian agriculture along western lines.

The Tsar intervenes

Such a debate about the hypothetical effects of abolishing serfdom could have gone on forever had it not been for the intervention of the new Tsar, Alexander II. A rather weak man and by nature as conservative as his father Nicholas I, who died in despair towards the end of the Crimean War, Alexander nevertheless had a genuine insight into the serf

In March 1861 serfdom was abolished at a stroke. The text was distributed throughout the land, and, since virtually all peasants were illiterate, it was ordered to be read out in church (above), to ensure that every serf would fully understand the proposals.

Emancipation did little to improve the everyday life of the peasants. They were technically free, but still bound to the land. When they received land it was often smaller than the allotment they enjoyed under the serf system. Many left the land (right) to seek a living in the towns.

Debate over abolition

Enlightened thinkers in Russia had long favoured the abolition of serfdom, and not just on moral grounds. They argued that the progress of Western Europe showed, beyond doubt, that free labour was far more productive than slave or serf labour. Everywhere, agricultural progress had gone hand in hand with the demise of serfdom, and it was precisely because she clung to such an anachronism that Russia lagged so far behind her western neighbours – and was falling further behind all the time. Free the serfs and Russia would overnight shake off her medieval past and take her rightful place in the modern world – to the benefit of all classes of society.

Reactionary landlords, they stated, merely betrayed their ignorance of the outside world by claiming that such a transformation would impoverish them. The landed aristocracy in England were the richest and most powerful in the world, and serfdom there was a far distant memory. It was agricultural productivity that created genuine wealth for those who possessed land, not the ownership of a few hundred down-trodden serfs.

Against this was a conservative view held with equal tenacity. Russia, it was claimed, was not like western Europe, in fact she was not really a European nation at all, and it would therefore be folly to emulate western institutions in the naive assumption that western prosperity would automatically follow. The lower orders in such countries as England and Germany were well known for their industriousness, and for their desire to better their material lot. The Russian

Alexander II enlisted the help of the liberal intelligentsia to reform his regime. These university students and literary men soon became impatient with the slowness of true change in Russian society. But, though politically frustrated, many enjoyed a leisurely and relatively idyllic existence (left) – underlining the deep rift in Russian society.

In 1864 local councils were elected to deal with welfare, public health and education. The painting below shows peasants waiting patiently for aid outside the local administration offices.

question. Brushing aside any moral considerations, he considered the system historically doomed, and in April 1856 he stunned an assembly of the Moscow nobility with the trenchant observation: 'It is better to abolish serfdom from above than to wait until it begins to abolish itself from below.'

It was in the nature of Russian society that once the Tsar had expressed a sentiment, action would follow. He was an absolute monarch, not constrained by the need to carry even his most powerful subjects with him along any path he chose to tread. From the moment of his historic utterance, therefore, it was a foregone conclusion that serfdom was on its way out, and sooner rather than later. All that had to be decided were the terms for abolition.

The serf had to be released from his bondage, but in such a way that he was not uprooted from the land. Otherwise there would be chaos, with millions of peasants milling about uncontrolled, uncared for and confused about their new role in society, if indeed they had one. Therefore, the freed serf had to be given some land, land that could only come from its existing owners, either the proprietors, or the state. And since it was no one's intention, least of all the Tsar's, to impoverish the aristocracy, there would have to be compensation.

For the next few years the government wrestled with the problem, which boiled down to three main questions. How much land should the serf get? On what terms? How should the previous owner be compensated for his loss? The results of these lengthy deliberations finally emerged in 1861 in the form of an Imperial decree abolishing serf law with immediate effect. A manifesto spelling out the essentials of the new deal was distributed throughout the land, and in recognition of the illiteracy of the peasantry it was ordered that the manifesto be read out in church.

Given the complexity of the issues, and the potentially disastrous consequences of botching the job, the terms of the emancipation were ingeniously simple. The serfs were freed and given protection under the law. As far as possible, the land they received was the land they customarily used for their own purposes under serfdom, with the self-governing peasant commune stepping in to fill the void left by the landlord in matters of everyday management.

The peasant was to compensate his ex-master for the land he received, but indirectly. The state itself advanced the agreed sum to the dispossessed landlord, and was to recover the money in a series of annual payments from the peasant, the responsiblity for making the payment as well as taxes resting with the commune.

That was the essence of what can fairly be described as an unprecedented piece of social engineering. At a stroke 40 million serfs became free, and while the bargain struck to give them that freedom was heavily weighted in favour of the existing order, that it was achieved at all and implemented comparatively smoothly was a great accomplishment. After all, the attempt by that most progressive of nations, the United States, to rid itself of black slavery had at that very moment plunged America into a terrible civil war.

Equally remarkable was the speed with which other major reforms were triggered by the abolition of serfdom. Removing the jurisdiction of the landlords left huge gaps in the legal system, and it was duly overhauled along western lines – independent courts sitting openly, trial by jury in criminal cases, irremovable judges, all those legally progressive institutions which had been sadly lacking under the old order. And while it would be quite wrong to suggest that as a result of all this the serf suddenly took his place as an equal in society, even in the limited sense that a free-born English farm labourer of the time enjoyed equality, it was nevertheless a firm step away from the medieval past. So, too, was the establishment of a representative system of local government.

Reforms of the 1860s

The results of the reforms of the 1860s were necessarily mixed, for both classes were directly affected. Some proprietors seized on the opportunities presented by the sudden windfall of capital and overhauled their shrunken estates in line with advanced agricultural methods, using machinery and free labour to work the land more productively. Others proved incapable of adjusting to the new realities and sank into self-pitying torpor. Still others cut and run – delighted to be able to clear their debts, lease off the remainder of their estates to the peasants and flee rural boredom for the urban pleasures of St Petersburg or Moscow.

The consequences for the peasantry were no less varied. They were now free, for example, to marry whom they chose, and to work where they wanted, although here their freedom was circumscribed by their obligations to the commune. For a while the commune had exercised considerable authority over its members, mainly in such practical agricultural matters as what crop was to be grown at what time of

Peasants who left the land to work in the factories were obliged to send back some of their wages to the communal council. Living conditions in the cities were often no better than in the communes, and these metal workers in St Petersburg (below) lived in the rented corner of a single room.

Great Composers

In the 18th century Peter the Great (below) and Catherine the Great (below right) had turned Russia from its essentially Asian aspect to look westward into Europe. This only served to create a divide between the 'westernizers' and the 'slavophils' – those who saw Russia spiritually, and culturally, as a part of Asia.

year. Now the commune was responsible for seeing that the individual peasant paid his dues to the state. Hence the 'free' peasant could only obtain permission to leave the commune if he could satisfy his fellows that he would continue to pay his share – by sending back some of his wages, for instance, if he wanted to move off and work in a factory.

The reforms brought no guarantee, however, that the ex-serf would be materially better off than he had been before. Many, in fact, ended up with smaller allotments of land than they had enjoyed under serfdom, in which case they were still obliged to work hard and long for the old master – as hired labour rather then enforced labour, but with the same practical effect.

Westernizers versus slavophils

Tsar Alexander might have been forgiven for thinking that by resolving the central issue of the age, however imperfectly, he had set Russia on a steady course towards future strength and prosperity, and all without undermining the sacred principle of autocracy and the unique qualities of the Russian way of life. In fact, he had done nothing of the sort. What he had

done was to focus attention on the deep, some wou say fathomless, divide in the Russian mind – a divi that went far beyond the immediate issue of reform the nature of the Russian experience itself.

There existed side by side, and for quite some tim two diametrically opposed visions of what Russia w and where her destiny lay. Two of the 18th century most forceful monarchs, Peter the Great and Catheri the Great, had virtually frogmarched Russia from Asian past into what they saw as its European futu Peter had built his magnificent new capital on t western frontier of his empire, so as to provide window by which the Russians might look into ci lized Europe'. Like Peter himself, who was near seven feet tall, St Petersburg was built on a coloss scale: immense palaces, public buildings and church vast squares and avenues, and all of it inspired t Peter's vision of what Russia should aspire to.

Under Catherine, the Europeanization of the Russi aristocracy reached its zenith. Anyone wi pretensions to being civilized spoke French fluentl and in preference to Russian, aped French fashions ar extolled the merits of French classical literature; short, a cultivated Russian put up as high a barrier as could between himself and what he viewed as t semi-barbarous society that he had been born into.

It is easy to mock such affectation, but underlying was a serious assumption: namely that Russia's pa was an unenviable one and that a great future was he only if she could become thoroughly westerniz from the top down. And it was this underlyi assumption, rather than the posturings of a few overl refined courtiers, that exposed those who we westernized to attacks from a rival school of thinke the so-called 'slavophils'.

Based mainly on the older pre-St Petersburg capi of Moscow, the slavophils looked at Russia and Russi history through the other end of the telescope. As th saw it, things had been going well enough until Pet the Great came along with his mad vision of western zation. Russia was geographically, spiritually a culturally an eastern, not a western, society.

Attempts to assassinate Alexander II were made in 1866, 1873, and in 1880. Finally on 13 March 1881, th terrorists achieved their aim. A bomb was thrown a the Tsar's carriage passed along the Catherine Canal (below). He was unharmed but as he attempted to comfort his wounded guards a secon fatal bomb fell at his feet (below right).

They considered that the principle of autocracy, with all power resting securely in the hands of the anointed Tsar, had saved Russia from the political upheavals and class struggles that had proved such a disfiguring feature of western life. Russia had been blessed with the Orthodox religion and thus spared the great Roman Catholic/Protestant schism that had overshadowed western Europe for centuries.

Tragically, they thought, large segments of the upper classes had been beguiled by the siren song of western materialism – the mania for progress at any cost, the flirtation with liberalism and the cult of the individual. But the peasantry, even after emancipation, were still mercifully untainted, and it was to them that the slavophils looked for a regeneration of traditional Russian values.

The young radicals

The long-standing rift between westernizers and slavophils began to take on a new dimension during and after the reform era of the 1860s. A new set of western ideas was thrown into the intellectual and political arena. These were radical notions which were as abhorrent to the cultured aristocrats as they were to diehard slavophils. The advocates of these new ideas were mainly young university-educated idealists, who believed that the reforms had gone nowhere near far enough, indeed were no more than a swindle since they left power and money with the few while the majority remained in abject poverty. The complete transformation of society was their aim, a true egalitarianism based on the natural socialism of the peasant commune.

During the 1860s small revolutionary groups began to appear. The outstanding figure was N. G. Chernyshevsky (above), a socialist writer, who was to influence a generation of young Russians.
The 1870s saw a revival of revolutionary activity – and a revival of harsh counter-measures enforced by military power (above left).

Their Utopian dream appeared as a hideous nightmare to all the established forces in Russian society, and the reaction set in swiftly. The authorities began cracking down heavily on the universities and on the press which disseminated radical thought. This had the predictable effect of goading the young radicals into greater defiance, both open and clandestine, and in 1866 there was the first of a succession of attempts on Alexander's life.

It was, of course, ironic that the 'Tsar Liberator' should become the focus of the radicals' hatred, since he himself had played midwife to the reform movement in the first place. Now, however, he began to take refuge in more traditional beliefs. The principles of autocracy and the established order were sacred to him, and the violent attack upon them – and upon his own person – showed that reform had gone far enough, if not too far already. It was time to call a halt, time to bring the nation to heel.

So began the era of the exile, the secret society and the bomb. Many of the radicals fled to the relative sanctuary of western Europe, mostly to Switzerland, and from there conducted a tireless war of words against the Russian state. Those who remained behind organized themselves into various secret societies,

After the death of Alexander II and the crowning of Alexander III (below) came the rejection of any plans to introduce elected representatives into the government structure. The re-establishment of virtual dictatorship succeeded in fermenting the revolutionary ideals that would explode in the Bolshevik revolution of 1917.

reflecting different shades of opinion about how to bring down the established order. And from within and without Russia endless terrorist plots were hatched, and not a few brought to deadly fruition.

The real target, however, remained Alexander himself, and on 13 March 1881, the terrorists finally achieved their aim. As the Tsar was driving along the Catherine Canal in St Petersburg a bomb was thrown at his carriage. He was unharmed, and got out of the carriage to comfort some of his Cossack guards who had been injured. Then a second assassin lobbed a bomb between his feet, which mutilated him dreadfully. He had time only to murmur 'Home to the palace, to die there', before he died.

The assassination of Alexander shocked Russia profoundly, and it widened even further the gulf between those who wanted more reforms whether of a liberal or revolutionary nature, and those who saw national salvation only through repression. The new Tsar, Alexander III, brought little comfort to progressives of any nature. The great Russian experiment – the attempt to achieve social and political harmony from above – had failed. The train of events that would culminate in the revolution of 1917 had been set firmly in motion.

Antonín Dvořák
1841–1904

At the height of his career, Antonín Dvořák was fêted from Moscow to the Mississippi. But he never forgot his Bohemian peasant childhood or the Czech people who inspired his music.

Great Composers

Antonín Dvořák was among the happiest of all composers. Unassuming, level-headed and natural, even at the height of his success, Dvořák – pronounced 'dVoorrshark' – suffered none of the mental anguish that seemed to afflict so many of the composers of the Romantic era, such as Tchaikovsky and Schumann. Throughout his life, despite many setbacks and reverses, Dvořák retained a simple, wholehearted delight in living, a delight that shines throughout his music and inspired deep affection in all who knew him.

In many ways, Dvořák is the spiritual heir of Schubert and their music has 'the same spontaneous and irrepressible flow of melody, the same delicate sense of instrumental colouring and the same instinctive command of the means of expression.' These words were actually used by Dvořák to describe Schubert, his favourite composer; but they apply equally well to himself.

Although during his lifetime he was fêted in London, Paris and New York, Antonín Dvořák remained at heart a country-loving man. The uncomplicated beauty of the Bohemian countryside (below and centre) was always a delight to him. It always gave him great pleasure to wander through the woodlands near his home at Vysoká – south of Prague, where from 1888 he spent his summers relaxing.

Dvořák's music is, like Schubert's, instantly approachable, and it was always his belief that music should above all entertain, not instruct. Indeed, few composers have had at their command such a rich fund of wonderful, memorable tunes, tunes that have become as familiar as brown bread. Pieces like the *New World Symphony* and the *Slavonic Dances* flew straight to the hearts of the public and have remained there ever since.

Although fairly tall, about five foot eleven, Dvořák had the solid, stocky build of all Bohemian peasants, and the same broad, squat features. When he was younger, wild dark hair and a thick, bushy beard combined with a piercing gaze to give an effect so strikingly outlandish that the famous German conductor Hans von Bülow declared that Dvořák reminded him of Caliban, the monstrous character from Shakespeare's play *The Tempest.* Von Bülow also described Dvořák as 'next to Brahms, the most God-gifted composer of the present day'.

Pictures of the composer also give an impression of what one critic called grim 'bulldog ferocity' and it is easy to get an impression of Dvořák as a wild, irascible Bohemian. Nothing could be further from the truth.

Dvořák was born in 1841 in the small village of Nelahozeves (right), north of Prague. Despite the fact that his musical talent was abundantly obvious, his father František Dvořák (far right) intended that he should follow in his footsteps and become a butcher. However, after completing his apprenticeship one of his uncles, Antonín Zdeněk, offered to finance his full-time musical studies in Prague. On his arrival there he stayed with several relatives, amongst whom was his father's sister, Josefina Dušková (far right).

middle-aged, Dvořák would stroll down to the Franz Josef station in Prague early every day just to see the trains and take down their numbers. Nothing would please him more than to make friends with an engine driver. If he was teaching, he would send one of his pupils to discover which engine was hauling the Vienna express that day.

Dvořák had many other passions apart from trains. He was fascinated by birds, for instance, and the theme for the third movement of the *String Quartet in F* is inspired by the song of the scarlet tanager. When he bought his country home in Vysoká, he was able to indulge a long-cherished dream and breed pigeons. But his greatest passion was, of course, music and his enthusiasm for the art never once dimmed.

The Village Inn
Dvořák's passion for music started young. He was

Dvořák could indeed be tenacious and extremely obstinate. He seems to have had quite a temper – and on big public occasions he smiled but rarely. But all Dvořák's friends testify ardently to the real sweetness and gentleness of his nature, and loved him deeply for it. They loved him too for the simple pleasure he took in life, and the great joy he found in telling people about these pleasures. Any slowness to smile was simply natural modesty and humility. When his stern face wrinkled in laughter or he launched enthusiastically into one of his pet subjects, oblivious to the world, few could resist his warmth and humour. Tchaikovsky, who befriended Dvořák in 1888, referred to him as *'simpatichniy chudak'* – the dear funny fellow – and the normally testy Brahms seems to have had an even deeper affection for him – an affection that lasted a lifetime.

For Dvořák, life was a wonderful, happy thing and he looked on the great inventions of man with the wide-eyed delight of a child. When he was nine, a railway was built through his native village of Nelahozeves, only 25 years after the opening in England of the Stockton-Darlington railway. The young country boy was spell-bound and ever after had a tremendous fascination for trains. Even when

born, on 8th September 1841, in a low-ceilinged room above the inn in the village of Nelahozeves on the River Vltava. His father, František Dvořák, like František's father before him, was the inn keeper and butcher for the sleepy village – the two trades often went hand-in-hand in this part of the world. His mother Anna was the daughter of the bailiff at the local castle. Both young Antonín's grandfathers had been simple peasants, working the land, but by enterprise and sheer hard work, they had improved their status a little.

František Dvořák was an attractive and solidly-built man, accomplished not only in dispensing fine ale and meat but also, like so many of his fellow country-men, a capable musician.

Music was in the blood of all Czechs and they burst into song and dance at every occasion. Dvořák once said of the English that they did not love music; they merely respected it. The Czechs certainly loved it.

There always seemed something to celebrate in Nelahozeves. Like so many Bohemian villages, it seemed filled with an air of gaiety and optimism even when the weight of the Austrian Empire was at its heaviest.

It was not long before little 'Toník' too was caught

by this exuberant musical spirit, and it seems that he was playing simple dance tunes on the fiddle for the benefit of customers in the inn before he was five years old. Before long, helped by the local schoolmaster and organist Josef Spic, Toník was playing alongside his father in the band at weddings and other local festivals.

Music soon became everything to the little boy. But when he was 11 years old and his time at the local village school came to an end, Toník was naturally apprenticed to his father in the butcher's trade. He took badly to the trade and dreaded going to fetch a heifer from the next village – the heifer invariably dragged him through the mud.

In the days of Austrian domination, it was essential to speak German if you wanted to get on in any trade. So after a year of apprenticeship at butchering, Toník was sent to stay in the small town of Zlonice, 15 miles away, with his uncle Antonín Zdeněk (Anna's

PRAGUE

brother). There, his parents hoped he would learn German from a teacher at the local school, Antonín Liehmann.

From Zlonice to Prague

Liehmann had a fiery temper and was a strict disciplinarian, but he was also a dedicated and highly competent musician. He was so delighted by his new pupil's rapid progress on organ, viola and piano, that he began to teach Toník harmony and counterpoint and invited him to join his small orchestra – the German studies were inevitably neglected.

Soon Toník may have tried his hand at composition. He was so proud of his first polka, so the story goes, that he took it back to Nelahozeves for the local band to play. Unfortunately, he had not realized that the cornet is a transposing instrument and music must be written in a different key from that in which it is to be played. Poor Toník's composing debut was slightly less harmonious than he anticipated.

After a year Toník's parents joined him when František took over The Big Inn in Zlonice. Toník's musical activities were curtailed a little, and, in 1856, he may have actually completed his apprenticeship as a butcher. A year in the Silesian village of Česká Kamenice improved his German (and his music) no end. But his father desperately needed his help in the inn, which was in difficulties because of the landlord's vindictive attitude towards a 'foreigner'.

Liehmann couldn't bear to see his star pupil's musical talent go to waste, so he persuaded Toník's Uncle Antonín Zdeněk to put up the money to send

the boy to the Organ School in Prague. Liehmann's pleadings were successful and, in late September 1857, Toník, then 16 years old, set out with his father and a hand cart piled with his belongings to walk the 26 miles south to the great city of Prague – they could not afford a train ticket.

The young musician was never really at ease in the imposing surroundings of the Organ School, partly because only those who spoke German well seemed to get favourable treatment. He acquired a rudimentary knowledge of the old classical masters, Mozart and Beethoven, but never seriously threw himself into the study of musical theory. At the end of his time at the school, his teachers described him as 'excellent, but inclined to show a more practical talent. Practical knowledge and accomplishment appear to be his aim; in Theory he achieves less.'

It was playing the viola in the St Cecilia Society Orchestra that he really enjoyed. The leader of this orchestra, Antonín Apt, was an ardent admirer of Richard Wagner, a composer whose work was frowned upon by the rather staid Organ School. Soon the impressionable young viola player was equally enthusiastic about Wagner's heady, intoxicating music. For Dvořák, the spell of Wagner's music was to last many years – he even wrote an opera, *Alfred,* in Wagnerian style about the Anglo-Saxon king Alfred the Great.

Until 1878 Dvořák relied on teaching as his main source of income. Then, as the result of sending a copy of his Moravian Duets *(below) to Brahms, his reputation spread. Brahms sent them to his publisher, Simrock, who published them and at once commissioned the* Slavonic Dances *(below right).*

The young musician

When Dvořák finished at the Organ School in 1860, his family was still desperately poor and unable to support him. Fortunately, a Prague band-leader Karel Komzák was in need of a viola player and Dvořák willingly accepted the job. The band was very popular in restaurants in Prague and was often asked to play at balls and classical concerts.

Meanwhile, as a sop to nationalist feelings the Habsburgs began to grant a few minor concessions to their subject nations. For the Czechs, this included the founding of a Czech National Theatre to stage Czech plays and operas and foreign operas in Czech translations. The Czech nationalist composer Bedřich Smetana was to play a key role in the theatre, and many of his operas, such as *The Bartered Bride* received their premières there.

Komzák's band was to form the nucleus of the orchestra at the theatre and so Dvořák actually played at many of these premières. During his nine years in the theatre orchestra, from 1862 to 1871, Dvořák played in a wide range of new and interesting works such as Gounod's *Faust* and Glinka's *Ruslan and Lyudmila* and more than made up in practical experience what he had failed to learn in theory at the Organ School. More importantly he was exposed to the works of Czech nationalist composers and shown just what potential there was in his own national heritage.

In his spare time, Dvořák composed and gave lessons to supplement his income. He told no one but his closest friends about his compositions, which included his first couple of symphonies. Although none of these early works receive much attention now, in their composition Dvořák was slowly but surely coming to grips with his craft. Yet after 12 years, there was still little to suggest he would be anything more than a minor composer.

During this time, one of Dvořák's music pupils was Josefina Čermáková, the pretty 16-year old daughter of a Prague goldsmith. Antonín fell deeply in love with her and wrote a song cycle, *Cypresses,* in her honour. Sadly, his ardour was not reciprocated. But as he continued to teach in the Cermák household over the years, his eye eventually fell upon her younger sister Anna. Anna had a fine contralto voice and, at the age of 16, began to sing in the chorus at the Provisional Theatre. Clearly there were plenty of occasions for the young couple to get together, and by the time Anna's father's objections to their marriage were removed (by his death in 1872), Anna was already pregnant.

Anna and Antonín were married on 17 November 1873, and their marriage was long and happy. Indeed, Dvořák's marriage coincided with a slow but steady upturn in the quality of his music and his fortunes as a composer. In 1874, he received his first major première, with Smetana conducting the overture to *King and Charcoal Burner* (a drastically revised version of the sub-Wagnerian opera *Alfred).* A year later, he was fortunate enough to win the Austrian State Stipendium offered to poor young artists in the Western half of the Empire.

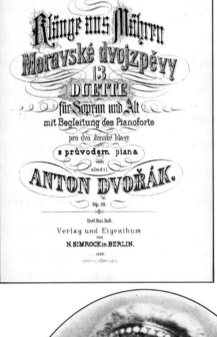

Dvořák's first invitation to conduct his own work abroad came from the Philharmonic Society in London. At the first of three public performances in March 1884 he conducted Stabat Mater *at the Royal Albert Hall (below).*

Encouraged by this success, Dvořák was spurred to a burst of creative activity and in four months a stream of beautiful music flowed from his pen, including various pieces of chamber music, the lovely *Serenade for Strings,* the *Moravian Duets* and his first symphony of real merit, No 5 in F Major.

The following year, Dvořák entered, and won, the Stipendium again and was freed from his main financial worries. But his music was still heard only by a small circle of Czech musicians. By chance, one of the panel judging the Stipendium was the composer Johannes Brahms. When Dvořák entered for the award for the fourth time in 1878, Brahms wrote to his publisher Simrock, recommending the *Moravian Duets.*

When you play them through you will be as pleased as I am, and, as a publisher, taken by their piquancy . . .Dvořák has written all kinds of music . . .and is very talented. He is also very poor! I beg you to think the matter over!

Simrock published the *Duets* widely and they were an instant success. He followed these up with Dvořák's *Slavonic Dances.* Western Europeans were charmed by the fresh, lyrical sound and exciting rhythms of this very Bohemian (to western ears) music and Dvořák was soon in terrific demand.

At that time, however, three events clouded his life, the deaths of his three children in quick succession, – Josefa two days after her birth in 1876, 11 month old Ružena by swallowing phosphorous, when accidentally left unsupervised in August 1877, and Otakar just three weeks later from smallpox. In his grief, Dvořák returned to and completed the *Stabat Mater,* a religious choral work first started three years earlier. It was this lovely and poignant work, more than anything, which was to consolidate his success abroad.

It was the *Stabat Mater* which was performed in the Albert Hall on 20 March 1884, giving Dvořák one of his greatest public triumphs.

As soon as I appeared, I received a tempestuous

welcome from the audience of 12,000. These ovations increasing, I had to bow my thanks again and again, the orchestra and choir applauding with no less fervour. I am convinced that England offers me a new and certainly happier future, one which I hope may benefit the Czech art.

Dvořák was right. The English had indeed taken him into their hearts. A round of banquets and receptions ensued and newspapers carried lengthy articles on him and Czech music. His popularity in England was assured and in all he made nine happy trips to England over the next 15 years.

After his great success in England Dvořák was at last financially secure and he celebrated by realizing a long-cherished dream – he bought a small house in the country where he and his family could spend the summer. The house was at Vysoká on land belonging to Count Kaunitz (who had married Dvořák's first love Josefina) and Dvořák's life here proved to be

In 1892 Mrs Jeanette Thurber (above left), founder of the National Conservatory in New York, invited Dvořák to be its Director. In all, Dvořák spent three years in America, mainly in New York, (above) where amongst other things he enjoyed riding on the 'El' – the over-head tram system! Very homesick, he arranged to spend his summer holidays in the Czech community of Spillville, Iowa. In the summer of 1893 he stayed in the house (below) on Main Street, Spillville.

Although the source of his inspiration was firmly rooted in the Bohemian countryside and people, Dvořák's international reputation established him as a celebrity far beyond its borders. Indeed, such was his popularity that he was, posthumously, included as a subject in a cigarette card series of Musical Celebrities issued in 1912 (above).

blissfully happy. Early every morning while at Vysoka, he went for long rambles through the woodlands. During the day, he composed in the summer house or pottered in the garden. In the evening, he went down to the village inn to drink, sing and tell stories with the peasants and miners.

Over the next nine years, his success was consolidated and he was showered with an increasing number of awards and honours, including the Austrian 'Iron Crown' and a Doctorate of Music at Cambridge, England. He continued to compose and wrote many masterpieces, great and small. His life was spent working in Prague – teaching at the Conservatory, composing or conversing in coffee bars; relaxing at home in Vysoká with the family; or performing on one of his many trips abroad. But in 1891, he received a telegram that was to change this routine.

WOULD YOU ACCEPT DIRECTOR NATIONAL CONSERVATORY OF MUSIC NEW YORK OCTOBER 1892 ALSO LEAD SIX CONCERTS OF YOUR WORKS

At first, he took little notice of this unusual telegram, but the sender persisted. The sender was Mrs Jeanette Thurber, the wife of a millionaire New York grocer, who had founded the American Opera Company and the National Conservatory of Music. Her aim in founding the Conservatory was to establish a national American school of composition, and Dvořák, the leading nationalist composer, seemed the ideal person to set the ball rolling. Dvořák was taken with the idea, particularly when he found that the Conservatory was open to all, regardless of means and colour. He was also taken by the salary, a princely $15,000. So, in September 1892, he set sail for New York.

Dvořák's time in America was immensely successful, and he found many new friends and fans and wrote much music, including the famous symphony *From the New World.* But he was never really happy there, away from his family and beloved country. So when Mrs Thurber ran into financial difficulties during his second period in New York and was unable to pay him, he was relieved to find an excuse to go home once again.

Among the many beautiful works that Dvořák wrote in the last eight years of his life are the operas *The Devil and Kate, Armida* and *Rusalka.* In these works, Dvořák finally realized his ambition to write a genuine Czech opera to match the masterpieces of Smetana. Both *The Devil and Kate* and *Armida* were relatively successful, but it was the beautiful, atmospheric *Rusalka,* based on a libretto by the Czech poet Kvapil, which was the real triumph. Rarely performed abroad, it is regarded with deep affection by Dvořák's fellow countrymen and holds a place of high honour in the national heritage. It was a fitting summation to a rich life's work.

Dvořák died suddenly on May Day 1904. After a month's illness, he had finally been given permission by the doctor to get up and join the May Day celebrations. But after the meal, he suddenly felt dizzy, and slumped in his chair unable to speak. He was carried to his room while the doctor was called, but moments later he had died. Few composers can have been so greatly missed by their fellow countrymen.

'Land of opportunity'

Pioneers of the American West

The America that greeted Dvořák was an exciting and ever-changing one. Brave and adventurous pioneers were pushing back the frontiers of the wild west, and a whole new world was opening up.

Spurred on by hope and the determination to reach a land that promised freedom and endless opportunity, countless emigrants crossed the vast continent of America, heading west by wagon train.

When the first European settlers walked ashore the Atlantic coast of America at the beginning of the 17th century, their every step demarcated a new western frontier. And for the next 300 years their descendents pressed on inexorably, establishing frontier after frontier until that vast sprawling continent was finally subdued.

By the end of the Civil War in 1865 this process of westward expansion had gone a long way. Few could remember a time when the Mississippi River had been the natural as well as national boundary on the west, and beyond it to the Missouri River and southwest into Texas pioneer farmers had created thriving communities. Some 1500 miles further on, far across the mighty Rockies and warmed by the waters of the Pacific lay gold-rich California and its splendid new city San Francisco. All along the coast from British Columbia in the north to Mexico in the south an energetic race of adventurers was forcing

the earth to yield its riches – most spectacularly so its mineral wealth, but there was an abundance of timber and agricultural wealth too.

Between these newly settled areas lay the final and most awesome frontier of all – the Great Plains. For long the Great Plains had stymied prospective settlers. That seemingly endless expanse of prairies, almost treeless and studded with bunch grass, scorched by sun and wind in summer and swept by blizzards in winter, where long stretches of killing drought were occasionally interrupted by torrential rains and hailstorms which could flatten a man. Then to the west these inhospitable prairies finally gave way to mighty mountains and canyons, majestic to behold, but the graveyard of many who had tried to struggle through them to reach fabled California. Through it all roamed bands of Indians, who had every reason to discourage yet one more intrusion on their shrinking homeland. Not for nothing was this whole region known in geography books of the time as the Great American Desert, or as Mark Twain put it, 'one prodigious graveyard'.

This then, was the setting for the great drama that was to be played out in a single generation following the Civil War: the taming of the American West.

Building the rails west

The years immediately following the Civil War were boom times in the victorious North. Crucially for the opening of the West, the railway industry was geared up for phenomenal expansion. The settled eastern part of the nation was already well served by the railway, and indeed the western fingers of this network probed very near the edge of the frontier from Texas north to Wisconsin. From there, however, transportation and all communication slowed to the pace of the horse. From the 1850s stagecoach services had been in operation, notably the Butterfield Overland Mail and the legendary Wells, Fargo & Co., but while these wonderfully cinematic four- and six-horse coaches competed bravely with terrain, distance and hostile Indians, they were really obsolete from the beginning. The technology and wealth were there to span the continent by rail.

The first of the great transcontinental lines was begun even as war raged, in 1863. One portion, then the Union Pacific, was laid westward from Omaha, Nebraska, while the other, the Central Pacific came eastward from Sacramento, California. As almost everywhere in the English-speaking world, the labour employed on the eastern section was mainly Irish. In the west, however, it was Chinese, an early indication of America's true geographical position in

The long and treacherous assault course to their western destination cost the lives of many pioneer men, women and children. For those who survived the harsh weather condition – from blizzards to droughts – there was always the terrifying prospect of being attacked by rampaging Indians (above).

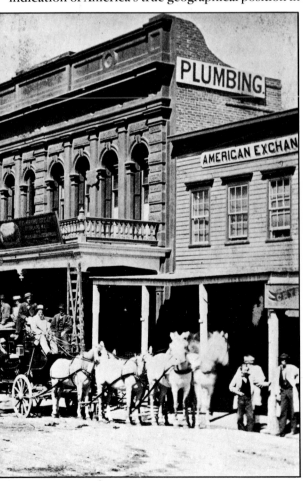

In its heyday, the famous Wells, Fargo & Co. stage-coach service was an invaluable means of transportation and communication. But even in 1866, when this photograph (left) was taken, its days were numbered – work on the great transcontinental railroad had begun.

the world.

On 10 May 1869 the two lines met at Promontory Point, some fifty miles west of Ogden, Utah, and as the famous golden spike was driven in the telegraph tapped out the message that the United States was finally spanned from sea to sea.

The building of the first transcontinental railway was one of the outstanding engineering achievements anywhere to that time, and others followed quickly behind, the Northern Pacific, the Great Northern and tens of thousands of miles of smaller lines spreading out across the West. A daunting vista still, but perhaps not quite so implacably hostile as had been assumed.

Home on the range

In 1865 something like five million unbranded longhorn cattle roamed the Texas prairie. Fierce, rangy creatures, these wild cattle were descended from breeds introduced by the Spanish centuries earlier. To destitute ranchers returning from defeat in the Civil War, these cattle were a resource of obvious potential, since there was an insatiable demand for beef in the urban north and east. But the means of cashing in on that resource were tantalizingly out or reach. How could they get the cattle to the market? Arduous drives to the distant slaughterhouses of Cincinatti, St. Louis and Chicago reduced the cattle to a near valueless state on arrival, and while some ranchers attempted this most settled for slaughtering thousands of these longhorns simply for tallow and hide.

Then in 1867 the situation changed overnight. The Kansas Pacific Railroad was building west from Kansas City, and a sharp-witted Illinois cattle dealer

An historic and memorable moment when East met West at Promontory, Utah, on 10 May, 1869 (above). The trains of the Union Pacific and the Central Pacific moved forward until they touched – the United States of America had been spanned by rail.

image to the real cowboy himself. What was life actually like on the trail? One thing it was not was romantic. As one chronicler has put it:

There was no romance in getting up at four o'clock in the morning, eating dust behind the trail herd, swimming muddy and turbulent rivers, nor in doctoring screw worms, pulling stupid cows from bog holes, sweating in the heat of summer, and freezing in the cold of winter.

These, then, were the physical elements the cowboy contended with. On top of all that, he lived in constant fear of the dreaded stampede. The sudden rearing of a horse, the barking of a distant coyote, the rumble of thunder, the crack of lightning, anything could galvanize thousands of terrified cattle into blind action. The suddenness and the violence of a stampede would shake even the most sanguine cowboy. As one recalled:

Sometimes the herd might get completely out of control and scatter for a hundred miles. While I was looking at him, this steer leaped into the air, hit the ground with a heavy thud, and gave a grunt that sounded like that of a hog. That was the signal. The whole herd was up and going – and headin' right for me. My horse gave a lunge, jerked loose from me, and was away. I barely had time to climb into an oak. It took us all night to round them up. When we got them quieted the next morning, we found ourselves six miles from camp.

named Joseph McCoy immediately realized the implications. Well to the west of established agricultural settlement but beside the newly laid tracks, he chose his spot: Abilene, 'a small dead place of about a dozen log huts'. There he built shipping pens large enough to hold 3000 head of cattle, a hotel and a livery stable. By the end of that year 35,000 head of cattle had been shipped out of the first of the legendary cowtowns, and 1.5 million were to follow over the next four years. The greatest cattle movement in history had begun, and with it the brief heyday of the quintessential American hero, the cowboy.

The popular image of the cowboy has been romanticised for so long now and in so many different ways that it is difficult to see through that

Turning from the hazards of the trail to the day-to-day organization and workload, the key figure that emerges is the trail boss. It was he who assigned the men their duties, and would rise first in the morning to wake them. He would ride ahead to make sure of water supplies and to choose the place to stop for a midday meal. And of course, he was responsible not only for the safety of the cattle but for the men themselves, for tending their injuries and settling their disputes.

The opening of the West brought prosperity to the white man, but for the American Indian it was the beginning of the end. With the new railroad crossing the Great Plains, more and more people ventured west to make a new life. En route, huge herds of buffalo were indiscriminately slaughtered for sport by travel-weary passengers (right) – and deprived the Indians of their life source of food, fuel and clothing.

Advertising the event to beat all events, this poster (left), sums up the excitement stirred up by the 'grand opening' of the Union Pacific. No sooner had the famous golden spike been driven into the rails at Promontory Point than the maiden run from Omaha to San Francisco took place.

Some 20 years later, the accent was more on luxury than on adventure as can be seen by the advertisement for the 'Great Palace Reclining-chair Route' (far left).

Following breakfast at 3.30 in the morning the cowboys would take up their positions around the herd, and the day's drive would begin. Herds varied in size, but the norm was 2-3000 with each cowboy allocated about 300. The technique was to keep the cattle moving in a loosely controlled pack, at a pace that ensured both progress and calm. At 11 a.m., the entourage would come to a halt and the men fed, the cattle grazed and then settled down for a nap. Roused for the afternoon drive, the herd would start to pick up speed as the cattle began to thirst for their evening watering holes. By sundown they were content to settle, although occasionally during the night they would stand to stretch. The men on night watch were as vigilant as any sailor.

The next day, the same routine – with, as always, the imminent possibility of storm, stampede and Indian attack. The duration of the journey varied widely, depending on weather conditions as well as the starting and finishing points, but something like two months from Texas to Abilene was average.

Having survived the rigours of the trail, the cowboy finally found himself at one of the trail and rail junctions scattered across the Plains – dusty towns with names that are part of folklore like Witchita, Cheyenne, Abilene itself, and most famous of all, Dodge City, 'Queen of Cow Towns'. There he might visit a barbershop for a haircut and an overdue bath, then outfit himself with new boots and perhaps a suit and hat. He would be careful, however, not to spend too much money on these preliminaries. For what he really wanted, and what the new cowtowns were well equipped to provide, was a few days' spree. Saloons, gambling halls, dance halls and brothels awaited his arrival with keen anticipation, and while cattle-brokers got on with the serious business of making money, he got on with the equally serious business of squandering it. The process rarely took long, however, and before he knew it the long trek back along the trail to Texas and another herd of longhorns was under way.

The mining bonanza

The discovery of gold in California in 1848 touched off the most feverish and famous 'rush' ever witnessed. But it was only the first of many fabulous strikes that turned the mountains of the American Far West into an Eldorado for fortune-seekers the world over. Next to California, the greatest of these strikes was the fabulous Comstock lode on the slopes of Mount Davidson in Nevada. Two Irish prospectors stumbled upon this unprecedently rich source of silver in 1859, and within a year the boisterous new town of Virginia City lay perched on the side of the mountain. A mining engineer's description of Virginia City in 1861 gives a fair indication of the conditions of life men will accept when bedazzled by the imminence of wealth.

Frame shanties pitched together as if by accident; tents of canvas, of blankets, of brush, of potato-sacks, and old shirts, with empty whisky barrels for chimneys; smoky hovels of mud and stone; coyote holes in the mountainside forcibly seized and held by men; pits and shafts with smoke issuing from every crevice; piles of goods and rubbish on craggy points, in the hollows, on the rocks, in the mud, in the snow, everywhere, scattered broadcast in pell-mell confusion, as if the clouds had burst overhead and rained down the dregs of all the flimsy, rickety, filthy little hovels and rubbish of merchandise that had ever undergone the process of evaporation from the earth since the days of Noah.

Over the next two decades major strikes of gold, silver and copper were made with wonderful regularity, and mining camps dotted the mountains and valleys from the Fraser River far to the north in British Columbia to Tombstone, on the edge of the Arizona Desert. Wherever they were, these mining camps, or mining towns as they became when the tents and shacks gave way to timber and brick buildings with false façades, were tough places – far tougher than the cattle towns further east. Many accounts are doubtless exaggerated: 'the roaring, raving drunkards of the bar-room, swilling fiery liquids from morning till night; the flaring and flaunting gambling-saloons, filled with desperados of

The lure of land ready for the taking brought many poor farming families out West. But life was tough for these homesteaders. Land was plentiful, but resources few and home was usually a simple cabin (above) made from the only building material available – prairie sod.

the vilest sort.' This is unlikely to be a description of the activities of all the inhabitants of Virginia City. But considering the fact that miners, unlike cowboys, were quite likely to have large sums of money about them when their luck was in it is not surprising that the lure of 'mining the miners' attracted as motley a crew of swindlers and cut-throats, thieves and whores as one could expect to encounter anywhere.

The pioneer on the plains

The cattle and mining kingdoms had an ephemeral, even vagrant quality about them, and they could never have claimed to 'tame' let alone settle the West. Only the establishment of settled farming communities could do that, and it was here that the westward urge came into the most direct conflict with the myth of the Great American Desert. It was one thing for free-spirited cowboys to endure the hardship of the open range, or for bold fortune-

A prominent figure in the 19th century western communities was the saloon owner (such as Jeff 'Soapy' Smith pictured above). Apart from a few 'good-time' girls, saloons were all-male enclaves and were often the only form of entertainment in town.

Roping a longhorn steer on the Texas prairie (right). The skill of the cowboy was constantly put to the test as keeping a herd under control was the only way to avoid the dreaded stampede.

seekers to put up with a few years in rowdy mining camps. It was quite another for young men and women, perhaps already with families, to carve out the stable, settled existence necessary for productive farming in the face of hostile conditions. Many thoughtful observers took the view that the Great Plains would never yield to settlement. The whole region, wrote Union General John Pope in 1866, 'is beyond the reach of agriculture, and must always remain a great uninhabited desert'.

At the same time, there were those who argued that the desert myth was precisely that, a myth, and that quite wonderful prospects lay in wait for those who were prepared to chance their arm. One traveller returned from northern Dakota to tell of soil 'of the richest sort and easily cultivated for there is neither stone nor stump to bother the plow'. A Kansas newspaper editor returned from a visit to the western part of that state in 1867 and waxed lyrical about an agricultural vista: 'rich as that on the banks of the far famed Nile . . .land before us, land behind us, land at the right hand, land at the left hand – acres, miles, leagues, townships, counties – oceans of land, all ready for the plough, good as the best in America, and yet lying without occupants.'

The truth lay somewhere in between such starkly contrasting views. Fertile land there was in abundance, and encouraged both by government and the new western railways, the final generation of

The real American cowboy (above) – dressed for the part, but here's where the resemblance to his celluloid counterpart ends – could tell a very different story about life on the trail: the workload, the danger and the harsh conditions that had to be endured as part of the job.

Fortunes were there to be made, but for many prospectors the only way to make a quick 'buck' was to try their luck at gambling (above) – a regular feature of saloon life.

American pioneers flooded onto the Great Plains in the years following the Civil War. But scanty rainfall and a climate of sometimes grotesque severity condemned these settlers to a life of toil and struggle – and for many the rewards were heartbreakingly meagre. It was particularly hard on the women. As farmers' wives they were used to the daily grind of domestic chores, but nothing back east had prepared them for the conditions on the plains. The hard water made washing almost impossible. During the long dry months of dust and wind the dust got everywhere. It stung the eyes and got into the hair and stayed there. It crept through windows and covered the furniture the moment it was dusted. Many women, exhausted by fighting a losing battle, gave up the struggle against the dust and dirt and let their sod houses deteriorate into squalor.

Drought, and plagues of grasshoppers frequently reduced the pioneers to abject misery – and the brink of starvation. In 1874, this twin calamity struck with particular ferocity, and the nightmare quality of the grasshopper invasion was forcefully expressed by the editor of the Witchita City *Eagle:*

'They came upon us in great numbers, in untold numbers, in clouds upon clouds, until their dark bodies covered everything green upon the earth . . .' A Kansas farmer, writing at the same time, wryly lamented, *'There has been no rain here of consequence for a couple of months, and between the drought, the cinch bugs and the grasshoppers we will be forced to go to Egypt or somewhere for our corn'.*

In fact, most of these first pioneers stuck it out, and successive waves of settlers followed them – from Europe as well as the eastern states. Improved farming methods and new machinery succeeded in bringing almost the entire expanse of the Great Plains under cultivation, thereby providing one of the foundation stones of 20th-century America's prosperity.

The Indian tragedy

For all the hardships they faced on the Great Plains, the white newcomers were there by choice and could not, in a general sense, blame their plight on anyone else. For the Indians it was quite different. For centuries they had been pushed further and further west by the white man, and the Great Plains was their last stronghold. Taking into account those inhabiting the Rockies and the intermountain region they numbered about 250,000, with another 50,000 or so in the Indian Territory, later to become Oklahoma. But the salient point about the plains Indians – notably the Sioux, the Blackfeet, the Crow in the north, the Cheyenne of the central plains and the Apache and Comanche in the south – is that they were nomadic and extremely warlike.

The reason for this is that they were almost totally

As gold fever spread rapidly, prospectors, such as the three old timers pictured below, came from all over America in the hopes of striking it rich.

The last of the Apache chiefs, the legendary Geronimo (above). After surrendering in 1894, he brought the surviving members of his Chiricahua tribe to a reservation at Fort Sill in the northern part of Red River Country which is now Oklahoma. He died in 1909 still a prisoner of war.

Custer's Last Stand (right). Ignoring orders, and heavily outnumbered by Sioux, Cheyenne and Arapaho warriors, General George Armstrong Custer led his men into battle. All but a single horse were killed.

A group of Ute Indians (below). At first this aggressive Rocky Mountain tribe looked on the white man as an ally who could help drive the Cheyenne off the plains of Colorado. But, although they traded, trusted and even fought alongside the white man, in the end they too were forced off their land onto a reservation.

dependent on the American bison, or buffalo. They used its flesh for food, its hide for clothing, blankets, footwear and teepees, its horns for domestic implements like cups and spoons, and its bones for ornaments. Its sinews provided bowstrings and the stitching for garments, and even its dung, dried, was used for fuel. For thousands of years the plains Indians had hunted the buffalo on foot, but the introduction of the horse to the New World by the Spanish in the 16th century transformed their way of life. The horse provided the perfect answer to buffalo hunting, and within time the plains Indians became astonishingly skilful horsemen. They became fearsome warriors too, as their wide-ranging pursuit of

the great buffalo herds brought them into conflict with other tribes, similarly equipped with horses and that primitive, deadly weapon, the bow and arrow. Riding bareback at top speed they could slide down the side of the horse and cling on by a heel, leaving both hands free to fire a stream of arrows from beneath its neck.

Westward expansion after 1865 led inevitably to conflict between the whites and the Indians, indeed to a series of wars as the US Army moved west with the settlers in order to protect them. In the long run, all the advantages lay with the army, which was quite prepared to match savagery with savagery – and with interest. Ironically, however, the most celebrated engagement in the twenty years of bitter fighting that settled the issue was an Indian victory of shocking totality: the Battle of the Little Bighorn.

In June 1876, thousands of Sioux, Cheyenne and Arapaho were congregated along the Little Bighorn River in southern Montana. This gathering of the tribes for the annual sun dance, the Indians' most important religious ritual, was protected by an estimated 2500 warriors. Regardless, the Army was determined on a show of force in order to bring the Sioux and their mighty chief Sitting Bull to heel. Cavalry from all sides converged on the Indians.

Following a skirmish to the south of the Little Bighorn, Lieutenant George A Custer of the Seventh Cavalry was despatched with about 600 officers and men to locate the main body of the enemy. A vainglorious, reckless man if a courageous one, Custer blithely ignored his orders, which were simply to reconnoitre the area. Instead he drove his men as hard as he could right into the enemy camp. Then, ignoring their exhaustion, he mounted his fateful attack on 24th June. Despite being hopelessly outnumbered, he divided his force, which meant that he and his battalion, thought to have numbered 225, stood alone against an onslaught of whooping

warriors led by chiefs Gall, Crazy Horse and Two
Moons. Custer and his men were annihilated – and
this bungled venture became immortalized as
Custer's Last Stand.

Even such a victory – and it was by no means the
only mauling they inflicted on the army – only
prolonged the Indians' agony, and by the middle of
the 1880s their resistance had been crushed. The
West was finally 'safe', safe, that is, for the white man.
For the Indian, it marked his final, enduring tragedy.
One of the defeated chiefs summed up the despair of
a permanently eclipsed race; 'The white man made
us many promises, but he only kept but one. He said
he would take our lands, and he did.'

The western myth

In the census of 1900 it was stated that the frontier
no longer existed. There were by then approx-
imately half a million farms in Kansas, Nebraska, the
Dakotas and Oklahoma Territory, and a flourishing
cattle industry further to the west and north, as far as
the foothills of the Rockies. The rail network was
virtually complete, and with the Indian population
subjugated Americans could come and go as they
pleased, subject only to the normal hazards of life.
The Wild West was a thing of the past.

The idea of the West, or really a succession of
Wests, had always exercised a powerful hold on the
imagination of Americans – as a place of freedom
from constraint, of boundless opportunity and the
chance to start afresh, of adventure pure and simple.
The final disappearance of the frontier did not and
has not to this day removed the emotional appeal of
the West and what it stood for.

*The rapid growth, wealth and prosperity that came
with the opening up of America, can be seen clearly
in these two very different views of San Francisco
(above and below). In little over 40 years this gold-
rich Californian city had become every bit as
sophisticated as anywhere 'back East'.*

Edvard Grieg
1843–1907

Ever genial and urbane, Edvard Grieg was the first great Norwegian composer and his music carried the beauty of his land to people all over the world.

Edvard Grieg was born in the busy and prosperous fishing town of Bergen (right) in June 1843. His father, Alexander Grieg (left) a wealthy merchant of Scottish origin, was the British consul at Bergen. Grieg's mother, Gesine Judith Hagerup (left), a talented musician, was his first music teacher.

The turning point in Grieg's hitherto informal musical education came in 1858, when Ole Bull (below) – one of the most important figures in the creation of a nationalist school of music in Norway – heard the young Grieg play the piano. Bull insisted that his parents send him to the Leipzig Conservatoire 'to become a musician'.

Grieg was born in Bergen in June 1843 and died there in September 1907. For the composer who was to become the best loved and most celebrated in Norway's history, Bergen was a fitting birthplace. It was both a lively cultural centre and a prosperous commercial town, and Grieg's parentage reflects both these advantages. His father, Alexander Grieg, was a rich merchant of Scottish origin, and his mother, Gesine Judith Hagerup, was a gifted poet and musician from a famous Bergen family.

The town, sandwiched between the sea and a steep mountain range, alive with the to-ing and fro-ing of its sea traffic and buffetted by capricious weather, had nurtured the talents of some of Norway's finest dramatists, poets, painters and musicians. Grieg, on his 60th birthday, made a speech acknowledging the special debt he owed to his home town:

My material has been drawn from the whole of the surroundings of Bergen. Its natural beauty, the life of its people, the city's achievements and activities of every kind have been an inspiration to me. I find the odour of the German Quay exciting; in fact I am sure my music has a taste of codfish about it.

At the age of six, Grieg began piano lessons with his mother and made rapid progress. Gesine Grieg's love of the keyboard music of Mozart, Beethoven, Weber and Chopin, which she played often was effectively communicated to Edvard. For him, routine practice was a chore, although he stuck to it well enough. But he loved to spend hour upon hour experimenting alone, drawing his own sounds out of the piano. These were his first voyages of discovery into the world of harmony, and many years later, in an essay called *My First Success,* he recalled one of these childhood experiments:

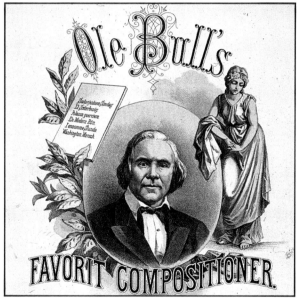

First a third, then a chord of three notes, then a full chord of four, ending at last with both hands. Oh joy! a combination of five – the chord of the ninth!

Grieg's spirit of adventure was not confined to music and he soon developed an intense dislike for institutional life. When the time came for him to go to school in Bergen, he rebelled, but had to accept his fate. At school, of course, scorn was poured on his sensitive, wayward nature and his early experiments in music met with derision. From the age of ten on, he thought of the most incredible ways of escaping.

Grieg's longed-for escape from school finally came just before his 15th birthday. In the summer of 1858, the Griegs were visited by a remarkable man, the 'Paganini of the North' Ole Bull, perhaps the most famous man in Norway. Part genius, part charlatan, and charismatic eccentric, the violinist Ole Bull had

become a folk hero, a symbol of the new Norway which had declared its independence half a century previously.

Edvard was asked to play for the distinguished guest. Bull was impressed and insisted that the boy be despatched to the Leipzig Conservatoire 'to become a musician'. In Leipzig, the finest piano masters in North East Europe were to be found. Grieg's parents were easily persuaded and, the following October, Grieg began the long journey to Leipzig, feeling 'like a parcel full of hopes'.

The young romantic

How those hopes were to be dashed! Leipzig turned out to be just as oppressive an institution for the boy from the north as school had been. Grieg's first teacher, Plaidy, far from allowing the young romantic his head prescribed a strict diet of fiendish piano studies by such worthy, but unexciting composers as Clementi, Kuhlau and Czerny — all of whom Grieg 'loathed like the plague'. But Grieg was lucky enough to study under Ignaz Moscheles as well. The kindly Moscheles, who had been a close friend of Mendelssohn and a piano virtuoso in his own right, was far more liberal — although even he preferred Mozart to Chopin.

Yet the composition tutor, Reinecke, made him jump through some impossible hoops. How was he to attempt string quartet and symphonic writing when he had no prior experience? He struggled miserably with his assignments, too young at the time to realize that his was a lyric rather than epic talent which would flower in exquisite songs and piano miniatures, rather than vast romantic forms. Further despondency set in during the summer of 1860 when a serious attack of pleurisy struck, presaging the respiratory troubles which would trouble him for the rest of his life.

Although he claimed to have 'left the institution as stupid as I entered it', a very different impression is given by his teachers and fellow students. He had come to be known as 'that lively Bergen fellow, outspoken, quick-witted and enthusiastic.' Reinecke, especially, wrote of Grieg's 'significant musical talent, especially for composition', while one of his piano teachers, Hauptmann, called him 'an outstanding pianist and among the best of our students.' If nothing else, a period spent with access to public music making at the famous Leipzig Gewandhaus — where on one occasion Grieg heard Clara Schumann perform her husband's piano concerto — must have been a musical education in itself.

In 1862, Grieg put the mixed blessing of his Leipzig career behind him, as soon as his course finished, and went home to Norway to face the task of building a professional reputation. He began by giving a concert in Bergen, which included perform-

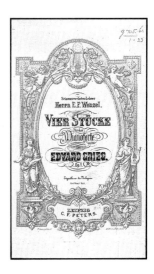

Grieg was 15 when he was enrolled as a student at the Leipzig Conservatoire (left). After a disappointing beginning with some indifferent tuition, he was taught by E. F. Wenzel, who had been a close friend of Schumann, and it was he who instilled in Grieg a deep love for Schumann's music. Before Grieg left the Conservatoire in 1862 one of his compositions (below), Vier Stücke (Four Pieces for Piano – dedicated to his teacher Wenzel) was performed at the students' examination.

In 1863 Grieg left Bergen to live in Copenhagen (right). Although Norway was independent of Denmark, Copenhagen was still the centre for Norwegian cultural and intellectual life, and here Grieg began mixing with a circle of musicians and literary figures, including Hans Christian Andersen.

In 1864 Grieg became engaged to his cousin, Nina Hagerup. A talented singer, she was both the inspiration and best interpreter of Grieg's songs, including 'I love thee' (above).

ances of studies by Moscheles, a sonata by Beethoven and three of his own *Four Piano Pieces,* Op. 1. The concert was very well received, although Grieg could hardly have foretold from this modest success that it marked the beginning of an internationally successful career as a concert pianist. That was for the future. In the meantime Grieg began to realize that it might not have been such a good idea to return to Norway so soon. The urge took him to go abroad again in search of fresh ideas and influences.

Copenhagen

Although Norway was tied to Sweden, the real melting pot of Norwegian intellectual and cultural life was still Copenhagen. Certainly for a composer in the making, a period of residence in the Danish capital was essential. So Grieg went to Copenhagen and immediately tried to engage the attention of two of the father figures of Scandinavian music. The leading Danish composer, Niels Gade, was hardly encouraging. J. P. E. Hartmann was much warmer and Hartmann's interest in Nordic legend was soon to inspire Grieg himself.

The three years Grieg spent in Copenhagen were a happy contrast to his term in Leipzig. He fell in with kindred spirits of his own generation, took pleasure in the stimulation of life in the capital, the idyllic gentleness of the surrounding countryside, the proximity of the sea – all providing a delightful setting for the leisurely life of a young artist whose personal life had just taken on a new and romantic dimension. Grieg had met his cousin, Nina Hagerup, another native of Bergen, who had spent most of her life in Denmark. They fell in love and became engaged in July 1864. As an engagement present Grieg wrote for Nina one of his most lyrical songs, *I Love thee,* setting verse by Hans Christian Anderson. From that time on, Nina's poetic sensitivity and enchanting voice were to be the inspiration for Grieg's songwriting.

Later that year, after returning from a summer holiday in Norway, visiting his parents and spending time with Ole Bull, Grieg experienced a new artistic awakening. It happened through the agency of a new friend, the 22-year-old Rikard Nordraak, to whom Bjornsen had paid the compliment, 'to be with him was a feast from beginning to end.' Grieg was immediately carried away by Nordraak's romantic and passionate belief in everything ethnically Norwegian – the sagas, the mountains, the fjords, the country people, and all. Nordraak bolstered Grieg's belief in the possibility of creating a true Norwegian nationalism in music and, together with a group of other musicians, they founded a society called Euterpe, which put on concerts of contemporary Scandinavian music.

The friendship between Grieg and Nordraak deepened and they cemented it by a firm pact to make it their lives' work to express in music the spirit of Norway and bring to fulfilment the work Ole Bull had begun. Sadly, their pact was to be broken by Nordraak's premature death only two years after their first meeting, but this, if anything, intensified in Grieg the zeal to raise the musical consciousness of Norway.

Return to Norway

Grieg's artistic mission was clear, but he delayed taking up residence in Norway to travel more widely in Europe. He and Nordraak had dreamed of Italy but Nordraak's fast declining health made it impossible

Grieg became a close friend of Rikard Nordraak (right), whom he met in Copenhagen in 1864-65. Nordraak, then aged 22, was the central focus of a movement to establish a school of Norwegian nationalist music. Grieg, inspired by Nordraak's enthusiasm for all things Norwegian, made a pact with Nordraak to express in music the spirit of Norway. This was broken by the premature death of Nordraak two years after their first meeting. Grieg, however, continued on what he saw as his true path – that of becoming a Romantic Nationalist composer. Prior to meeting Nordraak Grieg had spent the summer renewing his love for the Norwegian countryside (below).

for him to travel. Leaving his friend in the throes of tuberculosis, Grieg set out for Italy on his own.

He travelled widely, sightseeing in Rome, Naples, Capri, and Sorrento. He visited the archeological findings at Pompeii and heard 'appalling music in the Chiesa Nuova: Bellini, Donizett, Rossini!' He met a galaxy of cultural stars, was mildy scandalized by the sight of Liszt in philandering mood and Ibsen under the influence of the local wine. The one shadow cast on Grieg's Italian trip was the grief he felt upon receiving news of Nordraak's death. In his diary he noted the date with a black cross, and later that day he began to write a moving tribute to his friend, *Funeral March in Memory of Richard Nordraak*. He wrote a letter of sympathy to Nordraak's father expressing the determination within him to keep to the task they had assigned themselves:

his cause should be my cause, his goal mine. Do not believe that what he aspired to will be forgotten. . . .

Now determined to carve a future for Norwegian music on his own, Grieg returned to Norway to make a base in Christiania. At first, the capital city was unwelcoming and it seemed impossible to find a permanent job. He plucked up the courage to ask Ibsen to use his influence with Bjørnsen – Director of the Christiania Theatre – to persuade him to appoint the young composer to the vacant position of music director there. Disappointingly, Bjørnsen failed to respond.

In the face of such indifference, Greig decided to take his future into his own hands. On 15 October 1866, he managed to obtain a public concert with an all-Norwegian programme. Incredibly, this was an historic event in itself. Nina sang some songs by Nordraak, and, out of Grieg's portfolio came several songs with words by Hans Christian Andersen, some

piano music and his first violin sonata. Thanks to a generous article in a Christiania daily newspaper – written by the composer Otto Winter-Hjelm, the first Norwegian to compose a symphony – entitled *On Norwegian Music and Some Compositions by Edvard Grieg',* the concert was well attended, and finally turned out to be a commercial as well as an artistic success. Certainly it established Grieg as the bright new star of Norwegian contemporary music. He soon began to attract pupils and accepted an invitation to become the conductor of the city's orchestral society, the Harmoniske Selskab. Then, with the help of O. Winther Hjelm, Grieg launched the Norwegian Academy of Music in January 1867. It was an encouraging start.

The blissful summer

The following June, Grieg and Nina Hagerup were married. On 10th April 1868, Nina gave birth to their daughter, Alexandra. The Griegs spent a blissful summer in a rented cottage in Denmark. It was during these warm, happy days that Grieg conceived the work that to this day is a symbol of Norwegian

Nordraak's enthusiasm for the traditional elements of Norwegian life stimulated a similar passion in Grieg. Amongst other things Grieg was overwhelmed by the beauty of folk costumes (above) and by the simplicity of peasant life (above right).

romanticism, the Piano Concerto in A minor.

Yet despite this creative flowering, and his popularity in Christiania, Grieg was still far from achieving the widespread recognition he believed he deserved. Christiania was still very much a musical backwater. Grieg was itching for a new move. Then, in late 1868, he received a charming letter from Franz Liszt, praising his violin sonata (opus 8) in his most elegant French, and adding, 'I cordially invite you to come and stay for a while in Weimar so that we may have the opportunity of getting to know one another better.'

Unfortunately, Grieg could not immediately set out for Weimar, much though he wanted to. First the new concerto had to be premièred in Denmark and at home, followed by the summer vacation period at Grieg's family estate at Landås.

While he was at Landås, Greig made a very significant discovery for the future direction of his career. He found a book of Norwegian folk music, *'Older and Newer Mountain Melodies',* compiled by the organist Ludvig Lindemann who over 25 years, had amassed a collection of melodies from folk fiddlers and singers in the more isolated parts of Norway. Grieg began to appreciate for the first time the boundless wealth and diversity of his native traditional music, and at last he saw how he could incorporate folk music into his own art. He soon set to work at his own arrangements of Lindemann's tunes, dedicating the first collection to Ole Bull. From that time onwards, he was continually indebted to Lindemann's collection for new ideas.

Liszt and 'Peer Gynt'

At last, in February 1870, Grieg finally managed to visit Liszt – but in Rome, not Weimar. Grieg sent animated letters home telling how 'the Maestro' seized upon his portfolio and pulled out the G major sonata for violin and piano. There then ensued one of Liszt's remarkable feats of sight-reading. He played

the sonata through at sight, playing both piano and violin parts, with a perfect understanding of all the composer's intentions and with all the nuances and effects. Liszt disdained compliments, saying, 'I am an experienced musician and ought to be able to play at sight.' At another meeting, Liszt played the A minor piano concerto and his enthusiasm was impressive to behold. After playing the work through, again at sight, Liszt went back to the piano and played the ending again. Finally he said, in a strange emotional way, 'Keep on, I tell you. You have what is needed and don't let them frighten you.'

Liszt's admiration won immense prestige for Grieg at home. In 1874, a letter arrived which was to commission from Grieg his most famous work; it came from Ibsen requesting incidental music to his bewitching drama *Peer Gynt*.

At first Grieg had immense difficulty putting his mind to the task. He admired *Peer Gynt* as a literary work but thought it 'the most unmusical of all subjects' and it took him many months to finish the 22 movements that went to making up the *Peer Gynt* score. It was February 1876 by the time the weighty score was finished and the production went ahead, strangely enough, in the absence of both the dramatist and the composer. It was a success, running for 37 performances and only closing because the Christiania theatre was destroyed by fire. But Ibsen, who did not get round to seeing the play until a future production, was only fairly satisfied – though

While holidaying in 1869 on the family estate at Landås Grieg discovered a copy of 'Older and Newer Mountain Melodies' (above) compiled by an organist, Ludvig Lindemann. The collection of melodies of the more remote parts of Norway made Grieg increasingly aware of the boundless wealth of his native music.

In 1876 Grieg and a friend, John Paulsen, went to Bayreuth for the first complete performance of Wagner's Ring. Grieg was asked by a local Bergen newspaper to send back reviews. Of Götterdämmerung, a scene from which is shown left, he wrote: 'I can hardly venture to write about the music of this last gigantic work. It presents such a world of greatness and beauty that one is almost dazzled.'

Grieg's relationship with the dramatist Henrik Ibsen (heavily caricatured right) dated from 1874, when he wrote the music for Ibsen's Peer Gynt.

From the summer of 1877 until late in the autumn of 1888, the Griegs rented accommodation in the beautiful countryside of Hardanger. First they stayed on a farm, then they took a guest house owned by friends in Loftus (left). During this stay Grieg experienced one of the most creative periods of his life, producing among other things one of his finest works, The Mountain Thrall, for solo baritone, two horns and strings.

In 1885 Grieg and his family moved to the house that had been built for them in the Westland, at Troldhaugen. He lived there for the next 20 years and his life fell into a fairly regular pattern of composition, walking tours and concert-giving. He is photographed below in front of his house in 1903, with his friend, Bjørnsterne Bjørson, one of the most influential literary and political figures of the day.

he admitted that Grieg's music made the heavy, sophisticated drama much more accessible to the public.

A hut by the fjord

With the onset of summer 1877, the Griegs began a 14 month stay in the beautiful Hardanger country, at first on a farm, then at Lofthus, in a guest house owned by some friends. Grieg, who insisted on absolute peace while he was composing, moved into a little hut on the edge of the fjord, just big enough to hold a piano, a table and chair, and affording a spectacular view of the glacier above. Unfortunately the sound of the piano tended to attract passers by. Grieg became more and more annoyed. So one day, he laid on vast quantities of food and drink and persuaded 50 local men to carry the piano, hut and all down the road to a more secluded spot. In a letter, Grieg tells how the operation went:

Now, 'troops' were sent to do the job and after a short while they came galloping at full speed with the heavy case as if it were filled with feathers.

At Hardanger, Grieg found a rich creative vein. In the peace of his newly-positioned hut, he wrote a string quartet, some choral music and one of his finest works – *The Mountain Thrall* for solo baritone, two horns and strings, which is based on an old Nor-

wegian ballad. It was given a prestigious first performance, in the presence of royalty, in the spring of the following year at Copenhagen. A masterpiece of national romanticism, it was declared by Grieg to have been written with his heart's blood.

The 1880s ushered in a fever of touring interspersed with periods of tranquility at Lofthus. Grieg's expanding reputation abroad meant that his autumn and winter months were generally filled with extended concert tours. One Herculean stint included visits to Weimar, Dresden, Leipzig, Meiningen, Breslau, Cologne, Karlsruhe, Frankfurt-am-Main, Arnhem, the Hague, Rotterdam, and Amsterdam! No wonder by the end of the year Grieg was so exhausted he had to refuse invitations to extend the tour still further.

A home at Troldhaugen

By now Grieg had decided to settle permanently in the Westland and began building the beautiful house at Troldhaugen that was to be his permanent home for the rest of his life. In 1885, the Griegs took up residence in Troldhaugen and for the next twenty years Grieg's life conformed to a fairly regular pattern. The spring and early summer would be a time for composition, the later summer for mountain walking tours with friends, and then, come the autumn, back on to the concert schedule again, which, despite encroaching ill health, Grieg found so hard to resist.

Grieg began to be showered with distinctions from academic institutions all over Europe, including honorary doctorates from Oxford and Cambridge Universities, and Membership of the Institut de France. He was even made a Knight of the Order of Orange-Nassau, a distinction he accepted gladly, because, ever pragmatic as he wrote to a friend, 'orders and medals are most useful to me in the top layer of my trunk. The customs officials are always so kind to me at the sight of them.'

The Bergen festival

In 1898, an exciting event in Bergen provided Grieg with a wonderful opportunity. The town of Bergen had organized an exhibition of Norwegian arts, crafts and trade, to accompany a fishing congress that was planned for the summer. Grieg was invited to run a festival of Norwegian music at the same time. He did not hesitate to accept although a letter written to his friend Rontgen gives the impression that he might have repented at leisure:

The music festival is making my hair whiter than ever! The most incredible composers are arising out of the dark abyss and demanding in peremptory tone to be considered . . .

But in the end, as Grieg said himself, 'a lucky star reigned over the festival.' He kept performances of his own works to minimum, allowing such composers as Svensden, Selmer, Sinding, Nordraak and many others, to have their voice. For Grieg, the best reward was the sight of the audiences of country folk sitting 'as reverently as if they were in church, while the tears ran unchecked down their faces.' It was a great triumph and for Grieg represented the summit of his career and the realization of his earlier ambition to become a truly Norwegian composer.

In the early years of the new century Grieg's health, never robust, began to seriously deteriorate. Refusing to read the danger signals, he allowed his concert tours to take him as far afield at Prague, Warsaw and Paris.

In the summer of 1906 Grieg wrote what was to be his last work, *Fire salmer* (Four Psalms) which were inspired by folk melodies.

The last year

Finding that the climate of Troldhaugen was adversely affecting his lungs, Grieg grudgingly moved into a Christiania hotel during the winter months of 1906-1907, which were to usher in the last year of his life.

The following summer, an urgent invitation arrived from the Leeds Festival begging Grieg to participate. Against all advice he accepted, but, as he was about to begin the journey to England, a sudden heart attack forced him into hospital in Bergen. On arrival he said: 'This, then, is the end.' Overnight he died in his sleep.

His body lay in state as thousands of compatriots, foreign dignatories and representatives of the musical world filed past to pay their respects. He was given a spectacular state funeral befitting a national hero, and the urn containing his ashes was placed in a recess cut from bare rock overlooking his favourite view of the fjord at Troldhaugen. It bore no epitaph, although Grieg's own words would have served:

Artists like Bach and Beethoven erected churches and temples on the heights. I only wanted . . . to build dwellings for men in which they might feel happy and at home!

Grieg moved away from Troldhaugen in the last months of his life because of ill-health. He died in September 1907 in Bergen, just before he was due to set off for England. In April 1908 his ashes were placed in a carved recess in the rock overlooking his favourite view of Troldhaugen. When she died in 1935, Nina's ashes were also placed there.

Björnson og Grieg. Troldhaugen 1903.

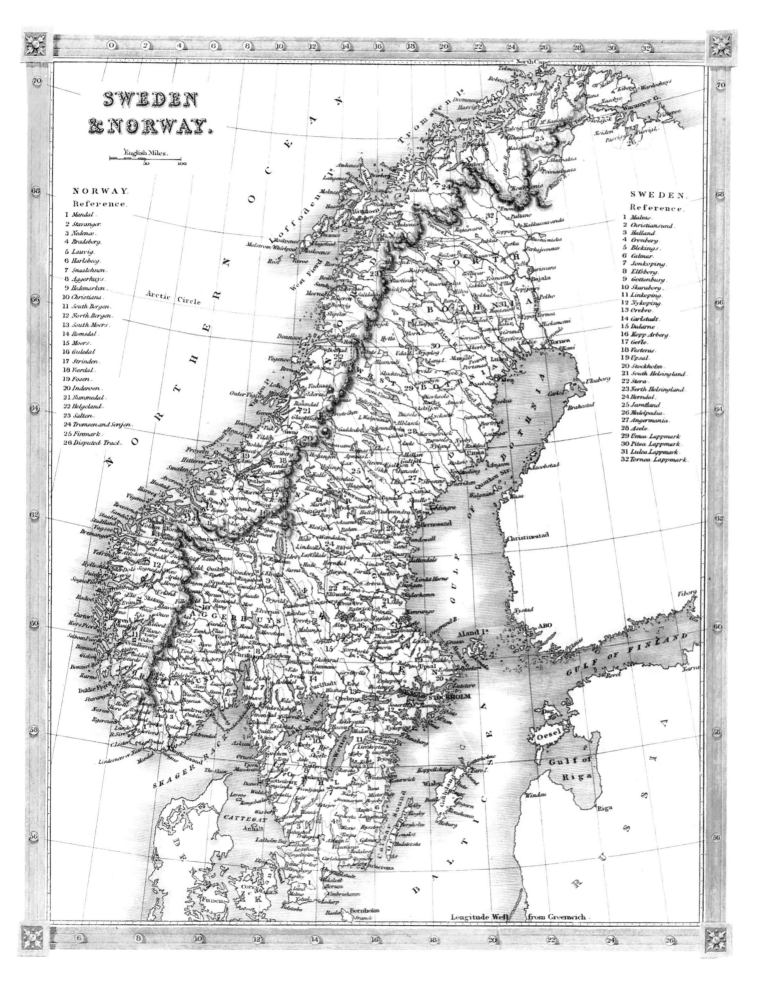

SWEDEN & NORWAY.

English Miles.
50   100

NORWAY.
Reference.

1 Mandal
2 Stavanger
3 Nedenæ
4 Bradsberg
5 Lauvig
6 Harlsberg
7 Snaalehnen
8 Aggerhuys
9 Hedemarken
10 Christiana
11 South Bergen
12 North Bergen
13 South Moers
14 Romsdal
15 Moers
16 Guledal
17 Strinden
18 Verdal
19 Fosen
20 Inderoen
21 Nummedal
22 Helgeland
23 Salten
24 Tromsen and Senjen
25 Finmark
26 Disputed Tract

SWEDEN.
Reference.

1 Malmœ
2 Christiansund
3 Halland
4 Orenberg
5 Blekings
6 Calmar
7 Jenkoping
8 Elfsberg
9 Gottenburg
10 Skaraborg
11 Linkoping
12 Nykoping
13 Orebro
14 Carlstadt
15 Dalarne
16 Kopp Arberg
17 Gefle
18 Vesterus
19 Upsal
20 Stockholm
21 South Helsingland
22 Stora
23 North Helsingland
24 Herndal
25 Jamtland
26 Medelpadia
27 Angermania
28 Asele
29 Umea Lappmark
30 Pitea Lappmark
31 Lulea Lappmark
32 Tornea Lappmark

Norwegian independence

For over 500 years, Norway was ruled by foreign powers, first Denmark, then Sweden. But the 19th century saw Norway's national pride re-kindled as the country strove for, and won independence.

As the terror of the Viking years slowly faded from the memories of the people of western Europe, so too did the glory of the kingdom of Norway and its kings of Bergen. Robbed of her trading riches by the power of the German Hanseatic League and decimated by the loss of almost two thirds of her already tiny population in the Black Death of 1349, Norway became almost a forgotten country quietly slipping into a subservient union with Denmark in 1380.

Over 400 years later, Norway was still so insignificant that it was again pushed into a similar union with Sweden. In the settlement of Europe following the defeat of Napoleon in 1814 – Norway was simply 'given away' as a reward for the king of Sweden's loyalty to the great powers. Yet over the next 90 years, the people of Norway were gradually to find their courage again and, in the art of such figures as Edvard Grieg, their voice as well. By 1905, they were able to declare with conviction that they were a free and independent nation once more.

The story of Norway's struggle for nationhood runs parallel to the great nationalist movements that flamed all over Europe throughout the 19th century and, indeed, there are many similarities. There is the same deeply romantic strain in Norwegian nationalism, the same passionate love of the country's natural beauty and the same commitment to the country's folk heritage. Yet in Norway, the struggle was uniquely, and remarkably, bloodless. While elsewhere in Europe, nationalism was marked by noisy and violent episodes, the waves of Norwegian nationalism beat steadily against the bastions of foreign domination, slowly but surely eroding away all resistance.

Of course, there had been bloodshed in the past, indeed there were peasant rebellions as early as 1436, but such incidents became increasingly isolated as the Danes contrived to take the fire out of Norwegian protest by a series of judicious concessions. Such protest as there was became vocal rather than physical and Danish culture gradually swamped the small Norwegian population. Even the written word lost its power as Norway's written language was steadily replaced by Danish and by 1814 only a tiny proportion of the population even spoke Norse.

Nevertheless, the desire for independence never quite died out, and throughout the four centuries of Danish rule there was a steady undercurrent of nationalist feeling. Then, in the 18th century, demand for Norway's timber and mineral resources from England gave the country a period of increasing prosperity, and the population almost doubled. The buoyant economy and the rising number of Nor-

wegians gave the people a new awareness of their own identity. Consequently, pressure for concessions built up and a number of external events conspired to help the cause. First, in September 1807, Britain hijacked the Danish fleet to stop it being used by Napoleon, and then proceeded to blockade Denmark. The result was that Norway was cut off from the king in Copenhagen, and a separate administration had to be set up in Oslo, headed by Prince Christian Augustus. The second event was the Russian invasion of Swedish Finland in 1808-9. During the ensuing crisis in Sweden, Norwegian nationalists nominated Prince Christian Augustus heir to the Swedish throne – which would have effectively taken Norway from under Danish rule.

In the rising tide of anti-nationalism after the Napoleonic Wars Norway was ceded to the kingdom of Sweden (left) by Denmark in 1814. The Norwegian spirit and separate national identity was not so easily crushed however, and its ethnic and cultural traditions were maintained in everyday life (below).

encouraged by Bernadotte, Norwegians were far from pleased. They made an immediate declaration of independence and established a representative national assembly at Eidsvoll to prepare their own constitution, based on American and French lines. The assembly defiantly adopted this constitution on May 17, 1814, and unanimously elected the Danish viceroy Christian Frederick as king of Norway.

Bernadotte reacted fiercely and sent in the Swedish troops, but negotiations started before there was any bloodshed. Norway contrived to keep the Eidsvoll constitution and its own legislative assembly, called the *Storting*. But despite this degree of progress the country was to remain under foreign domination – becoming part of a dual monarchy, presided over by the king of Sweden. Sweden held the power of veto over all the Storting's decisions, and Norway was to have no say whatsoever in foreign affairs. By this settlement the seeds of future conflict were clearly sown, for the Storting could pass legislation only to see it rejected out of hand by the Swedish king if he so chose. The Norwegians were in no position to object – the nationalist movement was not yet strong enough to resist.

However, one important concession for the Storting was wrung from the Swedes – namely that if three successive sessions in the Storting passed the same piece of legislation, the Swedish king lost his right of veto. The Norwegians immediately took advantage of this loophole and passed a bill abolishing its nobility in 1815. The Swedish king, of course, vetoed the bill. So they passed it again in 1818. Again the king vetoed it. In 1821, the Storting passed the bill for a third time, and Bernadotte, by then Charles XIV John, had, very reluctantly, to accept it as law. This tactic was to prove invaluable again in the future.

Unfortunately, Christian Augustus died suddenly in May 1810, leaving the Swedes open to a Danish claim to the throne. To prevent this, the Swedes adopted one of Napoleon's marshalls, Jean-Baptiste Bernadotte (later Charles XIV John), as heir to the throne, thereby hoping to neutralize any Danish ambitions.

The Storting

From this complex series of events, Norwegians gained nothing, but emerged with the conviction that it was no use looking to anyone else for help with their problems; they had to go it alone. So when the great powers awarded the sovereignty of Norway to Sweden under the Treaty of Kiel (January, 1814),

In the latter half of the 19th century, women's rights took a leap forward. Spurred on by the writings of Camilla Collett (above) vast improvements were made to the law regarding inheritance and in the employment of women. There were great achievements, too, in the field of education and in 1882 the first female student was admitted to the University of Christiania (top).

The move away from rural cottage industries towards urbanization and industrialization (right) marked the turning point for Norwegian nationalism. Enthusiasm for the nationalist cause spread rapidly through the new industrial urban communities and independence, came within sight.

Working men identified very closely with the cause of nationalism, and it is no coincidence that the transition from individualism to mass democracy provided the final thrust towards achieving the goal of independence: a goal which undoubtedly diverted the minds of the workers (right) from the miseries of poor social conditions in the industrialized towns.

After 400 years of Danish rule, the Norwegians set about creating an independent native language – landsmål (language of the land) – which was based on rural dialects and Old Norse. Men such as Peter Christian Asbjørnsen (above) resurrected collections of Norwegian folk tales and introduced many native words and phrases into printed text.

Old Norway

The early years of the union with Sweden were far from easy for Norwegians. During the long years of the Napoleonic wars, their economy had suffered dreadfully because of the restrictions on trade. Poverty was widespread and, even in 1814, the population was still pitifully small, barely 900,000. Added to these problems was Bernadotte's increasingly high-handed approach to his Norwegian subjects. As far as he was concerned, Norway was Swedish property and the Treaty of Kiel the title deed for it. No wonder, then, that he should be so put out when Norwegians had the temerity to celebrate the 15th anniversary of their independence on 17 May 1829. Troops were sent in to disperse the celebrants but, fortunately, there was no bloodshed. Even so, many Norwegians continued to regard the 1814 constitution as a sign of their own independence and the existence of the Storting gave them a degree of self-respect that they had lacked for many years, a self-respect that could overcome many hardships.

In the years after the union with Sweden, the nationalist movement burgeoned among romantic intellectuals. Painters like J. C. Dahl explored the Norwegian landscape for their dramatic canvasses. Poets like Henrik Wergeland believed passionately in the potential for a genuinely Norwegian culture and way of life, and not only wrote about it but carried the idea into politics.

Just as in so many other countries at the time, Norwegians started to explore their own folk herit-

age and rediscover the culture that had seemed all but lost in the long years of Danish rule. In many ways, the very sparseness of the population had helped to preserve the distinctively Norwegian way of life in remote country districts. So when researchers from the towns went out to the outlying villages, they found a rich and lively tradition still flourishing. Peter Asbjørnsen and Jørgen Moe recorded many of the folk tales in their *Norske Folkeeventyr* (1841–4); M. Landstad and L. Lindemann did the same for folk songs. And musicians like Ole Bull, the violinist who encouraged the young Grieg to become a musician, tried to promote international acceptance of Norwegian folk music.

Most important of all, perhaps, was the attempt to redevelop a native Norwegian language to replace Danish, using the language of the country folk as a base. In 1836, the young Ivar Aasen formulated *Landsmål,* meaning 'language of the land', based on a synthesis of rural dialects and Old Norse from the Middle Ages. The publication of folk tales and poems which included many native elements of vocabulary and style gave the movement to promote the adoption of Landsmål an important fillip, and the movement continued to flourish throughout the century. Eventually, Landsmål was to take its place alongside Dano-Norwegian *(Riksmål).*

Norwegian artists continued to draw inspiration from the folk heritage of their country throughout the century. Many of the playwright Henrik Ibsen's early works, notably *Peer Gynt,* and the 'peasant

Educated as a lawyer, Johan Sverdrup (left) led the Venstre party (a radical-liberal coalition) in the long fight against the government over the admission of ministers to the Storting (below). After the Venstre's victory he became the first Norwegian-elected prime minister within the newly empowered Storting. During his term of office (1884–1889) he introduced important reforms including trial by jury and the reorganization of the elementary school system.

Although under foreign rule for centuries, the spirit of Norway and the desire for independence lived on. The Norwegian people were passionately committed to the natural beauty of their land and to their own folk heritage (right).

tales' of Bjørnstjerne Bjørnson, are based on the myths and legends of old Norway. And musicians, from Grieg's young friend Rikard Nordraak, who composed the Norwegian national anthem, *Ja, vi elsker*, to Johan Svendsen and, of course, Grieg himself, mined the same rich vein.

The growing nation

At first, the nationalist movement in Norway was immensely popular amongst romantic intellectuals, but had little broadly-based support. Between 1840 and 1860, however, Norway underwent rapid industrialization. Both the economy and the population grew. By 1850, Norway's population increased to 1½ million, almost double the figure for 1815. As the concentration of people in the towns accelerated, so mass support for the nationalist cause grew in strength. Men and women working close together began to appreciate their common problems and identities.

Equally important was the work of the Storting in spreading democracy by showing just what could be done if the people governed themselves. At first, power in the Storting was very much in the hands of the old ruling class. But after 1830 the assembly began to draw the peasantry into the political fold. A major victory was won in 1837 when, despite initial opposition from the Swedish king, the Storting placed local government in Norway on a popularly-elected base. And from the mid-1830s onwards a peasant party was represented in the Storting.

Peasant and liberal representation in the Storting rose steadily throughout the century, and with it rose the political consciousness of the people. During the 1840s and 1850s many liberal reforms in the fields of civil rights, religious tolerance and penal

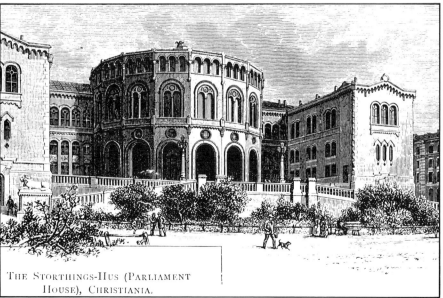

THE STORTHINGS-HUS (PARLIAMENT HOUSE), CHRISTIANIA.

reform were pushed through, despite the disapproval of the Swedish government, and Norwegians began to take great pride in their enlightenment. Norway pioneered many social reforms, including industrial accident compensation, and was well ahead of most European nations in extending the vote. Women's rights also took a step forward. An early campaigner for women's rights was Henrik Wergeland's sister, Camilla Collett, whose *The Country Governor's Daughter* highlighted the plight of middle class women forced into unhappy marriages by social pressure. The book was widely read, and had a great influence on Norwegian writers such as Ibsen and Jonas Lie. A great victory for women's rights was won in 1857 when women were given equal rights for inheritance and equal access to all forms of employment.

The rise of the Venstre
After 1870, the democratic base of the Storting continued to expand, and in the late 1870s, the city radical party, led by the great orator Johan Sverdrup, and the Peasant party united to form a broad left coalition (the Venstre) to push through further reforms. In particular, the Venstre wanted to move Norway towards full parliamentary government by bringing ministers, until then appointed by and responsible only to the Swedish king, under the control of the Storting. The Venstre brought in a bill to enforce ministers to attend sessions of the Venstre, and ensured that the bill was passed in three successive sessions, 1874, 1877 and 1880. But on the advice of the Conservative Prime Minister Stang, the king refused to accept the bill even the third time round.

After a sweeping victory in the 1882 elections,

Sverdrup and the Venstre felt strong enough to risk a showdown. Members of the cabinet were impeached for acting contrary to the wishes of the Storting. The king muttered vaguely about a coup d'état to bring the Norwegians into line, but he was restrained by Swedish Liberals. Sverdrup, then, took office as head of a Venstre ministry which clearly derived its authority from the Storting, and not the crown.

The final split
Now that internal freedom from Sweden had been achieved, an independent foreign policy, and thereby complete independence, became the goal. Norway's prosperity depended increasingly on her large merchant navy and Norwegians began to demand their own consular service to protect these trading interests. Then, in the general elections of 1891, the Venstre won an impressive majority on the issue of a separate foreign and consular service for Norway.

To make their intentions clear on the issue,

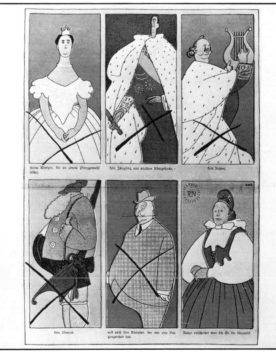

In the late 19th century anti-monarchical dramas, satires and cartoons (left) fuelled the republican as well as the nationalist cause. However, the republican cause never really became a strong force because of Norway's long-standing royalist traditions.

King Oscar (below), seated with members of the Swedish Royal family, was persuaded by Swedish liberals not to take repressive measures against Norway, which was then under Swedish control.

Norway abandoned the emblem of the Union from her merchant flag and began to build forts along the border with Sweden. When King Oscar refused to accept their bill establishing a Norwegian consular service, the entire Norwegian ministry resigned. Of course, the king was unable to appoint an alternative cabinet with the support of the Storting. So the Storting resolved that the monarchy had ceased to function. A proclamation to Oscar was prepared which ran:

The Storting authorises the members of the resigned ministry to continue as the Norwegian government . . . and to administer the authority granted to the King . . . The union with Sweden is dissolved in consequence of the King's ceasing to function as the King of Norway.

Members of the Storting voted unanimously for the resolution. The Prime Minister Christian Michelsen closed his address to the Storting in the early hours of 7 June 1905 with the words, 'God preserve our fatherland.' Crowds were ecstatic, and accompanied many of the Government leaders to their homes, drinking toasts to the 'New Norway'.

During the summer of 1905, the situation was tense with both sides mobilizing their armed forces. But an amicable agreement was soon reached. Sweden sensibly agreed to let Norway separate, and confirmed this by providing a 25-mile neutral border zone, which still exists today. Norway, as a conciliatory gesture, offered to accept a Swedish prince as head of the Norwegian monarchy and agreed to Swedish requests for a referendum on the issue of independence. The true force of Norwegian nationalism was revealed when a vote of 368,208 in favour of independence was recorded. Only 184 voted against.

There was some talk of a republic, as there had been for some years, but the traditions of Norway's former greatness were closely associated with the rise of monarchy, from the days of Olav the Saint, and a second referendum indicated a 4 to 1 majority in favour of a monarchy.

The aged King Oscar II of Sweden felt too deeply irritated to accept the Norwegian suggestion of a Swedish nomination. The Norwegians eventually accepted King Edward VII of England's nomination, his Danish son-in-law, who became King Haakon VII. Most important in Norwegian eyes was Haakon's two-year-old son, who would grow up in Norway and learn the history, traditions and language of his adopted country.

Edward Elgar
1857–1934

Edward Elgar rose from humble provincial origins to gain a knighthood for his services to music. He also became the first English composer in 200 years to win international acclaim.

Edward Elgar was born at Broadheath, just outside Worcester, in 1857. His father, William Elgar, originally from Dover, had settled in Worcester in 1841, and with his brother set up in business as a piano-tuner and music retailer. He was also organist of St George's Catholic Church, and some of Edward's earliest musical experiences were gained watching his father at work in the organ loft. His mother, Anne Elgar, was a well-read woman from whom he derived his background in literature.

When Edward was nearly three the family moved into Worcester, where they lived above the music shop – Elgar Brothers, at 10 High Street. Edward, however, often returned to Broadheath in his school holidays and came to know and love this part of the countryside. This love of rural surroundings was to stay with him for the rest of his lfe and was to make its way into much of his music.

Apart from the valuable musical background at home, Elgar had very little formal musical education

– in fact, he was largely self-taught. He played both the piano and the violin, and at one point had ambitions to study at the famous Leipzig Conservatoire. Unfortunately, when he left school in 1872, aged 15, his family could not afford to send him. His parents, knowing that the life of a professional musician could be insecure, proposed instead that he became articled in a solicitor's office. After a year he persuaded his parents that this was not where his ambition lay and, consequently, he was released from his articles. The business experience, however, was not wasted – he began to help with the accounts of the family shop where he had access to a wealth of music. He also began giving violin lessons and gradually built up a local reputation as teacher, performer, arranger and, on occasion, composer.

In 1877 he spent twelve days in London, taking a short course of lessons to improve his playing, with Adolphe Pollitzer, leader of the New Philharmonic Orchestra. Pollitzer, was impressed by his young pupil and urged him to return for further instruction, but Elgar eventually decided against a virtuoso performance career, feeling that his tone was too thin.

From 1879 he was a member, and later conductor, of the Worcester Glee Club. He also played the

Edward Elgar was born on 2 June 1857 in the cottage at Broadheath (above left). In 1860 the family returned to Worcester to live above Elgar Brothers shop at No 10, High Street (below). Elgar grew up there and with his family took part in the provincial but not insubstantial musical life of the Cathedral city of Worcester (above). Although he sought musical recognition beyond his home front he was always at his most creative when close to his beloved Malverns – the hills close to the city.

Up to this point most of what Elgar had composed was so-called 'salon music', and although he believed himself capable of greater things, his powers of more extended musical thought and composition had yet to be exercised. But during these early years he came into contact with the music of composers such as Wagner and Schumann who were to exert considerable influence upon him. In 1882 he spent three weeks in Leipzig where he attended the Opera and heard the famous Gewandhaus Orchestra.

In 1884, the Three Choirs Festival held in Worcester coincided with the 800th anniversary of Worcester Cathedral, and the celebration included a visit by Dvořák, who conducted his *Stabat Mater* and his *D Major Symphony* (now known as No. 6). Elgar, who played in the violins at the festival was enthralled by Dvořák's music.

The following year, 1885, brought the satisfaction of seeing his music in print for the first time, with the publication of violin pieces first by John Beare, then by Schott's. Also in that year he was appointed organist of St George's, succeeding his father who had retired.

Marriage to Alice Roberts

Among his many lady pupils was Caroline Alice Roberts, the only daughter of an Indian Army Major-General, Sir Henry Gee Roberts. When she began lessons, in October 1886, she was already 38 and, since the death of her father and the departure of her brothers to the Army, she had remained at home to look after her mother. She was a cultivated woman, with an interest in music which extended to singing in the local choir. The choir was often accompanied

bassoon in a wind quintet (which also included his oboist brother Frank) and during 1879–84 coached, played in and later conducted, the band at the County Lunatic Asylum at Powick – where the Superintendent had progressive ideas about the beneficial effects of music on his patients. In 1882 he became first violin in W. C. Stockley's Orchestra in Birmingham – Stockley's Popular Concerts were an established and well known feature of Midland musical life.

Early ambitions

Busy as he was, Elgar cherished ambitions far beyond those of a talented local musician. In any time that he was not conducting, performing or teaching he was composing, or listening to other people's work. He spent much of his earnings from teaching the violin and piano to the young ladies of Worcester and Malvern on travelling to London to hear August Manns' famous concerts at Crystal Palace. Manns, a German conductor was music director at the Crystal Palace and was responsible for providing good music at popular prices. Elgar's ambition to be recognized beyond his local boundaries had its first realization in July 1884 when the score of an orchestral work, *Sevillana*, shown by Elgar to Pollitzer, was sent to Manns, who included it in one of his Concerts.

Elgar wrote his early compositions for the woodwind quintet (right) which he formed together with three friends and his brother Frank. They are, from left to right, standing – William Leicester (clarinet), Edward Elgar (bassoon), Hubert Leicester (flute), and seated, Frank Exton (flute) and Frank Elgar (oboe).

by a string orchestra in which Elgar played. In 1887 Lady Roberts died and Alice, inheriting a small income, moved from the family home to lodgings in Malvern Link near Worcester. Her friendship with Edward prospered but when a year later their engagement was announced her aunts and cousins expressed strongly their disapproval of her involvement with a tradesman's son.

Regardless of the opposition, Alice and Edward were married in May 1889 at the Brompton Oratory in London; soon after they took up residence in London – moving first to Kensington, then Norwood and finally back to Kensington again. Both felt that London was the place to be to win the wider recognition he sought, since London was where the publishers and music promoters were based. With Alice's income to fall back on Elgar was able to devote more time and energy to composing and to keeping abreast of musical developments in the capital city. He did, however, return to Malvern once a week to fulfil teaching commitments.

In terms of publishing Elgar scored a notable success with a small piano piece called *Liebesgrüss* (Love's greeting), which was published by Schott under the title *Salut d'Amour*. It earned a great deal for the publisher but, unfortunately, Elgar had sold the manuscript outright and therefore had no financial share in its success. Although Manns performed *Salut d'Amour* and the *Suite in D* at Crystal Palace, wider public recognition of his own work remained elusive.

Family life in London was made happier by the arrival of their only child, Carice, in March 1890, but apart from this life in the city was not living up to the expectations Elgar had of it. City life also aggravated his health – he was susceptible to throat trouble throughout his life. Furthermore, neither commissions nor pupils were arriving in quantity as he hoped they would. It was decided that the family would return to Malvern where at least Elgar could earn a living as a teacher and compose at the same time. So, in June 1891, the Elgars moved back to Malvern.

Elgar and Caroline Alice Roberts (above left) were married in May 1889 despite great opposition from Alice's family, who felt that she was marrying beneath herself. Her love for Elgar lies behind the creation of most of his masterpieces, including The Dream of Gerontius *(final page of the score shown above). After her death Elgar produced no original work of any note.*

Return to the provinces

Finding himself in the round of teaching the violin to young ladies again, Elgar was naturally despondent, but in reality the return to Malvern was probably fortunate. Although publishers and critics were in London, the heart of English musical life was, at that time, to be found in the great oratorio festivals, in Leeds, Birmingham, Sheffield and cities which hosted the Three Choirs – Worcester, Gloucester and Hereford.

During the 1890s Elgar produced several cantatas – including *The Black Knight* and *Scenes from the Saga of King Olaf,* both inspired by works of the American poet Longfellow, a love of whose work he shared with his mother, and *Caractacus*. Back in his beloved Malvern Hills and surrounded by many friends it seemed that he had found the milieu that suited his creative impulse.

Elgar at last began to be rewarded with some measure of recognition. His works were greatly appreciated by those who performed them and, even if some critics continued to write patronizingly of him as a 'provincial' composer, the more enterprising conductors of the choral societies in the Midlands and the North began to show interest in his work and put on their own performances of it.

In 1897 the organizers of the Leeds Festival, then the leading platform for English composers, gave him a commission. Although Elgar would have preferred to write a symphony it was a cantata which they required. The result was *Caractacus* – a story of Britons and Romans, set in Elgar's Malvern Hills. Everything augured well for the first performance – Queen Victoria had accepted Elgar's dedication of the work to her and the first-night audience included

Elgar began work on what he planned to be a symphony in 1901, but the result was a concert overture, Cockaigne (In London Town), *(title page above). This was a series of variations inspired by the sights and sounds of London (left) – the city to which he had often travelled to attend concerts and hear new music.*

many celebrities, among them the French composer Gabriel Fauré, and many of Elgar's close friends. However, the performance was not as good as it might have been, and the critics concluded, once again, that Elgar was an up-and-coming composer, rather than one who had created a masterpiece.

Friends, old and new

The 1890s saw the strengthening of many old friendships and the growth of some new ones. In Malvern the Elgars' circle of friends included the Norbury sisters, Winifred and Florence (whose family estate adjoined Elgar's recently-acquired summer cottage, Birchwood), the architect Troyte Griffith, Alice's friends the Bakers and Dora Penny (Dorabella of the Enigma Variations), Lady Mary Lygon, Rosa Burley (a Malvern headmistress) and Dr George Sinclair, organist of Hereford Cathedral. One friendship which differed radically from the rest sprang from a professional association – that with August Johannes Jaeger, who had come to England from Düsseldorf and eventually taken a job as a production manager at the London music publishing house, Novello. Although employed at a relatively junior level, and not necessarily expected to exercise his musical judgement, Jaeger was quick to spot in Elgar's music the pointers to a new direction and sense of style which, coming from a continental tradition, he had found lacking in much of the music the firm already published. Jaeger recognized Elgar's talents and because of their close friendship was able to encourage him to greater musical heights than he might otherwise have attempted. Until Jaeger's death in 1909, the two men kept up a correspondence which reveals some of Elgar's most candid opinions and reflections on his music and his life.

By the end of the decade, Elgar had established a firm reputation as a composer of 'festival cantatas' and as such was increasingly in demand in the provinces. He was still depressed by the unappreciative attitude of Jaeger's superiors at Novello's. Although he was aware that his life in Malvern, particularly the time spent at the cottage at Birchwood, offered him the surroundings of country life which provided such a powerful stimulus to his creative spirit he still hoped for recognition further afield.

Fame, at last
In October 1898 Elgar wrote to Jaeger 'I have sketched a set of variations on an original theme: the variations have amused me because I've labelled 'em with the names of my particular friends . . .' This piece of music was the Enigma Variations. First performed on 19 June 1899 in London, the work at last brought Elgar the national acclaim he had so long yearned for.

The musical life of London, from bandstand to concert hall, attracted Elgar to moving there. However, although his Salut d'Amour was performed at Crystal Palace (below) he had a generally unsuccessful time. After only one year he returned with Alice and his new daughter Carice (bottom), to Worcester.

wrote many of his songs there, and it was through Schuster's fellow financier Edgar Speyer that Elgar met Richard Strauss who greatly admired Elgar's work. Another devoted friend, and wealthy patron of the arts, was Alfred Rodewald – a Liverpool textile magnate, who was also a talented conductor and double-bass player. His largely amateur Liverpool Orchestral Society achieved excellent standards and, in fact, later gave the first performance of the first two 'Pomp and Circumstance' marches, four days before they were played in London.

Lady Alice Stuart-Wortley, daughter of the Pre-Raphaelite painter Sir John Millais and the wife of Charles Stuart-Wortley, Conservative MP for a Sheffield constituency became a source of inspiration to Elgar and was a long-standing admirer of his

Elgar now stood on the threshold of a new chapter in his life. Along with his new-found fame came a number of new friends – friends who were to remain important to him for the rest of his life. Many of them were influential, either musically or financially, and belonged to the level of society to which Alice Elgar had been born. Accordingly, Alice encouraged her husband to move in 'society' circles as comfortably as she herself could. Elgar, however, sometimes found it hard to forget his own family background in 'trade', which, in the heavily stratified structure of Victorian and Edwardian society was considered respectable but socially inferior.

Among the new friends were the financier Frank Schuster, whose riverside home near Maidenhead, called 'The Hut', was a meeting place for musicians, painters and writers. His guests included Fauré, who

music. Their relationship was very close and there has been much speculation as to the extent of its intimacy. But it was essentially based on her response to his music and understanding of it – this naturally deepened to affection and provided him with an emotional creative impulse.

A second masterpiece
The turn of the century, then, saw a turn in Elgar's fortunes – even if he himself initially failed to see it ('All is flat, stale and unprofitable' – he wrote to Jaeger on 29 December 1899). One result of his improved circumstances was the move to a newly-built house (Craeg Lea) in Malvern Wells, where he began work on what was to become the oratorio – *The Dream of Gerontius*. Although he still continued some local teaching, he was now able to make more

frequent visits to London, to concerts, opera, art exhibitions or simply to lunch at Pagani's restaurant or at his club.

The first performance of *The Dream of Gerontius,* in Birmingham in 1900, was, however, a disaster. The chorus-master died halfway through rehearsals, and the conductor, the great Hans Richter, had failed to appreciate the difficulties which Elgar's adventurous choral writing would present to a typically conservative English choral society. Elgar was understandably bitter that another masterpiece had not had a decent first hearing. Happily, the element of misfortune was short-lived. Attending the première in Birmingham with Jaeger was Julius Buths, musical director of the city of Düsseldorf and, despite the bad performance, he quickly recognized the true stature

Back in sight of the Malvern Hills Elgar spent his time teaching, composing and enjoying the companionship of a circle of close friends (below). When not composing or with friends Elgar could often be found experimenting in his laboratory 'The Ark' (bottom right).

of the work. When he returned to Germany he began work on a German translation and *The Dream of Gerontius* was duly performed in Düsseldorf in December 1901, and again at the Lower Rhine Festival in May the following year. The Elgars were fêted on both occasions – Richard Strauss proposed a toast 'to the welfare and success of the first English progressive composer'.

Back in England, Elgar scored much more immediate success with the *Cockaigne Overture* and the first two *Pomp and Circumstance Marches.* The trio of the first 'March' contained 'Land of Hope and Glory' – a tune the public took to with such fervour that it became almost a second national anthem. Elgar had captured the popular patriotic mood of the country in its Empire days. Meanwhile, Elgar returned to work on a sequence of three oratorios the idea for

which dated back to his school-days. The first, *The Apostles,* was completed for performance in Birmingham in October 1903. The concentrated effort put into its completion left Elgar exhausted; he was also troubled by eye-strain and throat infections. That winter the Elgars went to Italy where Elgar was at his most relaxed. As he had done on previous holidays he recorded his impressions musically, in the concert overture *In the South (Alassio),* which received its first performance at a three-day Elgar Festival held at Covent Garden in March 1904.

The year of acclaim

1904 was indeed a year of recognition and acclaim. Apart from the Festival at Covent Garden where he was recognized as a new force in English music there was the command to dine with the King, membership of a famous London club, the Athenaeum, and a Knighthood. To Elgar, self-made and self-taught these honours must have vindicated the snubs of his wife's family. The family moved to a larger house, Plas Gwyn, near Hereford, where modern amenities included a telephone, and in 1905 Elgar, who had always been wary of the prominent 'academic' musical establishment, was invited to join its ranks as first Professor of Music at Birmingham University taking a chair endowed by businessman, Richard Peyton.

In the same year honorary doctorates from Oxford and Yale were conferred upon him and he travelled to the United States to receive the Yale doctorate. He returned on three later occasions to conduct his music in the United States. It was wearing his Yale robes, shortly after his return, that he made his way through Worcester in a ceremony in which he was granted the freedom of the city. As he passed along the High Street he paused to bare his head in greeting to his father who, too frail to attend the celebrations, watched from his window above the family shop.

Back at Plas Gwyn, Elgar busied himself with the second part of the trilogy he had earlier begun with 'The Apostles'. The second part, *The Kingdom,* was ready for the Birmingham Festival of 1906. It was his last oratorio – although he began sketches for the third part, the trilogy remained incomplete. He turned instead to orchestral music and in the next five years completed two symphonies and the *Violin Concerto.*

for the death of Edward VII than with the jubilant spirit of coronation of the new King George V. Not only was there nothing of the patriotic fervour which the audience of the time expected but also the performance difficulties for the orchestra were great and it was some years before the Second Symphony took its rightful place in the orchestral repertoire.

Back to London

Elgar was disappointed by its lack of immediate success but there were other rewards – he was awarded the Order of Merit in Coronation Honours of 1911 and also acquired a permanent London home. By 1912 the family was installed in the imposing and palatial Severn House in Hampstead. It had a music-room, a billiard-room, a picture gallery and several acres of grounds.

Settled in London, the Elgars led a busy life, both professionally and socially. Lady Alice was in her

The Elgars continued to spend the winters in Italy. As always, the experience of being in a new place provided valuable creative stimulus, although it was usually only on his return to Plas Gwyn that Elgar would finally settle to the task of composing, transforming his musical sketches into their final form. At home he could also indulge in his favourite country pursuits, including bicycle rides and bird-watching, and he also revived an earlier interest in chemistry, turning one of the outhouses into a laboratory called 'The Ark', where he amused himself with various experiments – on one occasion inadvertently blowing up a water-butt.

Unfitting as it might seem this was the milieu in which he composed what was acclaimed as his greatest work, his *First Symphony*. It received its first performance in 1908 – and in its first year was performed nearly 100 times in London, Vienna, Leipzig, St Petersburg, Sydney and the United States. At last the recognition which had eluded him in his early years as a composer now flowed in full measure.

Early in 1910 Elgar went to stay with the Schusters at 'The Hut' and here took up work on the *Violin Concerto*. Although himself doubtful of its quality, he was greatly encouraged, by his friends, the Stuart-Wortleys and the Speyers (Leonora Speyer was a professional violinist and played over parts of the new work for him).

Work on the concerto also resulted in a new friendship, with the violinist W. H. (Billy) Reed, later leader of the London Symphony Orchestra. Following a chance meeting in the street in London, Reed was invited back to Elgar's flat in New Cavendish Street to advise on bowings, fingerings and other technical aspects of the solo writing. Reed described how

on my arrival I found Sir Edward striding about with a number of loose pieces of manuscript which he was arranging in different parts of the room. Some were already pinned on the back of chairs, or fixed up on the mantelpiece ready for me to play . . .

It was the beginning of a firm friendship, which also became a professional association. By the time Elgar accepted an invitation from the London Symphony Orchestra to become its permanent conductor on Richter's retirement in 1911, Reed was its leader.

In May 1911 Elgar conducted his *Second Symphony* at its première in London. This symphony, reflective and elegiac in mood, was more in keeping with the previous year's national mood of mourning

element entertaining their many guests, and Sir Edward was busily engaged in conducting the London Symphony Orchestra as well as composing. In the capital city the Elgars were also able to indulge their love of the theatre. With the outbreak of war in 1914, however, Elgar's popularity rested in 'Land of Hope and Glory'. It was enormously popular but Elgar would have preferred that the sentiments expressed in the words provided by A. C. Benson were less swaggering. He himself worked hard both to sustain British music-making and at the same time to satisfy the public's appetite for suitable patriotic expression during the years of war. Apart from his commitment to the London Symphony Orchestra he also conducted the Hallé Orchestra in Manchester.

The war marked the decline of Elgar's popularity in Germany, not only for reasons of nationality, but also because many of the conductors and artists who had championed his early successes belonged to the

Elgar's friendship, in his later years, with the dramatist George Bernard Shaw (far left), renewed his interest in theatre, particularly after the death of his wife. In 1932 he met Yehudi Menuhin (right) then 16, who was the soloist for the 1932 recording of the Violin Concerto.

Elgar's life-long passion for the English countryside (below) and country pursuits, like cycling and walking, are reflected in the very 'Englishness' of his music.

generation now reaching old age and retirement. Elgar himself was approaching his sixties and, despite the outward successes of his wartime works – like *The Spirit of England* – he was neither happy nor in good health. Although he still gained pleasure from the company at Severn House, he began to long once again for the countryside. Alice Elgar, realizing her husband's need for peace and solitude, found a summer cottage, Brinkwells, near Fittleworth in Sussex. Elgar loved the new home which had a studio in the garden where he could work and was surrounded by woods in which he could walk for hours. Here he turned to chamber music, writing a string quartet, piano quintet and violin sonata. One other composition dates from the time at Brinkwells – the *Cello Concerto*. This was premièred in London in October 1919, and, as had happened before, in disgraceful circumstances. Part of the programme was conducted by Albert Coates, who overran his allotted rehearsal time by an hour. Elgar, greatest English composer of the day, who was to conduct his own work was not only kept waiting but also denied the opportunity of adequate rehearsal. The performance was consequently disastrous – as the critic Ernest Newman pointed out 'the orchestra made a lamentable public exhibition of itself'.

Swan-song

The *Cello Concerto* was in effect Elgar's swan-song. Although he lived for another fifteen years, he did not complete another major work.

The *Cello Concerto's* first performance was also the last witnessed by Lady Elgar, who died early in 1920. The effect of her death on her husband was shattering. For over thirty years it was she who had unfalteringly believed in him, who had supported and sheltered him, and seen the humble music-teacher she was disinherited for marrying, rise to become a national figure, sought-after by royalty, society and the British people.

Elgar survived Alice by 14 years but felt that his music vanished with her. He died on 23 February 1934 and is buried alongside her in the churchyard at St. Wulstan's, Little Malvern.

Life in the Raj
The British in India

Throughout Elgar's lifetime Britain was at the peak of her imperial power and ruled colonies the world over. And it was India, in the days of the Raj, that was 'the jewel in the imperial crown'.

British rule in India grew out of the British East India Company's commercial interests there in the 18th century. And, as the painting The East offering its riches to Britannia *(above) shows, India certainly had much to give. But by the mid-19th century simple trading involvement had grown into the belief that Britain had a 'sacred duty' to oversee the nation – by force, if necessary.*

Exotic goods (left), native craftsmanship and low labour costs made India a profitable marketplace for Britain.

At the stroke of midnight on 14 August 1947, British rule in India (The Raj) came to an end. For just under two centuries the huge subcontinent had been 'the brightest jewel in the royal crown', and far more than the countless other British colonies dotted around the world, it had been the very symbol of the British Empire.

British ascendancy in India fell into two chapters of nearly equal length. For the first century, British India was simply a commercial empire established and run by the East India Company. Known colloquially as 'John Company', it exercised control over three-fifths of the subcontinent by the fateful year of 1857. Then, seemingly out of the blue, came the greatest trauma of the Victorian era – the Indian Mutiny. The savagery of the Mutiny and the brutality of its suppression left permanent scars – on the British, who never again felt they could trust the Indians among whom they lived, and on the Indians, who were left in no doubt that the 'natural' authority of the British Empire, in the final analysis, rested on force.

From the ashes of the Mutiny emerged modern India – that is to say, the India that existed, more or less unchanged, until the end of British rule. On 1 November 1858, the responsibility for administering the subcontinent passed from the East India Company to the British Crown – in effect, the British Government acting through an appointed Viceroy, an Indian Civil Service and an overhauled Indian Army.

When, on New Year's Day 1877, Queen Victoria was proclaimed Empress of India, the imperial edifice was complete. The Raj was now an established fact of life – if one of the most improbable facts ever. From a small island off the west coast of Europe – Britain – something like 1000 officials administered for generations a vast area 6000 miles distant that teemed with 350 million people – then about one-fifth of the world's population. They did this, moreover, against a geographical landscape harshly unfamiliar, in a climate as unhealthy as it was uncomfortable, and in the midst of such varied races and cultures that to gain more than a passing knowledge of them would require the study of a lifetime. Above all, they did it free from self-doubt, secure in the belief that theirs was a noble duty.

Victorian notions of such a duty look suspiciously hypocritical to modern eyes. But not so very long ago, a great many people considered the British Empire to be almost divine in its foundation, and as likely to lead, through righteous administration, to the relief of the miseries and evils of the world. British rule in India was, therefore, considered a sacred trust, and one which would confer immense benefits on India itself. George Nathaniel Curzon, one of the ablest and most dedicated Viceroys (1899–1905) wrote without a trace of irony,

The sacredness of India haunts me like a passion. To me the message is carved in granite, hewn in the rock of doom: that our work is righteous and that it shall endure.

The social pyramid
The Viceroy stood at the pinnacle of the Anglo-Indian structure – a social structure far more tightly regimented than anything to be found in contemporary Victorian England. In fact, it has often been remarked that the social order of the Raj bore a marked resemblance to the Hindu caste system. Senior civil servants and administrators cor-

The British wrought radical social changes in India, such as the abolition of 'Suttee' – the burning of widows on their husbands' funeral pyres (a rite depicted with Victorian delicacy, below). Such practices reinforced the belief that Britain was 'obliged' to tame and civilize the country.

responded to the priestly class of Brahmins, and enjoyed special authority and privileges befitting their lofty status. Then came the military officers of both the British and Indian Army, equivalent to the Hindu warrior caste. Next came businessmen, plantation owners and others of middle class, corresponding to the low-caste Hindu merchants. Finally, the equivalents of the Hindu outcasts were the British Tommy and, still lower, the half-caste Eurasian.

Everyone knew precisely where he stood in the social order. He could find out where anyone else stood, too, by simply looking at the relevant Civil or Military Lists. The *India Office List* for 1899 comprised 700 pages of minute type, setting out the title, duties and salary of every British official in India, from haughtiest judge to humblest clerk.

This social pyramid had an effect on the behaviour of both British and Indians. The first thing a young man learned when he arrived was that he must conform to his status. In addition, he was a member of the ruling race, and he was to behave as such. This meant, above all, that his relations with native Indians were to be conducted along rigorously formal lines. The gravest sin possible was to 'go native': the penalty, ostracism from the Anglo-Indian community.

Fraternization was a theme much explored by Rudyard Kipling. Kipling was widely read, and so served to reinforce the taboo. In a preface to an unpleasant little parable entitled *'Beyond the Pale'*, he asserts,

A white man should, whatever happens, keep to his own caste, race and breed. Let the White go to the White and the Black to the Black. Then whatever trouble falls is in the ordinary course of things neither sudden, alien, nor unexpected. This is the

Until the Indian Mutiny of 1857, British army officers had no idea that Indian soldiers were capable of disloyalty. Side by side, British and Indian troops had fought together in countless battles (above), clearing India's borders of invading bands of brigands.

story of a man who wilfully stepped beyond the safe limits of decent everyday society, and paid for it heavily . . . He took too deep an interest in native life; but he will never do so again.

This cautionary tale speaks volumes about the insecurities that haunted the British in India. They abhorred the idea of integration. They were not settlers, much less immigrants. They came to India to do a job, and if they survived long enough, they went home to England in their retirement.

This estrangement of rulers from the ruled resulted, at best, in a high-minded paternalism on the part of the British official. He attempted to preserve public order, promote private justice, stamp out barbaric practices such as suttee (Hindu widows burning themselves to death on their husband's funeral pyres) and alleviating the effects of natural disasters such as famine. At worst, it led to a demoralizing hypocrisy. As one disenchanted Englishman put it in a letter back home: 'The English contempt proceeds in the main from English ignorance, and English ignorance is accompanied, as so often happens, by English bluster.'

Whether approached in a spirit of altruism or disdain, the task of uplifting the Indian masses to any extent was probably hopeless. The population was huge, the annual rainfall upon which its harvests relied were unreliable. Famine stalked the land. Between 1876 and 1878, for example, successive failures of the monsoon exposed some 36 million people to famine. Five million died. The famine of 1896–7 brought 62 million to the edge of starvation and again claimed about 5 million lives.

If famine was an ever-present threat, poverty and disease were ever-present realities. English sensibilities recoiled from conditions that condemned millions upon millions to mercifully short lives of squalor. In a Sanitary Survey made in 1896, the house drains in Calcutta were described as follows:

In a large number of cases, the downpipe was broken 5–15ft from the ground, and the water,

The responsibility for governing and implementing British policy in India was invested in the Viceroy. One of the ablest and most dedicated Viceroys was Marquis George Nathaniel Curzon (left), Viceroy between 1899-1905.

The Great Durbars were spectacular gatherings of British and Indian notables. These events were, essentially, public relations exercises organized to promote British prestige. The first Great Durbar was in 1876 when Queen Victoria was declared Empress of India (below).

urine and liquid sewage from the houses was simply splashing on the ground, fouling the whole gali (lane), and soaking the walls of the houses . . . Many of the interiors of the dwelling were pitch dark even in broad daylight; the rats ran about fearlessly as if it were the middle of the night. Walls and floors alike are damp with contamination from liquid sewage which is rotting, and for which there is no escape.

A crowded community awash in sewage: perfect conditions for cholera, and the stinking slums of Calcutta duly won the title 'world headquarters of cholera'. In India as a whole, 800,000 died of the disease in 1900 alone. Malaria and tuberculosis killed far more. And normally non-fatal afflictions like dysentery and diarrhoea took a dreadful toll. Plague, spread by rats, was endemic. In the quarter-century beginning 1896, it claimed 34 million victims.

Surviving these mass killers was no guarantee of health. At any given time, there were probably a million lepers and half that number blinded by infectious eye disease. An estimated 5 per cent of the adult population endured the ravages of venereal disease. Children readily fell prey to whooping cough, diptheria, meningitis and anything else that could grip a physique weakened by malnutrition and mired in filth. There was a desperate shortage of doctors, nurses and medical facilities.

The British in India were not indifferent to the plight of India's masses. They built thousands of miles of railway, which not only improved communication in general, but also made it possible for food to be transported more quickly from areas of plenty to those stricken by drought. Irrigation schemes, too, were undertaken as a means of improving yield and reducing poverty. In 1901 Lord Curzon appointed an Irrigation Commission, which

put forward a 20-year programme of development. By the end of that period more than 10 per cent of the total area of British India under cultivation – 20 million acres – was served by irrigation.

The scale of India's problems, however, would have defeated the most determined and sweeping efforts at social and economic reform, even if such reforms had been the purpose of the Raj. They were not. An article in the *Asiatic Review* for 1889 swept aside any such pretensions:

Let us have the courage to repudiate the pretence, which foreigners laugh at and which hardly deceives ourselves, that we keep India only for the benefit of their country and in order to train them for self-government. We keep it for the sake of the interests and the honour of England . . .

The great Durbars
The honour, more, the glory of imperial England reached its apogee in the great Durbars of the Raj. The Durbar was an old Mogul custom of holding court, and the British readily adapted it to their own needs. Normally, Durbars were simply made up of petitioners gathering outside an official's home or office each morning. At a more exalted level they were the various official gatherings held at the court of the Viceroy in the course of the year. On three occasions, however – in 1876, 1903 and 1911 – truly magnificent Durbars were staged outside Delhi.

The first of these great Durbars was to celebrate the proclamation of Queen Victoria as Empress of India. The second, to mark the coronation of Edward VII, was the ceremonial high point of Lord Curzon's tenure. In terms of scale and grandeur it far surpassed the coronation celebrations in London. Curzon and

The ordinary Indian lived in atrocious conditions of poverty and squalor (above left), yet the regional rajas and princes (above) were vastly wealthy. Indeed, it was from the latter that Queen Victoria received some of her richest tributes.

A tea planter, his wife and neighbours sit out (below) beyond the 'verandah' of their 'bungalow' (both words were added to the language during the Raj). Life for these ex-patriots was a mixture of adventure, formal socializing, and boredom.

his staff made their grand entrance on elephants, to take the salute in a march-past of 40,000 men of the Indian Army and the British Army in India. Scores of princes and maharajahs, bedecked with the most fabulous garments and jewels, came to pay homage to the King-Emperor, as represented by the Viceroy. And – a revealing touch, this – Curzon banned the hymn *Onward Christian Soldiers* from the religious service because of its seditious sentiments:

Thrones and crowns may perish,
Kingdoms rise and wane . . .

The third great Durbar, in 1911, even outshone Curzon's. It marked the accession of George V, and the King-Emperor and Queen Mary made the voyage from England for the occasion. An army of 20,000 workers prepared the site for the Durbar, and a fortune was spent building drains and polo grounds for 233 camps extending over 25 square miles. The

From the British point of view the Indian soldiers' virtues of loyalty and heroism drew a great respect, as the Victorian music hall song (title page, right), shows.

The British Army in India was made up of both Indians and British – usually Indian soldiers under British command (below right). This system could not have worked without a certain willingness of the native troops to submit to foreign domination.

This Song may be Sung in public without fee or Licence, except at Theatres and Music Halls.

HOW · INDIA · KEPT · HER · WORD.

Written by
J. P. HARRINGTON,

Composed by
GEORGE LE BRUNN,

CHORUS.
India's Reply in the days gone by,
To other nations may have been absurd,
But when Britain's flag unfurl'd, They prov'd to all the world,
How the Sons of India kept their word.

SUNG BY

LEO · DRYDEN.

The British soldier though he might work out his entire career in India, could never be more than an onlooker of Indian society (above). Due to the rigid rules of the social system, to mix with the natives was to risk being outcast by his fellow men.

royal camp alone spread across 85 acres, with green lawns, red roads, and roses from England.

The everyday life of a minor official

For the most part, life in the Raj was humdrum. A typical official would be posted to a remote up-country station, at least for the first few years of his service. If he was lucky, he would find himself in a favoured province such as Punjab or the United Provinces. If not, it might be the steamy jungles of Upper Burma, or the parched Sind Desert. The station itself would be broken down into self-contained communities – the native quarter on the 'wrong' side of the railway tracks, the British on the other, complete with church, offices, public buildings, and perhaps a public garden. Invariably, the station club and the best bungalows reserved for senior officials were at the centre, giving way towards the perimeter to lesser bungalows, police and military garrisons.

A typical bungalow was surrounded by a verandah; the rooms inside were spacious. At the rear, separate from the bungalow, stood the kitchen, with the servants' quarters nearby. There was no servant problem. A book describing Anglo-Indian Life, published in 1878, suggests 27 servants as appropriate for a reasonably affluent family in Calcutta, 14 as sufficient for a bachelor. Children, and sometimes even the family dog, had their own servant.

The first step a new arrival took, on reaching the station, was to don formal clothes and present his card at the door of senior officials. After an appropriate interval this would elicit a dinner invitation. He would also apply at once for membership of the station club.

In preparation for the day's work, he would rise early, taking tea and toast before six. This would allow a period of exercise – riding, in all likelihood – during the relative cool of the morning. Breakfast would be at nine, then the day's work began.

It was probably tedious. He was a tiny part of the largest bureaucracy in the world, and everything that bureaucratic machine did was committed to paper. Huge piles of written memoranda and minutes were carried by a horde of messengers from office to office across the land. Officials spent most of their working hours reading and writing, and, in consequence, it took an eternity to accomplish the most trivial task.

The working day ended at five, with dinner at seven followed by cards or billiards or reading. The dinner might be a dinner party; there might be a chukka of polo in the early evening. But the overwhelming pattern was one of deadly monotony. There was a great deal of heavy drinking.

The one great perk was The Tour, which was encouraged by most branches of the service. Freed from the boredom and red tape of the office, the *sahib* (gentleman) would set out to inspect his territory. It might be a huge area requiring weeks of

touring. Sleeping under canvas by night, enjoying the hospitality and deference accorded a VIP by day, it was the perfect way to savour the delights of India during the 'Cold Weather' – that is to say, the winter.

The young official on his first tour was certain to be a bachelor: it was frequently stipulated in his contract that he remain one for a certain period of time, or until he reached a certain status. During the 'Hot Weather' he would be unlikely, in any case, to encounter any unmarried young women, because they would have been packed off to the more temperate hills. When the Cold Weather came (mid-October) the situation changed overnight, just as summer clothing gave way to winter clothing regardless of the weather. For the next four months it was a whirl of dances: tea-dances and club-dances, dinner-dances and the Viceroy's Annual Ball.

If the young official failed to find himself a wife during the hectic match-making of the Cold Weather, he could always return to England to seek one (where the competition was less stiff), at the end of his first tour of duty. Such a tour of duty was usually an unbroken period of four or five years.

For his English bride, the sea voyage to India would be the beginning of an adventure for which she could not possibly be prepared. After the opening of the Suez Canal in 1869, the journey was reduced to four weeks from anything up to six months by the Cape route. It was a luxury cruise aboard one of the great ocean-going liners. But on disembarking at the gateway of India in Bombay, a new life began. She was now a *memsahib* (gentleman's lady).

She would live in a rented house with rented furniture, changing both maybe every year, without any say in the matter. All day long she was alone in the house with a clutch of servants who could understand her no better than she could understand them, and shared her unwillingness to break down the barriers to communication. If she was married to an army officer, she might be on her own for months while he was away on active service. When she had children, she could expect to nurse them through a host of illnesses and, assuming they survived to reach school age, send them away to England.

Such a bleak picture does not, of course, describe the Indian years of every young woman who made the voyage to Bombay. Many refused to succumb to the climate, or to the equally energy-sapping routine of a typical household. Many accompanied their husbands on tour, living in tents and eating whatever local concoctions were placed before them. Many, in the later years of the Raj, openly showed an interest in Indian society, concerned themselves in the welfare of their servants and the wider India beyond their own doorstep. Many seldom thought of England.

The end, when it came, was sudden, though nationalistic movements had existed for a hundred years. Ironically, a concerted struggle for independence only became possible because of the achievement of the Raj. Improved lines of communications meant that sympathetic political groups could communicate and unite. The use of English throughout the country meant that political debate could take place between intellectual Indians from whatever region. It also exposed the educated to the works of Western liberals who questioned imperialism and recommended democracy. Englishmen who could so fervently colonize foreign soil in the interests of their own flag taught Indians to think in nationalistic terms themselves. Once India had realized the possiblity of saying 'No' to British domination, there was no way that domination could profitably continue.

As the last Viceroy (Queen Victoria's great-grandson, Lord Louis Mountbatten) prepared to sign over the Raj, the Anglo-Indians packed their bags for the last voyage home. Their fairest epitaph has been provided by the historian who wrote: 'By and large, they meant well.'

The legacy of the Raj included a railway network on a scale to match the vast size of the country. The huge Victoria Rail Terminus, Bombay (above), built in a mixture of Victorian and Indian styles, reflects the scale of British involvement in India.

Claude Debussy
1862–1918

Debussy's life was chequered, to say the least, yet he was destined to rise, after inauspicious beginnings, to lead the world of music in a new and exciting direction.

The French composer Claude-Achille Debussy (left) was born in Paris and spent most of his adult life in the Bohemian quarter of Montmartre (below).

Claude-Achille Debussy was born in Paris on 22 August, 1862, the first of five children. The household was a poor one, his father, Manuel, being generally irresponsible in both money and family matters. His mother, Victorine, also regarded herself as a free spirit and spent most of her time trying to forget she ever had any children. Consequently, the young Claude and his brothers and sisters were frequently packed off to Cannes, where, in the home of their aunt and godmother, Clémentine, they were largely brought up. She not only gave them all much-needed love and attention, but was also the first to note Claude's attraction to music and arranged for his first piano lesson.

The unsettled nature of Claude's early life must have reached a climax in 1871, the year of the Paris Commune, when his father was arrested and imprisoned. During this period Manuel Debussy met Charles Sivry whose mother, Madam Antoinette-Flore Mauté, convinced him of his son's musical talent. This cultured and intelligent woman – the mother-in-law of Verlaine – immediately recognized the young boy's talent at the keyboard and declared that he must be trained for a concert career.

Manuel, seeing visions of a life of leisure being supported by his genius son, gave up his plan that Claude should be a sailor and enthusiastically agreed.

Debussy's parents expressed little concern for the welfare of their children and, in fact, passed much of the responsibility for their upbringing to Clémentine Debussy – the children's aunt and godmother. Consequently, Debussy and his brothers and sisters had an unsettled childhood moving between Paris and Cannes (left) where she lived. Here, Debussy spent much of his time until he entered the Paris Conservatoire.

During Debussy's student years his piano teacher, Marmontel, arranged summer work for him as house musician to various wealthy patrons. The first appointment was at the opulent Château de Chenonceaux (below) – the home of Madame Marguerite Wilson-Pelouze.

Debussy met Madame Blanche-Adélaide Vasnier (right), a singer, in 1881. It has been suggested, though not proved, that they had an affair. Undoubtedly, though, Debussy was deeply attached to her and dedicated to her many of his early songs.

So the nine-year-old Claude was groomed by Madam Mauté for entry into the Conservatoire. She lavished care and attention on him to such an extent that he became almost a grandchild to her, and he frequently stayed at her apartments.

Debussy responded well to such encouragement, passing the 1872 summer exams for entrance into the Conservatoire. A measure of Madame Mauté's achievement here is shown by the fact that to this date Debussy had received no formal schooling.

Early training
Debussy thus started his music training as a piano student with Antoine Marmontel, and for the first three years made good progress. At a Conservatoire concert of 1875 he was described as having 'a delightful temperament . . . this budding Mozart is a regular devil.' However, within three years he was to give up all pretensions to a career as a virtuoso, for he was rapidly becoming fascinated by composition. After a second prize for piano in 1877 there were no more pianistic awards.

As Debussy's piano studies waned, his music theory successes multiplied and he began to experiment with sounds and musical ideas in novel and often controversial ways. Although he was an unorthodox student interested in anything which challenged existing musical beliefs, he always made sure he did enough work on the basics to sustain high examination marks. Thus a first prize in 1880 for practical harmony enabled the eighteen-year-old to progress to the composition class.

Meanwhile, in the previous summer, 1879, his world had opened up in a new and exciting way. His old piano teacher, Marmontel, managed to find him a summer post as house musician to the cultured millionairess and Wagner fanatic, Madame Marguerite Wilson-Pelouze. He spent the summer months at her beautiful and opulent home, the Château de Chenonceaux.

The summer of 1880 found him in even more sumptuous surroundings, for Marmontel placed him

with Nadezhda von Meck, the wealthy Russian patroness of Tchaikovsky. For this and the following summers of 1881 and 1882, Debussy became part of the von Meck household, playing to the family, accompanying them, and tutoring some of Madame von Meck's substantial brood of children. He travelled throughout Europe with them, and seems to have been very popular as both accompanist and tutor.

Exposure to the leisurely and sophisticated lifestyle enjoyed by such wealthy people obviously stimulated Debussy greatly, and led him to dream of similar surroundings for himself. Not surprisingly, Madame von Meck was the first person to be presented with a composition by the ambitious young man. This she forwarded to Tchaikovsky for his comments. His judgement was crushing: 'It's a very nice thing but really too short; nothing is developed and the form is bungled.' Thus ended Debussy's first attempt at wider artistic recognition.

Montmartre life
Meanwhile, life and study continued back in Paris. His composition studies progressed to the satisfaction of his teachers, and Debussy gradually discovered a sympathetic circle of like-minded young artists with whom to spend his evenings. He frequented many of the new Montmartre cabarets with companions such as the composers Erik Satie and Paul Dukas, and the poet Raymond Bonheur. Together they encountered the new poetry of the great Symbolist writers such as Verlaine, Mallarmé and de Banville as it was being created. It was these poets, and others like them, who were to provide Debussy with inspiration for some of his greatest music in years to come.

It was around this time, particularly, that Debussy became acutely self-conscious of his appearance – he was short, swarthy and solidly-built, with a thick mop of black wavy hair and the most extraordinary forehead, caused by two protuberances formed by benign tumours on the bone. These crowned his

head at the hairline and attempting to hide them he combed locks of hair down over them in a 'girlish' fringe.

Another important friendship at this time was with the wealthy amateur singer, Madame Blanche-Adélaide Vasnier, a beautiful woman married to a civil servant eleven years her senior. Soon after their first meeting, Debussy was virtually living in the Vasniers' apartments. Many of his songs from this time were dedicated to Blanche, and it is often suggested that they had an affair. Whatever the case, their relationship was temporarily interrupted by Debussy's move to Rome.

In 1884 he entered, and won, the Conservatoire's *Prix de Rome.* Part of the prize was four years of subsidized study and unsupervised composition with accommodation at the Villa Medici in Rome. Although this was what he had wanted for years, shortly after his arrival he was implacable in his hatred of the villa, his fellow prize-winners from previous years, and Rome itself. Only one event stirred any enthusiasm in him: a meeting with the aged virtuoso Franz Liszt. Liszt encouraged Debussy to seek out performances of the music of Renaissance masters such as Palestrina and de Lassus in the little churches of Rome. When he finally made the effort, the young Frenchman was immediately won over. But from every other aspect he found Rome 'positively ugly – a town of marble, fleas and boredom'. At the start of his third year he could take no more. He hurriedly wrote a letter of resignation to the Conservatoire and bolted back to Paris and the Vasniers.

Back in Paris he produced the major work required of him by the rules of the *Prix de Rome,* the cantata *La damoiselle élue* set to a poem by Dante Gabriel Rossetti. This, his first mature work, was condemned by the Conservatoire though it appeared not to worry him as by then he had other things on his mind. He was practically penniless, and had no reason to believe things would improve. Nevertheless, he moved into his own Montmartre garret and began looking for wealthy patrons. He also

go further into the nostalgia and light (it) with subtlety, malaise and richness.' The work was successful across Europe and, though it brought in no money, it established Debussy's name outside Montmartre. He himself seemed totally unconcerned, continuing to live in penury with his mistress while relying on the generosity of a few friends such as Louÿs and patrons such as the publisher Hartmann. Thus thanks to their generosity he continued work on his new opera, *Pelléas et Mélisande,* and gradually gathered around himself most of the little comforts in life.

Marriage to Lily Texier

This lifestyle was to remain more or less the same up to the première of 'Pelléas' in 1902, but there were some decidedly desperate moments in between. Most of them involved his affairs with women. His relationship with the strong-willed, beautiful and passionate Gabrielle Dupont – his mistress – was a stormy one. More than once she left him, or he left her for a brief fling with someone else. In 1897 her discovery of just such a fling led to an attempted suicide with more than a hint of the melodramatic. By 1899 the pair had literally worn each other out, and when Debussy quietly slipped off with the

started to lead a cultured, Bohemian lifestyle in earnest, taking up all the latest literary, artistic and musical fashions, and arguing constantly among his friends about the relative merits of their contemporaries. Somehow he even found the time and money to go to Bayreuth (Bavaria) in 1888 to see Wagner's *Parsifal* and *Die Meistersinger,* yet his feelings towards Wagner's achievements were to remain deeply ambivalent for the rest of his life.

Oriental influence

However, the 1889 Paris World Exhibition was to expose Debussy to an influence he wholeheartedly embraced: Orientalism. At the exhibition, he was transfixed by the strange rituals of the Cochin China Travelling Theatre, and he spent hour after hour in the Javanese section 'listening to the percussive rhythmic complexities of the gamelan (xylophone) with its inexhaustible combinations of ethereal, flashing timbres'. This far-Eastern influence permeated much of his work and thinking for the next twenty years. In this he was not alone, for his contemporaries in art and literature, including such diverse figures as Gauguin, Zola and Manet, were just as enthusiastic in their appreciation.

The early 1890s, ironically, found Debussy irresolute and unproductive. It was 1893 before he produced a work, his *String Quartet op. 10.* But it was well worth the wait – one critic commenting at its première that Debussy was 'rotten with talent'. The Quartet hardly made him a household name, however, and he continued to live in an aimless and hedonistic fashion. During this time, though, he did make a string of notable aquaintances including the young poet and aesthete Pierre Louÿs, Oscar Wilde, and Marcel Proust.

Then, almost suddenly, the tide began to turn. His love of Mallarmé's poetry bore spectacular fruit with his *Prélude à l'après-midi d'un faune,* composed as a musical equivalent of Mallarmé's famous symbolist poem. This one perfect and revolutionary piece was enough to alter the course of music in France. Mallarmé himself marvelled at it: 'your illustration . . .
. presents no dissonance with my text; rather does it

Debussy won the **Prix de Rome** *in 1884 and was awarded four years of study in Rome. Although it was the realization of a long-held wish, he found little enjoyment in his stay. His one pleasure, though, was listening to the Renaissance music which could be heard in Rome's many small churches (above). After two years he abandoned the 'city of marble, fleas and boredom' and returned to Paris, taking up the Bohemian lifestyle of Parisian artistic society. Here he encountered, and was greatly inspired by, the poetry of a group known as the 'Symbolists' (right).*

In 1893 Debussy met the young poet Pierre Louÿs (right) who was to become one of his closest friends during the ensuing decade. Sadly, their friendship did not survive after Debussy (photographed by Louÿs, far right) left his first wife, Lily, to live with Emma Bardac, whom he subsequently married. Like many of Debussy's friends, Louÿs suspected that Debussy's motives were purely financial.

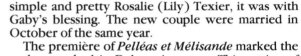

simple and pretty Rosalie (Lily) Texier, it was with Gaby's blessing. The new couple were married in October of the same year.

The première of *Pelléas et Mélisande* marked the real watershed in Debussy's career. This setting of Maurice Maeterlinck's symbolist play produced a completely new type of opera – one which had a poetic as well as a musical intention. Its effect was to make Debussy the composer of the moment, the leader of a new 'school' called 'Debussyism', and something of an institution. All of this he greeted with intense dislike, surliness and distrust, for he remained a deeply private man, committed to his own creative path, with no use for public curiosity.

Still, for better or for worse, his life was irrevocably changed. For one thing, he was no longer completely dependant on the charity of friends or on the income from the musical critiques he had begun to write for different journals in 1900 under the name of Monsieur Croche. 'Pelléas' was the start of his ascent to self-sufficiency. On the domestic front the changes were even more sweeping.

Debussy elopes

At the end of 1903 he met Emma Bardac, a beautiful and distinguished Jewish heiress with children from her first marriage and a seemingly wealthy future on the death of her millionaire uncle. Debussy fell madly in love with her and, in 1904, the two eloped – prompting Lily Debussy into a suicide bid.

Lily survived, as had Gabrielle Dupont in 1897, but Debussy's behaviour killed many of his closest friendships, including that of Pierre Louÿs, as his motives were seen as purely financial, considering Emma's own personal fortune. But two subsequent events bear witness to the inaccuracy of this accusation: one is the birth out of wedlock the following year of Claude-Emma (Chou-Chou). The other is their marriage in 1908: the year after Emma was disinherited by her uncle for taking up with a musician and four years after the start of bitter divorce proceedings by Lily.

'Debussyism'

Thus there was a considerable moral, financial and artistic strain on Debussy as he prepared for the première of a new work *La mer,* in 1905. Happily, the work was an immediate sensation, despite an inept performance at the première by a conductor who became lost in the score. Overnight, Debussy had created, and became the leader of, a new school – that of musical 'Impressionism'. However, Debussy did not follow an exclusive 'impressionist' line in his music – he was interested in the eternal mysteries evoked by nature as well as by its representation. In this he was more in step with his Symbolist contemporaries and it is significant that his greatest unfulfilled wish was to write an opera to the Edgar Allan Poe short story *The Fall of the House of Usher* – Poe was easily one of the greatest influences on the French Symbolists and Decadents.

The two years after this triumph, despite the security afforded by Emma's own resources, were a major trial to Debussy. During this period he saw the virtual disappearance of his old lifestyle, and most of his old friends with it. He was deeply disturbed by such wholesale loss, and wrote virtually no music at this time. His only compensations were Emma and Chou-Chou, to both of whom he was devoted.

The marriage, in 1908, though, seemed to galvanize Debussy into activity and from this time until his death, his creative fertility was astonishing, and he turned his hand to virtually every musical form. He also took up a career as a conductor of his own works, urged on by numerous requests from impresarios as well as by his own desire for financial independence. Unfortunately, he was a very poor conductor, and the constant rehearsals and concerts were an agony for him. Nevertheless, the public did not seem to notice his lack of conducting prowess and the concerts were a popular success.

By 1909 the first symptoms of cancer of the rectum had been discovered and from 1912 onwards Debussy suffered almost daily haemorrhages. Resorting to mixtures of cocaine and morphine to suppress the pain he persevered with the conducting tours, and also started accepting commissions for orchestral works in the hope of earning quick money, dedicated as he was to providing his wife and daughter with a real measure of security.

Debussy's revived creativity led to collaborations with two extraordinary personalities in 1911–12 – the impresario Sergei Diaghilev and the Italian playwright Gabriele d'Annunzio. Considering the impact of Diaghilev's *Ballet Russes* on Paris in 1909 it is not surprising to find Debussy eager to work with him. Yet it took them four years to mount an original ballet together. Their first project, a choreographing of *Prélude à l'après-midi d'un faune,* was a dismal failure which Debussy himself cordially detested.

The composer's collaboration with d'Annunzio hardly fared much better. D'Annunzio had arrived in Paris in 1911 in a blaze of publicity as the greatest living Italian playwright come to Paris, and he had come especially to write a 'mystery play' on the death and martyrdom of St Sebastian. In reality, he had fled from Italy to avoid paying his many creditors for his extravagant lifestyle. On his arrival he immediately recruited the famous actress Ida Rubinstein for the part of the saint, and asked Debussy to supply the musical interludes. Debussy's fine and often deeply moving score notwithstanding, the work was a disaster. The première itself seems to have been almost farcical in its failure. Even *Jeux,* the

ballet produced with Diaghilev in 1913, failed to win general acclaim. This, Debussy's last orchestral masterpiece, was made a nonsense of by Nijinsky's childish and narcissistic choreography. And within two weeks of its première it was more or less buried by the scandal and controversy surrounding the first night of a work by Debussy's friend Stravinsky: *The Rite of Spring.* In the orgy of critical recrimination provoked by Stravinsky, the more refined and delicate audacity of *Jeux's* score was completely overlooked.

During 1913, the year before the outbreak of the Great War, Debussy continued his battle against his illness, completing both a round of conducting engagements and new sets of compositions. Both books of *Preludes* for piano were completed, as well as the second of his two piano suites for his daughter, Chou-Chou. This in itself was significant, for it is clear that his domestic life was deeply fulfilling for him, both with his wife Emma and with his beloved daughter, who was by all accounts a beautiful and vivacious child.

Debussy's setting of one of Mallarmé's poems, Prélude à l'après-midi d'un faune, *was given its first performance to tumultuous acclaim in 1894. In 1909 Debussy collaborated with the impresario Sergei Diaghilev to produce a ballet to this music. The famous Russian dancer Nijinsky (above) danced the lead part at the ballet's première, but his choreography, rather than the music, contributed to its dismal failure.*

MADEMOISELLE MAGGIE TAYTE

Dans le rôle de Mélisande, du Pelléas et Mélisande de Claude Debussy et Maurice Maeterlinck, qu'elle vient d'interpréter, à l'Opéra-Comique, avec beaucoup d'art et un grand succès.

The impact of war

The outbreak of war in August 1914 put an immediate stop to Debussy's public engagements, and also temporarily stilled his creative impulse. His reactions to France's involvement were markedly ambivalent:

'I have nothing of the army spirit – I've never even held a rifle. My recollections of 1870 and the anxiety of my wife, whose son and son-in-law are in the army, prevent me from developing any enthusiasm.' In a later letter he wrote: *'if, to ensure victory, they are absolutely in need of another face to be bashed in, I'll offer mine without question . . . (however) . . . Art and war have never, at any period, been able to find any basis of agreement.'*

Debussy's publisher, Durand, aware of his reduced income brought on by the war, gave him a new edition of Chopin's works to edit in early 1915. This was to bear glorious fruit later that year when Debussy wrote the twelve *Etudes,* his crowning pianistic achievement. As the year wore on, other works in a new, severe style poured from his pen. Struggling as he was by this time against the cancer which had a terminal grip on him, he managed to complete two of a projected set of six chamber pieces, as well as *En blanc et noir,* a four-hand piano work of great emotional power. He wrote to a friend towards the end of the year 'I must humbly admit to the feeling of latent death within me. Accordingly, I write like a madman or like one condemned to die the next morning.'

By December 1915 an operation was deemed necessary, and although it was successful, the doctors discovered that the cancer was now irreversible. Debussy spent most of 1916 recuperating, and struggling to complete his *Violin Sonata.* This elegiac, bittersweet work, finished by the end of summer, was to be his last. During 1917 he found the effort of composition too much, and

contented himself with finishing the libretto to his projected Poe opera. The music was never written. That October, he wrote: 'Music has completely abandoned me.'

'Papa is dead'

By January 1918 he was confined to bed. On the 25th of March he died in his Paris apartment, at the height of the last great German bombardment of the city. In a moving letter sent to her half-brother Raoul Bardac, Debussy's twelve-year-old daughter summed up the family's feelings of loss:

The première of Debussy's opera, Pelléas et Mélisande *in 1902 (Mélisande from a 1908 production shown left) marked a watershed in his career. It was Debussy's only opera but with it he won fame and wider recognition.*

Debussy (below) with his daughter Claude-Emma (Chou-Chou) in 1916, just two years before his death.

'. . . sweetly, angelically, he went to sleep for ever. What happens afterwards I cannot tell you. I wanted to burst into a torrent of tears but I repressed them because of Mama . . . At the cemetery Mama of course could not hide her feelings. As for myself, I thought of nothing but one thing: 'You mustn't cry because of Mama.' And I gathered up all my courage which came – from where? I don't know. I didn't shed a tear: tears repressed are worth tears shed, and now it is to be night for ever. Papa is dead.'

To the sound of German guns rumbling in the background, and in the presence of a handful of mourners, Debussy was buried at the cemetery of Père-Lachaise in Paris on 28 March 1918.

Impressionism and Symbolism

French painting was thrust forward into the 20th century by the twin forces of Impressionism and Symbolism – and the reverberations shook the artistic world from literature to music.

The French 'Impressionist' painters of the late 19th century are among the most popular of all artists nowadays, and prints of paintings by the core of the group – Renoir, Monet, Pissarro and Sisley – adorn the walls of houses right across the world. The shimmering colours, the glorious sense of light, the simple, natural choice of subject and, above all, their tremendous zest for life give Impressionist paintings a charm and appeal that captivates even those with only a passing interest in art. And their major role in the development of modern art is now fully established – so established that they are sometimes dismissed as 'too safe'.

Yet in the 1870s, the revolutionary techniques and approach of the Impressionists were too much for the art establishment and public alike, and they were

It was this painting (right) by Claude Monet, called **Impression, Sunrise,** *that gave the Impressionists their name. The art critic Louis Leroy coined the word in his mocking review of the 1874 exhibition, intending it to convey the artists' 'sloppy' approach. The name stuck.*

An early champion of the Impressionists was the writer and critic Émile Zola (left), but he was out-spoken in his support.

villified and scorned for many years. Indeed, the idea of the struggling artist, starving for his art, his talent unrecognized, was fostered to a great extent by the trials and tribulations of the Impressionist painters. The winding streets of Montmartre in Paris may now seem a chic and picturesque artist's quarter, but for some of the painters who established its reputation, it was simply the only place they could afford to live. Even in 1894, 20 years after the first Impressionist exhibition, the bequest of 67 Impressionist paintings to the Louvre by the painter Gustave Caillebotte aroused enormous hostility and official embarassment. Typically, one member of the academic establishment ranted:

Only great moral depravity could bring the State to accept such rubbish. These artists are all anarchists and madmen!

One of the most shocking features of Impressionism was its apparent carelessness of execution. Paint seemed to be just slopped onto the canvas with no real attempt to draw the shapes clearly, no attempt to reproduce textures and forms accurately, and the pictures appeared to be merely rough sketches, not finished works of art – even the crude brush strokes were clearly visible. Indeed, there was no evidence of any of the traditional painterly skills at all.

Worse still, for the art establishment, was the thoughtlessness of it all. Instead of the established subjects worthy of artistic study, the Impressionists simply painted scenes from everyday life, scenes that anyone could see, at any time. Renoir painted people in the cafes of Montmartre; Sisley painted suburban street scenes. And there was no attempt to compose these scenes within the picture frame in the time-honoured manner. They were fleeting glimpses, moments caught not arranged. In Renoir's paintings, arms, legs, even faces disappear beyond the edge of the frame. Although candid photographic snapshots have made us familiar with such images, they seemed bizarre to people in the 1870s. Only recently has Renoir's true mastery of composition been appreciated. To cap it all, there was no message in the pictures. They had nothing to say; they just existed. No wonder the Impressionists appeared to have no talent at all and to some seemed to be frauds.

Oddly enough, all these individual criticisms had at least some foundation in truth, particularly amongst the less capable Impressionist painters, and it may be that this was why they found it so hard to gain recognition. But the critics completely missed the point, failing to understand what the Impressionists were trying to do.

When Monet painted *Impression, Sunrise* in 1872, he was trying to capture as accurately as possible the real visual effect of a misty morning sun upon water – the way he actually saw the interplay of light and colour, not an interpretation of the scene that revealed each object. Monet's advice to painters gives a clear indication of his approach.

Try to forget what objects you have before you – a tree, a house, a field or whatever. Merely think, here is a little square of blue, here an oblong of pink, the exact colour and shape, until it gives your own naive impression of the scene before you.

The word 'naive' is important, for Monet believed, along with the other Impressionists, that it was essential to approach the subject with a completely fresh, open mind, rid of preconception of what the scene should look like. Only this way could you be totally objective.

For the Impressionists, capturing the rapid changes of light and colour in the atmosphere, rather than telling a story, was the central aim of their art. To achieve it, they evolved a revolutionary method of painting on the spot with rapid brush strokes – for it would be impossible to sketch these subtle atmospheric effects in pencil and then recall them in the studio.

They combined this location painting method with a new way of building up colour that drew its

Claude Monet was, with Renoir, one of the two giants of Impressionism and this painting Coin de Jardin à Montgeron *(right) is typical of his work. It was of Monet that Paul Cézanne later said, 'he was only an eye – but, my god, what an eye!' and this painting, with its shimmering interplay of light and colour, shows that eye to marvellous effect. The picture is built up with short deft brush strokes of pure colour.*

The Entrée du village de Voisins *(below left) is one of Camille Pissarro's contributions to the 1874 exhibiton – Pissarro was the only painter to contribute to all eight Impressionist exhibitions – and owes much to the influence of Corot.*

Auguste Renoir's À la Grenouillère *(below right) shows one of his favourite subjects, a healthy young woman in a natural everyday pose – the kind of subject and pose that was unheard of before the days of Impressionism.*

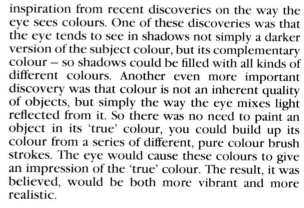

inspiration from recent discoveries on the way the eye sees colours. One of these discoveries was that the eye tends to see in shadows not simply a darker version of the subject colour, but its complementary colour – so shadows could be filled with all kinds of different colours. Another even more important discovery was that colour is not an inherent quality of objects, but simply the way the eye mixes light reflected from it. So there was no need to paint an object in its 'true' colour, you could build up its colour from a series of different, pure colour brush strokes. The eye would cause these colours to give an impression of the 'true' colour. The result, it was believed, would be both more vibrant and more realistic.

The origins of Impressionism

In many ways, Impressionism marks the logical and final development of a search that had been going on from the early 19th century, both in England and in France, to find a more truthful way of representing Nature. Throughout the previous century, French art had been dominated by the idea that only historical, religious or classical subjects were worth painting. This idea gained weight through the powerful institution of the French Academy of Fine Arts and its bi-annual official exhibitions in the *salon carré* of the

air rather than from the comfort of their studios, these artists set a powerful precedent for the Impressionists.

Yet despite this burgeoning of realistic landscape painting among the younger artists, the Salon still tended to feature the traditional subjects almost exclusively. Naturally this caused deep resentment, for the Salon had a crucial impact on public taste and sales of pictures. It came to a head in 1855, when some of Gustave Courbet's paintings were refused for the Salon at the Paris exhibition.

Courbet was the most influential of the younger painters and, although distanced from the Barbizon school, believed painting was the 'representation of real and existing objects'. He wanted to paint village funerals, stonebreakers and country people, not the traditional subjects. Faced with rejection by the Salon, Courbet staged his own rival exhibition called the 'Pavilion of Realism'. The impact of Courbet's fresh, bold paintings alongside the tired old works that hung in the Salon was remarkable. Courbet's exhibition set an important precedent which the Impressionists were later to follow. More importantly, it broke forever the stranglehold of traditional academic subjects.

The growing movement

Through the gap opened by Courbet came the whole Impressionist group, fathered in the 1860s, by Edouard Manet. Where Courbet had still used conventional techniques if not subjects, Manet developed a sketchy style, using pure colour to give a very realistic look even to studio subjects. The results, in works like *Déjeuner sur l'herbe* and *Olympia,* caused a sensation. The public could not come to terms with Manet's way of painting exactly what he saw. It seemed indecently and shockingly real! Manet too was shut out of the Salon, despite being championed by the outspoken art critic (later the novelist) Émile Zola. And, in 1867, he followed Courbet's example and organized his own exhibition – one-man exhibitions are one of our most notable legacies from the Impressionist era.

Louvre and the so-called Salons.

Remarkably, both the idea and the institution survived the revolution of 1789 intact, but amongst younger artists, the romantic movement and increasing urbanization and industrialization was fostering a passion for nature and growing preference for landscapes. The Salon, however, continued to favour the traditional subjects almost exclusively.

In England, though, landscape painting already had a long history and by the early 19th century was progressing in leaps and bounds with the paintings of John Constable and J M W Turner. In 1825, Constable's *The Hay Wain* was exhibited in Paris and its fresh colours and bold sketchy technique were a tremendous inspiration to young French painters. More important still was its simple, everyday subject and natural quiet landscape.

By the late 1830s and the 1840s, many young French painters were going out into the country to paint *real* landscapes in the open air. One village called Barbizon, situated on the edge of the forest of Fontainebleau, attracted a whole string of fine landscape painters – Camille Corot, Théodore Rousseau, Jean Millet, Charles Daubigny and many others, who thus became known as the Barbizon School. Observing and studying nature in the open-

Although not actually an Impressionist, Manet's anti-establishment stance made him the focus of the young group of artists who were to create the new movement. In the late 1860s, a whole group of artists would gather round Manet at the Café Guerbois in Paris to drink coffee and wine and discuss art vociferously. Among them were Degas, Monet and Renoir, Berthe Morisot and the photographer Nadar. Émile Zola was also a frequent visitor to the Café and, if he disagreed with their ideas, always resolutely defended the Impressionists. Another occasional participant was the poet Baudelaire.

It was from these sessions in the Café Guerbois that the idea for the first Impressionists exhibition emerged. For the previous decade, Monet and Renoir had worked side by side out of doors at La Grenouillère, a cafe and boating place on the Seine, and produced a series of paintings that, in their quick, definite brush strokes and informal subject matter, provided the basis for the full Impressionist style. By the early 1870s, Monet, Renoir, Sisley, Pissarro and others had developed this style to a

remarkable extent. But there was still no recognition from the establishment. So, in 1874, the group, now led by Monet and Pissarro, decided to stage their own exhibition at Nadar's studio near the elegant Boulevard des Capucines.

The exhibition, which opened on 15 April, caused a public and critical sensation. It was, in fact, one of the critics, Louis Leroy of the satirical journal *Le Charivari*, who gave the group their name. Faced with Monet's *Impression, Sunrise*, he called Monet an 'impressionist' in his mocking review to characterize his 'sloppy' style and the name stuck. Leroy went on to lament:

Oh Corot, Corot, what crimes are committed in your name! It was you who brought into fashion this messy composition, these thin washes, these mud-splashes in front of which the art lover has been rebelling for 30 years.

The impressionists remained undaunted by the abuse and lack of understanding, even if their material circumstances remained straightened. And

Despite the almost abstract style of some of his later work, Cézanne always painted his landscapes in the open air. One of his favourite views was of Mont Ste Victoire and the painting above is just one of a celebrated series he painted of the mountain. This re-working of the same subject was important as, although like the Impressionists Cezanne drew from nature, he painted not his first impression but a studied view.

they continued to develop their style. During the late 1870s, with Monet and Renoir working together at Argenteuil, Pissarro not far away at Pointoise and Sisley at Port Marly, some of the most characteristic examples of Impressionist painting appeared. Soon each artist found his own favourite subject. For Monet, water, with its continually changing reflections of light and colour, was especially attractive. Similarly, the myriad reflections from snow held a special fascination for Sisley. Renoir, after working with Monet on water and landscape themes found his challenge in the constant bustle of the boulevards of Paris and its cafes.

A dead end

Ironically, it was the very concern with the way the light and colour changed that proved to be the main reason for the short life of Impressionism – barely a decade. By 1880, the Impressionists and some of their followers had begun to sense that their treatment of light and colour did not tell the full story. More to the point, they began to feel, along with many others, that the search for complete realism was fruitless. The pursuit of realism, which had been going on since the Renaissance, seemed to have no further to go – painting reality was ultimately meaningless and the reaction to the most real imaginable picture could be 'So what?'

The problem was where to go. The Impressionists were not alone in their search. Realism, and its successor Naturalism, had played a significant part in all art forms at the time and was now beginning to ask the same questions. Influenced by the German philosophers, Schopenhauer, Hegel and Nietzsche, artists began to fall more in line with a new movement called 'Symbolism' which wanted art to

contain imaginative, spiritual and sensual ideas, conveyed in symbolic terms. There was also an increasing concern with dreams and allegorical visions – it is perhaps significant that it was at this time that Freud's main discoveries about dreams, symbols and the importance of sex were being made.

Not every artist followed the Symbolist line and, in painting, the urge towards imaginative expression took two main directions forward from Impressionism: that of Monet, Cezanne and Seurat who developed a kind of Post-Impressionism (Seurat's version was called 'Neo-Impressionism'), eventually transforming the Impressionist search for 'Truth to Nature' into an art based on the personal contemplation of nature; and that of the Symbolists like Gauguin and Van Gogh, Moreau and Puvis de Chavannes, who tried to explore themes of intensely personal symbols. The oddity is that though working from such totally different directions, the common ground that formed their point of departure, the discovery of colour, led in the end to paintings that in many ways were surprisingly similar. Between them these paintings were to revolutionize art in the early 20th century.

Post-impressionism

Of the original group of Impressionists, Monet found the only truly successful and consistent sytle in the years after 1880. His solution was to paint a series of pictures on exactly the same subject, seen at different times of the day and under different atmospheric conditions. There were first the 15 paintings of *Haystacks* in 1891, followed by six views of *Poplars on the River Epte* in 1891 and 1892, and then some twenty views of the facade of Rouen Cathedral.

But the ultimate and most astonishing develop-

Paul Gauguin's **Vision after the Sermon** *(right) painted in 1886 was his first great masterpiece in his 'new style'. In many ways, it was one of the first great 'symbolist' works. The picture shows the people of a Breton village recalling a sermon about Jacob wrestling with the angels, but it is neither visionary nor 'realistic'. Instead, it uses pure vivid colours like red, flat shapes and fluid outlines to create a new expressive form of art, a form that was to lead forward to the abstract art of the 20th century.*

ment of these ideas in Monet's art are the works that occupied him for the last 30 years of his life from 1895 onwards: the water gardens and lily ponds at his garden at Giverny. In these paintings, essentially one enormous series, Monet created a completely separate world of his own, of slowly moving water and undulating plants, with the world beyond known only by the vague reflections of sky and clouds above. Painted largely in his studio, the gardens became visions, half-seen, half-remembered in the mind's eye, the colour and brushstrokes being freed almost totally from the objects themselves in a way that, at times, resembles the much later techniques of 20th century Abstract Impressionism.

A similar change of direction overtook the work of Paul Cézanne. Of the same generation as the Impressionists, he had been very much slower to find his direction and never evolved a truly Impressionist style. By 1880 he had already become dissatisfied with its results, determined instead to try and find a way of translating his visual sensations when looking at nature into strong harmonious designs, that could stand comparison with the great compositions of the Old Masters and avoid the messiness and lack of structure that he felt so weakened Impressionism. He retreated from Paris to his home in Aix-en-Provence where he lived and worked in almost total isolation, working the problem out for the next quarter of a century.

Like Monet, Cézanne found working in themes or series a helpful way of exploring these sensations, the static qualities of table-top still lifes or the Mont Ste Victoire providing fixed points against which he could return time and again to record the gradual changes in his perceptions of them. In the Mont Ste Victorie paintings of the 1890s and 1900s, he can be seen steadily reversing the Impressionist argument, as the attempt to see the world becomes an intense act of contemplation. Each picture, with its brilliant mosaic of tightly interlocking colour, stands as a symbol of his feelings when painting it. Like Monet, hard observation became transformed into a profound meditation on nature.

The last and most puzzlingly eccentric of those artists who aimed at transforming rather than breaking with Impressionism is George Seurat. A man of scientific and logical frame of mind, he was deeply impressed by the contemporary scientific colour theory and he felt that the Impressionist difficulties lay in the fact that they had been too casual in their treatment of light and colour. He evolved a technique which he called 'divisionism' but which is commonly referred to as 'pointillism'. It involved painting each colour as little dots of pure colour which would be mixed by the eye to give the right colour. The effect, as seen in his great outdoor masterpiece *A Sunday Afternoon on the Island of the Grand Jatte* is paradoxically far more artificial and symbolic than any Impressionist painting. The treatment has a positive almost abstract sense of form which has a poetic, timeless feel and this made the work much admired by the younger Symbolist writer and artists in the later 1880s.

Symbolism

In 1886, two younger painters, Bernard and Anquetin, made a conscious decision 'to abandon the Impressionists in order to allow Ideas to dominate the techniques of painting'. It was a decision which was to have immense significance for the new anti-art-establishment movement of the late 1880s. They

wanted to find an art based on emotional experience rather than on visual analysis, a way of exploring the unconscious and instinctive parts of the mind as a source of ideas for painting. But it was Gauguin and Van Gogh who were to take this new symbolist idea into the forefront of European art. In the late 1880s, Gauguin and van Gogh both evolved a radical style in which bold, often unnaturalistic colour and strongly contoured decorative shapes were used to convey

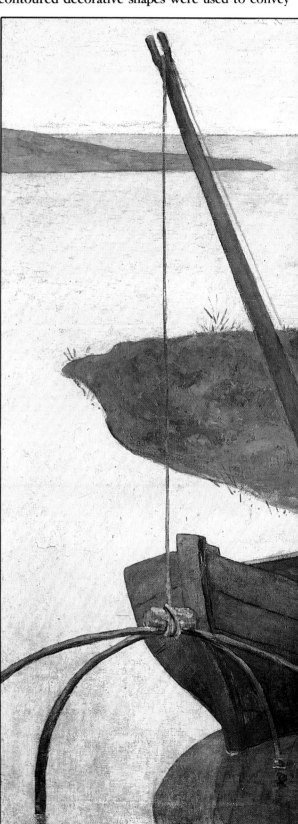

In his 'Symbolist Manifesto' of 1886, the poet Jean Moreas had talked about the need to clothe the 'Idea' in sensual form and to reject the spirit of realism that had produced both the Impressionists and the naturalist novels of Émile Zola. His ideas, which he continued to express in the symbolist journal (above), found an echo in the work of artists in many different fields.

expressive and highly charged spiritual messages.

By 1888, Gauguin had, in his first great masterpiece *The Vision after the Sermon,* painted in the remote countryside of Brittany, shown the main elements of the revolutionary art he was later to develop in the South Seas. It reveals priests and peasants emerging from the church, vividly recollecting in their imaginations the sermon they had just heard about Jacob wrestling with the angels.

The peasants and their thoughts are distinguished by areas of flat, unnatural colour. Heavily influenced by Japanese art and Medieval stained glass, Gauguin's style found a way of exploiting the expressive possibilities of colour and form most effectively, building on art that was to lead to the first explorations of abstraction in the early 20th century.

The search for a still more primitive expressive power led him to Tahiti and the South Seas. There the

In the 1880s, Puvis de Chavannes was a hero among the younger symbolist painters and this painting (Le Pauvre Pecheur) is one of his best (left). Unlike Gauguin, Puvis' background was the traditional academic style, not the avant garde of the Impressionists. By using allegory, Puvis and other painters of the older generation, like Moreau and Redon, tried to breath new life into the traditional forms with new symbolic meanings. His paintings had a profound influence on Gauguin, but Gauguin later commented, 'Puvis explains his idea but he does not paint it.' Only now is Puvis' work being re-evaluated.

colour harmonies became richer and more exotic, the symbolism more complex, especially in its allusions to primitive versus civilized societies. In a letter from the South Seas he wrote:

Colour which is vibration just as music, reaches what is most general and therefore vaguest in nature: its interior force . . .
Here in my hut, in complete silence, I dream violent harmonies in the natural scents which intoxicate me. A delight distilled from some indescribably sacred horror which I glimpsed of far off things . . .'

Gauguin had described the creative process as 'an eruption of intense feeling which flows like lava from the depths of one's being'. But it is Van Gogh who seems to epitomize this view of the creative process. A meeting with Gauguin in Paris had confirmed Van Gogh's growing belief that 'colour expresses something in itself'. Van Gogh hoped to develop an art that through the radiance of its coloured light would create images which in their 'heartbroken expression of our times' would help others as they had helped him. Like Gauguin, Cézanne and even Monet, he had found it necessary to go and work out these ideas on his own, spending the last three violently productive years of his life in Provence. The bold colours and shapes of his paintings, their writhing lines and the agitated brushwork convey a claustrophobic and oppressive atmosphere that it is impossible to mistake. As in Gauguin and Cézanne, the progression towards an art in which feeling was symbolized by colour and design was only achieved by great suffering. In Van Gogh's art there is the added sense of living on the edge of a precipice, in which painting becomes a lifeline to human comfort, a means of personal communication that makes him the true forerunner of 20th century Expressionism. But his sense of pictorial beauty prevented his style from fragmenting into non-representational art. Only as depression, despair and madness took a grip of him did his bright colours take on an overcast menace and his landscapes verge on chaos.

The road to 20th-century art

With Van Gogh committing suicide in 1890, Seurat dying and Gauguin departing for the South Seas the following year, most of the leading avant-garde artists of the 1880s were no longer in Paris. The vacuum was mostly filled by those who had worked with Gauguin in Pont-Aven, with even younger artists impressed and influenced by his ideas. Among the former, the most significant was Paul Serusier, who as an art student had in 1888 taken lessons direct from Gauguin in Brittany. The painting deriving directly from these lessons was a tiny landscape, painted on the back of a cigar box, known as *The Talisman.* It grew into an important symbol of his ideas, ideas which Serusier and a fellow student, Maurice Denis, actively propogated. With its flat areas of unmodelled yellows, blues and greens creating a surface pattern distinct from, and in tension with, the landscape they described, *The Talisman* was a revelation, in terms of the expressive, abstract power of colours and shapes, to the next generation of artists. A small group of artists calling themselves the Nabis – Hebrew for Prophet – met to discuss these ideas and soon established themselves as the most original of the new artistic groupings. Vuillard and Bonnard are the most striking artists of the group, their fascination with pattern and surface

composition being used to describe scenes from Parisian daily life. Vuillard's preoccupation was with people in interiors, like *Misa at the Piano and Cipa Listening,* where patterns of wall-paper, textiles and lamplight transform everyday experience into a subtle and ambiguous poetry. They are introverted pictures, showing people within their own environment. Bonnard by comparison is much more extrovert and out of doors as the witty painting of *Two Dogs Playing* shows, though the decorative patterning effect is very similar.

Taken together, therefore, the discoveries of Monet, Seurat, Cezanne, Gauguin and Van Gogh and the Nabis' own clear advances towards abstraction, all led inevitably forwards to 20th century Modernism – and Impressionism and Symbolism had done much to point the way.

In the swelling tide of rejection of realist and Impressionist art, the Symbolist Gustave Moreau suddenly found his mystical, sensual paintings highly fashionable. His painting of 'The Siren' (below) is typical of his decadent, dreamy interpretations of mythical figures.

Jean Sibelius
1865–1957

His imagination fired by the haunting beauty of his country and its past, Sibelius wrote music which not only won him acclaim abroad but also embodied the spirit of Finnish nationalism.

Jean Sibelius was born in Finland on 8 December 1865. At that time, Finland, under Russian rule, although supposedly autonomous, was a country with a precarious national identity. Swedish was the official language and the Finnish-speaking members of the population were regarded as second-class citizens.

His parents – Christian and Maria Sibelius – lived in the small garrison town of Hämeenlinna in south-central Finland. His father – a military doctor – died in a cholera epidemic when Jean was only two years old, and the three Sibelius children were brought up by their mother in the home of their maternal grandmother and spinster aunt. Summers were spent at the home of his other grandmother in Loviisa. He also paid regular visits to one of his uncles, Pehr, an eccentric bachelor with strong interests in music and astronomy who lived in the coastal town of Turku, but otherwise the influences on him during his early years were overwhelmingly female.

His ancestry was part Swedish and part Finnish,

Jean Sibelius (right), Finland's first internationally acclaimed composer, drew much of the inspiration for his music from his deep love of the countryside where he grew up (below).

but as members of the middle class the family was Swedish-speaking. Jean was taught some Finnish from the age of eight to prepare him for entry to the local grammar school, which was exceptional in being one of the few schools in the country where lessons were taught in Finnish. He had a small number of close friends but does not seem to have been naturally gregarious and had little liking for team sports and other group activities. He also found many of his lessons boring; he dreamed a lot of his time away and was really only stimulated by mathematics and natural history.

This close identification with nature remained with him to the end of his life and was the single most profound influence on his music. Above the published score of his last major composition, the tone-poem *Tapiola,* he wrote these lines:

Widespread they stand, the Northland's dusky forests,
Ancient, mysterious, brooding savage dreams;
And within them dwells the Forest's mighty God
And wood-sprites in the gloom weave magic secrets.

Sibelius's background ensured that he came into contact with music at an early age; families made their own entertainments, and it was the rule rather than the exception for children to learn to sing and play a musical instrument. Jean enjoyed listening to music and even composed a little piece for violin and cello called *Water Drops* at the age of ten, but this was not considered exceptional, though it shows

that he was keen to create his own music. It was only when he was presented with a violin at the age of 14 that he developed real enthusiasm; he took lessons with the local bandmaster and for the next ten years his ambitions were centred on becoming a virtuoso player. He also developed a more serious interest in musical form, especially after his discovery and study of Marx's *Kompositionslehre*. However, music-making was not really approved by the family as a profession so when he left the Grammar School in 1885 it was to read law at Helsinki University. He also enrolled at the Academy of Music as a special student to study violin and composition under the director, Martin Wegelius. It was soon clear that the legal studies were taking a back seat; he was visited one day by an uncle who noticed his text book lying open on the window-sill, its pages yellowed by months of exposure to the sun. Perceptively he advised Sibelius to take up music full-time.

A full-time music student
He acquitted himself well at the Academy of Music, although by the time he was due to leave he had probably concluded that he would never be a violinist of the top rank – he had after all made a fairly late start. He had received a lot of encouragement from Wegelius in composition and in his final term produced a String Trio in A Major and a String Quartet in A minor.

Perhaps more important than all the academic training he received at this time were the people with whom he came in contact. In 1888 Wegelius had engaged the brilliant young German–Italian Ferruccio Busoni as a piano teacher. Busoni was about the same age as Sibelius and in spite of

Sibelius was the second child of Christian and Maria Sibelius (above). From an early age his imagination was fired by the vast and overwhelming grandeur of his homeland (below).

differences in background and experience – Busoni had been hailed as a prodigy from early childhood – the two had an immediate rapport. Although he was basically shy, Sibelius would open out in the company of trusted friends and express his great capacity for enjoying food, wine and conversation. Many long evenings in Helsinki were spent at a favourite restaurant, Kämps, in the company of Busoni and two other friends, Adolf Paul and Armas Järnefelt (later his brother-in-law).

Adolf Paul had enrolled at the Helsinki Music Academy at the same time as Sibelius to study piano, and in the autumn of 1889 both young men went to Berlin to continue their studies. Paul soon decided that his main talents were literary rather than musical, and set about writing an autobiographical novel entitled 'A Book about a Man'. It contained a character called Sillen. Mercurial, passionate, extravagant, but with his energies still largely unfocussed, this is Sibelius in thin disguise.

Frequently indulging his natural generosity and taste for high living, after two months in Berlin Sibelius had exhausted his state grant and had to appeal for help from home. He had studied conscientiously enough under Albert Becker, but the teaching was unimaginative and he found little encouragement for his own individual talent. But all was not wasted – Berlin did offer him the opportunity to hear much more music. He attended the world premiere of Strauss's *Don Juan,* Bülow's performances of the Beethoven piano sonatas, and recitals by the Joachim Quartet.

Importantly for his own development as a nationalist composer he made the acquaintance in Berlin of Robert Kajanus. Kajanus was founder and

director of the Helsinki Philharmonic Orchestra, but because of the extraordinary feud between the Music Academy and the orchestra Sibelius had not met him earlier – Wegelius even forbade his students to attend their concerts. Kajanus was in Berlin to conduct his *Aino* Symphony – a tone-poem for chorus and orchestra based on legends from the Finnish national epic, the *Kalevala*. What Sibelius thought of the symphony we do not know, but the possibilities of the Kalevala as a source of musical inspiration were awakened in him.

In 1890 on his return to Finland, Sibelius spent much of the summer with his friend from the Academy, Armas Järnefelt, and his family. Armas came from a very distinguished background – his father, General August Järnefelt, was a famous soldier and government administrator and his mother was an aristocrat with a great interest in the arts. He had two brothers, Arvid and Eero, who were to become a writer and a painter respectively, and a younger sister, Aino. Still only eighteen, she fell for Sibelius at first sight and by the end of the summer they had become secretly engaged.

In the autumn Sibelius went to Vienna to continue his studies. He had a letter of introduction written by Busoni to Brahms, who, in his customary way, refused to meet him – but they did meet by accident in a cafe though nothing more came of this. Instead, Sibelius studied under two other leading Viennese musical figures, Karl Goldmark and Robert Fuchs. In 1891, his studies over, he returned to Finland and spent the summer in the family house at Loviisa.

Suddenly, during the space of a few months, everything seemed to work towards the realization of his ambitions. The visits to Berlin and Vienna may have

At the age of 20 Sibelius left Hämeenlinna and went to the bustling capital city of Helsinki (above) to study law – his family felt that a musical career was not respectable. However, he also enrolled as a part-time student at the Academy of Music. After only two terms he gave up his law studies to pursue his own cherished ambition to become a full-time music student.

Considering his late start in serious musical studies he acquitted himself well at the Academy. For his final term he composed a String Trio in A Major and a String Quartet in A Minor, accompanying the latter with an atmospheric pencil sketch (above).

As a student Sibelius, together with his Academy friends, frequented the many cafés of Helsinki, including Kämps Hotel (below). Although not active in Helsinki society he did come into contact with many members of Finnish cultural life. In Berlin (bottom), however, he indulged his taste for high living.

been valuable experiences in some respects, but creatively had offered him little. Back amongst the scenery he loved so much, and surrounded by family and friends, he relaxed and his musical plans took shape. But external events were to provide the prompt and inspiration for his work.

At this time, Russia was beginning to exert further control over Finland's already limited independence. In response, particularly among the young, a growing feeling of nationalism began to percolate through the country – a reaction against being swamped and lumped in with the sprawling giant of Russia. Sensing the mood and wanting to contribute to expressing Finland's identity, the idea of using legends from the Kalevala came back to him, and he

set to work with a new urgency.

By the spring of 1892 Sibelius had completed a massive five-movement tone-poem for soloists, chorus and orchestra which he called *Kullervo*. It was given its first performance by the Helsinki Philharmonic on April 29, 1892, with Sibelius himself conducting. He had at last found his own voice, and it brought him instant acclaim, yet, in a pattern to be repeated many times with other works, he was not satisfied with his composition and after a few performances he withdrew it for revision – indeed, he never allowed it to be performed again in his lifetime.

One effect of success was to pave the way for his marriage to Aino Järnefelt, which took place in June the same year. After a honeymoon in the Eastern province of Karelia, the couple went to Helsinki where Sibelius took up teaching posts at the Musical Academy and at Kajanus' Orchestral School.

During the next seven years, a number of orchestral compositions appeared, mostly inspired by Finnish legend – *En Saga,* the *Karelia Suite,* the *Lemminkäinen Suites* and finally, in 1899, *Finlandia.*

Under the so-called February Manifesto of 1899, the Russians virtually crushed Finnish independence by severely restricting the right of assembly and freedom of speech. A theatrical pageant was staged in Helsinki in November with a strong patriotic theme, and *Finlandia* was composed to accompany the final tableau, entitled 'Finland Awakes'. It immediately acquired the status of a second national anthem and has remained the composer's most famous piece. Much more significant though, in terms of his work and establishment of a personal musical language, was the appearance in the same year of the First Symphony.

Although firmly established as his country's leading composer, Sibelius still did not feel financially secure. He was by now in receipt of a state pension, awarded to him in 1897 as compensation for his

In 1888 Sibelius and the brilliant young German–Italian musician Ferruccio Busoni (above and right) became firm friends. Busoni, one of the first to realize and appreciate Sibelius's talent, was always an enthusiastic champion of Sibelius's international reputation.

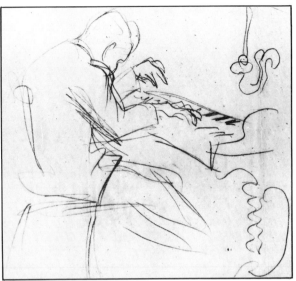

On his return from Berlin, Sibelius met and became engaged to Aino Järnefelt (far left) in 1890. Later, her brother, the painter, Eero Järnefelt, drew him at the piano.

failure to win the post of Professor of Composition at Helsinki University – the job went instead to Kajanus. The pension guaranteed him a basic minimum income and the gesture showed the esteem in which he was already held by his countrymen. His teaching also provided him with a steady income and although he was a somewhat unorthodox teacher his pupils rememberd him with warm affection. He also had very little business sense, accepting modest lump-sum payments for some of his compositions when a royalty arrangement would have made him a small fortune. However, matters improved somewhat after his introduction to the German publishing firm of Breitkopf and Härtel.

International reputation

Baron Axel Carpelan, together with Kajanus, organized a European tour by the Helsinki Philharmonic in 1900 which triumphantly introduced Sibelius' music to audiences outside Finland. Carpelan put 5000 marks towards the cost of a trip to Italy at his disposal. This meant that he could take time off from teaching to compose and during this extended holiday with his family in the spring of 1901 begin work on the Second Symphony. Later that year he was asked to conduct two of the *Lemminkäinen Legends* at the Heidelberg Festival. The Second Symphony had its premiere in March 1902 in Helsinki, and soon afterwards he was turning his thoughts to a violin concerto.

But although these were quite prolific years, Sibelius was in fact growing restless and discontented. Finding the city of Helsinki a disagreeable place for composition, he turned more and more inward in his search for inspiration. In the spring of 1904 he purchased some property on a wooded hillside just outside the village of Järvenpää, about 35 kilometers north east of Helsinki, and had a large traditional-style villa built there.

Although Järvenpää, which was his home for the rest of his life, provided the peaceful atmosphere he needed, he was by no means cut off from life outside. Helsinki was less than an hour away by train and he continued to visit his favourite restaurants and hotels and also to travel abroad when he could afford it. Between 1905 and 1908 he made several trips to England and said that he was so well entertained that he 'did not become acquainted with English coins'. In 1908 on the second of these trips he conducted his Third Symphony, which had been premiered in Helsinki the previous year.

During this time Sibelius was troubled by pains in the throat, and a tumour was diagnosed. After an initial examination in Helsinki, he travelled to Berlin for specialist treatment and after several operations a malignant tumour was successfully removed. The threat of recurrence remained and he was forbidden alcohol and cigars. The experience made him acutely aware of his own mortality and the music he composed over the next few years, especially the String Quartet *Voces intimae* and the Fourth Symphony, reflect this in their meditative mood.

Sibelius in America

In 1914 Sibelius made a trip to the United States at the invitation of a millionaire music-lover, Carl Stoeckel. Stoeckel had built a concert hall in the

Sibelius's international reputation began to take wing after a tour undertaken by the Helsinki Philharmonic Orchestra under Kajanus in 1900. They visited Stockholm, Lübeck, Hamburg and Paris, where the concerts they gave were part of the Finnish contribution to the Paris Exhibition (centre). In 1901, one of the patrons of the tour, Baron Axel Carpelan, a close friend of Sibelius, arranged for sufficient funds to be put at his disposal so that he could take a year off from teaching to spend time composing. He went with his family to Italy where he worked on the Second Symphony. On his return journey he visited Florence (above) where he considered the idea of setting part of Dante's Divine Comedy to music.

independent of Russia, but was overthrown in a left-wing coup a month later. Away from the capital, there were many violent incidents and Sibelius' own life was considered to be in danger, especially in view of the patriotic music he had written. His house was twice searched by soldiers. Eventually, he was persuaded to leave the countryside and take his wife and children to Helsinki to stay with his brother, who was a doctor at one of the city hospitals. Fortunately, by the summer hostilities had come to an end, an independent government had been restored and the family was able to return to Ainola.

Retirement and silence

The next few years saw the publication of his last two symphonies and he again went on travels abroad. But the appearance of a tone-poem *Tapiola* in 1926 effectively marked the end of his creative life. The publication of this work coincided with his retirement as a conductor. The thirty years which followed, for Sibelius lived to a great old age, have become known as 'The Silence from Järvenpää.

The reasons for his retirement were many: his instincts lay in more traditionally rooted music than that coming from more avant-garde composers like Schoenberg and Stravinsky. On a personal level he deeply felt the loss of his friend Axel Carpelan who had died, and his drinking had become a problem. It proved difficult for him to regain the position he had held in pre-war Europe. Sibelius did not leave Finland during the 1930s and so never felt at first hand the esteem in which he was held in Britain and

grounds of his estate at Norfolk, Connecticut, and every summer, in association with the Litchfield County Choral Union, he held a music festival there. The festival has been described as 'America's Bayreuth' but it lacked the latter's almost religious atmosphere. Sibelius composed and conducted a new tone-poem, *The Oceanides.* He was treated with great warmth and generosity, and after the festival was over he and Stoeckel travelled to a number of places of interest, including Niagara Falls, in Stoeckel's luxurious motor car or private Pullman coach. Sibelius's sole regret seems to have been that he was still too nervous about his throat condition to accept the fine wines and cigars which his host pressed upon him. Before he returned home he was presented with a Doctorate of Music from Yale.

Shortly after he came back, World War I broke out in Europe. Sibelius was depressed by the appalling news of the slaughter and there was the added irritation that communication with his German publishers became very difficult. Nonetheless, 1915 was a year of great celebration – his 50th birthday – and he marked it by conducting the premiere of his Fifth Symphony. The day was declared a national holiday and he was showered with gifts and tributes from all over the world. This symphony seems to have had particularly happy associations for him; he once said that his only memory of his father was of sitting on his knee and being shown a picture of a swan, and as he was completing the score of this symphony he was delighted to see a flock of swans rise from the lake and circle the house three times before flying away.

1918 was a hard year for Sibelius, and indeed for all his countrymen. Following the Russian Revolution of 1917, a bitter class struggle developed in Finland and both sides were soon taking up arms. In January 1918 the existing government declared the country

Following the Russian Revolution of 1917 and the bitter class struggle in Finland, in January 1918 the existing government declared Finland, represented in the political cartoon (above left) as an elk harried by the Russian wolf pack, free from intimidation and dominance by Russia. A left-wing coup ensued and during the bitter fighting in the countryside, Sibelius and his wife (above) were advised to take refuge in Helsinki. Later that year they returned to their beloved home, Ainola.

America.

Life in retirement was hardly quiet though, as Sibelius' five surviving daughters had all married and produced children, and there was an army of grand-children and great-grandchildren for whom he expressed interest and concern. Finally, there was the vexed question of the Eighth Symphony.

Whether this work ever existed is not known, but many musicians and journalists seemed to think that it ought to, and kept pestering Sibelius for information about it. He became adept at parrying these requests, remarking that to publish and to compose were two quite different things, but it seems likely that if there was a score, it did not meet his own exacting demands and was subsequently destroyed. The loss of creative ability caused him worry, even guilt, as he sometimes felt he was not justifying his generous state pension.

On September 20, 1957, Malcolm Sargent was conducting a performance of the Fifth Symphony in Helsinki. Normally, at least some members of Sibelius' immediate family would have been there, but that afternoon he had suffered a stroke and at a quarter to nine in the evening, he died. Two days earlier, watching the migrating cranes pass over his home, he had had a premonition of death. His body lay in state in Helsinki Cathedral before he was finally laid to rest at Järvenpää, in the grounds of his beloved Ainola.

'Of Gods and Men'
Scandinavia's mythological legacy

Renewed interest in their cultural heritage of myths and legends provided Scandinavians with a rich source of material which helped promote a profound sense of national pride and identity.

When time began, say the Scandinavian bards, the earth did not exist, nor did the oceans or the sky. Their creation was the starting point of a fantastic mythical world which inspired the early Scandinavian people and which lives on in a rich heritage of myths and legends.

The myths themselves are a unique cultural property. Just as the exploits of the Greek and Roman gods recalled the glories of the classical world to nineteenth-century resistance fighters, so the Scandinavian tradition inspired the northern races and gave them a powerful sense of history and racial identity. It is impossible to exaggerate the relief and pleasure they felt when they found that they too had a dramatic and particular national identity and, to this day, their myths and legends excite profound nationalistic sentiments.

A pre-Christian past

The stories themselves date far back to the long years of the Scandinavian Bronze Age (from about 1600 to 450 BC) and lasted well into the wild, adventurous days of the Vikings. But, as Viking raiding parties swept through western Europe, they came into contact with Christianity and, gradually, its teachings had an effect. Most of Scandinavia was converted to Christianity in the 10th century (though Sweden remained a stubborn outpost for almost 200 years longer) and many of the 'old beliefs' were irrevocably lost.

Archaeology, art and local place names provide scant insight into the early legends, while the writings of early travellers like the Roman historian Tacitus add valuable but limited detail. Other material lies in the Norse sagas and a small collection of Icelandic poems – the *Codex Regius*. Apart from these, the poems and stories gathered together survive almost entirely in manuscripts from later Christian sources.

Heroic inspiration

The central figure of northern legend is Siegfried (Sigurd), who inspired Richard Wagner's supreme operatic cycle, *Der Ring der Nibelungen* and was the hero of the *Volsung Saga* (translated by Eirikr Magnusson and William Morris). This saga was described as the 'Great Story of the North' and stirred fervent patriotism in the souls of many Scandinavians: in Finland, however, a mood of exultant nationalism was aroused by the publication of a quite separate collection – the *Kalevala*. The Kalevala was a collection of Finnish songs with a rich tradition of

myth, magic and folklore (compiled by the scholar, Elias Lönrot) which seemed to compensate for an absence of any other Finnish literature or independent history. History had a hand in its creation, however, for the annexation of Finland by Russia in 1809 led to a reawakening of a national consciousness that found its outlet partly through the burgeoning of Finnish literature. In 1831 *The Society of Finnish Literature* was founded and the pioneering work of a great statesman and national figure, J. V. Snellman (1806–81) gave further impetus to the movement.

Jean Sibelius, Finland's foremost composer, dipped into the Kalevala for inspiration many times: The hero of his first symphony (Kullervo) and Lemminkainen, whose deeds formed the centrepiece of others, were both major characters from its pages. Their appeal, when Finnish autonomy was threatened and the use of the Finnish language was a sensitive political issue, could not be overstated. It

According to Scandinavian legend, there once existed a land of fire in the south and a northern region of ice and snow (above). Sparks of fire slowly thawed the icy floes and, from the vapours, new life was mysteriously formed.

In the epic cycle of myths, the tragic story of Siegfried has achieved wide fame as the basis of Richard Wagner's great opera, The Ring. The adventures and disasters that beset the young hero begin when he slays a huge dragon (left) and so acquires the hoard of gold it protects. Unknown to Siegfried, however, the treasure includes a magic ring that puts a curse on all who possess it.

was proudly claimed that 'Finland can now say for itself: I too have a history'.

Although of central importance to the Finns, the mythology of the Kalevala was something of a side-show to the sombre tale of doomed gods which formed the theme of the cycle of stories in the rest of Scandinavia. Most of our knowledge of this cycle, which begins with the creation of the world and ends with the fall of the gods and total destruction, comes from poetry written in the tenth century. It is, therefore, closely associated with the Viking Age and its great emphasis on heroic virtue, even though the myths were widespread long before the first Viking ever put to sea. The acceptance of the transience of life and the inevitability of disaster sometimes seems shockingly gloomy, but it gives the gods of that pagan, warlike world an impressive, heroic dignity.

The dawn of time

The cycle begins with the creation of the world: a realm of clouds lay in the north and in the south was a land of fire; between them stood a mighty fountain which gorged out 12 icy rivers. As warm southern winds blew across the ice, droplets of melt water fell and formed the first of all beings – a massive giant.

From this creation, other giants were made but, in their bitter struggle for supremacy, they all but destroyed one another and most were killed. The gods used one of the fallen bodies to create land, mountains, trees and oceans, and the skull of the

One of the most ancient creation myths concerned the great ash tree Yggdrasill (above). Its roots were entwined with serpents, while its massive trunk passed through all the realms of creation.

Odin, was a fearsome Lord of Battle (right). He meted out victory or disaster, stirring up conflict with his huge spear, Gungnir.

333

Wielding his mighty hammer and wearing his Belt-of-Strength, Thor (above) was the champion of the gods – supreme in strength and scourge of all their enemies. He was renowned for his quick temper: those who crossed him were likely to have thunderbolts hurled above their heads or find their ships driven toward the rocks as his red beard bristled with anger!

In complete contrast to the awesome power and strength of Odin and Thor, Freyja (above right) was the beautiful and promiscuous goddess of love and fertility. She travelled across the sky in a carriage drawn by cats and lived in a sumptuous banqueting hall where she entertained heroes who had fallen in battle.

giant became the vault of the heavens. From sparks of fire, they then added the moon and galaxies of stars.

Further life was moulded from the rotting flesh of the giant corpse: dwarves were created to live in a subterranean world and, finally, the human race was created from the trunks of trees. Three great gods worked together in making man: Odin gave him breath, Hoenir gave him a soul and the ability to reason and Lodur gave him warmth and colour.

The world the gods created for man and the other beings was made up of nine realms. In the heavenly, upper world, lay three of them: Asgard, where Odin and the gods lived, Vanaheim where the fertility gods lived and Alfheim, the land of the 'light' elves. Below this heavenly strata was the realm of mankind (Midgard), which stood next to the land of the giants (Jotunheim) and was surrounded by a vast ocean, the home of a serpent whose coils encircled the world. Deep in the bowels of this middle level were the realms of the dwarves (Nidavellir) and the 'dark' elves (Swartalfheim). Below them was the home of the dead; a damp, dark place known as Mist-world (Niflheim). Its horrible citadel was presided over by a female monster, Hel. The entrance to the underworld was guarded by a monstrous hound (Garm), whose task it was to prevent any living soul from entering his domain. Growing through all three levels and sheltering all nine realms with its massive branches was the great tree of life, Yggdrasill.

The myths are not absolutely precise about the structure of creation and locations vary from one account to another. The creation part of the myth cycle is largely concerned with natural phenomena: the rainbow was called Bifrost – the fiery bridge between the world of men and the citadel of the gods, while the wind was caused by the wing beats of

Hraesvelg, a giant, corpse-eating eagle. Each part of the cosmos was explained as the result of action by the gods or the giants, and always with sinister reminders of approaching doom. In Asgard (home of the gods), for example, there lay a great plain where the army of gods and men would march out for their last great battle and would suffer defeat at the hands of giants and monsters. Among the halls and palaces of Asgard was Valhalla, where great heroes from the world of man, saved from Hel, waited for the day when they would fight alongside the gods. But however many they numbered and however heroically they fought, they were all destined to fail.

The pantheon of gods
The world painted in Scandinavian myth carries the seeds of its own destruction: but the day of Doom (Ragnarok) lies in the future. Before it dawned there would be a cycle of clashes between gods and giants which illustrated the powers and place of each god in the pantheon. Odin was the greatest of them all and, to some extent, was their ruler. But he was not the strongest or even the most trustworthy. He had powers to change shape and could oversee every action in all nine worlds when he sat upon his magic throne. He was immensely wise, but had made great personal sacrifices to gain this wisdom. He was one eyed, because he had given up an eye as a pledge when he drank from the Spring of Mimir, source of all wisdom. He even hanged himself in the tree of life in order to learn the knowledge of the dead. He loved warfare and was the god of battle. He decided which side would win – but his decision-making was capricious and he liked to stir up trouble. Finally, he had the gift of poetry and, like the ancient Greek gods, was a determined seducer (even raper) of

women.

Next to Odin in importance was his son Thor, who was a far more straightforward and better liked divinity. He was the strongest god – matchlessly strong – somewhat slow-witted but quick-tempered and with a vast, earthy appetite. He was the guardian of men and gods and constantly called upon to battle to the death with awesome giants – killing them with his indestructible hammer. Emotionally, he was the god of order, keeping the forces of chaos at bay and the myths made it clear that, if his strength was ever overcome by magic or if he lost the magic hammer, the giants would lose no time in storming Asgard and overrunning the world of men.

Among the fertility gods, the most important were Njord, guardian of ships and seafarers, and his two children, Freyr, god of plenty, and Freyja, most beautiful of the goddesses. Freyja plays quite a leading part in the myths, being portrayed as desirable and promiscuous – a goddess of battle as well as love.

Other deities in the pantheon included Tyr, bravest of all. He was the only god prepared to sacrifice his own hand so that a huge wolf could be captured. In the tale, the wolf had grown so strong and vicious that the gods feared for their own safety. They obtained magically strong but flimsy-looking chains (made by the dwarves) and cunningly challenged the wolf to prove his strength by being bound and then bursting his shackles. The wolf, however, was suspicious and demanded that one of the gods put a hand in his mouth as a surety that they would release him if his strength failed. Only Tyr was prepared to lose his hand as the price for capturing

Closely associated with Odin were the Valkyries (left), helmeted goddesses who carried slain warriors to the land of the gods. Astride flying steeds with dew and hailstones dripping from their manes, the Valkyries also had the power to transform themselves into gentle and graceful swan maidens. Among their number was the beautiful Brunnhilde (above), who thwarted Odin and, despite her desperate pleading, was stripped of her divine powers and condemned to live in the land of men. Lying in a magically induced slumber, she could only be saved by a hero who dared to ride through the ring of flames that encircled her. Such a hero finally came – and was none other than Siegfried.

the beast and he bravely volunteered.

Another of the more important gods was Heimdall, a sleepless watchman who would summon the host of Asgard on his horn when the day of reckoning approached. Most important of all was Heimdall's particular enemy, the treacherous, cunning, dynamic mixture of god and devil, Loki (he would lead the side of the the giants and monsters in their final battle). Although he was descended from giants, Loki appeared to be one of the gods and spent much of his time at Asgard. He was amusing and clever, the chosen companion of both Odin and Thor, but his nature was flawed. Too tricky for his own good, his many pranks often went sour and he nursed a growing hatred and resentment of those more powerful or popular than himself. It was this resentment that finally led him to commit the unforgivable crime of murdering one of the gods.

The enemy within

An early story illustrates perfectly how much Loki was identified with the gods and how far his sharp wits could cause them trouble. During one of the many battles against the giants, the walls of Asgard had been ruined and the task of rebuilding them was so great that they had been left unrepaired. One day a solitary horseman cantered over the rainbow bridge and offered to build impregnable walls around the entire citadel – in less than eighteen months. In exchange for this, he wanted the sun, the moon and the goddess Freyja.

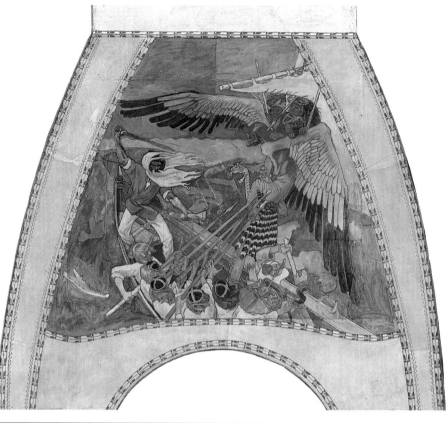

One of the liveliest heroes of the Kalevala is Lemminkainen, a debonair but reckless young man. To prove himself to his future bride, he is ordered to kill a particular swan but is betrayed by an old man. His body is torn to pieces and thrown into the river. But his enemy has reckoned without the magical powers of the hero's mother. Using her black arts, she rebuilds the lifeless body (right). She then enlists the help of a bee to bring her honey from beyond 'the highest heaven'. Anointed with this potent balm, Lemminkainen is finally revived.

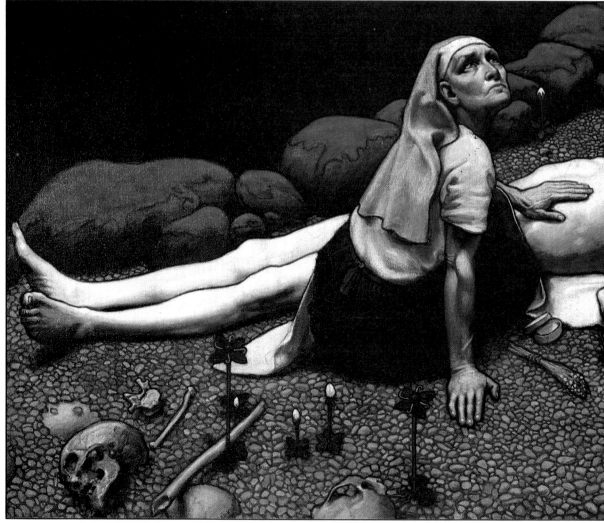

Full of strange and mystical events, one of the central stories in the Kalevala concerns the theft of a magic talisman, the sampo, crafted by the blacksmith (Ilmarinen) as a gift to his wife's family. The talisman proves to have great power and, after his wife's death, Ilmarinen and two friends resolve to steal it. Before the heroes can escape with their prize, however, they must fend off the fierce attacks of its rightful owners (left).

Kullervo (right) was one of the key figures in the Finnish sagas. He was an immensely strong but very bad-natured warrior who used his gifts for evil ends.

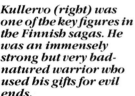

The gods at first rejected the offer outright, but Loki suggested that they agree to the price on condition that the work was completed within six months. His idea was that such a task would prove impossible but much of the work would be done and the gods would not be obliged to pay out anything. With some hesitation, the mysterious mason agreed to the terms, but only if he was allowed the help of his stallion. Loki eagerly pressed the case and the bargain was struck.

The stallion, however, turned out to be a trump card, hauling huge loads of rock for the tireless stranger to use. At this point, he was identified as a giant – a scheming enemy – and, worse still, he was working fast enough to win the prize. The gods were horrified to think that they would be deprived of light and warmth when they paid out with the sun and moon, and Freyja wept bitterly at the thought of being carried away to the land of the giants. Furiously, the gods rounded on Loki and made him swear to make the giant lose the wager. Just before completion of the wall, Loki changed himself into a mare and enticed the stallion away, so winning the day.

But the story does not end there. Knowing that he had failed, the giant threatened the gods with force and demanded his reward regardless. They had the good sense to send for Thor, however, who came running, eager for the fight and characteristically despatched the giant with one mighty blow of his hammer. As a postscript to the episode, Loki returned some months later, leading an eight-legged grey horse which he presented to Odin. He claimed to have conceived the horse by the giant's stallion, and said that no other steed could match his extra-ordinary offspring for pace.

The tale is impressively complete in its detail of the relationship between the various gods and in stressing the constant threat presented by the giants. It also makes the disturbing point that Loki was capable of changing sex as well as shape, and of bearing children as well as fathering them! By one means or another, this resulted in his having numerous progeny, including three of the vilest and most deadly monsters in creation: Hel, the rotting hag who owned the citadel of the dead; the wolf who had bitten off Tyr's hand (and was destined, one day, to kill Odin) and the giant serpent who encircled the world of men. It was this serpent who would confront Thor in the final battle, being crushed by his hammer blows but, in its death throes, spewing out venom that would kill Thor as well.

The story of the rebuilding of the walls of Asgard is only one of many myths which form a linked chain describing a system of religious beliefs but also warning of coming destruction. In many of the tales, the threat to the gods is only just averted. Their great weakness is that they are not immortal – they can be maimed or killed.

The gathering gloom

As the cycle proceeds, the shadows darken and Valhalla fills with heroes preparing for the final battle. A belief in fate pervades the religious message of the myths. When a man was born, his fate was decided and was inescapable. All he could hope to do was to choose the manner in which he met his end – bravely or otherwise. There is great stress laid on courage and strength: the best fate that could befall a man was to fall heroically in battle and so be borne to Asgard by the Valkyries – Odin's beautiful shield maidens – and to feast in Valhalla till Doomsday.

Just as men were fated, so were the gods. As time passed, Loki had changed from a slightly malicious joker to a bitter, tormented demon who was wildly resentful of those around him. Among the gods, the wisest and most beautiful was Balder, the son of Odin – a god whose sweet disposition made him universally

loved. Balder became wracked by frightening dreams that foretold his death and deeply alarmed the other gods. In a desperate attempt to forestall his fate, his mother visited everything in the nine worlds wringing out the promise that it would not harm him. Every animal, every plant, every stone and every illness promised in turn not to hurt the beloved god. When all the pledges were made, Asgard sighed with relief and the gods began a celebratory game of hurling rocks and weapons at Balder to watch them turn away from him and leave him unscathed.

Loki, however, found out that one object – the humble mistletoe – had been overlooked and he proceeded to fashion a deadly dart from its growth. Ever treacherous, he then went to Balder's blind brother, placed the mistletoe dart in his hand and urged him to join the sport by throwing it. Innocently the brother agreed and, with a single blow of the dart, Balder was struck dead. Amid the ensuing pandemonium, the distraught mother pleaded for a volunteer to go to the underworld and ask Hel to release Balder. One of the dead god's brothers volunteered and, after a horrifying journey, he persuaded Hel to agree – but she stipulated that everything in creation must first weep for the slain god. Once again the mother did her rounds and everything agreed to the condition. But it was to no avail! Loki, in the form of giantess, refused to weep and professed complete contempt for Balder.

After a rancorous argument with the other gods, Loki fled but was tracked down and made to face a severe punishment for his crimes. He was bound, face upwards, in a gloomy cave while a serpent dripped venom into his face. His faithful wife held a bowl over him to catch the stream of venom but, every time she turned to empty the bowl, the drip of stinging poison made Loki writhe in agony.

At this stage, the myth cycle had dealt solely with the past deeds of the gods but then it moves into the 'present' and a short period during which the gods still rule in Asgard. The last story, however, is a prophesy of coming doom. The earth will be wracked by wars and crimes and gripped by a bone-chilling cold spell of three terrible winters with no summer between them. The ground will shake and all bonds and fetters will burst, freeing Loki and the great wolf so that they can take part in the final battle. The end of each of the principal gods is described in a series of duels with terrible monsters and the heroes who march out of Valhalla in 540 columns of 800 men, are all destined to be killed in battle. The flaming sword of the giant Surt will set all creation on fire and the earth will sink below the sea. Following this titanic conclusion, the prophesy makes an unconvincing effort to foretell rebirth: a green earth will rise again from the sea, some of the minor gods will have survived and a man and woman will have hidden from destruction in the branches of the tree of life.

The idea of total and final destruction was perhaps, too much to bear and a message of hope was tacked on to the main body of stories. In a way, this contradicts the central theme of the myth cycle, which is one of the inevitability of fate. It makes a stirring and tragic tale, an epic in praise of courage and the defiance of a grim destiny and a message that inspired nationalists of a later age.

The Kalevala was not one complete written saga, but a collection of old Finnish ballads, songs and folklore handed down by word of mouth from one generation to the next (top). It was gathered together and first published as a single, epic story in 1835 (above).

Elias Lönnrot (below left) travelled the country gathering material from even the smallest villages and was eventually able to compile the Kalevala. The impact of his work was immediate and statesmen like Johan Vilhelm Snellman (below right) were quick to recognize its uniquely Finnish importance.

The Kalevala

The great myth cycle was not the only religious tradition of Scandinavia. Co-existing with it was a definitively Finnish collection of songs and stories that told a similarly robust but less gloomy tale of creation and magical adventure. The proponents were not gods – indeed they frequently prayed to a god who was somewhat like Thor in character – nor were they simply men who had the gift of magic. They were more nearly concepts that had been given personalities. The chief of them, Vainamoinen, for example, was the embodiment of wisdom, poetry and endeavour. His companion (Ilmarinen) was the archetypal craftsman, while another, Lemminkainen, was the soul of rashness and charm.

Their adventures, and many other pieces of folk-lore, were recorded in song: They are described as the people of a district called Kalevala and they are in frequent dispute with a neighbouring district, North Farm. North Farm itself appears to have been an immensely rich Viking Age-farm which suffered from the to-ing and fro-ing of the mythical Finnish heroes as they came to wage war, woo the daughter of its chieftain or pursue other ends. The purpose and origin of the tales is now rather obscure – but its importance to the Finnish people is paramount.

The songs were collected in the middle of the last century and have always had immense appeal to the national sentiments of the Finns – the name Kalevala is a poetic name for Finland and means 'Land of Heroes'. Apart from being in the Finnish language and telling tales of Finnish characters, they are entertaining and well composed. Almost every line spoken by the devil-may-care Lemminkainen, for instance, is redolent of his attitude to life. When he sets off to attend a wedding at North Farm, he dismisses complaints that he has not even been invited: 'Wretched people go by invitation, a good man skips along without one'. When he arrives, he behaves so badly that the provokes the master of the farm to a duel and kills him. He flees from vengeance and lands up in a remote island where he seduces so many of the girls that he once again has to flee – this time from their outraged fathers and husbands. He is the eternal, entertaining rogue.

Not all the tales are so full of zest and humour. There is also a sullen, tragic character who murders a friend's wife, seduces his own sister in a ghastly episode of mistaken identity and ends by committing suicide. Taken together, the stories are the great

Following her long years of acquiescence to Swedish domination, Finland seemed to awake with a start of national awareness after her annexation by Russia in 1809. This new awareness led to the founding of a Society of Finnish Literature (left) – an institution which played a significant role in raising the status of Finnish as a language of equal importance to Swedish: it was in this atmosphere of renewed pride and consciousness that the Kalevala was published.

Finnish national epic and yet they have more to offer besides: they also contain much folklore on bridal songs, farming lays and hunting charms which are invaluable parts of Finnish history. Though many of its key elements are no longer of any practical significance to Finnish people – the Kalevala is more than anything else, a sequence of poetry with magical and ritual incantations that give power over nature – the stories are richly detailed and enjoyable in their own right and, most importantly, they are a source of national inspiration to the Finns. The stirring epic fired the imaginations of one of Finland's greatest artists, Akseli Gallen-Kallela (1865–1931), her greatest musician, Jean Sibelius and, indirectly, the distinguished poet Eino Leino. Translated into 20 languages – the distinctive metre was even imitated by Longfellow in his North American epic, Hiawatha – its powerful appeal has extended far beyond the national boundaries of Finland and, like the main body of Scandinavian mythology, has provided pleasure and entertainment to people around the world.

Kept alive through the popular memories and traditions of her people, the myths and legends of Scandinavia are as much a part of the national heritage as her folk dances and local costumes (left). Scandinavian composers, inspired by these roots, blended the dramatic storylines with colourful peasant music to create new and profoundly nationalistic masterpieces.

Gustav Mahler

1860–1911

Mahler, a Jew living in a city poisoned by anti-Semitism, fought his way through a life punctuated by devastating blows. But in both his conducting and his extraordinary music his innovative and restless genius emerged triumphant.

Gustav Mahler was born to a Jewish family on 7 July 1860, in Moravia (now a province of Czechoslovakia). He was the second of 12 children born to Bernhard and Marie Mahler, five of whom died at an early age. Mahler was not exempt from the troubled legacy of the Jews living in the Austro–Hungarian empire, and the 19th-century persecution of the Jews had directly affected his family. Under the infamous *Familiengesetz* law introduced by Metternich, only the eldest son of a Jewish family was free to marry. Due to this law, Gustav's own father Bernhard had, in official terms, been born illegitimate – which was a great social burden to carry in those times.

Through sheer determination in the face of official interference and discouragement, Bernhard had managed to build up a comfortable liquor business (one of the few trades open to the Jews) and give the family a secure financial standing. A harsh and brutal authoritarian, Bernhard always insisted on a good education for all his children and, when young Gustav first displayed great musical talent, this was recognized and encouraged. By the age of six his vocation had already been decided upon and from that time on great sacrifices were made by the entire family to ensure Gustav's steady progress.

Youth and education

In 1875 a local administrator, Gustav Schwarz, heard the 14-year-old Mahler and was immediately convinced of his potential. Eager to help nurture the young boy's talent, he persuaded Bernhard to send his son

Marie Hermann, (above) married Bernhard Mahler in 1857. But he proved to be a brutal and domineering husband and her marriage was a sad and loveless one. Gustav (right, aged six) was devoted to his maltreated mother and was deeply saddened by her death in 1889.

Mahler's first home (above) was in the village of Kalište, Bohemia where he was born in 1860. But before the year was out the family moved to a larger house in the more prosperous town of Iglau.

for proper training at the Vienna Conservatory. Though this meant a complete break from his home in Iglau, his father realized the importance of thorough training and let the boy go. Arriving in Vienna in September 1875, Mahler quickly blossomed and threw himself into the hectic musical life of the city. In his three years there as a student, he wrote a number of compositions for piano (virtually all of which he destroyed later in life) and was soon in trouble for his radical ideas, pugnaciousness and unpunctuality.

In 1878, the year he graduated, Mahler began work on his first mature work, *Das klagende Lied* (The Song of Lament) and enthusiastically took up the lifestyle of a composer. For two years he was

supported by his family as he attempted to compose, but the isolation and privation led to depression, disillusionment and a complete dissipation of his energies. This was a crucial period for Mahler, for it proved he was not psychologically equipped to deal with such a solitary vocation. He decided to pursue the idea of becoming a conductor and by mid-1880 he had taken the first step to that end.

The start of a career

By the summer of 1880, Mahler had made his début in Bad Hall, near Linz, and his success there led to a position in Laibach (now Ljubljana), in the province of Carinthia (now Yugoslavia), for the 1881–2 season. His career had begun.

His next position took him, in early 1883, to the Stadttheater in Olmütz where his sure instincts, superhuman zeal and clever handling of the slenderest resources paved the way to his first appointment to a professional opera company. This was in Kassel, in Prussia, for the 1883 season. But the renowned Prussian mania for petty bureaucracy soon had Mahler embroiled in numerous disputes. Irritated by officialdom, the young conductor lasted only two of his three contracted seasons. In 1885 he moved on to Prague, then to Leipzig in 1886 with little to show for his Herculean labours. But at least while in Kassel he embarked on his first major love affair, with a young singer in the company, called Johanna Richter, and this had inspired him to write the first of his *Lieder eines fahrenden Gesellen* (Songs of a Travelling Companion), setting his love poems to music.

While his position as junior 'Kapellmeister' at the Leipzig Stadttheater was a boon for Mahler, his term there was clouded by scandal. In the summer of 1887 he was asked by Baron Carl von Weber, grandson of the composer Carl Maria von Weber, to complete a series of comic operatic sketches entitled *Die drei*

Pintos (The Three Pintos) which the great man had left in disarray on his death in 1826. This was a great honour and Mahler applied his customary zeal to the work. But a disturbing side-effect soon manifested itself – the young man became entangled in a torrid affair with Baron von Weber's wife, Marion. In a climate of increasing pain and difficulty, Mahler finished the opera, and it was later accorded success on the stages of Europe in 1888. But the price was high; an elopement was abandoned only at the last moment, and the Baron himself, unable to bear the emotional strain of the situation, had a long-lasting breakdown.

This scandal hurt Mahler and indirectly led to his resignation from Leipzig in 1888. But within a few weeks he was offered the position of new Director at the Royal Budapest Opera. This was a dazzling appointment for the 28-year-old Mahler and he was quick to prove equal to it.

The thrill of the appointment in Budapest, and his initial success with audiences, the opera company and music critics, was soon to be overshadowed. In February 1889 his father died, leaving Mahler with a heavy burden of financial and family worries. On top of this, his critics both inside and outside the opera were becoming hostile towards some of his innovatory work, and he was soon publicly attacked for every deficiency, whether or not it was actually his fault.

After a fitful summer break spent putting the finishing touches to his First Symphony, Mahler's life

Tasting the new crop's wine at open-air wine shops (left) was as popular a tradition in Vienna in the 1880s, when Mahler was there, as it is today. Mahler studied at the Vienna Conservatory from the autumn of 1875 to the summer of 1878 then, after a series of short-term jobs, was appointed junior 'Kapellmeister' at the Leipzig Stadttheater (below) in 1886. But personality clashes with other conductors there and involvement in a major romantic scandal forced him to resign within two years.

was shattered by the deaths of both his mother and his favourite sister, Leopoldine. With his sorrow scarcely contained, Mahler had to wind up his family's affairs in Iglau and re-house his younger brothers and sisters. The year of 1889 was perhaps the unhappiest of the composer's life.

Romantic interlude

In 1890, his life took on a happier note. In the autumn Mahler met Natalie Bauer-Lechner.

A young violinist, Natalie was recovering from a broken marriage when she and Mahler met. A tall and not unattractive woman, she proved to be attentive, inquisitive and devoted almost to a fault. She kept a journal relating every piece of information regarding Mahler during the years of their 'intimacy'. A scrupulous and gifted chronicler, her records are invaluable in giving later generations a true insight into Mahler's creative genius. It is true that the conductor was often irritated by her devotion and constant attentions, but he recognized her qualities. He had a real fondness for her and spent many summers with her and his sister Justine. Yet sadly for Natalie his emotions were never as passionately engaged as hers.

Also in November 1890 he came into contact, for the first time, with Johannes Brahms. Dragged unwillingly to see Mahler conduct *Don Giovanni*

In 1890 Mahler met and became close friends with Natalie Bauer-Lechner (above). She was well aware of his genius, unlike the general public or music critics who, in the previous year, had met his First Symphony (title page below) with considerable derision. The cartoon (right), printed shortly after the première with a one-word caption meaning 'effect', shows how little his adventurous composition was appreciated.

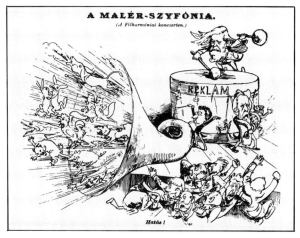

while in Budapest, Brahms was immediately won over by Mahler's interpretative genius, crying out 'Bravo' from his box. In later years, Brahms was to do much to help Mahler's career, though he never liked his compositions.

The road to fame

By the spring of 1891 things had come to a complete deadlock at the Royal Opera in Budapest, and Mahler's departure was only a matter of time. His new appointment as conductor with the Hamburg Opera was finally confirmed, and he took up the position with relish. He was to spend six years there and, although he was to battle continually with the Opera administration for higher standards and with German critics who were disdainful of innovative methods, it was a period when he finally assumed his position in the front rank of contemporary conductors. It was also a period during which he won the friendship of many great and famous musicians, such as the conductors Hans von Bülow and Willem Mengelberg.

The 1892 season gave him particular pleasure because he had the personal satisfaction of meeting

'One cannot imagine how beautiful and animated this city is', wrote Mabler to his sister (with bim, right) when he arrived in Hamburg (left) in March 1891. He was about to take up his most prestigious post yet, as first conductor with the Hamburg Opera company. His six years there were important and creative and included working with Tchaikovsky on his opera Eugene Onegin. Some of the stage sets for it were spectacularly grand (as below), but the opera itself was only a moderate success.

Tchaikovsky. After witnessing the rehearsals of his opera *Eugene Onegin,* Tchaikovsky gave Mahler the honour of conducting the première in his presence.

The following year also saw the flowering of Mahler's long friendship with Richard Strauss, a young man who was doing precisely what Mahler had always dreamed of by winning ecstatic reviews for both his conducting and his compositions. By contrast, Mahler's own composing was going slowly – he had just finished his Second Symphony – and his reputation in the field of composition was slight.

Emotional upheavals

As if Mahler and his family had not sustained enough blows already, a new misfortune beset them in early 1895. After a period of relative domestic peace, when his sisters Justine and Emma shared his Hamburg home with him, there came the tragic and unexplained suicide of their brother Otto in Leipzig. Gustav was so deeply affected by this loss that he never mentioned it for the rest of his life. And only after his own death did his widow, searching through an old trunk, find three symphonies and a collection of *Lieder,* all written by Otto, which Gustav had never been able to bring himself to look at again.

Perhaps it was this deeply-buried sorrow which expressed itself in the sudden and tempestuous affair he started later that year with a new young singer at the opera house, Anna von Mildenburg. Passionate and ill-concealed, the relationship was soon common knowledge throughout the company. The tortuous affair, which went to the brink of what would have been a suicidal marriage, dragged on for over a year, fed by Anna's jealous possessiveness and Mahler's inability to make a clean break.

The relationship finally came to an end when Mahler left Hamburg for a new position in mid-1897. He had been angling for the post of Director at the Imperial Vienna Opera for over a year, as his relationship with the Hamburg director Bernhard Pollini had been deteriorating drastically. He wanted nothing more than to leave the city which had witnessed disastrous attempts to introduce his own music (not one ticket had sold for the première of his Second Symphony), and scenes of open humiliation in front of his own company by Pollini, who loudly insinuated that his prized conductor was actually incompetent.

A break with the past
Early in 1897, the job in Vienna became available. But Mahler's appointment was only secured after he had resigned from Hamburg and had also taken the unusual step of converting to Catholicism. Mahler, who was not an orthodox Jew, realized that he would never otherwise get the Vienna appointment, anti-Semitism being rife in official circles, and he was willing to make the change. But although he was a deeply religious man, he never became a practising Catholic.

Vienna was the opera capital of the world at the time, and this appointment was a crowning achievement in Mahler's public career. His first season there was one of unqualified triumph, and with his fanatical dedication and inexhaustible dynamism he reversed

the previous decline in performing standards. He remarked to a colleague at the time, 'I am hitting my head against the walls, but the walls are giving way . . .'. So successful was he that by the end of spring 1898, when Hans Richter resigned from the post of Director of the Vienna Philharmonic, Mahler was invited to replace him.

Trials and tribulations in Vienna
But after the initial wave of success, public response began to change, and the old problem of critical publicity reared its head. At first it didn't concern Mahler as he was enjoying capacity audiences for his productions, and even for his stagings of complete, uncut Wagner operas (a rarity at this time). But a virulent and libellous smear campaign was mounted in the two anti-Semitic Viennese papers. He was even referred to as 'that dwarf Jew'. Sworn to dignified silence by his employers during the subsequent court case, Mahler could only fume. Even his new summer retreat at Wörthersee, where he completed his Fourth Symphony, and his hiring of brilliant new singers such as Franz Naval, couldn't compensate for the indignities he had suffered.

Events reached a climax in the winter of 1900–1, with the Viennese première of his First Symphony being roundly hissed and booed, and many of his opera productions being savagely attacked by the critics. Undoubtedly suffering from tension caused by those setbacks in his life, Mahler became seriously ill in the spring, and needed a long convalescence.

The Vienna Opera House (above) was the home of one of the world's greatest opera companies and Mahler was delighted when he became director in 1897. But after initial success the old problem of a critical and anti-Semitic press reared its ugly head. In the cartoon (left) he is the monkey who must ride on the back of his superior as they leave the theatre.

Mahler's Sixth Symphony had its première in Vienna on 4 January 1907. The caricature (above) pokes fun at his use of unusual percussion instruments. 'Good God!' Mahler is supposed to be saying, 'Fancy leaving out the motor horn! Now I shall have to write another symphony!'

Beautiful socialite Alma Schindler (above) met Mahler in the autumn of 1901. Her marriage, a few months later, to Vienna's most eligible bachelor was the talk of Viennese society (below).

This, plus a peaceful summer spent with Justine and Nathalie at Wörthersee, restored both his health and his creativity. He not only revised his Fourth Symphony, but wrote two huge movements of his Fifth, plus seven beautiful *Lieder* to the poetry of Friedrich Rückert.

A new romance

Mahler's return to Vienna in the autumn was the start of another hectic round of rehearsals, production headaches and critical sniping. On top of this the Munich première of his Fourth Symphony was disastrous – and was cruelly labelled by the critics as sheer 'musical madness'. So it was a depressed and lonely man who, in late November 1901, went to a party being held by an acquaintance. And it was here that he met the beautiful, 23-year-old society beauty Alma Maria Schindler for whom he conceived a violent passion.

Within a matter of days he found his feelings being returned, and their whirlwind courtship had started. By late December they were both sure enough of their feelings to announce their official engagement.

The news burst upon Vienna like a bombshell, for Mahler was the city's most famous bachelor, and he was fêted by his audience at the opera. Consumed with desire for each other, the pair became lovers in the new year, and Alma fell pregnant. The need for an early wedding gave Mahler concern over the future of his sister Justine, whom he still looked after. But happily, Justine took this opportunity to anounce her own engagement to her long-time beau, the violinist Arnold Rose. The two weddings took place one day apart, Gustav and Alma's on 9 March 1902, and Justine's the day after. One casualty of this sudden domestic revolution was Natalie Bauer-Lechner. There was a complete break between her and Mahler. She never married.

Mahler was now content as never before: working with his usual fanaticism in his post at the opera, writing during the summer at Maiernigg on Wörthersee, and leading a quiet, spartan existence at home in Vienna. The greatest event for the new couple in that first year was the birth of their first child, Maria Anna.

From the start she was doted on by her father, and this withdrawn, quiet child gave him more conver-

Mahler adored his first daughter Maria Anna (with him above) and he never really recovered from the shock of her death at the age of four.

sational pleasure than his social peers. This was not really surprising – since his marriage Mahler had become more and more anti-social, he rarely liked to entertain, and liked going out even less. His increasingly reclusive nature and the dictatorial regime he imposed on Alma was a great strain for her. He demanded absolute obedience and tact from her, especially when it came to his precious hours spent composing. This Alma gave him, just as Justine and Natalie had done before her, and as the whole Mahler family had done before that. But it wasn't easy for her; Alma was highly intelligent, had a large circle of friends, and had been creative in her own right before her marriage.

However, she was slowly able to introduce some of her friends into their small circle: the composer Arnold Schoenberg and the poet Gerhard Hauptmann, both brilliant men who eventually became very close to Mahler.

A creative period

In the summer of 1904, with Alma pregnant for a second time, Mahler completed work on his Sixth Symphony, a dark and tragic work, and his series of *Kindertotenlieder* (Songs on the Death of Children) based on poems by Friedrich Rückert. For a man of outward contentment, this music bore worrying

Mahler was very keen to put on Richard Strauss's new opera Salome *in Vienna. But the sensuous Salome (above) was considered too risqué for the opera ever to emerge from behind the ornate curtain of the Vienna Opera House (right). So Mahler had to be content to display his lively and progressive conducting (in silhouette below) on less controversial operas.*

indications of deep inner disturbance. Alma found it impossible to warm to the beautiful songs in the *Kindertotenlieder,* and felt that they were a dreadful temptation to fate. But time passed, the baby was born and all was well.

It was somehow fitting that Mahler's last complete year in Vienna, 1906, should have coincided with a series of performances celebrating the 150th anniversary of Mozart's birth. During the course of the year he gave new and brilliant productions of five great Mozart operas, all of them dear to his heart, as well as a special gala performance of *Cosi fan tutte* for the Royal Court in Salzburg.

He also had good reason to feel that, at long last, he had 'arrived' as a composer in the public eye. The past two years had seen increasing performances of his music all round Europe. But the time he needed to appear at these occasions became the direct cause of a split with the Vienna Opera in early 1907. His absences had led to bickering and unrest among the public and critics, and word was openly circulating in Vienna that the search was on for Mahler's successor. While this was not actually true, Mahler was tired of the constant battles, the excessive workload and the fickleness of his public. He tendered his resignation.

The year of 1907 was to prove decisive in ways that reached far beyond Mahler's work. That summer at Wörthersee, his younger daughter, Anna Justine, fell ill with scarlet fever. She recovered, only to pass on the infection to her sister Maria. But Maria contracted a secondary infection, failed to respond to treatment and, within days, was dead. Soon after this Alma's mother suffered a stroke. The strain of these two tragedies affected Alma's heart, and a doctor was called. He took the opportunity, while he was there, to check Mahler's heart, only to find that it was already diseased. The distraught couple had a new nightmare to contend with.

At the end of the year – having concluded a contract in New York at the Metropolitan Opera, for a huge salary and a shorter season than those in Vienna – Mahler made his farewell appearance in Vienna conducting *Fidelio.* It was a highly emotional occasion with a tearful audience giving 30 curtain-calls to the equally tearful Mahler.

The tempting of fate two years previously had borne bitter fruit and Mahler was a changed man. Death had been a constant presence in his family all his life: but the death of his daughter had the most devastating effect. He was forced to abandon all strenuous exercise – something he had always enjoyed – and live like a convalescent. This very nearly completely broke his spirit. From this time on, his priorities changed radically, as did his music.

The declining years

Mahler's time spent in New York, from his début at the Metropolitan on New Year's Day, 1908, at the age of 47, to his last performance in front of the New York Philharmonic in early 1911, was one of reduced vitality and an increased concentration on financial security and his later symphonies. He had a three-month commitment to an opera company with

Mahler made his last trip to America early in 1911 but his health failed and he was forced to return at the end of a month. The photograph (left) on his homeward journey was the last to be taken of him.

In August 1910, Mahler consulted Sigmund Freud (below left) to help sort out the marital and emotional difficulties which existed between him and Alma. From this meeting Mahler gained an understanding of these problems, as well as a deeper insight into his creative personality.

Mahler had started work on the score for his Tenth Symphony (a sample below) during the summer of 1909. But, as he had suspected, he was never to finish the work.

A last chance

In the summer of 1910, all Alma's years of self-sacrifice finally caught up with her: she exploded, telling Mahler she couldn't stand her life of isolation, total subjection to his will and increasing emotional coldness any longer. She demanded that he change. Luckily, he could see that she was right and acknowledged it. In August of that year he attended a private analytical session with Sigmund Freud.

During the session, Mahler felt he had made several great breakthroughs concerning his own mental state, and both men acknowledged that they found each other fascinating. Freud later commented: 'I had much opportunity to admire the capability for psychological understanding in this man of genius.'

This encounter resulted in a renewal of Mahler's love and passion for Alma. Before they made a return visit to New York in January 1911, Mahler made every effort to redress the years of unacknowledged sacrifice. The depth of his feeling is best shown in the dedication of the Tenth Symphony: 'To live for thee! To die for thee! Almschi!'

Unfortunately, this was the last opportunity he was to have, for within a short time of his starting the new season, Mahler's strength failed him. Within a month he was bedridden, rising only once to conduct a concert of music by his friend Ferruccio Busoni. It was to be his last. With his health now rapidly deteriorating, he and Alma returned to Europe.

Doctors in Paris confided to Alma that he had only a matter of weeks to live, perhaps just days. He was taken back to Vienna, frail and exhausted. The day after they arrived, 18 May 1911, he died – a few weeks short of his 51st birthday.

On his death, Mahler finally received the adulation from the people of his beloved Vienna that had been denied to him all his life. As if beset by a deep sense of guilt at the way the composer had been vilified, Vienna gave him a funeral as impressive as any it had given its past musical heroes, and obituaries were unanimous in their expressions of profound loss. Mahler had finally won.

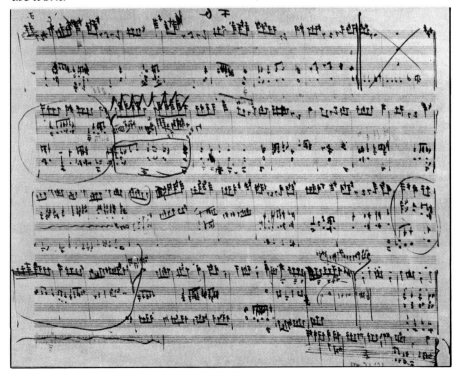

incomparable singers such as Caruso, but he had the misfortune of having a second-rate orchestra and the disadvantage of having to spend more time convalescing. Nevertheless the performances were brilliantly illuminated by his genius for two seasons, although he never gave his heart and soul to the New World. Always he longed to be back in Vienna, despite the incredible warmth the New Yorkers displayed.

It was back in Austria during the summers that he found the strength and inspiration to write his two heartfelt valedictory symphonies, *Das Lied von der Erde* and the Ninth. They were different from anything he had written before and, with the lack of the gigantic struggles which punctuated his earlier works before finding peace, showed signs that he had come to terms with mortality. He also made considerable progress with his Tenth Symphony but, like Beethoven and Schubert before him, felt he was doomed to complete only nine symphonies.

Unreal city

Mahler's Vienna

In 1900 Vienna was the cosmopolitan capital of the doomed Hapsburg Empire. Haunted by a sense of living on borrowed time, its anxious citizens found a refuge in art and music.

In 1900 Vienna was the capital of a huge, disintegrating empire. The forces of nationalism had been eating away at Austria-Hungary throughout the 19th century. To the south, the Italians had thrown Austrian troops out of Lombardy and Venice. To the north, Prussia had decisively ejected Austria from the sphere of German politics. Meanwhile, the Slavs, Czechs and Hungarians were clamouring for their own national parliaments – leaving the crisis-ridden administration in Vienna paralysed. The imposing two-headed eagle on the emperor's coat of arms symbolized the dual monarchy of Austria-Hungary, but to many it became a reminder of the ludicrous complexity of the Hapsburg civil service: how could a two-headed creature successfully govern such a vast and unwieldy state?

The Mayerling affair

Despite the nationalist ferments tearing at the empire's fabric during the 19th century, Vienna's liberal middle class had remained optimistic until two shocking crises permanently eroded morale. Wealthy, professional citizens (many of whom were Jewish) hoped that education, industrialization and the extension of voting rights would make their chaotic motherland evolve into a modern, multinational and democratic state. But their faith in the economic future was shaken by the stock market crash of 1873, which became known as Black Friday,

and a further blow came in 1889 with the shocking 'Mayerling affair'.

On 29 January 1889 the young heir to the throne, Crown Prince Rudolph, shot himself at his hunting lodge in the Vienna Woods and also killed his 17-year-old lover, Mary Vetsera. A hasty and inept attempt to pretend that he had died of heart failure was dropped when the old emperor, Franz Joseph, insisted on publishing the basic details of the whole tragic story. As the circumstances surrounding the Mayerling affair became public knowledge it became clear that, far from having been an able, humane and liberal young man, Rudolph had been very unsound mentally and he had lived in a world of sexual chaos.

The Mayerling affair was the last straw. Many Austrians had hoped that Rudolph's accession to the throne would bring a new vitality to the ailing empire, but now there was nothing to hope for. From this point on, they regarded the ageing Franz Joseph as the end of his line. After him, there would be nothing. The new heir to the throne, Archduke Franz Ferdinand, was widely distrusted. It was his assassination at Sarajevo that finally drove Austria over the abyss into the First World War, and yet there was little sorrow expressed at his death. On the afternoon of his murder, a hot Sunday in June 1914, a mild middle-of-the-road politician named Josef Redlich recorded the event in his diary. His entry concluded with the thought that perhaps God had

A typical street scene in turn-of-the-century Vienna (above). At the point where the tree-lined Ringstrasse meets Kärntnerstrasse, with the Opera House in the background, Viennese stroll, meet and gossip.

Emperor Franz Joseph mixed only with members of the huge imperial family. Court occasions (left) were usually restricted to the blue-blooded nobility, the diplomatic corps and officers on active service in Vienna. The 'Old Gentleman', as Franz Joseph was called, disapproved of Karl Lueger (below), the brilliantly opportunist politician who was mayor of Vienna from 1897 to 1910.

In 1889 all Vienna was scandalized when Crown Prince Rudolf (bottom), heir to the throne, shot himself and his teenage lover, Mary Vetsera (bottom left), at Mayerling.

been kind to the Austrians in sparing them an emperor who was said to possess 'the callousness and cruelty of an Asian despot'.

The death of liberalism

In France, the rise of the middle classes had destroyed the power of the court, and in Britain wealthy industrialists had married into the aristocracy to create a new alliance between traditional privilege and commercial wealth. But in Vienna this alliance failed. Through the complexities of official protocol, the court remained closed to the rising world of bourgeois power. In order to be presented at court, you had to trace your noble ancestry back through 11 generations. One wealthy American visitor to Vienna, Consuelo Vanderbilt, thought the hereditary rulers of Austria resembled an over-bred species of pedigree dog: 'The aristocratic Austrians I met looked like greyhounds with their long, lean bodies and small heads. It was, I thought, a pity that they could express their thoughts in so many languages, when they had so few thoughts to express.'

But despite the fact that the court establishment left them out in the cold, Vienna's middle class felt compelled to support the old regime, simply because what was threatening to succeed it was far more frightening. The working class was turning to socialism and to virulent strains of German nationalism, which were heavily tinged with anti-Semitism.

For the emperor's silver wedding celebrations in 1879 Hans Makart, the 'wizard' of the Ringstrasse era, organized a historical pageant (above). Dressed in a Rubens costume and mounted on a white charger, Makart himself rode at the head of the procession, which marched round the Ringstrasse.

After the demolition of the old city walls in the 1850s, the Ringstrasse (right), which girdled the inner city, became Vienna's principal thoroughfare.

Gustav Klimt, the leading painter of Mahler's day, had to free himself of Hans Makart's influence before he could establish his own distinctive style. Makart's sensuous ladies (below) loll in a typically cluttered and rich setting, but Klimt's client (right), the daughter of a rich Secession patron, is depicted with photographic realism against a stylized background.

Georg von Schönerer had organized the radical German nationalists in the 1880s and led them into extreme anti-Semitic politics. He never succeeded in forming a powerful party but he elevated anti-Semitism into a major disruptive force in Austrian politics. But Schönerer's political techniques influenced Karl Lueger, who did succeed in mobilizing the lower middle class as a political force, and he transformed this movement into the Christian Socialists in the 1890s. A skilled operator and a powerful leader, Lueger became the hero of the ordinary men and women of Vienna, who idolized him as *der schöne Karl* (handsome Karl) – the sworn enemy of financial speculators and Jewish bankers.

Three times Lueger was elected Mayor of Vienna before Franz Joseph (who deplored any trace of anti-Semitism) agreed to ratify his appointment. Eventually the emperor capitulated and from 1897 until his death in 1910, handsome Karl ruled over his beloved city. Although he was quick to denounce Jewish financiers for controlling the economy, he also included Jewish bankers among his supporters and advisers. When questioned about this contradiction, Lueger replied, 'I decide who is a Jew and who isn't.'

With the rise of Lueger, Vienna's wealthy middle class, who had once believed in progress and universal suffrage, found themselves propping up a moribund aristocracy while fearing the politics of the mob. More and more, this alienated middle class withdrew into the world of culture. They cultivated artists and musicians as heroes and saw in the realm of art an asylum from a hopeless present and a terrifying future.

Behind the façade

Vienna had been dramatically modernized in the second half of the 19th century. In 1857 Franz Joseph had ordered the medieval walls to be demolished and replaced by a great, circular road – the Ringstrasse – adorned with parks and lavish public buildings. By the time it was completed, in the 1880s, the Ringstrasse had become the showplace of liberal values, dominated by buildings that symbolized the modern secular state: parliament, university, art gallery and town hall. Historicism was the architectural style – a style that borrowed the most appropriate look from the history book. So the parliament looked like a Greek temple; the town hall looked suitably Gothic; and the opera house looked like a Venetian palace.

The leading artist of the Ringstrasse era was Hans Makart and he was a genius at historicism. He painted vast canvases overflowing with gorgeous costumes

and exotic props, and at his studio he and his friends loved to hold parties in historical fancy dress. Makart was the art director of the Ringstrasse era and the entire city of Vienna was stage managed by his elaborate designs.

For the modern artists who grew up in the late 19th century, the Ringstrasse came to epitomize everything they loathed about Vienna: it was phoney, it was pretentious, it was living in the past. 'We are the working people of today. We should be ashamed to live in the style of princes and patricians of yesterday. We are not the Baroque age, we don't live in the Renaissance. Why should we act as if we did?' wrote the critic Hermann Bahr.

A young architect, Adolf Loos, went even further. In his hard-hitting essay, *Ornament and Crime,* he argued that meaningless ornamentation was a form of degeneracy. Loos succeeded in designing one building in the centre of Vienna that was so free of ornamentation that he shocked the public, the critics and even the emperor. It was situated on the Michaelerplatz (opposite an entrance to the Hofburg, the imperial palace) and it had a simple

Members of the Vienna Secession at the Beethoven Exhibition of 1902 (above) – their first president, Gustav Klimt, is seated in the armchair. This, the 14th Secession Exhibition, was based on Max Klinger's status of Beethoven. The poster (right) was designed by Alfred Roller, who made his name as stage designer for Gustav Makart at the opera.

façade. Legend has it that Franz Joseph described this building as 'the house without eyebrows' and, having seen it once, he refused to use that entrance to his palace again.

The Secession

It was precisely this feeling of being smothered by the past that prompted Vienna's young artists to organize the Secession movement in 1898. They were aware of artistic developments abroad and they wanted to create an exhibition space and a public forum for modern art in Vienna. But it all began as a very polite form of artistic rebellion and the first president of the Secession movement, Gustav Klimt, invited Franz Joseph to open their first exhibition.

As a student Klimt had worked in Makart's studio and it was widely believed that he would be the heir to Makart's artistic empire. Through the 1890s Klimt continued to work successfully in the historicist tradition, painting frescoes for the Burgtheater and the Art Museum. But just as Klimt was confirming his role as Vienna's leading artist by initiating the Secession movement, an extraordinary scandal erupted around his latest Ringstrasse project.

He had been commissioned to paint frescoes representing justice, philosophy and medicine for the University of Vienna, but when the public and the critics took their first look at this work in progress, there was a storm of protest. Klimt had broken away from the style of Makart's historical pageants and created something much more disturbing. His image of philosophy showed a writhing column of naked people ascending one side of the picture, while on the other side a sphynx-like face peered through the clouds. What upset people most, however, was that the image seemed extremely pessimistic. 'This picture shows how humanity is no more than a dull mass, which in the eternal service of procreation is driven hither and thither, as if in a dream, from joy to sorrow, from the first stirrings of life to powerless collapse into the grave', said one newspaper.

The university scandal

Klimt was so angered by the public and political attack on his work that he altered the painting of jurisprudence that he was engaged on, to make it even more sinister. Klimt's image of justice showed a naked man arraigned in front of three predatory women, who resembled the Furies of Greek mythology, while a gigantic squid wrapped its tentacles around the wretched sinner. Eighty-seven faculty members signed a petition denouncing the work. After an outcry lasting five years, Klimt repaid the fee he had received from the Ministry of Culture, and the works were then bought by wealthy private collectors. By handing back his commission, Klimt was acknowledging that he could no longer work

A house designed by
Adolf Loos was an
extremely plain,
geometric structure
(below). In this
revolt against
ornamentation of any
kind, this radical
architect gave modern
utility a new, simple
beauty. Loos was a
close friend of the
painter Oskar
Kokoschka, whose
dynamic portrait of
him (left) is famous. As
a vigorously
Expressionist portrait
it is in keeping with
Adolf Loos's fervent
belief that whereas a
house had to appeal to
everyone, a work of art
needed no such
general approval.

The Secession included
architects and
craftsmen as well as
painters, and Otto
Wagner was the
movements's leading
architect. In this
interior (left) the
delicate wrought iron
of the banisters and lift
shaft is complimented
by the simple lines of
the stairs and walls.

with the state on this kind of public statement.

Klimt's paintings were the visual evidence that the artistic and intellectual community of Vienna had stopped believing in progress through education and justice. From now on, Klimt's work would be only for the cultivated middle class, a clientele with a strong Jewish element – hostile critics sometimes attacked Klimt's work as 'Jewish taste'. In his portraits of society ladies Klimt created some extraordinary images. He would set a face rendered with photographic realism against elaborately stylized surroundings that combined Byzantine mosaics, Cretan wall paintings and oriental metal work.

While Klimt and the artists of the Secession movement were turning Vienna's 19th-century heritage into elegant forms of modern art, Mahler was writing his epic symphonies and struggling to modernize the style of the Viennese opera. Mean-

while, Arnold Schoenberg and his pupils were beginning to compose atonal music, and the playwright Arthur Schnitzler and novelist Robert Musil were writing about a city that was troubled by identity problems. The affluent ladies who sat for Klimt also attended Mahler's operas, and when they were feeling anxious they could visit Sigmund Freud, who pioneered psychoanalysis in their city.

Twilight in Vienna

In its last 20 years as an imperial capital (before the outbreak of the First World War in 1914 brought about the long awaited disintegration of Austria-Hungary) Vienna produced an extraordinary flowering

Egon Schiele's paintings express the desperate, even violent, alienation of Viennese artists in the last years of the empire. In 'Agony' (below) he depicted himself and his mentor, Gustav Klimt (on the right of the painting), as suffering hermits. This guise was a symbol of their separation, from establishment Vienna.

of innovative talent. And partly because of their shared sense of alienation, there was a great deal of collaboration between artists of all kinds.

For their 1902 exhibition, they combined music and architecture in order to honour a statue of Beethoven which had been made by the German sculptor Max Klinger. They designed an elaborate pavilion for the statue and created a succession of murals and sculptures to lead the viewer into Beethoven's presence. Mahler arranged part of Beethoven's ninth symphony for a brass ensemble and conducted them at the opening ceremony. In the magnificent Beethoven frieze, which Klimt painted for this exhibition, there was a figure of a knight in armour that seemed to resemble Gustav Mahler. Certainly, Mahler and Klimt respected each other for they had both achieved the same dubious honour. Both men had risen to the highest artistic status and then found themselves denounced by newspapers and governments.

It was a common fate for Viennese intellectuals.

'Gustav Klimt is truly Viennese. One can see that from his pictures, but also from the fact that he is honoured throughout the world and attacked only in Vienna', wrote Felix Salten. When Loos published his book about the connections between architecture and morality, he gave it the title *Ins Leere Gesprochen* (Spoken into the Void) to convey his view that no one in Vienna was listening. And indeed many of Vienna's most radical thinkers felt compelled to leave the city that either ignored or vilified them. At the turn of the century Vienna had seen a brilliant concentration of talent in music and the arts, but gradually the artists withdrew into a private world, like Klimt, or simply left for other places. By 1914 many were gone from Vienna.

When Mahler left Vienna for America a small group of friends accompanied him to the station to bid him farewell. As the train steamed away into the distance, it was Gustav Klimt who uttered the word which hung over this group of artists and their audience: 'Finished!'

Sergei Rachmaninov
1873–1943

Sergei Rachmaninov, last of the great Russian Romantic composers, found himself out of step with his country's politics and music, yet he went on to produce some of this century's best-loved works.

For Sergei Rachmaninov's music we are deeply indebted to his father, Vasily. A spendthrift, gambler and womanizer, he broke up the family home, squandered the family fortune and made young Sergei's early life insecure and unstable. Yet, in doing so, he undoubtedly diverted his son from what would have been his natural family vocation – a career as a professional soldier – and, instead, indirectly set him on a musical course.

Against this background of emotional upheaval, the young Sergei, sensitive, moody and unruly, grew and developed. Though hailed early on by his teachers for his prodigious musical talent he sometimes showed a lack of self-confidence in terms of his creative ability and frequently found himself out of step with the music of the time. Despite all this his work came to be admired as containing some of the finest examples of late-Romantic music.

On leaving Russia in 1918 Rachmaninov believed that his future lay as a performer rather than as a composer. Indeed, his fame in his later years outside Russia rested on his career as a virtuoso pianist and recording artist. He is shown here at the Steinway piano given to him by the Steinway Company in America. During his first few months in America he gave nearly 40 concerts and recitals.

*Rachmaninov's
parents: father, Vasily
(top) and mother,
Lubov (below). They
separated in 1881.*

*After his parents'
separation, Sergei's
maternal
grandmother played
an active part in the
boy's life. She bought an
estate at Borivoso near
the river Volkhov and it
was here that Sergei
spent his summer
holidays swimming
and canoeing in the
countryside (right).*

Family turmoil

Sergei was born into an aristocratic Russian family on 1 April 1873. His father, a handsome, dashing army officer had done well for himself in marrying a wealthy general's daughter – Lubov Butakova – and had inherited a dowry of five large country estates. Devoted to the pursuit of pleasure, Vasily could now afford to indulge himself further and he left the army to lead the life of a gentleman landowner. Unfortunately for Lubov he also continued to indulge his bachelor ways. By the time Sergei was nine only one of the estates remained in the family's possession – the others had been sold to pay for his father's lavish taste for expensive women and his gambling debts. Soon, even the last estate had to go too and the family – which now included five other children besides Sergei – were forced to take a flat in St Petersburg.

There was no question, now, of expensive education for the children – alternatives had to be found, and quickly, for at home Vasily's and Lubov's marriage was breaking down under the strain of their straitened circumstances. Divorce, however was neither socially nor religiously acceptable so, instead, they separated. Vasily left the flat to Lubov and the children.

In the meantime, Sergei, who had shown considerable ability on the piano, having been taught since the age of five, was lined up for a musical education. Consequently, in 1882 Sergei entered the St Petersburg Conservatory on a scholarship.

Unfortunately, Sergei was not the best of students, which is hardly surprising considering the disruptive effect of his family background on his sensitive nature. He did only a minimum of work and frequently played truant – roaming the streets with gangs of boys instead of studying. When his reports came out he altered them to deceive his mother.

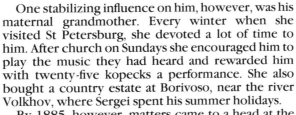

From the autumn of 1885 until the summer of 1892 Rachmaninov was a student at the Conservatory in Moscow (left). For the first four years in Moscow he lived under the strict regime of his tutor Zverev (seated, far right). Sergei (second from left) and a few other particularly gifted pupils lived at Zverev's home. With the help of his sister, Zverev supervised their education and saw that they were exposed to the finest musical talent in Moscow.

One stabilizing influence on him, however, was his maternal grandmother. Every winter when she visited St Petersburg, she devoted a lot of time to him. After church on Sundays she encouraged him to play the music they had heard and rewarded him with twenty-five kopecks a performance. She also bought a country estate at Borivoso, near the river Volkhov, where Sergei spent his summer holidays.

By 1885, however, matters came to a head at the Conservatory. Sergei's musical education had to some extent been mismanaged, as his teachers were so impressed by his technique and perfect pitch that they overlooked weaknesses in basic theory. His laziness in general subjects, though, was so unforgivable that, in 1885, they threatened to withdraw his scholarship. His mother turned for advice to her nephew, Alexander Siloti, himself a brilliant pianist, who advised a course with his own former teacher, Nikolai Zverev, in Moscow.

Sergei, apprehensive as any twelve-year-old boy might be about leaving home and family for the first time, was worried by the stories he heard regarding Zverev's stern discipline and insistence on hard work.

Studies in Moscow

The new régime was as strict as he had feared, but not unkind. Zverev, a distinguished teacher at the Moscow Conservatory, made a habit of taking a few particularly gifted pupils into his home where, with his sister's help, he supervised their whole education. His control over their lives was total — they were not even allowed home for the holidays — but no payment was expected and there were

frequent free outings to theatres and concerts. At the weekends it was open house to the finest musical talents in Moscow. In this way the pupils met, and played for, such famous musicians as Anton Rubinstein, Glazunov and Tchaikovsky.

In the summer of 1886 Zverev took his protégés to the Crimea, where they stayed on the estate of a Moscow millionaire whose children Zverev was teaching. They were accompanied by a professor of theory and harmony from the Conservatory, whose task it was to prepare them for next year's studies. Rachmaninov seems to have found this exciting and stimulating, for it prompted his first attempts at composition. The following year he produced an arrangement for two pianos of Tchaikovsky's Manfred symphony, which won the great composer's approval, and also presented a set of nocturnes for piano to Zverev. But Zverev's ambitions for him were centred on playing rather than composing and this was a source of disagreement between them which finally, when Rachmaninov was sixteen, reached a dramatic climax. Rachmaninov went to Zverev and asked that he be allowed a room of his own in which to compose and practise, instead of sharing with his fellow pupils as he had done for the past three years. How tactfully this request was put we do not know, but Zverev seems to have thought him arrogant and ungrateful as a result.

Although Rachmaninov stayed at the Conservatory quarters for another month, the situation became impossible, as Zverev refused even to speak to him and eventually he moved into the house of some relatives, the Satins, who lived nearby. Initially this was embarrassing, since Rachmaninov had hardly visited them at all during his time in the city. Nevertheless he found them welcoming and kind and they offered him the sort of intimate family atmosphere he had not experienced for some time.

Fortunately, Zverev had ceased to teach Rachmaninov personally, so his studies at the Conservatory were not seriously affected by the rift. However, in the spring of 1891, Siloti, who had been teaching him piano for three years, resigned his post

During the three years after the disastrous first performance in 1897 of his First Symphony (title page above) Rachmaninov found it impossible to compose. He spent his summers on the estate of relatives (left) and launched himself on a new career as an opera conductor with the Moscow Private Opera Company. Here he met and became a close friend of the singer Shalyapin (right).

after a disagreement with the new director. Rachmaninov did not want to be taught by anyone else and applied, successfully, to take his final piano examination a year early. This gave him only three weeks to prepare the set pieces, but nevertheless he passed with honours. The following year, 1892, he surprised his examiners in composition even more. The students were required to compose a one-act opera, *Aleko,* based on a· poem by Pushkin. Rachmaninov presented a fully orchestrated score within eighteen days and was awarded the Great Gold Medal, which had only been won twice previously in the history of the Conservatory. He was also reconciled with Zverev who, quite won over by the success of his former pupil, presented him with his gold watch in congratulation.

Rachmaninov had composed other works, including a piano concerto, during his last two years at the Conservatory and had also given his first public recital. On leaving the Conservatory he was introduced to the music publishers, Gutheil, who offered him five hundred roubles for a set of pieces including *Aleko.* Later that year he composed a *Prelude in C sharp minor for piano* which was to

become his most famous composition – he was obliged to play it, if only as an encore, at almost all his subsequent concerts. But he was not yet confident that he could earn a living from playing and composing, and for the next few years took on teaching work, which he heartily disliked. Then, about this time, his life entered another very disturbed and unsettled phase.

His stay with the Satins lasted only for a couple of years and he moved out, first to live with a fellow student and then for a while with his father, who had come to Moscow to work. He then rented a tiny furnished flat of his own for a few months, but by the end of 1894 he was back with the Satins, who offered him a bedroom and a studio in a new, larger house they had bought. He was upset by the deaths of Zverev and Tchaikovsky; the latter, who, despite the difference in their ages had been a real friend, and whose encouragement during his adolescent years had given him much confidence and security. Also at this time he developed an infatuation for a young married woman named Anna Lodizhensky. His feelings found expression in the restless and intense music of the *First Symphony,* which was dedicated to her.

In 1902 Rachmaninov married his first cousin Natalia Satina (left). Her family home (right) at Ivanovka became the focal point of their happy lives for the next ten years.

The first performance, in St Petersburg in March 1897, was under-rehearsed and badly performed, and Rachmaninov was so appalled by what he heard that he could not bear to sit in the concert hall. Next day, the St Petersburg critics, ever eager to attack a musician from the rival city of Moscow, savaged the work.

Rachmaninov was totally shattered by the rejection of a work into which he had put so much of himself, and composed nothing more for three years.

However, he was introduced to the millionaire industrialist Mamontov who ran the Moscow Private Opera Company and began another career, this time as a conductor for the company's 1897–8 season. He met the great singer Shalyapin who was to become a close friend for forty years. In the summer of 1898 he attended Shalyapin's marriage to the Italian ballerina Tornaghi. The bridal pair were serenaded at six the following morning by an improvised band playing household implements, conducted by Rachmaninov. Despite these diversions, on the whole, his mood was one of melancholy and his creativity was stifled.

Confidence returns

He made a visit to England in 1899, playing and conducting, and promised the London Philharmonic Society a new piano concerto, but he was unable to make any progress with it. In desperation, he consulted Dr Nikolay Dahl, a Moscow physician who specialized in treatment by hypnosis. The results were spectacularly successful; within a few months he had completed two movements of the new concerto, which were performed to an enthusiastic reception in Moscow in December, and in 1900 the finished concerto, the *Second Piano Concerto* was published and dedicated to Dahl.

As proof of confidence in him, Rachmaninov's cousin Siloti offered him a substantial loan, to be repaid over the next three years. With renewed confidence in his financial security and powers of composition, he asked his cousin Natalia Satina to marry him. Since marriage between first cousins was frowned upon by the Orthodox church, special permission of the Tsar had to be obtained. Eventually the wedding took place on 29 April 1902.

The next ten years or so were ostensibly the most successful of Rachmaninov's life, with his career advancing on all fronts and a happy marriage soon made happier by the births of two daughters.

During the decade he spent two seasons as

conductor of Moscow's Imperial opera. He travelled extensively, making his first trip to America in 1909, and then spending three successive winters in Dresden. He gave many concerts and recitals and composed much of his finest music, including the *Second Symphony,* the *Third Piano Concerto,* the symphonic poem *'The Isle of the Dead',* inspired by a picture by the Swiss artist Böcklin, and his choral symphony *The Bells,* based on a poem by Edgar Allan Poe. From 1910–1912 he was also vice-President of the Imperial Russian Music Society.

The pursuit of so many different activities imposed a heavy strain on his health, and he particularly resented the limits set upon his time for composition. He suffered severe pains in his head and back, and in his letters to friends constantly complained of ill-health and general tiredness, almost to the point of hypochondria. And in spite of his conspicuous success, he still remained a victim of his own self-doubt.

One unwavering consolation to him seems to have been his religion. Even from his childhood the services and especially the music of the Orthodox church had a deep effect on him. He composed two major religious works for unaccompanied choir, *The Liturgy of St John Chrysostom* and the *Vesper Mass.*

Into exile

As Rachmaninov moved into middle age, Russia became an increasingly turbulent place, with war outside its borders and revolution threatening within. He seems to have had uncertain feelings about the new political ideas which threatened the old règime. As early as 1905 he added his name to a declaration which stated that 'There is but one way out of this impasse: Russia must at long last enter the path of basic reforms'. And yet, as an aristocrat and landowner, he stood to lose most from these reforms. The hostile attitude of the peasants to him when he visited the Ivanovka estate in the spring of 1917 finally convinced him that things would never be the same again. As the year proceeded and the actions of government and governed became more extreme, he desperately sought some means of escape for himself and his family, even if on a temporary basis. The opportunity of a concert tour of Sweden presented itself in November 1917 and Rachmaninov snatched the chance; he obtained the necessary passes for his wife and children, and they crossed the Finnish frontier on 23 December, clutching a minimum of possessions and a gift of bread and caviar from Shalyapin. He was never to set foot in Russia again.

Although still only in his mid-forties, Rachmaninov had already composed 39 of his eventual 45 published works when he began his self-imposed exile. His main consideration was now to earn money and he realized that his best chance of doing this was as conductor and piano virtuoso.

After a few months in Stockholm and Copenhagen the Rachmaninovs moved to the United States of America where Sergei felt he would be more secure financially. His first few months there – he arrived in November 1918 – were spent giving concerts and making recordings. Although New York was to be his base for many years he kept his interests in Europe.

In the spring of 1926, just before the birth of his

first grandchild, Sergei and his wife had a family reunion in France with their daughters. Tragedy marred the event: his daughter Irina's husband, Prince Volkonsky died suddenly.

With the intention of helping his widowed daughter Rachmaninov set up a publishing house – TAIR, – which was to publish works by Russian émigré composers. The company was run by his two daughters.

From 1926 he spent more time in Europe. For a number of years he rented a villa in Clairfontaine, a village about an hour's drive from Paris, and there held court in the old Russian style. Russian-speaking company was not hard to find, as there were many exiles in Europe, including members of both the Siloti and the Satin families.

In 1930 he purchased some land beside Lake Lucerne and built a villa there which he named Senar. Although he loved its peace and seclusion, and also enjoyed trips across the lake in his new motor boat, he still travelled regularly to play and conduct, and continued to make historic recordings for the Victor Record Company. He would have nothing to do with radio broadcasting though, insisting stubbornly, though at the time perhaps correctly, that the sound quality was too poor to do justice to the music. He always preferred to play to a live audience.

In 1931 Rachmaninov put his name to an anti-Soviet manifesto published in the New York Times, and the Soviet government responded by banning performances of all his music in Russia. *Pravda* described him contemptuously as 'a composer who was played out long ago and whose music is that of an insignificant imitator and reactionary'. An overstatement, naturally, but not without a grain of truth; even while he still lived in Russia, his music was regarded condescendingly by the avant-garde, and Rachmaninov confessed himself quite out of sympathy with the trends in the twentieth century music represented by Prokofiev and Stravinsky. Nonetheless, he continued to compose – the *Third Symphony,* the *Rhapsody on a theme of Paganini* and the *Symphonic Dances* all date from the last decade of his life and prove that he still had a

Because of the turbulent political situation in Russia in 1918 Rachmaninov (left) and his family decided to leave Russia. They moved first to Stockholm and Copenhagen, but eventually decided to settle in America. He arrived in New York (above) in November 1918 and although he lived from time to time in parts of Europe, America became his home until his death in 1943.

distinctive, if unfashionable, voice.

As old age approached, so did more upheavals. In 1938 he lost his dear friend Shalyapin; he visited him twice a day as he lay in hospital in Paris, and was greatly shocked by his death. By the next year it was clear that there would be another war in Europe, and the house on Lake Lucerne, Senar, had to be abandoned. Rachmaninov sailed back to the United States in August 1939, accompanied by his wife, his elder daughter Irina and grandaughter Sophia.

Once back in America, he threw himself into his work, but it was impossible to forget the situation in Europe. His younger daughter Tatiana, her husband and their son Alexander, remained in France and news of them was almost impossible to obtain. The German invasion of Russia caused him great sadness though by donating the proceeds of many of his concerts to the Fund for Russian War Relief, he found himself in favour again with the Soviet government.

Early in 1943, he had to abandon a concert tour because of a sudden deterioration in his health and on 28 March 1943 he died of cancer in California. The funeral was held in Beverley Hills, but his remains were later taken to Kensico in New York State, where he lies buried in a quiet cemetery attached to a Russian orthodox church.

The Great War

and war artists

In their paintings, poems and novels, a generation of artists inspired by 'The Great War' of 1914–18, reflected the full horror and tragedy of the conflict.

As the August Bank Holiday sun sank behind the trees in London's St James's Park, in 1914, Sir Edward Grey, the British Foreign Secretary, stood thoughtfully at a window in the Foreign Office. Earlier that afternoon, he had almost wept as he saw 'the efforts of a lifetime go for nothing', and confessed, 'I feel like a man who has wasted his life'. Now all he could do was wait – wait for the German reply to Britain's ultimatum, a reply that might save the two countries from war. He knew it would not come. Germany's mobilization had gone too far. Then, as the sun finally dipped out of sight and the golden glow vanished from the room, he said quietly, 'The lamps are going out all over Europe; we shall not see them lit again in our lifetime'.

His plaintive comment has echoed down the years. For, with Britain's entry into a conflict that had already ensnared Russia, Austria-Hungary, Serbia, Germany, Belgium and France, Europe was plunged into the most terrible war the world had ever known. Over 10 million men and women were killed, more than 20 million seriously wounded; five million women were widowed, nine million children orphaned and 10 million people made refugees.

When war was declared, crowds thronged the streets, greeting the news with jubilation (right). Soon, though, the same young men were stumbling through a mire of horrors, having lost all sight of the war's purpose. Gassed (below) preserves the nightmare of battle.

Yet Sir Edward Grey and a few fellow statesmen were terrifyingly alone in their response to the outbreak of war. Over much of Europe, the great majority greeted the news not with despair but euphoria. In Germany, on the night of 31st July, thousands of people had thronged the streets of Berlin, awaiting Russia's reply to the German ultimatum. All next day they waited, crowding round the Foreign Office in Wilhelmstrasse and the Royal Palace. Then, at 5.30 pm, a policeman came to the palace gates and announced that mobilization had been ordered. Germany was at war. As the news passed from mouth to mouth, the crowds erupted in boisterous cheering and burst into a spontaneous chorus of *Now thank we all our God.*

It was the same in Britain on the night of 4th August. Men and women dressed in light summer clothes packed Parliament Square and the Mall, shoulder to shoulder in the warm evening air. When the declaration of war was announced, they began to cheer wildly and sing *Land of hope and glory* and, like the people in Berlin, went off into the night, still singing, to celebrate until the early hours. Similar scenes were witnessed all over Europe. War fever was in the air.

'Call to arms'

Thousands of British, young and old, answered Kitchener's 'Call to Arms' and rushed to enlist. Recruitment was entirely voluntary at first, but

throughout autumn and the following spring, an endless stream of volunteers waited patiently in queues, sometimes two miles long. On a single day in September 1914, 30,000 men joined up and, in the three months after the outbreak of war, no less than 700,000 volunteered. Many thousands more had arrived only to be turned down on grounds of ill-health or age. Britain did not need to introduce conscription until January 1916, by which time over four million men had offered themselves for service.

The will to fight was common to all classes. Most remarkably, it was prevalent among artists, intellectuals and socialists. Men and women who had been internationalists and revolutionaries were transformed overnight into ardent patriots willing to support their country's war effort to the death. The thriving political organization, the Socialist International, was pledged to oppose war. Suddenly it crumbled, as thousands of erstwhile revolutionaries all over Europe abandoned their cause. The Russian revolutionary Georgi Plekhanov, in exile in France, actually became a recruiting agent for the French army, recruiting men to fight against former socialist comrades conscripted into the German army. The Social Democrat party in the German Reichstag (the party founded by Marx and Engels) voted unanimously for the introduction of war credits. Lenin was so astounded ,when he heard this news that he convinced himself the newspapers containing the reports were forgeries.

Artistic idealists

In Britain, so many artists joined up that a batallion called the Artists' Rifles was formed. Painters such as John and Paul Nash and Charles Sergeant Jagger all saw active service in the Artists' Rifles. In his book, *Tommy goes to War,* Malcolm Brown quotes one artist's memories of the day after Britain joined the war:

Would they (the Germans) *invade us, I wondered. By George! If they should they'd find us a tougher nut to crack than they expected. My bosom swelled and I clenched my fist. I wished to do something desperate for the cause of England.*

Some were so keen to enlist that they lied about their age. The actor F. R. Benson gave his age as 34 – he was actually 56. 'Surely you're older than that?' asked the recruiting officer. 'Are you here to get soldiers or to ask silly questions?' Benson replied haughtily. He was turned down, but contributed to the war effort by giving performances of Shakespeare's patriotic *Henry V.* The royal portraitist John Lavery, then 58, was actually accepted into the Artist' Rifles, but the rigours of training proved too much:

. . . the second or third route march did for me. I had to call in the doctor whose verdict was, 'My dear sir, go back to your paint pots; you will do more for your country with your brush than with your rifle' . . . In the end, they went to the trenches and I went to bed.

Others did join up, from the painter Wyndham Lewis to the composer Vaughan Williams, while many *did* contribute to the war effort 'with their brushes'. Alfred Leete's famous poster showing Kitchener pointing out and saying, 'Your Country Needs You!' is believed to have encouraged many thousands of men to enlist. Another brilliant poster painter, Frank Brangwyn had his services rejected.

The Parliamentary Recruiting Committee turned Brangwyn down, even when he offered to work for nothing. They felt Brangwyn's work was too complex – and too realistic – to have the desired effect.

Of course, there were artists who dissented from this war mania from the start. Prominent among these were members of the 'Bloomsbury set', the fashionable circle of artists and writers who used to meet at the Bloomsbury house of Lady Ottoline Morrell. Lytton Strachey and Bertrand Russell, both

Both Germany and Britain chose the image of George and the Dragon (right) to symbolize the righteousness of their cause and to claim God for an ally. This heroic style of image was in keeping with the 'glamorous' image of war that prevailed in 1914. The poem of the moment ran:
Thou careless, awake! Thou peacemaker, fight! Stand England for honour, And God guard the Right!

members of the set, suffered for their pacifist views. Russell was fined for 'statements likely to prejudice the recruiting and discipline of His Majesty's forces'.

Playwright George Bernard Shaw condemned the war and the rabid patriotism sweeping the country. He wrote an article in the *New Statesman* suggesting that the best way to end the war was for the troops to shoot all the officers and go home. H. G. Wells dismissed Shaw as 'an idiot child screaming in hospital'.

Those artists who went off to the Front did so for a variety of reasons. Some sought the emotional stimulus for their work. 'You must not miss a war . . . You cannot afford to miss that experience,' wrote Wyndham Lewis. Some went because they were curious. Others went out of sheer bravado. But the predominant mood was of quiet idealism and patriotism.

The long, long trail to war

For 20 years, the fires of militarism had been fanned so ardently that the start of the war was almost a relief. Germany and England had been indulging in a race for naval superiority. In France, the concept of *revanchism* (revenge for their loss of Alsace and Lorraine to Germany in 1871), was so powerful that in 1913 compulsory military service was increased from two to three years by public demand. Young French people were taught in school that Germans were inferior and that Alsace and Lorraine had been cruelly wrenched away.

In Germany, patriotic, militarist pressure-groups advocated a build-up of arms. Like *revanchism* in France, these groups had considerable support among the young. In 1911, General von der Goltz had set up the *Jungdeutschlandbund* (Young Germans) to promote nationalist militarism among youth. The *Jungdeutschlandbund* glorified war. They said that when war came, as it inevitably would,

it wil be more beautiful and wonderful to live forever among the heroes on a war memorial in a church than to die an empty death in bed, nameless . . . let that be heaven for young Germany.

The Boy Scout movement in Britain, despite its peaceable nature nowadays, was very similar. The Boy Scout motto, 'Be Prepared', is actually a shortened version of Baden-Powell's exhortation to 'Be prepared to die for your country . . . so that when the time comes you may charge home with confidence, not caring whether you are to be killed or not!'

This was the kind of 'clean, healthy patriotism' that men like the poet Rupert Brooke carried into the

German Uhlans *(below left) – lancers reputed to ride down their enemies and die with a laugh – were the pride of the cavalry in 1914. But both cavalry and chivalry quickly disappeared in the mud and squalor of mechanized trench warfare, where the vast majority of soldiers were not professional but unskilled amateurs.*

Artist John Nash grew all too familiar with 'Going over the Top' *(below) and painted from experience.*

John Nash's brother, Paul (above), was an official war artist, perhaps best remembered for his picture, The Menin Road. *He and his brother both volunteered, and served in the battalion designated 'The Artists' Rifles'.*

war. His famous sonnet, *The Soldier,* reflects the dangerous innocence of it all:

If I should die, think only this of me;
That there's some corner of a foreign field
That is forever England . . .

The British public had been fed German invasion stories in popular fiction such as William le Queux's *The Invasion of 1910,* serialized in 1906 in *The Daily Mail* (then the most popular daily newspaper in the country), and Erskine Childers' *The Riddle of the Sands* (1903). Le Queux's story in particular so caught the public imagination that many people felt cheated when 1910 came and the war had not started.

The great escape
For some, war was a substitute for disappointed revolutionary hopes, removing men from a divided, unjust society to a community where all men were equal and shared a common fate.

Men like Robert Graves and T. E. Lawrence ('of Arabia'), jaded, disenchanted, middle-class sons saw in the army an escape from boredom, and a new purpose in life. The army would be 'real living'. In Germany, in particular, going off to war was seen as an escape from the industrial, urban society. Much art from the early war period has a distinctly pastoral flavour – almost as if war was a return to a healthy, open-air life. One of the most famous poems of the early months of the war is Julian Grenfell's *Into Battle,* published in *The Times* in May 1915. In this, battle is associated with natural images:

The naked earth is warm with Spring
And with green grass and bursting trees
Leans to the sun's gaze glorying
And quivers in the sunny breeze;
And life is colour and warmth and light,
And a striving ever more for these;
And he is dead who will not fight;
And who dies fighting has increase . . .

For millions of working men, going to war was to be an exciting break from the daily grind of work and poverty. The unemployed suddenly found a purpose in life.

The course of the war
Most expected the war to last a matter of months. 'It will all be over by Christmas,' they said. But they were terribly wrong.

The war began when two million German troops began to sweep westwards towards France. They advanced rapidly along a vast front stretching from the foothills of the Alps right into Belgium. (It was the fact that they marched through 'neutral' Belgium that brought Britain into the war.) The idea of their 'Schlieffen Plan' was to drive into France on this wide front and then wheel round on Paris from the north, like a hammerhead, to deliver the crushing blow. It was to be so quick that the French would have no time to resist; the war with France would be over in six weeks. The German forces would then be free to combat the massive Russian forces to the east – it was anticipated that Russia would take at least 60 days to mobilize her armies.

The plan failed. The Russians managed to get a makeshift army in the field in 15 days. Though they were soon beaten back by German troops, and suffered a terrible defeat at Tannenberg, their efforts had drawn valuable troops away from the crucial

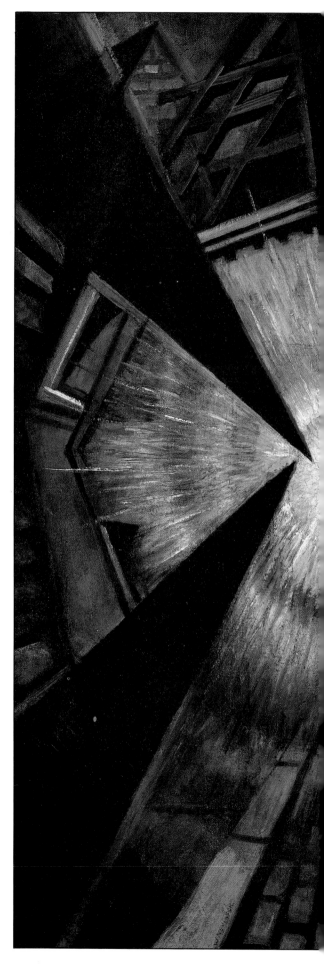

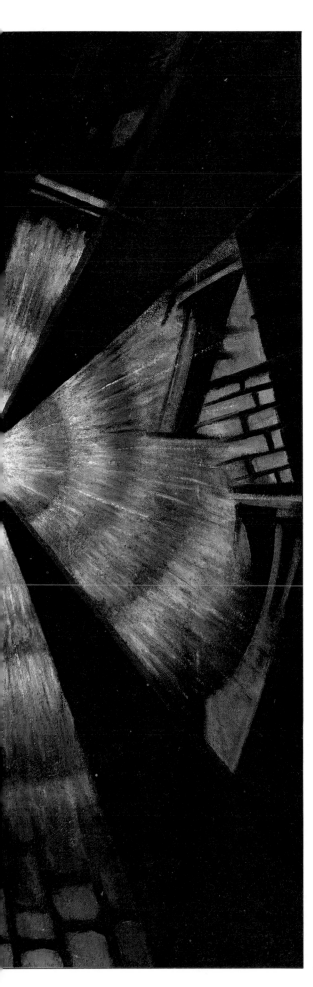

'hammerhead' in the west.

A second unforeseen factor was Britain's decision to join the war. Germany had not expected this, for in the build-up to hostilities Britain had seemed aloof, and they regarded the intervention as a betrayal.

However, for the first four weeks of the war, the Schlieffen Plan succeeded. By the end of August, the German armies had advanced far into France, and the French were retreating at breakneck speed. Then, on 5th September, the French armies commanded by Joffre decided to stand and fight. The two opposing forces were now barely 40 miles from Paris. The ensuing battle of the Marne was the most important engagement of the entire war, and was a decisive victory for the French, along with a small but well-trained force of British allies. The German advance was abruptly halted and they retreated to a line north of the River Aisne.

There, both sides dug themselves in. Two opposing lines of trenches, in some places barely 50 yards apart, stretched from the Alps to the sea. For the next four years, there was to be no further movement, except for the occasional 'push' as thousands of men were sacrificed to drive back the enemy at most a couple of miles on some short section of the Front.

Allied commanders were constantly launching 'pushes', the Germans less frequently. These futile attacks entailed 'going over the top' from trenches and stumbling across muddy ground, through shell-holes and ditches, before cutting rows of barbed wire – all the while under heavy shell and machine-gun fire. The numbers of men killed and wounded in the assaults were staggering. In the Allied offensive in Flanders, in the late summer of 1917, 400,000 men died in the mud around Passchendaele – many more were maimed for life. The offensive gained the Allies absolutely nothing.

The impact of reality

On the 'home front', the attitude was, for much of the war, 'business as usual'. People tried stoically to work in the same way they had in peacetime. Artists, too, tried to carry on painting and writing – though composers often found they could not muster a full orchestra. Many artists, however, felt drained of inspiration; the monumental terror of the war somehow belittled their work. Gustave Holst was rejected from the army when he tried to volunteer, and felt useless as a result. Although he completed *The Planets* in 1917, the war was a period of intense depression and small output for him. Vaughan Williams enlisted in the Royal Army Medical Corps in 1914 and, although he did not go to France until 1916, the war so absorbed him that he wrote hardly any music at all. Even Elgar wrote only a little chamber music.

For some at the front, however, the realities of war served as a grim inspiration. The idealism soon fell from the eyes of those exposed to the unimaginable horrors of the trenches. By the middle of 1915, many hundreds of men were sending home poems or small volumes of verse from Flanders, Egypt and Turkey, cataloguing the terrible events they were witnessing. The sheer horror turned ordinary men into poets as they sought to express the depth of their reactions to the appalling suffering. And those who were already poets achieved a profundity in their writing they had never had before.

Much of the work is lost, stored away in attics,

Perhaps because of the continual closeness of death, many entrenched soldiers experienced a heightened sensitivity to the sights they saw. And in the midst of destruction and horror they found elements of awesome beauty. 'Very' lights presented a nightly firework display above the trenches and white-hot bullets glowed like fireflies . . .
This strange beauty inspired Richard Nevinson to paint the stylized canvas, A Bursting Shell *(centre). Nevinson started the war with a dispassionate fascination in the power of conflict and mechanized warfare. He was eventually made an official war artist. In the meantime, however, he lost his belief in the dignity of war.*

buried in the French mud, or discarded long ago. Only the poems of the better-connected officers, such as Robert Graves, Isaac Rosenberg, Robert Nichols, Siegfried Sassoon and Wilfred Owen, survive. Realism and detailed description took the place of idealism, as in Rosenberg's *Dead Man's Dump:*

The wheels lurched over sprawled dead
But pained them not, though their bones crunched,
Their shut mouths made no moan.
They lie there huddled, friend and foeman,
Man born of man, and born of woman,
And shells go crying over them
From night till night and now.

Poetry like this was intended to prove to those back home that the glory of war was an illusion. It was intended to show what the men at the front were really suffering, and perhaps to act as a memorial to those who did not survive. It had its effect, but not as much as it might have – such poetry was not permitted, by government or media, to find wide publication – as witnessed by this passage from D. H. Lawrence's *Kangaroo:*

It was in 1915 the old world ended . . . The integrity of London collapsed and the genuine debasement began, the unspeakable baseness of the press and the public voice, the reign of that bloated ignominy, John Bull.

Not all artists found the experience of war so profoundly shocking or disillusioning. Futurist painters had, for a long time, found expressive power in the new machines of war like cars, guns and battleships and, in a way, gloried in the violence. Richard Nevinson, when rejected from the army as unfit, immediately joined the Belgian Red Cross and worked as an ambulance driver rather than be denied first-hand material for his paintings. But by the time he was employed as an official war artist, in 1917, even his belief in the 'beauty of strife' had been thoroughly shaken, and his paintings of the Western Front do not glorify mechanized war, but express human suffering instead.

Despair and protest

By 1917, the war showed little sign of ever stopping. The casualties and suffering and waste of life seemed increasingly futile. A note of anguished despair crept into the work of many artists; their calls for a halt to the fighting became more and more strident.

In 1916, the Frenchman Henri Barbusse had written *Le Feu,* protesting at a war that had cost the lives of hundreds of thousands of Frenchman defending Verdun against constant bombardment. Barbusse's book was translated into English in 1917 and profoundly affected poets, such as Siegfried Sassoon and Wilfred Owen.

Sassoon's poems were simple, spontaneous expressions of anger at the war and the almost blasé callousness of the commanders who constantly sacrificed thousands of men in futile offensives.

If I were fierce, and bald, and short of breath,
I'd live with scarlet Majors at the Base,
And speed glum heroes up the line to death.
You'd see me with my puffy petulant face,
Guzzling and gulping in the best hotel,
Reading the Roll of Honour. 'Poor young chap,'
I'd say – 'I used to know his father well;
Yes, we've lost heavily in this last scrap.'
And when the war is done and youth stone dead,
I'd toddle safely home and die – in bed.

Sassoon's protests became so vocal and so specific that he was in danger of being court-martialled for treason. Fortunately, the army side-stepped the issue – perhaps because of Sassoon's influential Bloomsbury friends – and invalided him out of the army to a hospital near Edinburgh. There he met Wilfred Owen.

Owen, like Sassoon, felt the need to protest. He wrote from the Front in 1917, 'The people of England needn't hope. They must agitate.' But it was not until he met Sassoon that he was confirmed in his resolve to speak out. Owen began to write a series of brilliant, searing indictments of the war and when his convalescence was over, he returned to the Front with almost missionary zeal. 'There I shall be better able to cry my outcry,' he wrote. In this verse from

The scale and power of war machines, seen for the first time during 1914-1918, inspired artists on both sides. Edward Wadsworth painted Dazzle-ships in Drydock *(right); a German,* Bayer, the armoured car *(bottom).*

Poets Siegfried Sassoon (below left) and Wilfred Owen (below). Owen was killed within days of Armistice.

Insensibility he echoes Sassoon's sentiments:

Happy are men who yet before they are killed
Can let their veins run cold.
Whom no compassion fleers
Or makes their feet
Sore on the alleys cobbled with their brothers.
The front line withers.
But they are troops who fade, not flowers,
For poets' tearful fooling:
Men, gaps for filling:
Losses, who might have fought
Longer; but no one bothers.

Tragically, Owen was killed less than three months later – and just one week before armistice. Today his poetry remains as a powerful epitaph to the horror, suffering and mindless waste of war.

The end of the war

In the end it was not any 'big push' on land that defeated the Germans, but the stranglehold of the British Navy on the seas. The British blockade was so effective that, despite remarkable ingenuity in finding substitute materials and food, the Germans were simply starved into submission. In a desperate attempt to break the blockade, they resorted to submarine warfare. The sinking of the American civilian liner, *Lusitania* in 1915 outraged America; and continued unrestricted warfare against American shipping finally brought America into the war against Germany in 1917. This intervention tipped the balance decidedly in favour of the Allies, and Germany, already reduced by the terrible news from the Front and the privations at home, began to crumble. Many Germans were actually starving. By the end of 1918, in the face of internal collapse, Germany was obliged to sue for peace.

Fighting ceased on 11th November 1918 after more than four years of bloody conflict.

Disillusionment and horror had long since dis-placed the heady idealism and had been replaced in turn by anger. When the armistice was finally signed in December 1918, those artists who had pent up their feelings, loosed them in a torrent, and the post-war months were punctuated by the publication of the memoirs of men determined to reveal the truth about war, and so prevent it ever recurring. Robert Graves' *Goodbye to All That,* Blunden's *Undertones of War,* Montague's *Disenchantment* and Erich Maria Remarque's *All Quiet on the Western Front* are among the best known works of the post-war period.

Other artists – particularly painters and those involved in the performing arts – adopted a hedonistic outlook in response to the proven transience of youth and pleasure.

Perhaps their feelings are summed-up best by Wilfred Owen's allegorical retelling of the biblical story of Abraham and Isaac, *The Parable of the Old Men and the Young.* Those responsible for the War and its mismanagement are likened to Abraham; the young soldiers to the son Abraham was prepared to sacrifice. But Owen's poem reaches a dramatic and poignantly different conclusion from the Bible story:

Then Abram bound the youth with belts and straps,
And builded parapets and trenches there,
And stretched forth the knife to slay his son.
When lo! an angel called him out of heaven,
Saying, Lay not thy hand upon the lad,
Neither do anything to him. Behold,
A ram, caught in a thicket by its horns;
Offer the ram of Pride instead of him.
But the old man would not so, but slew his son _
And half the seed of Europe, one by one.

Nine of Wilfred Owen's poems formed the structure of Benjamin Britten's *War Requiem,* first performed in 1962. And its power to stir a generation a lifetime removed from the horror of the Great War, reveals the massive cultural scar left by that 'war to end all wars'.

The skeleton of Chateau Woods, Ypres (left), laid bare by the attrition of massive daily bombardment. By the end of the War, artists, poets and writers were producing work as bleak and brutal as the battered landscape, in bitter protest at the cavalier and senseless squandering of life by commanders and politicians.

Gustav Holst
1874–1934

*Gustav Holst produced one of this century's most popular works with the magnificent **Planets**. But fame and acclaim rested uneasily on the shoulders of this shy, retiring composer.*

Great Composers

Adolphus Holst (right), pianist, organist and conductor, settled in Cheltenham (far right) in the 1890s. He married one of his pupils, Clara Lediard (above), and their first child, Gustav, was born in September 1874.

Gustav Holst was born on 21 September 1874 in a small Regency house in Cheltenham, Gloucestershire. He was named after his grandfather, a harpist and music teacher who had settled in Cheltenham in the 1840s. Holst's father, Adolphus, continued the musical traditions of the family – he was an excellent all-round musician. He gave piano lessons, played the organ on Sundays in a local church and gave recitals. In due course he married one of his pupils, a solicitor's daughter, Clara Lediard, and Gustav was their first child.

Gustav and his brother Emil (he later became an actor known as Ernest Cossart) found their father, the sound of whose virtuoso playing was a constant part of their childhood, to be an exacting teacher. When their hands were large enough to tackle 'five-finger exercises' they began music lessons and practised with him daily. He was held in great regard by his pupils and audiences but at home he was not really a family man. His grand-daughter, Imogen Holst, related that the family found him 'an uncomfortable man to live with'.

Gustav was a delicate child – short-sighted and prone to asthma and, although naturally boisterous, was not at all strong. His prediliction for indoor pursuits like reading and music is therefore not surprising. When he was eight his mother died and a few years later his father remarried another of his pupils, whose main interest was theosophy. Holst's own interest in religious philosophy developed later, although he might have heard many interesting discussions from his step-mother's friends.

From the age of 12 Holst began to try his hand at composition. Unfortunately his activities in this direction were hindered, rather than helped, by his father who discouraged composition and banned the music of Holst's favourite composer, Grieg, from the house. Holst had to continue his attempts – his 'early horrors', as he called them – in secret, late at night, and he could only air them on the piano when his father was out of the house. He learned his first principles of composition from his reading of Berlioz's *Treatise on Modern Instrumentation and Orchestration,* and from the practical experience he gained later conducting small choirs.

Holst (left) showed great musical promise early on and his father hoped he would become a concert pianist. Holst, however, became more interested in composition. He was a frail child, though, and before long his father realized that he just did not have the consititution for a performing career.

Unenthusiastic about his son's interest in composition, Adolph Holst did however nurture great hopes that Gustav might have a future as a concert pianist. Although Holst showed great promise from an early age he suffered increasingly from neuritis in his right arm and eventually his father had to face the fact that he would never be fit enough for a career as a virtuoso performer.

His first professional appointment after he left school, aged 17, was as organist and choirmaster, on pay of £4 per annum, to the village parish of Wyck Rissington, near Cheltenham. The following year he was invited to conduct the Choral Society of a neighbouring village, Bourton-on-the-Water. Once his father had realized that he would not be able to pursue a career as a performer he gave permission for his son to attend a two-month course in harmony and counterpoint in Oxford. After this it was decided that he would go to London to study composition at the Royal College of Music.

A student in London

Holst arrived in London in May 1893 and began life as a student at the Royal College of Music. At first he felt depressed since he had failed to win an open scholarship for composition and did not relish the fact that his father was paying his fees. Also his teacher of Composition, Stanford, was not always complimentary about his work. He corrected it heavily and constantly told Holst: 'It won't do, me boy'. However, in 1895 Holst was successful in winning a scholarship for composition thereby achieving financial independence from his father and acceptance as a serious composer.

During 1895 Holst met a fellow-student, Ralph Vaughan Williams. Vaughan Williams, himself destined to be a famous composer, became Holst's greatest musical confidant and lifelong friend. Later Holst recalled their student days when they sought each other out for mutual advice on their work:

What one really learns from college is not so much from one's official teachers as from one's fellow students. We used to meet at a little tea-shop in Kensington and discuss every subject from the lowest note of the bassoon to the philosophy of Thomas Hardy's 'Jude the Obscure'.

His second instrument at college was the trombone. Not only did learning this instrument help to cure his asthma but it also gave him an insight into orchestration from the viewpoint of the player. It also provided him with a means of income, as he played professionally in pier orchestras during his vacations, and in London theatres in winter.

The style of work which he showed to Vaughan Williams owed much to the music of Wagner – tickets for the standing room in the gallery of Covent Garden on Wagner nights were high on his list of priorities and soon after his arrival in London he had heard the Ring cycle. He was entranced by the startling new sounds, quite unlike anything he had heard before.

During these stimulating student days Holst was introduced to the work of contemporary poets such as George Meredith, Francis Thompson and Robert Bridges, and settings of some of their poems are found in his early works. Bridges, who became a great friend of Holst's, was the future poet laureate. Other writers whose work greatly influenced Holst's thinking and creativity were Walt Whitman, the American poet, and William Morris, artist, designer and socialist writer. It was after reading some of Morris's essays on Socialism that Holst decided to join the Hammersmith Socialist Club which met at Kelmscott House, Morris's Thameside home.

As it happened, the newly-formed Hammersmith Socialist Choir needed a conductor and Holst soon found himself in charge. In the course of rehearsals Holst met and fell in love with one of the sopranos,

Holst went to study composition at the Royal College of Music in London in 1893. He found student life there invigorating and made many strong friendships. One of these was with Ralph Vaughan Williams (below), who was later to become a famous composer.

Like most students Holst found that he needed extra money, and so he took to playing trombone (his second instrument) professionally. In summer he played in pier orchestras at the seaside and in the winter pantominme season he played in theatre orchestras in Leicester Square (below left).

In 1901 Holst married Isobel Harrison. They were unable to afford a honeymoon then, but in 1903 holidayed in Berlin (left). Their only child, Imogen (above), was born in 1907.

for his development as a creative artist there was little money to be made out of the publication of isolated short works, and for a while had to exist on what Isobel could earn as a dressmaker.

Music maker

Deliverance came in the form of a part-time teaching position at James Allens Girls' School in Dulwich. He gratefully accepted and made such a success of the job that he was invited to stay permanently. Two years later he took up the post of Director of Music at St Paul's Girls' School, Hammersmith, an appointment that he held until the end of his life. Many of his compositions were dedicated to the school: the most famous of the 'St Paul's' compositions – a piece for strings called *St Paul's Suite,* 1913, is not only one of Holst's finest works but also a testament to the high standard of the school orchestra.

Teaching was in Holst's blood and he took it very seriously and for his time was revolutionary in his methods. He hated harmony textbooks and compulsory examinations. He always believed in giving his pupils music that he was particularly fond of himself and not what he called 'the reams of twaddle' sent to him by publishers as 'suitable for girls'.

In keeping with the socialist ideal that art and

Isobel Harrison. He thought her the most enchanting girl he had ever met, and although it took some time to convince her of his own charms, he eventually persuaded her to marry him. At this stage he was about to leave college and it was clear to both of them that it would be some time before they could get married.

An oriental outlook

After leaving college he became interested in Indian literature, and was captivated by the rich poetry of the ancient texts of the Hindu *Rig Veda,* which he read in translation. He set some passages from this to music – enrolling at the London School of Oriental Languages, so that he could learn enough Sanskrit to make his own translations. His lessons there, from Dr Mabel Bode, made a lasting impression on him and he adopted certain oriental beliefs in his own outlook on life.

To finance himself after leaving college in 1898 Holst took up the trombone in a more serious way. He joined the Carl Rosa Opera Company as principal trombone and rehearsal pianist, and later did some touring with the Scottish Orchestra. In London he occasionally worked in the White Viennese Band. Members of the Band had to dress in a white and gold uniform and were under strict orders to put on Austrian accents for the benefit of the audience!

In 1901 he and Isobel were married and set up home in a couple of furnished rooms above a shop in Shepherds Bush. They could not afford a honeymoon, but in 1903 with the help of a legacy from his father's estate, Holst and Isobel decided to take a holiday in Germany. They stayed with Holst's second cousin, Mathias, in Berlin and were introduced to the concert life of the city and to a large circle of musicians and music lovers. Holst was amazed by the passion Germans had for new music.

When he returned to England Holst gave up his trombone-playing career and decided to turn his attentions to serious work as a composer. In any case, life as a touring musician had been tiring and had left him no time for composing. Although it was better

education should be available to everybody irrespective of income, Holst began teaching evening classes in 1907 at Morley College – an adult education centre for working-class people. Among Holst's students were cab-drivers, tram conductors, policemen, ladies' maids and even a cricket bat maker! The Morley College orchestra began life with two violins, one flute, three clarinets, all at the sharp pitch, a cornet and a piano. But before long they had improved their resources and standards enough to be able to give the first performance since 1697 of Purcell's masque, *The Fairy Queen.*

Teaching had brought employment, enjoyment and relative prosperity into Holst's life. Just after their daughter Imogen was born in 1907 the Holsts could afford to rent an elegant terraced house in Barnes, overlooking the river, and they moved there in 1908. Now Holst's only problem was that such a punishing teaching schedule left very little time for composition. Only on Sundays and during the school holidays could he manage to escape to the large airy music room at the top of the house where he could work in perfect peace. But he rarely complained about his teaching responsibilities and often declared that writing music for his pupils to sing meant a great deal to him.

A luke-warm reception

Out of school Holst's works fared less well. Few people were prepared to put money into new music at the time and Holst frequently became discouraged. The first piece to be composed in his new music room was inspired by Sanskrit literature – the opera *Savitri,* based on the old legends of the Mahabharata. Although it was the first chamber opera to be composed in England since Purcell's day it did not have a performance until eight years later. Another 'Indian' work – *The Cloud Messenger* was given a performance in 1913, but it was poorly received. In the spring of 1913, the sponsor of the concert where *The Cloud Messenger* was performed, the composer Balfour Gardiner, rescued Holst from his misery with the invitation to a holiday in Spain with his friends, the brothers Arnold and Clifford Bax. On this holiday he was to find the enthusiasm to write a large orchestral work – *The Planets* – which was to become his best known work.

Music at Thaxted

From 1913 the Essex town of Thaxted became the scene of family life for the Holsts. When not at work composing, Holst spent his time taking long walks, or music making at the local church. He spent much effort on the little choir, which was already rather good at plainchant and which, with encouragement from Holst, soon learnt to give passable performances of music by Byrd and other 16th-century English composers. One day it occurred to Holst that it would be a splendid idea to import the Morley and St Paul's Choirs to Thaxted for an informal festival of early music. The first Festival was arranged for Whitsun 1916, and was a huge success.

Everyone who took part in or attended the

Before he became established as a composer, Holst became music master at St Paul's Girls' School, Hammersmith, a post which he held until the end of his life. In the sketch above he is shown conducting a section of the school orchestra. Teaching brought relative prosperity to Holst and in 1908 the family moved to No 10, The Terrace, Barnes (left – their house second from right).

Holst was found unfit for combat but, in 1918, was sent to Salonika (shown in the postcard above, which he sent to his wife) as music master for the YMCA's army education scheme

The sketch above (featuring Holst, batted and conducting), captures the busy atmosphere of amateur music-making at the Whitsun Festivals. Holst initiated annual festivals of music at the Essex village of Thaxted, where he lived after 1914. Later, these were held in St Albans, Canterbury and Chichester.

Thaxted Festival felt it was worth repeating, and so, for the following two years, the forces regathered to sing at Whitsuntide. Holst wrote music especially for the Thaxted combined choir and one of the pieces is the now famous carol *This have I done for my true love*.

There was no festival in 1919 as Holst was posted abroad. Although not fit for combat himself, he was sent to do educational work among the troops who were about to be demobbed. In the autumn of 1918 he was posted to Constantinople and Salonika as Musical organizer for the YMCA army education scheme.

Holst returned home to England in the summer of 1919 and went back to his accustomed routine of teaching all week and composing on Sundays. Public interest in his music was now stirring and there were more opportunities for performances of his works. In March 1920 he had a memorable performance of his choral work *Hymn of Jesus* and a few months later came the first complete public performance under his own baton of *The Planets*.

It did not take him long to discover the disadvantages of fame. He was an unworldly man with no idea how to handle either the press or admirers and was often accused of looking sullen when taking a bow. His chief objection to all the attention was the potential danger he felt it represented to his art. He wrote to his friend Clifford Bax, 'Some day I expect you will agree with me that it's a great thing to be a failure. If nobody likes your work you have to go on for the sake of the work. And you are in no danger of letting the public make you repeat yourself. Every artist ought to pray that he may not be a success.'

During the early years of the 1920s up to 1923, Holst's popularity was at its peak. Performances of his work conducted by himself were invariably sold out. Apart from his performing engagements, his teaching commitments had also increased. He was professor at the Royal College of Music and was appointed to the staff of University College Reading. It was at Reading in February 1923 while conducting the student orchestra that an accident occurred which was to result in serious illness. He fell backwards off the podium and was concussed. He appeared to recover very quickly and his doctor allowed him to go ahead with plans to travel to America on a lecturing tour. However, not long after his return to England he began to suffer from sleeplessness and pains in the head which were probably the delayed effects of the concussion.

A complete rest was prescribed, so he cancelled all engagements for 1924 and retired to Thaxted, where, in the words of a letter he wrote to a friend he felt he led 'the combined lives of Real Composer and Tame Cat!'

Return to London
At the beginning of 1925 Holst was allowed back to London life and a limited resumption of his teaching activities. Outwardly he appeared in good health, but it was to be a long while before he could tolerate traffic noise or crowds. Although he was only 50

years old he seemed older – his hair was almost completely white, and he had lost the usual spring in his step. Craftily, though, he used his discomfort to his best advantage – as an excuse to miss the social functions which he found tedious.

One benefit, though, was that he found more time to enjoy the company of close friends. Ralph Vaughan Williams, still his closest friend, was a constant companion although musically they seemed to be growing apart.

Another friend was the novelist Thomas Hardy, whose novels and poetry had appealed to Holst in his student days. In the 1920s, after setting some of Hardy's poems as songs, Holst sent the works to the poet. Hardy received them warmly and over the ensuing years their friendship grew. Hardy was to provide Holst with the subject of his orchestral work, *Egdon Heath.* Holst felt the work grew out of a sentence in Hardy's novel *The Return of the Native.* In it the heath is described as 'A place perfectly accordant with Man's nature – neither ghastly, hateful nor ugly; neither commonplace, unmeaning nor tame, but like Man, slighted and enduring, and, withal, singularly colossal and mysterious in its swarthy monotony.'

The work was performed in Cheltenham Town Hall where it was well-received, but the first London performance was disastrous. Holst, however, was not discouraged, for although his popularity had declined since its peak in 1923, he knew he was producing better music than ever.

One of Holst's most important works after the The Planets *was* Egdon Heath, *which he dedicated to Thomas Hardy (left). According to Holst (shown above in the last photograph taken of him),* Egdon Heath *grew out of a sentence in Hardy's novel* The Return of the Native *and he personally considered it his best piece of music.*

During the next five years he was very productive. Works from these years include the opera *The Wandering Scholar,* the *Double Concerto* for two violins, the *Choral Fantasia,* written for the three Choir Festival, *Hammersmith,* a tone poem full of the sounds and sights of riverside London, and the *Lyric Movement* for viola and small orchestra. They all add up to what is possibly the finest testimony to creativity that he could have had in his last years.

In 1932 Holst spent six months enjoying the great honour of being guest lecturer at Harvard University. This gave him the opportunity to conduct highly successful performances of his music with the Boston Symphony Orchestra. Unfortunately, just before leaving Harvard for a tour of Canada he fell ill with a stomach complaint caused either by a duodenal or gastric ulcer. He had to spend several weeks convalescing but was well enough to attend a concert of his work given as a tribute by the University.

Back in England Holst seemed to be making a full recovery, but in early 1933 he suffered a relapse and from then on spent most of his time in and out of hospitals. Throughout 1934, the last year of his life, despite constant pain, he managed to keep cheerful and, although with great difficulty, managed to go on writing music until the end.

He died on 25 May 1934, and at the request of one of his friends, Bishop Bell, his ashes were buried in the north aisle of Chichester Cathedral. As a tribute to him the choir sang his lovely Thaxted carol, 'This have I done for my true love.'

'Votes for Women'

Holst's ancestral homeland, Sweden, was among the first European countries to enfranchize its womenfolk. In Britain, only a long struggle earned women the vote and their rightful social status.

From time immemorial to the late 19th century, most women had little or no say in the society in which they lived, and none had the right to vote. But with the arrival of industrialization large numbers of working women were brought together for the first time (left), marking the beginning of their development as a social force.

Holman Hunt's Awakening Conscience *(right) says much about the prevailing 19th-century attitudes to women – attitudes which long delayed women's suffrage. Full of symbolism, the picture preaches a visual sermon on the morality of the man and mistress relationship, via the woman's awakening to the dangers and vulnerability of her position. The picture thus exposes the hypocrisy of a society which condemns such a woman to ruin and shame while her seducer escapes without reproach.*

A cartoon (right) in the magazine Punch *speculated, in 1852, on the social repercussions of English women adopting the American 'habit' of bloomers. Its tone is derisive, and for many years derision was the only weapon men needed to quash women's emancipation.*

Women's rights – social equality and the right to vote (suffrage) – were advocated well over 2000 years ago by the Greek philosopher Plato. But women the world over had a long wait, in many cases until the early years of the 20th century, to find a place in society on an equal par with men. Even when the right to vote was granted it was most often after a long struggle on their part – women's right to vote was won rather than freely given. And nowhere was the battle for women's rights harder or longer fought than in Britain, where the suffragette movement campaigned for 25 years before seeing their dream of votes for all women realized.

The struggle for votes was generally just part of a wider movement towards the re-appraisal of women's place in society. And this movement had its roots at least 100 years deep in history.

When Mary Wollstonecraft wrote *The Vindication of the Rights of Woman*, in 1792, she was mocked by Horace Walpole (novelist, M.P. and arbiter of public taste) as a 'hyena in petticoats'. There were then a great many things women lacked besides the vote: they could not receive a University education or become doctors; until 1870, a married woman could not own property; nor did she have the right to divorce her husband in the event of his adultery. These were more pressing injustices than the lack of a vote. After all, only two out of three men had the vote themselves.

In Britain the issue of votes for women was first

seriously proposed by the philosopher John Stuart Mill in the 1860s, but elsewhere women were making practical strides. In America, they were attracted to the campaign to abolish slavery, and to the powerful temperance movement. In Wyoming, on the American frontier, women were given the vote as equals; and in Sweden, women were enfranchized for Municipal elections in 1862.

Working women and the oldest profession

On the whole, women's employment opportunities, an important key to greater equality, remained poor throughout the 19th century. In the countryside, unmarried women could make a little extra money by spinning at home (hence the term 'spinster') but many of those who married had to work in the fields all day as well as keeping house, just to keep the family above the poverty line. The work and the strain of child-bearing sent many to a premature grave.

In the towns, too, things were bad. Only the lucky few could find factory jobs, working for a pittance as sweated labour. Trapped between few jobs and poor wages, many women turned to prostitution.

This was a dangerous occupation, with a great risk of contracting venereal disease. On the other hand, Bernard Shaw's play of the 1890s, *Mrs Warren's Profession,* was undoubtedly correct in asserting that working class girls were better off working as prostitutes than in the white-lead factories where many died from phosphorous poisoning.

Absurd views about sex prevailed. For example, in 1870 American medical science suggested that men should not make love to their wives more than once a month. Indulgence was thought to be both sinful and harmful. Besides, contraceptives were primitive (and thought to be immoral), the birth rate was often more than the mother's health could stand and more than the father's wage could support. As a result, the demand for prostitutes was high.

It has been estimated that one in ten Americans was afflicted with venereal disease at the turn of the century. The situation was not much better in Britain. The government sought to reduce the problem by introducing the Contagious Diseases Act, which allowed for the compulsory medical inspection of women suspected of being prostitutes. Women displayed remarkable solidarity in opposing this Act. Thousands joined Josephine Butler's campaign which secured its repeal after a 15-year struggle. This victory showed women that they could win concessions from a male-dominated world. But though the campaign succeeded, the double standard remained: the prostitute was a social outcast, her clients were not.

This exemplifies the entrenched inequality of the sexes against which the suffragettes had to fight. Examples of male attitudes make amusing reading today. One eminent doctor suggested in *The London Times* that half the female population went mad as a result of the menopause, and he regarded the Suffragette Movement as proof of it: 'There are no good women, but only women who have lived under the influence of good men.' An early criminologist, Lombroso, went further and stated, 'even the normal woman is a half-criminaloid being'.

However, the women's cause was not helped by some of the equally extreme statements of its leaders. One suffragette wrote '. . . sterilization is a higher form of human achievement than reproduction.' Such expressions left the movement open

to accusations of lesbianism and unnaturalness.

In America, some preoccupations of the women's movement worked against it. It was staunchly in favour of the temperence movement and advocated the prohibition of alcohol. Many felt that 'votes for women' was synonymous with prohibition for men.

Many men were satisfied with the prevailing state of affairs. Enfranchizing women did not promise any improvement. Nevertheless, important inroads were being made on their complacency. An attack on the existing structure of marriage was beginning. Ibsen's play, *The Doll's House,* poured scorn on the hypocrisy of an outwardly happy marriage where the husband was head of the household, and the woman's place was in the home. In *Dance of Death* (1901), August Strindberg portrayed the misery of an unhappy marriage. E. M. Forster described, in *The Longest Journey* (1907), a man whose soul is destroyed by marriage.

Many marriages were unhappy, of course, and extremely difficult to dissolve. In England, for example, adultery by the husband was only grounds for divorce when accompanied by cruelty. The problem was worst for the middle classes. The upper classes could manage financially, if not socially, with the cost of ending a marriage; many of the urban

The introduction of typewriters to offices and the employment of thousands of young, literate women to operate them, originally helped many to find social and financial independence, as well as entry into the previously closed world of commerce.

working classes did not bother with a formal wedding ceremony, so there was no need for a formal divorce if the relationship soured. The movement for easier divorce, advocated as much by men as by women, achieved early success in America and France.

H. G. Wells' *Ann Veronica* told of the story of a young woman's struggle for independence, equality with men, and sexual freedom. The old attitudes about sex had at last come into question. The Victorian ethos found it desirable that a respectable woman knew nothing about sex; she was certainly not supposed to enjoy it. But the turn of the century brought new ideas. Havelock Ellis, the outspoken psychologist, wrote that women had erotic feelings of their own. Freud's psychological work gradually aroused public interest. Thus, easier divorce, a growing awareness of birth control and freedom from repressive sexual guilt, all added up to women's greater independence.

Trailblazers

The success of individual Victorian women in making a name for themselves also paved the way for later success. Florence Nightingale was one such woman. By organizing hospitals in the Crimea during the war of 1854–56, and later by becoming an adviser to the government on nursing, she made a significant step forward for women.

Amantine Dupin under her pen-name George Sand gained fame for her novels. Sarah Bernhardt

Mrs Emmeline Pankhurst (below), founder of the Women's Social and Political Union, fought militantly for women's right to vote. She undoubtedly captured attention though her violent enterprises jeopardized wider public support.

attracted great fame as an actress, and Elizabeth Garratt Anderson fought a long but successful battle to be admitted by Edinburgh University to study medicine. She qualified in 1865.

Such notable individuals showed what was possible, but the grass roots of the suffragette movement grew as a result of growing job opportunities for middle-class women. The 1871 Education Act created many jobs for women, as teachers.

High standards of respectablity were demanded of women teachers. The expectation was for them to be unmarried and to behave as though they had taken vows of poverty, chastity and obedience. Some teacher training colleges in the 1880s refused to install baths on the grounds that it would be unwise to give the teachers a standard of living they would never again be able to afford. Nevertheless, the large number of women employed in teaching played an important part, later on, in the fight to gain the vote.

The fundamental change came, however, with the expansion of office work. The advent of the

H. H. Asquith (below), took the post of Prime Minister in 1908, with a strong personal antipathy to the Women's Movement. He held power for eight years, and though he gradually accepted women's suffrage as inevitable, he staved it off for a decade.

typewriter drew thousands of women into offices. The introduction of the telephone also created a demand for switchboard operators. Office work in the 20th century replaced domestic service as the main employer of women. More jobs, and the new nature of those jobs, meant more independence.

In the home, the advent of tinned food, electric light, floor sweepers and soap flakes all lessened the drudgery of housework. And so at last, social and economic changes over a long period of time had created an environment in which the fight for the vote stood a reasonable chance of success.

Catching the public eye

The birthplace of the movement was the radical centre of Britain – Manchester. In 1903, a 45-year-old widow named Emmeline Pankhurst formed the Women's Social and Political Union (WSPU). 'Social' did not signify a programme of tea-parties, but referred to Pankhurst's socialism: the WSPU was allied to the Independent Labour Party.

The WSPU realized that polite lobbying of MPs was useless. Public opinion had first to be aroused. In October 1905, Emmeline Pankhurst, her eldest daughter Christabel and Annie Kenny were charged with attempting to cause a disturbance at a political meeting. They chose to be imprisoned rather than pay a small fine. For the first time, the public and press took notice.

At the general election of January 1906 the Liberal Party won a landslide victory. Believing the Liberals would be more sympathetic to the cause of the WSPU, the Pankhursts moved to London. They organized a procession from the statue of Queen Boudicca on Westminster Bridge to 10 Downing Street for the benefit of Prime Minister Sir Henry

The first instances of suffragette violence sparked off no more than the predictable laughter, as a postcard of 1908 shows (top left). When the women began to reap much worse violence in return at the hands of the authorities, they attracted far more sympathy for their cause. The government's clumsy methods – force feeding, and the cat-and-mouse release and re-arrest act – proved self-defeating. Suffragette campaigners were not slow to exploit their suffering, in pamphlets and electioneering posters (left).

In 1914, a suffragette protester slashed a canvas in the National Gallery. She chose Velazquez' Rokeby Venus (left), a priceless art treasure but one which epitomizes the age-old masculine view of women – simply objects of desire.

Campbell-Bannerman. Campbell-Bannerman was sympathetic, but the Cabinet was divided on the issue. The main opposition centred on Chancellor Herbert Asquith.

Then came heartening news from overseas. In 1905 Norway gave women the vote. In 1907 Finland followed suit. Ellen Kay, a Swedish social reformer received a favourable response to her calls for state maternity benefits – benefits explicitly extended to unmarried mothers. Such successes did a lot to sway British public opinion. The strength of the suffragette movement came not with more and more activists and demonstrations, but in the groundswell of supporters.

Setbacks and schisms
The movement suffered a serious setback in 1908. Campbell-Bannerman resigned on grounds of ill-health and died almost immediately. Asquith took his place. However, he was well aware that the WSPU would pose a threat to the prestige and electoral position of his Government if the question was ignored. The fact remained that women could not be given the vote without affecting the political situation. Clearly extended suffrage might have to include all the voteless men as well.

The Conservative Party opposed the idea since so many poor people would be enfranchized. The Liberals also feared it would encourage the growth of the Labour Party. On the other hand, they were opposed to the Conservative idea of extending the vote only to a few property-owning women.

The WSPU itself, despite its professed socialism, was quite prepared to gain votes on the lines suggested by the Conservatives, feeling that votes for all women would follow, once the principles had been established. Policy and tactics within the WSPU were dominated by the Pankhurst family, though the political issue split even them. A younger daughter, Sylvia, remained convinced that the WSPU should remain a socialist, not just a feminist, movement.

In the summer of 1908, the WSPU held a series of impressive demonstrations. Emmeline and Christabel Pankhurst were arrested along with another leader, Mrs Drummond, in Trafalgar Square, and again chose to be imprisoned rather than bound over. In Bristol, one suffragette tried to attack Home Secretary Winston Churchill with a dog-whip, another hid inside the organ at the Albert Hall hoping to leap out during Asquith's speech. Another locked herself into Lloyd George's car and gave the Chancellor a long lecture before he was able to escape.

Prisoners and martyrs

Suffragettes became more of an embarrassment to the authorities when imprisoned campaigners started hunger strikes. Initially, the government released them rather than offend public opinion by letting women starve. But this course seemed too weak. Force-feeding the women prisoners was suggested as the only solution. Churchill was cautious. He wanted to retain the support of Irish MPs, some of whom had experienced such handling as political prisoners of the 1880s. No matter how well supervized, force-feeding was a terrible business: a tube forced up the nostrils by one doctor and food poured down it by another. At least one prisoner was driven insane by the process.

The government line softened. Asquith had enough problems in facing two elections in 1910. During the run up to the December election, he promised to introduce a bill to extend male franchise, with an amendment to include women as well. In 1911, the WSPU called off its campaign of violence and looked forward to the Liberals fulfilling their promise. But Asquith seemed to be wavering again. And radicals in the WSPU bridled at the thought of votes for women passing into law as an afterthought. Emmeline Pankhurst returned from a tour of America and incited a large meeting of women in Parliament Square to go out and smash windows in protest. A week later, the idea was put into effect. In the early hours of 1 March 1912 around 200 women smashed most of the shop windows in London's Piccadilly, Regent Street and Oxford Street. Emmeline Pankhurst herself went to Downing Street to break Asquith's. Most of the women were arrested. Christabel Pankhurst, her mother in prison, fled to Paris.

In April 1912, the Commons rejected the Bill to extend franchise. The window smashing episode had lost vital support. More to the point, however, the Irish MPs had changed their mind and opposed the Bill, since they felt it would cost so much parliamentary time as to jeopardize Home Rule for Ireland.

The main body of support for the women's cause inside Parliament came from the Labour Party. One Labour member, George Lansbury even resigned his seat and stood for re-election as a WSPU candidate. Politically, he had cut his own throat: he failed.

After Lansbury's failure, many in the WSPU began to feel that alliance with the Conservative party might at least win them a limited extension of the vote to women property-owners. This feeling grew when Asquith withdrew a second bill to enfranchize all men (with women included in an amendment) on a technicality. In her prison cell, Emmeline Pankhurst felt betrayed.

In early 1913 the suffragettes turned to violence more stridently. They burnt a few country railway stations; put a bomb into a house being built for Lloyd George; mutilated the greens of golf clubs with acid; poured acid into post boxes; and slashed the Rokeby Venus in the National Gallery. Fortunately, no-one was killed as a result of their actions, or the movement could have been irrevocably destroyed.

Such militancy led to further arrests and, in turn, more hunger strikes. The Government dealt with the

This picture – originally captioned 'The Amazons-of-the-Vote are expelled from the Palace of Westminster' (right) – was published in the Italian press in 1906. Europe watched, with vested interest, the evolution of women's suffrage in Britain.

Protest turned to tragedy at the 1913 Derby when suffragette Emily Davidson threw herself in front of the galloping field and was trampled to death by the King's horse, Anmer (right). She was looked upon by her fellow suffragettes as a heroine and a martyr.

The heroic efforts of women who took over the jobs of men during World War I, particularly in the munitions factories (right), proved once and for all their equality and natural right to the vote. During the war years virtually all suffragette protest stopped, which perhaps helped smooth the path to suffrage when it finally came in 1918.

embarrassment by releasing hunger strikers and rearresting them when they had recovered their strength: the law was nicknamed the 'Cat and Mouse Act'. Emmeline Pankhurst was constantly rearrested after release: she had been reduced by her efforts to such a state of weakness that she had to be released after only a day or two's hunger strike. She also suffered from a gastric complaint which worsened her health. The authorities were terrified in case she died in custody. Her death would fuel the fury of the women's movement without robbing it of a leader: it could be run from the safety of Paris by Christabel.

However, the suffragettes got their martyr in the summer of 1913. Emily Davidson – one of the first suffragettes to be arrested, for trying to set fire to a post box – had almost died for the cause while on hunger strike in Manchester. She had barricaded herself into her cell and been half drowned by warders who directed hose jets through the bars of her cell. On 4 June, Emily took a train to Epsom for the Derby – the most popular horse race in the sporting calendar. At Tattenham Corner she slipped under the railings and threw herself in front of a group of racing horses. She felled – almost certainly by chance – King George V's horse, Anmer, and was trampled to death.

Perhaps she did not expect to die: among her possessions the police found half a ticket, for the return train journey. Emmeline Pankhurst was rearrested when she attempted to attend the funeral, but despite her absence it was a great suffragette demonstration. The bands played solemn music by Chopin and Handel as the funeral cortege made its way from Victoria to Kings Cross railway station. The coffin, draped in the purple, green and white colours of the suffragettes, was put aboard the train, for burial at the Davidson's home in Northumberland. At a service at St George's, Hanover Square, the suffragettes sang the hymn *Fight the Good Fight*.

Briefly the women's movement was united by Emily's sacrifice. But while Emmeline and Christabel Pankhurst moved progressively to the political right, Sylvia Pankhurst was preaching socialism in the East End of London. Mother and elder sister felt that such idealism detracted from the movement and deterred many of the more middle class suffragettes who contributed to the movement's funds. Sylvia was therefore expelled from the WSPU by her mother. But when, in June 1914, Asquith at last agreed to receive a suffragette delegation, the invitation was extended to Sylvia Pankhurst's East London Federation for Women's Suffrage, not the WSPU. Asquith, who was gradually accepting the inevitability of women's suffrage, had decided to

Members of the Women's Social and Political Union (WSPU) gather round a portrait of Christabel Pankhurst, daughter of Emmeline and heiress apparent to the WSPU leadership.

court popularity with working class women, in the hope they would vote Liberal, not Labour. The Prime Minister did not commit himself: he simply succeeded in giving the impression that the Government would shortly introduce a Bill for Universal Suffrage.

Women at war

Then, world events overtook both women and Government. Almost out of the blue, Britain was at war with Germany. World War 1 had begun.

The women's movement plunged into the war effort. The WSPU leadership were prominent in patriotic activity and ready to shelve the vote. No doubt they felt, like everyone else, that the war would be a short interlude, 'over by Christmas'.

In the event, the war delayed votes for women for four long years. But at the end of it, in 1918, six million women were enfranchised. It has been suggested that women received the vote because of their contribution to the war effort. But their war efforts only added the finishing touches. Women were admired for working in the munitions industries, running the risk of being blown to pieces. But the war was not the first time women had contributed to industry and they had worked in far worse conditions before the war.

When Parliament again considered the vote for women in 1918, so many men had been killed in the trenches that universal suffrage would have meant women voters outnumbering men. It was therefore suggested that all men should have the vote at 21, but women should not receive it until they were 30. Many of the leaders of the movement stood as candidates in the 1918 election, but only one woman MP was returned to Parliament: Countess Makievicz was elected as Sinn Fein member for South Dublin by electors with causes other than feminism on their minds. Women did not vote to see women elected: they tended to fall in line with their husbands: people went on voting according to their class.

The 30-year age limit remained in force till 1928 when complete equality was achieved. Emmeline Pankhurst died on 4 June 1928, just as Royal Assent was given to the Act.

No doubt the suffragettes would have been disappointed to see the poor representation of women in government, commerce and industry today. But their fight for votes did demonstrate to women that this and similar goals could be achieved in a male dominated society. Gradually, greater (though not complete) equality with men has been achieved. Undoubtedly these advances owe much to the efforts of the suffragettes and their brave forerunners.

Maurice Ravel
1875–1937

Maurice Ravel, the impeccable, cultivated gourmet of the Parisian musical scene, helped lead French music forward into the 20th century with his smooth, precise but strikingly original compositions.

Maurice Ravel (below), on the quayside in front of the house where he was born in the French Basque town of Ciboure. All his life Ravel felt deeply drawn to the Basque and Spanish heritage of his mother, a Basque, born in the Pyrenees (right), who had spent much of her childhood in Spain.

Brought up in Paris and living nearly all his life in France, Maurice Ravel was claimed by the French wholeheartedly, and completely, as their own. But the composer himself felt his roots lay elsewhere, in the homeland of his parents.

Ravel's father's family had for many generations lived in the French Haute-Savoie, near the Swiss border, and his father Pierre-Joseph Ravel had actually been born in Switzerland. His mother Marie Deluarte, however, was Basque, from the Pyrenees, and had spent much of her childhood in Madrid. It was this Basque and Spanish heritage to which the adult Ravel felt drawn so strongly.

Indeed, Pierre-Joseph and Marie first met in Aranjuez in Spain, although they were actually married in Paris in April 1873, and Maurice, their first child, was born in Basque country, in Ciboure, on 7 March 1875. Three months later, however, the family moved permanently to Paris where Pierre-Joseph had found employment as an engineer. They settled in a small house in Montmartre where their second and last child, Edouard, was born in 1878.

The family was an unusually close one, and Maurice remained devoted to them all his life. He was closest to his mother, and his relationship with her was probably the single most important emotional attachment in his life. His adoration was amply reciprocated. Through his mother Ravel inherited a deep love of the Basque country and Spanish music and, perhaps also, the rigorous repression of outward emotions that was to characterize the mature man. This trait he proudly told friends was directly attributable to his Basque descent, for it is a Basque tradition to feel deeply but show no one.

Ravel's aptitude for music was noticed early by his father, and by the time he was seven his parents had found him his first piano teacher. Four years later, as the boy's proficiency increased, a harmony teacher was also procured. Young Maurice had a happy and carefree attitude toward life and was not a particularly diligent pupil. He was never forced by his parents to practise, but still managed to make reasonable progress. By the age of 12, he was already

trying his hand at composition, writing pieces his tutor Charles-René later described as 'works of real interest, already indicating . . . an impeccable, elevated style'.

At this time, Ravel had long hair and looked like a 'Florentine page'. In 1888, he met a Spanish boy with equally long hair, Ricardo Viñes, and the two boys were to become firm friends. Ricardo also played the piano and he and Maurice would often play music together while their mothers talked in Spanish.

Both boys passed the entrance exam to the Paris Conservatoire of Music on the same day in November 1889. They spent many illicit hours at the piano together, discovering much music outside of the Conservatoire's strict curriculum. Such tendencies in the two boys were only encouraged by

EXPOSITION UNIVERSELLE — LE PHONOGRAPHE

The Edison phonograph (left) was one of the many inventions displayed at the Paris International Exposition of 1889. Although Ravel must have followed the early development of sound recording in the last decades of the 19th century it was only in the late 1920s that he first committed his music to disc. He was in no doubt about the opportunities afforded by the gramophone, realizing that recording would 'constitute a real document for posterity to consult . . .'

Ravel met Ricardo Viñes (above, left), when they were both young boys in 1888. Ricardo was also a pianist and in 1889 both Ravel and Viñes were admitted to the Paris Conservatoire of Music. Both found music outside the Conservatoire's strict curriculum more to their liking, and together explored new avenues in music as well as other contemporary arts.

the exotic music from all round the world show-cased at the Paris Universal Exhibition. Their explorations were not restricted to music though, and they made contact with many works of contemporary Parisian artists and writers such as Baudelaire, Mallarmé and Verlaine.

In 1893, the two young musicians were taken to meet Emmanuel Chabrier, a highly original French composer and pianist. The meeting made a profound impression on Ravel, and later that year he composed *Sérénade grotesque* in Chabrier's style. The same year, Ravel's father introduced him to another French composer whose influence was to be even more potent, the eccentric Erik Satie. Satie at this time was a penniless and largely self-taught 27 year-old playing piano at the café *Chat Noir* in Montmartre. They must have made an odd pair, Satie a bizarre mixture of frock-coat, pince-nez, goatee beard and general tattiness, while Ravel even at this stage was exhibiting the extreme dandyism of dress which was to remain with him all his life. Both were small men. Indeed Ravel, even when fully grown, was hardly more than five feet. Although his body was well-proportioned, his head was a little too large for its frame; a situation Ravel was not slow to try to compensate for by growing various luxurious

stylings of facial hair before yielding to fate and remaining clean-shaven for most of his adult life.

Satie was to have an important shaping influence on Ravel, just as he did on so many French composers during his lifetime, right up to his death in 1925. For the young Ravel, his importance lay in his ability to point the way towards a new and exotic simplicity based on studies of the old Greek modes, and in strikingly unresolved harmonic progressions.

All this found its place in Ravel's music in the next few years, just as the literature he avidly devoured, that of the French Symbolists and Decadents who were his contemporaries, was to provide him with texts for his songs for years to come. In this, the composer's very real concern to keep abreast of his own age is very much in evidence.

The young composer spent six years at the Conservatoire absorbing as much as he deemed necessary from his academic mentors, while continuing to explore the music of such mavericks as Chabrier and Satie in his free time. The inevitable result was that he became lax, inattentive and irregular in his attendance. He was bored, and being a talented youth indulged by his parents, he did not hesitate to show it. Predictably enough, in 1895 he was dismissed from his harmony and piano classes;

As a young composer Maurice Ravel (right) spent six years as a student at the Paris Conservatoire, where he absorbed in a selective way what he felt was necessary to his musical development. At the same time he continued to explore the music of his contemporaries in his determination to keep abreast of his own age.

not that this was the last he was to hear of them, or they of him, for that matter.

First successes

By 1897 the erstwhile student was feeling sufficiently contrite to approach the Conservatoire for more tutoring. He was accepted into the advanced composition class given by the composer Gabriel Fauré. This, plus private study with André Gédalge, gave Ravel the finishing touches he deemed necessary for his compositional technique. An indication of his continuing interest in the exotic was the unfinished opera on the subject of Scheherazade, of which only the overture was ever performed. At the première of this overture, Ravel remained unmoved at the furore the work caused. A letter to his friend Florent Schmitt reveals a deep irony.

'Schéhérazade' was violently whistled at . . . D'Indy, whose attitude toward me was perfect, exulted over the fact that the public could still get excited over anything. As far as I could judge from the podium, I was satisfied with the orchestra.

This concert placed Ravel firmly in the camp of the new composers, of whom Debussy was the acknowledged leader. The critics were to remain hostile for years to come, looking in vain for what they considered would be the saving grace of a Germanic influence.

Ravel's next composition made him famous, although it did not make him rich, or alter his student status. It was the *Pavane pour une Infante défunte.* The title and the stately dance rhythm showed the composer's love of all things antique and Spanish, with its conjuring of a princess from another age.

The Menuet antique *for piano (title page below), the first of Ravel's compositions to be published, was dedicated to his friend Ricardo Viñes.*

Ravel later tired of the piece, especially after hearing performances of it which caused him to exclaim, 'It is the princess who is dead, not the Pavane!'

The newly-successful composer entered the next century as a man secure in his opinions, possessed of a ready wit and discerning taste, still living with his parents but with a wide circle of friends in Parisian society. Yet, remarkably, he was still a student at the Conservatoire, and in 1900 failed even to qualify for the final round of the Prix de Rome, the Conservatoire's highest honour. The following year was even worse: he failed a compulsory exam for fugue writing and so was expelled from Fauré's class as a matter of course.

This setback left no public impression. He composed his first pianistic masterpiece, *Jeux d'Eau,* in the same year (he dedicated it to Fauré, with whom he had a strong friendship despite his expulsion), and in the next couple of years continued to write startling new works. And in his private life he was as independent as ever. Asked by a rich music-lover to play piano duets with him, Ravel replied, 'as long as we play no Beethoven, no Schumann, no Wagner or any other romantic music . . . in fact, as long as we play only Mozart.'

Chat-Noir — La première des projections d'ombres de « L'Epopée » dessinée par Caran d'Ache (1886)

In 1893 Ravel met the eccentric French composer Erik Satie, whose influence on him was to be profound. Through him Ravel was introduced to the much-celebrated café society of Montmartre. Together they frequented the famous Chat Noir *(above) which was also the haunt of many other artistic figures such as Emile Zola (at the centre table).*

From 1898 to 1903 Ravel studied composition under the composer Gabriel Fauré (right). Although thirty years Ravel's senior, a close friendship developed between the two.

The 'Apaches'

As the early years of the century went by, Ravel's life was increasingly devoted to the artistic community which met regularly at painter Paul Sordes' house. Within a short space of time his keen intelligence and his refusal to become embroiled in petty disputes had made him the unofficial central figure of the group which in 1903, the year he returned to the Conservatoire, picked up the nickname of 'the Apaches'. This had come about through the group returning en masse from a concert, dressed outrageously (as was so often the custom for Parisian intellectuals, and especially these aesthetes) and arguing very loudly among themselves as to the relative merits of what they had just heard. A poor newspaper boy selling his wares took fright at their approach, turning and running off bellowing 'beware the Apaches!' to amazed bystanders. The group were so amused by the incident that they adopted this as their name.

It was the Apaches who in these years attended the première of Debussy's *Pelleas and Melisande,* indulged in countless soirées together, participated in the authorship row between Debussy and Ravel over a harmonic and rhythmic device both had used, and finally, in 1905, helped to bring 'l'affaire Ravel' to boiling point.

The scandal came about through Ravel's dogged pursuit of the Prix de Rome, which by this time had become more a point of honour than anything else, for the composer was already recognized in the larger world. 1905 was the last year Ravel would be eligible, for when he turned 31 the following March, he would be barred from the competition. And in 1905, the judges, headed by arch-conservative Théodore Dubois, eliminated Ravel before even the finals. Such shoddy treatment was inexcusable, and the outcry soon reverberated beyond the small circle of the Apaches and Ravel's few supporters in the establishment such as Fauré and Massenet. It spilled over into the daily papers, moving even the famed novelist Romain Rolland to write a letter of protest to the Académie des Beaux-Arts. The furore only died down with the resignation of Conservatoire Director Dubois, and the appointment of Fauré in his place.

Ravel's reaction to all this public venting of spleen was typical. He refused to comment at any stage of the scandal, and, at its conclusion, accepted an invitation to go on a long cruise of Europe's rivers with two close friends. Any private relief he might have felt was concealed even from his most intimate friends. Perhaps Rolland's words had been enough,

Ravel entered the Prix de Rome not as a student, but as a composer who has already passed his examinations. I am astonished at the composers who dared judge him. Who will judge them in their turn?

Ravel saw little change in his life in the next three years. He continued to live at his parents' home in Paris, and earned little or no money from his composing. Only his father's death, after a lingering illness in 1908, disturbed this pattern. Though nothing like the blow his mother's death would be ten years later, the loss was still keenly felt, and the family turned in upon itself for support. Ravel, as usual, never mentioned it to anyone. Only the deepening emotional commitment in his works gave a clue to what he felt at this time.

A costume designed by Leon Bakst for the 1912 Ballets Russes production of Daphnis and Chloé (above). Ravel was commissioned by the director of the Ballets Russes, Sergei Diaghilev, to write the music for the ballet.

The Ballets Russes

The next event to impinge on his ordered and cultured existence was the arrival of Sergei Diaghilev's Ballets Russes in Paris. The troupe's sensational debut in 1909 with Mussorgsky's *Boris Godunov* had ensured that the group, then operating as both a ballet and opera company, would take Paris by storm. And of course Ravel and his group, as well as people such as the young Jean Cocteau, Picasso, Debussy and others were quickly drawn into Diaghilev's schemes and productions. But it was Diaghilev himself who introduced the then-unknown Igor Stravinsky into this impressive circle. Stravinsky was to become a close friend of both Debussy and Ravel, inspiring both men to further artistic experiments and encouraging them to take up fresh challenges. At his prompting, both Frenchmen began to study the works of Arnold Schoenberg and his Viennese circle, and readily agreed with Diaghilev to produce a ballet score on the theme of Daphnis and Chloe.

The ballet was premièred in 1912 after years of struggle with the score and bickering with the Ballets Russes and its director. The première was a disappointment, and the work was dropped. Happily,

though, a revival soon after saw it claim its rightful place as one of this century's great ballet scores. Soon after this, Europe began the dark descent into the Great War of 1914–18.

The Great War

Like so many artists, Ravel found the war a horrific experience. He was shaken to the core not only by the terrible waste of lives but also by the sense of impending doom hanging over a culture he had done so much in the previous ten years to define. Being a man wholly caught up in questions of aesthetics, and who strove for 'balance and clarity in all things', Ravel's first reaction to the war was predictably non-partisan. He knew how much the strength of European culture relied on the cross-fertilization of ideas between nations and so refused to condemn all Germans and Austrians, as many were doing. At the same time he was aware how dear France was to him.

But what clearly gave him most heartache was the problem of leaving his mother at home while both he and his brother were at the front. Edouard had already volunteered and been accepted by September 1914, and Maurice, after agonies of indecision, volunteered a month later, only to be rejected as

Ravel worked on the score for the ballet music of Daphnis and Chloé *(set design above) for about three years. When the ballet was first performed it had a disappointing reception but when revived shortly afterwards it received great acclaim.*

Like many of his contemporaries Ravel found the Great War of 1914–18 a shattering experience. He volunteered in 1914 but was rejected because he was underweight. In 1915, however, he was accepted in the army and was posted as a truck driver (above right) to the Verdun front.

underweight – he weighed just seven stone. By this time, however, his resolve had hardened, and he was tenacious in his efforts to be inducted. He was finally accepted in 1915, and was posted as a truck driver behind the Verdun front. He said on another occasion 'One must have a head and have guts, but never a heart.' Here, in a strange way, he had lived up to his words.

The war did not cost Ravel or his family as dear as it did most of his contemporaries. Both he and his brother survived intact, Maurice himself being invalided out in March 1917 with dysentery. He remained cheerful and communicative with his friends back in Paris, and was quick to comment publicly on the jingoistic and myopic thinking behind the establishment in 1916 of the National League for the Defence of French Music. He commented.

It would actually be damaging to French composers to ignore the output of their foreign colleagues . . . Our art of music, at present so rich, would soon degenerate and restrict itself to obsolete academic formulas.

The greatest single tragedy of Ravel's war was the

death of his mother in 1917, while he was still recovering from dysentery. He was immediately discharged from the army, and after the funeral was thrown into deep despair. The years after the war found him at a low ebb, and he began to suffer from the insomnia which was to progressively worsen for the rest of his life. His private grief was expressed in the piano work, *Le Tombeau de Couperin,* while *La Valse* is a seeming valedictory glance at an irretrievable world.

Le Belvédère

From 1921 onwards he divided his life between the Paris home of his now-married brother, and a little house he bought, christened Le Belvédère, in a village called Montfort-l'Amaury, with a truly magnificent view over the Ile de France. The developing of this shell-like house into the eccentric and immaculate home it became, slowly helped pull Ravel out of his long depression.

Ravel decorated the house lovingly, designing and painting elaborate friezes in the rooms, and filling the house with finely crafted ornaments. He had a cultivated taste for the exotic, and Japanese prints and mechanical birds figure heavily in the perfect, polished rooms. Ravel's fascination with clockwork toys was legendary – so much so that Stravinsky was inclined to believe that they inspired his music. The composer of *The Rite of Spring* derided Ravel as 'a Swiss watchmaker'. But Ravel had a mischievious sense of humour, deliberately mixing real master-pieces with blatent imitations in his decorations, and his artifice in music may well have the same knowingness.

Ravel was immensely happy at Le Belvédère, but increasingly found himself isolated from the world. So many of his contemporaries had already gone, including Debussy, and a new generation of com-posers was emerging who looked not to him, but to Erik Satie once again. And, as a man who retained his

From 1921 onwards Ravel divided his time between the Paris home of his brother Edouard and a house which he had bought in the village of Montfort-l'Amaury. His interest in the house (right), called Le Belvédère, *helped pull him out of a long depression after the death of his mother in 1917.*

In 1925 Ravel completed the music for a work in which he collaborated with the novelist Colette – L'enfant et les sortilèges, *the title page of which is shown below. In the work, the magical world of childhood is re-created.*

anti-establishment stance, even to the point of refusing to accept the Legion of Honour awarded him in 1920 – he claimed no one asked him first – he had no other natural social group to fall in with.

It is difficult to know entirely how Ravel felt at this time, for he remained all his life an intensely private, almost secretive, man, retaining the total reserve he claimed to have inherited from his mother. His sexual life, just as his compositional techniques, remain a complete mystery. There was some speculation that he was homosexual, but there is no evidence either way. While we cannot say that he had a physical liaison with either a man or a woman, we cannot say that he did not either.

Outwardly he remained a refined, extremely cultured, affable man – a man who derived tremendous pleasure and amusement from the best things in life. His lack of widespread acceptance never seemed to bother him at all. Ravel was quite happy entertaining his close friends with his legendary gourmet meals, as impeccable and original as his music, and smoking his beloved Caporal cigarettes.

The 'twenties'
The following decade was to see a number of important compositions flow from the composer's pen, such as the Violin Sonata, the Two Piano Concertos, and the opera *L'Enfant et les Sortilèges.* A

great many of these works were influenced by the jazz craze that swept through Europe in the 1920s. Ravel loved the spontaneous spirit of jazz and its expressiveness, and adopted its rhythms in many of his works.

Another important influence on Ravel was revealed in the opera, *L'Enfant et les Sortilèges* which was written in collaboration with the famous novelist Colette, whom he had first met in 1900. In it Ravel basked in the world of childhood fantasy which it conjured up, giving it all his tenderness and love. For in a sense, Ravel never grew up, holding on tenaciously to every aspect of his own happy childhood as long as he could.

Still, there was a living to be made, and the premières of these works, plus the series of concert tours which he embarked upon in 1922 in London and continued every year up to 1926 in Europe, certainly helped Ravel to become more self-sufficient than at any other time in his life. He even played *La Valse* in Vienna, where he stayed as a guest of Mahler's widow Alma. Although she did not find his dandyism overwhelmingly attractive she appreciated his elegance. She recalled that 'he was a narcissist . . . who came to breakfast rouged and perfumed . . . and related all things to his bodily and facial charms. Though short, he was so well-proportioned, with such elegance and such elastic mobility of figure that he seemed quite beautiful.'

It was during the late 1920s that his music was first committed to disc with his own approval. His String Quartet was recorded in accordance with his own

composer continued to work on both his music and his concert commitments. The change in economical climate occasioned by the 1929 crash had very little effect on him, and he continued to live his refined existence. He was still capable of acts of great warmth towards his friends, however. When the pianist Paul Wittgenstein, who had lost his right hand in the war, approached him for a work, Ravel responded with the inspired and moving *Concerto for the Left Hand.*

This and its companion concerto from the same year, 1931, attests to the composer's artistic and personal well-being; and there seemed no reason to doubt that this state of affairs would continue indefinitely. Tragically, this was not to be the case.

A tragic accident

In October 1932 he was in a taxi which collided with another vehicle. He received head injuries which at

In 1928 Ravel (above) made a highly successful tour of the United States. During the visit he gave both private and public performances at venues ranging from Carnegie Hall to private homes (above right). Although he was thrilled by his reception and impressed by the generosity and hospitality of his hosts Ravel was glad to return to France. Over the next few years his artistic and personal well-being continued to grow. Sadly, however, after a motor accident in 1932 his health gradually declined and he died after an operation in 1937.

views, and he was quick to see the opportunities offered by the gramophone:

It will constitute a real document for posterity to consult . . . if only we had gramophone records approved by Chopin himself! Even with Debussy a great chance was lost.

The following year, 1928, saw his first tour of the United States of America. It went phenomenally well. Travelling with a wardrobe which included 50 silk shirts and 20 pairs of pyjamas, Ravel was fêted on both seaboards, and thoroughly enjoyed all but two aspects of the trip. Being a committed gourmet, used to the best in French cooking, he was often affronted by food that was either second-rate or not highly seasoned enough. He was also increasingly at the mercy of crippling insomnia. And as the tour progressed, for it lasted five months, his health deteriorated rapidly. So, regardless of the huge financial and personal success of the tour, he was greatly relieved to reach France again.

The rest of the year proved to be just as profitable for him. His new orchestral piece, *Bolero,* proved wildly popular, and made him a household name. Ravel was pleased, but unemotional. He commented, 'I have written just one masterpiece, and that is the *Bolero.* Unfortunately, it is devoid of music.' However, he was pleased to accept an honorary D. Mus. from Oxford University, in recognition of his achievements.

In this period of increasing fame and security, the

the time seemed no more than slight concussion. But later, it became clear something was deeply amiss. He was unable to concentrate properly any more, and towards the end of the following year his bodily movements were no longer under the control of his brain. As the condition worsened, he lost proper control even over the power of speech. Saddest of all was the fact that he never wrote another composition after the accident.

What made this doubly tragic was that his brain continued to function perfectly inside his increasingly unreliable body. He was trapped inside his own infirmities, leaving him sometimes in impotent rages, at other times with a resigned equanimity.

In his last years Ravel stayed at his house at Montfort or with friends. He seemed happiest walking alone, or attending concerts. During this time his close and devoted friends did their utmost to help distract him from his suffering.

Finally, after a harrowing summer in 1937, it was decided that an operation should be risked. In December he was opened up and his brain examined. No irregularity was found. He regained consciousness, only to fall into a coma a few hours later from which he never recovered. He died on 28 December.

The cruellest blow perhaps was the fact that the man who had once said 'basically the only love affair I have ever had was with music' was unable to release the music he'd heard inside his head for the last five years of his life.

The romance of Spain

After years of political upheaval, 19th-century France entered a period of rich artistic expression inspired by the passionate individuality of her impoverished neighbour – Spain.

Throughout the 19th century, Spain stood out as the poor and battle-weary cousin of the European family. Unlike her wealthy neighbours (particularly Britain and France), she was almost totally without any kind of 'middle class' to provide a buffer between the extremes in her society. Political issues were decided by three main interest groups: landowners, clergy and the military, but resentment was growing. The spent wealth of many lesser nobles led to discontent and jealous rivalries among their ranks and, at the bottom of the scale, the peasants were involved in frequent uprisings and outbreaks of civil disorder.

Together these factors provided the ingredients for a total collapse of the social order and, on top of everything else, the country was wracked by bitter disputes over the legitimate succession to the throne. Having no sons, the ruling king, Ferdinand VII, 'changed the rules' so that his infant daughter (Isabella) could succeed him. After his death in 1833, the three-year-old princess was duly proclaimed queen, with her mother as regent. But the new edict was bitterly resented and rival factions clashed head on – opposition to the queen being spearheaded by supporters of her uncle, Don Carlos. Clinging to power, Isabella remained queen until 1868, when her blighted rule was ended by violent revolution. Continued disputes over the vacant throne embroiled not only Spain, but the external interests of France and Britain as well. In an effort to

The wild, free spirit of Spain – a country of rugged beauty, dazzling sunshine and earthy passions – enthralled the 19th-century French romantics and became a major source of artistic inspiration.

fill the vacuum, the Spanish crown was at first offered to an Italian prince (Amadeo), but his moderate rule ended in an abrupt abdication. The brief spell of republicanism which followed soon gave way to the royalists – this time led by the supporters of Isabella's son Alfonso – and the monarchy was once more restored.

Such endemic civil war, coupled with continuous interference from outside (and mostly Anglo-French) interests contrived to make Spain one of the unhappiest countries in Europe; as her neighbours grew in power and wealth, the contrast with her poverty and instability was made even sharper. In general, the population of Europe had almost doubled over the preceding century, thanks to improvements in areas like agriculture, science and medicine and, in Britain, the heralds of the industrial revolution, even greater prosperity and urbanization pointed the way to the future. But in more isolated areas such as Spain, these developments made little impact – her agriculture continued to be backward and her industry was almost non-existent.

Universal nationalism
Despite her wealth, France too suffered from political upheaval through much of the 19th century. The radical republicanism that led to Louis-Philippe's downfall in 1848, also led, within three years, to the coup d'état by Louis Napoleon (Emperor Napoleon III). After defeat by the Germans in 1870, the emperor in turn was replaced by the anarchic Paris Commune, before relative stability was at last achieved by the Third Republic. During its short period of success, the Second Empire was, nevertheless, a time of brilliant artistic achievements and considerable opulence, especially in Paris. The 1850s and 1860s saw a rich profusion of art and music, while the contrasting styles of different but outstanding generations overlapped to produce interest, controversy and inspiration.

Many Frenchmen were still deeply imbued with Revolutionary ideals of individualism, anticlericalism and, above all, the right to freedom of expression and thought. Under this impetus, and in an inevitable reaction to the 19th century obsession with 'scientific method', a new surge of romanticism was born. The mood was later summed up by the French artist Renoir:

Nowadays they want to explain everything. But if they could explain a picture it wouldn't be art. Shall I tell you what I think are the two qualities of art? It must be indescribable and it must be inimitable . . . A work of art must seize hold of you, enfold you, carry you away. It is the means by which the artist conveys his passion; it is a current which he transmits and which sweeps you up in his passion.

The idealists recognized no frontiers to expression, no limit to artistic treatment and, by experimenting freely with all or any inspiration, they sought new ideas from around the world – so coining the phrase 'universal nationalism' (a nationalism, for example, based on Spanish folk music but developing it within the sophisticated techniques of the French or Italian tradition).

One result of this was the artistic exploration of a formerly ignored source – the people. Their every-day lives, their struggle for survival and the earthy passions in their lives brought to light a world unfettered by the artificial value of the bourgeois

élite. The French also proved susceptible to another source – the new international contacts of the post-Napoleonic period. They eagerly absorbed influences from Germany, the Orient, Japan, the Arab world and Russia, but most of all they looked to Spain. Here, the arts had never been straitjacketed by minority tastes and, for example, would have rejected outright the rigid rules of an institute like the French Academy.

The lure of the South
The rugged, romantic appeal of her people and their seemingly indomitable spirit provided enchantment and allure: here was a land where the arts sprang directly from the soil, where the people had a fiery, pugnacious character and compulsive individualism. More than any other European country, it seemed that the history of Spain was the history of individuals, from the legendary conquistadores who had created the 16th-century Spanish empire to the local militias and rebel bands who had put up fierce and heroic resistance to the French in the Peninsular War of 1808–1814.

Spain, too, was unique in its rich tradition of folk music, songs and dances and in the tenacity with which she guarded this inheritance. The tradition was due in part to a long-established cycle of seasonal festivities associated with peasant life (and

Because of its enormous regional diversity, Spain boasted a uniquely rich tradition of folk music, song and dance. The colour and vibrancy of the flamenco fiesta (above) was just one of the many elements of peasant life that captured the imagination of Spain's more sedate neighbours.

little disrupted by the 'modernization' that was affecting other European countries) and partly to geography. To this day, the Iberian peninsula has a wealth of regional diversity thanks to the mountain chains which divide it and which provide remarkably effective cultural barriers. Like all countries, Spain has also experienced influences from various historic migration and invasions; in the 16th century, for example, the first gypsies crossed her borders, bringing with them the explosive vibrancy of Flamenco. In later years, fresh impetus resulted from her cultural ties with South America and her close proximity to France.

Proximity too, played its part in drawing the French south. There was a blurring of the frontier across the Pyrenees, where Basque and Catalan country spilled over into southern France and where local impulses were readily transmitted from one side to the other. As early as the 15th century, French literature had been directly influenced by Spanish

Whether in the sober portraits of the aristocracy (below) or in his gruesome emotive works depicting both real and imaginary horrors, Goya's works had a tremendous impact in France.

romances and folk stories and these ingredients reappeared in the 17th-century works of Corneille and Molière. In the 19th century, an upsurge of interest led to the classic Spanish story of Don Quixote being translated into French and it, in turn, provided rich material for many French composers. The Spanish 'romanceros' – folk poems of Spanish history and legend – were freely tapped by French writers and dramatists: Victor Hugo, Prosper Mérimée and Emile Deschamps were just some of the luminaries who used them as sources, thus injecting a fresh though savage vigour into French literature.

Even the world of the visual arts had little immunity to the infectious charm of these influences. An early but profound impact was made by the works of Francisco Goya y Lucientes (1746–1828). Goya had led a curious double life, producing orthodox portraits for members of the Spanish court on one hand, yet also creating deeply charged canvasses to highlight the piteous waste and cruelty of war and the gruesome fantasies from a black world of witches and warlocks.

The brutality and terror in Goya's work, its technical boldness, the rough, hasty texture and strong use of colour, gave a new, if uncomfortable jolt to the art world and deeply impressed French artists such as Eugène Delacroix (1798–1863) and, in later years, Edouard Manet (1832–1883).

Tourist Spain

Manet, the innovator and leader of the so-called Impressionist movement in art, was an ardent devotee of the Spanish master and was also deeply influenced by the 17th-century Spaniard, Velasquez. He was even accused of imitating directly their 'brilliant light effects and garish colours'.

Until 1865, however, Manet had never been to Spain: his was a culture acquired second-hand and, conveniently, out of context. Many of the subjects he painted were based on the colourful and picturesque troupe of Spanish dancers who visited Paris in 1862 and more than ever excited his enthusiasm for the 'tourist' Spain they represented. His whole attitude and approach was dramatically altered when he finally visited the country and was confronted by the harsh reality behind the glamorous façade so popular in Paris. After his return, Manet painted three bullfight scenes, but his Spanish phase was almost at an end – the poverty, dirt, illiteracy and preoccupation with death that he had encountered made far less attractive subjects than popular imaginings!

Bullfights, too, provided unexpected inspiration for one of France's great musicians, Debussy. Like Manet, Debussy only knew Spain from reading translations of great works, from pictures in the Paris galleries or from songs and dances performed by visiting troupes. At the Paris Exhibition of 1889/1890, he wandered about, listening intently to the extraordinary musical sounds gathered from around the world. But for him, Spanish music, especially from Andalusia, was outstanding. Curiously, he only crossed the borders into Spain on one occasion – to watch a bullfight in the frontier town of San Sebastian – yet he remembered the experience all his life. He vividly described the contrasting patterns of light falling across the ring, with one half in bright sunshine, the other deep in shade. These mixtures of light and shade, together with the drama of the fight itself, were transported into his music to create a powerful but purely

Edouard Manet 'the father of Impressionism' was an ardent fan of Goya and was greatly influenced by themes of 'tourist' Spain. Consequently he eagerly took full advantage of the visit of the Spanish Ballet (above) to Paris in 1862, making its members the subjects of several paintings.

Two centuries after Miguel Cervantes penned his humorous tales of Don Quixote and his 'faithful' servant Sancho Panza, the French public were just getting to know this curious couple. Their reputation even earned them pride of place in the works of Honoré Daumier (one of his many paintings of the pair, shown right), the 19th-century French painter and caricaturist.

imaginary evocation of Spain. Debussy, like Manet and so many other writers and musicians of his day, was not so much attempting to write 'Spanish' music, or create 'Spanish' paintings, rather he was translating into his own idiom the powerful associations that traditional images of Spain had aroused in him.

The triumph of Romance

While art and music were experimenting with new ideas and techniques, French literature and drama were also ready to explore fresh ground and many French writers looked across the Franco-Spanish borders for new ideas and romantic story lines. Victor Hugo (1802–1885) was a master of many forms; poetry, novels and drama. In the latter form, his aim was to conjure up Olympian visions of Man and History and his immediate model was

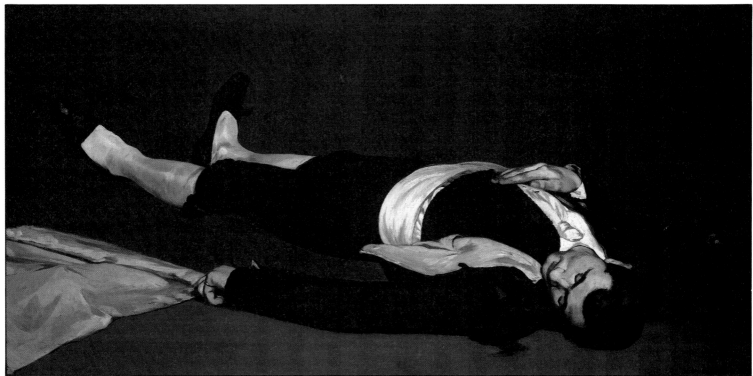

Cham's caricature Incident in the Bull Ring *(right) appeared in a French satirical magazine in 1864. It shows us what Manet's painting of the same name may have looked like (one of the two remaining portions of the work is the poignant* Dead Toreador *(below), but obviously the cartoonist did not share the painter's romantic view of Spain.*

Shakespeare. But, for his source material, Hugo turned to the Spanish romanceros and it was here that he found a basis for this melodramatic and highly controversial verse-play, *Hernani.*

Hernani was Hugo's assault on the decayed neoclassicism of the 18th-century French theatre. This antiquated convention had perpetuated the image but not the substance of the elegance and refinement achieved by the likes of Corneille, Molière and Racine. Their golden age had long passed, but the strict, formal rules of classical tragedy were still applied so rigidly that they debased character, action and credibility and, above all, had no relevance to human conditions. By the late 1820s, further barriers had been thrown up by restraints on the freedom of the press and by the severe censorship imposed by King Charles X. One of Hugo's plays (*Marion de Lorme*) had already fallen foul of the official censors and, for his riposte, Hugo presented French theatre-goers with a new and sensational drama – *Hernani.*

In the play, the hero is a disgraced nobleman, Hernani, whose lover is also courted by both the King of Spain and a powerful grandee (Don Gomez). The king unsportingly abducts the unfortunate señorita, leaving the hero to plan her rescue through an unlikely alliance with his remaining rival, Don Gomez. The price of the rescue is high, however, and Hernani has to promise that he will kill himself at the moment when Don Gomez sounds a golden horn. The young lovers are duly married but, on their wedding night, Don Gomez sounds the signal for suicide. The distraught bride faithfully shares her husband's cup of poison and Don Gomez, overcome with remorse, throws himself onto his sword.

The drama (which Giuseppe Verdi converted into his first successful opera, *Ernani* in 1844) was marked by high passion, fiery poetry and, for the ill-fated lovers, passages of great elegaic beauty. All this strength and heat so shocked the adherents of classicism that the first two performances – at the Comedie Française theatre in February 1830 –

resulted in violent clashes with Hugo's student supporters. The students were led by two flamboyant poets, Petrus Borel and Théophile Gautier (whose cherry-coloured doublet caused almost as much sensation as the play itself!) This rowdy band outclapped, outcheered and generally outmatched the staid supporters of classicism, won the day resoundingly for Hugo and helped to bring about a complete break with the past in terms of theatrical presentation.

Hugo's 'Cénacle' (literary circle) included a less volatile genius, Prosper Mérimée (1803–1870), one of France's greatest short story writers and a noted Hispanophile. Mérimée's strength in short fiction lay in his powerful delineation of characters and of situations in which they were driven to extremes by the strength of their own emotions. Spain, with its highly strung sense of personal honour, its under-lying violence and Moorish fatalism, seemed tailor-made for him. In addition to fiction, he wrote the scholarly *History of Spain* and a stylish biography of King Pedro I, (a 14th-century king of Castille) which is still considered a masterpiece. Like Hugo, Mérimée was drawn by the Spanish romanceros and these were the source of his series of plays, *Theatre de Clara Azul* (1825) and his most celebrated story, *Carmen* (1845). Thirty years later, Georges Bizet took this story of gypsy sensuality, love, revenge and murder and the work he created from it did as much for opera as Hugo's *Hernani* had done for the theatre.

Despite the emotional force of Bizet's music, the libretto was a somewhat sanitized version of the Mérimée original. Mérimée's Carmen was a sluttish, unwashed gypsy, her husband was a deep-dyed villain and the Basque, Don Jose, far from being a lovelorn victim driven to desperation by Carmen's infidelity, was a thoroughgoing and murderous rascal in his own right.

On its publication in 1845, the novel was received by a reading public well versed in the dramatic realities of Romanticism; the reaction to the opera was far less sophisticated. Even before the first performance, Bizet's work was pilloried as obscene, immoral and unplayable, and the first choice for the title role refused the part because Bizet would not tone down the 'very scabrous side' of his heroine. The ultimate Carmen (Galli-Marie) performed the role with all the brazen sensuality required, only to be abused by critics who thought her interpretation deserving of police prosecution! Theatre goers and critics alike were stupefied by the scenes of unbridled passions now unveiled on the stage of the Opera Comique.

Honouring a debt

Even before he wrote Carmen, Bizet had been moving towards the Spanish idiom with his operas, but none of his music was 'Spanish' in a sense that any Spaniard would recognize. Carmen may be an opera about Spain, but it is a French opera nevertheless. Still decidedly French, but nearer the Spanish spirit, were the works of Maurice Ravel and Claude Debussy. Both composers had a natural empathy for the traditional folk music of regions like Andalusia and the idiosyncratic tones of their songs and dances. Debussy, in fact, interpreted more faithfully than any of his compatriots, the essence of flamenco – that vibrant mix of French café singer and Moorish rhythm, colourful costumes, violent movement and whirring castanets (which, like guitars, were Moorish instruments).

Hugo's sensational drama, Hernani, *based on Spanish romanceros, shocked French theatre goers by breaking every rule in the 'classical tragedy' book. Reaction was so strong that riots broke out during the first two performances (left).*

LES ROMAINS ÉCHEVELÉS A LA 1ᵉ REPRÉSENTATION D'HERNANI.

The drama of Spain and its colourful spectacles such as the bullfight (below) inspired the works of French musicians, particularly Ravel and Debussy.

Events finally seemed to come full cycle, when Debussy was praised by one of Spain's outstanding composers, Manuel de Falla, who openly admired the authenticity and power of the Frenchman's music. Debussy had communicated his 'impressionistic' music to the young de Falla, influencing his work and advising him not to neglect the invaluable musical heritage of his native Andalucia. In 1920, two years after Debussy's death, de Falla acknowledged his obligation to and regard for the composer by writing a *Homage* to him, a piece of guitar music with echoes of Debussy's *Iberia*.

Debussy, Dukas, Vincent d'Indy, Camille Saint-Saens, Jules Massenet and other French composers were, in fact, remarkably hospitable to their Spanish counterparts – most notably Granados, Albeniz and de Falla – not simply as teachers or mentors but as performers championing their music and lifting their careers. Most vital were the practical returns that the Spaniards enjoyed from facilities which barely existed in Spain. At home there was no established musical infrastructure, no great opera house, no permanent orchestra of any size, no profusion of strong ensembles, no network of concert halls and no influential entrepreneurs. All these and more were made available in France and many personal as well as professional friendships flowered as a result of the exchange.

Manuel de Falla readily acknowledged his debt and regarded Paris as his second home; the seven years he spent in France (from 1907–1914) were crucial to his career. Without France and its opportunities, de Falla later said, he could have achieved nothing. He even went so far as to suggest that Debussy was not just a benevolent mentor and friend, but the virtual creator of modern Spanish music technique. To an extent this is true, though it took the talents of de Falla and Albeniz to wed 'impressionism' to the peculiar flavour of their native music before a truly distinctive Spanish mood emerged.

A new protégé

Towards the end of the century, the close contacts between France and Spain were about to produce yet another outstanding protégé. In 1896, a 16-year-old Spaniard called Pablo Picasso wrote to a friend:

If I had a son who wanted to paint, I wouldn't let him live in Spain. And I don't think I would send him to Paris (where I would love to be myself), but to Munik (I don't know if it is spelt that way). It is a town where painting is studied seriously, without paying attention to such fashions as pointillism, which I am not against but for the fact that other painters copy the originator if he is successful. I am not in favour of following any particular school, because it only results in being copied by supporters . . .

The young Picasso's wish was granted when, four years later, he was given an exhibition of his works in Paris.

After years of Spanish-found inspiration, there is little doubt about the role played by the French in fertilizing the seedbed of Spanish self-fulfilment. Through France, Spanish composers came to develop and enhance the long-cherished traditional music that surrounded them and one of the world's greatest artists found recognition and support. And, in the long history of French fascination for Spain, no feedback could have been more felicitous.

The writer and noted Hispanophile, Prosper Mérimée brought to life the most famous gypsy of them all – Carmen (above). His story of passion and death later provided Bizet with the sensual heroine of his famous opera.

It was through the work of Claude Debussy that Spanish composers such as Isaac Albeniz and Manuel de Falla were to become fully aware of the power and true worth of their own native music. De Falla (the frontispiece of his El Amor Brujo *is shown on the right) is quoted as saying '. . . if Debussy used Spanish folk music to inspire some of his greatest works he has generously repaid us and it is now Spain which is indebted to him'.*

Béla Bartók
1881–1945

Neglected, misunderstood and even notorious during his lifetime, Béla Bartók was hailed internationally as one of the most popular modern composers within a few years of his death.

Hungary's indigenous music, history and traditions were rooted deep in the countryside (left) and exerted a powerful and early influence on Bartók who was born into an agricultural community.

After the death of Bartók's father the family moved home several times as his mother sought to find work for herself and a good education for her children. Bartók was eventually enrolled, in 1899, at the Budapest Academy of Music (below).

Béla Bartók was born in the small town of Nagyzentmiklós in South-East Hungary on 25 March 1881. He was born into a musical family: his mother, formerly a teacher, was a particularly gifted pianist and his father, headmaster of the agricultural school, was also a talented cello player.

Béla's interest in music was evident very early on and by the age of five he had begun piano lessons. In 1888, when he was seven, his father died after a short illness, aged only 33. Bartók's mother, Paula, in order to support her family, was forced to resume the teaching career she had abandoned on her marriage. Bartók's musical ability continued to mature and his mother was determined to see it properly nurtured by first-rate teachers. Accordingly, she took leave of absence from her school in 1892 and removed the family to Pozsony (now Bratislava) where she hoped to find a new post. When, at the end of her year's absence, she had not found anything suitable she was transferred to a post at Beszterce where, although she found work, there was no suitable music teacher for Bartók. In April 1894 the family returned once more to Pozsony where Paula found a job at a teacher-training college and Béla settled down to five years of uninterrupted musical studies at the Pozsony Gymnasium.

Musical student in Budapest

By 1899 Béla had completed his secondary schooling and it was decided, although he was offered a place at the Vienna Conservatoire, that he should continue his musical studies at the Budapest Academy of Music instead. During his first few months he was dogged by ill-health but he did finish the academic year successfully. However, he was unable to continue his studies in his second year due to a severe bout of pneumonia which he contracted in August 1901. He recuperated at home with his

mother for several months before resuming his studies in April 1901. He had been a frail sickly child and ill-health was to recur throughout his student years.

During his years at the Academy Bartók's musical horizons were increasingly widened but it was after attending a première of *Also sprach Zarathustra* that he discovered the music of Strauss, which was to renew in him his earlier interest and enthusiasm for composition. His first compositions – waltzes and polkas – were produced when he was nine. A few years later aged 11, he had made his début as performer and composer with *The course of the Danube*. The influence of Strauss's music unleashed a creativity which had not been stirred by the traditional techniques of the Academy.

Bartók completed his studies at the Academy in June 1903. His teachers saw him as a pianist with a

In 1905 Bartók went to Paris to compete for the Prix Rubinstein – a prize open to gifted young pianists. Although he was disappointed in the outcome – he came second – and there were one or two clashes over the 'performability of his music', he enjoyed being in Paris. He was particularly taken with the night-life and character of the cabarets and bars of seamy Montmartre (right).

brilliant career ahead of him and he was given the opportunity to perform at many Academy concerts, where he played some of his own earlier compositions. Such was his talent as both a pianist and composer that the final examination at the Academy was waived: 'the general opinion is that this is superfluous', he related in a letter to his mother.

In the winter of 1903 Bartók moved around Europe and achieved recognition as a composer with his symphonic poem *Kossuth,* which was premièred in Budapest and Manchester, and the *Violin Sonata.* He also established a reputation as a performer, playing his own and other people's compositions at concerts in Budapest, Vienna and Pozsony.

The inspiration of folk songs

From April 1904 he spent several months staying with his sister in the Hungarian countryside. It was here that, quite by chance, he first heard authentic Hungarian folk music, sung by a local girl in the village. After his return from Paris where, in 1905, he had competed for the Rubinstein Prize, Bartók began organizing his first information-gathering tour

While he was at school in Pozsony Bartók met the son of one of his teachers, Ernö von Dohnányi (left), who was to become a lifelong friend. Dohnányi, later to become a distinguished composer himself, had a considerable influence on Bartók's taste and ideas during his early musical development.

around Hungary. 'As I went from village to village', he later wrote, 'I heard the true music of my race . . . This music was a revelation to me . . .' Before this journey he made contact with Zoltan Kodály, a composer and expert on the study of folk song.

Both men, destined to be great composers in their own right, originally looked upon this material as a source of inspiration for their own compositions. But over many trips in the next few years their prime concern became the preservation and study of the music itself. The first fruits of this work were co-authored and published in 1906 as *Twenty Hungarian Folksongs.*

The following year, in January 1907, Bartók was appointed to the staff of the Budapest Academy of Music, taking the position of teacher of the advanced piano class. In the two years leading to this appointment, he had been so occupied with his research into and collection of folk music that he had composed nothing of his own. With his interests drifting ever further from a concert career, the Academy post was both a vocational and financial godsend.

During 1907 he embarked on an intense relationship with a girl seven years younger than himself, the virtuoso violinist Stefi Geyer. The affair was doomed from the start, Stefi being a devout Catholic whereas Bartók was an atheist. The strain of trying to accommodate such opposite views eventually destroyed the relationship, but not before they had exchanged a series of deeply-felt letters, and Bartók had written some remarkable compositions, including the first *Violin Concerto* and the *Two Portraits (The Ideal* and *The Grotesque),* especially for Stefi.

Marriage to Márta

It was in the emotional aftermath of their affair that Bartók met his future wife. Called Márta Ziegler, she was just fourteen when they met (Bartók was 26). Within a few months of their meeting they had become greatly attracted to each other, and in 1908 Bartók made his first dedication to her, a little piano piece called *Picture of a Girl.*

The events of these years had given a new emotional maturity to Bartók, both in his life and in his work. His orchestral pieces found a wider audience throughout Europe, causing controversy at every turn. Many critics heard in his works only tonal chaos, and for much of his career he found himself either neglected or notorious as a composer of brash atonal music.

In 1909, at a simple and very private wedding, Bartók and the 16-year-old Márta were married. After the upheavals of the preceding years, Bartók's life finally took a more ordered turn. Márta gave birth to a son, also named Béla, in 1910.

Bartók continued with his work at the Academy and further consolidated his compositional progress. The following year, 1912, saw the completion of his only opera, *Duke Bluebeard's Castle,* which reflects the high-water mark of Debussy's influence on his work. By the end of 1912 both he and Kodály were at the receiving end of rough treatment from both critics and the public. As a result Bartók gave up all public musical activity and threw himself wholly into his folk researches. By the end of 1913 he had travelled through all of Hungary, parts of Romania, Transylvania and parts of North Africa. His articles on these researches were published all over the world and still stand today as models of careful research.

All this activity was abruptly curtailed in 1914 by Hungary's entry into World War I on the side of Austria. Bartók hated the war and lamented Hungary's involvement, seeing disaster as the only possible outcome. Luckily for him, he was found unfit for military service, and remained at the Academy for the duration of the war.

Renewal of activity

One indirect benefit of the war for him was an apparent renewal of his creativity, for, apart from the scholarly *Romanian Folksong Arrangements,* he completed the *Piano Suite Op. 14,* the second *String Quartet* and the ballet *The Wooden Prince* in the next three years. In 1917, against great opposition, the Italian conductor Egisto Tango brought *The Wooden Prince* to its Budapest première. He put his heart and soul into the production, defeating every sabotage attempt by the dancers and orchestra who had all pronounced it undanceable and unplayable before

Tihany mit dem Balaton-See

Bartók's desire to find the 'real' spirit of his homeland's people and music led him on a series of travels, after 1904, all over rural Hungary (left). What he discovered of the land, its people and music contrasted sharply with the Romantic notion of Hungary (above), as expressed in the music of composers such as Brahms and Liszt.

giving it a chance, and brought off a great success. Bartók remained eternally grateful to Tango who, the following year, also mounted the première of *Duke Bluebeard's Castle,* seven years after it was written. Bartók dedicated *The Wooden Prince* to him in appreciation of his effort.

The period after the end of the war brought increasing chaos and suffering to an already exhausted Hungary. Although both Bartók and Kodály were made Deputy Directors of the Academy under the new Provisional Government in 1919, the worsening political situation left no-one safe from the turmoil. At one point during the darkest days of Béla Kun's Communist terror, Béla and Márta were forced to flee their Budapest home, taking as many of their possessions as they could carry. When the Communists were overthrown and a rigidly conservative government installed, everyone feared for the positions given them by the former regime. Bartók survived, but Dohnányi, who had been Director, was removed. Kodály knew that he was a possible target, but his rigorously non-political public stance saved him from any reprisals.

Despite the turmoil, Bartók completed two *Sonatas for Violin and Piano,* and in 1922 he embarked on a highly successful concert tour of England, France, Germany and Italy, where the First Sonata in particular was given a warm reception, and his superlative piano playing was commented upon by many observers.

Before he set off on the tour he was beset by emotional problems. His marriage to Márta was fast disintegrating. In 1921 he had met his future second wife, Ditta Pásztory, in circumstances identical to his meeting of Márta: she came to him as a 19-year-old student and, as did most female students, developed a 'crush' on this handsome, quiet tutor and was thrilled to find her passion reciprocated. It is not known whether Bartók's marriage was in trouble before this; nor is it known why the marriage didn't survive the advent of Ditta. Strangely, when the split came in 1923, it was Márta who suggested a divorce so that Béla could marry Ditta. After a period of separation he and Márta met in August of that year to agree on the details.

The whole resolution of this episode was curiously painless, and after the marriage Márta remained a friend and was a frequent visitor to the new Bartók household. Ditta was 21, Bartók 41, when they married. Within a year she gave birth to a son, Peter. At the same time the contented Bartók returned to orchestral composition and produced the joyful *Dance Suite* – today one of his most popular pieces.

For the following few years Bartók's life settled into a welcome pattern of hard work and consistent inspiration in both his academic and creative fields. Piano pieces such as the *Sonata* (1926) and the *Out of Doors Suite* (1926) proved to be the equal of anything he had yet achieved, and the publication in 1924 of a book based on his researches, *Hungarian Folksong,* met with universal acclaim. In addition, Bartók kept up his concert-tour commitments, being well-received in both Italy and at the International Festival in Prague in 1925, where the *Dance Suite,* in particular, was a great success.

In 1927 a tour of the United States was arranged. Bartók managed sufficient leave from teaching to complete the long and arduous tour, but it was not

The title page, below, is from Bartók's piano pieces **For Children.** *This was first published in 1909 and was the result of one of his collecting tours of folk music in Slovakia and Romania.*

Zoltan Kodály (left) was involved in similar folk research to Bartók. Together they revolutionized the study of folk music and between them collected thousands of folk songs. Many of these were recorded by Bartók on Edison cylinders (below).

At the end of World War 1 Hungary was plunged into a period of political turmoil. During the worst days of terror inflicted by the communist government of Béla Kun many Hungarians were dispossessed and made homeless (right). At one point Béla and Márta Bartók fled from their Budapest home taking with them as many of their possessions as they could carry. It was some months before they returned to the city.

Bartók's only opera, **Duke Bluebeard's Castle** *(set design below) was completed in 1912, but only given its première in Budapest in 1918. It was conducted by the Italian, Egisto Tango, who had conducted the première of Bartók's ballet,* **The Wooden Prince,** *so successfully in the previous year.*

nationalist aggression stemming from Germany and Italy during the 1930s. He made his point of view felt by refusing to include these countries in his concert tours or allowing his concerts to be broadcast there. Although intensely patriotic he found the blatant chauvinism and anti-semitism around him in Hungary impossible to condone. Yet while many of his colleagues all over Europe fled to America, Bartók remained in Budapest. Then, in 1938, Hitler entered Austria. The event was depressing enough in itself but it also meant that Bartók lost all his royalties since his publisher was in Austria and all payments were stopped by the Nazis.

Bartók could clearly foresee the takeover of Hungary by Germany, yet he was in a real quandary whether to stay or flee. He regarded exile as tantamount to artistic suicide, as so many of his creative links were with his own people. And there was also his mother to consider: he was adamant in his refusal to abandon her, and was committed to stay in Hungary while she was alive to prevent reprisals of any sort being taken against her.

War broke out in August 1939 and three months later his beloved mother died. In the light of these two events, he used his concert tour of America in early 1940 to sound out the possibility of migrating there. He found himself welcomed, and his tour with Hungarian expatriate violinist, Joseph Szigeti, was a real success. In October 1940, he and Ditta again left Hungary for America, officially to complete another concert tour, but all their friends knew the stay would be indefinite.

the success he had hoped for. Part of the reason was that he was just not the larger-than-life personality, either on or off stage, that the public takes to its heart. That he was simply a brilliant pianist and composer was not enough for the public at that time. His music was also 'difficult', and despite the support of such conductors as Mengelberg and Reiner, the reviews were hostile.

The tour was exhausting and Bartók was relieved to return to Hungary. However, the following year he entered his *Third String Quartet* in a Philadelphia competition and was rewarded with joint first prize.

Although in official music circles he received scant recognition at home, abroad his reputation grew not only as a performer and composer but also as a musicologist. He undertook a successful tour of Russia in 1929, playing to enthusiastic audiences in Kharkov, Odessa and Leningrad. In 1931 he was a guest at the Geneva Congress of Human Studies and that same year in honour of his 50th birthday he was made a Chevalier of the Legion of Honour in France. In an attempt to match this honour the Hungarian authorities awarded him the Corvin Wreath. However, because of his increasing disquiet over the fascist tendencies of the government, he declined to attend the ceremony.

For several years Bartók immersed himself in his researches and compositions. The result was a string of new works, including the brilliant *Second Piano Concerto,* and a major new publication in 1934 on Hungarian and neighbouring folk music. That same year he finally gave up teaching at the Academy. Along with his old friend Kodály he took up a research post offered by the Hungarian Academic Sciences to prepare for the publication of a folksong collection.

Though not actively involved in politics, Bartók became increasingly distressed by the mounting

In 1921 Bartók met Ditta Pásztory (left), then a 19-year-old student. Two years later his first wife, Márta, suggested a divorce and in August 1923 he and Ditta were married.

The caricature (left) from a New York publication during Bartók's first visit to America in 1928 expresses the reception his 'difficult' music had there. One critic wrote that 'Bartok's music of last night is amoral, beyond good and evil, but hardly of Nietzschean expansiveness'.

Exile in America

The story of Bartók's five years in America is a bleak and distressing one. Although he had regular employment on a small wage for the first two years at Columbia University in New York, his health was never good and his presence as a composer and concert artist was virtually ignored. At home he and Ditta feared for their son Peter's survival, as he was still in Hungary. Added to that, they were both desperately homesick and out of place in New York.

It is no surprise to find that Bartók attempted no creative work before 1942, but this did not mean that he was idle. With admirable practicality, he immersed himself in further research. Bartók had received a fellowship from Columbia University to work on the Milman Parry collection of Serbo-Croatian folk music at Harvard. Parry had made more than two thousand recordings mainly of epic songs in Yugoslavia. Bartók was assigned to transcribe and annotate the music, a task which obviously delighted him. On 25 November, 1940, he received an honorary doctorate from Columbia and although he was employed at a salary of $3000 per year he didn't feel secure, since the post was renewable each term.

The personal pressures were eased at least in early 1942 when Béla and Ditta were reunited with their son, Peter, who had managed to reach the States through war-torn Europe. But although American friends continued to help Bartók find suitable work his music was still not being performed.

From April 1942 Bartók's health began to deteriorate rapidly. He suffered from high temperatures and weight loss – but for the time being, the leukaemia which was to kill him remained undiagnosed. Despite his ill health he struggled to find new work and on 21 January 1943 he gave his last concert performance. At the suggestion of one of his former pupils the American Society of Com-posers, Authors and Publishers agreed to finance his medical treatment. At about the same time, secretly prompted by some of his friends who concealed all trace of what the independent-minded Bartók might see as charity, the conductor Serge Koussevitsky, commissioned him to compose an orchestral piece.

Though initially reluctant to start the work, Bartók finally flung himself into it and, as a startling rejection of the pain and desolation of his circumstances, he wrote the joyful and forward-looking *Concerto for Orchestra*.

By the end of the year he had met Yehudi Menuhin and accepted a commission from him for the *Solo Violin Sonata*. This was completed by early 1944, and premiered by Menuhin in New York later that year. That year saw an immense change in his composing fortunes, as commissions began to flow in, some of which he reluctantly turned down, concerned as he was with conserving his diminishing energies. One commission he did accept, from William Primrose, was for a *Viola Concerto*. But it was to remain unfinished at his death.

By this time it was clear to all that he was a dying man, although he himself refused to acknowledge it. He worked constantly on his third *Piano Concerto* and the *Viola Concerto*, fighting against a complete collapse of his health.

Peace in Europe brought with it news of his former wife, Márta, son Béla, and his friend and collaborator Kodály, all of whom had survived.

Bartók rested for most of the summer at Lake Saranac, working on his last two compositions, and was too ill to take up an invitation from the Menuhins to travel to California. By early September 1945 he had finished the draft of the *Viola Concerto* and the beautiful *Piano Concerto* was virtually completed. On his return to New York, however, his health finally gave way, and he spent his last few days in Mount Sinai Hospital and the West Side Hospital where he was transferred. He died on 26 September 1945. One of his last comments made to a hospital doctor sadly emphasizes his late period of creativity:

'I am only sorry that I have to leave with my baggage full.'

The final irony was that within the next few years he was to become one of the most internationally popular modern composers.

The origins of modern art

Bartók's 'modern music' was scorned as incoherent and ugly. The same response greeted Modern Art, which broke with old techniques and values in an attempt to express something new.

Henri Matisse (above), leader of the first new movement in 20th-century art – Fauvism.

In the short but dynamic period between 1905 and 1925 'Modern Art' was born. And the innovations in European art that came about in this time laid the foundations for nearly all the creative developments which followed over the years, right to this day.

As the 20th century opened the world of art was dominated, as it had been throughout the latter part of the 19th century, by French artists and the influences of Impressionism and Symbolism – movements which were themselves the forerunners of the 'new' art of the 20th century. Then, in 1905, in an attempt to break new ground, the Fauves and Expressionists burst on the scene, followed by the Cubists, the Suprematists and abstract painters, the Dadaists and, finally, the Surrealists.

Not all these movements are clearly defined – artists changed direction and often became part of several different movements. The whole period is one of cross-fertilization and change, but after Fauvism, there was no looking back.

Forerunners of modern art

For about 500 years until the advent of the Impressionists, almost all artists had been striving to portray the world in a representational way – trying to capture on canvas the image of a scene, a face, an object, in the way the eye sees it, as accurately as possible. Then, around the mid-19th century, with the advent of popular photography, the artist's world changed. The camera blinked its automatic eye and, suddenly, the representational artist seemed to be left without a role – there was little point in using paints to record scenes and faces in a straightforward way when the camera could do a better job. What, then, could the artist do that the camera could not? For the Impressionists, the answer lay in trying to capture the fleeting effects of light and atmosphere and analysing the way colours work together. With Post-Impressionist and Symbolist artists however, came a more fundamental step in the development of artistic styles designed to show not only what they saw but also how they *felt* about the world around them. Theirs was a passionate attempt to use paint in an attempt to *express* their own emotional response to what they saw. Van Gogh (1853–90) was perhaps the most significant predecessor of modern art in this respect. He looked constantly to the use of colour to convey his feelings, and in colour he found a means of expression – 'instead of trying to record what I see, I use colour arbitrarily to express my feelings forcibly.'

Gauguin and Cezanne had also experimented

The Fauves artists paid scant attention to the form of their subject material. They looked instead to the use of colour to express and convey the feeling they had for their subjects – as in this painting (left) by Matisse, entitled Interior.

413

Georges Braque (above) at the age of 67. As a young man, he and Picasso worked together 'roped like mountaineers climbing Everest', and became joint founders of Cubism.

along similar lines in the 1880s and 1890s but it was left to the artists of the early 20th century to develop these ideas further.

The Wild Beasts

In 1905 the French art critic Louis Vauxcelles went to view the work of some young painters exhibiting at the Salon d'Automne. Shocked by the violence of the colours in their fiercely painted canvases he labelled the artists 'Les Fauves' – The Wild Beasts – and so baptised the first major artistic movement of the 20th century. The principal Fauvists – Matisse, Derain and Vlaminck, all French, owed much to Van Gogh in their approach to their painting. Their paintings were executed in a 'primitive' almost naive way – only the raw form of their subjects were recognizable – and then sometimes barely so – but it was in their use of colour that they sought to express the meanings in their work. And in this they went further than anything their predecessors had attempted. Matisse, leader of the Fauves, stayed longest with the movement and continued painting in this style into the 1920s. Many others, including Vlaminck and Derain began to change course as early as 1908, as other movements modified or stimulated different methods of expression.

In Germany, around the same time as Fauvism sprang up in France, German artists were working concurrently along similar lines. Here, Nolde, Kirchner and Kandinsky became the chief exponents of what was to develop into Expressionism.

Matisse once wrote that he was 'unable to distinguish between the feeling I have for life and my way of expressing it'. Contemporary philosophical thinking already placed increased importance on intuition and the subconscious when talking about the creative process. Matisse believed that these intuitive feelings were best explored through colour and design. The German Expressionists, however, had strong feelings about the artist's responsibility as a critic of society.

Nolde and Kirchner in Dresden, Kandinsky and Marc in Munich, felt that their paintings should express the problems of modern man, the dangerous materialism of contemporary society. In short, the subject of a picture dictated how it was to be painted, not the other way round.

Kandinsky and his abstract vision

The greatest achievement of the German school, however, was to lay the foundations of abstract art.

No need to distort everyday reality, they concluded, colours and forms are expressive in themselves. The artist who first made this breakthrough was Vassily Kandinsky (1866–1944). Though Russian born and raised, Kandinsky spent most of his working life in Germany. His youth in Russia had given him an intense interest in music, and he was fascinated by the expressiveness of pure colour and pure sound.

It took him some 15 years as a painter to see that abstract art was the best way for him to explore the spiritual world. His first abstract paintings appeared in 1910. His work has been described as 'pure visual music' – a metaphor Kandinsky would have greatly appreciated. For he combined colours and forms in much the same way as a composer orchestrates by setting different instruments against each other.

Cubism

Meanwhile, in Paris, around 1908 there had been an equally revolutionary development: the invention by Picasso and Braque of Cubism. Louis Vauxcelles was again responsible for the name: he said that Braque 'reduced everything . . . to cubes'. Cubism is probably the most complex and misunderstood movement of modern art. Its basic premise was that painting gives an opportunity to study, dismantle and reassemble an object's form and to exploit the infinite scope it offers for invention. Why should an artist restrict himself to one point of view? Why not incorporate what he *remembers* about an object, as well as what he can see of it? Picasso and Braque took still-lifes and figures and used them as starting points for this approach.

The work of Vassily Kandinsky led the way, via Expressionism, to abstract art. His painting Cossacks *(left) is one of a series called* Compositions, *painted between 1910 and 1914, and these mark the transition from Expressionism to abstraction. Here, a castle, five cossacks, their sabres and lances and a flight of birds are all discernible. But the arrangement of shapes and the clash of colours carry the weight of Kandinsky's abstract message.*

415

Many works were in monochrome, or a very restricted range of colours. This was partly in reaction to the gaudy Fauvists, partly to concentrate attention on structure and form.

Braque employed a 'mobile perspective', moving round his subjects and simultaneously recording different views from different angles, from near-to and far away, with features both remembered and seen. Certain elements are in sharp focus, some are quite blurred – the equivalent, perhaps, of how we recall objects to mind.

Picasso once said, 'I paint my figures as I think them, not as I see them.' The original subject is sometimes very difficult to recognize. Figures melt into the space that surrounds them. The space therefore becomes just as important as the subject.

This relationship between the object and the

space around it fascinated contemporary artists. The next logical step was to do without the object altogether. Thus the Cubists' fascination with form, and Kandinsky's fascination with colour brought them by different routes to abstract art.

In Russia, many collectors bought up the works of Gauguin, the Post-Impressionists, then Matisse and Picasso, almost as soon as the paint was dry. These huge collections had an immense impact on young Russian artists who, between 1910 and 1920, evolved a school of abstract, geometric art in advance of anything in Europe. The most important of these artists was Malevich. He, like the Cubists and Expressionsits, felt there was nothing to be gained from studying the visible world, the future lay in finding visual equivalents to conscious and unconscious states of mind.

The style he evolved he entitled Suprematism – shorthand for 'the supremacy of feeling in creative art'. Suprematism was based on the square, which he placed against a white background – the 'white sun of infinity'. So the first Suprematist work was a black square against a white background, though Malevich quickly built up from this an elaborate, highly distinctive vocabulary. Rectangles, squares, circles and lines painted in elementary colours correspond to a whole range of feelings. Squares and rectangles of unequal sizes and shapes, variations of angle and

direction, float against a background to suggest depth. Malevich was hugely influential, both in Russia and, later, in the West.

In wartime Holland, the great proponent of abstract art was Mondrian. Again growing out of Cubism, his was a style more austere than Malevich's, based simply on the square, the rectangle and the right-angle. He used only black and white and the three primary colours, equating these fundamentals of art with the fundamental forces underlying nature. He claimed to seek a purer reality that lay beyond mere superficial appearance. A dynamic tension between lines, shapes and colours animate the canvases. And within his wilfully limited means, he achieved extraordinary variety – just as a jazz musician can create many variations on a theme. (Mondrian was, in fact, an excellent jazz musician.)

Pablo Picasso (far left) was infinitely versatile, contributing to several quite separate schools of art. Co-founder of Cubism and artist of Seated Nude (centre) he pursued Cubism to its ultimate conclusion in abstract expressionism. He did not even confine himself to painting – his pottery is hugely prized.

Dada

Mondrian was appalled by the horrors of World War I. He hoped that his art would help create a better society where such things could not happen. Other artists reacted to the devastation, waste and folly of the war in a different way: with Dada.

Dada was not a person. It was not even a school of art. It was two separate political protest movements – one in New York, one in Zurich – which chose to adopt a child's nonsense word as its name and which violently rejected all established artistic values.

One parent of the rowdy Dada child was the 'Functionalist', Vladimir Tatlin, who argued that fine-art belonged to the capitalist's culture and that artists of conscience should give it up in favour of making chairs and building houses.

The other parent was perhaps the Futurist Movement in Italy, where a new generation of dis-

Composition in Grey, Red, Yellow and Blue (above) was painted by Piet Mondrian between 1920 and 1926. As early as 1917, he abandoned the landscape painting that had made his reputation, and concentrated on the pursuit of 'pure reality', equating pure colour with the fundamental forces in nature. As time passed, he grew increasingly severe – permitting himself only the use of primary colour blocks.

417

The Dada and Futurist movements were scornful of the art establishment and the past, as the quotation splashed across the Dada magazine cover above suggests: 'I don't even want to know if there were any men before me.'

Surrealism took many different forms but its object was always the same – to explore the fantasy world of the imagination and present it as a psychological document. Salvador Dali chose to express himself in an almost photographic style – beautiful, but always slightly grotesque and disturbing – as in The Metamorphosis of Narcissus *(1934) (right).*

Dali's later career was split between painting and making films in the tradition of the 'Theatre of the Absurd'. The still below is from the Surrealist film Le Chien Andalou, *1929.*

contented artists – Boccioni, Balla and Severini – called for museums to be torn down and for artistic taste to stop fawning slavishly on the Old Masters. A work of art was nothing if it was not *relevant*. A work of art was nothing if it did not say anything *original*. Their subjects were often urban and, since cities are full of movement, so were the paintings. Dynamism was all-important. Canvases look like delayed-exposure photography, with a multiplicity of flying limbs. Some subjects are too fragmented by movement to be recognisable. One late convert to Futurism was Marcel Duchamp. When Futurism died in the war, Duchamp's savagery found its outlet in Dadaism.

In New York in 1915, Duchamp and Picabia (both French) were central to the Dada protest movement. They made their protest by ridiculing conventional sensibilities. Man was being depersonalized by the machine: as a protest Duchamp produced his 'ready-

One important name to emerge from Dada was that of Jean (Hans) Arp. He became intrigued to know how the laws of chance affected the creation of a work of art, suspecting that the subconscious mind is heavily involved. His first work, *Collage with squares arranged according to the laws of chance,* was created by tearing up pieces of coloured paper and letting them fall haphazardly on to another sheet of paper, then fixing them where they fell, with additional shapes added as suggested by the initial pattern.

Towards 1918, the two Dada movements met, merged and became closely identified with the revolutionary left-wing politics of the time. But, whereas to sow confusion and dismay in bourgeois minds was an end itself to some Dadaists, others had more positive aims. Arp, for instance, said: 'We were looking for an elemental art that would, we thought, save mankind from the raging madness of those times.'

Cynicism and scorn eventually exhaust themselves when there is nothing left to deride. The shocking ceases to shock. So, in about 1920, Dada died though its ghost has been seen many times since World War 2. The positive offshoot that grew out of it was Surrealism. This movement, too, encompassed more than painting. Its first manifestation was written, its first proponent André Breton, who wrote the *Surrealist Manifesto* in 1924. He defined Surrealism as 'thought's dictation, free from any control by reason'.

Surrealism and Naivety

Shedding the desire to shock and protest, the Surrealists retained an obsession to get to the origins of art, to recover spontaneity and honesty, and purge themselves of superficial sophistication. The art of other cultures, particularly primitive cultures,

mades'. Everyday things like a typewriter, a comb or a urinal were given new and mysterious titles, signed by the artist and thereby made into 'artistic objects'. A snowshovel, for example, was retitled *In Advance of the Broken Arm.*

In Zurich, Dada centred on the Café Voltaire, an artistic club-cum-cabaret where, for two years, a demi-monde of literary and musical figures contributed to all kinds .of explosively original performances, demonstrations and exhibitions. Dada found outlets in poetry and literary presentation as well as painting and sculpture. Many of the typefaces now used by printers, for example, date back to that era. Design as a whole benefitted greatly from Dada's determination to startle and catch the eye. Dada directed a savage wit at contemporary culture. It interested itself in the subconscious, the childish and the irrational. Its art contrasted garishly with austere Cubism.

Whereas many of the radical, experimental artists abandoned perspective as an outmoded convention, Georgio de Chirico (right), allied to the Italian Futurists and a precursor of Surrealism, used it in the creation of deeply disturbing landscapes peopled by weird figures. Close enough to reality to be recognizable, surreal enough to be unsettling, his paintings are like bad dreams.

suddenly found an admiring Western audience. African, Indian and Oriental influences crept in. Naive painters, such as Henri Rousseau, who had been quietly ploughing their own furrows, were feted for their childlike spontaneity and richly primitive qualities.

But above all the Surrealists built on the artistic possibilites of the mind's subconscious – of dreams and Freudian impulses – trying to isolate the nature of thought from the cultural clutter of morality, intellect or aesthetics.

Under the movement's title are grouped vastly different styles. There were Orthodox Surrealists, such as Salvador Dali, Rene Magritte and Max Ernst. Their 'hand-painted dreams' pervade the art of the 1920s and 1930s. Equally, such abstract artists as Miro and Paul Klee accounted themselves Surrealists.

Paul Klee exhibited at the first Surrealist exhibition in Paris, 1925. He claimed to be 'possessed by colour', and entrusted his work to the demon 'intuition', refusing to decide on a theme or title until a work was finished. His work is compulsive – but not haphazard: his preoccupation is in placing symbols in a pure formal harmony with one another. In this respect he can be allied to Miro.

Before the dust settles

Almost all the movements that have arisen since can be traced back to the experiments in the first years of the century: black and white Op-Art to Malevich's geometric Suprematism; Warhol's crushed soup tins (countlessly reproduced or vastly enlarged) to Duchamp's 'Urinal'; Henry Moore's semi-abstract sculptures to those first Cubist invitations to examine 'the spaces in between'; Marc Rothko's rectangles of colour to Matisse's blocks of counterbalanced primary paints . . .

The determination to wrest art from the art gallery and the bourgeoisie has taken the form of Environmental Art (canvases too large to be displayed in a gallery) and even Destruction Events in which works of art are themselves obliterated. Ironically, the 'man-in-the-street' has been the first to condemn such *avant-garde* art, the dilletante bougeois the first to invest it with monetary value.

Only with hindsight can the genuine achievements of any movement be appreciated. As Herbert Read has written: an era 'leaves behind it, when the dust has settled, a few genuine works of art'. The dust is only beginning to settle over the first half of the 20th century.

Elements that concerned the artistic innovators of the early 20th century are all reflected in the work of Henry Moore, the British sculptor. His sculptures do not seek beauty, but admire rather the brute forces in Nature and in the human body in particular. He touched briefly on abstract means of expression, but was drawn more towards Surrealism. Like the Cubists, he invites the viewer to observe the spaces between the mass, volume and texture. All of this is contained in the 'Family group', right.

Igor Stravinsky
1882–1971

*An intellectual, cosmopolitan Russian emigré,
Stravinsky rocked the world with his startling,
dynamic music, but came to be acknowledged as
the greatest 20th-century composer.*

Stravinsky remains the great giant of 20th-century music, the man who, more than anyone, assured the break with the romantic traditions of the 19th century and led music forward into the modern world. He lived a Frenchman and died an American, but he was born in Russia and during years of exile he grieved – in life and in his music – for the country of his birth. Likewise he remained true to the Russian Orthodox faith, keeping icons, observing feast days and dedicating his most profoundly religious works to 'the Glory of God' – though, he admitted, 'like those of Haydn, all my works are so dedicated.' Out of Russian Orthodoxy came a lifelong fascination for ritual and order, a fascination which inspired such works as *The Rite of Spring,* and instilled a general respect for convention that meant he could never be 'even the nicest anarchist!'

Physically, Stravinsky was small and slight with disproportionately large hands – craftsman's hands, as he called them – and, despite a rather awkward frame, he was a graceful, charismatic figure. His intellect was sharp but logical and he had a highly organized 'world view'. Not content simply to be well-informed, he craved a specialist's knowledge of every subject and was an avid reader – his Los Angeles library contained 10,000 books! But however weighty the topic, his impish sense of humour was always near the surface and he was a gifted raconteur, especially under the influence of alcohol. (He was extremely partial to wine and whisky; he spurned water as only useful 'for the feet'!!)

He worked tirelessly, sometimes for 18 hours at a stretch, despite being plagued with ill health all his life. Tuberculosis, typhus, bleeding ulcers, hernias, crippling headaches and insomnia all afflicted him at one time or another. The range of pill bottles surrounding his plate at the dinner table once provoked the comment from W. H. Auden that 'the most stable business in the world would be a pharmacy next door to Stravinsky!' But time and again his titanic energy and love of life won through illness, spurring him on into a productive old age.

A Russian childhood

Stravinsky was exposed to music from the day he was born on 17 June 1882. His father, Fyodor Ignatievitch, was a famous opera singer with the Mariinsky Theatre who had impressed Glinka and Rimsky Korsakov with his performances. His mother,

When this picture was painted in 1915, Igor Stravinsky was only 33, yet he was already internationally acclaimed as one of Europe's brightest and most original composers.

Great Composers

Anna Kyrillovna also sang, and played the piano exquisitely. It was from her, as Stravinsky's memoirs relate, that he 'inherited the valuable ability to read orchestral scores at sight.'

But it was not until he was nine that Stravinsky began to study the piano and music theory and clearly preferred improvising his own pieces rather than struggling with routine practice. These improvizations sowed the seeds of the musical revolution he was to create later.

During his years at the Gurevitch School in St. Petersburg, he made few friends and was, by his own account, a very poor pupil. Invention at the keyboard banished loneliness, as did the yearly summer expeditions to join his cousins on the family country estates at Pechisky and, later, Ustilug where he could enjoy music-making, painting, and the kind of friendship he was never able to find at school.

Nevertheless, his interest in music was far from the consuming passion it was to be later. And in 1901, Stravinsky followed his parents' advice and enrolled in St Petersburg University to read law. Yet it was not long before music began to assume a more important role in his life. His early efforts at improvisation flowered into serious experiments in composition, and criminal law and legal philosophy started slipping into the background of his life. The idea of being a composer took hold firmly. He began to

wonder whether to enrol in the St Petersburg Conservatoire.

It was at this time that Stravinsky became friendly with a fellow student, Vladimir, the youngest son of the great Russian composer Rimsky-Korsakov. Then in 1902 Stravinsky met Rimsky-Korsakov himself. On hearing Stravinsky play, Rimsky-Korsakov advised Stravinsky not to go to the St Petersburg Conservatoire, where he might become discouraged by the rigid academic approach − 'Instead' wrote Stravinsky later, 'he made me the precious gift of his unforgettable lessons.'

The master-pupil relationship developed into close friendship and Rimsky-Korsakov took on a fatherly role in Stravinsky's life, particularly after the death of Fyodor in 1902. Friendship with Rimsky-Korsakov also gave Stravinsky an entreé to St Petersburg musical life and he began to attend soirées and 'Evenings of Contemporary Music' held to air new works by German and French as well as Russian Composers. He was particularly fascinated by the music of Debussy which seemed to inhabit its own unique sound world. But Rimsky-Korsakov warned: 'better not listen to him; one runs the risk of getting accustomed to him and one would end by liking him.'

Stravinsky's parents, Fyodor and Anna (left), provided a rich musical background for the young composer. From his nursery, Igor would hear his father practising for his many operatic roles, and as he grew older he was allowed to explore his father's extensive library of music.

In the summers of 1891 and 1892, the Stravinsky family stayed in the country at Pechisky (bottom left). It was here that Igor met his cousin Katerina, the girl who became his dearest friend and later his wife.

Triumph and tragedy

In 1905, he graduated successfully in law from the St Petersburg School, but he had no intention of following a legal career. He was now 23 and, as he later wrote, 'at this time, my adolescence came to an end'. He made two important decisions. The first was a total commitment to music. The second was his engagement to his cousin, Katerina Nossenko. Throughout Stravinsky's unhappy school days Katerina's kindness and affection had been a vital support and, over the years they had become very close. They married the following year, and the couple set up home in St Petersburg but during the summer they returned, as they always had, to the family at Ustilug where Stravinsky found he could work in peace. Their first child, Fyodor was born in 1907 and their second, Ludmilla, the following year.

The year 1908 was to hold a sad as well as a happy event for Stravinsky. Early in the summer, he completed an orchestral fantasy called *Fireworks,* to honour the forthcoming wedding of Rimsky-Korsakov's daughter, Nadieshda. Stravinsky posted the completed manuscript to Rimsky-Korsakov from Ustilug, seeking his approval. But the parcel crossed with a telegram from St Petersburg informing Stravinsky of his mentor's death. Shortly afterwards the parcel came back unopened and marked 'Not delivered on account of the death of the addressee'. Stravinsky hurried to join the family for the funeral and later said:

It was one of the unhappiest days of my life. But I was there, and I will remember Rimsky in his coffin as long as memory is. He looked so very beautiful I could not help crying.

Fireworks was later given a public performance in St Petersburg and among those present in the audience was the dazzling impresario Sergei Diaghilev. Diaghilev had, in 1908, successfully staged Russian music and opera in Paris and was now planning to introduce Parisians to Russian ballet. On hearing *Fireworks* Diaghilev immediately became

convinced that Stravinsky was the composer he needed to complete his team.

Stravinsky was quite happy to orchestrate the music for the opening season of Diaghilev's new ballet company in 1909. Then in 1910, Diaghilev found himself without a composer for his ballet on the legend of the Firebird after Anatol Liadov pulled out. It was Stravinsky who came to the rescue and created the score that was to make him the toast of Europe.

The 1910 première of *The Firebird* was greeted ecstatically by the Paris audience. After the final curtain Diaghilev came up to Stravinsky supporting a man on his arm whom he introduced as Claude Debussy. Thus began a friendship which was to last until Debussy's death.

'Petrushka' and 'The Rite of Spring'

The name 'Petrushka' or 'Little Pierrot' came to Stravinsky one day while he was walking along by the sea at Clarens. Typical of his less than solemn approach to musical tradition, he pictured 'a puppet suddenly endowed with life, exasperating the patience of the orchestra with diabolical cascades of arpeggios.'

In Paris, on 13 June 1911, Petrushka, the pierrot who survived murder to jeer and taunt the audience, was premièred with even greater success than the

Stravinsky's cousin Katerina (right) gave him the warm companionship he badly needed throughout his youth. As he explained later, 'I was a deeply lonely child, and I wanted a sister of my own. Catherine . . . came into my life as a kind of long-wanted sister in my tenth year. We were from then until her death extremely close, and closer than lovers sometimes are, for mere lovers may be strangers though they live and love together all their lives.'

Some of the world's leading avant garde artists designed sets for Stravinsky's ballets, from Picasso to David Hockney. The sets for the 1928 production of 'Petrushka' by the Krolloper in Berlin were designed by Ewald Duhlberg. Shown left is his sketch for the set for the opening scene in the fairground. Duhlberg's design was innovative in that it broke away from the traditional Russian setting of the story and showed instead a more cosmopolitan world.

Firebird. Debussy's praise was unstinted, 'Dear Friend, thanks to you I have passed an enjoyable Easter Vacation in the company of Petrushka, the terrible Moor and the beautiful ballerina . . . You will go much further than 'Petrushka', it is certain, but you may be proud of the achievement of this work.' These were prophetic words, for within two years Stravinsky had created one of the undisputed monuments of 20th century music, his controversial ballet score *The Rite of Spring.*

'And here', as the composer's son has written, 'let us stop a moment and consider. Is not the astounding creative vitality of this young 30-year-old musician a

Stravinsky met Vera de Bosset (right) when she was acting in 'The Sleeping Beauty' in London in 1923. Vera was married to the Russian artist Soudekeine at the time but her relationship with Stravinsky flourished and, 17 years later, she became his second wife.

and *Mavra* a comic opera based on a Pushkin story.

Stravinsky was not alone in his grief for Russia. His compatriots from the Ballets Russes shared his exile – Nijinsky, Massine, Fokine, and, of course, Diaghilev, to whom Stravinsky dedicated the work that most expressed his longing for his homeland – *Les Noces* (The Wedding). It was a ballet of peasant custom and religious ritual, born of the same spirit as *The Rite of Spring.* Stravinsky, ever fascinated by the subject of ritual, later recalled sounds of religious rite echoing in his mind as he wrote. And when he played parts of *Les Noces* to Diaghilev on the piano, the great impresario wept, saying it touched him more than

In 1942, the Ringling Brothers circus, with an eye for publicity, commissioned Balanchine and Stravinsky to score a ballet for them. The 'ballerinas' for 'The Circus Polka' were to be elephants! The performances in Madison Square Garden (programme cover right) were, needless to say, a massive success.

matter for wonder? In three years, 1910–13 he has written the three masterpieces that are to place him at the peak of his reputation – *Firebird, Petrushka* and *The Rite of Spring* – and at the same time, like any patriarch, he has made provision for the upkeep of a family living in a perpetual state of nomadism.'

Exile

As it happened, the nomadic state was soon to be terminated by the outbreak of war. Switzerland, which had so far been an occasional temporary refuge, now became home. With the onset of war, commissions from the Ballets Russes dried up, Stravinsky's publishers were out of reach in enemy territory and he could no longer depend on the income from his Russian estate.

'But, throughout the whole period when we were waiting to go back to Russia it was my Russian past which preoccupied me most,' declared Stravinsky, and after his death his son Fyodor reminisced: 'I think he realized in his heart he would never go back to Russia, so his love for his country and his homesickness increased.' A stream of Russia-inspired compositions resulted. He wrote Russian songs and choruses and a number of his best loved works included *The Soldier's Tale* based on a Russian folk tale – a colourful shoestring entertainment for war –

anything he had ever heard.

Although his family had now settled down at Morges in Switzerland, Stravinsky himself was always on the move, always possessed by the urge to travel. Though exiled from Russia, he had become a celebrated international artist.

'But after a while', as Stravinsky recalled, 'I became tired of the provincial life in Switzerland. I felt drawn back to the centre of things. Paris!' And in 1920, he moved his family to the French countryside where he was able to work peacefully in between frequent trips to Paris. As ever life involved constant travel, and in 1921, Stravinsky joined the Ballets Russes on tour in Spain and England, where he heard the concert première of *The Rite of Spring.* While in London, Diaghilev planned a revival of *The Sleeping Beauty* at the Alhambra Theatre, and Stravinsky agreed to help with the score. In the cast, playing the non-dancing role of the Queen was Vera de Bosset. Stravinsky was enchanted by the young Russian actress and Vera was captivated by the charismatic composer. Soon they were spending as much time as possible in each other's company. Surprisingly, despite his passion for Vera, he did not neglect his wife and family. And Katerina, devoted as she was, showed saint-like understanding, even to the point of befriending Vera.

On Tour

The 1920s saw Stravinsky travelling continuously all over Europe and as far afield as the USA where he was given a tremendous welcome. This meant that he had little time to devote to the Ballets Russes, and he accepted no more commissions after *Pulcinella* (1920).

But Diaghilev was not happy to lose a grip on his protégé. Nor was he especially mollified by the present of one of Stravinsky's greatest works, the Latin opera-oratorio *Oedipus Rex.* On the contrary, he called it 'a very macabre gift'. Then Stravinsky accepted a commission from Ida Rubinstein to write the ballet *The Fairy's Kiss,* based on music by Tchaikovsky. To Diaghilev, Stravinsky's use of 'classical' material was little short of treason, but there was no opportunity to heal the breach for when, in August 1926, Diaghilev died in Venice, the two men had not spoken for six months. Stravinsky was mortified for, despite many quarrels, they had been close: 'I gave myself up to mourning a friend, a brother, whom I should never see again.'

In June 1934, Stravinsky's naturalization papers came through and he became a French citizen. The following year he published his autobiography *Chronicles of my Life* written in French. But Stravinsky was beginning to realize that it was not in France but the USA that his music was finding most sympathy. In 1935 he toured America, again, to great acclaim, and received an invitation to compose the ballet *Jeu de Cartes* (Cardgame) for the newly-formed American Ballet. Other commissions rolled in from America including the chamber concerto *Dumbarton Oaks* and the *Symphony in C.*

These commissions came at a significant moment. Europe was again poised on the brink of World War, and Stravinsky had been shaken deeply by the deaths through tuberculosis of first his daughter Ludmilla, then his wife Katerina and his mother, within months of each other. As if this were not enough, Stravinsky fell victim to the disease himself. He tried to combat ill-health and his terrible grief by throwing himself into his work. By the time war broke out his health

It was Aldous Huxley (left), the English writer, who suggested to Stravinsky that the poet W. H. Auden (below) should write the libretto for 'The Rake's Progress'. Stravinsky was absolutely delighted with the results.

During his life, Stravinsky met and made friends with many of the world's most famous artists and political figures. The picture above shows Stravinsky and his second wife, Vera, meeting President John Kennedy and his wife Jacqueline at the White House in 1962 at a dinner party given in the composer's honour. Stravinsky later remarked that the President and his wife were 'nice kids!' When Kennedy was assassinated on 22 November, 1963, Stravinsky was deeply upset and wrote a unique intimate tribute. His 'Elegy for JFK' was a small piece for baritone and three clarinets, a setting of four verses in 'haiku' style with words by W. H. Auden.

had improved, and he decided to move to America.

Stravinsky called 1939 'the tragic year of my life', but the end of the year was to usher in the sunniest period of his entire life. He lived in a little bungalow in the Hollywood Hills, gladly relinquishing his nomadic existence to feel, at last, part of a community. Then, in 1940, he married Vera de Bosset, and they began a life of happiness together that was to last until Stravinsky's death.

The Rake's Progress

Stravinsky and his wife took American nationality in 1945. By then he was able to say: 'I feel very well, I feel America is my second country.' The same year he signed an exclusive contract with Boosey and Hawkes, the publishers, which brought to an end a long history of copyright and financial problems. It also meant that Stravinsky could, at last, afford the luxury of working without the constant need for commissions. Stravinsky had long wanted to compose a full-length opera, and now seized the opportunity to devote three years to the project. Moreover, he had a subject. While visiting the Chicago Art Institute he had been delighted by a set of Hogarth engravings depicting the Rake's Progress. The combination of crooks and rogues, love and the devil, seemed to suggest a perfect storyline.

On the advice of his friend, the writer Aldous Huxley, Stravinsky asked the poet W. H. Auden to write the libretto. The collaboration was a success beyond Stravinsky's wildest dreams.

The Venice première of the opera was to take place during the International Festival of Contemporary Music 1951, under the baton of the composer himself. The rehearsals went far from

Unlike many 20th century composers, Stravinsky loved taking the baton at concerts of his own music, and continued to do so until he was an old man. Here he is seen during the 1960s (right).

smoothly but the opera survived its first performance and delighted the Venetian audience.

One summer's day in 1948, a letter arrived from a 23-year-old musician called Robert Craft, asking if he could borrow a score for a Stravinsky concert he wanted to conduct in New York. Stravinsky not only lent the score, but generously offered to conduct parts of the concert himself, and the following spring, Craft met the composer to discuss arrangements. The collaboration was remarkably successful and grew into a close friendship.

The involvement of Robert Craft in his life also meant that he could return to the conducting tours

For the 1975 revival of 'The Rake's Progress' at Glyndebourne, David Hockney echoed Stravinsky's original inspiration for the opera, the paintings of Hogarth, in his design for costumes and set (left).

Stravinsky always yearned to return to the country of his birth, but it was not until 1962, 50 years after he first left, that he set foot in Russia once more – he was welcomed ecstatically (below).

He had often made such declarations as, 'the greatest crisis in my life was losing Russia', or 'I speak Russian, I think Russian, and, as you hear in my music, I am Russian'. And, as Robert Craft observed in his Russian diary, 'To be recognized and acclaimed as a Russian in Russia, and to be performed there has meant more to him than anything in the years I have known him.'

By 1967, Stravinsky's health was beginning to fail. That year he made his last recording and conducted his last concert – a performance of the *Pulcinella* suite. When he at last became physically incapable of composing he satisfied his need for music by listening to records, taking pleasure in being able to 'listen to and love the music of other men in a way I could not do when conducting my own.' On 6th April 1971, Stravinsky died at his home in New York. His body was carried across an ocean and a continent, then conveyed across the Venetian lagoon to its final destination, the island of San Michele, where he lies buried in the Russian Orthodox corner, close to his friend Diaghilev.

that he had previously enjoyed so much. As old age began to encroach on his strength he was unable to undertake all the work himself, but Craft, who had learnt the interpretation of Stravinsky's music at the composer's side, could prepare an orchestra in advance for Stravinsky's final rehearsal and performance. This way the three companions, Stravinsky, Vera and Craft, travelled extensively.

1962 marked Stravinsky's return to Russia after nearly half a century's absence, to conduct concerts of his music in Moscow and Leningrad. He was given a hero's welcome, and, according to his niece, thirty thousand people queued for the Leningrad concerts.

The Ballets Russes

**Sergei Diaghilev, 'the collector of geniuses',
gathered around him dancers, artists and
composers, and created a company that astounded
the world of art – the Ballets Russes.**

'It is my firm belief that human society is divided into three distinct castes: Russian dancers, dancers, and very ordinary people.' With these words Arnold Haskell opened his book *Balletomania* in 1934 – and he was not alone in his opinion. The Russian dancers he referred to were the dancers of the Ballets Russes who reigned over the world of ballet so supremely that, for hundreds of thousands of Europeans and Americans, they stood as giants even in a time of artistic 'greats'. Yet they owed their elevated position to much more than their own dancing abilities. In fact, they owed much to the brilliant overall staging of the ballet productions in which they danced – the productions of the Ballets Russes Company. And behind this great and revolutionary dance company was one man: the creator, organiser and director of it – Sergei Diaghilev.

For the 20 years between Diaghilev's first

Sergei Diaghilev (left) called himself a charlatan and a charmer, with no real talent, but he found his true vocation as an impresario. His first achievement was to open Russian minds to Western art with The World of Art *magazine (below right). His next was to expose the West to a generation of exceptional Russian artists. 'Remember, remember the ugliness, the triteness, the mediocrity at the beginning of the century,' wrote Emile Henriot in praise of the changes Diaghilev wrought on traditional ballet (below).*

presentation of the Ballets Russes, in 1909, until his premature death in 1929, Diaghilev set the world of art aflame. His vision was to bring together a huge assembly of talent from all the fields of art and unite them to present a balanced, rounded world of illusion and entertainment. This he did with unparalleled success in his Ballets Russes Company.

After Diaghilev's death the spirit of the Ballets Russes lived on in the form of other Ballets Russes Companies, but it was his original idea that was to revolutionize the world of art and dance.

'The World of Art'

Long before Diaghilev set up the Ballets Russes he had showed his individual ideas and his flair for organization. In his home city of St Petersburg, Diaghilev and his circle of friends founded, in 1899, a magazine called *The World of Art* (in Russian, *Mir Iskusstra*). This gives early clues to his ideas and to his unique sense of artistic presentation. The purpose behind the magazine was to fight Russian prejudice against Western art as, at the time, all art within Russia was dominated by a policy of 'Russian themes for Russian Art'. A notable example of this was classical Russian ballet. This had been the focus of the world as far as ballet was concerned yet it seemed to Diaghilev too claustrophobic – Russian ballet dancers, Russian themes and Russian music. Diaghilev set out to change this nationalist policy by championing 'art for art's sake' and introducing Russia to 'Western' art. In turn he introduced the West to the best of Russian art. He also organized a series of exhibitions in St Petersburg (now Leningrad) which featured Western paintings. And due to the theatrical flair with which he presented them they enjoyed considerable success.

Other exhibitions, even those with exclusively Russian themes, were also a revelation to those who saw them. These reached a climax in 1905 with his exhibition of historical Russian portraits. But in the same year, *The World of Art* ran out of funds and closed. Diaghilev thus turned his attentions abroad. He looked to Paris in particular to forward his ideas,

and took a major exhibition of Russian painting there in 1906, a series of concerts of Russian music in 1907 and a season of Russian opera in 1908. All these became, in turn, the talk of Paris.

Back in St Petersburg at the subsidized Mariinsky Theatre, under the patronage of Duke Vladimir, Diaghilev set to work on the repertoire for a new season of opera and ballet that would be presented in Paris in 1909. Working in committee with his associates Fokine the choreographer, Benois the set

Bakst's superb and exotic programme for the 1911 Ballets Russes season in Monte Carlo (below) shows the kind of design detail which was so typical of the Ballets Russes.

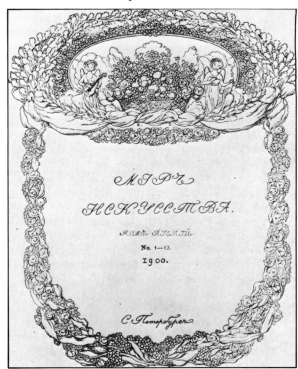

designer and Leon Bakst the costume designer, they began to gather ideas. The repertoire included the ballets *Les Sylphides, Le Pavillon d'Armide* and *Cleopatre,* and the operas *Ivan the Terrible, Prince Igor, Russlan and Ludmilla, Judith* and *Boris Gudonov.* Then, just as the repertoire was finalized Duke Vladimir died and the subsidy was withdrawn. All appeared lost until Diaghilev saved the day by calling on financial help from his friends in Paris. This, however, changed the whole situation vis-a-vis Diaghilev's position and his influence on the repertoire. Consequently, the opera was cut to the bare minimum and the ballet emphasized – with Diaghilev changing pieces and introducing others to reflect what he thought the Paris public wanted, as Paris, rather than Russia, seemed to point to the way forward for the company.

Gathering the very best artists and dancers from around him, Diaghilev and his company set off for the 1909 season in Paris.

The Ballets Russes opens
The opening night of the *Ballets Russes* in the Thêátre Chatelet, which Diaghilev had had specially

redecorated and refurbished, was a sensation. A few Russian dancers had been seen, and admired, before in the West. But the impact of a united company, harnessing unmatched artistic talents, staggered the Parisian audience. No Western artists had ever worked together with such commitment and intensity. These ballets were not mere vehicles for virtuoso dancing solos, they were overall images, presented as a unified whole. Maurice Brillant wrote of that first dazzling season: 'All artists understood that this was more than exotic entertainment.'

In due course, Petrushka was danced by Nijinsky to Stravinsky's music and Fokine's choreography, with Benois' designs. In *The Three-Cornered Hat,* Leonide Massine and Tamara Karsavina danced to Massine's choreography and the music of Spain's great composer Manuel de Falla, within vivid yellow sets designed by Pablo Picasso. *The Firebird, The Rite of Spring, Les Noces, Les Biches* and *Apollo* followed, and all were hugely successful.

Even when Diaghilev failed, he failed magnificently. Jean Cocteau, Satie and Picasso combined forces to attempt a 'union of painting and the dance' entitled *Parade.* It scandalized its audiences, But then, to an

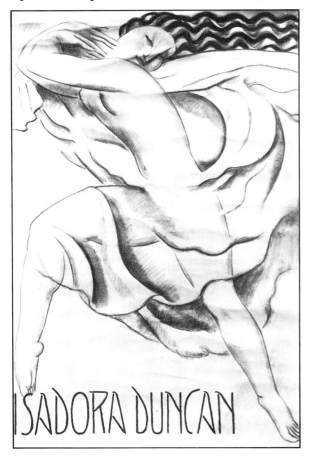

The American dancer Isadora Duncan (below) visited Russia early in the 1900s and rocked artistic society. She had no technique, no morals, she lacked sex appeal, and her prancing verged on the ridiculous. But her stage dress and use of non-ballet music had a dramatic and influential impact.

ISADORA DUNCAN

Vaslav Nijinsky and Anna Pavlova in Le Pavillon d'Armide *(right), selected for the first Ballets Russes season. Pavlova finally left the company when she felt it was stifling her stardom. Nijinsky, however, stayed on to become both dancer and choreographer.*

extent, the public relied on Diaghilev to shock them. They could forgive almost anything but conservatism. The man himself tired of the English who were doggedly complimentary about everything he did. But he tired, too, of the Parisians who wanted some new outrage to capture their attention every season.

Nijinsky – 'an angel, a genius'

Though the Ballets Russes did not rely for popularity on the cult of the star dancer, it must owe much of its glory to the quite exceptional talent available at the time of its creation. Destined to become the most famous male dancer of all time, Vaslav Nijinsky was among the artists who travelled to Paris for that first triumphant season. With him was Tamara Karsavina – 'the most exquisite daughter of classical choreography'. She stayed with Diaghilev through thick and thin: through financial instability, internal rifts, and ice ages of critical opinion.

Nijinsky – immensely energetic, unambiguously masculine, and with the on-stage illusion of good looks – was able to fulfill Diaghilev's ambition to put the lead male dancer back on par with the prima ballerina of classical ballet. Women had tiptoed their way towards monopolizing the Western ballet. Now Nijinsky leapt to the centre of the stage and captured the posters, the programmes, and the admiration of his astonished audience.

He captured Diaghilev, too, who needed the

Stravinsky shelved The Rite of Spring *to write* Petrushka *in time for the 1911 season. The design of costumes and scenery (above) was entrusted to Benois, and the ballet was hailed as a sublime unification of dance and painting. Fokine (seen left in* The Firebird *with Karsavina) was both dancer and choreographer in* Petrushka.

The artist Jean Cocteau made dozens of lightning sketches (like that showing Stravinsky, Diaghilev, himself and Satie, left) capturing the creative ferment surrounding Diaghilev.

The fly-poster below demonstrates what an ambitious and varied repertoire the Ballets Russes undertook.

companionship and potential of a golden protégé more than he needed an alliance with a woman. He encouraged Nijinsky's secondary career as a Ballets Russes choreographer, and showed great personal kindness to a young man who cut quite a helpless figure off stage. Tragically, Diaghilev's possessiveness soured the golden partnership even before its dreadful end in 1929 when Nijinsky suffered total mental collapse.

New dances to old music
The first choreographer whom Diaghilev used for his Ballets Russes was Mikhail Fokine (1880–1942). This determined and passionate young choreographer did his first work with dance students at the school attached to the great Mariinsky Theatre in St Petersburg. For in choreographing works set in ancient Greece, such as *Acis and Galatea* or *Daphnis and Chloe*, Fokine insisted on abandoning

conventional ballet tutus and pointework in favour of presenting a convincingly 'Greek' image. He wanted his student dancers to dance barefoot, though at the Mariinsky was thwarted in this by the strictly observed niceties of ballet convention. However, this radical approach was pre-empted by the revolutionary American dancer Isadora Duncan. In 1904 she had outraged and amazed St Petersburg with her dancing. Grand yet simple, it was set to great classical music by Chopin, Schubert and the like. She performed in bare feet and in a light, flowing, short Greek dress. The idea of dancing to music that had not been intended for the dance inspired others. In 1905 Fokine had set *The Dying Swan,* for the ballerina Anna Pavlova, to music from Saint-Saens' *Carnival of the Animals.* Then, perhaps inspired by Duncan, he made an entire ballet to orchestrated works by Chopin, revising it in 1909. A Romantic poet dances by moonlight with a winged sylph. In Russia, this version is still danced under the title *Chopiniana.* Later, in 1909, Diaghilev capitalized on the idea and took a modified version of it to Paris. For the Ballets Russes repertoire he

Pablo Picasso's painted set design for the ballet Pulcinella (below) was used to promote the performance. It appeared on posters and on the programme cover beneath the bold words Serge Diaghilev. By 1923 Diaghilev's reputation was such that his name featured prominently, whereas in the early days he kept it out of sight.

Ballets Russes *became synonymous with the lavish and the shocking. It has been suggested the company contributed to the decadence of the 1920s, but it may have simply reflected the taste of* avant garde *society and the artistic world, for exotic sensuality. At the same time as he was designing the orgiastic* Scheherazade, Leon Bakst painted The Pink Sultana (left).

commissioned new designs and gave it a new title to emphasize its Romanticism – *Les Sylphides.* Today it remains one of the most widely performed around the world of all ballets.

Fokine's *Scheherazade* of 1910 for the Ballets Russes was set to a work by Rimsky-Korsakov, and one familiar to concert-hall audiences. He omitted one movement, and though his story was taken from the world of the *Thousand and one Nights,* it used none of the specific tales which had inspired Rimsky-Korsakov's music. Instead, Fokine responded to the structure and the lavish colour of Rimsky's score. The harem setting was designed by Bakst in colours that had never been combined before – great expanses of emerald green against stretches of purple and orange, with cushions and hanging drapes. On the opening night the audience burst into spontaneous applause at their first glimpse of it. Indeed, the production inspired a new vogue in fashionable eastern interior decorations throughout Western Europe before World War 1. Its central performances by Ida Rubinstein as the glamorous and imperious Zobeide, and by Nijinsky as the Golden Slave, became legends of the theatre. Nijinsky, his skin daubed blue-black, stunned the audiences with giant bounds that covered over half the stage.

New music

Of the sixty-eight ballets that Diaghilev presented in 21 years, many were made to existing scores from the concert-hall, or to existing ballet music. The first 1909 season featured no ballet scores written specially for the Ballets Russes. But Sergei Diaghilev, a man of immense foresight and daring, could see the way ahead. He began to commission new scores, looking more and more, with the passage of time, to Western artists and composers. Ravel, Debussy, Richard Strauss, Satie, de Falla, Poulenc, Georges Auric, Daniel Milhaud, Constant Lambert, Henri Sauguet, Lord Berners and Vittorio Rieti all provided scores for new Diaghilev ballets. As for Russian composers – Serge Prokofiev was to provide scores for three ballets, including the last new work Diaghilev would present – *The Prodigal Son.* But by far the most important composer to Diaghilev, and to this century's music, was Igor Stravinsky.

Ida Rubinstein (below) was a pupil of Fokine's and the only non-Russian dancer to go to Paris with the first Ballets Russes. She later studied under Sarah Bernhardt to become an actress (seen here in Secrets of the Sphinx). Later still, she began a rival ballet company, purloining (as Diaghilev saw it) his artists.

Stravinsky and Diaghilev – a two-way debt

Stravinsky was involved in the Ballets Russes almost from the start. He was one of several composers whom Diaghilev asked to reorchestrate Chopin's music for *Les Sylphides* in 1909. He was also the first to compose a new score for Diaghilev – *The Firebird* — in 1910. And he worked with Diaghilev right through to 1929.

Diaghilev's audacious taste made the Ballets Russes an ideal vehicle for Stravinsky's rapidly changing musical style. In fact, his next major work for Diaghilev, presented in 1913, was *The Rite of Spring*. The first night was marked by the most violent scenes in the stormy history of Parisian

The Firebird (set design right) was the Ballet's first wholly original creation, with music, design and choreography all specially commissioned for it. It was an immediate and lasting triumph, made Stravinsky's name, and proved Diaghilev's theatricality, vision and daring.

In 1929, in an attempt to spark some memory in the vacant mind of Nijinsky after his mental breakdown, Diaghilev brought him on to the stage of the Paris Opera House at the curtain call of Petrushka (below). Tragically, Nijinsky remembered nothing. From the left: Benois, Karsavina, Diaghilev, Nijinsky, Serge Lifar.

theatre. Acid critics lambasted it. But Stravinsky wrote that after that tempestuous première Diaghilev took him and Nijinsky to dinner and remarked, 'Just what I wanted.'

The New Classicism

Before the Great War, the Ballets Russes were stylized representations of specific subjects. Several of these subjects were themselves Russian – *Firebird, Petrushka, Rite of Spring,* and the *Polovtsian Dances* from *Prince Igor.* The combination of Russian subjects and Russian artists had a vigour and exoticism that conquered the West. But slowly a new attitude emerged. Subjects became less important, style more so. Diaghilev asked several of his collaborators to revise old music as part of this 'neo-classical movement'. Tommasini worked on Scarlatti themes, Respighi worked on Rossini tunes, and in 1920 Stravinsky worked on Pergolesi music to make *Pulcinella:* old fabric, new styles.

Diaghilev was not solely concerned with novelty. To the great surprise of many admirers, he organized in 1921 a major revival of the great Tchaikovsky-Petipa ballet, *The Sleeping Beauty,* staging it in London at the Alhambra Theatre under the title *The Sleeping Princess.* There were lavish new decor and costumes by Bakst, some revised choreography by

(Above) Nijinsky at the height of his glory, in the role of Golden Slave in Scheherazade. *Over the years his dressers made considerable sums from selling fragments of his costumes.*

435

Bronislava Nijinska, and the Tchaikovsky music was subtly rescored by Stravinsky.

Not restricting himself to ballets, Diaghilev mounted (though rather grudgingly) the première of Stravinsky's opera *Oedipus Rex* in 1927. But he could not always afford to commission new works from Stravinsky, who occasionally provided compositions for organizations other than the Ballets Russes. Tremendously jealous and possessive, Diaghilev bitterly resented the fact that Stravinsky (like Ravel, Massine and Nijinska) did work for the Ida Rubinstein ballet company. He was also annoyed,

to find that in 1928, Stravinsky was making a ballet score for a première in Washington, DC. Stravinsky appeased him by offering the European première of the work to the Ballets Russes. The ballet was *Apollon Musagete,* also known as *Apollo, Leader of the Muses,* or just *Apollo.*

The score was given to Diaghilev's latest choreographer, George Balanchine. Twenty-four years old and musically trained, Balanchine would later say of the music that it changed his life.

Stars and a star-maker

This list of Diaghilev's designers for the Ballets Russes reads like a *Who's Who* of 20th century art: Benois, Bakst and Roerich from Russia; Picasso, Andre Derain, Marie Laurencin, Georges Braque, Coco Chanel, Maurice Utrillo, Max Ernst, Jean Miro, Giorgio de Chirico and Georges Rouault from the fertile West.

Diaghilev worked with five choreographers during the 21 years (all of them Russian): Fokine, Nijinsky and his sister, Bronislava Nijinska, Massine and George Balanchine.

Star dancers, star designers, star composers, star choreographers . . . it sounds like a recipe for success. But Diaghilev knew that art must not be subordinated to the stardom of one or other of its contributors. He was jealous that Ida Rubinstein could bring Nijinska and Massine together with Ravel and Stravinsky. But when he saw the finished product, he realized that she lacked the genius for synthesis, for fusing the separate elements into a whole. Though he described himself as having no real gift – and made light of his role, likening himself to a bartender who had invented a recipe for cocktails – those who worked with him never doubted his genius.

Diaghilev did not need stars. He called himself a 'collector of geniuses', but could build stardom himself. Great ballerinas like Pavlova and Kschessinkskaya appeared with his company, but because they preferred to be the centre of the ballet they did not stay. While he admired their artistry, he did not regret losing them. Dancers who worked with him – Nijinsky, Karsavina, Lydia Lopokova, Massine, Olga Spessivtseva – were artists who could lend their gifts interpretatively to the ballets around them, and who were prepared to direct their talents towards each ballet as a whole. Choreographers such as Nijinsky and Massine, who had little or no previous experience, were guided and coached by Diaghilev towards maturity.

Astonish me!

Diaghilev is often remembered as an impresario who liked to shock audiences and to be shocked himself. 'Etonne-moi!' ('Astonish me!') he said to Jean Cocteau. But he was all the while a man in earnest; he was concerned with tradition, not as unchanging, but as something which should be constantly renovated and developed.

When, in 1929, celebrations were proposed for the twentieth anniversary of the Ballets Russes, he said, 'I'm afraid I abhor jubilees in general and my own in particular . . . I wish to remain always young.' It sounds like the remark of a dandy, an aesthete. He was one. But that same year he died, an exhausted man, aged only 57. And as we look at the work of the Ballets Russes, we see how, at the expense of his own youth and vitality, he rejuvenated the whole world of art and dance.

George Gershwin
1898–1937

From Tin Pan Alley to Carnegie Hall, via Broadway, George Gershwin's career as composer and performer of both serious and popular music was typical of 'rags to riches' stories of American life.

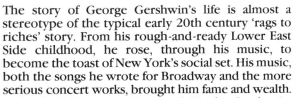

The story of George Gershwin's life is almost a stereotype of the typical early 20th century 'rags to riches' story. From his rough-and-ready Lower East Side childhood, he rose, through his music, to become the toast of New York's social set. His music, both the songs he wrote for Broadway and the more serious concert works, brought him fame and wealth.

Gershwin's parents, Rosa and Moishe Gershovitz migrated from St Petersburg in Russia to New York in 1891 and the family name was Americanized as Gershvin and later adapted to Gershwin. Their first son Israel (Ira) was born in 1896 and George, their second son, was born on 26th September 1898.

Ira, George's older brother, was the family scholar and in 1910 his mother purchased a piano for him, but it was George who quickly took to it, playing popular melodies on it. Unknown to the rest of the family, George had become interested in music after hearing a school friend, Maxie Rosenzweig (Max Rosen) play the viola in a school recital. George had been standing outside the school hall; was over-whelmed by the sound and made inquiries until he established who the player was. Then he arranged to meet Maxie. They became firm friends, their shared interest in music being the bond between them.

George's exceptional natural ability on the piano was soon recognized and his parents arranged for him to have lessons. After suffering at the hands of several bad teachers he became a pupil, in 1912, of a particularly able musician and gifted teacher, Charles Hambitzer. Hambitzer realized that George had a great talent and set about organizing his musical knowledge.

Inspired by his teacher's orderly and enthusiastic approach to both old and modern classics, George for a time entertained notions of becoming a concert pianist. Given his lack of interest in academic prowess his parents made a last ditch attempt to give him a stable career and arranged for him to go to an

Born in 1898 George Gershwin (left, shown with, from left to right, his younger brother Arthur, the maid, his mother and older brother, Ira), grew up in the seedy Lower East Side of New York City (above).

accountancy school. However, in 1914 the fifteen-year-old Gershwin persuaded his mother to allow him to leave school to take a job as a song salesman or plugger, promoting the popular song music of the Tin Pan Alley song publisher, Remick's. Tin Pan Alley – its name is thought to derive from the 'tinny' sound of pianos – was the Mecca for popular music. For Gershwin it was an important stepping stone, as it put him in close touch with popular music.

A novice in Tin Pan Alley

His starting salary at Remick's was $15 a week. The job was arduous, had long hours and consisted mostly of playing the piano in a little booth, either accompanying amateur singers or demonstrating the latest Remick songs to parlour pianists. One positive aspect of the job was that it developed his dexterity and stylistic scope. He was successful and was soon in demand with regular clients. Remick's asked him to record some piano rolls for them at $5 a roll, something which he did for them and other publishers for a number of years, to supplement his income.

His ambition, at this stage, was to have some of his own songs published. Remick's were not interested in their top song plugger being a songwriter as well. Not deterred, Gershwin hawked his songs from this period round Tin Pan Alley and by 1917 had a few songs published. Then, too, Remick's decided to publish one of his songs, a Gershwin/Will Donaldson ragtime piano piece, *Rialto Ripples*.

Soon after this George decided on a career on Broadway. He later wrote that 'The popular-song racket began to get definitely on my nerves. Its tunes somehow began to offend me . . . Jerome Kern was

the first composer who made me conscious that most popular music was of inferior quality and that musical-comedy was made of better material.'

The lure of Broadway

Given this attitude, it was no surprise when he left Remick's in March 1917 to make his way into the musical comedy world. He soon found work as an accompanist on small shows, all of which proved to be financial disasters for their producers. This didn't seem to matter to George – he used the shows as a means to meet the right people and to put himself about to the best of his ability. His outgoing, confident personality, coupled with his talent for improvisation on the piano made him a popular man on the productions he worked on.

Word soon got around Broadway that here was someone to be watched. Gershwin came to the attention of Max Dreyfus, the head of Harms publishing house. Dreyfus, an astute man, had a gift of recognizing song-writing talent, and he saw the potential in George Gershwin. In February 1918 Dreyfus signed him to a deal where he was paid $35 per week just to write songs. The immediate result of this was George's first collaboration with his brother Ira in the song *The Real American Folk Song*. It was premièred in a show in 1918 but only published 40 years later when it was recorded by Ella Fitzgerald.

Meanwhile George kept up his work for various productions and occasionally his songs were accepted for inclusion in musicals. He realized that only the composer credited with the music for whole shows made any money on Broadway.

In 1919 he had two important firsts: his first complete Broadway score and his first big song hit. The show was the moderately successful *La La Lucille,* which was also the first production for Alex Aarons, the producer of so many later Gershwin smash successes. The hit song was *Swanee.* Hardly a typical Gershwin tune, it was thrown together by Gershwin and lyricist Irving Caesar in an attempt to cash in on the popularity of a piece of music called *Hindustan.* The song was a flop when it first appeared on Broadway in the show *Capitol Review,* but it was later picked up by Al Jolson who heard Gershwin playing it at a party. Jolson put it into his current show, *Sinbad,* and it quickly became a sensation. With this song, which was to be the single biggest hit of his career, Gershwin had arrived. Al Jolson recorded the song in 1920, sold millions of discs, and boosted the sales of the sheet music tremendously.

Still only 22, Gershwin was a tall, well-developed man. Although not handsome – he had a broken nose, a receding hairline and a thrusting jaw – he seemed to ooze sex appeal. His reputation as a ladies' man grew as he moved into wider and higher circles of New York, Broadway and Hollywood. Conquests came easily to him as he became the darling of the social set. He was always to be seen with a different female companion, and it was common knowledge that as well as having many affairs he was also a

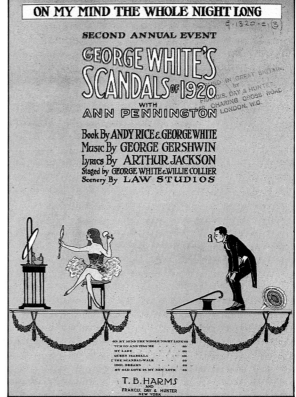

The annual Ziegfeld Follies (publicity material for the 1936 MGM film, The Great Ziegfeld, *left) started in 1907 was the brainchild of impresario Florenz Ziegfeld. These revues celebrated American femininity in a programme of song and dance both spectacular and extravagant. In 1919 a dancer, George White, formed a rival to the Follies, and from 1920 for four years George Gershwin wrote songs for George White's Scandals (above).*

frequent visitor to brothels. Although he had no difficulty in having casual sexual encounters he was never successful in finding a deep romantic attachment of a permanent nature. Despite his reputation Gershwin had many friends both male and female with whom he had companionable relationships. Outwardly a buoyant and exuberant man, his close friends knew that there were times of anxiety and depression, when he worried about his work and career. He developed a physical problem, which he described as 'composer's stomach'. As a result he became obsessed with his diet and resorted to all sorts of food fads to try to cure himself.

Gershwin's career after his hit with *Swanee* was one of increasingly rapid strides to the top of his profession. He was commissioned in 1920 to write the score for the second annual appearance of *George White's Scandals* show – the rival to the spectacular *Ziegfeld Follies* – the musical revues with which Florenz Ziegfeld had wowed Broadway. Gershwin was to write the score for another four of these shows.

During the years he was involved with George White's Scandals Gershwin still kept his hand in with many other Broadway productions. In 1923 he travelled to England for the first time to give his first revue there, *The Rainbow*. It was hardly a triumph but he fell in love with London Society and it with him.

Into the concert hall

By now he had established himself as an experienced show professional but since *Swanee* he had not had any major successes on Broadway. He now had his sights set further afield, not only in theatre but in the concert hall. Here in November 1923 he had a spectacular success, when he accompanied the Canadian soprano, Eva Gauthier in a programme entitled *'Recital of Ancient and Modern Music for Voice'*. Max Jaffee accompanied her in the classical selections and Gershwin in the Modern American section, where two of the songs featured were his own compositions. This section proved to be the hit of the evening and it marked the entry of jazz into the concert hall, as well as the triumph of Gershwin as composer and performer.

Gershwin's attempts to combine jazz and the popular song, and popular music with the concert hall were consolidated in 1924 by the overwhelming success of a work written as a concert piece in the jazz style, *Rhapsody in Blue*. So great was its success that it was obvious to all that Gershwin had arrived not only as a performer, but also as a serious composer. The momentum generated from the triumph of *Rhapsody in Blue* spilled over into Gershwin's next project – the score for his next Broadway hit, starring Fred and Adele Astaire, *Lady, Be Good!* This show, when it opened in November, was a tremendous hit, and had some of Gershwin's most memorable songs. It was also the first show written solely by George and his brother, Ira Gershwin. They had collaborated before but Ira, a more retiring personality than George used a pseudonym. He had not wished to be making his way in show business on his brother's bandwagon. As a bonus to his triumph, earlier in the year, George's second visit to London, for the show *Primrose,* was also a runaway success.

In 1925 Gershwin repeated his triumphs of the previous year with the *Concerto in F.* On Broadway his hit for the year was *Tip-Toes,* again written with Ira. From then until the great commercial and financial upheavals of the Depression, which began in Sep-

Paul Whiteman (shown above, with his orchestra) commissioned George to write a jazz symphony for a concert held at the Aeolian Hall, New York, on 22 February 1924. The work, Rhapsody in Blue, *was a great success. Later that year George's concert-hall triumph was further consolidated with the Broadway show,* Lady, Be Good! *The show marked the first appearance of the brother and sister partnership of Fred and Adele Astaire (right) in a Gershwin musical. The show was significant, too, as the first major Broadway hit for both George and his older brother, the lyricist, Ira Gershwin (far right). They had found the perfect working partnership to produce the glittering musical comedies much in demand on the stages of Broadway (centre). The brothers, opposites in personality (George was bouncy and gregarious, while Ira was quiet and retiring) worked together until George's death in 1937. Ira continued in showbusiness, writing for stage and screen until 1954.*

tember 1929 Gershwin went from strength to strength. *Oh, Kay!* in 1926, *Funny Face* in 1927 and *Rosalie* in 1928 were all hugely successful. In 1928 he moved from the large house on 103rd Street which he had bought some years previously for his family to very swish bachelor apartments at 33 Riverside Drive. From childhood he had often sketched and drawn caricatures but in 1927 he became interested in water colour painting. He proved to have a natural talent, and received much help and encouragement from his cousin and friend Henry Botkin. Botkin also assisted him in amassing a very impressive collection of modern masters.

Success abroad

A trip to Europe in 1928 confirmed his international stature – he was lauded and fêted in London, Paris and even in Vienna, where he met and became friendly with the composer Alban Berg. While he was in Paris Gershwin sketched out his next orchestral composition, a tone poem for orchestra, *An American in Paris*. Later that year it was orchestrated and it was premièred at Carnegie Hall on December 13 1928. At a party after the performance Gershwin was honoured by friends who acknowledged him as a leader of young America in music.

The Depression, when it did break, had little material effect on Gershwin's life or career. By this time he was a national hero, his finances were on a firm footing and the hits kept coming. Hollywood was the next goal on the horizon and in 1930 George and Ira made their Hollywood début. They spent four luxurious months writing the music for a determinedly second-rate feature film, *Delicious*. For this they were paid $100,000 and George, in addition, collected $50,000 for giving his permission to use *Rhapsody in Blue* in *The Paul Whiteman Story*. In Hollywood, when he was not actually composing, George spent his time golfing, partying and having flings with starlets. On his return to New York, he wrote the *Second Rhapsody for Orchestra with Piano*. After delays due to the hope that Toscanini might première the work, it was given its first performance in 1932 by Koussevitzky and the Boston Symphony Orchestra, with Gershwin playing the piano part. It was another raging success. However, although he had survived the effects of the bad economic climate his luck seemed to change and in 1933 he and Ira were associated with the ill-fated

In 1928 Gershwin made a trip to Europe. While in Paris he sketched out his next orchestral work, An American in Paris. *It was premièred at Carnegie Hall in December 1928. The following year the ballet choreographed by Harriet Hoctor (right) to the music appeared in the Broadway show,* Show Girl. *Despite lavish musical items in the show, including a spot for Duke Ellington and his band,* Show Girl *was not a box-office success.*

and poorly-backed show, *Pardon My English.* Not even George's golden touch could save it. This failure seemed to make no impression on him, however, for in the same month he moved to a cavernous apartment, considerably more spacious and luxurious than Riverside Drive.

In the autumn of 1933 Gershwin was pulled up short by another Broadway flop. *Let 'Em Eat Cake,* a sequel to *Of Thee I Sing,* despite its superior music, died very quickly. Up to this point only George's enormous prestige had kept his Broadway shows solvent. Broadway, in general, was having a disastrous time in the Depression. The series of box-office disasters, although they may not have altered his financial situation, certainly affected his equilibrium, and may have led to his decision to undergo psychoanalysis with Dr Gregory Zilboorg in 1934.

Still, creatively he had little to worry about. 1934, for example, was the year he began work on the opera he had been wanting to write for years. He and author Edwin DuBose Heyward, the writer of the novel *Porgy,* had long been planning an opera of it. Gershwin and DuBose Heyward started work on the project, with the help of Ira for the lyrics.

George, to get the uninterrupted peace he needed for such a sustained creative effort, spent two months, dispensing with all social comforts, on Folly Island with Ira and Heyward. There was not even a phone on the island. The isolation worked, and George returned to New York in autumn 1934 with a huge slab of the opera drafted out. By January 1935, working steadily, George completed the orchestration of the opera in time for the Boston opening, in September 1935. Ever since that Boston opening and the following New York opening in October, the full-length opera has aroused criticism and controversy. The New York Post reviewer summed up a general reaction by stating that the opera was 'a hybrid, fluctuating constantly between music-drama, musical comedy, and operetta. It contains numerous 'song-hits' . . . Yet they are too 'set' in treatment, too isolated from the pitch of opera for us to accept them

as integral parts of a tragic music-drama.'

Gershwin's reply was to claim *Porgy and Bess* as a folk-opera, written in a new form faithful to the cultural traditions of the folk it portrayed. Be that as it may, Gershwin and Heyward's opera was not destined to be successful on stage until, in 1942, five years after his death, a considerably reworked version was a hit on Broadway. Even though the songs were individually successful and their sheet music sold well, *Porgy and Bess* was Gershwin's third flop in a row in the theatre.

It was probably his third failure which prompted both George and Ira to look to Hollywood again. On 9 and 10 July 1936, George played two consecutive nights at New York's Lewishon Stadium. It was an all-Gershwin programme; and it was also his last live appearance in his native city.

For a number of years George Gershwin lived in a cavernous penthouse apartment at 33 Riverside Drive, New York. Every room, including the living room (above) was filled with Gershwin's collection of art treasures and stylish furniture.

Gershwin read Edwin DuBose Heyward's novel Porgy *in 1926, and at once wrote to him, saying that he wanted to compose an opera based on it. It was not until nine years later that Gershwin and Heyward actually collaborated on the opera,* Porgy and Bess, *(a lobby poster for the 1959 film is shown left). The opera opened in Boston on 30 September 1935 and in New York on 10 October. The critics were not whole-heartedly in favour of Gershwin's mixed use of opera and operetta and the show went on the road. After Gershwin's death it was more successful and by the early 1950s had been seen all over the States and Europe, including the Soviet Union.*

Although he had a reputation as a ladies' man Gershwin did make one or two deeper emotional attachments to women. At least two of these more serious relationships, however, were with married women; women who through their circumstances protected him from having to make a commitment to them. Paulette Goddard (left), for instance, at the time when Gershwin met and fell in love with her, was married to Charles Chaplin.

Return to Hollywood

The second Hollywood sojourn was a distinct artistic and financial success for the Gershwin brothers: they wrote scores for two Fred Astaire movies; *Shall We Dance,* and *A Damsel in Distress.* Both were full of the very best in quality music. Not only did George find creative fulfilment in Hollywood but a rake to the end, he also had many affairs. Despite these he did have one or two more serious relationships; one with Simone Simon, the French actress. By early 1937, he and Ira were into their third movie, *Goldwyn Follies,* and George was in love with Paulette Goddard, Charlie Chaplin's wife. He was deeply hurt when she refused to leave Chaplin.

During June 1937, previously noticed but isolated warning signs that all was not well with this usually robust and healthy person became more persistent. He began to experience frequent dizzy spells and headaches. Since his doctors could find no irregularities, he put these down to stress of overwork and continued to live his life as usual and rejected the idea of having a spinal tap to check for a possible brain tumour. However, over the following month his symptoms recurred with greater frequency and intensity until, on 9 July, 1937 after being weak and dazed for days, he fell into a coma.

A spinal tap performed the following day established the presence of a brain tumour, and it was decided that an emergency operation was the only hope. Early on 11 July this took place, and part of the tumour was removed. About five hours later, Gershwin died without regaining consciousness. Two gigantic funeral ceremonies, one in Hollywood and one in New York, on 15 July 1937, demonstrated the loss felt by Americans at his passing.

The Jazz Singer

How could it fail? The first 'talkie', a box-office star, and a title to whet middle-class appetites: **The Jazz Singer!** *Jazz (though nowhere to be seen in the film) was white America's latest discovery.*

The nightclub audience applauded rapturously as Al Jolson belted out the final lyric of *Toot, Toot, Tootsie, Goodbye!* As film extras on the set of *The Jazz Singer* they were paid to do so. Not so the New Yorkers who gazed up at the silver screen on the evening of 6 October 1927, watching the film's première. They had paid handsomely to see the fabulous Jolson's cinematographic performance. But without any doubt they got their money's worth.

The applause was cut short by Jolson himself. Looking directly into the camera, he broke into speech. In that rasping, strident voice familiar to generations of vaudeville fans, he blurted out, 'Wait a minute! Wait a minute! You ain't heard nothin' yet!' The lucky New York audience, in hearing that, had heard the 'somethin'' they were waiting for – they had just witnessed the birth of the 'talkie', and the greatest transformation in the brief history of the cinema was suddenly no longer a dream but a thrilling reality. The greatest barrier had been crossed.

The sound of the silents

In retrospect, it may seem surprising that talkies took so long to arrive. The cinema was some 30 years old by 1927, and had reached very high technical and artistic standards. Sound reproduction, too, was long past its infancy. The idea of combining sound with film was simple enough in theory: as early as the 1880s, Thomas Edison had tried to harness his recently-invented phonograph machine to the moving pictures of his brand-new Kinetoscope – a peepshow forerunner of cinema. He was balked, however, by the problem of synchronization. He simply could not match sound to the moving pictures with enough precision – and as is known to anyone who has seen sound and pictures go even slightly awry, the results are simply laughable. Others tried and failed, too. So it was that the industry, and Hollywood in particular, matured and flourished within the somewhat limited conventions of silent film.

'Silent' is something of a misnomer. No one ever watched a silent movie in silence. From the beginning, live music accompanied the flickering images on screen. Even the humblest little cinema houses had a piano, while the grand picture palaces in big cities installed massive Wurlitzer organs and even small orchestras. On occasion, distinguished composers were commissioned to write original scores. Saint-Saens, for example, provided one for the celebrated film *L'Assassinat du Duc de Guise* in 1908.

Sound effects, too, accompanied the action on the screen. Horses' hooves clattered, waves crashed against the shore, steam locomotives puffed along the rails. As with music, though, the cinema owner was constrained by the money he could afford to spend on equipment and the skill of those he could employ to work it. There was much variation in quality: badly-produced sound effects could detract from a film, rather than adding to the audience's enjoyment of it.

Thomas Edison had achieved rudimentary sound synchronization with his Kinetoscope (an animated peepshow), left, linked to a phonograph by string. He called it the Kinetophone (right).

The only way of achieving anything like uniformity of performances was to devize a means of reproducing sound mechanically. By the 1920s the gramophone was no longer the primitive, hand-wound instrument invented by Edison, but a machine essentially similar to the one we know today. The music was both recorded and reproduced electrically. At the same time, the rapid development of radio was giving impetus to the whole field of sound projection. The giant electrical companies were quick to see the implications for the cinema and, by the middle of the 1920s, were urging rival systems of sound reproduction on the studios in Hollywood in a bid to be a vital part of that lucrative industry.

Hollywood submits to sound

The vast majority of people involved in film-making would have liked to ward off talkies. They had good reason. Having persuaded an entire generation to accept the conventions of silent film, and having perfected the art, why change? Why tamper with a winning formula, especially when to do so would present a host of problems and cost a mint of money, and might not meet with public favour?

They had no choice. Radio posed a mortal threat to the cinema, just as television would do to both a generation later. The novelty value of being able to hear a disembodied voice in the comfort of the living room showed no signs of wearing off. The public had acquired a taste for sound. Steeply declining box-office figures proved it. There could be no ignoring this new trend – Hollywood would have to adapt or die.

Warner Brothers moved decisively in 1926. Using a synchronized disk system – Vitaphone – developed by Western Electric, they produced the silent classic *Don Juan* with a fully synchronized musical score. The film was warmly received, and Warners were sufficiently encouraged to commit themselves publicly to sound in the future. All they needed was the right vehicle with which to launch the revolution. The found it in the Broadway smash hit, *The Jazz Singer*.

The Jazz Singer is a sentimental tale about an immigrant cantor's son who forsakes home and synagogue for the bright lights of the theatre. His rebellion, his father's rage and his mother's pleas are finally reconciled as the old cantor lies dying. Then the mother proudly watches her son perform

It took the threat of radio, and wholesale closure of cinemas, to jolt silent-movie makers out of their complacency. Al Jolson, left, a huge star of music hall, must have been similarly conscious of the threat to his livelihood.

The problems involved in filming with microphones were enormous. At first, the cameras were so noisy that they had to be operated from inside a padded booth, below, eliminating all movement. And since the cameras could not move, neither could the actors.

triumphantly on stage. The story is very loosely based on the early career of the star of the film, Al Jolson.

In casting Jolson himself in the title role, Warners guaranteed themselves a box office success. Modestly billing himself as 'the world's greatest entertainer', Jolson was at the peak of one of the most phenomenal careers in the history of show business. A string of hit records had made him a household name across America, among them *Swanee, My Mammy* and *California, Here I Come*. As a stage performer he was unrivalled: he simply mesmerized his audience. Robert Benchley, a witty and trenchant critic, was left groping for words to describe a Jolson performance he witnessed at New York's Winter Garden in 1925:

When Jolson enters it is as if an electric current had been run along the wires under the seats . . . the house comes to tumultuous attention. He speaks, rolls his eyes, compresses his lips, and it is all over. You are a member of the Al Jolson Association. He trembles his underlip and your heart breaks with a loud snap. He sings a banal song and you totter out to send a night letter to your mother. Such a giving out of vitality, personality, charm and whatever all those words are, results from a Jolson performance.

The Jolson magic

Most of *The Jazz Singer* was shot as a silent film with separate musical accompaniment, but Jolson's songs were recorded synchronously. Since these were songs he had already made famous, they could hardly fail. What sent the audiences into ecstasy, however, were the two occasions when Jolson actually spoke on film. 'You ain't heard nothin' yet!' had been Jolson's catchphrase for 25 years and it brought the house down wherever *The Jazz Singer* played. When, after crooning *My Mammy* on bended knee, Jolson cries out to his mother in the audience, 'Did you like that, Mama?', there wasn't a dry eye in

Stars like Gilbert and Garbo, above, had to speak or die. Greta Garbo had a voice which matched, even enhanced, her image. Her greatest fame was still to come (right). John Gilbert, with his 'Mickey Mouse' voice, plunged to obscurity almost overnight.

cinema houses anywhere.

The overwhelming success of *The Jazz Singer* decided the future of the motion picture industry. Virtually overnight, the silent cinema became obsolete, as all the major studios worked frantically to re-equip. During 1928 about 80 feature films were made with at least some kind of sound component. But the transition was every bit as fraught as the film industry had feared. It was hideously expensive. MGM practically rebuilt their huge studios — complete with a huge *Quiet Please* notice painted on the roof of the (supposedly) sound-proofed studio in the hope of discouraging aircraft. Universal Studios laid out two million dollars on conversion, and it was estimated that Hollywood as a whole, by the middle

Metro-Goldwyn-Mayer PRÉSENTE

GRETA GARBO · RO TAY

dans

Le roman de Marguerit

avec LIONEL BARRYMORE

ELIZABETH ALLAN · JESSIE RALPH · HENRY DANIELL · LENORE ULRIC
Réalisation de GEORGE CUKOR

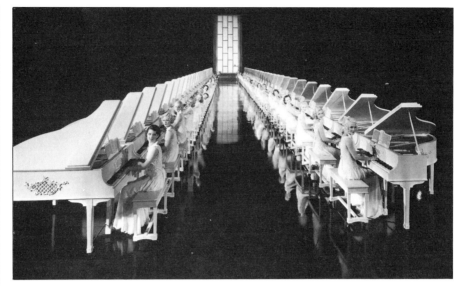

One of the all-time box-office hits, Singin' in the Rain, bottom, could afford to look back at the genesis of sound – the elaborate sound-rigging, the humiliation of silent-screen-goddesses – and laugh. Cinema had survived to see a new golden era, dazzling with the musical spectaculars of Buzby Berkeley, left, the epics of Cecil B. de Mille, below left, and a galaxy of stars.

of 1929, had spent about $50 million.

Inside the new studios, cutting out unwanted sound was a nightmare. The Vitaphone microphones were sensitive enough to pick up the whirring of the cameras and the hiss of the arc lights. Camera and camera operator had to be shut up in a tiny, sound-insulated cabin, with the lens poking out of a sound-proofed tube. This was not only a gross inconvenience for the cameraman; it badly restricted the scope of his craft.

Directors, too, had problems. On silent-film sets they could direct the actors while the cameras were running. Although most adapted to the need for silence, there were attempts to continue with the older methods: when Lionel Barrymore was directing *Madame X* in 1929, he attached fine wires to his stars' bodies so that he could, by small electric shocks, signal to them during filming.

Silent film sets had been bedlam – directors bellowing instructions, propmen hauling scenery about, carpenters hammering, bit players chattering off-camera. All that had to end. 'Quiet! Quiet!' became the command repeated endlessly, the echo fading away into an eerie total silence. The actors found this silence almost unendurable – director Frank Capra recalls that many of them could not stop shaking as they faced the camera's unblinking eye amid tomb-like stillness.

Equipment was such that the actor was obliged to address the microphone directly, at close quarters. So the microphone had to be concealed in a strategic

place for every scene. It might be taped to the back of an actor who then stood rooted to the spot for the entire scene, or it might be stuck in a flower vase, forcing the actors into inexplicably strange movements and positions. The results were often unintentionally comic.

But these purely technical difficulties were quickly overcome. The camera cabin could be fitted on wheels or castors. Then camera mobility was restored completely by the development of soundproof camera casing. Fixed microphones gave way to the boom – a pole with the microphone at one end, which could be moved around, out-of-camera, above the actors' heads.

The human factor

The biggest challenge for the actors, however, was not so simply met; for many it meant the swift and inglorious end to a glittering career. For those who had no live-stage experience, it could be the first time in their professional lives that they had had to *speak*.

Today, the skill of delivering dialogue effectively is so much a part of our notion of acting that it is difficult to imagine the collective shudder that ran through the Hollywood acting fraternity at the prospect of it. That classic film, *Singin' in the Rain* affectionately parodies the crisis that confronted the

luscious-looking but vinegar-voiced stars.

Courses in elocution were the rage, while some of the more prudent stars took a brief respite from films to work in repertory theatres and vaudeville to polish their vocal skills. For many, the transition proved impossible. John Gilbert was probably the most notable casualty. Gilbert, a silent-screen superstar, was idolized by millions of women and envied by as many men for his good-looks. But his voice slightly resembled Mickey Mouse's, and his career faded quickly. The dilemma of those such as Gilbert was neatly expressed in a little rhyme of the time:

> *I cannot talk – I cannot sing*
> *Nor screech nor moan nor anything.*
> *Possessing all these fatal strictures,*
> *What chance have I in motion pictures?*

Stars rising

Some of the greatest silent stars took the sound revolution in their stride, however. Greta Garbo managed it with ease, turning her heavy Swedish accent to her advantage. Laurel and Hardy found that it suited their comic gifts perfectly. And even the greatest exponent of silent cinematography, Charlie Chaplin, succeeded with sound when he finally came to accept that he must do so or give up film-making.

To swell the ranks of Hollywood actors who could handle speech, came a host of talented stage actors from New York's Broadway and from Britain. Their arrival coincided with the technical improvements that made possible realistic screen drama and which ushered in Hollywood's second golden age. In the 1930s came the stars: James Cagney, Edward G. Robinson, Clark Gable, Charles Laughton, and a whole galaxy more whose films continue to thrive thanks to television.

The sound cinema, ushered in by Al Jolson's 'You ain't heard nothin' yet!' had reached maturity with

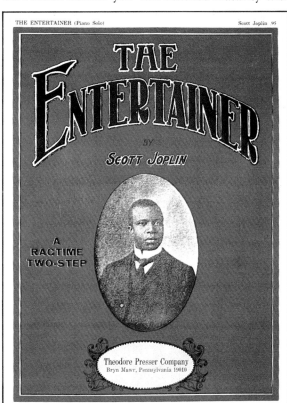

Folk jazz found a new form in New Orleans where, for the first time, it was orchestrated for professional bands, in such unsalubrious surroundings as Canal Street, above. Such places are now revered as the cradles of jazz and immortalized in the music 'written' there: Canal Street Blues, *for instance.*

Ragtime syncopation brought a complexity and irresistible bounce to jazz melodies that won a great many converts. Its finest exponent was the blind pianist/composer, Scott Joplin whose work had the quality to endure.

King Oliver's Jazz Band, right, was one of the first to hit the 'big time'. All its members were virtuoso musicians, none more so than (Daniel) Louis Armstrong (centre, on trumpet). His story was typical: a self-taught orphan waif from New Orleans who rose to fame in a society which, 10 years before, would not have spared him a dime.

astonishing speed – outpacing even D. W. Griffith's bold prediction: Griffith, perhaps the greatest of silent film directors, gave a warmer welcome to sound than many of his peers:

Talkies, squeakies, moanies, songies, squawkies ... just give them 10 years to develop and you're going to see the greatest artistic medium the world has known.

Jazz without Jolson

For all its significance in the history of the cinema, *The Jazz Singer* had no significance at all to jazz-lovers. Indeed, the title is completely misleading: Jolson's singing had nothing to do with jazz, either in style or content. The blacked face that was Jolson's trademark was, at best, an unconscious insult to the cultural tradition from which jazz came. Presumably, the title was chosen to titilate without alarming white middle-class Americans: the word 'jazz' was risqué, loaded with sexual and (worse still) *black* connotations. But everyone knew it was really only Al Jolson with his face blacked, singing catchy, sentimental and highly respectable numbers.

Whites who disliked jazz and all it stood for – 'booze, brothels and blues' was a familiar jibe – were woefully ignorant about this vibrant, new musical form. But they knew it for a black creation and they knew it to be the music of the poor.

The roots of jazz

The origins of jazz lie in African percussive rhythms, which somehow stayed alive among black Americans during generations of slavery. Work songs and chants from the cottonfields, negro spirituals and blues gradually fused with European melodies, particularly folksong. Blues songs combined spontaneous improvization with a fixed form. Always three lines long, the second simply repeats the first, allowing the singer time enough to think up a third line – a comment on the first. Frequently the comment is doleful, but it is often infused with a wry humour:

'Gwine lay my head right on de railroad track,
'Gwine lay my head right on de railroad track,
If de train come 'long, I'm 'gwine to snatch it back.

The greatest exponent of the blues was W. G. Handy (1873–1958). He was both an archivist, preserving and publishing anthologies of blues and spirituals, and a talented composer. Handy was blind from the age of 30, but from 1903 to 1921 he led his own orchestra and composed a number of blues classics, most notably *Memphis Blues,* and *St Louis Blues* with its haunting reflections on lost love:

I hate to see de ev'nin' sun go down,
I hate to see de ev'nin' sun go down,
Cause my baby he done lef' dis town.

Ragtime and Dixie

Another important influence on the development of jazz was ragtime, brought to a high level of excellence by the brilliant composer and pianist, Scott Joplin (1868–1917). Joplin's intricate compositions have enjoyed a tremendous revival in recent years, combining melody with an infectious rhythm based on syncopation (described in a contemporary joke as 'uneven movement from bar to bar'). As such, it was a staple ingredient of jazz.

Ironically, neither Handy nor Joplin was from New Orleans, traditionally considered the home of jazz. The New Orleans style, as it was called, was the original orchestral jazz, and its first great exponents were the members of the original Dixieland Jazz Band of 1917. The rollicking, good-natured Dixieland sound provided background music in the notorious 'red-light' district of Storyville. When Storyville was closed down by the US Navy in 1918, Dixieland jazz began to move north.

Big city jazz

The exodus from Storyville at the end of World War I had a crucial effect on jazz. Brothel music was never likely to gain a wide listening public. But people were prepared to lend an ear to the jazz bands which established themselves along the Mississippi River in Memphis, St Louis, Louisville and beyond. Other jazz musicians moved farther north still, to Detroit, to New York's Harlem district and, most significantly of all, to Chicago.

In the early 1920s Chicago established itself as the headquarters of jazz. Many would claim that this was jazz's finest hour and many exhilarating performances were preserved on gramophone records. King Oliver's Creole Jazz Band was at the top of the tree, with the young Louis Armstrong playing second trumpet to the great 'King' himself. A little later, Armstrong displayed the full range of his virtuosity with his own groups, the Hot Five and the Hot Seven. 'Jelly Roll' Morton and his Red Hot Peppers were there at the same time, playing, in a more formal

Great Composers

style, music of irresistible charm, and so, too, was the marvellous pianist, Clarence Smith.

By 1930 the rough edges were being smoothed off jazz, something lamented by jazz purists. There are several possible reasons. Many of the great originals wore themselves out with hard living, a phenomenon repeated by a later generation of pop musicians. Secondly, the tendency towards bigger and bigger bands had the effect of sweetening music – making it better for dancing to, but robbing it of much of its vitality. This trend coincided with a change in public taste, and jazz became caught up in that change. As the music became less raucous, more refined, it became more respectable, too. Whatever their original reaction to jazz, large numbers of whites had come to accept and enjoy jazz rhythms.

This is not to say that jazz music of the 1930s was utterly harmless. Though dominated by white tastes, it still possessed great black performers and composers in the vanguard of the new, 'sophisticated' jazz – in particular the supremely gifted Duke Ellington. White musicians of great originality were also now working within the idiom. The splendid cornetist, 'Bix' Beiderbecke had already demonstrated that to be white was no bar to jazz brilliance, as the clarinetist Benny Goodman and a host of others would later prove. Popular composers like Irving Berlin and Jerome Kern found in jazz a rich mine for their melodic invention, while George Gershwin aspired to greater heights. He not only took jazz seriously, as a legitimate form of American folk music, but he set himself the task of making it the basis of serious symphonic works of lasting value. The result was *Rhapsody in Blue*.

Edward 'Duke' Ellington, composer and jazz pianist, left, was the acme of sophistication. His was the acceptable face of black jazz, and 'The Duke' bridged that gulf between the raw, hot-blooded music of the Deep South and the glossy, big-band music white Americans called jazz. The brand Benny Goodman played, (below), swept the nation and was an irreversible influence on all subsequent popular music. Purists would say that 'trad jazz' lost touch with its origins, but then the whole essence of jazz is in its continuous evolution.

HH-86

Listening Guide

This is not meant to be a complete list of the works of the composers; rather, it is a suggested selection, chosen to give a comprehensive view of the progress and scope achieved in the course of their careers. Works are listed by dates of composition.

Johann Sebastian Bach

1700-1708:	Prelude and Fugue in E Minor for organ, BWV 548
1708-1717:	Fantasia and Fugue in G Minor for organ, BWV 542
	Toccata and Fugue in D Minor for organ, BWV 565
	Passacaglia and Fugue in C Minor for organ, BWV 582
1717-1723:	Violin Concerto in A Minor, BWV 1041
	Double Violin Concerto in D Minor, BWV 1043
1721:	Brandenburg Concertos
	No 1 in F for violin, piccolo, three oboes, two horns, bassoon, strings and continuo, BWV 1046
	No 2 in F for violin, flute, oboe, trumpet, strings and continuo, BWV 1047
	No 3 in G for strings and continuo, BWV 1048
	No 4 in G for violin, two flutes, strings and continuo, BWV 1049
	No 5 in D for clavier, violin, flute, strings and continuo, BWV 1050
	No 6 in B Flat for strings, BWV 1051
1722:	*The Well-Tempered Clavier,* Book I
1729:	*St Matthew Passion* for soprano, contralto, tenor and bass soli, double chorus, double orchestra and continuo
1734:	*Christmas Oratorio,* six cantatas for solo voices, chorus, orchestra and organ, BWV 248
1742:	*The Goldberg Variations* for double keyboard and harpsichord, BWV 988
1744:	*The Well-Tempered Clavier,* Book II
1747:	*A Musical Offering* for flute and violin with continuo, BWV 1079
1748-1750:	*The Art of the Fugue,* BWV 1080
Undated:	Orchestral Suite No 2 in B Minor for flute, strings and continuo, BWV 1067
	Suite No 3 in D for oboes, bassoons, trumpets, timpani, strings and continuo, BWV 1068

George Frideric Handel

1715-1717:	*Water Music* Suite in D
	Water Music Suite in F
c. 1720:	*Acis and Galatea,* secular cantata
1727:	*Zadok the Priest,* coronation anthem
1738:	Organ Concerti, Op 4
	Xerxes, opera, includes Handel's *Largo*
1739:	*Ode for St Cecilia's Day*
	Saul, oratorio
1740:	Concerti Grossi, Op 6
1741:	*Messiah*
1749:	*Music for the Royal Fireworks*
1752:	*Jephtha,* oratorio

Wolfgang Amadeus Mozart

1772:	*Lucio Silla*, opera
1775:	Violin Concerto No 5 in A, K 219
1777:	Piano Concerto No 9, K 271
1778:	Flute and Harp Concerto in C, K 299
	Flute Concerto in G, K 313
1780:	Symphony No 34 in C, K 338
1781:	*Idomeneo,* opera
1782:	Serenade No 7, *'Haffner'*, K 250
	Horn Concerto in D, K 412
	Il Seraglio, opera
1785:	String Quartet No 19 in C, *'Dissonance'*, K 465
	Piano Concerto No 20 in D Minor, K 466
	Piano Concerto No 21 in C, K 467
	Piano Concerto No 22 in E Flat, K 482
1786:	*Le Nozze de Figaro (The Marriage of Figaro),* opera
1787:	String Quintet in G Minor, K 516
	Serenade in F, *'A Musical Joke'*, K 522
	Serenade in G, *'Eine kleine Nachtmusik'*, K 525
	Don Giovanni, opera
1788:	Symphony No 40 in G Minor, K 550
	Symphony No 41 in C, *'Jupiter'*, K 551
1790:	Clarinet Quintet in A, K 581
	Cosi fan tutte, opera
1791:	Piano Concerto No 27, K 595
	Clarinet Concerto in A, K 622
	Requiem in D Minor, K 626
	La Clemenza di Tito, opera
	Die Zauberflöte (The Magic Flute), opera

Joseph Haydn

after 1770:	Piano Concerto in G
1783:	Cello Concerto in D
pre-1790:	Violin Sonata No 1
1791:	Symphony No 94 in G, *'Surprise'*
1794:	Symphony No 101 in D, *'The Clock'*
1796:	Trumpet Concerto in E Flat Major
1798:	*The Creation,* oratorio
1799:	String Quartets Nos 76-81

Ludwig van Beethoven

1799:	Piano Sonata No 8 in C Minor, *'Pathétique'*, Op 13
1802:	Piano Sonata No 14 in C Sharp Minor, *'Moonlight'*, Op 27
1803:	Romance in G for violin and orchestra, Op 40
1804:	Symphony No 3 in E Flat Major, *'Eroica'*, Op 55
	Triple Concerto in C for piano, violin, cello and orchestra, Op 56
	Piano Sonata No 23 in F Minor, *'Appassionata'*, Op 57
1805:	Romance in F for violin and orchestra, Op 5
	Symphony No 5 in C Minor, Op 67
1806:	Piano Sonata No 22 in F, Op 54
	Violin Concerto in D, Op 61
1807:	String Quartets Nos 7-9 in F, E Minor, C, *'Razumovsky'*, Op 59

1809:	Symphony No 6 in F, *'Pastoral'*, Op 68
	Piano Concerto No 5 in E Flat, *'Emperor'*, Op 73
1810:	*Egmont,* overture, Op 84
1811:	Piano Sonata No 26 in E Flat, *'Les Adieux'*, Op 81a
1817:	Symphony No 9 in D Minor, *'Choral'*, Op 125
1818-1819:	Piano Sonata No 29 in B Flat, *'Hammerklavier'*, Op 106

Franz Schubert

1816:	Symphony No 5 in B Flat Major
1819:	Piano Quintet in A, *'The Trout'*, Op 114
1822:	Symphony No 8 in B Minor, *'Unfinished'*
1823:	*Die Schöne Müllerin,* song cycle, D 795
	Rosamunde, incidental music, D 797
1824:	String Quartet No 14 in D Minor, *'Death and the Maiden'*
1827:	*Die Winterreise (Winter Journey),* song cycle, D 911
1828:	Symphony No 9 in C, *'The Great'*, D 944
	String Quartet in C, D 956

Felix Mendelssohn

1825:	String Octet in E Flat Major, Op 20
1826:	*A Midsummer Night's Dream,* overture, Op 21
1830:	*The Hebrides ('Fingal's Cave'),* overture, Op 26
	Symphony No 5 in D, *'Reformation'*
1831:	Piano Concerto No 1 in G Minor
1832:	*Calm Sea and Prosperous Voyage,* concert overture, Op 27
1833:	*The Tale of the Fair Melusina,* overture, Op 32
	Symphony No 4 in A, *'Italian'*, Op 90
1839:	*Ruy Blas,* overture, Op 95
1842:	Symphony No 3 in A Minor, *'Scottish'*
1842-1843:	Cello Sonata in D
1844:	Violin Concerto in E Minor, Op 64
1846:	*Elijah,* oratorio, Op 70

Fryderyk Chopin

1829:	Étude in C Minor, *'Revolutionary Study'*, Op 10 No 2
	Étude in E, Op 10 No 3
	Piano Concerto No 2 in F Minor, Op 21
1830-1831:	Nocturne No 2 in E Flat Major, Op 9
1830-1833:	Nocturne No 5 in F Sharp Major, Op 15 No 2
1831:	Grande Valse Brillante No 1 in E Flat Major, Op 18
1832:	Scherzo No 1 in B Minor, Op 20
1834:	Fantasie-Impromptu in C Sharp Minor, Op 66
1834-1836:	Étude in G Flat Major, Op 25 No 9
1835:	Ballade No 1 in G Minor, Op 23
1839:	Piano Sonata No 2 in B Flat Minor, Op 35
1842:	Polonaise No 6 in A Flat Major, Op 53
1843:	Berceuse in D Flat Major, Op 57 (revised 1844)
1846-1847:	Valse No 6 in D Flat Major, Op 64 No 1
	Valse No 7 in C Sharp Minor, Op 64 No 2

Robert Schumann

1838:	*Kinderscenen (Scenes of Childhood),* 13 short piano pieces
1841:	Symphony No 1 in B Flat Major, *'Spring',* Op 38
1841-1845:	Piano Concerto in A Minor, Op 54
1842:	Three String Quartets in A Minor, F, A
1849:	Overture in E Flat Minor, *'Manfred',* Op 115
1850:	Symphony No 3 in E Flat Major, *'Rhenish',* Op 97
	Cello Concerto in A Minor, Op 129
1851:	Violin Sonata in A Minor

Franz Liszt

1830-1849:	Piano Concerto No 1 in E Flat Major
1839:	Piano Concerto No 2 in A Minor
1843:	Valse Impromptu in A Flat Major
1850:	*Liebstraüme,* piano nocturnes
1852:	Hungarian Rhapsodies Nos 1-15
1853:	Piano Sonata in B Minor
1859:	Rigoletto Paraphrase
1880:	Hungarian Rhapsodies Nos 16-20
1881:	Mephisto Waltz

Jacques Offenbach

1858:	*Orphée aux enfers (Orpheus in the Underworld),* operetta
1864:	*La Belle Hélène,* operetta
1866:	*Bluebeard,* operetta
	La Vie Parisienne, opera
1868:	*La Périchole,* operetta
1878:	*Madame Favart,* operetta
1881:	*The Tales of Hoffman,* operetta

Johann Strauss II

1867:	*The Blue Danube* waltz
1868:	*Tales from the Vienna Woods* for orchestra
1874:	*Die Fledermaus,* operetta
1885:	*Der Zigeunerbaron (The Gypsy Baron),* operetta
Undated:	*Egyptian March*
	The Hunt
	Perpetuum Mobile
	Pizzicato Polka
	Roses from the South
	A Thousand and One Nights
	Voices of Spring
	Wiener Blut

Johannes Brahms

1854-1858:	Piano Concerto No 1 in D Minor, Op 15
1870:	*Alto Rhapsody* for alto, male chorus and orchestra, Op 53
1873:	Variations on a theme by Haydn, *St Anthony,* for orchestra, Op 56a
1876:	Symphony No 1 in C Minor, Op 68

1878:	Violin Concerto in D, Op 77
1878-1881:	Piano Concerto No 2 in B Flat, Op 83
1879:	Two Rhapsodies for piano, No 1 in B Minor, No 2 in G Minor, Op 79
1880:	*Academic Festival Overture,* Op 80
1884-1885:	Symphony No 4 in E Minor, Op 98
1887:	Double Concerto for violin, cello and orchestra in A Minor, Op 102
1891:	Clarinet Quintet in B Minor, Op 115
1892:	Six Piano Pieces (intermezzi, ballade, romance), Op 118
1896:	Four Serious Songs, Op 121

Pyotr Tchaikovsky

1869:	*Romeo and Juliet,* fantasy overture (revised 1880)
1872:	Symphony No 2 in C Minor, *'Little Russian',* Op 17
1874-1875:	Piano Concerto No 1 in B Flat Minor
1875:	*Swan Lake,* ballet
1876	*Slavonic March* for orchestra, Op 31
	Variations on a Rococo Theme for cello and orchestra, Op 33
1877:	*Francesca da Rimini,* symphonic fantasy after Dante, Op 32
	Symphony No 4 in F Minor, Op 36
1878:	Violin Concerto in D, Op 35
1879:	*Capriccio Italien* for orchestra, Op 45
	Eugene Onegin, opera
1880:	Serenade in C for string orchestra, Op 48
1882:	*1812,* overture, Op 49
	Piano Trio in A Minor, Op 50
1885:	*'Manfred'* Symphony, Op 58
1888	Symphony No 5 in E Minor, Op 64
	The Sleeping Beauty, ballet
1892:	String Sextet in D Minor, *'Souvenir de Florence',* Op 70
	The Nutcracker, ballet
1893:	Symphony No 6 in B Minor, *'Pathetique',* Op 74

Antonin Dvořák

1862:	String Quartet No 1 in A
1865:	*The Cypresses,* ten love songs for string quartet, later for voice and piano
1875:	Serenade for Strings in E, Op 22
1879-1880:	Violin Concerto in A Minor, Op 53
1889:	Symphony No 8 in G, Op 88
1893:	Symphony No 9 in E Minor, *'From the New World'*
	String Quartet in F, *'American'*
1895:	Cello Concerto in B Minor, Op 104
1901:	*Rusalka,* opera

Edvard Grieg

1867:	Violin Sonata No 2
1867-1901:	Lyric Pieces for piano, Books 1-X
1869:	Piano Concerto in A Minor
1875:	*Peer Gynt,* incidental music
1885:	*Holberg Suite* for strings or piano, Op 40
1898:	*Symphonic Dances* for orchestra
1906:	*Moods* for piano

Edward Elgar

1898-1899:	*Enigma Variations* for orchestra
1900:	*The Dream of Gerontius,* oratorio
1901:	*Pomp and Circumstance Marches 1-4*
1902-1913:	*Falstaff,* symphonic study in C Minor
1907-1908:	Symphony No 1 in A Flat Major
c. 1909-1910:	Violin Concerto
1918:	String Quartet in E Minor
1919:	Cello Concerto in E Minor
1930:	*Pomp and Circumstance March No 5* for orchestra

Claude Debussy

1890:	*Suite Bergamasque* for piano (includes *'Clair de lune'*)
1893:	String Quartet in G Minor
1894:	*Prélude à l'après-midi d'un faune* for orchestra
1897:	*Trois chansons de Bilitis*
1900:	*Nocturnes* for orchestra
1902:	*Pélleas et Mélisande,* opera
1904:	*La Mer,* three symphonic sketches
1909-1910:	Preludes for piano, Book I
1913:	Preludes for piano, Book II
1915:	Cello Sonata in D Minor

Jean Sibelius

1892:	*En Saga,* symphonic poem, Op 9 (revised 1901)
1894:	*Spring Song,* symphonic poem
1900:	*Finlandia,* symphonic poem, Op 26
1901:	Symphony No 2 in D, Op 43
1903:	Violin Concerto in D Minor, Op 47 (revised 1905)
1908:	String Quartet in five movements, *Voces Intimae*
1911:	*Rakastava Suite* for orchestra
1914-1915:	Symphony No 5 in E Flat Major, Op 82
1926:	*The Tempest,* incidental music

Gustav Mahler

1888:	Symphony No 1 in D, *'The Titan'*
1894:	Symphony No 2 in C Minor, *'Resurrection';* final movement for soprano and contralto, choir and orchestra
1895:	Symphony No 3 in D Minor, *'A Summer Morning's Dream';* final movement for contralto, boys' and female choruses and orchestra
1902:	Symphony No 5 in C Sharp Minor
	Rückert-Lieder, five songs
1905:	Symphony No 7 in E Minor, *'Song of the Night'*
1908:	*Das Lied von der Erde (The Song of the Earth),* song cycle of symphonic dimensions
1909:	Symphony No 9 in D

Sergei Rachmaninov

1890-1891:	Piano Concerto No 1 in F Sharp Minor
1893:	Suite No 1, *Fantasy,* for two pianos
1901:	Cello Sonata in G Minor
	Piano Concerto No 2 in C Minor
1907:	*The Isle of the Dead,* symphonic poem
	Symphony No 2 in E Minor
1934:	*Rhapsody on a Theme by Paganini,* variations for piano and orchestra
1936:	Symphony No 3 in A Minor
1941:	*Three Symphonic Dances* for orchestra, Op 45

Gustav Holst

1897:	*A Winter Idyll* for orchestra
1906:	*Two Songs Without Words*
1908:	*Savitri,* opera
1914-1916:	*The Planets,* orchestral suite in seven movements
1927:	*Egdon Heath,* symphonic poem
1929:	Concerto for two violins
1930:	*Hammersmith,* prelude and scherzo for orchestra
1933:	*Lyric Movement* for viola and strings

Maurice Ravel

1899:	*Pavane pour une infante défunte,* for piano
1901:	*Jeux d'eau* for piano
1905:	*Miroirs: Alborada del gracioso* for piano
1906:	Introduction and Allegro for harp, flute, clarinet and string quartet
1907:	*Rhapsodie espagnole* for orchestra
1908:	*Gaspard de la nuit* for piano
1912:	*Daphnis et Chloé,* ballet with chorus
1920:	*La Valse,* choreographic poem for orchestra
1925:	*L'enfant et les sortilèges,* opera
1928:	*Bolero* for orchestra
1931:	Piano Concerto for the left hand

Béla Bartók

1905:	Suite No 1 for Orchestra
1908:	String Quartet No 1 in A Minor
1914:	*The Wooden Prince,* ballet
1922:	Violin Sonata No 2
1923:	Dance Suite for orchestra
1926:	Piano Sonata
1928:	Rhapsody No 1 for cello and piano
1943:	Concerto for orchestra
1945:	Piano Concerto No 3

Igor Stravinsky

1910:	*The Firebird,* ballet
1911:	*Petrushka,* ballet
1913:	*The Rite of Spring,* ballet
1914-1923:	*Les Noces,* ballet
1918:	*The Soldier's Tale* for speakers, dancer and ensemble
1930:	*Symphony of Psalms* for chorus and orchestra
1938:	*Dumbarton Oaks,* concerto in E Flat for chamber orchestra
1940:	Symphony in C
1944:	Elegy for unaccompanied viola
1945:	*Ebony Concerto* for clarinet and jazz ensemble
1948-1951:	*The Rake's Progress,* opera

George Gershwin

1924:	*Lady, Be Good,* musical
	Rhapsody in Blue for piano and orchestra
1925:	Concerto in F for piano and orchestra
1927:	*Funny Face,* musical
1928:	*An American in Paris* for orchestra
1932:	*Cuban Overture* for orchestra
1934:	*'I Got Rhythm' Variations* for piano and orchestra
1935:	*Porgy and Bess,* opera
1936-1937:	*Shall We Dance,* film score

Index

Entries in **bold** refer to featured composers and articles.
Page numbers in *italics* refer to illustrations.

PICTURE CREDITS

by Antoine Jean Gros CFL, 107(b) 'The Campaign of France' by Ernest Meissonier, Louvre/Lauros, 132 Carnavalet, 151(t) Malmaison/Lauros, 153(b) Lauros, 155(bl) Carnavalet/Telarci, 155(br) Carnavalet/Lauros, 157(b) Carnavalet/Lauros, 158(br) Louvre/Lauros, 159(l) Private Collection, 159(r) Versailles, 161(t) Carnavalet, 163(b) Carnavalet/Lauros, 164 Lauros, 184 Musée Carnavalet/Lauros, 202(b) Lauros, 225(r), 316 Manet 'Émile Zola' Louvre, Paris/Lauros, 316/7 Monet 'Impression Sunrise' Musée Marmottan, Paris/Lauros, 319 Renoir 'À la Grenouillère' Louvre, Paris Garanger, 320 Cézanne 'La Montagne Sainte-Victoire' Kunsthaus, Zurich, 390/1 Roux 'The Universal Exhibition at Night' Carnavalet, Paris/Lauros, 392/3 P. Merwart 'Inside the Chat Noir', Carnavalet, Paris/Lauros, 421 Jacques Émile Blanche/Musée d'Orsay, Lauros DACS 1989, 436 Bayer 'Portrait of Serge Lifar' Private Collection © ADAGP Paris 1989. **The Granger Collection:** 267(tl), 268/9, 270(b), 271(l), 274(b). **Hamlyn Group Picture Library:** 31 Philippe Mercier 'Portrait of Handel', Private Collection. **Robert Harding Picture Library:** 188(t) Bethnal Green. **Photo Harlingue-Viollet:** 150(t), 152(tr), 156(r), 171(b). **Reproduced by Gracious permission of Her Majesty the Queen:** 26, 34/5, 130(r), 140, 141(b), 142, 142/3, 146/7, 148. **Hispanic Society of America:** 403(b), Sorolla 'Sevilla. The Bullfight'. **Historisches Archiv, Köln:** 198(tl). **Historisches Museum der Stadt Wien:** 50(b), 53(t), 64(r), 66/7, 126(t), 350 Hans Makart, Mick Gold Archiv, 354 Alfred Roller 'Poster for the 14th Exhibition of the Secession'. **Historisches Museum, Vienna:** 91, 110(b). **David Hockney 1975:** 426/7. **Michael Holford:** 57(t) MOD, National Maritime Museum, London, 58/9 National Maritime Museum, London. **Holst Birthplace Museum:** 374(tl,b), 375, 376, 377, 378, 378/9, 379(t). **Angelo Hornak:** 355(bl). **Hungarian National Gallery, Budapest:** 406(t) Károly Ferenczy 'March Evening'. **Imperial War Museum, London:** 364/5 John Singer Sargent 'Gassed', 366(t), 367(t), 367(bl) John Nash 'Over the Top', 372, 387(b). **Innes Archive:** 280(tr). **Iowa State Historical Society Des Moines Register:** 266(b). **Kunsthalle, Hamburg:** 284 Schmidt-Rottluff/'Loftus' © ADAGP 1989. **Kunstsammlungenzuweimar:** 18/9 Christian Richter 'Interior of the Himmelsburg Castle Chapel'. **Keystone:** 409(br). **The Kobal Collection:** 438/9, 440(b), 443(t), 444, 445(b), 446/7, 447(t,c). **Kommunes Kunstamlinger, Munich-Museet:** 289(t) Edvard Munch 'Workers returning home', Oslo. **Kunsthalle Hamburg:** 95, 96, 100. **Courtesy of the Lefevre Gallery, London:** 441(l) Edward Burra 'Show Girls' Private Collection. **Courtesy of Library and Museum of the Performing Arts, Lincoln Center:** 448. **Ljubljana Galerija:** 124 J. Tominc 'Moskonove'. **Lüneberg Museum/Presse Foto Makovec:** 10(tr). **Malvisi Archives:** 47(t) Mozarteum, Salzburg, 49(t) Mozarteum, Salzburg, 49(br) Abbey of St Peter, Salzburg, 49(c) Mozarteum, Salzburg, 50(t) Mozarteum, Salzburg, 50(tr) Mrs Beasley, Brighton, 50(br), 51(l) Mozarteum, Salzburg, 51(b) Mozarteum, Salzburg, 52(r) Villa Betramka, Prague, 72(r) B.G. Pesci 'Esterháza' National Museum Budapest, 74(r) Vigée-Lebrun 'Princess Marie Hermenegild' Palais Liechtenstein. **Mansell Collection:** 107(t), 111(t), 121(t,b), 122, 197, 207, 252, 264(tr), 265(br), 270(t), 275(t), 282, 290(b), 302(b), 305(tl,b), 307(t,b), 310(t), 313(tr), 335(b), 381(b), 382, 383, 384(t), 386/7, 387(t). **Courtesy of the Map House, London:** 184/5(l), 230/1, 237(t). **Foto Meyer:** 192(t) Johann Franz Greippel 'Performance of Gluck's II Parnasso Confuse' Holburg, Vienna. **Motley Books:** 200, 200/1, 306, 394/5, 395, 433. **Mozarteum Salzburg:** 68(b). **Musée Grenoble:** 309(b) Sisley 'View of Montmartre'. **Museo Carolino Augusteum, Salzburg:** 46(r), 66(t). **Museum der Stadt Wien:** 70 Schutz 'The Kohlmarkt', 213, 214, 216(t) Richard Moser 'Dommayer in Hietzing', 218/9, 219(b), 220/1. **Museum für Hamburgische Geschichte, Hamburg:** 11(t). **The Museum of London:** 384(bl,br). **National Film Archive:** 418(b), 447(b). **National Gallery of Art, Washington, Widener Collection 1942:** 402(b) Manet 'The Dead Toreador'. **National Gallery of Canada, Ottowa:** 371 Edward Wadsworth 'Dazzled Ships in Drydock, Liverpool'. **The National Gallery, London:** 384/5, 401(b) Daumier 'Don Quixote and Sancho Panza'. **National Gallery, Oslo/Jacques Lathion:** 287(l) Adolph Tidemand 'Woman at the Loom' (detail), 288(b) Wilhelm O. Peters 'From Hjula Weaving Mill', 290(t) Christian Krohg 'Johan Sverdrup' (detail), 332/3 Harold Sohlberg 'Rondane at night'. **National Gallery of Scotland, Edinburgh:** 321 Gauguin 'The Vision After the Sermon'. **National Maritime Museum, London:** 54, 56/7, 58, 61(r),

62(b). **National Museum of Finland, Helsinki:** 328(t,br), 338(b), 339(t,b) A. Hartmann 'The Society of Finnish Literature'. **By courtesy of The National Portrait Gallery:** 15 Philips Wouwermans 'Cavalry making a sortie from a Fort on a Hill', 34(t), 41(t,l), 44(t), 367(br) R. Lee 'Paul Nash', 373 M. Woodforde 'Gustav Holst', 379(b) R. G. Eves 'Thomas Hardy', 382/3 Georgina Brackenburg 'Emmeline Pankhurst'. **Nationalgalerie, Prague:** 130/1. **Nationalmuseum, Stockholm:** 340 Anders Zorn 'Midsummer Dance'. **Natural History Museum, London:** 57(b). **New York Public Library:** 442(t). **Peter Newark's Western Americana:** 266(tr), 268, 269, 271(r), 272(t), 272/3, 274(t), 275(b), 276(b). **Novosti:** 245, 246(tl), 249(t), 250, 251(t), 253(t) N. Kasatkin 'The Poor Picking Coal' Russian Museum, 255, 257, 259(tl) V. Makovsky 'Convicted', 359, 361. **Oslo Bymuseum:** 288(c). **Osterreichische Galerie, Vienna:** 127 F. F. G. Waldmuller, The Kerzmunn Family. **Osterreichische Nationalbibliothek:** 53(b) Musik-Sammlung, 131(t), 215, 216(b), 217(t), 219(t), 220(t), 220(t,b), 234(l), 341, 342(tl,tr), 344(b), 344/5(b) Anton Brioschi 'Stage Design for Eugene Onegin: a ballroom', 345, 347(r), 354(l). **Courtesy of the Paton Collection:** 376/7 S. Kay 'Barnes Terrace'. **Philadelphia Museum of Art:** 404(t) Manet 'Emilie Ambre in the Role of Carmen'. Given by Edgar Scott. **The Phillips Collection, Washington:** 401(t) Manet 'Ballet Espagnol'. **The Photo Source:** 426(t). **Popperfoto:** 441(r), 446, 448/9. **Private Collection:** 349(r). **Mauro Pucciarelli:** 60 Bibliothèque Nationale, 76/7 Antonio Francesco Callet 'Louis XVI' Prado Madrid, 154(tr), 158(bl), 183, 186(cl), 189(t), 193(b), 312 Pirelli 'Santa Mariadell Anima' Museo di Roma, 315(t), 318/9 Monet 'Corner of the Garden at Montgeron' Hermitage Leningrad, 329(b) Gallery of Modern Art, Rome, 393, 396/b), 399 Sorolla 'Festival in Valencia' Hispanic Society of America, 404(b) Bibliothèque Nationale, courtesy Chester Music. **Réunion des Musées Nationaux:** 26/7 L. N. Blarenberghe 'Battle of Fontenoy' Versailles, 312/3 Fantin-Latour 'A corner table' Louvre, Paris, 318 Camille Pissarro 'Entrance to the Village of Voisins' Louvre/Paris, 322/3 Puvis de Chavannes 'The Poor Fisherman' Louvre, Paris, 324 Gustave Moreau 'The Sirens' Musée Gustave Moreau Paris, 400 Goya 'La Marquise de la Solana' Louvre, Paris. **Rijksmuseum, Amsterdam:** 28(c). **Ringling Bros/Barnum & Bailey Circus:** 424/5. **Royal College of Music:** 157(t), 182(l), 184/5 David Parker, 192(b). **The Royal Opera House Archives:** 434/5. **Royal Opera House, Covent Garden:** 218(b). **Salmer:** 85, 87(t), 130(l) Venice Correr Museum, 162/3 Carnavalet. **Sammlung der Gesellschaft der Musikfreunde in Wien:** 63(t). **Scala:** 29(b), 46/7 Mozarteum, Salzburg, 71(t), 82 J. M. Moreau 'Robespierre' Versailles, 105 'The Empress Josephine' by Pierre Paul Prud'hon, Louvre (detail), 106(b) 'Coronation of Napoleon' by Louis David, Louvre, 235(tl). **Sibeliusmuseum, Abo, Finland:** 325(t), 326(b), 327, 329(tr). **Society for Cultural Relations with the USSR:** 247(c), 256, 358, 360(l), 360/1. **Staatliche Museen Preussischer Kulturbesitz, Berlin:** 25(t) Adolph Menzel 'Das Flötenkozen', 97(t), 100/1, 128(b), 191, 209, 355 Kokoschka 'Adolph Loos'. **Courtesy of Steinway and Sons/ Photo by Christopher Barker:** 357. **Stockholms Universitet:** 334/5 Nils Johan Olsson Blemmier 'Freya seeking her husband'. **Theodore Stravinsky:** 422(t), 423. **The Tate Gallery, London:** 368/9 R. Nevinson 'Bursting Shell', 381(t) William Holman Hunt 'The Awakening Conscience', 414/5 Vassily Kandinsky 'Cossacks' 1910 © ADAGP Paris 1989, 416/7 Pablo Picasso 'Seated Nude' 1900-10 © DACS 1989, 417 Piet Mondrian 'Composition with Grey, Red, Yellow and Blue' 1900-26 © DACS 1989, 418/9 Salvador Dali 'Metamorphosis of Narcissus' 1934 © DACS 1989, 420 Henry Moore 'Manquette for Family Group'. **By courtesy of the Trustees of The Tate Gallery, London:** 151(b). **Theatermuseum, Köln:** 422/3(b). **Theatre Collection, Museum of the City of New York:** 442(b). **Troldhaugen Museum:** 285. **Courtesy of the United Grand Lodge of England/David Parker:** 63(b), 64(l), 65, 66(br). **Universitetsbibliotheket i Oslo:** 278(t), 280(b), 281, 284/5, 289(b). **Victoria and Albert Museum:** 28(b) Michael Kitcatt, 201(bl), 230(tl), 432/3 © DACS 1984. **Roger Viollet:** 153(t), 154(b), 188(b), 201(br), 203(b), 204(r), 246(tr), 316/7, 322(t), 390(tl), 408(b), 414, 416, 419, 424, 425(t), 430(l) Poster by van Dongen, 432 © DACS 1989, 434(b). **Walker Art Gallery, Liverpool:** 104/5 'The Death of Nelson' by Daniel Maclise. **Reg Wilson:** 248(t). **Zefa:** 86(b). **Ziolo:** 389 P. Trela, 392(t) P. Trela.